CONCEPTS AND CONTEXT

Modern Administrative Law in Australia provides an authoritative overview of administrative law in Australia. It clarifies and enlivens this crucial but complex area of law, with erudite analysis and thoroughly modern perspectives. The full range of the subject is explored, from first principles to the cutting edge of controversies and concerns unfolding today.

The contributors – including highly respected academics from 11 Australian law schools, as well as eminent practitioners including Chief Justice Robert French AC and Justice Stephen Gageler of the High Court of Australia – are at the forefront of current research, debate and decision-making, and infuse the book with unique insight.

The book examines the structure and themes of administrative law, the theory and practice of judicial review, and the workings of administrative law beyond the courts. Each chapter addresses an important conceptual or procedural concern within administrative law with reference to current issues and trends, including human rights, environmentalism, immigration, privacy and integrity in government.

Administrative law affects innumerable aspects of political, commercial and private life, and yet is often considered difficult to understand. *Modern Administrative Law in Australia* unravels the intricacies and reveals how they are applied in real cases. Illuminating and engaging, it is an essential reference for students and practitioners of administrative law.

Matthew Groves is an Associate Professor in the Law School of Monash University, where he teaches and researches in administrative law. He is also a member of the Commonwealth Administrative Review Council, the peak body that advises the federal government on administrative law and policy.

MODERN ADMINISTRATIVE LAW IN AUSTRALIA

CONCEPTS AND CONTEXT

Edited by

Matthew Groves

CAMBRIDGE UNIVERSITY PRESS

University Printing House, Cambridge CB2 8BS, United Kingdom

One Liberty Plaza, 20th Floor, New York, NY 10006, USA

477 Williamstown Road, Port Melbourne, VIC 3207, Australia

4843/24, 2nd Floor, Ansari Road, Daryaganj, Delhi - 110002, India

79 Anson Road, #06-04/06, Singapore 079906

Cambridge University Press is part of the University of Cambridge.

It furthers the University's mission by disseminating knowledge in the pursuit of education, learning and research at the highest international levels of excellence.

www.cambridge.org
Information on this title: www.cambridge.org/9781107692190

© Cambridge University Press 2014

This publication is in copyright. Subject to statutory exception and to the provisions of relevant collective licensing agreements, no reproduction of any part may take place without the written permission of Cambridge University Press.

First published 2014 (version 2, January 2017)

Cover designed by Sardine Design

A catalogue record for this publication is available from the British Library

A Cataloguing-in-Publication entry is available from the catalogue of the National Library of Australia at www.nla.gov.au

ISBN 978-1-107-69219-0 Paperback

Reproduction and communication for educational purposes

The Australian *Copyright Act 1968* (the Act) allows a maximum of one chapter or 10% of the pages of this work, whichever is the greater, to be reproduced and/or communicated by any educational institution for its educational purposes provided that the educational institution (or the body that administers it) has given a remuneration notice to Copyright Agency Limited (CAL) under the Act.

For details of the CAL licence for educational institutions contact:

Copyright Agency Limited
Level 15, 233 Castlereagh Street
Sydney NSW 2000
Telephone: (02) 9394 7600
Facsimile: (02) 9394 7601
E-mail: info@copyright.com.au

Reproduction and communication for other purposes

Except as permitted under the Act (for example a fair dealing for the purposes of study, research, criticism or review) no part of this publication may be reproduced, stored in a retrieval system, communicated or transmitted in any form or by any means without prior written permission. All inquiries should be made to the publisher at the address above.

Cambridge University Press has no responsibility for the persistence or accuracy of URLs for external or third-party internet websites referred to in this publication, and does not guarantee that any content on such websites is, or will remain, accurate or appropriate.

It is an enticing book title – *Modern Administrative Law in Australia*. Why is it modern? How is it different from the system of Australian administrative law that has been familiar over decades to practitioners, teachers and students?

There are three characterising or long-standing elements of Australian administrative law. The first is the constitutional foundation. The separation of powers in the *Australian Constitution* both anchors the judiciary's role in controlling the legal exercise of executive power and places implied constraints on legislative freedom to immunise executive power from judicial scrutiny. Section 75 supplements that arrangement by giving the High Court a guaranteed jurisdiction to adjudicate legal claims against the Commonwealth and to restrain unlawful conduct by Commonwealth officers.

The second feature is that many foundation principles of Australian administrative law are drawn less from the *Constitution* than from the common law. Key concepts – the principle of legality, natural justice, principles of statutory interpretation, remedies and standing – were well developed before constitutional essentials became more pronounced in the last two decades. Indeed, books on Australian administrative law written before that time devoted little attention to the *Constitution* and focused instead on common law principles of judicial review, with a strong emphasis on landmark decisions of British courts.

The third feature is that Australian parliaments significantly expanded the scope of administrative law from the 1970s onwards. New institutions were created to which the community could turn to challenge or question government administrative action. Well-known examples are administrative tribunals, Ombudsmen and commissioners with specialist functions in areas such as human rights, corruption prevention and information regulation. Australian parliaments also enacted a range of new administrative law rights, such as the right to reasons, access to government information, protection of personal information, and whistleblower protection.

Modern Administrative Law in Australia, containing essays by leading jurists, practitioners and writers, presents a fourth element of administrative law. It evolves, changes and adapts to the changing face of government and community expectations. This is a unifying thread of all essays in this book. Together they provide a vivid picture of how administrative law values, doctrines and structures are dynamic and compelling. A few themes stand out.

One is that the *Constitution* has become, as Groves and Boughey observe, a 'major force that has shaped Australian administrative law in more recent years'. This influence is seen in many ways. The *Constitution* draws attention to overarching values and principles that now receive greater attention in administrative law jurisprudence, as they do in the essay by Chief Justice French. Essays dedicated to jurisdictional error, by Justice Gageler and Professor Aronson, similarly reflect how the *Constitution* has set a new doctrinal agenda – albeit one, as both observe, in which ambiguity is played out in case law and academic analysis. The inclusion in this book of a separate chapter on privative clauses conveys a similar message about the new constitutional agenda (Young). The development of the constitutional review jurisdiction has also sparked a lively debate about whether the *Administrative Decisions (Judicial Review) Act 1977* (Cth) has been overtaken or sidelined (Billings and Cassimitas).

A more intense focus on statutory interpretation is another contemporary administrative law theme, taken up in many essays, including in a separate essay by Barnes. The exquisite range of interpretive problems that can arise when the legislature seeks to codify a fundamental administrative principle – the right to a fair hearing – is examined by Pearson, in a discussion of judicial review of decisions by migration tribunals. This is also taken up in the essay by Groves, who explores the expanding breadth of natural justice doctrine and legislative attempts to exclude or confine it.

The newer structural elements of administrative law have evolved in interesting ways that reflect a greater complexity and sophistication. The institution of Ombudsman, as Stuhmcke discusses, now has many different forms and discharges a range of functions beyond complaint handling. There has been a comparable proliferation in the diversity, jurisdiction, procedure and caseload of administrative tribunals, described by Creyke as the effective face of justice to most Australians. Freedom of information legislation has moved from a first to a second generation model of providing public access to government information (Bannister). Privacy protection, once a neglected area of administrative law, has fast become a core concern for both government and the community (Paterson). Drawing these threads together, Brown examines the options for acknowledging the development of a fourth or integrity branch of government.

Administrative law has grown in scope and now plays a larger role in reviewing the exercise of public power. Should it go further still? Some essayists question whether Australian administrative law fulfils its potential to protect human rights (Duxbury), to review the exercise of coercive powers that have a national security dimension (Saul), or to provide standing to community groups to seek judicial review of environmental and planning decisions (Edgar). Are judicial review principles too procedurally focused, or should they provide redress against substantive unfairness (Weeks)? And is Australian administrative law unduly constrained by a classic but diminishing distinction between public and private power (Finn)?

Modern Administrative Law in Australia is a fitting title for an excellent collection of scholarly essays that convey the richness, growth and vigour of Australian administrative law. A particular strength of the book is that it is sure to play a central role in the next phase of development.

Professor John McMillan
Australian Information Commissioner

Foreword	*v*
Author biographies	*ix*
Table of statutes	*xii*
Table of cases	*xix*

PART 1   THE STRUCTURE AND THEMES OF ADMINISTRATIVE LAW — 1

1 Administrative law in the Australian environment — 3
Matthew Groves and Janina Boughey

2 Administrative law in Australia: Themes and values revisited — 24
Chief Justice R S French AC

3 The public/private distinction and the reach of administrative law — 49
Chris Finn

4 Human rights and judicial review: Two sides of the same coin? — 70
Alison Duxbury

5 Security and fairness in Australian public law — 93
Ben Saul

6 Statutory interpretation and administrative law — 119
Jeffrey Barnes

7 Standing for environmental groups: Protecting public and private interests — 140
Andrew Edgar

PART 2   JUDICIAL REVIEW — 163

8 The constitutional dimension — 165
Hon Stephen Gageler

9	Australia's codification of judicial review: Has the legislative effort been worth it? *Peter Billings and Anthony Cassimatis*	180
10	The evolution and entrenchment of natural justice *Matthew Groves*	205
11	Holding government to its word: Legitimate expectations and estoppels in administrative law *Greg Weeks*	224
12	Jurisdictional error and beyond *Mark Aronson*	248
13	Privative clauses: Politics, legality and the constitutional dimension *Simon Young*	276

PART 3   BEYOND THE COURTS — 299

14	The integrity branch: A 'system', an 'industry', or a sensible emerging fourth arm of government? *AJ Brown*	301
15	The Ombudsman *Anita Stuhmcke*	326
16	Freedom of information: A new era with old tensions *Judith Bannister*	348
17	Privacy *Moira Paterson*	370
18	Tribunals and merits review *Robin Creyke*	393
19	'Fair is foul and foul is fair': Migration tribunals and a fair hearing *Linda Pearson*	416

Index — 440

Mark Aronson is an Emeritus Professor in the Law Faculty at the University of New South Wales. He has written extensively on issues in administrative law, Crown liability, evidence and procedure, and recently published Aronson and Groves, *Judicial Review of Administrative Action* (Thomson Reuters, 5th ed, 2012).

Judith Bannister is a Senior Lecturer in the Law School at the University of Adelaide. Judith teaches and researches in intellectual property, particularly copyright and confidential information, and the regulation of information access. She has published many books and articles in these areas. Judith is currently completing her book, *Government Accountability: Australian Administrative Law* (with Gabrielle Appleby, for Cambridge University Press).

Jeffrey Barnes is a Senior Lecturer in the School of Law at La Trobe University. He teaches and researches in administrative law and has also published widely on statutory interpretation. He is a former Project Officer with the Administrative Review Council and former part-time legal member of the Social Security Appeals Tribunal.

Peter Billings is a Senior Lecturer in the TC Beirne School of Law at the University of Queensland, before which he taught at the University of Southampton and the University of the West of England, Bristol. He holds a Bachelor of Laws degree and a PhD in law, both from the University of Southampton. He has published widely on administrative law. In 2010 he edited and contributed to a special issue of *Law in Context*, entitled 'Indigenous Australians and the Commonwealth Intervention' (Federation Press).

Janina Boughey is a PhD candidate in the Law Faculty at Monash University. She researches and teaches in Australian and Canadian public law. Prior to commencing her PhD, Janina worked in administrative law policy at the Commonwealth Attorney-General's Department and as a researcher at the Australian Senate. She has published a number of articles on comparative administrative law.

AJ Brown is Professor of Public Policy and Law in the School of Government and International Relations at Griffith University. He is also program leader in public integrity and anti-corruption in the Centre for Governance and Public Policy, and a director of Transparency International Australia. His former roles include senior investigation officer for the Commonwealth Ombudsman and Associate to the Hon G E Tony Fitzgerald AC, President of the Queensland Court of Appeal. He researches, consults and teaches in public accountability, integrity, governance, federalism and intergovernmental relations. His authored and co-authored books include *Whistleblowing in the Australian Public Sector* (2008) and *Whistling While They Work* (2011, both ANZSOG/ANU E-Press), and the biography *Michael Kirby: Paradoxes and Principles* (Federation Press, 2011).

Anthony Cassimatis is an Associate Professor of Law in the TC Beirne School of Law at the University of Queensland, where he teaches and researches in public international law and administrative law. Anthony has published many books and articles on international law, administrative law and legal advocacy. He has also supervised the Jessup Mooting teams from the TC Beirne School of Law, including its world champion Jessup Moot team of 2005.

Robin Creyke is a Professor in the College of Law at the Australian National University. She is currently on leave while she acts in the role of Senior Member of the Commonwealth Administrative Appeals Tribunal. Robin's main research interest is administrative law, particularly the position of tribunals in our system of government. She has published many books and articles about administrative law, the most recent of which is Creyke and McMillan, *Control of Government Action* (LexisNexis Butterworths, 3rd ed, 2012).

Alison Duxbury is an Associate Professor in the Melbourne University Law School. She teaches and researches in international law, military law and public law. Alison has published widely in those areas, most recently *The Participation of States in International Organisations: The Role of Human Rights and Democracy* (Cambridge University Press, UK, 2011).

Andrew Edgar is a Senior Lecturer in the Law School at the University of Sydney. He teaches and researches in administrative and environmental law. Andrew's research focuses on judicial and merits review of environmental decisions, and he has published a wide range of articles and book chapters in that area.

Chris Finn was recently appointed as an Associate Professor at the Curtin Law School, before which he worked for many years in the Law Schools at the University of Adelaide and then the University of South Australia. Chris has published many articles and book chapters in administrative law.

Chief Justice R S French AC is the Chief Justice of the High Court of Australia. Prior to his appointment to the High Court, his Honour was a Justice of the Federal Court of Australia. Justice French has also held many other appointments, including the office of President of the National Native Title Tribunal (1994-98) and President of the Australian Association of Constitutional Law.

Hon Stephen Gageler is a Justice of the High Court of Australia. At the time of his appointment he was Solicitor-General of Australia. Prior to that appointment he maintained a practice in the New South Wales Bar in constitutional, administrative and revenue law, specialising in appeals to the Federal Court and the High Court. Before he was called to the Bar, Justice Gageler worked in both private practice and government, and was Associate to Sir Anthony Mason. He has published widely in the areas of public law and federal jurisdiction.

Matthew Groves is an Associate Professor in the Law Faculty at Monash University, and is a member of the Commonwealth Administrative Review Council. Matthew is co-author of the leading Australian work on judicial review, Aronson and Groves, *Judicial Review of Administrative Action* (Thomson Reuters, 5th ed, 2012). He has also published widely on administrative law. The editing of this book was assisted by a publications grant from the Faculty of Law, Monash University.

Moira Paterson is an Associate Professor in the Law Faculty at Monash University. She teaches and researches in the field of information law, with a focus on freedom of information and privacy. Moira has published the book *Freedom of Information and Privacy: Government and Information Access in the Modern State* (LexisNexis, 2005), and many articles and book chapters on information and privacy. She is a member of the Board of the Australian Privacy Foundation.

Linda Pearson is a Commissioner of the Land and Environment Court of New South Wales and a member of the Commonwealth Administrative Review Council. She was previously a senior lecturer in the Faculty of Law, University of New South Wales, and has extensive experience in a number of tribunals, both Commonwealth and State, including the Migration Review Tribunal. Linda has written widely in administrative law and environmental law.

Ben Saul is a Professor of International Law at the Sydney Centre for International Law at the University of Sydney. He has published many books and articles in terrorism, human rights, the law of armed conflict, and international criminal law. His current research includes several projects funded by large competitive grants, including an Australian Research Council Future Fellowship on the emerging international law of terrorism.

Anita Stuhmcke is a Professor in the Law School at the University of Technology, Sydney. Her doctorate was an in-depth empirical study of the office of the Commonwealth Ombudsman. Anita has published widely in Australia and internationally on all aspects of the institution of the Ombudsman. She also teaches and publishes on the law of torts and legal research.

Greg Weeks is a lecturer in the Faculty of Law at the University of New South Wales, where he teaches administrative law. Greg's research interests are primarily related to judicial review, on which he has published a number of articles, and to the availability of private law remedies against public authorities. His recently completed doctoral thesis is on the remedies available when public authorities fail to adhere to their own soft law instruments.

Simon Young is a Professor of Law in the Law School at the University of Western Australia. He specialises in public law (particularly administrative law) and indigenous law and policy (notably native title). He has published several books, book chapters and articles in these areas.

TABLE OF STATUTES

Commonwealth

Acts Interpretation Act 1901, 261
 s 2B, 375
Administrative Appeals Tribunal Act 1975, 11, 406
 Pt IV Div 3, 397
 s 2A, 11, 411, 417
 s 25, 403, 418
 s 27, 154
 s 28, 349
 s 33, 411
 s 39A, 117
 s 39B, 117
 s 43, 12, 268
Administrative Appeals Tribunal Bill 1975, 132
Administrative Decisions (Judicial Review) Act 1977, 8–11, 15, 19, 56, 81–2, 152, 169–70, 181–2, 182–4, 185–9, 194, 195, 196, 199, 201, 203, 204, 260–1, 272, 275, 281, 353
 s 3, 285
 s 3(1), 76
 s 3(4), 75
 s 4, 285
 s 5, 10, 37, 77, 188, 189, 400
 s 5(1)(b), 190, 260
 s 5(1)(c), 261
 ss 5(1)(c)–(d), 191
 s 5(1)(f), 189, 260
 s 5(1)(h), 189, 200, 260
 s 5(1)(j), 10, 191, 261
 s 5(2)(f), 194, 194
 s 5(2)(g), 196
 s 5(2)(j), 10, 261
 s 5(3), 200, 260
 ss 5–6, 10
 ss 5–7, 260
 s 6, 10, 77, 188, 189, 261
 s 6(1)(b), 190, 260
 s 6(1)(c), 261
 ss 6(1)(c)–(d), 191
 s 6(1)(f), 189, 260
 s 6(1)(h), 189, 200, 260
 s 6(1)(j), 191
 s 6(2)(f), 194
 s 6(3), 200, 260
 s 7, 188
 s 13, 9, 136, 152, 188, 202, 349
 s 13A, 9
 s 16, 203
 sch 1, 97, 184, 281, 285, 285
Archives Act 1983, 351, 379
 s 3(7), 365, 369
 s 22A, 365
Australian Capital Territory Government Service (Consequential Provisions) Act 1994, 373
Australian Information Commissioner Act 2010, 14, 386
Australian Security Intelligence Organisation Act 1979, 96, 100, 110
 Pt 4, 96
 s 4(a), 96
 s 4(aa), 96
 s 4(b), 96
 s 35, 96
 s 36, 96, 97
 s 37(2), 96, 101
 s 38, 96, 101
 s 54, 96, 101
Broadcasting Services Act 1992
 s 4, 129
 s 122, 128
 s 122(2)(b), 128
 s 122(4), 128
 s 160, 129–30
 s 160(d), 128, 129
Competition and Consumer Act 2010
 s 46, 66
 s 80, 157
Constitution, 4, 5, 16–21, 21, 22, 30–1, 107, 110, 157, 166, 166–8, 179, 192–3, 206, 242, 247, 253, 265, 270
 Ch I, 167, 177
 Ch II, 167, 177
 Ch III, 105, 167, 174, 177, 287, 396, 400
 Ch V, 167
 s 7, 272
 s 61, 31
 s 71, 168

s 73, 20, 287
s 73(ii), 167, 168, 173, 174, 175
s 75, 97, 183, 204
s 75(iii), 183, 204
s 75(v), 4, 9, 20, 29, 33, 75, 86, 167, 168, 169,
　170, 172, 173, 175, 183, 188, 192, 244,
　245, 260, 281, 282, 283, 284, 286, 287,
　288, 289, 291, 293, 426
s 106, 28
s 109, 30
*Corporations (Aboriginal and Torres Strait
　Islander) Act 2006*
　s 487-10(1)(a), 133
Crimes Act 1914, 386
　Pt VIIC, 372
*Data-matching Program (Assistance and Tax)
　Act 1990*, 385, 386
Endangered Species Protection Act 1992
　s 131, 153
*Environment Protection and Biodiversity
　Conservation Act 1999*, 154
　s 475, 153
　ss 475(6)–(7), 153
　s 475(7), 153
　s 487, 153
　ss 487(2)–(3), 153
　s 487(3), 153
Evidence Act 1995, 286
　s 17(2), 265
　s 130(1), 104
Family Law Rules 2004
　Pt 6.3, 417
Federal Court of Australia Act 1976
　s 23, 170
Federal Magistrates Act 1999, 8
*Federal Magistrates (Consequential
　Amendments) Act 1999*, 8
Freedom of Information Act 1982, 14, 60, 349,
　352, 354, 358, 375, 383, 384
　Pt IV, 356, 361
　Pt IV Div 3, 358
　Pt V, 353
　s 3, 355
　s 3(3), 352
　s 4, 356
　s 8(g), 356
　ss 8–8E, 360
　s 10, 356
　s 11, 356
　s 11A(4), 358
　s 11A(5), 60, 358, 366

s 11B(3), 61
ss 11B(3)(b)–(c), 61
s 11B(4), 368
s 11C, 356
s 21, 366
s 23, 361
s 29(5), 360
s 34, 364
s 43, 60
s 43(1), 60
s 43(1)(c), 60
s 47G, 60, 366
s 54M(3), 361
s 55K, 362
sch 1 pt I, 356
sch 2 pt II, 356
*Freedom of Information (Removal of Conclusive
　Certificates and Other Measures) Act 2009*,
　354
*Freedom of Information Amendment (Reform)
　Act 2010*, 14
*Freedom of Information (Charges)
　Regulations 1982*
　r 5, 360
*Hazardous Waste (Regulation of Exports and
　Imports) Act 1989*
　s 58A, 153
Income Tax Assessment Act 1936, 385
　s 177, 42
Judiciary Act 1903, 183–4
　s 38B, 188
　s 39B, 9, 97, 169, 170, 183, 186, 188,
　　189, 204
　s 39B(1), 183
　s 39B(1A), 183, 188
*Law Enforcement Integrity Commission
　Act 2006*, 312
Legal Services Directions 2005, 397
Marriage Act 1961
　s 111A, 225
Marriage Amendment Act 1976
　s 23, 225
Migration Act 1958, 19, 25, 34, 75, 97, 220,
　420
　Div 4, 424
　Pt 5 Div 5, 425, 435
　Pt 7 Div 4, 37, 435
　Pt 8, 281
　s 4, 423
　s 5E, 285
　s 6A(1)(c), 136

s 51A(1), 223
s 97A(1), 223
s 118A(1), 223
s 127A(1), 223
s 198A(1), 80
s 198A(3)(a), 80
s 353, 412, 420, 424, 425, 426
s 357A, 425, 434
s 357A(1), 223
s 357A(3), 424, 425, 426, 438
s 360, 420, 426, 427
s 360(1), 427
s 363(1)(b), 437
s 366A, 419
s 366C, 431
s 414, 418
s 420, 412, 420, 425
s 420(1), 424
s 422B, 434
s 422B(1), 223, 424
s 422B(3), 424, 438
s 425, 422, 423, 424, 427, 429, 434, 438
s 427(7), 431
s 462A, 422
s 474, 42, 281, 284
ss 474(1)–(2), 281
s 474(2), 285
s 476, 97, 285, 425, 434
s 476(1)(b), 434
s 476(1)(c), 434
s 476(1)(e), 434
s 476(2)(b), 198
s 476A, 285
s 486A, 284
s 500A(11), 252
Migration Legislation Amendment (Consequential Amendments) Act 1989, 169
Migration Legislation Amendment (Judicial Review) Act 2001, 19
Migration Reform Act 1992, 19
Migration Regulations 1994
    cl 202.211, 135
    cl 300.214, 122
    sch 4, 97
Military Rehabilitation and Compensation Act 2004
    ss 344–59, 33
National Health Act 1953, 386
National Security Information (Criminal and Civil Proceedings) Act 2004, 104, 117

Ombudsman Act 1976, 13, 15, 329
    s 3, 331
    s 3A, 331
    s 5, 331
    s 5(1)(a), 13
    s 5(1)(b), 13
    s 6, 331
    s 9, 334
    s 13, 334
    s 14, 334
    s 15, 332
    s 15(1), 328
    s 16, 335
    s 17, 335
    s 35A, 323, 335
    s 35B, 323
    s 35C, 323
    s 36, 334
Patents Act 1990
    s 51, 34
    s 109, 34
Privacy Act 1988, 371, 372–6, 384, 385, 386, 390
    Pt IIIB, 385
    Pt V, 387
    Pt VIII, 389
    s 2A, 373
    s 6(1), 374, 375, 378, 379
    s 6C, 375
    s 7A, 376
    s 13G, 388
    s 16(2), 377
    s 16A(1), 376
    s 16B, 377
    s 28, 386
    s 28A, 386
    s 28B, 386
    s 33C, 387
    s 33D(1), 387
    s 33D(3), 387
    s 33E, 388
    s 33F, 388
    s 36, 387
    s 38, 387
    s 40, 387
    s 40A, 387
    s 41, 387
    s 51(1A), 389
    s 52, 387
    s 52(1), 389
    s 55A, 387, 389

s 62, 387, 389
s 80W, 388
s 93, 389
s 96, 388
s 96(1)(c), 389
s 98, 389
Privacy Amendment Act 1990, 373
Privacy Amendment (Enhancing Privacy Reform) Act 2012, 373
Public Service Act 1999
s 13(10), 351
Public Service Regulations 1999
r 2.1, 351
Safety, Rehabilitation and Compensation Act 1988, 397
Social Security (Administration) Act 1999
ss 124Q–189, 33
s 142, 418
Statute Law (Miscellaneous Provisions) Act (No 2) 1983, 9
Superannuation (Resolution of Complaints) Act 1993
s 37(4), 409
s 37(6), 409
Taxation Administration Act 1953, 385
s 14ZZ, 34
Telecommunications Act 1997, 386
Telecommunications (Consumer Protection and Service Standards) Act 1999
s 128, 63
Telecommunications (Interception and Access) Act 1979, 371
Trade Marks Act 1995
s 35, 34
s 55, 34
s 67, 34
s 84D, 34
s 104, 34
Trade Practices Act 1974, 58
s 46, 57
s 80, 157
Veterans' Entitlements Act 1986
s 135, 418
Wheat Marketing Act 1989
s 57(3B), 58

Australian Capital Territory
ACT Civil and Administrative Tribunal Act 2008, 405
Div 5.3, 397
s 8, 411
s 9(1)(b), 404
s 9(2), 404
s 26, 411
s 81(3), 403
Administrative Decisions (Judicial Review) Act 1989, 11, 182, 189
s 4, 285
s 5, 400
s 5(1)(f), 272
s 6(1)(f), 272
Freedom of Information Act 1989, 352
Health Records (Privacy and Access) Act 1997, 390
Human Rights Act 2004, 86, 104
s 30, 87
s 32, 88
s 40A, 89
s 40B, 89, 90
Listening Devices Act 1992, 371
Ombudsman Act 1989, 329
s 3, 331
s 5, 331
s 6, 331
s 18, 332

New South Wales
Administrative Decisions Tribunal Act 1997, 405
Pt 4, 397
s 24(1), 403
s 63(1), 408
s 73(3), 411, 412
s 113(2), 403
s 115(1), 408
Civil and Administrative Tribunal Act 2013, 406
Environmental Planning and Assessment Act 1979, 158–9, 160
s 4, 156
s 98, 156, 159
s 123, 157, 158
s 123(1), 158
Freedom of Information Act 1989, 352
Government Information (Information Commissioner) Act 2009
s 30, 362
Government Information (Public Access) Act 2009, 354
Pt 3, 356
s 3, 355
s 5, 357

s 9(1), 357
s 12, 357, 358
s 13, 61
s 14, 61
s 14(1), 358
s 14(1), Sch 1, 361
s 14(2), 357, 366
s 15, 357, 368
ss 25–26, 356
ss 27–35, 61
s 32, 61
s 92, 362
s 106, 362
sch 1, 358
sch 1 cl 2, 364, 365
sch 4, 61
Guardianship Act 1987, 417
Health Records and Information Privacy Act 2002, 391
Independent Commission Against Corruption Act, 1998
   s 301, 322
Industrial Relations Act 1996
   s 179, 286
Ombudsman Act 1974, 329
   s 5, 331
   s 26, 332
   ss 12–14, 331
Privacy and Personal Information Protection Act 1998, 371, 391
State Records Act 1998
   s 50, 365, 369
Supreme Court Act 1970
   s 69, 272
   ss 69(3)–(4), 286
Surveillance Devices Act 2007, 371
Uniform Civil Procedure Rules 2005, 417
   r 7.18, 42

Northern Territory
Information Act 2002, 329
Ombudsman Act 2009, 331
   s 3, 331
   ss 10–14, 332
   s 14, 371
Ombudsman (Northern Territory) Act 1978, 329
Surveillance Devices Act 2000, 303, 308, 311, 315, 323

Queensland
Crime and Misconduct Act 2001, 352
Freedom of Information Act 1992, 371, 391
Information Privacy Act 2009, 372
Invasion of Privacy Act 1971, 11, 58, 182, 189
Judicial Review Act 1991, 188
   Pt 5, 400
   s 4, 285
   s 18, 190
   s 20(2)(b), 272
   s 20(2)(f), 200
   s 21, 272
   s 21(2)(f), 400
   s 31, 329
Ombudsman Act 2001, 331
   ss 7–10, 331
   ss 14–16, 331
   s 18, 332
   s 49, 329
Parliamentary Commissioner Act 1974, 405
Queensland Civil and Administrative Tribunal Act 2009, 397
   Pt 6 Divs 2–4, 397
   s 4(b), 408
   s 20(1), 411
   s 28, 412
   s 28(2), 404
   s 42(1), 397
   s 69, 397
   s 75, 403
   s 166(1), 396
Queensland Civil and Administrative Tribunal Bill 2009, 354
Right to Information Act 2009, 357
   s 23, 361
   ss 30–1, 357
   s 44(4), 357
   s 47(2)(a), 357
   ss 47–48, 357
   s 48(1), 357
   s 49, 357
   s 49(1), 357
   s 49(4), 356
   ss 78–78B, 362
   s 105, 357
   sch 3, 365
   sch 3 cl 2, 357
   sch 4, 368
   sch 4 pt 1, 366
   sch 4(7), 366
   sch 4(8), 131

South Australia
Co-operative and Community Housing Act 1991
   s 84(1), 131
Development Act 1993
   s 38(12), 156
   s 86(1)(b), 131
District Court Act 1991
   s 7, 397
   ss 31–2, 354, 361
Freedom of Information Act 1991, 362
   s 39(11), 322
Freedom of Information (Miscellaneous) Amendment Act 2004, 352
Independent Commissioner Against Corruption Act 2012, 322
   sch 2, 329
   s 3(3), 322
   s 7(4)(a)(i), 323
   s 25, 323
   s 54, 323
   s 54(2)(j), 323
   s 56, 322
Ombudsman Act 1972, 331
   s 3, 331
   s 5, 331
   ss 13–15, 332
   s 25, 327
   s 32, 352

Tasmania
Freedom of Information Act 1991, 11, 182, 189
Judicial Review Act 2000, 400
   s 4, 285
   s 15, 272
   s 17(2)(f), 203
   s 43, 372
Listening Devices Act 1991, 406
Magistrates Court Act 1987
   s 15AE, 329
Magistrates Court (Administrative Appeals Division) Act 2001, 130
Ombudsman Act 1978, 331
   s 3, 331
   s 4, 331
   s 12, 331
   ss 14–16, 332
   s 28, 371, 391
Personal Information Protection Act 2004, 354
Right to Information Act 2009, 359
   Pt 3 Div 1, 359

Pt 3 Div 2, 365
s 26, 362
s 47(1)(k), 359
sch 1, 359, 368
sch 2, 203
Rules of the Supreme Court
   r 623, 126

Victoria
Administrative Law Act 1978
   s 2, 272
   s 10, 285
   s 12, 144
Archaeological and Aboriginal Relics Preservation Act 1972, 133
Charter of Human Rights and Responsibilities Act 2006
   s 4, 87
   s 7(2), 87
   ss 8–27, 88
   s 28, 87
   s 32, 89
   s 36(5)(b), 89
   s 38, 90
   s 38(1), 91
   s 39, 90
   s 39(1), 91
   s 39(2), 122, 123
Children's Services Act 1996
   s 36, 123
   s 36(1), 122, 123
   s 36(1)(f), 122, 123
   s 46, 352
Freedom of Information Act 1982, 354
Freedom of Information Amendment (Freedom of Information Commissioner) Act 2012, 391
Health Records Act 2001
   sch 1, 322
Independent Broad-based Anti-corruption Commission Act 2011
   s 117(1), 371, 391
Information Privacy Act 2000, 391
   sch 1, 329
Ombudsman Act 1973, 331
   s 2, 331
   s 13, 331
   s 14, 332
   s 23, 130
Planning and Environment Act 1987
   s 57, 156
   s 82, 137

Right to Information Act 2009
  s 3, 372
Surveillance Devices Act 1988, 405
Victorian Civil and Administrative Tribunal Act 1998, 397
  Pt 4 Div 5, 411
  s 52(1)(c), 410, 412
  s 98(1), 411
  s 98(1)(d), 352

Western Australia

Freedom of Information 1992, 44
Mining Act 1978, 329
Parliamentary Commissioner Act 1971, 331
  s 4, 331
  s 4A, 331
  s 13, 331
  s 14, 332
  s 25, 405
State Administrative Tribunal Act 2004, 397
  Pt 2 Div 4, 412
  s 2(2)(b), 408
  s 27(2), 411
  s 32(2), 372
Surveillance Devices Act 1998, 240, 245

Canada

Canadian Charter of Rights and Freedoms, 206
  s 7, 10, 190
Federal Courts Act 1985
  s 18.1(4), 115
Immigration and Refugee Protection Act (2001)
  s 85, 31

United Kingdom

Agricultural Marketing Act 1958, 86
Human Rights Act 1998, 87
  s 3(1), 88
  s 4, 89
  s 6, 90
  s 6(1), 89
  s 6(3), 90
  s 8, 127
Senior Courts Act 1981
  s 31(3), 132
Special Immigration Appeals Commission Act 1997
  s 6, 73

South Africa

Constitution
  s 33, 73

New Zealand

Immigration Act 2009
  s 263, 81, 86
New Zealand Bill of Rights Act 1990, 89
  s 3(a), 89
  s 3(b), 206

United States of America

Administrative Procedure Act 1946, 166
Constitution, 206
  5th Amendment, 206
  14th Amendment, 81

United Nations

Convention on the Rights of the Child, 82
  Art 3(1), 81
Declaration of the Rights of the Child, 81, 87
International Covenant on Civil and Political Rights, 84
  Art 2(3)(a), 79, 112, 114
  Art 9, 84, 86
  Art 9(4), 114
  Art 13, 112, 114
  Art 14, 72
  Art 14(1), 371
  Art 17, 73

Council of Europe

Charter of Fundamental Rights of the European Union
  Art 41, 113
European Convention for the Protection of Human Rights and Fundamental Freedoms
  Protocol 7, 73, 87
European Convention on Human Rights, 112
  Art 5, 112
  Art 6, 73
  Art 6(1), 73

Australia

A v Hayden (No 2) (1984) 156 CLR 532, 103
ABC Developmental Learning Centres Pty Ltd v Secretary, Department of Human Services (2007) 15 VR 489, 122–4, 123, 138, 139
Abebe v Commonwealth (1999) 197 CLR 510, 19, 281, 285
Access For All Alliance (Hervey Bay) Inc v Hervey Bay City Council (2007) 162 FCR 313, 149, 152
Accused A v Callanan [2009] QSC 12, 189
ACT Health Authority v Berkeley Cleaning Group Pty Ltd (1985) 7 FCR 575, 57
ACTEWAGL Distribution v Australian Energy Regulator (2011) 123 ALD 486, 194
Ainsworth v Criminal Justice Commission (1992) 175 CLR 564, 212, 213, 221
Ainsworth v Ombudsman (1988) 17 NSWLR 276, 328, 335–6
Alister v R (1983) 154 CLR 404, 103, 104, 107, 109
Al-Kateb v Godwin (2004) 219 CLR 562, 79, 99
Alliance to Save Hinchinbrook v Cook [2007] 1 Qd R 102, 155
Annetts v McCann (1990) 170 CLR 596, 46, 219, 220–1, 212, 213, 216, 217, 218
Apache Northwest Pty Ltd v Agostini (No 2) [2009] WASCA 231, 47
Apache Northwest Pty Ltd v Department of Mines and Petroleum [2012] WASCA 167, 363
Applicant NAFF of 2002 v Minister for Immigration and Multicultural and Indigenous Affairs (2004) 221 CLR 1, 438
Applicant NAHF of 2002 v Minister for Immigration and Multicultural and Indigenous Affairs (2003) 128 FCR 359, 424
Applicant VEAL of 2002 v Minister for Immigration and Multicultural and Indigenous Affairs (2005) 225 CLR 88, 99, 100, 216, 412
Applicant WAFV of 2002 v Refugee Review Tribunal (2003) 125 FCR 351, 43
Applicants A1 and A2 v G E Brouwer (2007) 16 VR 612, 279
Ashley v Southern Queensland Regional Parole Board [2010] QSC 437, 197
Attorney-General (Cth) v R (1957) 95 CLR 529, 167
Attorney-General (NSW) v Quin (1990) 170 CLR 1, 17, 21, 23, 26, 47, 77, 124, 130, 170–1, 196, 198, 206, 207, 208, 216, 228, 242, 243, 244
Attorney-General's Department v Cockcroft (1986) 10 FCR 180, 363
Australian Broadcasting Corp v Lenah Game Meats Pty Ltd (2001) 208 CLR 199, 272, 372
Australian Broadcasting Tribunal v Bond (1990) 170 CLR 321, 23, 37, 45, 169, 185–6
Australian Communist Party v Commonwealth (1951) 83 CLR 1, 29, 171
Australian Conservation Foundation v Commonwealth (1980) 146 CLR 493, 72, 141, 143–4, 146, 148, 153, 155, 159, 161, 162
Australian Conservation Foundation v Forestry Commission (1988) 19 FCR 127, 155
Australian Conservation Foundation v Minister for Resources (1989) 76 LGRA 200, 75, 158
Australian Conservation Foundation v South Australia (1990) 53 SASR 349, 149, 155
Australian Education Union v Department of Education and Children's Services (2012) 285 ALR 27, 137
Australian Film Commission v Mabey (1985) 6 FCR 107, 57
Australian Heritage Commission v Mount Isa Mines Ltd (1997) 187 CLR 297, 201
Australian Institute of Marine and Power Engineers v Secretary, Department of Transport (1986) 13 FCR 124.161

Australian National University v Burns (1982) 64 FLR 166, 56
Aye v Minister for Immigration and Citizenship (2010) 187 FCR 449, 127, 285
Baba v Parole Board of New South Wales (1986) 5 NSWLR 338, 221
Baker v Commonwealth [2012] FCAFC 121, 265
Banks v Transport Regulation Board (Vic) (1968) 119 CLR 222, 212
Bankstown City Council v Alamdo Holdings Pty Ltd (2005) 223 CLR 660, 43
Bateman's Bay Local Aboriginal Land Council v Aboriginal Community Benefit Fund Pty Ltd (1998) 194 CLR 247, 146, 157, 161
Batterham v QSR Ltd (2006) 225 CLR 237, 279, 291
Bayley v Osborne (1984) 4 FCR 141, 57
Berowra Holdings Pty Ltd v Gordon (2006) 225 CLR 364, 254
Bickle v Chief Executive, Department of Corrective Services [2008] QSC 328, 198
Birdseye v Australian Securities and Investment Commission (2003) 76 ALD 321, 406
Blyth District Hospital Inc v South Australian Health Commission (1988) 49 SASR 501, 215
Bodruddaza v Minister for Immigration and Multicultural Affairs (2007) 228 CLR 651, 272, 279, 284, 286, 292, 294
Booth v Dillon (No 2) [1976] VR 434, 333–4
Botany Bay City Council v Minister of State for Transport and Regional Development (1996) 66 FCR 537, 160
Brandy v Human Rights and Equal Opportunity Commission (1995) 183 CLR 245, 16, 396
Brettingham-Moore v Warden, Councillors and Electors of Municipality of St Leonards (1969) 121 CLR 509, 218, 221
Brickworks Limited v The Council of the Shire of Warringah (1963) 108 CLR 568, 242
Bridgetown/Greenbushes Friends of the Forest v Department of Conservation and Land Management (1997) 93 LGERA 436, 153
Brodyn Pty Ltd t/as Time Cost and Quality v Davenport (2004) 61 NSWLR 421, 56
Bromby v Offenders' Review Board (1990) 22 ALD 249, 212
Bropho v State of Western Australia (1990) 171 CLR, 40
Budworth v Repatriation Commission [2001] FCA 317, 408
Building Insurers' Guarantee Corporation v Owners – Strata Plan 60848 [2012] NSWCA 375, 278
Building Professions Accreditation Corporation Tasmania Ltd v Minister for Infrastructure, Energy and Resources [2005] TASSC 73, 193, 197
C Cockerill & Sons (Vic) Pty Ltd v County Court of Victoria [2007] VSC 182, 390
C Inc v Australian Crime Commission (2008) 251 ALR 424, 47
Cairns City Council v Commissioner of Stamp Duties [2000] 2 Qd R 267, 197
CECA Institute Pty Ltd v Australian Council for Private Education and Training (2010) 30 VR 555, 54, 289
Chairperson, Aboriginal and Torres Strait Islander Commission v Commonwealth Ombudsman (1995) 63 FCR 163, 334, 336
Chase Oyster Bar Pty Ltd v Hamo Industries Pty Ltd (2010) 78 NSWLR 393, 55, 56, 289
Chiropedic Bedding Pty Ltd v Radburg Pty Ltd (2008) 170 FCR 560, 132
Chu Kheng Lim v Minister for Immigration, Local Government and Ethnic Affairs (1992) 176 CLR 1, 79
Church of Scientology v Woodward (1982) 154 CLR 25, 103, 104, 105, 107, 109, 171
Clancy v Butchers' Chop Employees Union (1904) 1 CLR 181, 277, 279
Clarence City Council v South Hobart Investment Pty Ltd [2007] TASSC 16, 193
Clyde Group Incorporated v Minister for Primary Industries and Water [2007] TASSC 95, 149
Coal and Allied Operations Pty Ltd v Australian Industrial Relations Commission (2000) 203 CLR 194, 259
Coco v R (1994) 179 CLR 427, 40, 78

Cole v Whitfield (1988) 165 CLR 360, 179
Coleman v Power (2004) 220 CLR 1, 134
Collector of Customs (NSW) v Brian Lawlor Automotive Pty Ltd (1979) 24 ALR 307, 268, 408
Comcare v Etheridge (2006) 149 FCR 522, 406
Commissioner for Railways (NSW) v Cavanough (1935) 53 CLR 220, 269
Commissioner of Police v Ombudsman (Unreported, NSW Supreme Court, 9 September 1994), 328
Commissioner of Taxation v Futuris Corporation Ltd (2008) 237 CLR 146, 256, 265, 269, 271, 272, 291, 292, 293, 294, 295
Commissioner of Taxation v Indooroopilly Children Services (Qld) Pty Ltd (2007) 158 FCR 325, 130
Commonwealth v Anti-Discrimination Tribunal (Tas) (2008) 169 FCR 85, 400
Commonwealth v Colonial Combing, Spinning & Weaving (1922) 21 CLR 421, 103
Commonwealth v Northern Land Council (1993) 176 CLR 604, 364
Commonwealth v Verwayen (1990) 170 CLR 394, 225
Commonwealth of Australia v John Fairfax & Sons (1980) 147 CLR 39, 351, 372
Condon v Pompano Pty Ltd [2013] HCA 7, 286
Cooper Brookes (Wollongong) Pty Ltd v Commissioner of Taxation of the Commonwealth of Australia (1980) 147 CLR 297, 132, 133, 138
Corporate Affairs Commission (NSW) v Yuill (1991) 172 CLR 319, 38
Corporation of the City of Enfield v Development Assessment Commission (2000) 199 CLR 135, 18, 21, 133, 177, 255
Craig v South Australia (1995) 184 CLR 163, 6, 18, 21, 178, 256, 259, 272, 283, 289
Crime & Misconduct Commission v Assistant Commissioner J P Swindells [2009] QSC 409, 198
Croome v Tasmania (1997) 191 CLR 119, 146
Cunliffe v Commonwealth (1994) 182 CLR 272, 23
Curragh Queensland Mining Ltd v Daniel (1992) 34 FCR 212, 200
Curruthers v Connolly [1998] 1 Qd R 339, 279
D and Wentworthville Leagues Club [2011] AICmr 9, 388
Daihatsu Australia Pty Ltd v Federal Commissioner of Taxation (2001) 184 ALR 576, 43
Darling Casino Ltd v New South Wales Casino Control Authority (1997) 191 CLR 602, 47, 282, 285
Davis v Commonwealth (1998) 166 CLR 79, 32
Day v Pinglen Pty Ltd (1981) 148 CLR 289, 142
Daycorp Pty Ltd v Parnell [2011] SADC 191, 367
Department of Immigration and Ethnic Affairs v Ram (1990) 69 FCR 431, 83
Dietrich v R (1992) 177 CLR 292, 72
Director of Housing v IF [2008] VCAT 2413, 89
Director of Housing v Sudi [2011] VSCA 211, 91
Dossett v TKJ Nominees Pty Ltd (2003) 218 CLR 1, 131
Drake v Minister for Immigration and Ethnic Affairs (1979) 2 ALD 60, 12, 132, 407, 409
Drake v Minister for Immigration and Ethnic Affairs (1979) 46 FLR 409, 408
Dranichnikov v Minister for Immigration and Multicultural Affairs (2003) 197 ALR 389, 22, 207, 257
Drummond v Telstra Corporation Limited (Anti-Discrimination) [2008] VCAT 2630, 89
D'Souza v Royal Australian and New Zealand College of Psychiatrists (2005) 12 VR 42, 54
Dunghutti Elders Council (Aboriginal Corporation) RNTBC v Registrar of Aboriginal and Torres Strait Islander Corporations (2011) 279 ALR 138, 133
E & J Gallo Winery v Lion Nathan Australia Pty Ltd (2010) 241 CLR 144, 43
Eccleston and Department of Family Services and Aboriginal and Islander Affairs (1993) 1 QAR 60, 350
Edelsten v Federal Commissioner of Taxation (1989) 85 ALR 226, 126
Edelsten v Health Insurance Commission (1990) 27 FCR 56, 126

Edwards v Santos Ltd (2011) 242 CLR 421, 144, 146
Electrolux Home Products Pty Ltd v Australian Workers' Union (2004) 221 CLR 309, 40
Elias v Director of Public Prosecutions (NSW) [2012] NSWCA 302, 263
Evans v New South Wales (2008) 168 FCR 576, 78
Ex parte Hebburn Ltd; Re Kearsley Shire Council (1947) 47 SR (NSW) 416, 258
Ex parte Helena Valley/Boya Assn (Inc); State Planning Commission and Beggs (1990) 2 WAR 422, 149
FAI Insurances Ltd v Winneke (1982) 151 CLR 342, 30, 73, 212
Fares Rural Meat and Livestock Pty Ltd v Australian Meat and Livestock Corp (1990) 96 ALR 153, 197
Fish v Solution 6 Holdings Ltd (2006) 225 CLR 180, 290
Fisher v Gaisford (1997) 48 ALD 200, 96
Flack v Commissioner of Police, New South Wales Police [2011] NSWADT 286, 357
Francis v Attorney-General (Qld) (2008) 100 ALD 600, 126, 126
Franklins Limited v Penrith City Council and Campbells Cash & Carry Pty Limited [1999] NSWCA 134, 159
G J Coles & Co Ltd v Retail Trade Industrial Tribunal (1986) 7 NSWLR 503, 278
Garland v Chief Executive, Department of Corrective Services [2006] QSC 245, 200–1
Gedeon v Crime Commission (NSW) (2008) 236 CLR 120, 257, 265
Geelong Community for Good Life Inc v Environment Protection Authority (2008) 20 VR 338, 47
General Newspapers v Telstra (1993) 45 FCR 164, 57
Gerlach v Clifton Bricks Pty Ltd (2002) 209 CLR 478, 31
Gibson v Minister for Finance, Natural Resources and the Arts [2012] QSC 132, 193, 196, 197
Gilligan v Nationwide News Pty Ltd 101 FLR 139, 103
Glenister v Dillon [1976] VR 550, 333
Gribbles Pathology (Vic) Pty Ltd v Cassidy (2002) 122 FCR 78, 209
Griffith University v Tang (2005) 221 CLR 99, 58–9, 181, 183, 187, 188, 213
Gypsy Jokers Motorcycle Club Inc v Commissioner of Police (2008) 234 CLR 532, 103, 105, 400
Habib v Commonwealth (2010) 183 FCR 62, 74
Haj-Ismail v Minister for Immigration and Ethnic Affairs (No 2) (1982) 64 FLR 112, 103
Haoucher v Minister for Immigration and Ethnic Affairs (1990) 169 CLR 648, 47, 213
Harris v Great Barrier Reef Marine Park Authority [2000] FCA 603, 221
Harrison v Melhem (2008) 72 NSWLR 380, 131
Hicks v Ruddock (2007) 156 FCR 574, 74
Hill v Green (1999) 48 NSWLR 161, 221
Hot Holdings Pty Ltd v Creasy (1996) 16 WAR 428, 44
Hot Holdings Pty Ltd v Creasy (1996) 185 CLR 149, 31
Hot Holdings Pty Ltd v Creasy (2002) 210 CLR 438, 48
Humane Society International Inc v Kyodo Senpaku Kaisha Ltd (2006) 154 FCR 425, 161
International Finance Trust Co Ltd v New South Wales Crime Commission (2009) 240 CLR 319, 29, 110, 206, 209, 216
J & MD Milligan Pty Ltd v Queensland Building Services Authority [2012] QSC 213, 196
J v Lieschke (1987) 162 CLR 447, 221
James Richardson Corporation v Federal Airports Corporation (1992) 117 ALR 277, 57
Jarratt v Commissioner of Police for New South Wales (2005) 224 CLR 44, 218
Jemena Gas Networks (NSW) Ltd v Mine Subsidence Board (2011) 243 CLR 558, 135
Johns v Australian Securities Commission (1993) 178 CLR 408, 212, 218
Jomal Pty Ltd v Commercial & Consumer Tribunal [2009] QSC 3, 400
K-Generation Pty Ltd v Liquor Licensing Court (2009) 237 CLR 501, 400
Kable v Director of Public Prosecutions (NSW) (1996) 189 CLR 51, 16, 29, 32, 265, 396, 400

Keach v Minister for Health and Human Services [2006] TASSC 28, 204
Khan v Minister for Immigration, Local Government and Ethnic Affairs (1987) 14 ALD 291, 194–5
Khuu & Lee Pty Ltd v Adelaide City Corporation (2011) 110 SASR 235, 52
Kioa v West (1985) 159 CLR 550, 10, 37, 47, 80, 95, 125, 126, 169, 189, 206, 212–3, 214, 215, 216, 218, 227, 228, 258, 260, 349
Kirk v Industrial Court (NSW) (2010) 239 CLR 531, 20, 29–30, 34, 86, 173–4, 175, 176, 185, 203, 246, 254, 255, 256, 258, 259, 260, 262, 264, 265, 267, 269, 272, 278, 279, 284, 286–8, 288–9, 291, 293, 294
Kirk v Industrial Relations Commission of New South Wales (2008) 173 IR 465, 289
Lacey v Attorney-General (Qld) (2011) 242 CLR 573, 39
Lark v Nolan [2006] TASSC 12, 198
Leghaei v Director General of Security [2005] FCA 1576, 97–8, 108, 109
Leghaei v Director-General of Security [2007] FCAFC 37, 98, 114
Lim v Minister for Immigration, Local Government and Ethnic Affairs (1992) 176 CLR 1, 79
Little v Commonwealth (1947) 75 CLR 94, 42
Lodhi v R [2007] NSWCC 360, 104
Long v Minister for Immigration and Multicultural Affairs [2000] FCA 1172, 432
M v P [2011] QSC 350, 204
Macquarie International Health Clinic Pty Ltd v University of Sydney (1998) 98 LGERA 218, 159
Magee v Delaney [2012] VSC 407, 88
Mahmoud v Sutherland [2012] NSWCA 306, 256
Maitland City Council v Anumbah Homes Pty Ltd (2005) 64 NSWLR 695, 285, 288
Malika Holdings Pty Ltd v Streeton (2001) 204 CLR 290, 40
Margarula v Minister for Environment (1999) 92 FCR 35, 158
Masu Financial Management Pty Ltd v Financial Industry Complaints Service Ltd (No 2) (2004) 50 ACSR 554, 54, 55, 56
Mazhar v Minister for Immigration and Multicultural Affairs [2000] FCA 1759, 434, 433
MBA Land Holdings v Gungahlin Development Authority (2000) 206 FLR 120, 52
McGinty v Western Australia (1996) 186 CLR 140, 265, 265–6
McGuirk v NSW Ombudsman [2008] NSWCA 357, 336
McKinnon v Secretary, Department of Treasury (2006) 228 CLR 423, 354, 362, 363
McLelland v Burning Palms Surf Lifesaving Club (2002) 191 ALR 759, 64
McWilliam v Civil Aviation Safety Authority (2004) 142 FCR 74, 187
Melbourne Corporation v Barry (1922) 31 CLR 174, 78
Metro West v Sudi (Residential Tenancies) [2009] VCAT 2025, 89
Michael James Austen v Civil Aviation Authority (1994) 33 ALD 429, 390
Mickovski v Financial Industry Ombudsman Service Ltd [2011] VSC 257, 55
Mickovski v Financial Industry Ombudsman Service Ltd (2012) 91 ASCR 106, 55
Mills v Commissioner of the Queensland Police [2011] QSC 244, 190
Minister for Aboriginal Affairs v Peko-Wallsend Ltd (1986) 162 CLR 24, 30, 80, 82, 124, 156, 160, 193
Minister for Arts, Heritage and Environment v Peko-Wallsend Ltd (1987) 15 FCR 274, 51, 73, 127, 215, 271
Minister for Immigration v Kurtovic (1990) 21 FCR 193, 195
Minister for Immigration v SGUR (2011) 241 CLR 594, 412
Minister for Immigration v SZMDS (2010) 115 ALD 248, 199
Minister for Immigration and Citizenship v Le (2007) 164 FCR 151, 197, 431
Minister for Immigration and Citizenship v Li (2012) 202 FCR 387, 425–6
Minister for Immigration and Citizenship v Li (2013) 297 ALR 225, 21, 33, 35, 45, 240, 245, 256, 257, 259–60, 423, 426–7, 430, 435, 437

Minister for Immigration and Citizenship v MZYHS [2011] FCA 53, 427
Minister for Immigration and Citizenship v SZGUR (2011) 241 CLR 594, 257, 428, 429
Minister for Immigration and Citizenship v SZIAI (2009) 111 ALD 15, 35, 197, 257, 418
Minister for Immigration and Citizenship v SZIAI (2009) 259 ALR 249, 439
Minister for Immigration and Citizenship v SZIZO (2009) 238 CLR 627, 19
Minister for Immigration and Citizenship v SZJSS (2010) 243 CLR 164, 22, 208, 257
Minister for Immigration and Citizenship v SZMDS (2010) 240 CLR 611, 22
Minister for Immigration and Citizenship v SZMOK [2009] FCAFC 83, 424, 425, 426, 438
Minister for Immigration and Citizenship v SZNVW (2010) 183 FCR 575, 423, 424
Minister for Immigration and Citizenship v Yucesan (2008) 169 FCR 202, 121–2, 124, 137, 138, 139
Minister for Immigration and Ethnic Affairs v Kurtovic (1990) 21 FCR 193, 196, 231, 233, 236, 243
Minister for Immigration and Ethnic Affairs v Mayer (1985) 157 CLR 290, 136
Minister for Immigration and Ethnic Affairs v Pochi (1980) 4 ALD 139, 12
Minister for Immigration and Ethnic Affairs v Teoh (1995) 183 CLR 273, 79, 81, 82, 92
Minister for Immigration and Ethnic Affairs v Wu Shan Liang (1996) 185 CLR 259, 45
Minister for Immigration and Multicultural Affairs v Anthony Pillai (2001) 106 FCR 426, 45
Minister for Immigration and Multicultural Affairs v Bhardwaj (2002) 209 CLR 597, 209, 268, 425
Minister for Immigration and Multicultural Affairs v Epeabeka (1999) 84 FCR 411, 45
Minister for Immigration and Multicultural Affairs v Eshetu (1999) 197 CLR 611, 35, 45, 285, 411, 420, 425
Minister for Immigration and Multicultural Affairs v Miah (2001) 65 ALD 141, 45
Minister for Immigration and Multicultural Affairs v Rajamanikkam (2002) 210 CLR 222, 200, 260
Minister for Immigration and Multicultural Affairs v SCAR (2003) 128 FCR 553, 421, 422, 423, 424, 428, 430, 433, 436
Minister for Immigration and Multicultural Affairs v SZFDE (2006) 154 FCR 365, 421–2, 436, 438
Minister for Immigration and Multicultural Affairs v Teo (1995) 183 CLR 273, 47
Minister for Immigration and Multicultural Affairs v W64/01A [2003] FCAFC 12, 195
Minister for Immigration and Multicultural Affairs v Yusuf (2001) 206 CLR 323, 19, 259, 260, 281
Minister for Immigration and Multicultural Affairs; Ex parte Applicant S20/2002 (2003) 198 ALR 59, 281
Minister for Immigration and Multicultural and Indigenous Affairs v SGLB (2004) 207 ALR 12, 429
Minister for Immigration and Multicultural and Indigenous Affairs v Yusuf (2001) 206 CLR 323, 420
Minister for Immigration, Multicultural and Indigenous Affairs v Al-Masri (2003) 126 FCR 54, 78, 79
Minister for Natural Resources v New South Wales Aboriginal Land Council (1987) 9 NSWLR 154, 131
Minister of State for Immigration and Ethnic Affairs v Teoh (1995) 183 CLR 273, 208, 227
Mitchforce Pty Ltd v Industrial Relations Commission of New South Wales (2003) 57 NSWLR 212, 279, 282, 286, 288, 291
Momcilovic v R (2011) 245 CLR 1, 21, 88, 265, 266
Mooney v Commissioners of Taxation (NSW) (1905) 3 CLR 221, 253
Muin v Refugee Review Tribunal (2002) 190 ALR 601, 260, 272
Mutual Life & Citizens' Assurance Co Ltd v Evatt (1968) 122 CLR 556, 225
MZXOT v Minister for Immigration and Citizenship (2008) 233 CLR 601, 279, 284, 285
MZYRX v Minister for Immigration and Citizenship [2012] FMCA 723, 435–6
N0500729, N9701858 [2010] MRTA 327, 102

NAAP v Minister for Immigration and Multicultural and Indigenous Affairs [2002] FCA 805, 43
NAAQ v Minister for Immigration and Multicultural and Indigenous Affairs [2002] FCAFC 300, 43
NAAV v Minister for Immigration and Multicultural and Indigenous Affairs (2002) 123 FCR 298, 282
NADR v Minister for Immigration and Multicultural and Indigenous Affairs (2002) 124 FCR 465, 43
NAFF v Minister for Immigration and Multicultural and Indigenous Affairs (2004) 221 CLR 1, 227
NAIS v Minister for Immigration and Multicultural and Indigenous Affairs (2005) 228 CLR 470, 257
NAKF v Minister for Immigration and Multicultural and Indigenous Affairs (2003) 199 ALR 412, 43
NAMJ v Minister for Immigration and Multicultural and Indigenous Affairs (2003) 76 ALD 56, 428–9, 431
Nation v Repatriation Commission (No 2) (1994) 37 ALD 63, 12
Neat Domestic Trading Pty Ltd v AWB Ltd (2003) 216 CLR 277, 55, 57–8, 183, 187, 207
New South Wales v Bardolph (1934) 52 CLR 455, 32
New South Wales v Kable (2013) 298 ALR 144, 258, 268
Nicholson v Federal Privacy Commissioner [2010] FMCA 716, 376
North Australian Aboriginal Legal Aid Service Inc v Bradley (2004) 218 CLR 146, 400
North Coast Environmental Council Inc v Minister for Resources (1994) 55 FCR 492, 75, 152, 153, 154, 155, 156, 158, 162
Northbuild Construction Pty Ltd v Central Interior Linings Pty Ltd [2012] 1 Qd R 525, 203
Ogle v Strickland (1987) 13 FCR 306, 75
Onesteel Manufacturing Pty Ltd v Whyalla Red Dust Action Group Inc (2006) 94 SASR 357, 149
Onus v Alcoa of Australia Ltd (1981) 149 CLR 27, 75, 144–5, 145, 147, 152, 153, 159, 162
Origin Energy Electricity Ltd v Queensland Competition Authority [2012] QSC 414, 195, 196
Orthotech Pty Ltd v Minister for Health [2013] FCA 230, 195
Oshlack v Richmond River Council (1980) 193 CLR 72, 30
Osland v R (2008) 234 CLR 275, 350
Osland v Secretary, Department of Justice (2008) 234 CLR 275, 361
Osland v Secretary, Department of Justice (No 2) (2010) 241 CLR 320, 254, 361
O'Sullivan v Farrer (1989) 168 CLR 210, 30
O'Toole v Charles David Pty Ltd (1991) 171 CLR 232, 280
Owen v Menzies [2012] QCA 170, 396, 400
P&O Automotive & General Stevedoring Pty Ltd v Chief Executive, Department of Justice and Attorney-General [2011] QSC 417, 200
Pape v Federal Commissioner of Taxation (2009) 238 CLR 1, 31, 32
Parisienne Basket Shoes Pty Ltd v Whyte (1938) 59 CLR 369, 176
Parkin v O'Sullivan (2009) 260 ALR 503, 103, 105
Paull v Munday (1976) 9 ALR 245, 121
Peninsular Anglican Boys' School v Ryan (1985) 7 FCR 415, 127
Perder Investments v Lightowler (1990) 21 ALD 446, 194
Perera v Minister for Immigration and Multicultural Affairs (1999) 92 FCR 6, 431, 432–3, 434
Petrie v Queensland Community Corrections Board [2006] QSC 282, 197
Phillips v Military Rehabilitation and Compensation Commission [2006] FCA 882, 390
Plaintiff M47/2012 v Director-General of Security (2012) 292 ALR 243, 99–100
Plaintiff M61/2010E v Commonwealth (2010) 243 CLR 319 (*Offshore Processing Case*), 54, 214, 217, 290, 417, 435
Plaintiff M70/2011 v Minister for Immigration and Citizenship (2011) 244 CLR 144, 80
Plaintiff S10/2011 v Minister for Immigration and Citizenship (2012) 290 ALR 616, 125, 126, 138, 139, 214, 217, 219–20, 229, 417
Plaintiff S157/2002 v Commonwealth (2003) 211 CLR 476, 6, 20, 33, 34, 75, 76, 78, 92, 172, 175, 222, 271, 280, 281–5, 288, 290, 291, 292, 293, 294, 294–5
Port of Brisbane Corporation v Commissioner of Taxation (2004) 140 FCR 375, 131

Potter v Minahan (1908) 7 CLR 277, 40, 218
PQ v Australian Red Cross Society [1992] 1 VR 19, 411
Prasad v Minister for Immigration and Ethnic Affairs (1985) 6 FCR 155, 197
Precision Data Holdings Ltd v Wills (1991) 173 CLR 167, 178
Project Blue Sky Inc v Australian Broadcasting Authority (1998) 194 CLR 355, 127–30, 138, 139, 269, 272, 291
Public Service Association of South Australia Inc v Industrial Relations Commission (SA) (2012) 289 ALR 1, 174, 288, 293
Public Service Board of New South Wales v Osmond (1986) 159 CLR 656, 9, 201, 349
Qantas Airways Ltd v Gubbins (1992) 28 NSWLR 26, 35
QCoal Pty Ltd v Hinchcliffe [2011] QSC 334, 199
R (on the Prosecution of Freeman) v Arndel (1906) 3 CLR 557, 253
R v Australian Broadcasting Tribunal; Ex parte 2HD Pty Ltd (1979) 144 CLR 45, 30
R v Australian Broadcasting Tribunal; Ex parte Fowler (1980) 31 ALR 565, 269
R v Bersinic [2007] ACTSC 46, 103, 104, 104
R v Coldham; Ex parte Australian Workers' Union (1983) 153 CLR 415, 179, 253, 282, 283
R v Commonwealth Conciliation and Arbitration Commission (1967) 118 CLR 219, 280
R v Commonwealth Rent Controller; Ex parte National Mutual Life Association of Australasia Limited (1947) 75 CLR 361, 279
R v Hickman; Ex parte Fox and Clinton (1945) 70 CLR 598, 20, 173, 280, 282, 293
R v Khazaal [2006] NSWSC 1061, 105
R v Kidman (1915) 20 CLR 425, 32
R v Kirby; Ex parte Boilermakers' Society of Australia (1956) 94 CLR 254, 16, 167, 283, 396
R v Lodhi (2006) 65 NSWLR 573, 104
R v MacKellar; Ex parte Ratu (1977) 137 CLR 461, 212
R v Murray; Ex parte Proctor (1949) 77 CLR 387, 42, 280, 282
R v Richards; Ex parte Fitzpatrick and Browne (1955) 92 CLR 157, 167
R v Taylor; Ex parte Professional Officers' Association-Commonwealth Public Service (1951) 82 CLR 177, 178
R v Toohey; Ex parte Northern Land Council (1981) 151 CLR 170, 73, 271
R v War Pensions Entitlement Appeals Tribunal; Ex parte Bott (1933) 50 CLR 228, 411
R v Watt [2007] QCA 286, 432
Re Bolton; Ex parte Beane (1987) 162 CLR 514, 131
Re Control Investments and Australian Broadcasting Tribunal (No 3) (1981) 4 ALD 1, 409
Re Costello and Secretary, Department of Transport (1979) 2 ALD 934, 408
Re Dennison and Civil Aviation Authority (1989) 19 ALD 607, 409
Re Ditfort; Ex parte Deputy Commissioner of Taxation (1988) 19 FCR 347, 31
Re Eccleston and Department of Family Services, Aboriginal & Islander Affairs [1993] 1 QAR 60, 368
Re Epifano and Privacy Commissioner [2010] AATA 489, 389
Re Gee and Director-General of Social Services (1981) 3 ALD 132, 411
Re Greenham and Minister for Capital Territory (1979) 2 ALD 137, 409
Re Howard and Treasurer of the Commonwealth (1985) 3 AAR 169, 367
Re MacTiernan; Ex parte Coogee Coastal Action Coalition Inc (2005) 30 WAR 138, 149, 152
Re McBain; Ex parte Australian Catholic Bishops Conference (2002) 209 CLR 372, 269, 272
Re Minister for Immigration and Multicultural Affairs; Ex parte Applicant S20/2002 (2003) 198 ALR 59, 10, 178, 182, 190, 199, 249, 261
Re Minister for Immigration and Multicultural Affairs; Ex parte Lam (2003) 214 CLR 1, 47, 83, 92, 100, 176, 208, 216, 226, 228, 230, 235, 238, 240, 241, 243, 244, 245–6, 258, 266, 272, 438
Re Minister for Immigration and Multicultural Affairs; Ex parte Miah (2001) 206 CLR 57, 40, 126, 218, 221, 222, 258

Re Minister for Immigration and Multicultural Affairs; Ex parte Palme (2003) 237 CLR 146, 291
Re Minister for Immigration and Multicultural and Indigenous Affairs; Ex parte Akpata [2002] HCA 34, 283
Re Minister for Immigration, Multicultural Affairs; Ex parte Applicant S20/2002 (2003) 198 ALR 59, 198
Re Minister for Immigration and Multicultural and Indigenous Affairs; Ex parte Applicant S134/2002 (2003) 211 CLR 441, 260, 439
Re Mullett and Attorney-General's Department [2012] AATA 103, 368
Re Pastoral Lease No 531 (1970) 17 FLR 356, 408
Re Ranger Uranium Mines Pty Ltd; Ex parte Federated Miscellaneous Workers' Union of Australia (1987) 163 CLR 656, 178
Re Refugee Review Tribunal; Ex parte Aala (2000) 204 CLR 82, 46, 46, 172, 216, 218, 253, 255, 256, 269
Re Rent to Own (Australia) Pty Ltd and Australian Securities and Investment Commission (2011) 127 ALD 141, 408
Re Residential Tenancies Tribunal (NSW); Ex parte Defence Housing Authority (1997) 190 CLR 410, 32
Re Roche & Commonwealth of Australia (1998) 16 ALD 787, 411
Re Rummery and Federal Privacy Commissioner (2004) 85 ALD 368, 387–8, 389
Re Scott and Commissioner for Superannuation (1986) 9 ALD 491, 132
Re Secretary, Department of Social Security and Diepenbroeck (1992) 27 ALD 142, 132
Re Visa Cancellation Applicant and Minister for Immigration and Citizenship [2011] AATA 690, 408
Re Wakim; Ex parte McNally (1999) 198 CLR 511, 269
Re Western Australian Planning Commission; Ex parte Leeuwin Conservation Group Inc [2002] WASCA 150, 155
Right to Life Association (NSW) Inc v Secretary, Department of Human Services and Health (1995) 56 FCR 50, 152
Rivera v Australian Broadcasting Corporation (2005) 144 FCR 334, 375
Rivers SOS Inc v Minister for Planning (2009) 178 LGERA 347, 160, 213
Riverside Nursing Care Pty Ltd v Bishop (2000) 100 FCR 519, 126, 221
Roads Corp v Dacakis [1995] 2 VR 508, 45
Robb & Dale v Chief Commissioner of Police (2005) 23 VAR 244, 209
Roche Products Pty Ltd v National Drugs and Poisons Schedule Committee (2007) 163 FCR 451, 124
Ruddock v Taylor (2005) 222 CLR 612, 268
Ruddock v Vadarlis (2001) 110 FCR 491, 85
Rush v Commissioner of Police (2006) 150 FCR 165, 47, 244
SAAP v Minister for Immigration and Multicultural and Indigenous Affairs (2005) 228 CLR 294, 19, 216
Sabet v Medical Practitioners Board of Victoria (2008) 20 VR 414, 89, 90, 91, 192
Saeed v Minister for Immigration and Citizenship (2010) 241 CLR 252, 35, 125, 216, 218, 219, 223, 266, 292, 296, 417, 420, 435
Sagar v O'Sullivan (2011) 193 FCR 311, 106, 107, 109, 117
Salemi v MacKellar (No 2) (1977) 137 CLR 396, 47, 212, 218, 227
Salisbury City Council v Biganovsky (1990) 54 SASR 117, 334
Sankey v Whitlam (1978) 142 CLR 1, 364
SBBS v Minister for Immigration and Multicultural and Indigenous Affairs [2002] FCAFC 361, 43
SBEG v Secretary, Department of Immigration and Citizenship [2012] FCA 277, 117
Schwennesen v Minister for Environment & Resource Management [2010] QCA 340, 187

Scurr v Brisbane City Council (1973) 133 CLR 242, 156
SDAV v Minister for Immigration and Multicultural and Indigenous Affairs (2003) 199 ALR 43, 176, 259
Seiffert v Prisoners Review Board [2011] WASCA 148, 126
Sellars v Woods (1982) 69 FLR 105, 57
Seven Network (Operations) Ltd v Media Entertainment and Arts Alliance (2004) 148 FCR 145, 389
Shahi v Minister for Immigration and Citizenship (2011) 283 ALR 448, 135
Shepherd v South Australia Amateur Football League Inc (1987) 44 SASR 579, 64
Shergold v Tanner (2002) 209 CLR 126, 361
Shi v Migration Agents Registration Authority (2008) 235 CLR 286, 12, 408, 409, 418
Shop Distributive and Allied Employees Association v Minister for Industrial Affairs (1995) 183 CLR 552, 149, 161
Shorten v David Hurst Constructions Pty Ltd (2008) 72 NSWLR 211, 131
Sidhu v Minister for Immigration and Multicultural and Indigenous Affairs [2007] FCA 69, 47
Sieffert v Prisoners Review Board [2011] WASCA 148, 292
Sinclair v Mining Warden (1975) 132 CLR 473, 155
Soh v Commonwealth (2008) 101 ALD 310, 98
State of South Australia v Lampard-Trevorrow (2010) 106 SASR 331, 131
State of South Australia v O'Shea (1987) 163 CLR 378, 126, 127
State of South Australia v Slipper (2004) 136 FCR 259, 221
State of South Australia v Totani (2010) 242 CLR 1, 110, 174, 288
STBP v Minister for Immigration and Multicultural and Indigenous Affairs [2004] FCA 818, 433
Stuart v Kirkland-Veenstra (2009) 237 CLR 215, 226
Sunol v Collier (No 1) [2012] NSWCA 14, 400
Sunshine Coast Broadcasters Pty Ltd v Australian Communications & Media Authority (2012) 130 ALD 589, 195
SZADC v Minister for Immigration and Multicultural and Indigenous Affairs [2003] FCA 1497, 192
SZBEL v Minister for Immigration and Multicultural and Indigenous Affairs (2006) 228 CLR 152, 100, 208
SZFDE v Minister for Immigration and Citizenship (2007) 232 CLR 189, 19, 48, 436
SZKUO v Minister for Immigration and Citizenship (2009) 180 FCR 438, 269
SZLBE v Minister for Immigration and Citizenship [2008] FCA 1789, 421
SZLDY v Minister for Immigration and Citizenship [2008] FMCA 1684, 433
SZMSA v Minister for Immigration and Citizenship [2010] FCA 345, 429–30
SZMSF v Minister for Immigration and Citizenship [2010] FCA 585, 431, 438
SZNKO v Minister for Immigration and Citizenship [2013] FCA 123, 198–9
SZOOR v Minister for Immigration and Citizenship (2012) 202 FCR 1, 199
SZQUH v Minister for Immigration and Citizenship [2012] FCA 265, 434
Tasman Quest Pty Ltd v Evans (2003) 13 TAS R 16, 203
Tasmanian Conservation Trust Inc v Minister for Resources (1995) 55 FCR 516, 158
Telstra Corp Ltd v Australian Competition and Consumer Commission (No 2) (2007) 240 ALR 135, 221
Theo v Secretary, Department of Families, Community Services and Indigenous Affairs [2007] FCAFC 72, 195
Theophanous v Herald & Weekly Times Ltd (1994) 182 CLR 104, 39, 137
Thomas v Mowbray (2007) 233 CLR 307, 108
Thorpe v Commonwealth (1999) 144 ALR 677, 74
Tickner v Chapman (1995) 57 FCR 451, 156, 160
Tien v Minister for Immigration and Multicultural Affairs (1998) 89 FCR 80, 83

TNT Skypack International (Aust) Pty Ltd v Federal Commissioner of Taxation (1988) 82 ALR 175, 406
Toulmin v Tasmanian Racing Appeal Board [2009] TASSC 115, 201
Trust Co of Australia (t/a Stockland Property Management) v Skiwing Pty Ltd (t/a Café Tiffany's) (2006) 66 NSWLR 77, 400
Truth About Motorways Pty Ltd v Macquarie Infrastructure Investment Management Ltd (2000) 200 CLR 591, 145, 157
Tunchon v Commissioner of Police, New South Wales Police Service [2000] NSWADT 73, 366
Twist v Randwick Municipal Council (1976) 136 CLR 106, 221
United Mexican States v Cabal (2001) 209 CLR 165, 34
United States Tobacco Company v Minister for Consumer Affairs (1988) 20 FCR 520, 155
Upham v Grand Hotel (SA) Pty Ltd (1999) 74 SASR 557, 221
Victoria v Master Builders Association (Vic) [1995] 2 VR 121, 52–3, 54, 56, 65, 215
Victorian Stevedoring and General Contracting Company Co Pty Ltd and Meakes v Dignan (1931) 46 CLR 73, 177
Videto v Minister for Immigration and Ethnic Affairs (1985) 69 ALR 342, 197
Wainohu v State of New South Wales (2011) 243 CLR 181, 206, 286, 288
WAIZ v Minister for Immigration and Multicultural and Indigenous Affairs [2002] FCA 1375, 433
Waltons Stores (Interstate) Ltd v Maher (1988) 164 CLR 387, 225
Water Conservation and Irrigation Commission (NSW) v Browning (1947) 74 CLR 492, 30
Waterside Workers' Federation of Australia v JW Alexander Ltd (1918) 25 CLR 434, 167
Waugh Hotel Management Pty Ltd v Marrickville Council [2009] NSWCA 390; (2009) 171 LGERA 112, 131
WBM v Chief Commissioner of Police (2010) 27 VR 469, 137
Weinstein v Medical Practitioners Board of Victoria (2008) 21 VR 29, 411, 412
Western Fish Products Ltd v Penwith District Council [1981] 2 All ER 204, 352, 354, 371, 391
Wide Bay Conservation Council Inc v Burnett Water Pty Ltd (No 8) (2011) 192 FCR 1, 161
Wiggington v Queensland Parole Board [2010] QSC 59, 194
Wijayaweera v Australian Information Commissioner [2012] FCA 99, 389
Wilderness Society Inc v Turnbull (2007) 166 FCR 154, 160
Williams v Commonwealth (2012) 288 ALR 410, 31, 254
Wilson v Minister for Aboriginal and Torres Strait Islanders Affairs (1996) 183 CLR 1, 16
Wingecarribee Shire Council v Minister for Local Government [1975] 2 NSWLR 779, 278
Woolworths Ltd v Maryborough City Council (No 2) [2006] 1 Qd R 273, 133
Wort v Whitsunday Shire Council [2001] QCA 344, 196
X v Minister for Immigration and Multicultural and Indigenous Affairs (2002) 116 FCR 319, 209
X7 v Australian Crime Commission (2013) 298 ALR 570, 33
Yang v Minister for Immigration and Multicultural and Indigenous Affairs (2003) 132 FCR 571, 9
Zheng v Cai (2009) 239 CLR 446, 39
ZMSF v Minister for Immigration and Citizenship [2010] FCA 585, 429

Canada

Baker v Canada (Minister of Citizenship and Immigration) [1999] 2 SCR 817, 239, 264
Canada (Attorney General) v Mavi [2011] 2 SCR 504, 236
Charkaoui v Canada (Citizenship and Immigration) [2008] 2 SCR 326, 114
Doré v Barreau du Québec [2012] 1 SCR 395, 262
Dunsmuir v New Brunswick [2008] 1 SCR 190, 262, 264
Mount Sinai Hospital Centre v Quebec (Minister of Health and Social Services) [2001] 2 SCR 281, 238–40, 244
R v Conway [2010] 1 SCR 765, 262
Re British Columbia Development Corp v Friedmann [1984] 2 SCR 447, 333

European Court of Human Rights

A v United Kingdom (2009) 49 EHRR 625, 112, 112–13
Al-Nashif v Bulgaria (2003) 36 EHRR 655, 114, 115
Chahal v United Kingdom (1996) 23 EHRR 413, 115, 116

European Union

Case 54/65 *Compagnie des Forbes de Châtillon, Commentry et Neuves-Maisons v High Authority of the ECSC* [1996] ECR 185, 226–7

New Zealand

Attorney-General v Udompun [2005] 1 3 NZLR 204, 209
Drew v Attorney-General [2002] 1 NZLR 58, 209
Furnell v Whangarei High Schools Board [1973] AC 660, 218
Hosking v Runting [2003] 3 NZLR 385, 372
Tavita v Minister for Immigration [1994] 2 NZLR 257, 81

United Kingdom

A v Secretary of State for the Home Department [2005] 2 AC 68, 114
Anisminic Ltd v Foreign Compensation Commission [1969] 2 AC 147, 18, 250–1, 251, 254, 256, 279
Associated Provincial Picture Houses Ltd v Wednesbury Corporation [1948] 1 KB 223, 46, 193, 197, 235
Attorney-General for Ceylon v AD Silva [1953] AC 461, 241
Attorney-General of Hong Kong v Ng Yuen Shiu [1983] 2 AC 629, 235, 245
AXA General Insurance Limited v HM Advocate [2012] 1 AC 868, 147
Bagg's case (1615) 77 ER 1271, 206
Bank of Australasia v Harding (1850) 9CB 662, 255
Belfast City Council v Miss Behavin' Ltd [2007] 1 WLR 1420, 71
Boddington v British Transport Police [1999] 2 AC 143, 251
Boswell's case (1606) 77 ER 326, 206
Breen v Amalgamated Engineering Union [1971] 2 QB 175, 31, 227
British Oxygen Co Ltd v Minister for Technology [1971] AC 610, 194
Calvin v Carr [1980] AC 574, 267
Campbell v MGN [2004] 2 AC 457, 372
Case of Proclamations (1611) 12 Co Rep 74, 271
CCSU v Minister for Civil Service [1985] AC 374, 73
Chief Constable of North Wales v Evans [1982] 1 WLR 1155, 269
Connock Chase DC v Kelly (1978) 1 WLR 1, 42
Council of Civil Service Unions v Minister for the Civil Service [1985] AC 374, 51, 127, 190, 215, 271
Davies v Price [1958] 1 WLR 434, 254
E v Secretary of State for the Home Department [2004] QB 1044, 263
Eba v Advocate General for Scotland [2012] 1 AC 710, 251
Ex parte Mwenya [1960] 1 QB 241, 84
Fisher v Keane [1879] 11 Ch 353, 64
Free Church of Scotland v Overton [1994] AC 515, 42
Ghaidan v Godin-Mendoza [2004] 2 AC 557, 87
Howell v Falmouth Boat Construction Co. [1951] AC 837, 231
HTV Ltd v Price Commission [1976] ICR 170, 232–3
Huntley v Attorney-General for Jamaica [1995] 2 AC 1, 221

In Re Racal Communications Ltd [1981] AC 374, 178
Inland Revenue Commissioners v National Federation of Self-Employed and Small Businesses Ltd [1982] AC 617, 146, 146, 147
John v Rees [1970] Ch 345, 208
Jones v First Tier Tribunal [2013] 2 AC 48, 263
Kanda v Government of Malaya [1962] AC 322, 209
Kruse v Johnson [1898] 2 QB 91, 240
Lazarus Estates Ltd v Beasley [1956] 1 QB 702, 48
Lever (Finance) Ltd v Westminster Corp [1971] 1 QB 222, 232
Local Government Board v Arlidge [1915] AC 120, 47
Mahon v Air New Zealand Ltd [1984] AC 808, 99
Maritime Electric Co Ltd v General Dairies Ltd [1937] AC 610, 232, 242
McLaughlin v Governor of the Cayman Islands [2007] 1 WLR 2839, 269
Norwich v Financial Ombudsman Service Ltd [2002] EWHC 2379, 338
Padfield v Minister of Agriculture, Fisheries and Food [1968] AC 997, 31
Pearlberg v Varty [1972] 1 WLR 534, 218
Pearlman v Harrow School [1979] 1 QB 56, 251, 262
Prohibitions del Roy (1607) 12 Co Rep 63, 271
R (Abdi and Nadarajah) v Secretary of State for the Home Department [2005] EWCA Civ 1363, 237
R (Anufrijeva) v Secretary of State for the Home Department [2004] 1 AC 604, 233
R (Bancoult) v Secretary of State for Foreign and Commonwealth Affairs (No 2) [2009] 1 AC 453, 271
R (BAPIO Action Ltd) v Secretary of State for the Home Department [2008] 1 AC 1003, 207
R (Bibi) v Newham London Borough Council [2002] 1 WLR 237, 237
R (Cart) v Upper Tribunal [2011] QB 120, 264
R (Cart) v Upper Tribunal [2012] 1 AC 663, 251, 264
R (Grimsby Institute) v Chief Executive of Skills Funding [2010] EWHC 2134 (Admin), 241
R (Jackson) v Attorney-General [2006] 1 AC 262, 71
R (Lumba) v Secretary of State for the Home Department; R (Mighty) v Secretary of State for the Home Department [2012] 1 AC 245, 234, 235, 268
R (Mullen) v Secretary of State for the Home Department [2005] 1 AC 1, 207
R (on the application of Begbie) v Department of Education & Employment [2000] 1 WLR 1115, 235, 243
R (on the application of Bhatt Murphy (a firm)) v The Independent Assessor [2008] EWCA Civ 755, 230
R (Roberts) v Parole Board [2005] 2 AC 738, 221
R v Board of Inland Revenue; Ex parte MFK Underwriting Agencies Ltd [1990] 1 WLR 1545, 234, 236–7
R v Bolton (1841) 1 QB 66, 254
R v Devon County Council; Ex parte Baker [1995] 1 All ER 73, 234
R v East Sussex County Council; Ex parte Reprotech (Pebsham) Pty Ltd [2003] 1 WLR 348, 207, 230, 232, 233, 241
R v Governor of Brockhill Prison; Ex parte Evans (No 2) [2001] 2 AC 19, 268
R v Hull University Visitor; Ex parte Page [1993] AC 682, 251
R v Inland Revenue Commissioners; Ex parte Preston [1985] AC 835, 233
R v Inspectorate of Pollution; Ex parte Greenpeace (No 2) [1994] 4 All ER 329, 150, 161
R v Ministry of Agriculture, Fisheries, Food; Ex parte Hamble (Offshore) Fisheries [1995] 2 All ER 714, 234
R v Nat Bell Liquors Ltd [1922] 2 AC 128, 254
R v North and East Devon Health Authority; Ex parte Coughlan [2001] QB 213, 207, 237, 238, 239, 243–4, 245, 246
R v Panel on Take-overs and Mergers; Ex parte Datafin Plc [1987] QB 815, 53–4, 54, 56, 65, 270, 289

R v Secretary of State for Foreign and Commonwealth Affairs; Ex parte World Development Movement Ltd [1995] 1 WLR 386, 147
R v Secretary of State for Home Department; Ex parte Pierson [1998] AC 539, 40
R v Secretary of State for the Home Department; Ex parte Simms [2000] 2 AC 115, 266
R v Secretary of State for the Home Department; Ex parte Tarrant [1985] 1 QB 251, 209
Rahmatullah v Secretary of State for Defence [2012] 1 WLR 1462, 85
Ridge v Baldwin [1964] AC 40, 212
Robertson v Minister of Pensions [1949] 1 KB 227, 231
Schmidt v Secretary of State for Home Affairs [1969] 2 Ch 149, 226, 231
Secretary of State for Foreign and Commonwealth Affairs v Rahmatullah [2012] 3 WLR 1087, 86
Secretary of State for the Home Department v AF (No 3) [2010] 2 AC 269, 113, 209
Southend-on-Sea Corporation v Hodgson (Wickford) Ltd [1962] 1 QB 416, 232, 242
W (Algeria) v Secretary of State for the Home Department [2010] EWCA Civ 898, 113
Walton v Scottish Ministers [2012] UKSC 44, 147, 155, 272
Wells v Minister of Housing and Local Government [1967] 1 WLR 1000, 231–2
Western Fish Products Ltd v Penwith District Council [1981] 2 All ER 204, 232, 241, 352, 354, 371, 391
Westminster Corporation v London and North Western Railway Company [1905] AC 426, 42
Wiseman v Borneman [1971] AC 297, 221
Wood v Woad [1874] LR 9 Ex 190, 64
YL v Birmingham City Council [2008] 1 AC 95, 89, 207

United States of America

Association of Data Processing Service Organisations Inc v Camp 397 US 150 (1970), 145
Boumediene v Bush 553 US 723 (2008), 85
Chevron USA Inc v Natural Resources Council Inc 467 US 837 (1984), 18
City of Arlington, Texas v Federal Communications Commission 569 US __ (2013), 177
City of Yonkers v United States 320 US 685 (1944), 175
Hunt v Washington State Apple Advertising Commission 432 US 333 (1977), 150, 161
International Union, United Automobile, Aerospace and Agricultural Implement Workers of America v Brock 477 US 274 (1986), 150
Lujan v Defenders of Wildlife 504 US 555 (1992), 146, 157
Marbury v Madison 5 US 87 (1803), 17, 18, 130, 146, 170, 171, 177
Sierra Club v Morton 405 US 727 (1972), 145, 149
Summers v Earth Island Institute 555 US 488 (2009), 145
United Food and Commercial Workers Union Local 751 v Brown Group Inc 517 US 544 (1996), 150
United States v LA Tucker Truck Lines Inc 344 US 33 (1952), 175

PART 1

THE STRUCTURE AND THEMES OF ADMINISTRATIVE LAW

ADMINISTRATIVE LAW IN THE AUSTRALIAN ENVIRONMENT

Matthew Groves and
Janina Boughey

Introduction

In 2008 the now late Professor Michael Taggart argued that Australian administrative law was in many ways 'exceptional' amongst common law jurisdictions.[1] He was right to suggest that Australian public law, especially perhaps administrative law, 'stands apart' from other common law jurisdictions. Indeed that trend has continued, and it seems that Australian administrative law is becoming increasingly distant from its counterparts in the United Kingdom, Canada and New Zealand.[2] Taggart and others have noted that much of what is exceptional about Australian public law can be traced to our written constitution.[3] The *Constitution* and its implications are now the dominant force shaping Australian administrative law at the federal and state levels.[4] The separation of powers doctrine implied from the division of the *Constitution* into three chapters, and the express protection in s 75(v) of the High Court's original jurisdiction to remedy unlawful administrative action, have been instrumental in driving the direction of Australian administrative law.

The growing influence of the *Constitution* has diverted attention from our unique statutory framework of administrative law, which also sets Australia apart from most other jurisdictions. The reforms made in Australia during the 1970s and 1980s, resulting in what is widely known as the 'new administrative law', developed a modern and 'comprehensive system of administrative law'[5] which sought to shift focus from the courts as the central institution responsible for executive accountability, by creating several new systems and agencies of administrative review.

This chapter provides a snapshot of the evolution and current state of Australian administrative law. It is by no means an exhaustive analysis of the Australian administrative law environment, which, as readers will come to appreciate by the end of this book, is vast, complex and intertwined with many other areas of law. This chapter presents a context for the more detailed discussion of specific topics

---

1 Michael Taggart, 'Australian Exceptionalism in Judicial Review' (2008) 36 *Federal Law Review* 1.
2 See, eg, Ben Saul's discussion of the distinctions between the Australian, UK and Canadian approaches to procedural fairness in national security decision-making in Chapter 5 of this book; Greg Weeks' analysis of the different approaches to legitimate expectations in various common law countries in Chapter 11; and Mark Aronson's discussion of the continued importance of jurisdictional error in the Australian context in Chapter 12.
3 Taggart, above n 1, 5; B Selway, 'The Principle Behind Common Law Judicial Review of Administrative Action – the Search Continues' (2002) 30 *Federal Law Review* 217, 229.
4 See, eg, J J Spigelman, 'The Centrality of Jurisdictional Error' (2010) 21 *Public Law Review* 77. See also the chapter by Chief Justice French in this book.
5 A phrase used by the Kerr Committee to describe its vision for Australian administrative law: Commonwealth Administrative Review Committee, *Commonwealth Administrative Review Committee Report*, Parliament of the Commonwealth of Australia Paper No 144 (1971) (Commonwealth) ('Kerr Report'), 71.

contained in later chapters. It begins with an overview of the 'new administrative law' reforms of the 1970s and 80s, and how those reforms continue to affect modern administrative law in Australia. The chapter then considers the major force that has shaped Australian administrative law in more recent years – which is, ironically, far older than the 'new administrative law' – the *Constitution*. The final section examines some of the most recent and developing implications of the way in which the *Constitution* is seen to interact with administrative law in Australia.

The reforms of the 'new administrative law'

The various pieces of federal legislation comprising the 'new administrative law' package of reforms are now almost 40 years old, but remain central to the Australian public law landscape. The reforms were enacted in response to the reports of three committees which investigated administrative law during the late 1960s and early 70s. The first committee, the Commonwealth Administrative Review Committee, chaired by Sir John Kerr ('Kerr Committee'), was asked to report on: the judicial review jurisdiction for the proposed new Federal Court; the grounds on which review may be sought, and associated procedures; and the desirability of Australia introducing legislation along the lines of the United Kingdom's *Tribunal and Inquiries Act 1958*.[6] In its 1971 report, the Kerr Committee noted that the size and powers of executive government – including Ministers, government departments and statutory authorities – had expanded dramatically over the 20th century.[7] It concluded that this burgeoning government power – particularly discretionary power – should be balanced by adequate mechanisms which would ensure that the executive government exercised its powers and discretions in a fair rather than arbitrary manner.

The Kerr Report found that the three main avenues available to Australians to challenge adverse government decisions were significantly limited. The first avenue involved a check on executive power by the judicial arm of government. Individuals affected by a government official exercising discretionary functions could seek judicial review from the relevant superior court (the High Court of Australia if the decision-maker was a Commonwealth officer, or the respective State Supreme Court for decisions of State officials). The Kerr Committee found that judicial review

---

6 Ibid. The UK legislation was enacted on the recommendation of the Franks Committee (*Report of the Committee on Administrative Tribunals and Enquiries*, Cmnd 218 (1957)).
7 Kerr Report, above n 5, 5.

of administrative action at common law was uncertain and complex.[8] The common law was based around the judicial remedies – the prerogative writs of mandamus, certiorari and prohibition, and equitable remedies of injunction and declaration – but these remedies carried a range of technicalities. For instance, each had different standing rules, time limits in which they could be issued, decisions they could remedy, and grounds on which they could be sought.[9] American Professor Kenneth Culp Davis famously described judicial review at common law as follows:

> An imaginary system cunningly planned for the evil purpose of thwarting justice and maximising fruitless litigation would copy the major features of the extraordinary remedies. For the purpose of creating treacherous procedural snares and preventing or delaying the decision of cases on their merits, such a scheme would insist upon a plurality of remedies, no remedy would lie when another is available, the lines between the remedies would be complex and shifting, the principal concepts confusing the boundaries of each remedy would be undefined and undefinable, judicial opinions would be filled with misleading generality, and courts would studiously avoid discussing or even mentioning the lack of practical reasons behind the complexities of the system.[10]

The second mechanism designed to achieve executive accountability, which is also built into Australia's constitutional structure, is responsible government. The principle of ministerial responsibility was intended to ensure that Ministers were accountable to the Parliament for the actions of their departments through various parliamentary processes, but it provides no clear means for individuals to bring complaints directly to Parliament or to force a Member to do so on their behalf. Parliament itself does not have the time or resources to review all administrative decisions alleged to be erroneous.[11] The doctrine of responsible government was therefore a political one, offering no direct rights to individuals who wished to challenge the expanding power of governments.

Finally, the Commonwealth Parliament had recognised the need for additional accountability mechanisms in some areas where it had established boards or tribunals to review or oversee the exercise of executive discretion in areas including

---

8 See, eg, S A de Smith, *Judicial Review of Administrative Action* (Stevens, 1st ed, 1959) 17, 29.
9 Kerr Report, above n 5, 9–20. Some of these aspects of the common law have now relaxed slightly. As Andrew Edgar notes in Chapter 7, there is increasingly a single standing test for each of the remedies, focused on 'interest'. Similarly, the range of decisions to which each remedy applies, while still different, is at least broader because of the expanded notion of jurisdictional error following *Craig v South Australia* (1995) 184 CLR 163 and *Plaintiff S157/2002 v Commonwealth* (2003) 211 CLR 476. Mark Aronson discusses these developments in Chapter 12 of this book.
10 K C Davis, *Administrative Law Treatise* (West Publishing, 1st ed, 1958) 388.
11 Kerr Report, above n 5, 7–8.

taxation, veterans' entitlements, and film censorship. The Kerr Report noted that these review mechanisms were far from universal.[12] There were no clear principles or policies governing external review of administrative discretions. The areas where the Parliament had established specialist tribunals to review administrative decisions revealed no uniformity in the procedures the various tribunals followed.[13] Though this flexibility had the benefit of each tribunal being able to develop procedures that suited its own decision-making context, the Kerr Committee noted that this created 'a situation in which there is a lack of publicity and ignorance of procedure which is a handicap not only to legal advisors but to litigants generally'.[14]

The Kerr Committee took on the monumental task of addressing the gaps in accountability that existed under Australian law. It considered reforms and suggestions from the UK, New Zealand, the US and France, and recommended a suite of reforms drawing elements from each of those jurisdictions but adding new ideas. The reforms were intended to produce a 'comprehensive system of administrative law', rather than the ad hoc accountability provided by existing mechanisms.[15] The system envisaged by the Kerr Committee included:

- conferring jurisdiction on the proposed new Federal Court to review the lawfulness of administrative decisions;[16]
- enacting legislation to simplify, and in some cases extend, the judicial review jurisdiction of the new Federal Court;[17]
- establishing a new generalist Administrative Review Tribunal to replace the many specialist tribunals;
- establishing an Administrative Review Council to conduct research on discretionary powers and advise the governments on the review and oversight of such powers;[18]
- establishing a 'General Counsel for Grievances' to investigate complaints that were either outside the scope of administrative and judicial review, or otherwise 'not worth litigating before a tribunal or a court'.[19]

Following the Kerr Report, the government established two more committees to further examine aspects of the proposed reforms. The Committee of Review of

---

12 Ibid, 5–7.
13 Ibid, 26.
14 Ibid.
15 Ibid, 71.
16 At the time of the Kerr Report, the Federal Court of Australia had not yet been established. The Committee recommended that, if the plans for the Federal Court did not proceed, a specialist administrative court should be created: Kerr Report, above n 5, 73–4.
17 Kerr Report, above n 5, 76.
18 Ibid, 83–5.
19 Ibid, 93.

Prerogative Writ Procedures ('Ellicott Committee') considered the proposed judicial review legislation. It agreed with the Kerr Report's recommendations.[20] The Committee on Administrative Discretions ('Bland Committee') largely supported the Kerr Committee's proposals for a generalist tribunal and Counsel for Grievances, and fleshed out those reform suggestions.[21] Australian administrative law was completely refashioned by the enactment of these recommendations. While the full force of those changes can only be understood by their cumulative effect, it is useful to note their key individual elements.

Administrative Decisions (Judicial Review) Act 1977 (Cth)

The *Administrative Decisions (Judicial Review) Act 1977* (Cth) ('ADJR Act') confers judicial review jurisdiction on the Federal Court of Australia and the Federal Circuit Court of Australia (previously the Federal Magistrates Court).[22] It also adopts many of the Kerr and Ellicott Committees' recommendations to simplify, codify, and in some cases expand, common law judicial review. The ADJR Act was a radical and innovative reform. It quickly became the primary vehicle for federal judicial review, and the Federal Court was the main venue for those cases.[23] That changed when migration cases were largely excluded from the ADJR Act. Migration applicants were left with only one avenue of review – the original jurisdiction of the High Court. As migration cases flowed into the High Court, attention quickly shifted from statutory review in the Federal Court to constitutionally based review in the High Court. This change has led to criticism about the value of the ADJR Act, but the many benefits of the Act, as described below, should not be forgotten.

1 Establishing a single, simple procedure for judicial review

The ADJR Act creates a single procedure for judicial review, which applies regardless of the grounds used or the remedy being sought. The Act also contains a unified test for standing. The ADJR Act process is therefore

---

20 Committee of Review of Prerogative Writ Procedure, *Report of the Committee of Review of Prerogative Writ Procedure*, Parliament of the Commonwealth of Australia Paper No 56 (1973) ('Ellicott Report') 5, 11.
21 Committee on Administrative Discretions, *Final Report of the Committee on Administrative Discretions*, 1973 ('Bland Report').
22 Originally, jurisdiction was only conferred on the Federal Court. The Federal Magistrates Court was established in 1999 by the *Federal Magistrates Act 1999* (Cth), and the ADJR Act was amended to confer jurisdiction on the Federal Magistrates Court at the same time by the *Federal Magistrates (Consequential Amendments) Act 1999* (Cth).
23 Mark Aronson and Matthew Groves, *Judicial Review of Administrative Action* (Lawbook, 5th ed, 2013) 60.

significantly more straightforward than applications made under the common law or the *Constitution*. Cassimatis and Billings explain in Chapter 9 that the jurisdictional formula of the ADJR Act has proved difficult to apply and has perhaps created as much complexity in Australian judicial review as it resolved. The ADJR Act applies to decisions 'of an administrative character' and made 'under an enactment',[24] which provides a narrower jurisdiction than s 75(v) of the *Constitution*. This difference meant that some cases not covered by the ADJR Act could only be heard in the High Court. In 1983 the Commonwealth Parliament sought to rectify this situation by conferring additional jurisdiction on the Federal Court, which matched the High Court's constitutional jurisdiction.[25] Thus the Federal Court has two sources of judicial review jurisdiction, each with slightly different coverage: the ADJR Act; and s 39B of the *Judiciary Act 1903* (Cth). Cassimatis and Billings explain how the gaps between the two avenues of judicial review have increased as the ADJR Act jurisdiction has been interpreted more strictly. The result has seen the Federal Court's s 39B jurisdiction – originally intended only to supplement the ADJR Act – overtaking the ADJR Act in usage and importance. The Administrative Review Council ('ARC') recently recommended that the scope of the ADJR Act be expanded to ensure that the Act could continue to do the job of simplifying judicial review.[26]

2 Establishing a right to reasons

Decisions are almost impossible to challenge if no reasons are given, yet there is no general right to reasons under Australian common law.[27] Both the Kerr and Ellicott Committees recommended that people with standing to seek review of a decision should have a right to obtain reasons for that decision.[28] The ADJR Act adopted this recommendation in s 13, which enables anyone entitled to apply for review under the Act to request reasons from the decision-maker. Although there are some limits to the right to reasons under the ADJR Act,[29] s 13 has been described as 'the most significant right introduced into law by the [ADJR] Act'.[30] That is because a right

---

24 ADJR Act, s 3(1).
25 Commonwealth, *Parliamentary Debates*, House of Representatives, 21 September 1983, 1046 (Lionel Bowen, Minister for Trade), discussing the *Statute Law (Miscellaneous Provisions) Act (No 2) 1983* (Cth) which inserted s 39B into the *Judiciary Act 1903* (Cth).
26 ARC, *Federal Judicial Review in Australia*, (Report No 50, 2012) 77.
27 *Public Service Board of New South Wales v Osmond* (1986) 159 CLR 656.
28 Kerr Report, above n 5, 78–9; Ellicott Report, above n 20, 8.
29 For example, the decisions listed in Schedule 2 are excluded from ss 13 and 13A of the ADJR Act. Decision-makers are also not obliged to provide certain confidential information.
30 *Yang v Minister for Immigration and Multicultural and Indigenous Affairs* (2003) 132 FCR 571, 583.

to reasons 'changes the balance of authority between the citizen and the state in a way the common law never recognised'.[31]

3 Codifying the grounds of review

Perhaps the most controversial feature of the ADJR Act is its codified list of the grounds of review. While other statutes around the world also do this, the level of detail in the ADJR Act grounds is unmatched.[32] Section 5 of the ADJR Act sets out a comprehensive, though not exhaustive, list of seventeen grounds.[33] These grounds were intended, and have been found, to restate the grounds available under common law.[34] The one exception is the 'no evidence' ground of review, which goes beyond the common law ground, although its precise scope remains unsettled.[35]

The English administrative law expert Sir William Wade cautioned the Ellicott Committee that codification might frustrate 'judicial development of additional grounds'.[36] The Ellicott Committee ultimately favoured codification but took heed of Wade's advice and recommended that the list of grounds include an open ended ground. The result was two 'catch all' grounds: that a decision is 'otherwise contrary to law';[37] or was an 'exercise of power in a way that constitutes abuse of the power'.[38] Neither ground has been widely used, perhaps because the enumerated grounds are sufficiently flexible to accommodate common law developments.[39] Justice Kirby suggested that the codified grounds of review in the ADJR Act had impeded common law development of the grounds of review.[40] He thought that Australia had not matched the expansion of a number of common law grounds of review in the UK since the 1970s because of the rigidity of the ADJR Act's grounds.[41] But others argue that codification of the grounds of review has made judicial review more accessible, both to lawyers and the wider public.[42]

---

31 J J Spigelman, 'Foundations of Administrative Law: Toward General Principles of Institutional Law' (1999) 58 *Australian Journal of Public Administration* 3, 8.
32 Eg, Canada's *Federal Courts Act*, RSC 1985, c F-7 sets out the grounds on which the Federal Court of Canada can review decisions in s 18.1(4). The six grounds set out are much broader articulations of the common law grounds than those set out in ss 5–6 of the ADJR Act.
33 Section 6 of the ADJR Act does likewise with respect to 'conduct' that may be challenged.
34 *Kioa v West* (1985) 159 CLR 550, 567 (Gibbs CJ), 576 (Mason J), 625 (Brennan J).
35 Aronson and Groves, above n 23, 248–53.
36 Ellicott Report, above n 20, 9.
37 ADJR Act, s 5(1)(j).
38 ADJR Act, ss 5(1)(j), 5(2)(j).
39 M Aronson, 'Is the ADJR Act hampering the development of Australian Administrative Law?' (2004) 15 *Public Law Review* 202, 214–16.
40 *Re Minister for Immigration and Multicultural Affairs; Ex parte Applicant S20/2002* (2003) 198 ALR 59, 94–5.
41 Ibid, 97.
42 ARC, above n 26, 127–8. See also Aronson, above n 39.

The ARC has concluded that the Act has had an overwhelmingly positive impact on judicial review in Australia, by improving the quality of government decision-making since 1980 and elevating respect for the rule of law in government.[43] A measure of the success of the Act is the fact that it has provided the model for statutory reform in the ACT, Queensland and Tasmania.[44]

Administrative Appeals Tribunal

The Kerr and Bland Committees were enthusiastic about the benefits of an administrative or 'merits'[45] review process – whereby an administrative decision can be appealed to an independent tribunal or board – to the quality of decision-making and to the cost of challenging administrative decisions.[46] Both committees noted that the proliferation of specialist tribunals was inefficient, confusing and inequitable, and recommended that these specialist tribunals be amalgamated into a single generalist tribunal.[47] The Administrative Appeals Tribunal ('AAT') was established by the *Administrative Appeals Tribunal Act 1975* (Cth) ('AAT Act') and has the express objective of providing 'a mechanism of review that is fair, just, economical, informal and quick'.[48] Unlike courts, the AAT must have jurisdiction expressly conferred upon it by legislation – there is no automatic right to appeal to a tribunal. The AAT now has jurisdiction to review decisions made under more than 400 Commonwealth Acts and legislative instruments. Its major areas of jurisdiction include tax, social security, workers' compensation for various Commonwealth employees, and veterans' entitlements.[49] The AAT also has jurisdiction over areas as diverse as space licences, fisheries management, trade marks and patents.

Although the AAT sometimes appears to function very much like a court and is sometimes criticised as too 'court-like',[50] its role is fundamentally distinct from judicial review. While courts ask only whether a decision-maker has acted within the legal limits of their power, the AAT asks whether the decision is 'the correct

---

43 Ibid, 73.
44 See, respectively, the *Administrative Decisions (Judicial Review) Act 1989* (ACT), *Judicial Review Act 1991* (Qld) and *Judicial Review Act 2000* (Tas).
45 The Kerr Report distinguished between review 'on the merits' and judicial review at a number of places – [58], [89], [90], [225], [289] – but did not elaborate on what the former entailed. Nor does the AAT Act use the phrase 'merits review'. As Robin Creyke explains in Chapter 18 of this book, the concept has largely been developed by the AAT itself.
46 See Bland Report, above n 21, 23.
47 See Bland Report, above n 21, 23–5.
48 AAT Act, s 2A.
49 Administrative Appeals Tribunal, *Annual Report 2011–12*, 22–6.
50 ARC, *Better Decisions: Review of Commonwealth Merits Review Tribunals*, Report No 39 (1995) 29.

or preferable one on the material before the Tribunal'.[51] The AAT is often said to 'stand in the shoes' of the original decision-maker because, like original decision-makers, the AAT may consider law, facts and policy, and may exercise discretion to determine the best decision in all the circumstances.[52] This metaphor is not completely accurate because the AAT usually also considers any new evidence or arguments from parties.[53] In other words, parties can lead evidence that was not before the original decision-maker. The AAT can also issue remedies that courts cannot, notably altering an original decision or making a new one.[54] Such powers mean merits review is more likely than judicial review to offer the different outcomes that applicants want.

The different function of tribunals means that they fall squarely within the executive arm of government, at least from a constitutional perspective. The situation at the State level is a little different – the separation of powers doctrine is not as strict.[55] This is another notable point of distinction from the UK, where tribunals are seen as a part of the judicial system.[56] Despite being creations of the Parliament and sitting within the executive arm of government, most tribunals have deliberately been set up with a significant level of independence from government, which is crucial for maintaining public confidence in them.[57] This independence is why many commentators suggest that tribunals are part of a fourth 'integrity' arm of government, along with the various other independent oversight bodies established in recent decades, such as Ombudsmen and anti-corruption bodies.[58] As AJ Brown notes in Chapter 14, independence is a key quality of the institutions which are part of the integrity arm of government.

Commonwealth Ombudsman

The Kerr Report noted that its proposals for the ADJR Act and AAT would not be sufficient to create a comprehensive system of administrative law because

---

51 *Drake v Minister for Immigration and Ethnic Affairs* (1979) 2 ALD 60, 68 (Deane J).
52 *Minister for Immigration and Ethnic Affairs v Pochi* (1980) 4 ALD 139, 143 (Smithers J); *Nation v Repatriation Commission (No 2)* (1994) 37 ALD 63, 68.
53 *Shi v Migration Agents Registration Authority* (2008) 235 CLR 286.
54 AAT Act, s 43.
55 Thus the generalist tribunals in the States and Territories exercise a mix of judicial and administrative functions.
56 W Wade and C Forsyth, *Administrative Law* (Oxford University Press, 10th ed, 2009) 776–83.
57 Gabriel Fleming, 'Tribunals in Australia: How to Achieve Independence' in Robin Creyke (ed) *Tribunals in the Common Law World* (Federation Press, 2008) 86.
58 This idea was first mentioned by the eminent Canadian scholar Professor David Mullan, in 'Administrative Tribunals: Their Evolution in Canada from 1945 to 1984', in I Bernier and A Lajoie (eds) *Regulations, Crown Corporations and Administrative Tribunals* (University of Toronto Press, 1985) 155.

not all administrative discretions were appropriate for merits review, and judicial review is 'necessarily limited in scope'.[59] The Report added that 'some complaints against administrative action are not justiciable at all or not, for reasons of cost, worth litigating before a tribunal or a court'.[60] The Kerr Committee recommended the creation of a General Counsel for Grievances, empowered to investigate and resolve complaints or steer them towards other appropriate avenues. The government ultimately accepted a slightly scaled-back approach recommended by the Bland Committee. The Bland Report suggested that the Commonwealth follow the lead of New Zealand, the UK, Western Australia and South Australia (which had in turn copied the idea from Sweden) and establish an Ombudsman.[61] The office of the Commonwealth Ombudsman was established by the *Ombudsman Act 1976* (Cth). Although Australia emulated many elements of overseas Ombudsman models, unlike most other models, which tend to locate the position as an officer of the Parliament, the Commonwealth Ombudsman sits within the executive.[62] Nevertheless, like the AAT, the federal Ombudsman has considerable independence from the executive.

Anita Stuhmcke explains in Chapter 15 how the role of the Commonwealth Ombudsman has evolved over time.[63] Its current role has been described by the former Ombudsman, Professor McMillan, as comprised of three main functions: investigating individual complaints received from members of the public about 'a matter of administration';[64] a proactive function of investigating matters on the Ombudsman's own motion, which tend to be matters of systemic maladministration;[65] and an ongoing audit/inspection role to ensure that law enforcement agencies in particular are complying with their legislative requirements.[66] The Ombudsman may only investigate the actions of agencies, not Ministers. On completion of an investigation (whether arising from an individual complaint or from the Ombudsman's own motion), if the Ombudsman finds that errors have occurred, they will report to the relevant agency and may make recommendations as to appropriate remedies, including that the agency apologise to an individual, pay compensation, change its procedures or policies, or that the Parliament amend the law.[67]

---

59 Kerr Report, above n 5, 93.
60 Ibid.
61 Bland Report, above n 21, 7–14.
62 Anita Stuhmcke, 'Privatisation and Corporatisation: What Now for the Commonwealth Ombudsman?' (2003) 11 *Australian Journal of Administrative Law* 101, 104.
63 See also ibid.
64 *Ombudsman Act 1976* (Cth), s 5(1)(a).
65 *Ombudsman Act 1976* (Cth), s 5(1)(b).
66 John McMillan, 'The Ombudsman, Immigration and Beyond' (Speech delivered to IPAA Seminar, Canberra, 25 October 2005), 1 <http://www.ombudsman.gov.au/files/25_October_2005_The_Ombudsman_immigration_and_beyond.pdf>.
67 Stuhmcke, above n 62, 105.

Government information: Freedom of information and privacy

The *Freedom of Information Act 1982* (Cth) ('FOI Act') did not form part of the Kerr, Bland and Ellicott proposals; however, because of the important roles it plays in supporting those reforms and government accountability more generally, plus the fact that it was introduced at around the same time, the FOI Act is generally considered part of the 'new administrative law' package. Australia drew inspiration for its FOI Act from the United States, but over time has developed its own unique approach to government information. The FOI Act was intended to make the federal government more accountable by providing individuals with a legally enforceable right to access government information. However, by the mid-1990s it was clear that the Act was not working as well as it could be to promote a culture of transparency and accountability within government.[68]

Judith Bannister explains in Chapter 16 the significant changes made, in 2010, to reform FOI.[69] These changes sought to reboot FOI by introducing a proactive publication scheme which requires government departments and agencies to publish certain documents, rather than making individuals request it. A public interest test was introduced for most categories of exempt documents, which means that documents can only be withheld if they fall within an exemption category and a public interest in withholding them is shown to outweigh the interest in disclosure. These changes also established an FOI Commissioner, to act as a champion for FOI issues within government and promote a pro-disclosure culture.

The 2010 amendments also recognised the important intersection between FOI and privacy, and amalgamated the new FOI Commissioner's office with the Privacy Commissioner into a new agency – the Office of the Australian Information Commissioner ('AIC'). The AIC's role is to oversee and advise the government on information policies and practices. The AIC also has a merits review function over decisions by government agencies about the release of documents under the FOI Act, and an investigative role under the *Privacy Act 1988* (Cth).

---

68 See, eg, M Paterson, 'Transparency in the Modern State: Happy Birthday FOI or Commiserations?' (2004) 29 *Alternative Law Journal* 10.
69 By the *Freedom of Information Amendment (Reform) Act 2010* (Cth); and the *Australian Information Commissioner Act 2010* (Cth).

A comprehensive system of administrative responsibility

The former Chief Justice of New South Wales argued that the effect of the new administrative law system arose from the cumulative impact of its individual parts. In other words, the sum total of the package contains more than its individual parts. Spigelman CJ explained that this was partly because the reforms had created a system of 'administrative responsibility'. According to this view, the individual elements of administrative law, such as freedom of information legislation and the availability of judicial and merits review over a wide range of decisions, have, in combination, introduced a distinct new form of accountability. Spigelman CJ explained:

> The cumulative impact of this entire body of reform... has been to introduce a new and distinctive character to our mechanisms of governance. What we now have, operating in parallel to the system of ministerial responsibility – both individual and collective – is a system that is appropriately characterised as 'administrative responsibility'... a system by which public servants have a direct responsibility for their conduct, not merely a derivative responsibility, through their minister and parliament.[70]

The importance of administrative responsibility was its consequence. Instead of seeking advice and support from their local MP, people can now easily launch their own challenge. Administrative responsibility does not cast off wider forms of political accountability. It instead acknowledges the right and legitimacy of people to directly challenge adverse government decisions. Another important feature of the new administrative law system is the complementary nature of its individual parts. Both the ADJR Act and Ombudsman legislation allow for the scrutiny of administrative decisions, but do so using different criteria. The ADJR Act allows for review of administrative decisions by fairly black letter legal principles. The more holistic criteria used by the Ombudsman consider whether administrative action is fair or just. Neither forum has the power to remake a decision that is found to be wrong. That is precisely the power given to the AAT. The apparent gaps in each part of the new administrative law system can only be understood in light of other parts. What cannot be achieved in one part can always be achieved in another.

---

70 Spigelman, above n 31, 7.

The rise and rise of the *Constitution*

Although the 'new administrative law' reforms have been somewhat overshadowed in the last two decades by a focus on constitutional aspects of judicial review, they continue to play a crucial role in shaping the relationships between the branches of government. Indeed a former Chief Justice of NSW has suggested that the institutions and laws of the new administrative law are so important that they form part of Australia's constitutional framework in a broader sense.[71] Others have suggested that we should reconceive the separation of powers, to recognise and accommodate the important role that many bodies outside the courts, such as Ombudsmen and Auditors-General, play in maintaining the division and allocation of power in our system of government.[72] The common theme in these and other attempts to incorporate newer aspects of our administrative law system within a revised conception of the separation of powers doctrine is that all assume the fundamental role of that doctrine.

The cornerstone of the Australian version of the separation of powers doctrine can be traced to the *Boilermakers'* case.[73] That and subsequent cases entrenched a two-fold approach to the separation of powers which prohibits the conferral of judicial powers on non-judicial bodies and the conferral of non-judicial powers on judicial bodies. One immediate consequence of these complementary limitations is the limitations imposed on both courts and non-judicial bodies. Administrative tribunals, for example, cannot make orders which are enforceable in the binding manner of court orders.[74] The corresponding restrictions upon courts and judges mean they cannot be invested with functions that are incompatible with the judicial function, such as conducting an investigation to provide advice to government ministers.[75]

These distinctions underpinned the new administrative law package because the AAT was created to perform a task placed beyond the reach of the courts by the *Boilmakers'* doctrine – the exercise of administrative power. A key feature

---

71 Ibid, 8.
72 J McMillan, 'Rethinking the Separation of Powers' (2010) 38 *Federal LR* 1.
73 *R v Kirby; Ex parte Boilermakers' Society of Australia* (1956) 94 CLR 254.
74 A point established in *Brandy v Human Rights and Equal Opportunity Commission* (1995) 183 CLR 245.
75 That was the function accepted by the judge in *Wilson v Minister for Aboriginal and Torres Strait Islanders Affairs* (1996) 183 CLR 1. That same year, the High Court declared invalid legislation conferring jurisdiction upon a Supreme Court to perform a non-judicial task: *Kable v Director of Public Prosecutions (NSW)* (1996) 189 CLR 51. The combined effect of *Wilson* and *Kable* is restrictions protecting the institutional integrity of judges and courts.

of merits review is the power to make a new decision. The AAT does this by assuming the same powers held by the administrative official whose decision is under review. Our separation of powers doctrine prohibits courts or judges from assuming that defining feature of merits review, but the courts eventually began to draw upon those wider principles to also explain the principles that underpin judicial review.

A convenient modern starting point is *Attorney-General (NSW) v Quin*,[76] in which Brennan J adopted a conception of judicial review aligned with the landmark American case of *Marbury v Madison*.[77] In the American case the US Supreme Court explained that in a system of government containing a written constitution which divided and allocated power between the three arms of government, the 'province and duty' of the courts was to declare and apply the law. The Supreme Court reasoned that this function enabled it to review legislation and, where appropriate, declare statutes invalid on constitutional grounds.[78] *Marbury* explained the division of power and functions between the courts and legislature. In *Quin's* case, Brennan J explained a similar division of power and functions between the courts and the executive. The result articulated the purpose and scope of judicial review of administrative action within a constitutional framework. Brennan J explained:

> The duty and jurisdiction of the court to review administrative action do not go beyond the declaration and enforcing of the law which determinates the limits and governs the exercise of the repository's power. If, in doing so, the court avoids administrative injustice or error, so be it; but the court has no jurisdiction to simply cure administrative injustice or error. The merits of administrative action, to the extent that they can be distinguished from legality, are for the repository of the relevant power alone and, subject to political control, for the repository alone.[79]

Several important consequences flowed from this reasoning. Perhaps the most important was an acceptance that the role of the courts in judicial review is a mixture of constitutional duty and limits. The function of the courts is to decide questions of law. Accordingly, their role in judicial review of administrative action is limited to questions of legal validity. It does not extend to reviewing or correcting the factual merits of administrative decision-making.[80]

---

76 (1990) 170 CLR 1.
77 1 Cranch 137; 5 US 137 (1803).
78 This jurisdiction marked a radical break from English law.
79 *Attorney-General (NSW) v Quin* (1990) 170 CLR 1, 35–6.
80 Research shows judicial review still affects final outcomes because successful judicial review applicants have a much greater chance of ultimately securing a more favourable decision after their judicial review case has ended: R Creyke and J McMillan, 'Judicial Review Outcomes – An Empirical Study' (2004) 11 *Australian Journal of Administrative Law* 82.

The High Court took another important step in *Craig v South Australia*,[81] where it endorsed, or arguably revived, the concept of jurisdictional error as a guiding principle for courts to determine the constitutional limits upon the jurisdiction of tribunals and administrative officials.[82] *Craig* was important for other reasons. It made clear that superior courts would be especially vigilant to correct jurisdictional errors made by administrative tribunals and officials. *Craig* also adopted a vague and open ended approach to jurisdictional error, which has provided the basis for a relentless expansion in the scope of errors which can be categorised as jurisdictional.[83]

An important further step was taken in *Corporation of the City of Enfield v Development Assessment Commission*,[84] when the High Court rejected a pragmatic exception to the separation of powers doctrine adopted by the US Supreme Court in *Chevron USA Inc v Natural Resources Council Inc*.[85] The so-called *Chevron* doctrine allows courts to sometimes defer to the interpretation of statutes by administrative agencies. The doctrine provides an exception to the *Marbury* principle by allowing administrative agencies to decide the meaning of laws in some cases. The issue in *Enfield* was the slightly different one of deference to findings of fact (in that case it was a jurisdictional fact) by administrative agencies, but the High Court took the occasion to bluntly reject any American style of softening of the *Marbury* doctrine. The High Court held that questions about the existence of jurisdictional facts were ultimately legal ones over which the courts had the final say. It also made clear that this approach reflects broader limits on both the executive and the courts. Administrative officials and bodies cannot trespass into the judicial realm of declaring and law, but courts are similarly prohibited from entering the executive terrain of the merits of administrative decisions.[86]

These and other cases signalled the development of a more coherent explanation of the purpose and place of judicial review within our constitutional framework. They also hinted at an underlying assumption that judicial review of administrative action would always be available. If successive federal governments had realised and accepted that assumption, they may not have lost so many migration cases. Migration law became the key battleground in administrative law when successive

---

81 (1995) 184 CLR 163.
82 *Craig* can be said to have revived jurisdictional error because the distinction between jurisdictional and non-jurisdictional errors was largely discarded by the House of Lords in *Anisminic Ltd v Foreign Compensation Commission* [1969] 2 AC 147.
83 As Mark Aronson notes in Chapter 12, the open ended nature of the jurisdictional error doctrine has been crucial to its expansion.
84 (2000) 199 CLR 135.
85 467 US 837 (1984).
86 *Corporation of the City of Enfield v Development Assessment Commission* (2000) 199 CLR 135, 152–4.

federal governments sought to restrict review rights of refugee claimants. The ADJR Act influenced this battle in two ways. First, refugee and other claimants were excluded from the ADJR Act. That change quickly turned attention to the previously neglected original jurisdiction of the High Court. Second, the exclusion of ADJR Act review was replaced for refugee cases by several grounds listed in the *Migration Act 1958* (Cth).[87] The ADJR Act thus provided the initial point of reference, from which certain grounds were stripped away.

The High Court accepted the validity of these restricted grounds of review, mainly because they limited the grounds in Federal Court but not High Court proceedings.[88] The High Court also held that the errors which could be regarded as jurisdictional for the purposes of the procedures governing migration decisions were not limited to the examples of jurisdictional error provided in *Craig*.[89] This last finding meant that, even if the Commonwealth could limit the available grounds of judicial review, it would struggle to limit the basis upon which those grounds could be sought. The High Court threw many other spanners into the machinery of migration legislation. An especially difficult issue arose about the consequences of failures to observe the exact detail of the ever increasing procedures governing migration decisions, which were, ironically, introduced to clarify and exhaustively state the duties of decision-makers. Some cases held that statutory procedures governing important issues, such as rights of notice and appearance at hearings, were so central that any breach of them would normally constitute jurisdictional error.[90] Others held that a finding of jurisdictional error depended on satisfaction of the substance rather than form of procedures.[91] These decisions illustrate the analysis of Linda Pearson in Chapter 19 of the difficulty in providing a fair hearing in migration cases. They also show that attempts to codify hearing procedures, or to limit the grounds upon which decisions could be reviewed, cause as many problems as they resolve.

The Commonwealth responded by enacting a privative clause which sought to exclude judicial review from a wide range of decisions, purported decisions and

---

87 These and other reforms were introduced by the *Migration Reform Act 1992* (Cth), which was eventually repealed by the *Migration Legislation Amendment (Judicial Review) Act 2001* (Cth).
88 *Abebe v Commonwealth* (1999) 197 CLR 510.
89 *Minister for Immigration and Multicultural Affairs v Yusuf* (2001) 206 CLR 323, [81]–[85].
90 See, eg, *SAAP v Minister for Immigration and Multicultural and Indigenous Affairs* (2005) 228 CLR 294, 321–2 (McHugh J), 345–6 (Kirby J), 353–4 (Hayne J); *SZFDE v Minister for Immigration and Citizenship* (2007) 232 CLR 189, 201, 205–7 (per curiam).
91 See, eg, *Minister for Immigration and Citizenship v SZIZO* (2009) 238 CLR 627, 640 where French CJ, Gummow, Hayne, Crennan and Bell JJ explained that a detailed scheme to provide notice to refugee claimants was 'not an end in itself'. Their Honours held no jurisdictional error occurred if the provisions were not followed exactly but applicants still received all required information.

related conduct. The clause was carefully drafted by reference to a long-standing decision of the High Court, which appeared to accept the validity of privative clauses so long as they met a series of specific requirements.[92] Simon Young explains in Chapter 13 how the High Court adopted reasoning which held that the clause was constitutionally valid but left it with little effective operation. The High Court also invoked constitutional principles when it reasoned that privative clauses must be interpreted in light of the 'minimum entrenched provision of judicial review' introduced by s 75(v) of the *Constitution*. The Court reasoned:

> The centrality and protective purpose of this jurisdiction of this Court ... places significant barriers in the way of legislative attempts to impair judicial review of administrative action. Such jurisdiction exists to maintain the federal compact by ensuring that propounded laws are constitutionally valid and ministerial and other official action lawful and within jurisdiction ...[93]

Such reasoning confirmed the constitutional entrenchment of judicial review and also the central function of jurisdictional error in demarcating the limits of administrative powers and the reach of supervisory review. The result was a devastating judicial response to privative clauses. It was all the more devastating, or unyielding, because of its constitutional rationale. The constitutional function of the courts was to detect and correct any jurisdictional error. The constitutional basis of that role precluded the enactment of privative clauses that limited or excluded this judicial function. At the same time, the nebulous and expanding nature of jurisdictional error meant that legislatures could never be sure when it might be invoked. The only certain thing about privative clauses now is their inevitable failure.

The most recent notable step, though certainly not the last, occurred in *Kirk v Industrial Court (NSW)*,[94] when the High Court essentially extended the principles developed at the federal level to State judicial review. The High Court held that the single integrated judicial system established by s 73 of the *Constitution*, which invests the High Court with appellate jurisdiction from the State Supreme Courts, presumed among other things that those State courts would continue to exist and exercise their core function of supervisory review over State executive or administrative action. The High Court held that function of the State Supreme Courts existed to enable them to detect and prevent jurisdictional error at the State level. It followed that legislation seeking to remove or diminish that jurisdiction was invalid on constitutional grounds.

---

92 *R v Hickman; Ex parte Fox and Clinton* (1945) 70 CLR 598.
93 *Plaintiff S157/2002 v Commonwealth* (2003) 211 CLR 476, 513–14.
94 (2010) 239 CLR 531.

The reasoning in *Kirk* surprised most observers and is not supported by either the text or history of the *Constitution*, but it arguably represents a logical step in Australian law. After all, the key cases of *Quin*, *Craig* and *Enfield* were appeals from State courts about State law. They gave rise to broad constitutional principles which drew no significant distinction between the judicial review doctrine applicable to State and federal courts. If the judicial review jurisdiction of State and federal courts is governed by the same constitutional fundamentals, the step required to place State courts in the same constitutionally protected position is a relatively small and arguably natural one.

Conclusion – *Constitution*, common law and statute

The road down which the High Court has travelled to explain the entrenched nature of its own supervisory jurisdiction, and now also that of the State Supreme Courts, has not been a one way journey. Just as the High Court has emphatically asserted that the *Constitution* secures the supervisory role of the courts, it has also conceded that constitutional principles necessarily keep the courts away from some areas. The constitutional security granted to judicial review weakens as its grounds move closer to merits review. It is for this reason that the High Court has disapproved of the more expansive grounds of review accepted in other jurisdictions, such as the English doctrine of substantive unfairness. As Greg Weeks explains in Chapter 11, substantive unfairness and doctrines such as estoppel are unlikely to be adopted in Australia because they require a qualitative rather than procedural approach to fairness. Such reasoning appears too close to merits review for the comfort of Australian courts. Proportionality may suffer a similar fate because the various expressions of that ground require a balancing process between the infringement of rights and the legitimacy of any official objective for infringement. That also smacks of merits review.[95]

A closer inspection of many cases suggests that dividing lines drawn on constitutional principles do not always translate into precise principles of review. While the High Court has affirmed the fundamental nature of the review/merits divide, it often explains grounds of review in a way that allows a more open

---

[95] There is an added problem: that no clear explanation of proportionality in judicial review arose from *Momcilovic v R* (2011) 245 CLR 1. Proportionality seemed to be endorsed, albeit in passing, by Hayne, Kiefel and Bell JJ in *Minister for Immigration and Citizenship v Li* (2013) 297 ALR 570, [73]–[74]. Their Honours described giving 'excessive weight – more than was reasonably necessary' to a matter as 'an obviously disproportionate response' which could support a finding of unreasonableness.

consideration of the facts and merits of cases. Gummow and Callinan JJ, for example, have accepted that the failure of a decision-maker 'to respond to a substantial, clearly articulated argument relying upon established facts' is a denial of natural justice.[96] Examining whether decision-makers have responded to an argument could easily invite consideration of whether they have done so adequately. In another case, Crennan and Bell JJ explained that illogicality or irrationality (and therefore invalidity) could be established:

> [i]f only one conclusion is open on the evidence, and the decision maker does not come to that conclusion, or if the decision to which the decision maker came was simply not open on the evidence or if there is no logical connection between the evidence and the inferences or conclusions drawn.[97]

Such examples presume some cases are so clear cut that examination of the reasoning process and its outcome is possible without a descent into merits review. In truth, any judgement to label a case as clear cut, or one on which reasonable minds could only reach one conclusion, requires an assessment of the evidence and value judgements that veer towards merits review.

The *Constitution* is not the sole influence on the scope of judicial review. The creation of a merits review tribunal with a wider jurisdiction than any other tribunal in the common law world must have had *some* influence on judicial review, but the exact influence of the AAT is unclear. Some argue that the AAT has served to formalise and confine the scope of judicial review. Cane argues that the theory and practice of merits review are quite different, and that merits review operates as a thinly disguised form of judicial review in which the AAT performs a quasi-judicial role.[98] He suggests that Australian 'judicial review would probably have developed to cover all or most of the ground now occupied by merits review' if the AAT had not been created.[99] If merits review is a veiled form of judicial review, one might question whether the AAT really has frustrated the evolution of judicial review. It may have simply enabled the more adventurous parts of judicial review that developed in other common law jurisdictions to be rebadged within the work of the AAT.

The courts sometimes allude to the AAT's role when exercising their own jurisdiction. The AAT has been variously invoked as one of several 'powerful

---

96 *Dranichnikov v Minister for Immigration and Multicultural Affairs* (2003) 197 ALR 389, [24]. This passage was endorsed by a unanimous High Court in *Minister for Immigration and Citizenship v SZJSS* (2010) 243 CLR 164, 177.
97 *Minister for Immigration and Citizenship v SZMDS* (2010) 240 CLR 611, 649–50.
98 P Cane, *Administrative Tribunals and Adjudications* (2009) 179.
99 P Cane, 'Merits Review and Judicial Review – The AAT as Trojan Horse' (2000) 28 *Federal Law Review* 213, 243.

considerations' why courts should adopt a cautious approach to fact-finding in judicial review,[100] and why the grant of very wide discretionary powers is difficult to impeach on constitutional grounds.[101] Some judges have also acknowledged that tribunals may be better suited for those tasks which lie at the heart of merits review. Sir Gerard Brennan conceded that courts were not well suited to formulating or evaluating policy, and appeared relieved that the AAT was assigned this task and was 'armed with authority to apply whatever policy it thinks appropriate'.[102] Sir Gerard also accepted that the courts were fenced out of the 'lush field of policy'.[103] Later, in *Quin's* case,[104] he saw the green grass of merits review as a 'forbidden field'.

Any such clear division between judicial and merits review begs the question of which came first – the chicken or the egg? Does the courts' acceptance that the new administrative law package divided judicial and merits review mean that the two would necessarily have merged under an expansive conception of judicial review if we did not have the AAT? Was the rigid Australian distinction between judicial and merits review caused or simply recognised by the creation of the AAT? Such questions highlight the likely influence of the statutory elements of our administrative law system upon the development of constitutional principles. The same is true of the common law. The lack of a general common law right to reasons, for example, may be explicable by the existence of the rights to reasons created by the AAT and ADJR Act.

If both the common law and constitutional principles are informed by the statutory elements of our administrative law system, and that statutory system is itself fashioned about wider constitutional principles, each part of the system affects and is affected by the other. Perhaps then we should question the idea that the exceptional nature of Australian administrative law is a criticism. An explanation of the unique nature of our administrative law system also demonstrates why it is exceptional in a desirable way.

---

100 *Australian Broadcasting Tribunal v Bond* (1990) 170 CLR 321, 341 (Mason CJ).
101 *Cunliffe v Commonwealth* (1994) 182 CLR 272 (Mason CJ), 303 (Brennan J).
102 G Brennan, 'Purpose and Scope of Judicial Review' (1986) 2 *Australian Bar Review* 93, 111.
103 Ibid, 110.
104 *Attorney-General (NSW) v Quin* (1990) 170 CLR 1, 38.

ADMINISTRATIVE LAW IN AUSTRALIA: THEMES AND VALUES REVISITED

Chief Justice
R S French AC

Introduction: The search for simplicity

The search for a simple pattern underlying apparent complexity is the perennial quest of science. It is rewarded from time to time when, from masses of apparently uncorrelated data, a pattern is discerned and underlying rules deduced. The periodic table of elements and the standard model in particle physics are examples. Law, whether statutory or judge-made, is the product of untidy historical processes. Simple patterns are not so readily discernible. Sir Owen Dixon, writing in 1933, saw 'the methods of a modern representative legislature and its pre-occupations' as an obstacle to 'scientific or philosophical reconstruction of the legal system'.[1] It is still the position that much important legislation is the result of political compromises between interests and purposes which are in tension with each other. Legislation affecting the jurisdiction and powers of courts in the supervision of executive action sometimes reflects such tension. A leading example can be found in the history of the provisions relating to judicial review of decisions made under the *Migration Act 1958* (Cth).

The common law is the product of a historical process whereby legal doctrines and principles emerge out of judicial decisions on particular cases. The pragmatic and non-systematic processes by which the common law evolves can generate a degree of obscurity in its doctrines, its principles and their terminology.

In the field of administrative law, and specifically judicial review of administrative action, the jurisdiction, powers and remedies exercised and granted by courts have been burdened by sometimes arcane-sounding terminology and taxonomy. On the other hand, it is possible to have a sensible conversation about what constitutes the essential elements of administrative justice and the proper boundaries of judicial intervention in support of it.

The student of administrative law should aspire to an understanding of the origins and history of its principal doctrines and the remedies for which it provides. It should not be necessary to that understanding to embroider the doctrines with undue complication. As Sir Robin Cooke wrote in 1986:

> Obscure concepts hinder progress. So to attempt more direct and more candid formulations of principle has more than a sematic purpose.[2]

---

1 O Dixon, 'Science and Judicial Proceedings' in Woinarski (ed) *Jesting Pilate* (2nd ed, 1997) 11–23.
2 R Cooke, 'The Struggle for Simplicity in Administrative Law' in M Taggart (ed) *Judicial Review of Administrative Action in the 1980s* (Oxford University Press, 1986) 5.

In administrative law, it is possible to identify simply stated 'themes and values' which should engender at least an instinctive awareness that a public law question has arisen. These themes and values can also inform a wider understanding of the way in which the rule of law operates in contemporary society. They are lawfulness, good faith, rationality and fairness. They can be taken as reflecting community expectations that representative and responsible government in a democracy will act within the law, honestly, sensibly and fairly in its dealings with the people of that democracy. These requirements are closely related to the grounds upon which administrative decisions may be reviewed in the courts. As Brennan J said in a frequently quoted passage from his judgment in *Attorney-General (NSW) v Quin*:[3]

> The essential warrant for judicial intervention is the declaration and enforcing of the law affecting the extent and exercise of power: that is the characteristic duty of the judicature as the third branch of government... The duty and jurisdiction of the court to review administrative action do not go beyond the declaration and enforcing of the law which determines the limits and governs the exercise of the repository's power. If, in so doing, the court avoids administrative injustice or error, so be it; but the court has no jurisdiction simply to cure administrative injustice or error.[4]

When the field of administrative law is more widely defined than by reference to judicial review, there are larger themes and values which come into play. They include 'accessibility', 'openness', 'participation' and 'accountability'.[5] As Professor Paul Craig has written,[6] there is much diversity of opinion about the nature and purpose of administrative law:

> For some it is the law relating to control of government power, the main object of which is to protect individual rights. Others place great emphasis upon rules that are designed to ensure that the administration effectively performs the tasks assigned to it. Yet others see the principal object of administrative law as ensuring government accountability, and fostering participation by interested parties in the decision-making process.[7]

Wade and Forsyth take as the first approximation to a definition of administrative law the statement that 'it is the law relating to the control of governmental power'.[8] There are, of course, a variety of mechanisms for the control of governmental

---

3 (1990) 170 CLR 1.
4 Ibid, 35–6.
5 M Aronson, B Dyer and M Groves, *Judicial Review of Administrative Law* (Lawbook, 3rd ed, 2004) 1.
6 P Craig, *Administrative Law* (Sweet & Maxwell, 7th ed, 2012).
7 Ibid, 3.
8 H W R Wade and C F Forsyth, *Administrative Law* (Oxford University Press, 10th ed, 2009) 4.

power in a representative democracy. Judicial review is but one of them. Wade and Forsyth take as their second approximation that administrative law is 'the body of general principles which govern the exercise of powers and discretions by public authorities'.[9] If the reference to 'general principles' is taken as a reference to 'judicial principles' then the second approximation falls within the scope of this chapter.

It is the purpose of this chapter to offer an overview of the thematic and normative ideas in contemporary administrative law in Australia. If the exercise has any value, it lies in providing an occasion for reflection upon the nature of administrative law, the simplicity of the principles which underlie it and the desirability of their connection to widely held community values. Each of these themes, however, finds its place under the overarching concept of the rule of law which, in Australia, is supported by constitutional remedies against unlawful official action.

Administrative law and the rule of law

The Australian legal system operates upon the assumed application of the rather numinous concept of the rule of law.[10] It is a term descended from English constitutional discourse. Parliamentary sovereignty and the rule of law were described by Professor A V Dicey as two characteristic features of the political institutions of England since the Norman conquest. Parliament inherited the royal supremacy. The rule of law was expressed in what Dicey called 'the old saw of the courts':

> La ley est le plus haute inheritance, que le roy ad; car par la ley il même et toutes ses sujets sont rulés, et si la ley ne fuit, nul roi, et nul inheritance sera.

The Diceyan vision involved 'at least three distinct though kindred conceptions'. They were, in summary:

1. ... no man is punishable or can be lawfully made to suffer in body or goods except for a distinct breach of law established in the ordinary legal manner before the ordinary courts of the land.[11]

---

9 Ibid, 5.
10 R H Fallon, 'A celebrated historic ideal, the precise meaning of which may be less clear today than ever before', '"The Rule of Law" as a Concept in Constitutional Discourse' (1997) 97 *Columbia Law Review* 1, 1.
11 Ibid, 174.

2. Every man whatever be his rank or condition, is subject to the ordinary law of the realm and amenable to the jurisdiction of the ordinary tribunals.[12]
3. …the general principles of the constitution (as for example the right to personal liberty, or the right of public meeting), are with us the result of judicial decisions determining the rights of private persons in particular cases brought before the courts.

Dicey's formulation has been much criticised, but judicial elaboration of the rule of law has been described rightly as '[p]erhaps the most enduring contribution of our common law'.[13] Jeffrey Jowell, who so described it, saw the rule of law as supplying the foundation of a new model of democracy in Britain that limited governmental powers in certain areas even where the majority preferred otherwise:

> It is a principle which requires feasible limits on official powers so as to constrain abuses which occur even in the most well-intentioned and compassionate of governments. It contains both procedural and substantive content, the scope of which exceeds by far Dicey's principal attributes of certainty and formal rationality.[14]

The dominant requirement of the rule of law in Australia is that the exercise of official power, whether legislative, executive or judicial, be supported by constitutional authority or a law made under such authority. A secondary principle is that disputes about the limits of legislative and executive power in particular cases can only be determined in a final and binding manner through the exercise of judicial power.

The rule of law in Australia operates within a framework set by written constitutions. The *Australian Constitution* defines, separates and limits the legislative executive and judicial powers of the Commonwealth. Each of the States has its own constitution inherited from that which it had as a colony before federation, which was supported by specific or generic Imperial statutes, and which was continued in force by s 106 of the *Australian Constitution*. The State constitutions do not provide in a formal way for the separation of powers. Generally that doctrine is applied by way of convention. It has been suggested that it may be possible for State legislatures to confer judicial power upon themselves and/or the Executive.[15] However there may also be irremovable implications in State constitutions which prevent their Parliaments from so doing.[16]

---

12 Ibid, 180.
13 J Jowell, 'The Rule of Law Today' in J Jowell and D Oliver (eds) *The Changing Constitution* (Oxford University Press, 6th ed, 2007) 24.
14 Ibid, 25.
15 A Twomey, *The Constitution of New South Wales* (Federation Press, 2004) 203–4.
16 Ibid, 204.

In the *Australian Communist Party* case, Sir Owen Dixon spoke of the *Australian Constitution* as framed in accordance with many traditional conceptions, some of them given express recognition and effect. An example is the separation of judicial power from other functions of government. Other traditional conceptions are assumed. Dixon CJ said:

> Among these I think that it may fairly be said that the rule of law forms an assumption.[17]

The rule of law is constitutionally supported, in respect of official decision-making by Commonwealth officials, by s 75(v) of the *Constitution*, which directly confers upon the High Court original jurisdiction in all matters:

> in which a writ of Mandamus or prohibition or an injunction is sought against an officer of the Commonwealth.[18]

The subject is thus provided with a mechanism to challenge the lawfulness of the exercise of official power. Its construed extension to Ministers of the Crown also provides the States with 'a significant means of requiring observance by the Commonwealth of the federal system'.[19]

The rule of law is also supported, in relation to the exercise of powers and discretions by State officials, by implications drawn from Ch III of the *Constitution* relating to the continuance, jurisdiction, powers and functions of State Supreme Courts and State courts generally. As explained in a number of decisions of the High Court beginning with *Kable v Director of Public Prosecutions (NSW)*,[20] State legislatures cannot abolish State Supreme Courts nor impose upon them functions incompatible with their essential characteristics as courts, nor subject them, in their judicial decision-making, to direction by the Executive.[21] Nor can State legislatures immunise statutory decision-makers from judicial review by the Supreme Court of the State for jurisdictional error.[22] In a joint judgment, six Justices of the Court said in *Kirk v Industrial Relations Commission (NSW)*:

> There is but one common law of Australia. The supervisory jurisdiction exercised by the State Supreme Courts by the grant of prerogative relief or

---

17 *Australian Communist Party v Commonwealth* (1951) 83 CLR 1, 193.
18 See the reference by Gleeson CJ to s 75(v) as providing in the *Constitution* 'a basic guarantee of the rule of law' in M Gleeson, *The Rule of Law and the Constitution* (Boyer Lectures 2000, ABC Books) 67.
19 W M C Gummow, *The Constitution: Ultimate Foundation of Australian Law?* (2005) 79 *Australian Law Journal* 167, 179.
20 (1996) 189 CLR 51.
21 See *International Finance Trust Co Ltd v New South Wales Crime Commission* (2009) 240 CLR 319.
22 *Kirk v Industrial Court (NSW)* (2010) 239 CLR 531.

orders in the nature of that relief is governed in fundamental respects by principles established as part of the common law of Australia. That is, the supervisory jurisdiction exercised by the State Supreme Courts is exercised according to principles that in the end are set by this Court. To deprive a State Supreme Court of its supervisory jurisdiction enforcing the limits on the exercise of State executive and judicial power by persons and bodies other than that Court would be to create islands of power immune from supervision and restraint. It would permit what Jaffe described as the development of 'distorted positions'. And as already demonstrated, it would remove from the relevant State Supreme Court one of its defining characteristics.[23]

Thus:

Legislation which would take from a State Supreme Court power to grant relief on account of jurisdictional error is beyond State legislative power. Legislation which denies the availability of relief for non-jurisdictional error of law appearing on the face of the record is not beyond power.[24]

It is fundamental to the rule of law in the *Australian Constitution* that there is no such thing as an unfettered discretion. Any Commonwealth statute conferring discretionary power is confined by the requirement that it be a law with respect to a head of legislative power conferred by the *Constitution*. A statute conferring an unfettered power upon an official would be unconstitutional, for an unfettered power would know not even constitutional limits. The laws of the States and Territories are not limited to specific heads of power as are those made by the Commonwealth Parliament. But they must operate within the limits imposed by the *Constitution* on the legislative competence of the States and the legislative supremacy of Commonwealth laws established by s 109 of the *Constitution*. They must also operate within their entrenched limitations at least as to manner and form of making certain classes of law. All laws, Commonwealth and State, are affected by interpretive principles which prevent, as a matter of their internal logic, the creation of unfettered discretions.

Every statutory power is confined, under its inherent logic, by the subject matter, scope and purpose of the legislation by which it is conferred.[25] This inescapable interpretive principle has a constitutional dimension, for the subject

---

23 Ibid, 581 [99].
24 Ibid, 581 [100].
25 *Water Conservation and Irrigation Commission (NSW) v Browning* (1947) 74 CLR 492, 505 (Dixon J), 496 (Latham CJ); *R v Australian Broadcasting Tribunal; Ex parte 2HD Pty Ltd* (1979) 144 CLR 45, 49–50; *FAI Insurances Ltd v Winneke* (1982) 151 CLR 342, 368 (Mason CJ); *Minister for Aboriginal Affairs v Peko-Wallsend Ltd* (1986) 162 CLR 24, 40 (Mason J); *O'Sullivan v Farrer* (1989) 168 CLR 210, 216, *Oshlack v Richmond River Council* (1980) 193 CLR 72, 84.

matter, scope and purpose of a statute, within which the power conferred by it must be exercised, define the criteria by which the constitutional legitimacy of the statute can be measured. As Kirby J has observed:

> No Parliament of Australia could confer absolute power on anyone.[26]

Even absent a written constitution, discretions conferred by law are necessarily limited by the laws which confer them. When the Minister of Agriculture in Britain claimed an unfettered discretion under the *Agricultural Marketing Act 1958* (UK), his claim was rejected by the House of Lords. It spoke of the judicial control over the Executive:

> namely that in exercising their powers the latter must act lawfully and that is a matter to be determined by looking at the Act and its scope and object in conferring a discretion upon the Minister rather than by the use of adjectives.[27]

And as Lord Denning MR observed in a later case:

> The discretion of a statutory body is never unfettered. It is a discretion which is to be exercised according to law.[28]

It has sometimes been contended by the Executive both in England and Australia that the exercise of prerogative or executive power is not justiciable. But as Gummow J pointed out in 1988:

> [E]ven in Britain, the threshold question of whether an act in question was done under the prerogative power will be for the court to decide, the point being that if it was, the court may then decide it will not inquire further into the propriety of that act... To decide whether a question is 'non-justiciable' is not to decide the alleged non-justiciable question itself.[29]

Under the *Australian Constitution* the executive power of the Commonwealth is conferred by s 61. The scope and content of s 61 was considered by the High Court in *Pape v Federal Commissioner of Taxation*[30] and in *Williams v Commonwealth*.[31] It extends to:

---

26 *Gerlach v Clifton Bricks Pty Ltd* (2002) 209 CLR 478, 503–4 [69]–[70]. See also *Hot Holdings Pty Ltd v Creasy* (1996) 185 CLR 149, 171.
27 *Padfield v Minister of Agriculture, Fisheries and Food* [1968] AC 997.
28 *Breen v Amalgamated Engineering Union* [1971] 2 QB 175, 190. And see generally the discussion in Wade and Forsyth, above n 8, 297–302.
29 *Re Ditfort; Ex parte Deputy Commissioner of Taxation* (1988) 19 FCR 347, 368–9.
30 (2009) 238 CLR 1.
31 (2012) 86 ALJR 713.

- powers necessary for or incidental to the execution and maintenance of a law of the Commonwealth;[32]
- powers defined by reference to such of the prerogatives of the Crown as are properly attributable to the Commonwealth;[33]
- powers defined by the capacities of the Commonwealth common to legal persons;[34]
- inherent authority derived from the character and status of the Commonwealth as the national government.[35]

It is sufficient for present purposes to say that the question of the limits of the executive power under the *Constitution* is justiciable.

There are three species of official power for which the *Australian Constitution* provides. The first is the law-making power vested, under Chapter 1, in the Federal Parliament. The second is the Executive power vested, under Chapter 2, in the Queen and exercisable by the Governor-General through his or her appointed Ministers of State. The third is the judicial power vested, under Chapter 3, in the High Court, such other federal courts as the Parliament creates and such other courts as it invests with federal jurisdiction. In the constitutions of the States of Australia, which trace their ancestry to colonial constitutions predating federation, there are delineations of legislative, executive and judicial power similar to those found in the *Australian Constitution*, but not so well defined in their separation of one from another. The State constitutions inherited the 'United Kingdom model under which the extent to which a separation of powers was observed was conventional rather than compelled by any constitutional mandate'.[36]

The great common law remedies against unlawful official action came to Australia from the courts of England. The prerogative writs, certiorari to quash jurisdictional error, mandamus to require the performance of official duty, and prohibition to restrain excess of official power, together with habeas corpus against unlawful restraints on liberty, form a historical foundation for administrative justice in Australia. The principles underpinning their application have a constitutional character which does not depend upon the existence of a written constitution. The

---

32 *R v Kidman* (1915) 20 CLR 425, 440–41 (Isaacs J); *Re Residential Tenancies Tribunal (NSW); Ex parte Defence Housing Authority* (1997) 190 CLR 410, 464 (Gummow J).
33 *Farey v Burvett* (1916) 21 CLR 433, 452 (Isaacs J); *Barton v Commonwealth* (1974) 131 CLR 477, 498 (Mason J), 505 (Jacobs J); *Davis v Commonwealth* (1998) 166 CLR 79, 93–4 (Mason CJ, Deane and Gaudron JJ), 108 (Brennan J).
34 *New South Wales v Bardolph* (1934) 52 CLR 455, 509 (Dixon J); *Davis v Commonwealth* (1998) 166 CLR 79, 108 (Brennan J); *Pape v Federal Commissioner of Taxation* (2009) 238 CLR 1, 60 [126] (French CJ).
35 *Pape v Federal Commissioner of Taxation* (2009) 238 CLR 1, 63 [133] (French CJ), 87–8 [228], 91–2 [242] (Gummow, Crennan and Bell JJ), 116 [328]–[329] (Hayne and Kiefel JJ).
36 *Kable v Director of Public Prosecutions (NSW)* (1996) 189 CLR 51, 79 (McHugh J).

writs of prohibition and mandamus for which s 75(v) of the *Australian Constitution* provides, in relation to officers of the Commonwealth, are commonly referred to as 'constitutional writs' rather than as prerogative writs.[37] They are concerned with enforcing limits on governmental power. In the 9th edition of Wade and Forsyth's *Administrative Law* it is said that:

> The British Constitution is founded on the rule of law and administrative law is the area where this rule is to be seen in its most active operation.[38]

The vessels of administrative law – administrative and judicial review

Administrative law is particularly concerned with the exercise of executive power, whether conferred by statute or derived from a constitution or Crown prerogative. The exercise of such power is subject, in Australia, to various kinds of checking when challenged. In the front line, and bearing the highest volume of decision-making, are mechanisms of administrative review primarily concerned to ensure that when official decisions are disputed, the decision made on review is the correct or preferable decision having regard to the relevant law, the facts of the case and any applicable policy. Many government departments and authorities have internal review procedures which may not have a specific statutory basis. External administrative review may be provided by tribunals, and there may be more than one level of such review. A multi-tiered process applies to decisions under the Social Security legislation, which may be reviewed internally, then by the Social Security Appeals Tribunal, and thereafter by the Administrative Appeals Tribunal.[39] Decisions under the Veterans Affairs legislation may also go through multiple stages of such review which end in the Administrative Appeals Tribunal.[40] Similar administrative review arrangements exist in a number of the States.

---

37 See, eg, *X7 v Australian Crime Commission* (2013) 298 ALR 570 [59] (French CJ and Crennan J); *Minister for Immigration and Citizenship v Li* (2013) 297 ALR 225 [51] (Hayne, Kiefel and Bell JJ); *Plaintiff S157/2002 v Commonwealth* (2003) 211 CLR 476, 507 [80] (Gaudron, McHugh, Gummow, Kirby and Hayne JJ).
38 Wade and Forsyth, above n 8, 17.
39 See *Social Security (Administration) Act 1999* (Cth), Pt 4, ss 124Q–189.
40 See *Military Rehabilitation and Compensation Act 2004* (Cth), Ch 8, ss 344–59.

Tribunals which provide administrative review are themselves subject to judicial review. Judicial review may be expressly provided for in the statute establishing the relevant tribunal and may be on specified or limited grounds. It may be left to the prerogative writs (in State jurisdiction). It may be left to the constitutional writs of mandamus and prohibition in relation to Commonwealth tribunals, with certiorari invoked as an incidental remedy. These general remedies and those of the declaration and injunction may co-exist with specific statutory remedies.

Administrative review is sometimes generically referred to as 'merits review' and distinguished from 'judicial review'. Ultimately both are concerned with the merits of the case. A decision which is bad in law is bad on its merits. A better distinction might be drawn by using the terms 'factual merits review' and 'legal merits review'.

The principal object of judicial review is to ensure that when official action affecting the subject is challenged in the courts, it has been taken within the boundaries of constitutional, statutory or executive power, and to set it aside and require its reconsideration if it has not. Judicial review may apply to first-line decision-making such as that of a Minister or the Minister's delegate. It may apply to a tribunal which has made a decision in the exercise of an administrative review function. There are some species of judicial review which have a factual merits review character about them. Examples are statutory 'appeals', so-called, from administrative decision-makers to the Federal Court in the exercise of its original jurisdiction. Appeals from the Commissioner of Taxation,[41] the Commissioner of Patents[42] and the Registrar of Trade Marks[43] fall into that category. The review by the Federal Court of decisions of magistrates, acting administratively, about eligibility for extradition,[44] although confined to the materials before the magistrates, has a merits review aspect in that it is not confined to review for error of law or failure to follow necessary procedures.

Judicial review can be constrained by specific statutory provisions. These may take the form of privative clauses which seek to exclude or limit its scope. The considerable difficulty facing legislative attempts to exclude review for jurisdictional error were illustrated, in relation to the *Migration Act 1958* (Cth), by the decision of the High Court in *Plaintiff S157/2002 v Commonwealth*[45] and, in relation to State Supreme Courts, by the decision of the High Court in *Kirk*.[46] Some privative clauses

---

41 *Taxation Administration Act 1953* (Cth), s 14ZZ.
42 *Patents Act 1990* (Cth), ss 51, 109.
43 *Trade Marks Act 1995* (Cth), ss 35, 55, 67, 84D, 104.
44 *United Mexican States v Cabal* (2001) 209 CLR 165.
45 (2003) 211 CLR 476.
46 *Kirk v Industrial Court (NSW)* (2010) 239 CLR 531.

may seek to codify the grounds of review. In the Migration Act there are sections which are calculated to limit the content of procedural fairness by confining the natural justice hearing rule to specific mechanisms for which the Act expressly provides.[47]

Administrative law operates within a constitutional framework. Judicial review of administrative action requires a focus upon that framework in a way that does not arise to the same extent with factual merits review. Review by administrative tribunals, albeit reactive to application by aggrieved parties, is part of the continuum of administrative decision-making. In one sense, it may be more useful to an applicant for review than judicial review because it can offer a complete answer on the merits which is not available through the courts. It can do so more economically and expeditiously than judicial review. Tribunals may act in an inquisitorial rather than adversarial way.[48] Typical statutory formulae require administrative review tribunals, in reviewing decisions, to be 'not bound by technicalities, legal forms or rules of evidence' and to 'act according to substantial justice and the merits of the case'. Although there have been attempts to invoke those statutory directions as grounds for judicial review, they have generally been interpreted as 'facultative, not restrictive' and intended 'to free tribunals, at least to some degree, from constraints otherwise applicable to courts of law, and regarded as inappropriate to tribunals'.[49] Administrative tribunals may not necessarily be bound by the rules of evidence. They can also address questions of legality, but not in a way that delivers a final and binding determination.

While the focus of this chapter is on judicial review, it is important for lawyers concerned with administrative law not to let its power and trappings 'divert their gaze from more fundamental, if less glamorous mechanisms to redress citizens' grievances and call government to account'.[50] The assessment of the state of administrative justice in Australia requires acknowledgement of the full range of 'less glamorous mechanisms'. Professor Robin Creyke has written of the Australian administrative law system that it:

> provides a wide variety of remedies with different levels of access and costs for users.

---

47 *Saeed v Minister for Immigration and Citizenship* (2010) 241 CLR 252.
48 For a discussion of the inquisitorial function of the Refugee Review Tribunal see *Minister for Immigration and Citizenship v SZIAI* (2009) 111 ALD 15.
49 *Minister for Immigration and Multicultural Affairs v Eshetu* (1999) 197 CLR 611, 628 [49] (Gleeson CJ and McHugh J); see also 635 [77] (Gaudron and Kirby JJ), 643 [109] (Gummow J). As to the direction to 'act according to equity, good conscience and the substantial merits of the case without regard to technicalities and legal forms' see *Qantas Airways Ltd v Gubbins* (1992) 28 NSWLR 26, 29–31 (Gleeson CJ and Handley JA), 41–2 (Kirby P). See generally the recent decision of the High Court in *Minister for Immigration and Citizenship v Li* (2013) 297 ALR 225.
50 R Cranston, *Law, Government and Public Policy* (Preston Hall PTR, 1987) 176.

And picking up the different functions of its components:

> Judicial review of legality with its precedential value is matched by merits review and its ability to provide substantive outcomes. Alongside these adjudicative bodies are institutions which operate principally by means of investigation and recommendation, such as ombudsmen, information, privacy and other commissioners. Finally, there are particular rights — such as the right to reasons, to access information and to require government to keep to itself personal information supplied by an individual — which protect important interests. The system can be said to provide a comprehensive package of institutions and principles, each component designed to provide 'justice to the individual'.[51]

Neither judicial review nor tribunal-based factual merits review are means by which administrative policies can be developed. They do not provide mechanisms for general supervision or review of administrative programs. They are remedial in character and respond to particular disputes about or challenges to official action. Courts can only hear and decide the disputes which are brought before them. They are necessarily reactive. Federal jurisdiction, whether exercised by federal courts or by State courts, only arises if there is a 'matter' before the Court for determination. That is to say, there must be a 'controversy'. State courts exercising jurisdiction under State laws or the common law are similarly but not as tightly confined because of their character as judicial institutions.

Judicial review, however limited in its accessibility, supports in the most direct way the basic themes and values of administrative law identified earlier. It provides, in a way no other process can, the mandate to executive authorities to be lawful, to act in good faith, to be fair and to be rational.

Themes and values: A taxonomical choice

Ultimately, administrative justice, reflecting the rule of law, requires official action to be authorised by law. Put another way, all official action must lie within the boundaries of power created by law. This is perhaps the most fundamental theme of administrative law, from which all others may be derived. Within that framework,

---

51 R Creyke, 'Performance of Administrative Law in Protecting Rights' in Campbell, Goldsworthy and Stone (eds) *Protecting Rights without a Bill of Rights* (Ashgate, 2006) 127.

themes and values of administrative justice in the sense administered by the courts may be identified as follows:

1. Lawfulness – that official decisions are authorised by statute, prerogative or constitution.
2. Good faith – that official decisions are made honestly and conscientiously.
3. Rationality – that official decisions comply with the logical framework created by the grant of power under which they are made.
4. Fairness – that official decisions are reached fairly, that is impartially in fact and appearance and with a proper opportunity to persons affected to be heard.

The identification of these elements of administrative justice is a little like the identification of 'fundamental' particles in physics. When pressed, they will transform one into another or cascade into the traditional grounds of review developed at common law.[52] A decision-maker may be affected by actual bias which constitutes a breach of the requirements of procedural fairness. Such bias, if directed against an attribute of the person affected by the decision, such as race or gender or sexual orientation, may mean that the decision is made by reference to irrelevant considerations or for improper purposes and therefore is beyond power. A serious enough bias may lead to dishonest decision-making. Bad faith has a similar character. Professor Craig has written of it as 'synonymous with improper purposes or relevancy' and noted that it is difficult to conceive of bad faith that would not automatically render applicable one of those two traditional grounds of review.[53] Lack of rationality may manifest in illogicality that fails to take into account mandatory relevant considerations. In such a case there may be an error of law for failure to apply statutory criteria or an improper exercise of power. Or it may yield a decision so unreasonable that no reasonable person could have made it. A factual finding without any evidentiary base may be irrational and reviewable on the so-called 'no-evidence' ground. Unfairness following from a failure to hear from a party to be affected may also constitute a failure to comply with express statutory procedures conditioning the exercise of the power.[54] These examples indicate the interdependence of the themes and values set out above. They nevertheless form a convenient taxonomy, not least because they are capable of being broadly understood by a wider audience than lawyers or judges, in terms of widely accepted community values.

---

52 To a large extent reflected in the statutory grounds for judicial review set out in s 5 of the *Administrative Decisions (Judicial Review) Act 1977* (Cth) and its State counterparts: *Kioa v West* (1985) 159 CLR 550, 567, 576, 594, 625, 630; *Australian Broadcasting Tribunal v Bond* (1990) 170 CLR 321, 356–8.
53 Craig, above n 6, 576.
54 See, eg, Part 7, Div 4 of the *Migration Act 1958* (Cth).

Statutory interpretation: Where themes and values are embedded

The themes and values of administrative law are brought to bear upon its practical application first through the process of statutory interpretation. In Australia, most official decisions affecting the subject are taken in the exercise of a power conferred by a statute or some form of subordinate legislation. In such cases, the question whether an official has acted within the limits of his or her power will depend upon the interpretation of the statute or delegated legislation conferring that power. A decision to grant or refuse a benefit or privilege will require a consideration of statutory criteria and conditions to be satisfied before such grant or refusal is made. The lawfulness of the exercise of the power will depend critically upon the interpretation of its scope and limits. Good faith, rationality and fairness all apply within the framework and to the extent defined by the statute. In administrative law, statutory interpretation is always a threshold issue, even if not contested.

Whether a statutory power is exercised in good faith will depend upon whether there is an honest and conscientious attempt by the decision-maker to discharge the function conferred by the statute. That necessarily involves identification of the function by reference to the interpretation, informed by legislative purpose, of the statute. Every exercise of power under a statute must be carried out in accordance with its internal logic, which defines the range of considerations relevant to the exercise of the power. That is a matter of interpretation and imposes a framework of rationality within which the decision-maker must operate. So too, the application and content of the requirements of procedural fairness in the exercise of the power will depend upon the nature of the function conferred by the statute and the extent to which explicitly or implicitly it qualifies, limits, excludes or codifies those requirements.

Those who are subject to the law, those who invoke it and those who apply it are entitled to expect that it means what it says. This is a rule of fairness. So the courts, as a rule, take as their starting point the ordinary and grammatical sense of the words used:

> [T]hat rule is dictated by elementary considerations of fairness, for, after all, those who are subject to the law's commands are entitled to conduct themselves on the basis that those commands have meaning and effect according to ordinary grammar and usage.[55]

---

[55] *Corporate Affairs Commission (NSW) v Yuill* (1991) 172 CLR 319, 340 (Gaudron J).

Statutory words are a direct expression of the outcome of parliamentary deliberation. Their binding interpretation is a judicial function. It requires the application of statutory and common law rules of interpretation. A purposive approach is mandated by Commonwealth and State Interpretation Acts. Also in play is the concept of legislative intention. That concept is a construct. It has recently been considered by the High Court in *Lacey v Attorney-General (Qld)*.[56] The joint judgment of six Justices in that case said of legislative intention:

> The legislative intention...is not an objective collective mental state. Such a state is a fiction which serves no useful purpose. Ascertainment of legislative intention is asserted as a statement of compliance with the rules of construction, common law and statutory, which have been applied to reach the preferred results and which are known to parliamentary drafters and the courts.[57] (footnotes omitted)

In an earlier decision, *Zheng v Cai*,[58] the Court highlighted the constitutional dimension of judicial conclusions on legislative intention:

> [J]udicial findings as to legislative intention are an expression of the constitutional relationship between the arms of government with respect to the making, interpretation and application of laws...[T]he preferred construction by the court of the statute in question is reached by the application of rules of interpretation accepted by all arms of government in the system of representative democracy.[59] (footnotes omitted)

The themes and values of administrative law, reflecting as they do broadly accepted community values, are part of the background of interpretation. As McHugh J said in an often quoted passage:

> The true meaning of a legal text almost always depends on a background of concepts, principles, practices, facts, rights and duties which the authors of the text took for granted or understood, without conscious advertence, by reason of their common language or culture.[60]

Part of this background is the concept of the rule of law.

Legislative power is exercised in Australia, as in the United Kingdom from which it has drawn much of the common law relevant to judicial review, in the setting of a 'liberal democracy founded on the traditions and principles of the

---

56 (2011) 242 CLR 573.
57 Ibid, 592 [43].
58 (2009) 239 CLR 446.
59 Ibid, 455–6 [28].
60 *Theophanous v Herald & Weekly Times Ltd* (1994) 182 CLR 104, 196.

common law'.⁶¹ The importance of those traditions and principles in statutory interpretation in Australia is reflected in the interpretive approach to the interaction between statute law and common law. This may be traced back to the judgment of O'Connor J in *Potter v Minahan*,⁶² in which he cited the 4th edition of Maxwell on *The Interpretation of Statutes*:

> It is in the last degree improbable that the legislature would overthrow fundamental principles, infringe rights, or depart from the general system of law, without expressing its intention with irresistible clearness; and to give any such effect to general words, simply because they have that meaning in their widest, or usual, or natural sense, would be to give them a meaning in which they were not really used.⁶³

A presumption against the modification or abolition of common law rights and freedoms has been repeatedly restated by the High Court of Australia.⁶⁴ It is expressed as a presumption that Parliament does not intend to interfere with common law rights and freedoms except by clear and unequivocal language for which Parliament may be accountable to the electorate. It requires that statutes be construed, where constructional choices are open, to avoid or minimise their encroachment upon rights and freedoms at common law.⁶⁵ The rights and freedoms covered by the principle have often been qualified by the adjective 'fundamental', although there are difficulties with that designation.⁶⁶ The term 'fundamental' offers little substantive guidance to the class of rights and freedoms which inform an interpretive principle which, after all, does not constrain legislative power. The principle does apply to the interaction between statute law and the rules of procedural fairness. In *Re Minister for Immigration and Multicultural Affairs; Ex parte Miah*,⁶⁷ McHugh J spoke of the common law rules of natural justice as part of the background principles upon which legal texts depend:

> They are taken to apply to the exercise of public power unless clearly excluded.

---

61 *R v Secretary of State for Home Department; Ex parte Pierson* [1998] AC 539, 587.
62 (1908) 7 CLR 277, 304.
63 Maxwell, *The Interpretation of Statutes* (4th ed) 121.
64 *Bropho v State of Western Australia* (1990) 171 CLR 1, 18; *Coco v R* (1994) 179 CLR 427, 437.
65 *Bropho v Western Australia* (1990) 171 CLR 1, 18 (Mason CJ, Deane, Dawson, Toohey, Gaudron and McHugh JJ); *Coco v R* (1994) 179 CLR 427, 436–7 (Mason CJ, Brennan, Gaudron and McHugh JJ); *Electrolux Home Products Pty Ltd v Australian Workers' Union* (2004) 221 CLR 309, 329 [21] (Gleeson CJ).
66 P Finn, 'Statutes and the Common Law: The continuing story' in S Corcoran and S Bottomley (eds) *Interpreting Statutes* (Federation Press, 2005) 52, 56–7, and see *Malika Holdings Pty Ltd v Streeton* (2001) 204 CLR 290, 298–9 [27]–[29] (McHugh J).
67 (2001) 206 CLR 57, 93.

In the context of administrative law, it is helpful to go back to Wade and Forsyth for a useful statement of the way in which interpretive principles affect the limits of administrative power:

> It is presumed that Parliament did not intend to authorise abuses, and that certain safeguards against abuse must be implied in the Act. These are matters of general principle, embodied in the rules of law which govern the interpretation of statutes. Parliament is not expected to incorporate them expressly in every Act that is passed. They may be taken for granted as part of the implied conditions to which every Act is subject and which the courts extract by reading between the lines. Any violation of them, therefore, renders the offending action ultra vires.[68]

The rules governing the interpretation of statutes, and particularly those which raise barriers against the abrogation of common law principles and rights and freedoms under common law, mean that the themes and values of administrative law are logically anterior to the way in which official power is exercised. Some aspects of those themes and values emerge from the very nature of statutes, which does not depend upon common law principles. Others concerned with the requirements of procedural fairness and the limits of power against fundamental common law rights and freedoms will require the assistance of the interpretive principle described above. The themes and values of administrative law have a part to play in defining the terms of the instruments by which power is conferred, and so are linked to the societal origins of those statutes which in Australia is a representative democracy governed by the rule of law.

Good faith

Good faith is difficult to define but is entrenched in statutes, the common law and equity. It appears in no less than 154 Commonwealth Acts. It has a core meaning, in ordinary usage, of honesty with fidelity and loyalty to something – a promise, a commitment or a trust.[69] It is therefore a relational concept. But its elements do

---

68 Wade and Forsyth, above n 8, 30. See also C F Forsyth, 'Of Fig Leaves and Fairy Tales: The Ultra Vires Doctrine, The Sovereignty of Parliament and Judicial Review' (1996) 56 *Cambridge Law Journal* 122. For a perspective on administrative law principles as judicial creations see J Laws, 'Law and Democracy' (1995) *Public Law* 72. See also M Elliott, *The Constitutional Foundations of Judicial Review* (Hart Publishing, 2001) 109–10. Cf P Craig, 'Competing Models of Judicial Review' (1999) *Public Law* 428, 446, and T R S Allan, 'The Constitutional Foundations of Judicial Review: Conceptual Conundrum or Interpretive Inquiry?' (2002) 61 *Cambridge Law Journal* 87.
69 Shorter Oxford English Dictionary – 'faith'; Black's Law Dictionary (West Group, 7th ed, 1999) 701.

not diminish from one legal application to another. It is imposed as a statutory obligation upon company directors and officers. It conditions, in bankruptcy, the validity of certain antecedent dispositions of property. It has long been identified as a positive obligation attaching to the exercise of official power. In 1905, Lord Macnaghten said of the exercise of statutory power by a public body:

> It must keep within the limits of the authority committed to it. It must act in good faith. And it must act reasonably. The last proposition is involved in the second, if not in the first.[70]

It is also well established that in instruments which create powers there is a condition implied 'that the powers shall be used bona fide for the purposes for which they are conferred'.[71]

Good faith and honesty of purpose are closely linked. Sir Owen Dixon spoke of good faith as 'an honest attempt to deal with a subject matter confided to the tribunal and to act in pursuance of the power of the tribunal in relation to something that might reasonably be regarded as falling within its province'.[72]

Bad faith is generally taken to imply dishonesty, but is often regarded as akin to an allegation of fraud by a decision-maker. The requirement of good faith is not necessarily satisfied by mere absence of dishonesty. So much appears from Lord Macnaghten's reflection upon the interdependence of good faith and reasonableness. This has given rise to confusion when public authorities are found to act in bad faith because they have acted unreasonably or on improper grounds:

> Again and again it is laid down that powers must be exercised reasonably and in good faith. But in this context 'in good faith' means merely 'for legitimate reasons'. Contrary to the natural sense of the words they import no moral obliquity.[73]

That criticism has been echoed in some English decisions.[74] Good faith has not figured prominently in Australian administrative law, save where its asserted absence has been invoked to defeat privative clauses which seek to exclude judicial review.[75] There has been debate about its scope. It has been equated to

---

70 *Westminster Corporation v London and North Western Railway Company* [1905] AC 426, 430.
71 *Free Church of Scotland v Overton* [1994] AC 515, 695 (Lord Lindley).
72 *R v Murray; Ex parte Proctor* (1949) 77 CLR 387, 400. See also *Little v Commonwealth* (1947) 75 CLR 94, 108 (Dixon J).
73 Wade and Forsyth, above n 8, 352.
74 *Connock Chase DC v Kelly* (1978) 1 WLR 1; *Western Fish Products Ltd v Penwith District Council* [1981] 2 All ER 204, 215.
75 Eg, *Income Tax Assessment Act 1936* (Cth), s 177; *Migration Act 1958* (Cth), s 474.

a requirement for 'an honest or genuine attempt to undertake the task'.[76] A wider formulation proposed that recklessness and capriciousness in decision-making will demonstrate its absence.[77] On that wider view, an honest attempt to exercise official power is not demonstrated merely by the absence of dishonesty or malice. What is required is an honest and conscientious approach to the statutory task.[78] A decision-maker who deliberately makes no attempt to conform to statutory duty will not be acting in good faith.[79]

The term 'good faith' appears in so many statutory contexts[80] that, notwithstanding its relational character, it must be seen by those who draft statutes as having a core meaning capable of a degree of practical application. Applying its essential elements, good faith requires, in the exercise of a statutory power, honest action and fidelity to the purposes and criteria that govern the exercise of the power. Good faith would seem to require that attention be paid by the decision-maker to those criteria and purposes and that the decision-maker honestly and conscientiously attempt to exercise the relevant power in accordance with them.

To wilfully and deliberately make a decision without attempting to carry out the relevant statutory duty, such as by tossing a coin without reading the file, or finding in favour of every third applicant, or rotating applicants from different countries, would amount to a want of good faith.[81] In these examples, want of good faith is expressed in conduct which would support judicial review on other grounds. A decision made on the toss of a coin is likely to be a decision made by reference to an irrelevant consideration. So too would be a decision based on the chance fact that the favoured applicant is the third in line after the last favoured applicant.

---

76 *NAAP v Minister for Immigration and Multicultural and Indigenous Affairs* [2002] FCA 805 [41] (Hely J); *NADR v Minister for Immigration and Multicultural and Indigenous Affairs* (2002) 124 FCR 465; *NAAQ v Minister for Immigration and Multicultural and Indigenous Affairs* [2002] FCAFC 300.
77 *SBBS v Minister for Immigration and Multicultural and Indigenous Affairs* [2002] FCAFC 361.
78 *Applicant WAFV of 2002 v Refugee Review Tribunal* (2003) 125 FCR 351, 371. Cf *NAKF v Minister for Immigration and Multicultural and Indigenous Affairs* (2003) 199 ALR 412, 420 [24] where Gyles J rejected the notion that good faith could be constituted by recklessness in the sense of negligence.
79 *Daihatsu Australia Pty Ltd v Federal Commissioner of Taxation* (2001) 184 ALR 576, 587 (Finn J).
80 For recent examples considered by this Court see *Bankstown City Council v Alamdo Holdings Pty Ltd* (2005) 223 CLR 660, 674–5; *E & J Gallo Winery v Lion Nathan Australia Pty Ltd* (2010) 241 CLR 144, 168–9.
81 *NAKF v Minister for Immigration and Multicultural and Indigenous Affairs* (2003) 199 ALR 412.

A process of rotational choice would also indicate an irrational basis for decision-making because it is founded on irrelevant considerations.[82]

Rationality

Rationality has been described as 'a common law standard of good administrative decision-making'.[83] It may be put higher than that. In the exercise of statutory power, rationality is demanded by the very assumptions upon which the power rests. Professor Galligan, in his text *Discretionary Powers: A Legal Study of Official Discretion*,[84] states that the requirement that officials exercising discretion comply with canons of rationality means that their decisions must be reached by reasoning which is intelligible and reasonable, and directed towards and related intelligibly to the purposes of the power.

Administrative decision-making requires the identification of the relevant rule of law, the ascertainment of facts which engage the application of the rule, and the application of the rule to the facts. That application may involve or precede the exercise of a discretion. If there is a discretion, then its exercise will be confined in all cases by the purposes of the statute and, in some cases, by a specific requirement to have regard to particular matters. Rationality here reduces to lawfulness – that is, compliance with the legal requirements for the exercise of statutory power.

Rationality, in the sense of decision-making according to law, does not necessarily permit only one possible outcome, although there may be cases in which it does. Nor does it mandate a single pathway of reasoning for any particular case. Rationality at this level is an envelope which can cover a family of alternative pathways, each of which may lead to what could properly be called a rational decision.

The High Court has drawn a distinction between judicial and administrative decision-making so far as it relates to the ascertainment of fact:

> Where facts are in dispute in civil litigation conducted under common law procedures, the court has to decide where, on the balance of probabilities, the truth lies as between the evidence the parties to the litigation have thought it in their respective interests to adduce at the trial. Administrative

---

82 Sometimes the toss of a coin, figuratively speaking, is a good faith way to proceed. Decision-making between applicants for a single benefit who cannot be otherwise distinguished may be conducted by ballot without complaint – see the process under the *Mining Act 1978* (WA) of holding a ballot between competing applicants for an exploration licence, upheld by the Full Court of the Supreme Court of Western Australia in *Hot Holdings Pty Ltd v Creasy* (1996) 16 WAR 428.
83 G Airo-Farulla, 'Rationality and Judicial Review of Administrative Action' (2000) 24 *Melbourne University Law Review* 543–75.
84 D Galligan, *Discretionary Powers: A Legal Study of Official Discretion* (Clarendon Press, 1986).

> decision-making is of a different nature. A whole range of possible approaches to decision-making in the particular circumstances of the case may be correct in the sense that their adoption by a delegate would not be an error of law.[85]

The materials before a decision-maker may permit more than one inference to be drawn about matters of fact. If an inference on a matter of fact relevant to the decision is drawn by the decision-maker, the fact that another inference is open, and may even be preferable or more persuasive from the point of view of a court, does not render the decision-maker's inference irrational. Some people apply the words 'irrational' or 'illogical' to inferences with which they disagree. If a challenged inference is open on the materials then it cannot be said to fall within either of those categories. But there is authority for the view that, even if the particular reasoning taken to reach such an inference may have been illogical, it may yet be unreviewable. A person affected by a decision cannot show error of law simply by showing that the decision-maker inferred the existence of a particular fact by illogical reasoning:

> [A]t common law, according to the Australian authorities, want of logic is not synonymous with error of law. So long as there is some basis for an inference – in other words, the particular inference is reasonably open – even if that inference appears to have been drawn as a result of illogical reasoning, there is no place for judicial review because no error of law has taken place.[86]

Where there is no evidence to support a particular finding of fact by a decision-maker, then the factual finding will involve an error of law. The question whether there is any evidence of a particular fact is treated as a question of law. Whether a particular inference *can* be drawn from facts found or agreed is also treated as a question of law. For, before the inference is drawn, a preliminary question arises whether the evidence reasonably admits a different conclusion. So making findings and drawing inferences in the absence of evidence is an error of law which is judicially reviewable.[87]

In Australia, 'unreasonableness' is a ground for judicial review. As the plurality recently observed in *Minister for Immigration and Citizenship v Li*,[88] a standard of reasonableness in the exercise of discretionary powers given by

---

85 *Minister for Immigration and Ethnic Affairs v Wu Shan Liang* (1996) 185 CLR 259, 282; see also *Minister for Immigration and Multicultural Affairs v Eshetu* (1999) 197 CLR 611, 656 (Gummow J).
86 *Australian Broadcasting Tribunal v Bond* (1990) 170 CLR 321, 355–6 (Mason CJ, Brennan, Toohey and Gaudron JJ agreeing); *Roads Corp v Dacakis* [1995] 2 VR 508, 517–29, approved in *Minister for Immigration and Multicultural Affairs v Epeabeka* (1999) 84 FCR 411; see also *Minister for Immigration and Multicultural Affairs v Anthony Pillai* (2001) 106 FCR 426, 437 [42].
87 *Minister for Immigration and Multicultural Affairs v Miahi* (2001) 65 ALD 141, 149 [34].
88 *Minister for Immigration and Citizenship v Li* (2013) 297 ALR 225, 246–7 [64] (Hayne, Kiefel and Bell JJ).

statute was required by the law long before the first statement of 'Wednesbury unreasonableness' in *Associated Provincial Picture Houses Ltd v Wednesbury Corporation*.[89] Their Honours referred, with approval, to the observation of Gaudron and Gummow JJ in *Re Refugee Review Tribunal; Ex parte Aala*[90] that 'the requirement of reasonableness represents the development of legal thought which began before federation and accommodates s 75(v) to that development'. In so saying, their Honours acknowledged that there is an area within which a decision-maker has a genuinely free discretion, but that area resides within the bounds of legal reasonableness:

> Properly applied, a standard of legal reasonableness does not involve substituting a court's view as to how a discretion should be exercised for that of a decision-maker.[91]

The *Wednesbury* test is a test which allows for curial visitation upon an administrative decision where the decision is, on the face of it, absurd. No underlying error needs to be identified in order to characterise such a decision as beyond power simply because it is beyond the pale. The language of the test imposes a constraint. It is only to be applied in extremis and therefore in rare cases.

Rationality is an inescapable requirement of official decision-making which underpins most of the traditional grounds of review. An irrational decision will often be unlawful because it fails to comply with the substantive requirements of the decision-making power as defined explicitly or implicitly by the statute which is its source.

Fairness

When a statute empowers a public official to adversely affect a person's rights or interests, the rules of procedural fairness regulate the exercise of the power unless excluded by plain words.[92] It is a matter which goes to power:

> [I]f an officer of the Commonwealth exercising power conferred by statute does not accord procedural fairness and if that statute has not, on its proper construction, relevantly (and validly) limited or extinguished any obligation to afford procedural fairness, the officer exceeds jurisdiction in a sense necessary to attract prohibition under s 75(v) of the Constitution.[93]

---

89 [1948] 1 KB 223, 230.
90 (2004) 204 CLR 82, 100–01.
91 *Minister for Immigration and Citizenship v Li* (2013) 297 ALR 225, 246–7 [66].
92 *Annetts v McCann* (1990) 170 CLR 596, 598.
93 *Re Refugee Review Tribunal; Ex parte Aala* (2000) 204 CLR 82, 101 [41].

Procedural fairness supports rational decision-making in two ways. As already noted, bias in a decision-maker is likely to inform reviewable error. A failure to give a person affected by a decision the right to be heard and to comment on adverse material creates a risk that not all relevant evidence will be before the decision-maker, who may thereby be led into factual or other error. Apparent or apprehended bias is likely to detract from the legitimacy of a decision and so undermine confidence in the administration of the relevant power. The requirements of procedural fairness, particularly in relation to the right to be heard, are ambulatory. They will vary from one legal context to another and from one fact situation to another. They must be practical. They do not require the imposition on administrators of highly prescriptive requirements of the kind appropriate to a judicial proceeding. The assumption that the methods of natural justice are necessarily those of the courts is 'wholly unfounded'.[94]

Procedural fairness may apply where there is a legitimate expectation of a particular approach to decision-making based, for example, upon a statement or undertaking or regular practice followed by the decision-maker.[95] That is to say, a decision-maker who has committed himself or herself to a declared procedure or policy or a regular practice may not fairly depart from that commitment, policy or practice without first giving persons to be affected an opportunity to be heard on the question whether there should be a departure. This is a process requirement. It does not create, in Australia, substantive rights to the subject matter of the expectation.

The extension of the legitimate expectation principle to compliance, by Australian officials, with obligations under international conventions to which Australia is a party, was made in *Minister for Immigration and Multicultural Affairs v Teoh*[96] but has been called into question in *Re Minister for Immigration and Multicultural Affairs; Ex parte Lam*.[97] In the end, legitimate expectation is probably best regarded as a tool for the analysis of the requirements of procedural fairness in particular classes of case.[98]

---

94 *Local Government Board v Arlidge* [1915] AC 120, 138.
95 *Kioa v West* (1985) 159 CLR 550; *Salemi v MacKellar (No 2)* (1977) 137 CLR 396; *Haoucher v Minister for Immigration and Ethnic Affairs* (1990) 169 CLR 648; *Attorney-General (NSW) v Quin* (1990) 170 CLR 1; *Darling Casino Ltd v New South Wales Casino Control Authority* (1997) 191 CLR 602.
96 (1995) 183 CLR 273.
97 (2003) 214 CLR 1.
98 *Re Minister for Immigration and Multicultural Affairs; Ex parte Lam* (2003) 214 CLR 1, 21 [67] (McHugh and Gummow JJ), 48 [48] (Callinan J); *C Inc v Australian Crime Commission* (2008) 251 ALR 424, 437–8 [53]–[58] (Reeves J); *Geelong Community for Good Life Inc v Environment Protection Authority* (2008) 20 VR 338, 342–5 [15]–[20] (Cavanough J); *Sidhu v Minister for Immigration and Multicultural and Indigenous Affairs* [2007] FCA 69 [125]–[126] (Lander J); *Rush v Commissioner of Police* (2006) 229 ALR 383, 403 [82]; *Apache Northwest Pty Ltd v Agostini (No 2)* [2009] WASCA 231 at [117] (Buss JA).

Fairness is sufficiently valued as an attribute of administrative decision-making that a decision can be quashed for want of fairness even though the decision-maker has acted entirely fairly. The unfairness may be attributable to the conduct of a third party. An official who is expected to provide a tribunal with all papers in the possession of the government department responsible for the primary decision may, deliberately or inadvertently, withhold material favourable to the applicant for review. In that case, unfairness can result despite the fact that the tribunal is unaware of the true situation. Alternatively, a third party may present misleading material to a tribunal or decision-maker without its knowledge. As Gleeson CJ said in *Hot Holdings Pty Ltd v Creasy*:

> Procedural unfairness can occur without any personal fault on the part of the decision-maker.[99]

Fraud and circumstances analogous to fraud may also vitiate administrative decisions which they affect, notwithstanding that there is no fault on the part of the decision-maker or of the party affected by the decision.[100] Of course, it is also true that a decision procured by the fraud of the party benefited by it will be a nullity. Generally speaking, third-party fraud adversely affecting the subject of a decision necessarily involves procedural unfairness. But fraud has its own long-established vitiating quality. Fraud 'unravels everything'.[101] It is, however, difficult to establish. The case law on administrative decisions induced or affected by fraud is sparse. The vitiating quality of fraud is, in a sense, implicit in the themes and values of administrative law already identified, although for the most part they relate to the standards imposed upon official decision-makers.

Conclusion

The themes and values of administrative law identified in this chapter are useful heads for the discussion of its essential elements. Perhaps more importantly, they form a bridge of intelligibility between what administrators, judges and lawyers do in the pursuit of administrative justice and what the wider community is entitled to expect of them. The pursuit of intelligibility through simple statements of basic themes and values is important to establish and maintain confidence in administrative justice in contemporary Australian society.

---

99 (2002) 210 CLR 438, 448.
100 *SZFDE v Minister for Immigration and Citizenship* (2007) 232 CLR 189.
101 *Lazarus Estates Ltd v Beasley* [1956] 1 QB 702.

THE PUBLIC/PRIVATE DISTINCTION AND THE REACH OF ADMINISTRATIVE LAW

Chris Finn

Introduction

Writing in 1992,[1] Geoffrey Airo-Farulla offered a strong critique of the 'public-private' distinction and its inability to clearly define the reach of administrative law. He described the dichotomy between the public and private spheres as 'formalist' and as 'one of the basic premises of traditional liberal political philosophy'.[2] Airo-Farulla argued that this distinction was untenable and should be replaced by a focus on 'the appropriate decision making standards that should be applied by (and to) bureaucracies generally'.[3]

This critique of the public/private divide came in the wake of the privatisation and outsourcing movement which began in the United Kingdom in the 1980s and swept through Australia in the 1990s. The ideology of 'new managerialism' and the mantra of 'private sector efficiency' which accompanied those changes gave birth to many other academic calls to reconsider the proper scope of administrative law.[4] Despite these calls, however, little has changed in the 20 years since this challenge to the traditional conception of the reach of administrative law. Government continues to reinvent itself and thus to challenge traditional understandings of the public/private divide. Courts continue to wrestle with an all-or-nothing classification of organisations as either 'public' or 'private', rather than recognising, as Airo-Farulla hoped, that they actually lie along a continuum, from the highly public to the very private, with many bodies comprising a mixture of each. At the highest, courts have occasionally grappled with the idea that the 'public' or 'private' classification might not be wholly determined by the proximate source of the power being exercised. Even here, however, their ultimate conclusions have seldom strayed from the traditional.

Statutory conferrals of review jurisdiction to courts and tribunals have generally followed the same all-or-nothing pattern. Courts and tribunals have rarely been granted power to review exercises of non-statutory power. Even the jurisdiction to review statutory powers has been interpreted increasingly narrowly by the courts, wherever there has been a hint of the 'private' about the body exercising the power in question. Similar difficult issues have arisen in the application of Freedom of Information (FoI) legislation. Where, for example, information is sought about significant government tenders or major outsourcing projects, the legislative

---

1 G Airo-Farulla, '"Public" and "Private" in Australian Administrative Law' (1992) 3 *Public Law Review* 186.
2 Ibid, 187.
3 Ibid, 200.
4 M Aronson, 'A Public Lawyer's Responses to Privatisation and Outsourcing' in M Taggart (ed) *The Province of Administrative Law* (Hart Publishing, 1997) 40; C Saunders and K Yam, 'Government Regulation by Contract: Implications for the Rule of Law' (2004) 15 *Public Law Review* 1; M Allars, 'Public Administration in Private Hands' (2005) 12 *Australian Journal of Administrative Law* 126.

prescription has usually allowed 'private' notions of commercial confidentiality to trump 'public' values such as democratic accountability. Neither courts nor legislatures have been able to provide a principled answer to the basic question of how administrative law should respond to the evolving nature of government.

The limits of common law judicial review jurisdiction

The scope of common law judicial review is an appropriate starting point as this form of review has long been available for exercises of statutory power, subject to various limiting doctrines such as justiciability, the need for a plaintiff with appropriate standing, and the possibility of Crown immunity in some instances. Despite these limitations, it has been largely non-controversial that exercises of statutory power are quintessentially 'public' in nature and hence reviewable, at least in principle.

It is now widely accepted that exercises of prerogative power, at least in the narrow sense defined by Blackstone, are also reviewable in principle.[5] Prerogative powers in this narrow sense are possessed exclusively by government and are also regarded as 'public' for that reason. They may still escape review because of particular subject matter immunities, but are not automatically outside the purview of judicial review.[6]

It is otherwise, however, with exercises of power which partake of the 'public' in a range of ways but are not sourced directly to either statute or the prerogative powers of government. Exercises of common law power such as the capacity to enter into contract or other consensual forms of agreement, to buy and sell property and exercise the property rights of owners, or to enter into various forms of association, have largely been classified as 'private' and hence outside the scope of judicial review.

This is most controversial in the case of powers exercised by government, for clearly governmental purposes, and admittedly in pursuit of the public interest, but where those powers are not exclusive to government, such as contractual powers.

---

5 See Blackstone, *Commentaries on the Laws of England* (first published 1765, 3rd ed, 1768) Bk I, Ch 7, 239. Compare with the broader view of Dicey that '[e]very act which the executive government can lawfully do without the Act of Parliament' was to be viewed as an exercise of prerogative power: A V Dicey, *Introduction to the Study of the Constitution* (10th ed) 424–5.

6 *Council of Civil Service Unions v Minister for the Civil Service* [1985] AC 374; *Minister for Arts, Heritage and Environment v Peko-Wallsend Ltd* (1987) 75 ALR 218. See F Wheeler, 'Judicial Review of Prerogative Power in Australia: Issues and Prospects' (1992) 14 *Sydney Law Review* 432.

The most obvious example is the use of contractual powers by government in pursuit of a range of outsourced service delivery arrangements, whereby services are delivered to citizens by contractors on behalf of government and under its direction and control. In such instances, government seeks to achieve by contractual means what it might otherwise implement by legislation.

What is clear is that the exercise of contractual powers by government wears a dual aspect and straddles the purported divide between 'public' and 'private'. These exercises of power are 'public' in the sense that they are used to accomplish public purposes, and indeed may provide an alternative means of accomplishing what might otherwise be achieved by the exercise of statutory powers. But they are also 'private' in that they may be seen simply as an exercise of legal personality by government – a legal personality which it shares with other legal entities, and which includes the ability to enter or not to enter into contractual relationships. Australian courts have assumed that the dual nature of such powers compels a bifurcated choice one way or the other, and have largely opted to treat such exercises of power as 'private'.[7] The practical outcome has most commonly been the non-availability of judicial review jurisdiction, which leaves plaintiffs to whatever contractual remedies might exist.

There have been some cases where governmental exercises of contractual power have been held amenable to judicial review. For example, in the *Gungahlin Development Authority* case,[8] Higgins J was prepared to allow common law judicial review, on the basis of a denial of procedural fairness in a tendering process. Review was held to be justified due to the fact that the authority was obliged under its legislation to perform its functions in a manner which advanced the interests of the public.[9] Higgins J placed weight on the earlier decision of the Victorian Court of Appeal in the *Master Builders* case.[10] In that 1995 decision, Tadgell, Ormiston and Eames JJ held that review was available, again on procedural fairness grounds, of a decision made by a Building Industry Taskforce to compile and publish a 'black list' of building contractors with whom the government would not enter into future contracts. The taskforce was non-statutory in nature, but had been set up by the Victorian government to counter questionable tendering practices. The court held the taskforce to be essentially an extension of government, which was performing a public duty. Tadgell J observed that the taskforce 'directly represents the State of Victoria, being, as it were, its alter ego'.[11] The compilation of the black list was 'part and parcel of a scheme designed to induce former contractors and tenderers

---

7 See, eg, *Khuu & Lee Pty Ltd v Adelaide City Corporation* (2011) 110 SASR 235.
8 *MBA Land Holdings v Gungahlin Development Authority* (2000) 206 FLR 120.
9 Ibid, 147.
10 *Victoria v Master Builders Association (Vic)* [1995] 2 VR 121.
11 Ibid, 137.

(successful and unsuccessful) to atone for their presumed past misconduct'.[12] Eames J commented that:

> It would be unrealistic to pretend that the actions of the executive in this case, through administrative agencies of the state, concerned merely private functions akin to those which might be exercised by any private citizen. The integrity, and efficiency, of the building industry is plainly a matter of immense public importance.[13]

On this basis, the Court held that there was a sufficient public element in the actions of the taskforce to attract judicial review.

There are rarer instances where judicial review has been granted of exercises of power which are arguably 'public' in nature, even though the entity exercising the power in question is *not* a direct emanation of government. These cases involve a shift of focus from the source of the power being exercised to its 'nature', or of the public 'function' or 'duty' being performed. Such was the case in the celebrated *Datafin*[14] decision in the United Kingdom. In that case, the UK Take-over Panel, an unincorporated association which performed a self-regulatory function in relation to takeovers and mergers, was held amenable to common law judicial review by the English Court of Appeal because the panel exercised 'undoubtedly public law functions',[15] and its activities contained a 'public element'[16] or had 'public law consequences'.[17]

Sir John Donaldson MR described the Panel as being 'without visible means of legal support' but concluded that it was performing 'public functions'.[18] One rationale was that had the Panel had not been in existence, it would have been necessary for the government to have stepped in and performed its functions. Other factors leading to the conclusion that the Panel was amenable to review included the historical performance of those functions by government, de facto recognition of the Panel's existence in relevant legislation, and the performance of similar functions by government in other jurisdictions.[19] The court held the panel amenable to judicial review, although the claim ultimately failed.

Datafin is now an accepted element of English public law, though often distinguished. The same acceptance is not clear in Australia where the courts have struggled with the case as they respond to the challenges of the modern

---

12 Ibid.
13 Ibid, 164.
14 *R v Panel on Take-Overs and Mergers; Ex parte Datafin plc* [1987] QB 815.
15 Ibid, 836 (Donaldson MR), 847 (Lloyd LJ).
16 Ibid, 838 (Donaldson MR).
17 Ibid, 847 (Lloyd LJ), 852 (Nicholls LJ).
18 Ibid, 824 (Donaldson MR).
19 Ibid, 835 (Donaldson MR).

administrative state. *Datafin* has been cited with apparent approval in some cases but questioned just as frequently in others. This uncertainty can only be resolved when the High Court finally finds it necessary to determine the issue.[20]

One case that appeared to accept the applicability of *Datafin* in Australia was *Masu v FICS*.[21] The body that was ultimately held susceptible to judicial review, the Financial Industry Complaints Service (FICS), was a registered corporation operating as a complaints resolution body for the financial services industry. FICS had determined that Masu had provided deficient financial advice. Shaw J held that FICS was a 'public' body, and hence judicially reviewable, due to many factors. These included government involvement in the constitution of both the FICS Board and any complaint hearing panels it set up, and the establishment of FICS as a part of a regulatory scheme envisaged by legislation. *Datafin* arose in a very different area in *D'Souza*,[22] where a doctor challenged the decision of a surgical college to deny him specialist accreditation. Ashley J steered something of a middle course. He held that the decision was potentially 'public' and therefore reviewable, but ultimately found that the existence of a contract between the practitioner and the college removed any such 'public' element. Ashley J also noted that '*Datafin* ha[d] not been applied, in Australia, to a case where the pertinent relationship between the parties was contractual'.[23]

CECA v ACPET[24] raised a series of related issues. CECA, a private education provider, applied for membership of ACPET and its tuition assurance scheme. This was a prerequisite for CECA obtaining the necessary registration to provide educational services to overseas students in Australia. The application was ultimately refused by ACPET. Kyrou J applied *Datafin* and *Master Builders* to hold that a decision of a private body may be amenable to judicial review if made in the performance of a 'public duty' or in the exercise of a power which has a 'public element'.[25] However, Kyrou J then held that the decision fell outside the scope of the *Datafin* principle because no public law consequences flowed from the decision. Strictly speaking that was true, because ACPET was one of several bodies providing a pathway to the registration which CECA ultimately sought, so that its refusal had no necessary consequences for that registration.[26] Kyrou J also held that

---

20 *Datafin* was the subject of extensive submissions by the parties but not mentioned once by the High Court in its unanimous decision in the *Offshore Processing case*: *Plaintiff M61/2010E v Commonwealth* (2010) 243 CLR 319.
21 *Masu Financial Management Pty Ltd v Financial Industry Complaints Service Ltd (No 2)* (2004) 50 ACSR 554.
22 *D'Souza v Royal Australian and New Zealand College of Psychiatrists* (2005) 12 VR 42.
23 Ibid, 58.
24 *CECA Institute Pty Ltd v Australian Council for Private Education and Training* (2010) 30 VR 555.
25 Ibid, 570, 576.
26 Ibid, 578.

the availability of judicial review and the applicability of the hearing rule were not co-extensive. ACPET was obliged to comply with the latter, and its failure to do so led to declaratory relief being granted and an order that CECA's application be considered according to law.[27] Thus, 'private law' remedies effectively provided a functional substitute for judicial review on this occasion.

The most recent litigation examining the amenability of 'private' bodies to judicial review in Australia was *Mickovski*.[28] The decision-maker in this Victorian case was the Financial Ombudsman Service Ltd (FOS), which had decided that it lacked jurisdiction to deal with a complaint made out of time. FOS was the successor body to the FICS body whose amenability to review had been considered in *Masu*. It was a private company and its powers derived from consensual submission by its members.

At first instance, Pagone J held that the balance of the authorities suggested the *Datafin* principle was part of Victorian law. However, his Honour concluded that the principle could not apply to the case because the actions of FOS lacked the necessary public duty or public element.[29] His Honour was influenced by the fact that submission by the parties to the FOS jurisdiction was voluntary. Mr Mickovski was not obliged to use the FOS or be bound by its decisions.

The Victorian Court of Appeal was more circumspect on the *Datafin* principle. Whilst describing that principle as 'appealing' and 'logical',[30] the Court of Appeal deferred to what they considered to be the 'clear implication' of the views expressed by the High Court in *Neat Domestic Trading Pty Ltd v AWB Ltd*:[31] that any decision on the matter should be deferred until a case arose in which it was necessary to decide the point.[32] On this occasion, the Court of Appeal agreed with Pagone J that this was not a case falling within the ambit of *Datafin*. Contract was the source of any power that FOS held over its members, and its arbitrations were not supported by any public law sanctions. These factors, combined with the fact that members of the public did not need to use the FOS scheme, were sufficient to confirm that its decisions lacked the necessary public element.[33] Overall, the *Mickovski* litigation is not unfavourable to the *Datafin* principle but, like so many cases in which the principle has been considered, it does not stand as clear authority for its adoption in Australia.

Other cases are less favourable to the reception of *Datafin* in Australia. In *Chase Oyster Bar*,[34] the decision-maker was an arbitrator, who was held to exercise statutory power and hence was amenable to the issue of certiorari on normal

---

27 Ibid, 587.
28 *Mickovski v Financial Industry Ombudsman Service Ltd* [2011] VSC 257.
29 Ibid, [12].
30 [2012] VSCA 185, [31].
31 (2003) 216 CLR 277.
32 (2012) 91 ASCR 106, [32].
33 Ibid, [33].
34 *Chase Oyster Bar Pty Ltd v Hamo Industries Pty Ltd* (2010) 78 NSWLR 393.

principles, despite some surprising earlier authority to the contrary.[35] Discussion of *Datafin* was therefore unnecessary to the decision, but Basten JA explored the point at some length and concluded that there was 'an absence of authority' on the point. His Honour considered that neither the decision of Shaw J in *Masu* nor the *Master Builders* decision provided clear authority for the acceptance of that principle, as neither case had turned upon its application.[36] With respect, this seems an unduly narrow view of those cases.[37]

Statutory conferrals of judicial review jurisdiction

Statutory conferrals of judicial review jurisdiction might have been thought to have clearly indicated the limits to reviewability, and hence to have escaped the toils of the 'public/private' debate. The *Administrative Decisions (Judicial Review) Act 1977* (Cth) ('ADJR Act')[38] and similar legislation confer jurisdiction to review decisions 'made under an enactment', and not otherwise. Thus, it might have been thought that exercises of statutory power were to be judicially reviewable under such legislation, and other governmental exercises of power were not. Whilst the latter proposition has held good, the former has proven to be capable of a steadily shrinking interpretation. Wherever it has been possible to argue that an exercise of power, even though ultimately sourced to statute, was in some significant sense 'private', courts have been willing to accept that it might therefore not be susceptible to review. This steady constriction of judicial review jurisdiction can be traced in a series of landmark ADJR cases, which have taken increasingly restrictive views as to the meaning of the phrase 'made under an enactment'. Again, where faced with decisions of a 'dual' character, the courts have preferred to classify the exercise of power in question as 'private' and hence outside the scope of judicial review.

In *ANU v Burns*,[39] the Federal Court held that while a decision to *enter into* a contract (in that case an employment contract) would be a decision made *under the relevant statute*, a subsequent decision to *terminate* employment was made *under the contract*, and was therefore an exercise of non-reviewable contractual power.[40] For some years following this case, decisions by statutory bodies to enter into

---

35 *Brodyn Pty Ltd t/as Time Cost and Quality v Davenport* (2004) 61 NSWLR 421.
36 *Chase Oyster Bar Pty Ltd v Hamo Industries Pty Ltd* (2010) 78 NSWLR 393, 411–13.
37 The contrary view was expressed by Kyrou J, writing extra-judicially, in E Kyrou, 'Judicial Review of Decisions of Non-Governmental Bodies Exercising Governmental Powers: Is Datafin part of Australian Law?' (2012) 86 *Australian Law Journal* 20.
38 *Administrative Decisions (Judicial Review) Act 1977* (Cth).
39 *Australian National University v Burns* (1982) 64 FLR 166.
40 Ibid, 174 (Bowen CJ and Lockhart J, Sheppard J).

contracts were considered to be made under the enactment which conferred the general power to do so.[41] Accordingly, decisions to enter contracts were judicially reviewable but subsequent decisions made in accordance with the terms of a contract were not.[42]

That position was changed by the decision of the Full Federal Court in *General Newspapers v Telstra*.[43] The plaintiff in that case complained of a flawed tender process which led Telecom (as it then was) to enter into a contract for the printing of telephone directories with another company. The Federal Court could have simply applied *ANU v Burns* and held that the decision of Telecom to *enter* the contract was indeed made under an enactment. Instead, the Court held unanimously that the relevant legislation merely conferred the capacity to contract. Any decision to enter (or not to enter) into particular contractual arrangements was an exercise of that contractual power, rather an exercise of statutory power. Davies and Einfeld JJ held that:[44]

> The contracts were not relevantly authorised or required by and were not made under an enactment. The validity of the contracts and of the acts done was governed entirely by the law of contract, not by the statutes. Thus, the ADJR Act had no application to the conduct or to the alleged decisions.

The impugned tendering process occurred when Telecom was still a fully publicly owned body and faced only limited competition in the telephone directories market.[45] Telecom was engaging in the same activities as many private law companies, but its functions and unique commercial position clearly owed much to its statutory foundation and government ownership. There was therefore a good case that Telecom, and its tendering decisions, could reasonably be characterised as both 'public' and 'private'. The Federal Court opted decisively for the latter, taking a broad view of contractual power and a correspondingly narrowing view of both 'public' power and any judicial review of its exercise. Only a decision that was clearly 'authorised or required' by the statute would be regarded as being 'made under' the relevant enactment.[46]

The phrase 'made under an enactment' was further limited in scope in two subsequent High Court decisions. In *Neat Domestic Trading*,[47] the plaintiff had

---

41 *ACT Health Authority v Berkeley Cleaning Group Pty Ltd* (1985) 7 FCR 575; *James Richardson Corporation v Federal Airports Corporation* (1992) 117 ALR 277.
42 *Sellars v Woods* (1982) 69 FLR 105; *Bayley v Osborne* (1984) 4 FCR 141; *Australian Film Commission v Mabey* (1985) 6 FCR 107.
43 (1993) 45 FCR 164.
44 Ibid, 173 (Davies and Einfeld JJ).
45 Ibid, 191. The court held that Telstra held a position of market power but had not breached s 46 of the *Trade Practices Act 1974* (Cth) because its actions lacked any of the purposes proscribed by s 46.
46 Ibid, 170 (Davies and Einfeld JJ).
47 *Neat Domestic Trading v AWB Ltd* (2003) 216 CLR 277.

made repeated applications to export wheat. All had been refused. The nominal statutory decision-maker, the Wheat Export Authority, was required by legislation to withhold its consent unless AWBI, the 'single desk' wheat exporter, consented to the approval.[48] In effect, AWBI was able to veto the entry into the relevant market of any potential competitors, and it chose to do exactly that. Behaviour which might well have been seen as anti-competitive in normal circumstances was expressly permitted by legislation.[49]

Again, the decision wore both 'public' and 'private' aspects and might plausibly have been characterised as either. The 'private' characterisation arose from the fact that AWBI was a corporate entity, controlled by wheat growers rather than the government, and pursuing its own private commercial interests. This characterisation was ultimately the dominant one for McHugh, Gummow and Callinan JJ, who held that AWBI's decision to withhold consent was not made under an enactment. Although the legislation provided a veto power to AWBI, their Honours held that its powers arose from its status as a private corporation and its own constitution. As a 'private' corporation, AWBI was entitled, indeed obliged, to maximise its own commercial returns to the exclusion of other considerations.[50] McHugh, Gummow and Callinan JJ concluded that there was 'no sensible accommodation' that could be made between the relevant public and private considerations.[51] Their Honours felt that the latter must prevail because AWBI was required to act in its own commercial interests. It did not matter that this requirement, or many other features of AWBI, arose from statute.

Griffith University v Tang[52] further restricted the scope of statutory judicial review. In that case, a doctoral candidate alleged denial of procedural fairness in a decision made by the university to terminate her candidacy. A majority of the High Court held that the decision was not 'made under an enactment' and hence statutory judicial review was not available.[53] The majority held that review would not be available simply because a decision was expressly or impliedly required or authorised by the relevant enactment. Gummow, Callinan and Heydon JJ reasoned that there was an additional, cumulative, requirement that the decision 'must itself confer, alter, or otherwise affect legal rights or obligations'.[54] The decision-making might be thought to have worn a dual aspect in that the university's powers to

---

48 *Wheat Marketing Act 1989* (Cth), s 57(3B).
49 AWBI was in fact expressly exempted from the scope of the *Trade Practices Act 1974* (Cth).
50 (2003) 216 CLR 277, 299.
51 Ibid, 300.
52 *Griffith University v Tang* (2005) 221 CLR 99.
53 Review was sought under the *Judicial Review Act 1991* (Qld), which has identical terms to the federal ADJR legislation in all relevant parts.
54 (2005) 221 CLR 99, 130–31.

exclude Ms Tang were, at least in a broad sense, derived from its enabling statute. But, consistently enough with the earlier decision in *Neat*, the majority viewed the decision as an essentially 'private' one made by the university, and outside the scope of judicial review. The decisions in both *Neat* and *Tang* are much criticised,[55] albeit occasionally defended.[56]

Freedom of information and commercial confidentiality

Whilst much of this discussion has focused upon common law and statutory avenues for judicial review, other accountability mechanisms encounter similar issues of scope. For example, the appropriate reach of Freedom of Information legislation has posed difficult questions both for legislatures and, subsequently, for courts. Where should the line be drawn, for example, in relation to commercially sensitive information that is relevant to the performance of government contracts, particularly where those contracts relate to the outsourced delivery of utility services or the operation of 'private' prisons and detention centres on behalf of government? Should the 'private' nature of commercial information and the commercial interests of the contracting service providers prevail, meaning that such information is exempt from disclosure? Or should the fact that services are delivered either to government, as in the case of prison and detention centre management, or to citizens on behalf of government, as in the management of various utility services, indicate that information as to the cost of such services and their effectiveness is of a public nature? Should considerations of democratic accountability dictate that such material be publicly available?

At one level, such questions are resolved by the courts as ordinary questions of statutory interpretation. But this is simply to refocus the question on the normative question to be addressed by policymakers, and legislators in particular. Should legislation protect commercially sensitive material, even where it relates to matters of public interest and accountability, or should the 'public interest' prevail, with the

---

55 Mark Aronson commented in 2007 that: 'There have been over 25 articles and comments so far, the great bulk of them extremely critical of the majorities' reasoning, both in doctrinal and policy terms': M Aronson, 'Private Bodies, Public Power and Soft Law in the High Court' (2007) 35 *Federal Law Review* 1, 2–3.
56 P A Keane, 'Judicial Review: The Courts and the Academy' (2008) 82 *Australian Law Journal* 623.

legislative consequence that disclosure is part of the cost of doing business with government?[57]

Different legislatures have drawn the public/private line in relation to disclosure in slightly different places. That line can shift. For example, the Commonwealth FoI Act,[58] until amendments in 2010, fully exempted from disclosure:

a. trade secrets;

b. any other information having a commercial value that would be, or could reasonably be expected to be, destroyed or diminished if the information were disclosed; or

c. information (other than trade secrets or information to which paragraph (b) applies) concerning a person in respect of his or her business or professional affairs or concerning the business, commercial or financial affairs of an organization or undertaking, being information:

   i. the disclosure of which would, or could reasonably be expected to, unreasonably affect that person adversely in respect of his or her lawful business or professional affairs or that organization or undertaking in respect of its lawful business, commercial or financial affairs; or

   ii. the disclosure of which under this Act could reasonably be expected to prejudice the future supply of information to the Commonwealth or an agency for the purpose of the administration of a law of the Commonwealth or of a Territory or the administration of matters administered by an agency.

There was no balancing of private and public interests to be performed under that legislative regime. The private interests prevailed. Section 43 was repealed in 2010 by amendments that introduced a new s 47G which varied the approach in some instances. Full immunity from disclosure was preserved for some categories of business documents, including trade secrets. However, exemption from disclosure was made conditional, and subject to a public interest test, in relation to documents falling within the old s 43(1)(c).

Section 11A(5) of the amended legislation set out the approach to be applied in relation to documents which were 'conditionally exempt' from disclosure, and provided that:

> The agency or Minister must give the person access to the document if it is conditionally exempt at a particular time unless (in the circumstances) access to the document at that time would, on balance, be contrary to the public interest.

---

57 See N Seddon, 'Commercial-In-Confidence and Government Contracts' (2000) 11 *Public Law Review* 51; C Finn, 'Getting the Good Oil: Freedom of Information and Contracting Out' (1998) 5 *Australian Journal of Administrative Law* 113.

58 *Freedom of Information Act 1982* (Cth), s 43(1).

Section 11B(3) now sets out a list of factors that are statutorily designated as relevant and irrelevant to the question of whether disclosure of 'conditionally exempt' documents would be contrary to the public interest. Factors in favour of disclosure include that such disclosure would inform debate on a matter of public importance, or promote effective oversight of public expenditure.[59] This legislative change is compatible with a shift towards recognition of the 'public' nature of at least some commercial information in the context of government contracting, and hence an extension of the reach of the FoI Act in this field.

The various State Acts strike the balance in differing ways. In New South Wales, for example, s 13 of the *Government Information Act*[60] sets out an 'overriding public interest test', to the effect that disclosure of government information is prohibited if (and only if) the public interest considerations against disclosure, on balance, outweigh those in favour of disclosure. The table to s 14 of the Act provides that the public interest considerations which may weigh against disclosure include, *inter alia*, that the disclosure may: reveal the commercial-in-confidence provisions of a government contract; diminish the competitive commercial value of any information to any person; prejudice any person's legitimate business, commercial, professional or financial interests; or prejudice the conduct, effectiveness or integrity of any research by revealing its purpose, conduct or results (whether or not commenced and whether or not completed). This is an extensive list, although none of these factors make non-disclosure of information mandatory. The NSW legislation also provides for a public register of government contracts,[61] whilst excluding confidential information, which is extensively defined, from that register.[62]

These two examples indicate the complexity of this aspect of the interface between public and private interests. The newer legislative provisions are more complex than their predecessors and do not mandate non-disclosure of all commercially sensitive information. That said, it is uncertain whether they will result in significantly higher levels of disclosure. It is probably fair to say that protection of private interests continues to dominate in this legislative scheme, although not as absolutely as in earlier schemes.

---

59 *Freedom of Information Act 1982* (Cth), ss 11B(3)(b)–(c).
60 *Government Information (Public Access) Act 2009* (NSW).
61 Sections 27–35.
62 Section 32. See also Schedule 4, which defines the 'commercial in confidence' provisions of a contract to include any provisions of the contract that disclose the contractor's financing arrangements, cost structure or profit margins, full base case financial model, any intellectual property in which the contractor has an interest, or any matter the disclosure of which would place the contractor at a substantial commercial disadvantage in relation to other contractors or potential contractors, whether at present or in the future.

Difficulties with the distinction

Against this backdrop, the landscape of Australian public administration has been altered beyond recognition in the last twenty years or so. The move towards privatisation, outsourcing and other forms of 'public/private partnership' is widely recognised. No-one could fail to notice the privatisation of utility services, or the contractual engagement of private sector bodies in the delivery of welfare and employment services, and the management of prisons, detention centres and even refugee visa assessments. The public service itself has also been reformed along private sector lines, to take account of managerialist dictates.

Most responses to these changes have originated from the legislatures rather than the courts. These responses have taken a number of forms. In areas such as the delivery of employment and welfare services, one response has been to preserve entitlements to both merits and judicial review that would have existed where the services were delivered directly by government agencies. For example, decisions may be 'deemed' to have been made by the government agency that has in fact contracted them out. This approach can make outsourcing more politically palatable to the public, but can be criticised for creating a bifurcation of decision-making between private sector contractors and government agencies that blurs accountability. Equally, the 'private' nature of the bodies making the substantive decisions makes it more difficult to access the information upon which a successful review might be based.[63] These criticisms aside, it would be unfair not to acknowledge that such statutory extensions of review to private agencies delivering services under contract can at least ameliorate what would otherwise be a substantial accountability deficit flowing from the shift to 'private' delivery.

A second response to the privatisation wave has been the emergence of a raft of 'private' industry ombudsmen and dispute resolution bodies. Examples include the Telecommunications Industry Ombudsman (TIO), a range of State energy industry ombudsmen such as the Energy and Water Ombudsman of Victoria (EWOV), and financial industry consumer protection bodies such as FICS and its successor body, FOS. These bodies straddle the traditional 'public/private' divide in interesting ways. Typically, they are not actually created by statute, but the relevant regulatory scheme requires that there be such a body, albeit set up and funded by industry members. The regulatory statute does not usually mandate the existence of any

---

[63] R Bacon, 'Rewriting the Social Contract?: The SSAT, the AAT and the Contracting Out of Employment Services' (2002) 30 *Federal Law Review* 39. Bacon argues that merits review of decisions made within the federal 'jobs network' is difficult for unemployed people because the system is hard to access, it fragments responsibility for delivering services, and it divides the decision-making process between contracted providers and government. These problems make it hard to establish who has made a decision.

particular body, merely that there be one (or more), but may require membership of a scheme as a mandatory condition of licensing. The regulatory scheme may set out to some extent the roles and powers of the contemplated body.[64] The body itself may be a corporation, an unincorporated association or a company limited by guarantee. When these bodies are duly created by their members, they possess enforcement powers, but these derive from contractual agreement between the members rather than from statute. These bodies may therefore be seen as consensual in nature, and hence 'private', but for the statutory prescription that such a body exist. A factor tending to a 'public' classification is that they perform an accountability function in terms of the enforcement of Customer Service Guarantees and consumer protection that might otherwise fall to a more recognisably 'public' body. In truth, however, as Airo-Farulla recognised, such bodies are neither 'public' nor 'private'. They are hybrid in nature. To force them into either of the opposed camps for the sake of conceptual simplicity is to misunderstand their nature. This hybrid nature was recognised in McGill's analysis of financial services complaints bodies, which concluded that these bodies were not amenable to judicial review but were still required to observe procedural fairness.[65]

There are other bodies which are hybrid in nature. How should we classify housing associations and cooperatives? It might be argued that these are simply private consensual bodies, albeit regulated by statute. But that regulation is extensive and frequently imposes a duty to observe the requirements of procedural fairness. Some statutes impose further requirements for decision-making, such as a prescription that decisions not be unreasonable, oppressive or unjust.[66] Their decisions in general may be subject to a wide range of merits review regimes. The functions of these bodies are significant. They frequently control a great deal of publicly owned real estate, sometimes worth millions of dollars, and are themselves accountable to 'public' regulatory bodies for the care and maintenance of that property. They assist in the provision of a scarce resource (public housing), usually to disadvantaged people, which surely entails a direct public interest. Again, it seems that any simple classification of such bodies as wholly 'public' or 'private' is likely to be unhelpful.[67]

---

64 In the case of the TIO, s 128 of the *Telecommunications (Consumer Protection and Service Standards) Act 1999* (Cth) requires providers of telecommunications services to enter into the Telecommunications Industry Scheme. Section 128 also provides that the TIO must have power to investigate and determine complaints from consumers of telecommunication services, and that there must be only one TIO scheme.
65 D McGill, 'Are the Financial Services External Complaints Resolution Schemes Subject to Judicial Review?' (2006) 26 *Companies and Securities Law Journal* 438.
66 *Co-operative and Community Housing Act 1991* (SA), s 84(1).
67 See discussion in K McEvoy and C Finn, 'Private Rights and Public Responsibilities: The Regulation of Community Housing Providers' (2010) 17 *Australian Journal of Administrative Law* 159.

Such bodies are closely analogous to a range of 'private' consensual bodies which have long dwelt at the fringe of judicial review, such as sporting bodies, professional associations and unions. These bodies derive their often considerable powers from neither statute nor prerogative, but from the consent of their members. Prima facie, this would suggest they would not be susceptible to judicial review, but their power over their members is often extensive. In fact there are many cases, extending at least back to the 19th century, where such bodies have been held amenable to review on procedural fairness grounds.[68] Typically, where this has been the case, it has been on the basis that the body in question, albeit consensual in nature, regulated access to a means of livelihood, or to a resource that a member of the public would ordinarily expect to be entitled to access. Expulsion from such a body has therefore been seen as the loss of an interest that is sufficient to require fair decision-making processes.[69]

Judicial review in this area has rarely extended beyond the procedural fairness ground.[70] The remedies granted have not extended to the prerogative writs, but 'private' equitable relief has been granted. Again, such bodies may be seen to sit awkwardly between traditional conceptions of 'public' and 'private'. The consensual basis to their power, with little or no governmental involvement, speaks powerfully to their 'private' nature. However, where such bodies hold effective monopolies over livelihood in their particular field, it is much more difficult to argue that their activities fall wholly outside the purview of 'public' accountability.

Attempting to redefine the public/private divide

The existence of this range of hybrid legal bodies has generated varying responses from courts and scholars. Those responses have tended to look for a reformulated notion of the boundary between public and private, rather than abandoning the attempt to see the spectrum of legal bodies as one form or another of dualism. These attempts to recast the public/private divide have not been conspicuously successful.

---

68 *Wood v Woad* [1874] LR 9 Ex 190; *Fisher v Keane* [1879] 11 Ch 353.
69 It has generally been accepted, however, that it is possible for members of a 'private' association to contract out of the requirements of procedural fairness. See, eg, the discussion by Campbell J in *McLelland v Burning Palms Surf Lifesaving Club* (2002) 191 ALR 759, 780–86.
70 *Shepherd v South Australia Amateur Football League Inc* (1987) 44 SASR 579 (denying disproportionality as an available ground to a sporting club).

One such attempt, flowing from *Datafin*, is an attempt to identify the 'public function' or 'public element' present in that case and justifying review in it and other similar sets of circumstances. These attempts have generated a list of factors, the presence of a sufficient number of which has been argued to give rise to the necessary 'public element'. These include a social necessity that the function be performed,[71] or a public interest in the work of a body;[72] a legislative requirement that such a body (or bodies) exist, and consequent enmeshment in regulatory schemes;[73] or the involvement of government in appointments to the body in question.[74]

Viewed through that particular lens, the Takeover Panel in *Datafin* was classified as 'public' on the basis of several of these factors. It did not matter that its *source* of power was neither statutory nor prerogative. The precise source of power being exercised by the building industry taskforce in the *Master Builders* case was equally obscure, but the taskforce itself was undoubtedly an emanation of government and established to pursue a public purpose. Hence, judicial review was held to be available.

This approach has some appeal but can be criticised. As Campbell points out, none of the suggested factors appears decisive, and each can be questioned as providing insufficient justification for the classification of a body as 'public' and therefore open to judicial review.[75] Importantly, each of the factors is indeterminate in scope and none would be capable of easy application. For example, what exactly is a 'public' function? History provides little guidance. There are a range of activities which have been the domain of public bodies in recent history, such as the delivery of utility services, but this seems little more than historical accident. One might argue that it is in the public interest that essential utilities such as electricity and water be delivered by the state, but this has not always been the case. In some instances, one sees historical cycles of private supply, followed by public ownership and control, itself subsequently overturned by fresh privatisation. Such cycles make it difficult to argue convincingly that many utility services are inherently either 'public' or 'private' in nature.

The privatisations and outsourcings of the late 20th century have demonstrated afresh that many traditional 'governmental' activities can be carried out capably enough with major private sector involvement. Even the operation of prisons

---

71 *Datafin* [1987] QB 815, 835 (Donaldson MR).
72 *Victoria v Master Builders Association (Vic)* [1995] 2 VR 121, 164.
73 As in the case of industry ombudsmen.
74 *Masu* (2004) 50 ACSR 554.
75 C Campbell, 'The Public/Private Distinction in Australian Administrative Law' in M Groves and HP Lee, *Australian Administrative Law: Fundamentals, Principles and Doctrines* (Cambridge University Press, 2007).

and detention centres, seemingly at the centre of truly coercive 'governmental' activity, can be carried out by private contractors, albeit again under a measure of governmental regulatory control. Where this occurs, 'private' activity under management contracts is interwoven with a layer of accountability to the government initially under those contractual arrangements, supplemented by broader public accountability to the extent that this is provided for, either by contractual agreement or statutory prescription.

Those difficulties are only increased when a multi-factor approach is taken. The result will at best be impressionistic conclusions as to whether a body is indeed sufficiently 'public' in nature to justify judicial review of its decisions. Such indeterminacy is not uncommon in the law, but it contrasts unfavourably with the relative simplicity of the more traditional approach that limits judicial review to exercises of statutory and prerogative power.

Campbell himself suggests a different approach, with a focus on the exercise of monopoly power. This resonates, at least in part, with Airo-Farulla's suggestion that attempts to distinguish between 'public' and 'private' should be replaced by a focus on the exercise of power by large bureaucracies. A focus on monopoly power has some appeal, and may explain the long-standing judicial willingness to extend at least a measure of judicial review to sporting and professional bodies, particularly where these bodies function as gatekeepers to one form or another of livelihood. Given the significance of the interests at stake to an affected party, it seems inappropriate that those interests could be adversely affected without the grant of basic process rights, such as a fair hearing. Such cases can be distinguished from those where membership of an association is purely consensual and where expulsion does not affect livelihood, either because membership is not a prerequisite or because there are alternative avenues of securing the same livelihood. Perhaps, however, a focus on monopoly power per se goes too far. It has gained no traction in the courts. Critics of such an approach might also note that private monopoly power is already subject to statutory restrictions in the form of competition law sanctions for certain proscribed misuses of that power.[76] To subject such bodies to judicial review would be to impose an additional burden.

One is forced to conclude that attempts to provide a new basis for the division between public and private, no longer based upon the source of the power being exercised, have made little progress. The second and deeper problem with attempts to reformulate the public/private distinction in this fashion is that these proposals remain inherently dualist. Airo-Farulla recognised that legal entities are arrayed across a continuum. It follows that a simple dualist set of categories,

---

76 *Competition and Consumer Act 2010* (Cth), s 46. This test applies where the threshold of 'market power' is crossed.

however formulated, cannot adequately respond to that diversity. A radical reconceptualisation of public and private in terms of the presence or absence of monopoly power remains ultimately a new form of this dualism. This suggests that the public/private distinction should not be reformulated; it should be abandoned. But this does not seem likely.

Public/private values and the liberal tradition

The public/private distinction has such deep roots in western political philosophy that its abandonment may not be feasible. English, and hence Australian, administrative law has its origins in the political philosophies of J S Mill and John Locke. For these thinkers, the state was a necessary evil, and an intrusion into freedom of action, the state of nature otherwise to be enjoyed by individuals. This tradition tolerated the existence of the state but regarded it with suspicion. The state was to be curbed, for fear of excessive use of its powers to tax, to regulate and otherwise control the lives of citizens. Flawed as this conception of the relationship between citizens and the state may be, it is deeply entrenched in the common law tradition. Administrative law became the lawyer's weapon of choice in that tradition and was essentially conceived of as a weapon against government.

Modern administrative law has superimposed the language of 'democratic accountability' and representation upon this pre-existing conceptualisation of the relationship between citizen and the state. That democratic rationale perhaps makes individuals feel more than ever justified in questioning the actions of government, not merely because those actions may be perceived as threatening to themselves, but because democratically elected governments source their legitimacy from the consent of the governed, periodically renewed via the electoral process. Citizens therefore feel justified in calling 'their' government to account, via demands for information and participation, greater avenues of review and electoral sanctions. Modern conceptions of administrative law have expanded to include this broader range of forms of public accountability, but they have not altered the basic focus of those accountability mechanisms upon the doings of the state and its agents. Thus 'public' law, and administrative law in particular, is redolent with ideas of restraining, restricting and controlling the use of the power of executive government. This is most evident in notions of ultra vires and excess of jurisdiction, which have limited counterpart in the 'private' sphere. In short, the essential reason that administrative law is unlikely to abandon the public/private distinction is that it depends on that very distinction. Administrative law generally, and judicial review in particular, is conceived of as a defence of a cherished realm of individual privacy and freedom of action from unjustified governmental intrusion. Most modern statutory accountability mechanisms have followed closely in this tradition.

The tradition of the private sphere is of course central to the common law, with its core values of liberty and freedom of action. In that private realm, relationships, absent the unilateral coercive force of government, have long been, albeit ideally, conceived of as free and consensual. While government has increasingly become required to show lawful authority for its exercise of power, that burden is reversed for individuals, whose actions are presumptively lawful. Where individuals enter into contracts, they are considered to do so freely and equally, despite often enormous inequalities of bargaining power. The ideology is one of formal equality, despite any substantive differences between the parties. Judicial review is seen as inappropriate due to the absence of coercive force in any decision-making processes. Where relationships are genuinely consensual, simple withdrawal of consent provides a sufficient remedy for abuse of that relationship.

'Public' and 'private' are thus fundamentally interrelated in the common law worldview. In that worldview, it is the 'private' sphere of free and untrammelled consensual association that takes logical precedence, and falls to be protected from undue interference from the 'public' activities of government. The prospect that such a fundamental set of common law values will be abandoned is slight. A more useful focus would therefore seem to be on incremental change, both judicial and legislative.

For the courts, a particular focus might be on a more nuanced approach to the availability of judicial review, looking at the availability of particular grounds of review, rather than the availability of judicial review as a whole. Such developments are likely to be cautious, with a gradual extension of the scope of the procedural fairness doctrine perhaps the most probable.

As noted above, the cases suggest that the scope of this doctrine ought not to be seen as co-extensive with judicial review more generally. Rather, a more nuanced approach, consistent with a body of existing case law, may allow the grant of injunctive or declaratory relief, particularly on the basis of a denial of procedural fairness, in circumstances where 'judicial review' more generally might not be available, and the prerogative remedies in particular would not be granted. Administrative law, it is suggested, should not be seen as monolithic. Nor should judicial review be seen as 'all or nothing'. Instead, it may be appropriate to respond to bodies whose status straddles the public/private divide with an intermediate level of review, where perhaps denial of procedural fairness and manifest excess of power grounds were available, but other grounds such as error of law, relevant/irrelevant considerations, irrationality or unreasonableness were not. Where one of this limited range of grounds was made out, it might be sufficient to respond with equitable relief. The result might be that the public/private line would be drawn in different places for different purposes, allowing a more flexible response to bodies and decisions that have elements of both the 'public' and 'private' about them.

A similar approach might be taken to legislative prescriptions of the limits of statutory accountability mechanisms. There is no particular reason why statutory judicial review, merits review, or the scope of FoI schemes and ombudsmen should be co-extensive. Their availability need not be approached in an 'all-or-nothing' fashion. Information rights might be appropriately extended to a wide range of bodies delivering services to citizens on behalf of government. That does not mean judicial review should also be available.

Conclusion

The 'public/private' question presents itself in many guises and can therefore admit to many answers. The key is context. When it is recognised that a body, or its decisions, may be 'public' for one purpose, yet better viewed as 'private' for another, it is possible to respond in ways that better reflect the nature of the body or decision in question. For example, incorporated bodies possessing common law legal personality may generally be unconstrained by considerations of ultra vires when exercising normal incidents of that personality, such as entering contracts. Procedural fairness constraints might be appropriately imposed wherever a body possesses an effective monopoly and, therefore, has a greater capacity to make decisions directly affecting rights, interests and expectations.

However such measures develop, it seems highly unlikely that the public/private divide will cease to demarcate the limits of administrative law. This divide is not a single 'bright line' but a series of lines, drawn in differing places and for different purposes. A clearer delineation of where these particular lines are drawn will require a clearer articulation of the distinct underlying values that each of the different administrative law mechanisms serve. Airo-Farulla's vision of an abandonment of 'public' and 'private' terminology seems unlikely, but a more nuanced response to the continuum of bodies that straddle that divide is not.

HUMAN RIGHTS AND JUDICIAL REVIEW: TWO SIDES OF THE SAME COIN?

Alison Duxbury*

* The author thanks Tessa Plueckhahn for her helpful research assistance, Associate Professor Julie Debeljak for her comments on an earlier draft, and the Centre for Comparative and Public Law at the University of Hong Kong, where the work for this chapter was undertaken.

Introduction

> The role of the court in human rights adjudication is quite different from the role of the court in an ordinary judicial review of administrative action. In human rights adjudication, the court is concerned with whether the human rights of the claimant have in fact been infringed, not with whether the administrative decision-maker properly took them into account.[1]

> There is a distinction to be made between the framework for judicial review...and the substantive question of whether particular human rights should be taken into account by administrative decision makers. There is a further question of the distinction between judicial review and human rights review – human rights review is concerned with the substantive question of whether rights have been infringed, while judicial review focuses on decision making procedure.[2]

These two statements – one by a Law Lord (now a Justice of the Supreme Court of the United Kingdom) and the other by members of the Administrative Review Council in Australia – contrast judicial review (largely focused on procedure) and human rights review (concerned with the substance of rights protection). When viewed in isolation such comments leave the reader with the lingering impression that judicial review is different from, and perhaps inferior to, human rights review. After all, procedural safeguards never sound quite as desirable as substantive rights. However, it is clear that the authors of both statements do not hold this view – Baroness Hale has equated the removal of judicial review of governmental action which affects individual rights to subverting the rule of law,[3] and the first line of the Administrative Review Council's discussion paper, *Judicial Review in Australia*, notes that judicial review is important in ensuring the accountability of public officials.[4] Both accountability and the rule of law are dear to human rights lawyers – without these overarching principles, human rights protections would languish.

The purpose of this chapter is to analyse the way in which human rights principles interact with judicial review of administrative action in Australia. It will examine three main areas: access to the courts; the substantive arguments made in judicial review proceedings (the grounds of review); and remedies. Although the main focus will be on judicial review at the federal level, developments in jurisdictions with statutory human rights regimes will also be discussed briefly. At

---

1 *Belfast City Council v Miss Behavin' Ltd* [2007] 1 WLR 1420, 1430 (Hale LJ).
2 Administrative Review Council, *Judicial Review Consultation Paper* (2011) [1.20].
3 *R (Jackson) v Attorney-General* [2006] 1 AC 262, 318.
4 Administrative Review Council, above n 2, 7.

the outset it is important to note that the phrase 'human rights' as used in the title of this chapter may refer to a number of different issues, including international human rights law (as articulated in the numerous treaties to which Australia is a party), general humanitarian values, and common law or fundamental rights. A distinction should also be drawn between decisions of courts in judicial review applications that may enhance an individual's rights and judgments where the court actually applies or utilises international human rights law. While the first possibility is uncontroversial (many perceive it as an aim of judicial review),[5] the second has excited much discussion.

This chapter will not enter into the debate as to the merits (or otherwise) of a statutory or constitutional rights instrument at the federal level. It is axiomatic that without a bill of rights, individuals cannot directly challenge government action for failure to comply with human rights norms.[6] Despite this lacuna, many Australian cases demonstrate the relevance of human rights principles to judicial review proceedings. Most of these cases have arisen in migration law – particularly refugee applications – where human rights concerns are acute.[7] These cases illustrate the 'convergence' of values between human rights law and judicial review[8] and demonstrate that, although judicial review in Australia is different from human rights review, it can provide similar (sometimes greater) protections to people who challenge government action.

Access to the courts

The *International Covenant on Civil and Political Rights* ('ICCPR') provides extensive fair trial guarantees for those charged with a criminal offence, but is virtually silent on rights accorded to individuals engaged in other court actions.[9] In response to this gap, in 1995 Professor Bradley drew upon developing European human rights law and formulated a potential human right to administrative justice on the basis of

---

5 A Mason, 'The Importance of Judicial Review of Administrative Action as a Safeguard of Individual Rights' (1994) 1 *Australian Journal of Human Rights* 1.
6 *Dietrich v R* (1992) 177 CLR 292, 305.
7 The principles articulated in refugee cases are discussed in J Boughey, 'The Use of Administrative Law to Enforce Human Rights' (2009) 17 *Australian Journal of Administrative Law* 25, 27–9.
8 For a discussion of the similarities (and also differences) between the underlying values of human rights law and administrative law see B Saul, 'Australian Administrative Law: The Human Rights Dimension' in M Groves and HP Lee (eds), *Australian Administrative Law: Fundamentals, Principles and Doctrines* (Cambridge University Press, 2007) 50, 51–2.
9 Article 14(1) of the ICCPR provides that '[i]n the determination of any criminal charge against him, *or of his rights and obligations in a suit of law*, everyone shall be entitled to a fair and public hearing' [emphasis added].

a similar (although not identical) provision of the *European Convention on Human Rights and Fundamental Freedoms* ('ECHR').[10] The first component of this right was that an individual should be 'entitled to seek judicial review of government decisions which adversely affect them'.[11] Although there is no separate right to administrative justice in international human rights law,[12] the ability to launch an application in the courts challenging executive action is fundamental to prevent governmental excesses of power and to protect individual rights. Three elements of judicial review have the potential to restrict an individual's ability to access the courts: justiciability; standing; and privative clauses. The approach of Australian courts to all three 'gatekeepers' has ensured that individuals can challenge a broad range of government decisions, thus enhancing a 'right' to administrative justice.

The doctrine of justiciability places a limit on those decisions considered appropriate for judicial review – if a decision is non-justiciable then it is not considered amenable to legality review by the courts, as 'the decision-making function lies within the province of the executive'.[13] This doctrine has been used to suggest that decisions made pursuant to the prerogative powers are beyond legality review, but the courts have slowly eroded this principle.[14] In *CCSU v Minister for the Civil Service*,[15] Lord Diplock stated that the fact that a decision-making power was 'derived from the common law and not a statutory source' was not a reason to quarantine it from judicial review. This approach has been adopted in Australia, where courts have looked to the 'subject matter' of the prerogative to determine its reviewability.[16] The result is that the mere fact that a power is vested in a particular person, such as the Governor-in-Council,[17] or is based on the prerogative rather than statute, is no reason to deny a court's ability to intervene. Certain areas are considered to be beyond judicial review – for example, decisions made in the realm of foreign affairs, such as the power

---

10 A W Bradley, 'Administrative Justice: A Developing Human Right?' (1995) 1 *European Public Law* 347. Article 6(1) of the ECHR provides (in part) that '[i]n the determination of his civil rights and obligations or of any criminal charge against him, everyone is entitled to a fair and public hearing within a reasonable time by an independent and impartial tribunal established by law'.
11 Bradley, above n 10, 351.
12 The right to just administrative action is included in the South African Bill of Rights: *South African Constitution* (1996), s 33. A right of 'good administration' is located in the Charter of Fundamental Rights of the European Union, article 41.
13 Mason, above n 5, 8.
14 Review of prerogative powers is discussed in F Wheeler, 'Judicial Review of Prerogative Power in Australia: Issues and Prospects' (1992) 14 *Sydney Law Review* 432.
15 *CCSU v Minister for Civil Service* [1985] AC 374, 410.
16 *R v Toohey; Ex parte Northern Land Council* (1981) 151 CLR 170, 220; *Minister for Arts, Heritage and Environment v Peko-Wallsend Ltd* (1987) 75 ALR 218, 249.
17 *FAI Insurances Ltd v Winneke* (1982) 151 CLR 342, 349–50.

to ratify treaties and declare war and peace.[18] By narrowing the scope of non-justiciable decisions, the courts have increased the ability to challenge executive actions. However, the continued acceptance by courts that executive decision-making in the fields of foreign affairs and international relations remain beyond judicial review leaves some cases with human rights implications beyond the reach of the courts. *Thorpe v Commonwealth*[19] was such a case. The applicant sought to require the Australian government to ask the United Nations General Assembly for a resolution requesting an advisory opinion from the International Court of Justice on the 'separate rights and legal status' of aboriginal people. Kirby J held that these issues were matters of international relations and thus reserved to the executive government.[20] Nevertheless, the courts do not accept such claims without question. A claim that matters are non-justiciable because they impact on matters of international relations and related principles, such as the Act of State doctrine, will be examined by judges to determine whether it is properly beyond the reach of the courts.[21] The power of the courts to determine whether a case actually involves non-justiciable issues means that the executive government will encounter some level of judicial scrutiny even when such a claim ultimately succeeds.

The second method by which access to the court may be restricted is through the tests for determining an individual's or group's standing to bring an action. Restrictive rules of standing decrease the ability of an individual or group to challenge government actions, whereas more liberal rules provide greater access to the courts. In order to obtain the general law remedies, an individual must demonstrate standing according to the test prescribed for the relevant remedy.[22] The Australian Law Reform Commission has noted that there has been a move towards applying a 'special interest in the subject matter' test across all general law remedies and a 'more liberal application of the criteria for determining whether a "special interest" exists'.[23] The statutory standing test of 'a person aggrieved' in the *Administrative Decisions (Judicial Review) Act 1977* (Cth) ('ADJR Act') has developed along similar lines. For the purposes of the ADJR Act, a 'person aggrieved' is defined as 'a person whose interests are affected' by a decision, conduct leading

---

18 *R v Toohey; Ex parte Northern Land Council* (1981) 151 CLR 170, 219–20.
19 *Thorpe v Commonwealth* (1999) 144 ALR 677.
20 Ibid, 690–91.
21 See *Hicks v Ruddock* (2007) 156 FCR 574, 586–7; *Habib v Commonwealth* (2010) 183 FCR 62, 96–7, 101.
22 M Aronson and M Groves, *Judicial Review of Administrative Action* (Thomson Reuters, 5th ed, 2013) Ch 11.
23 Australian Law Reform Commission, *Beyond the Doorkeeper* (Report 78, 1996) [3.3]. The 'special interest' test articulated by the High Court is explained in Chapter 7.

to a decision, or a failure to make a decision.[24] The major developments in this area have concerned the ability of organisations with a diverse range of interests to obtain standing to challenge government decisions. This test has been applied to enable environmental groups to challenge decisions within their area of expertise,[25] priests to challenge the classification of an allegedly blasphemous film,[26] and members of an Aboriginal community to challenge a decision to allow works to be undertaken on land where Aboriginal relics were located.[27] Although access to the courts has increased by the slow relaxation of the standing rules, those rules do not allow judicial review in all circumstances.[28] The Australian Law Reform Commission has recommended that the test for standing be further liberalised to enable any person to commence public law proceedings, unless it can be demonstrated that there is a legislative intention to the contrary or it would unreasonably interfere with another person's private rights.[29] This recommendation has not been adopted, demonstrating that although access to the court has increased, it is not open to all individuals or groups to challenge any executive action.

Finally, access to the courts may be restricted through the inclusion of a privative clause in a statute excluding judicial review and the grant of public law remedies. Bradley has suggested that legislation which seeks to exclude judicial review 'runs the risk of infringing a fundamental human right'.[30] The immediate problem faced by Parliament when it inserts such clauses in federal legislation is that s 75(v) of the *Commonwealth Constitution* protects the jurisdiction of the High Court to grant the remedies of prohibition, mandamus and injunction. This constitutionally entrenched jurisdiction has been described as securing 'a basic provision of the rule of law'.[31] Much controversy has surrounded the privative clause in the *Migration Act 1958* (Cth) ('Migration Act'), where the Parliament has sought to restrict judicial review in the context of decisions concerning refugee status. Although the High Court has held that privative clauses are constitutional, the approach of courts to the insertion of privative clauses generally has been to regard them with 'a mixture of incredulity, hostility, and thinly disguised disobedience'.[32] In *Plaintiff S157/2002 v Commonwealth*,[33] the High Court held

---

24 ADJR Act, s 3(4).
25 For example, *Australian Conservation Foundation v Minister for Resources* (1989) 76 LGRA 200; *North Coast Environmental Council Inc v Minister for Resources* (1994) 55 FCR 492.
26 *Ogle v Strickland* (1987) 13 FCR 306.
27 *Onus v Alcoa of Australia Ltd* (1981) 149 CLR 27.
28 See Chapter 7.
29 ALRC, above n 23, 5.25.
30 Bradley, above n 10, 353.
31 *Plaintiff S157/2002 v Commonwealth* (2003) 211 CLR 476, 482 (Gleeson CJ).
32 Aronson and Groves, above n 22, 940.
33 (2003) 211 CLR 476.

that such clauses must be interpreted against the presumption that Parliament does not intend 'to abrogate or curtail fundamental rights or freedoms unless such an intention is clearly manifested by unmistakable and unambiguous language'.[34] This presumption will be discussed further in Chapters 10 and 13, but the importance of preserving an individual's access to the courts, particularly in the context of decisions concerning refugee status, was underlined by Gleeson CJ's statement that 'people whose fundamental rights are at stake are ordinarily entitled to expect more than good faith. They are ordinarily entitled to expect fairness'.[35] In *Plaintiff S157/2002*, the High Court held that the privative clause could not oust the Court's jurisdiction over jurisdictional errors.[36] Although the concept of jurisdictional error has yet to be comprehensively defined by the Court, it appears to include a wide range of errors, including a failure to accord natural justice.[37] Once more, the High Court's restrictive interpretation of such clauses has enlarged the ability of an individual to challenge the legality of government actions.

These three 'gatekeepers' to the courts are not the only potential limits on judicial review of executive action. For example, an applicant for review pursuant to the ADJR Act must demonstrate that a decision is of 'an administrative character' and made 'under an enactment'.[38] The interpretation of both phrases by the courts has excluded administrative actions from judicial review.[39] However, the approach of the courts to standing, justiciability and privative clauses demonstrates that judges are suspicious of any attempt to restrict an individual's ability to challenge the legality of executive action. Returning to the distinction outlined at the beginning of this chapter, the courts' decisions in this area have enhanced individual rights and the rule of law – aims of both administrative law and human rights law. But it should be recognised that these decisions do not represent the enforcement of human rights law through the courts, not the least since international human rights law does not explicitly deal with an individual's right to challenge administrative action. Although they do not represent examples of the replication of rights in administrative law and human rights law, nevertheless they demonstrate the confluence of values between the two areas.

---

34 Ibid, 492 (Gleeson CJ). See also 516 (Callinan J).
35 Ibid, 494 (Gleeson CJ).
36 Ibid, 491 (Gleeson CJ), 506–8 (Gaudron, McHugh, Gummow, Kirby and Hayne JJ).
37 Ibid, 490 (Gleeson CJ). See also R Creyke, 'The Performance of Administrative Law in Protecting Rights' in T Campbell, J Goldsworthy and A Stone (eds), *Protecting Rights Without a Bill of Rights* (Aldershot, 2006) 122.
38 ADJR Act, s 3(1).
39 The phrase 'administrative character' has excluded quasi-legislative decisions from the ambit of the Act, and the phrase 'under an enactment' has excluded decisions which have no explicit statutory basis or which involve the exercise of private power. See Chapter 9.

Substantive arguments in judicial review proceedings

Once an individual or group has gained access to a court they must establish the substantive grounds of judicial review, that is, the legal basis on which the decision is to be invalidated. Government actions must be based on the law – through either legislative or executive power[40] – and judicial review provides a mechanism for ensuring legality is maintained. The second element of Bradley's right to administrative justice requires that a court 'apply the substantive grounds of judicial review'.[41] The grounds of review at the common law, and as listed in ss 5 and 6 of the ADJR Act, are extensive but also restricted in the sense that they only encompass legality, and not merits, review. In Australia, this distinction is reinforced by the constitutional separation of power between the executive and the judiciary. This was noted by Brennan J in *Attorney-General (NSW) v Quin*[42] when he stated that '[t]he duty and jurisdiction of the courts to review administrative action do not go beyond the declaration and enforcing of the law which determines the limits and governs the exercise of the repository's power…[T]he court has no jurisdiction simply to cure administrative injustice or error'. This section will not examine the way in which all the grounds of review may enhance an individual's ability to challenge executive action, but instead will focus on three grounds where fundamental rights or human rights arguments have been raised, specifically: that a decision is not supported by a statutory power, that the decision-maker has failed to take into account a relevant consideration, and that the decision was not made in compliance with the rules of natural justice. Despite Brennan J's comment in *Quin*, it will be seen that the courts perceive the breach of these standards 'as leading to administrative injustice' – a form of legal error.[43]

Statutory interpretation

French CJ has noted that '[o]ur legal universe today is dominated by innumerable statutes and varieties of delegated legislation and legislative instruments made under those statutes'.[44] Fundamentally, when courts consider whether a power has

---

40 Creyke (2006), above n 37, 103.
41 Bradley, above n 10, 351.
42 (1990) 170 CLR 1, 35–6.
43 R Creyke, 'Administrative Justice – Towards Integrity in Government' (2007) 31 *Melbourne University Law Review* 705, 714.
44 Robert French, 'Litigating in a Statutory Universe' (unpublished speech, 18 February 2012) 2.

been exercised in accordance with the statute, they are ensuring that the executive remains within the limits of the powers granted by Parliament and thus preserving the rule of law. When interpreting statutory powers, courts have invoked common law or fundamental rights and also international human rights law in the form of international treaties and declarations.

Although a number of presumptions of statutory interpretation may impact on an individual's rights,[45] in the field of judicial review the one most frequently stated and applied is the presumption that legislation does not interfere with fundamental rights without clear and unambiguous language. In *Coco v R*,[46] the High Court held that '[t]he courts should not impute to the legislature an intention to interfere with fundamental rights. Such an intention must be clearly manifested by unmistakable and unambiguous language'. In *Evans v New South Wales*,[47] the Full Court of the Federal Court stated that '[i]t is an important principle that Acts be construed, where constructional choices are open, so as not to encroach upon common law rights and freedoms'. Both statements express the same sentiment, although using slightly different language.

The question then becomes 'What rights are considered worthy of the badge "fundamental"?'. *Coco* concerned the right to non-interference with property, whereas *Evans* applied the presumption to protect freedom of speech. The list of rights would appear to include (among others) freedom of movement,[48] access to the court[49] and personal liberty.[50] Meagher has highlighted that 'what rights and freedoms are recognised as fundamental at common law is ultimately a matter of judicial choice'.[51] To date, courts have not expressly used international human rights law as the touchstone for developing the list of common law rights, although the similarity between common law rights falling within this principle and international human rights law has been noted.[52]

The principles of international human rights law have greater relevance when applying a second presumption – that Parliament intends to legislate in conformity with international law. If there is an ambiguity in a statute which has been enacted

---

45 Including the presumptions that penal provisions are strictly construed and that Parliament does not abrogate the privilege against self-incrimination.
46 *Coco v R* (1994) 179 CLR 427, 437.
47 *Evans v New South Wales* (2008) 168 FCR 576, 593.
48 *Melbourne Corporation v Barry* (1922) 31 CLR 174, 200–01.
49 *Plaintiff S157/2002 v Commonwealth* (2003) 211 CLR 476, 492–3.
50 *Minister for Immigration, Multicultural and Indigenous Affairs v Al-Masri* (2003) 126 FCR 54, 76.
51 D Meagher, 'The Common Law Principle of Legality in the Age of Rights' (2011) 35 *Melbourne University Law Review* 449, 459.
52 J Spigelman, 'The Application of Quasi-Constitutional Laws' (second lecture in the 2008 MacPherson Lectures Statutory Interpretation and Human Rights, 11 March 2008), 10; Meagher, above n 51, 466.

pursuant to a treaty obligation, 'a court should favour a construction which accords with Australia's obligations'.[53] This is because it is presumed that Parliament 'prima facie, intends to give effect to Australia's obligations under international law'.[54] Furthermore, a court should interpret a statute 'as far as its language permits, so that it is in conformity and not in conflict with the established rules of international law'.[55] In this context it has been argued that the power of mandatory detention in the Migration Act should be construed with reference to Australia's obligations pursuant to article 9 of the ICCPR (a provision which prohibits arbitrary detention).[56] Such an approach was favoured by the Full Court of the Federal Court in *Minister for Immigration, Multicultural and Indigenous Affairs v Al-Masri*.[57]

But these *presumptions* are just that and can be displaced by the words of the relevant statute. In *Chu Kheng Lim v Minister for Immigration, Local Government and Ethnic Affairs*,[58] Brennan, Deane and Dawson JJ accepted that, where legislation is ambiguous, the court should favour construction which accords with Australia's international obligations, but found that a requirement in the Migration Act that 'boat people' (as designated in the Act) be held in custody was unambiguous. Similar reasoning was adopted by a majority of the High Court in *Al-Kateb v Goodwin*,[59] which concerned the detention, pursuant to the Migration Act, of a stateless person who had been denied refugee status and yet had no prospect of being removed from Australia. The majority found that the Act provided for mandatory detention in unambiguous terms and could not be interpreted in conformity with Australia's obligations under the ICCPR.[60] The minority used a combination of the presumptions discussed above to interpret the Act in a way that would have protected Mr Al-Kateb from indefinite detention.[61]

These presumptions of statutory construction enhance the protection of common law rights and also the rights located in international human rights treaties; however, *Al-Kateb* is a reminder that they are merely presumptions. Absent constitutional protection, they cannot override an express parliamentary intention to deprive an individual of these rights. The impact of statutory charters or bills

---

53 *Minister for Immigration and Ethnic Affairs v Teoh* (1995) 183 CLR 273, 287.
54 *Lim v Minister for Immigration, Local Government and Ethnic Affairs* (1992) 176 CLR 1, 38.
55 *Teoh* (1995) 183 CLR 273, 287.
56 *Minister for Immigration, Multicultural and Indigenous Affairs v Al-Masri* (2003) 126 FCR 54, 89.
57 Ibid, 92.
58 (1992) 176 CLR 1, 38.
59 (2004) 219 CLR 562.
60 Ibid, 581 (McHugh J), 642 (Hayne J, Heydon J agreeing), 661 (Callinan J).
61 Ibid, 577 (Gleeson CJ referring to the presumption that Parliament did not intend to interfere with fundamental rights – in this case personal liberty), 616–17 (Kirby J referring to the presumption that legislation should be construed in accordance with Australia's international obligations).

of human rights on these presumptions of interpretation will be discussed later in this chapter.[62]

Relevant considerations

Administrative decision-makers must take into account relevant considerations, and not take into account irrelevant considerations, when exercising their powers. In *Minister for Aboriginal Affairs v Peko-Wallsend Ltd*,[63] Mason J held that this ground of review 'can only be made out if a decision-maker fails to take into account a consideration which he is bound to take into account in making that decision'. The list of express and implied considerations which are relevant for the purposes of this ground of review can be determined by construing the relevant statute.[64] In the context of the relationship between human rights and judicial review the question arises whether international human rights law principles could be considered mandatory relevant considerations. In Australia, the answer to this question would appear to be 'no', unless they are expressly incorporated into the relevant statute.

An example of express incorporation can be found in the parts of the Migration Act which enable the Minister to make a declaration with respect to a particular country. Once a declaration is made, offshore asylum seekers can be removed to that country.[65] Section 198A(3)(a) enables the Minister to declare that the relevant country meets four conditions in order for the power of removal to operate: that is, the country provides asylum seekers access 'to effective procedures for assessing their need for protection', 'provides protection for persons seeking asylum, pending determination of their refugee status', 'provides protection for persons who are given refugee status', and 'meets human rights standards in providing that protection'. In *Plaintiff M70/2011 v Minister for Immigration and Citizenship*,[66] the High Court held that these criteria were jurisdictional facts requiring an examination of the relevant country's legal obligations as well as the actual situation on the ground – that is, a combination of human rights law and the human rights conditions prevailing in the relevant country (in that case, Malaysia).

Attempts to argue that international human rights instruments may be relevant considerations, absent statutory incorporation, have not been successful. In *Kioa v West*,[67] it was argued that a relevant consideration in determining whether a man could be deported was the impact of the deportation order on his child – as the

---

62 See 'Impact of statutory bills of rights on judicial review' in this chapter.
63 (1986) 162 CLR 24, 39.
64 Ibid.
65 *Migration Act 1958* (Cth), s 198A(1).
66 *Plaintiff M70/2011 v Minister for Immigration and Citizenship* (2011) 244 CLR 144, 181–3 (French CJ), 200–02 (Gummow, Hayne, Crennan and Bell JJ), 232–6 (Kiefel J).
67 (1985) 159 CLR 550, 603.

child was entitled to the 'the concurrent enjoyment of the care of her parents and of the fruits of her citizenship in Australia' in accordance with the United Nations Declaration of the Rights of the Child. While Wilson J concluded that there was no evidence that the child's circumstances had not been taken into account,[68] Gibbs CJ expressly discounted the possibility that the provisions of the Declaration (or the ICCPR) could be relevant considerations that the delegate was bound to take into account, on the basis that there was 'no legal obligation on the Minister's delegate to ensure that his decision conformed with the Covenant or the Declaration'.[69] Brennan J also dismissed this argument, stating that the exercise of power cannot be set aside merely because the decision-maker 'does not take into account a matter which he was entitled to, but not bound, to take into account'.[70] In *Minister for Immigration and Ethnic Affairs v Teoh*[71] ('*Teoh*'), Mason CJ and Deane J accepted that the Minister could take into account a provision in the Convention on the Rights of the Child in a decision to deport a father (that is, the Convention was not an irrelevant consideration), but did not go so far as to state that the Convention was a relevant consideration that must be taken into account.[72]

This approach has not been universally endorsed outside Australia. In a New Zealand deportation case with similar facts to *Teoh*, it was argued that the Minister for Immigration did not have to take into account the Convention on the Rights of the Child and the ICCPR (in relation to a New Zealand child) as it was not incorporated into domestic law.[73] Cooke P described the Minister's argument as 'unattractive',[74] giving rise to the suggestion that the unincorporated treaty obligations may be mandatory relevant considerations. Subsequently, the Minister changed the departmental policy to ensure that the interests of children were taken into account in immigration decisions.[75]

In Australia, the report of the National Human Rights Consultation recommended that the ADJR Act 'be amended in such a way as to make the definitive list of Australia's international human rights obligations a relevant consideration in government decision making'.[76] This proposal has a worthy objective but appears

---

68 Ibid, 604.
69 Ibid, 570–71.
70 Ibid, 630.
71 (1995) 183 CLR 273.
72 Ibid, 285. Discussed in M Allars, 'One Small Step for Legal Doctrine, One Giant Leap Towards Integrity in Government: *Teoh's* Case and the Internationalisation of Administrative Law' (1995) 17 *Sydney Law Review* 204, 228.
73 *Tavita v Minister for Immigration* [1994] 2 NZLR 257.
74 Ibid, 266. This case was heard prior to the introduction of the *New Zealand Bill of Rights Act 1990* (NZ).
75 Discussed in M A Poole, 'International Instruments in Administrative Decisions: Mainstreaming International Law' (1999) 30 *Victoria University of Wellington Law Review* 91, 94.
76 National Human Rights Consultation Committee, *National Human Rights Consultation Report* (2009), Recommendation 11, xxxii.

to misconstrue the nature of the ADJR Act, which facilitates judicial review of administrative decisions rather than conditioning each exercise of statutory power. As explained by Mason J in *Peko-Wallsend*, the considerations which condition the exercise of a power must be gleaned from the scope, subject matter and purpose of the statute in which the power is located.[77] Mandating that all administrative decision-makers must take into account the provisions of all human rights treaties to which Australia is a party, without indicating the articles which are relevant to the exercise of a particular statutory power or the weight to be given to such legal provisions, would not appear to enhance the objectives of either administrative law or human rights law.[78]

Procedural fairness, legitimate expectations and the concept of unfairness

The greatest controversy concerning the relationship between international human rights law and judicial review has occurred in procedural fairness. In *Teoh*,[79] a case that has been described as 'dramatic',[80] potentially an example of 'backdoor incorporation'[81] of treaty obligations, or 'puzzling',[82] depending on the point of the view of the commentator, the High Court held that an unincorporated treaty could give rise to a legitimate expectation for the purposes of the law relating to procedural fairness. Mason CJ and Deane J stated that ratification of an international convention provided 'adequate foundation for a legitimate expectation, absent statutory executive indications to the contrary, that administrative decision makers will act in conformity with the Convention'.[83] If a decision-maker intended to act inconsistently with that expectation, 'procedural fairness requires that the person affected should be given notice

---

77 *Minister for Aboriginal Affairs v Peko-Wallsend Ltd* (1986) 162 CLR 24, 39.
78 The proposal is discussed in M Groves, 'Statutory Judicial Review and Human Rights' (forthcoming).
79 (1995) 183 CLR 273, 291.
80 Allars, above n 72, 204.
81 D Dyzenhaus, M Hunt and M Taggart, 'The Principle of Legality in Administrative Law: Internationalisation as Constitutionalisation' (2001) 1 *Oxford University Journal of Commonwealth Law* 5, 11.
82 E Handsley, 'Legal Fictions and Confusion as Strategies for Protecting Human Rights: A Dissenting View on *Teoh's Case*' (1997) 2 *Newcastle Law Review* 56, 65.
83 Above n 79. The relevant treaty obligation was article 3(1) of the Convention on the Rights of the Child, which provides that 'in all actions concerning children...the best interests of the child shall be a primary consideration'.

and an adequate opportunity of presenting a case against the taking of such a course'.[84] Gaudron J broadly agreed but placed greater significance on the child's Australian citizenship, holding that 'any reasonable person' would assume that the best interests of a child would be a primary consideration in administrative decision-making which impacts on their welfare.[85] Despite a vigorous dissent from McHugh J on the ability of international treaties to give rise to a legitimate expectation,[86] the decision constitutes the most obvious example of the explicit use of a provision of international human rights law in a ground of review in the Australian courts.

Although the majority in *Teoh* found that the international human rights law obligation only gave rise to a procedural obligation (or further hearing rights) rather than a substantive right, the executive response to the decision was swift. The Minister for Foreign Affairs and Trade and the Attorney-General issued a joint statement stating that merely entering into a treaty, without further parliamentary action, would not raise a legitimate expectation that administrative decision-makers would act in accordance with the treaty's provisions.[87] The joint statement made particular reference to the need to incorporate human rights treaties if they are to have domestic effect.[88] The legal effect of the joint statements is doubtful,[89] but stronger shadows were cast over *Teoh* by the High Court in *Minister for Immigration and Multicultural Affairs; Ex parte Lam*.[90] Although the impact of international treaties on the exercise of administrative discretion was not directly in issue in *Lam*, several members of the High Court described the reasoning in *Teoh* as a 'curiosity'[91] and expressed obvious displeasure at the 'elevation of an Executive ratification of an un-enacted Convention'.[92] Although *Teoh* was not expressly overruled, it was strongly doubted and now can be seen as the high point in the relevance of unincorporated human rights conventions to judicial review in Australia.

---

84 (1995) 183 CLR 273, 291–2.
85 Ibid, 304.
86 Ibid, 315–18.
87 Joint Statement by the Minister for Foreign Affairs and the Attorney-General, *International Treaties and the High Court decision in Teoh*, 10 May 1995. A similar statement was made in 1997 by the new Attorney-General and Minister for Foreign Affairs for the Coalition Government. Legislation seeking to overturn the decision in *Teoh* was introduced into Parliament by both the ALP and Coalition governments but lapsed on both occasions.
88 These parts of the statement are reproduced in *Tien v Minister for Immigration and Multicultural Affairs* (1998) 89 FCR 80, 103.
89 *Department of Immigration and Ethnic Affairs v Ram* (1990) 69 FCR 431, 437–8.
90 (2003) 214 CLR 1.
91 Ibid, 33 (McHugh and Gummow JJ).
92 Ibid, 49 (Callinan J).

Remedies

As there is no separate right to administrative justice in international human rights law, it is difficult to determine if the remedies for a successful judicial review application in Australia coalesce with the remedies for human rights review. Article 2(3)(a) of the ICCPR provides that the state must provide an 'effective remedy' for the violation of the rights listed in the Covenant. The diverse remedies for breaches of international human rights law include reparations, restitution, compensation, and guarantees of non-repetition of the relevant acts.[93] These remedies are all directed to the substance of rights claims. Remedies in judicial review are limited to ensuring that the decision-maker reaches a decision in accordance with the law rather than directing the actual content of that decision. Compensation is not available as a remedy in Australian judicial review proceedings. The most common remedy in a successful application is an order that a decision be quashed and returned to the decision-maker to be remade in accordance with the law. The fact that judicial review remedies are directed at the procedural aspects of decision-making, rather than the substance of administrative action, has led the UK Ministry of Justice to suggest that a successful claim 'may only result in a pyrrhic victory'.[94] Such statements are strongly disputed by commentators, who emphasise the importance of the government exercising its powers lawfully in society based on the rule of law.[95] In addition, a 10-year study into the outcomes of judicial review before the Federal Court and High Court found that in around three-quarters of cases reconsideration by the relevant agency resulted in a favourable outcome to the applicant.[96] This would suggest a victory for both the rule of law and an individual applicant.

There is one remedy that a superior court can grant that is closely analogous to international human rights law – the writ of habeas corpus, which was been described as 'the most efficient protection ever invented for the liberty of the subject'.[97] A writ of habeas corpus enables the release of a person from illegal detention. It is similar to article 9(4) of the ICCPR, which provides that '[a]nyone who is deprived of his liberty by arrest or detention shall be entitled to take proceedings before a court, in order that that court may decide without delay on the lawfulness of his detention and order his release if the detention is not

---

[93] See Human Rights Committee, General Comment No 31 [16].
[94] Ministry of Justice (UK), *Judicial Review: Proposals for Reform,* Consultation Paper (2012) [32].
[95] Centre for Public Law, University of Cambridge, Response to Ministry of Justice Consultation Paper, *Judicial Review: Proposals for Reform* (2012) [7].
[96] R Creyke and J McMillan, 'Judicial Review Outcomes – An Empirical Study' (2004) 11 *Australian Journal of Administrative Law* 82.
[97] *Ex parte Mwenya* [1960] 1 QB 241, 292 (Lord Evershed MR).

lawful'. An applicant for habeas corpus must show that a person has been illegally detained, and the writ must be directed to a person who can obey an order to release the individual.[98]

Habeas corpus has no standing requirement – anyone can seek the writ of habeas corpus on behalf of someone who is detained. This was illustrated by *Ruddock v Vadarlis*[99] where the Commonwealth did not dispute the standing of the Victorian Council for Civil Liberties and a solicitor (Vadarlis) to seek habeas corpus to secure the release of asylum seekers who had been rescued at sea by a Norwegian vessel (the M/V *Tampa*) and transferred to an Australian naval vessel. Although standing was not disputed, two aspects of the case led the Full Court of the Federal Court to refuse the writ. First, the lawful authority to hold the asylum seekers was provided by prerogative power enabling the government to prevent the entry of non-citizens into Australia and to undertake such actions as are necessary to effect exclusion. Those powers authorised the restraint on the liberty of the asylum seekers.[100] Second, the court held that the acts of the Commonwealth in preventing the landing of the rescuees did not constitute detention for the purposes of the writ of habeas corpus because 'nothing done by the Commonwealth amounted to a restraint on their freedom'.[101] Accordingly, there was neither the 'detention' nor 'unlawfulness' required to issue the writ.

Habeas corpus has been prominent in cases arising from the 'war on terror' in the United Kingdom and the United States, where it is alleged that detainees have been held in breach of international human rights law standards. It is the remedy sought by those seeking to secure their release from detention in Guantánamo Bay.[102] In 2011, the English Court of Appeal granted habeas corpus to release a Pakistani man who was being held in US custody in Afghanistan after having been transferred from UK custody.[103] It was argued on behalf of the applicant, Mr Rahmatullah, that a Memorandum of Understanding between the UK and US governing the transfer and treatment of prisoners in Iraq essentially gave the UK enough influence over Mr Rahmatullah's fate to gain his transfer to the UK (and release) by the US government.[104] The majority of the Court of Appeal held that

---

98 Aronson and Groves, above n 22, 858–64.
99 *Ruddock v Vadarlis* (2001) 110 FCR 491, 509, 518.
100 Ibid, 543–4.
101 Ibid, 548. Black CJ dissented on the issue of whether the actions of the Commonwealth amounted to detention for the purposes of the writ: 511–13.
102 The most prominent US Supreme Court decision on the question of whether habeas corpus is available to Guantánamo Bay detainees is *Boumediene v Bush* 553 US 723 (2008).
103 *Rahmatullah v Secretary of State for Defence* [2012] 1 WLR 1462.
104 Clause 4 of the Memorandum of Understanding (2003) provided that '[a]ny prisoners of war, civilian internees, and civilian detainees transferred by a detaining power [the UK] will be returned by the accepting power [the US] to the detaining power without delay upon request by the detaining power': Ibid, 1479.

this influence was sufficient to meet the requirement of 'control' for the purposes of habeas corpus.[105] The United States thought otherwise and refused to cooperate. Following this refusal, the case was returned to the Supreme Court, where the judges upheld the decision to issue the writ.[106] Lord Kerr distinguished habeas corpus from the remedies of judicial review by stating that the issue of the remedy was not discretionary – if the unlawfulness of the detention can be demonstrated, the writ issues as of right.[107] Viewed in light of article 9(4) of the ICCPR, the non-discretionary nature of habeas corpus is important from a human rights perspective.

In Australia, the security of the remedy is reinforced by the suggestion in *Kirk v Industrial Relations Commission (NSW)*[108] that one of the defining features of the Supreme Courts is their ability to issue habeas corpus. The position of the writ at the federal level is less clear. Habeas corpus is not referred to in s 75(v) of the *Commonwealth Constitution*, although some judges have hinted that the remedy may be constitutionally entrenched.[109]

Impact of statutory bills of rights on judicial review

The above analysis is focused on the position in Australia at the federal level, where there is no constitutional or statutory bill of rights. When investigating options for improving the promotion and protection of human rights in Australia, the National Consultation on Human Rights recommended that the Commonwealth Parliament introduce a statutory bill of rights.[110] The question is to what extent the introduction of a statutory bill of rights, enabling an individual to challenge executive actions for breaching enumerated human rights, has impacted on this analysis in other jurisdictions. Statutory bills of rights have been enacted in the United Kingdom, New Zealand, Victoria and the Australian Capital Territory (ACT).[111] These Acts are not constitutional bills of rights, but nevertheless they enable an individual to challenge executive actions which infringe their human rights. The human rights set out in such statutes include the traditional civil and political rights, similar to

---

105 Ibid, 1485.
106 *Secretary of State for Foreign and Commonwealth Affairs v Rahmatullah* [2012] 3 WLR 1087, 1107.
107 Ibid, 1110.
108 *Kirk v Industrial Court (NSW)* (2010) 239 CLR 531, 581.
109 See Aronson and Groves, above n 22, 839–40.
110 National Human Rights Consultation Committee, above n 76, Recommendation 18, xxxiv.
111 The relevant Acts are: *Human Rights Act 1998* (UK); *New Zealand Bill of Rights Act 1990* (NZ); *Human Rights Act 2004* (ACT); *Charter of Human Rights and Responsibilities Act 2006* (Vic).

those contained in the ICCPR, as well as an acknowledgement that such rights may be limited in certain circumstances. For example, ss 8–27 of the *Charter of Human Rights and Responsibilities Act 2006* (Vic) ('the Victorian Charter') includes a wide-ranging list of rights, while s 7(2) acknowledges that 'reasonable limits' can be placed on a human right as 'demonstrably justified in a free and democratic society'. These statutes enable courts to undertake certain action in the event that a legislative provision is found to be incompatible with human rights, or an infringement of human rights has been found to have occurred – the precise actions that a court may take depend on the particular statutory scheme in question. However, there are limitations on these models which indicate that the remedies available for judicial review still have an important role to play in rectifying executive action which infringes individual rights.

The statutory bills of rights govern the way in which courts (and other entities) undertake the role of statutory interpretation. For example, s 32 of the Victorian Charter provides that 'so far as it is possible to do so consistently with their purpose, all statutory provisions must be interpreted in a way that is compatible with human rights'.[112] The equivalent provision in the *Human Rights Act 1998* (UK) provides that '[s]o far as it is possible to do so, primary legislation and subordinate legislation must be read and given effect in a way which is compatible with the Convention rights'[113] – the Convention being the ECHR. Unlike the Victorian Act and the *Human Rights Act 2004* (ACT),[114] the *Human Rights Act 1998* (UK) does not refer to the 'purpose' of a statute.[115] As has been highlighted by Justice Spigelman (extra-judicially), the critical issue is to what extent the court can modify a statute and 'still be undertaking a task that can be correctly identified as one of "interpretation"'.[116] The judiciary will be legitimately criticised 'if it strays into the territory of judicial legislation, as this undermines the preservation of parliamentary sovereignty'.[117] The interpretative obligation in the *Human Rights Act 1998* (UK) has been described by the House of Lords as 'unusual and far-reaching' in that it may require the court to depart from the intention of Parliament in enacting the legislation.[118] Charlesworth has noted that the first four years of practice under

---

112 Section 30 of the ACT statute is similar to s 32 of the Victorian Charter.
113 *Human Rights Act 1998* (UK), s 3(1).
114 *Human Rights Act 2004* (ACT), s 30.
115 Interestingly, the Victorian Human Rights Consultation Committee believed that the proposed wording of s 32 codified the English jurisprudence on s 3(1) of the UK Act: Human Rights Consultation Committee, Government of Victoria, *Rights Responsibilities and Respect: The Report of the Human Rights Consultation Committee* (2005) 83.
116 Spigelman, above n 52, 18.
117 J Debeljak, 'Parliamentary Sovereignty and Dialogue Under the Victorian *Charter of Human Rights and Responsibilities*: Drawing the Line between Judicial Interpretation and Judicial Law-Making' (2007) 33 *Monash University Law Review* 9, 47.
118 *Ghaidan v Godin-Mendoza* [2004] 2 AC 557, 571 [30] (Lord Nicholls).

the UK Act 'seems...to give priority to human rights-compatible interpretation of legislation over parliamentary intent'.[119]

In the ACT and Victoria, there has been much debate as to the correct method of applying the interpretative provisions. In *Momcilovic v R*,[120] a majority of the High Court held that s 32 of the Victorian Charter was valid as it does not require courts to go beyond established methods of statutory interpretation and undertake a task of 'judicial legislation'.[121] French CJ equated the task required by the Charter to the application of the common law presumption that legislation is not intended to interfere with fundamental rights without clear words to the contrary.[122] However, the judges differed on the role of s 7(2) in this process. Gummow, Hayne and Bell JJ believed that when interpreting legislation, the human rights listed in the Charter were to be considered, taking into consideration the 'reasonable limits' provision in s 7(2).[123] French CJ, Crennan and Kiefel JJ concluded that s 7(2) only became relevant after the interpretative task in s 32 was completed.[124] Heydon J dissented and held that both s 32 and s 7(2) required the court to undertake a legislative, rather than judicial, task, which was incompatible with its role as a court, and that consequently the Charter was invalid.[125] It is difficult to discern a single coherent approach from these differing judgments. Kyrou J conceded that problem in *Magee v Delaney*.[126] His Honour adopted the approach of French CJ, Crennan and Kiefel JJ, while acknowledging that applying the different approaches in *Momcilovic* may not necessarily result in different outcomes. Thus, a human rights-compatible interpretation pursuant to the Charter is both the same as, and also different from, the task of statutory interpretation in traditional judicial review proceedings.

In the event that legislation cannot be interpreted consistently with a human right, the statutory bills of rights in the United Kingdom, Victoria and the ACT enable a court to issue a statement of inconsistent interpretation.[127] Such statements are not judicial determinations that a legislative provision is invalid, but rather statements to the relevant legislature that a provision is not capable of being read in accordance with human rights principles. The final word is left with Parliament to determine whether it will amend or repeal the relevant provision. The constitutionality of the

---

119 H Charlesworth, 'Human Rights and Statutory Interpretation' in S Corcoran and S Bottomley (eds), *Interpreting Statutes* (Federation Press, 2005) 114.
120 *Momcilovic v R* (2011) 245 CLR 1.
121 The phrase 'judicial legislation' was used by Heydon J in his dissenting opinion in *Momcilovic*: Ibid, 183.
122 Ibid, 50.
123 Ibid, 91–2 (Gummow J, Hayne J agreeing), 250 (Bell J).
124 Ibid, 44, 50 (French CJ), 218–20, 224 (Crennan and Kiefel JJ).
125 Ibid, 163–75 (s 7(2)), 178–84 (s 32).
126 *Magee v Delaney* [2012] VSC 407, [163].
127 *Human Rights Act 1998* (UK), s 4; *Human Rights Act 2004* (ACT), s 32; *Charter of Human Rights and Responsibilities Act 2006* (Vic), s 28.

Supreme Court of Victoria's role in issuing such statements has been upheld by the High Court,[128] but many questions about its operation were left unsettled. Leaving aside the role of Parliament, Victorian statements of inconsistent interpretation do not assist an individual in particular proceedings who claims that their rights have been breached.[129]

Of greater assistance to an individual is the fact that each of the statutory bills of rights applies human rights principles to the executive branch of government.[130] The reach of these Acts is also extended to bodies that undertake public functions, potentially encompassing a broader range of bodies than are traditionally encompassed within the notion of the executive government.[131] In Victoria, the Director of Public Housing, Metro West (an independent contractor with delegated statutory powers to provide social housing to vulnerable people) and the Medical Practitioners Board of Victoria have been held to be 'public authorities' for the purposes of the Charter, while the view has been taken that Telstra does not fulfil the definition as it is 'a company limited by shares carrying on a commercial business'.[132] In the leading authority on the interpretation of the phrase 'of a public nature' in the United Kingdom, *YL v Birmingham*,[133] the majority took a narrow view of the phrase to hold that a privately owned independent nursing home which provided accommodation and care to elderly people (such care being arranged and paid for by the local authority in some cases) did not undertake a function of a 'public nature'.[134] Commentators have suggested that this decision has 'led to a serious protection gap for vulnerable individuals in relation to public services procured from the private sector'.[135] Such debates are familiar to international human rights lawyers given that international human rights treaties too place obligations on the state, rather than on private entities.

---

128 *Momcilovic v R* (2011) 245 CLR 1.
129 *Charter of Human Rights and Responsibilities Act 2006* (Vic), s 36(5)(b).
130 *Human Rights Act 1998* (UK), s 6; *New Zealand Bill of Rights Act 1990* (NZ), s 3(a); *Human Rights Act 2004* (ACT), s 40B; *Charter of Human Rights and Responsibilities Act 2006* (Vic), s 38.
131 *Human Rights Act 1998* (UK), s 6(3); *New Zealand Bill of Rights Act 1990* (NZ), s 3(b); *Human Rights Act 2004* (ACT), s 40A; *Charter of Human Rights and Responsibilities Act 2006* (Vic), s 4.
132 See *Director of Housing v IF* [2008] VCAT 2413 [49]; *Metro West v Sudi (Residential Tenancies)* [2009] VCAT 2025 [165]; *Sabet v Medical Practitioners Board of Victoria* (2008) 20 VR 414, 431; *Drummond v Telstra Corporation Limited (Anti-Discrimination)* [2008] VCAT 2630, [73].
133 *YL v Birmingham City Council* [2008] 1 AC 95.
134 The case did not provide a single coherent principle to determine this issue because most of the Lords adopted a multi-factorial approach to determine whether a function was public.
135 John Wadham et al, *Blackstone's Guide to the Human Rights Act 1998* (6th ed, 2011) 59.

The two Australian statutory bills of rights provide that it is unlawful for a public authority to 'act in a way that is incompatible with a human right' or 'in making a decision, to fail to give proper consideration to a relevant human right'.[136] This phrasing gives rise to the possibility that an applicant in a judicial review proceeding could argue that a public authority has failed to take into account a relevant consideration (the relevant consideration being a human right), or that a public authority has acted unreasonably in not giving appropriate weight to a human rights consideration.[137] Although the first option is suggested by the wording of both the Victorian and ACT statutes, the second option is less certain, not least as it could give rise to the suggestion that proportionality (that the decision of a public authority was disproportionate to a legitimate aim) is a 'free-standing' ground of review.[138] In *Sabet v Medical Practitioners Board of Victoria*, Hollingworth J accepted that a doctor who applied for judicial review of a decision by the Medical Practitioners Board to suspend his registration could argue that the Board had failed to give proper consideration to a relevant consideration (the presumption of innocence in s 25(1) of the Charter).[139] In that case, the argument was ultimately unsuccessful as it was held that even if the presumption of innocence had direct application to the Board's hearings, there was no evidence that it had been unreasonably or unjustifiably limited.[140] In *Sabet* the applicant also argued that the Board's decision was disproportionate. Hollingworth J rejected the applicability of proportionality in Australia as an independent ground of review separate from the more onerous test required by *Wednesbury* unreasonableness, stating that such a change in Australian law would be for an appellate court.[141]

The utility of applicants for judicial review making these arguments depends on whether it will result in a remedy. In the event that a public authority has violated human rights in the United Kingdom, a court with appropriate jurisdiction is able to grant the remedies available in judicial review, and in addition, may award damages or compensation in civil proceedings.[142] In Victoria, the precise relationship between the remedies for judicial review and the Victorian Charter is unresolved. Section 39(1) of the Charter provides that:

---

136 *Charter of Human Rights and Responsibilities Act 2006* (Vic), s 38(1); the *Human Rights Act 2004* (ACT), s 40B. Section 6(1) of the UK *Human Rights Act 1998* provides that it 'is unlawful for a public authority to act in a way which is incompatible with a Convention right'.
137 J Debeljak, 'Human Rights Responsibilities of Public Authorities Under the *Charter of Rights*' (presented at the Law Institute of Victoria Charter of Rights Conference) 18 May 2007, 13.
138 Ibid, 13.
139 *Sabet v Medical Practitioners Board of Victoria* (2008) 20 VR 414, 430.
140 Ibid, 441–2.
141 Ibid, 424.
142 *Human Rights Act 1998* (UK), s 8.

> If, otherwise than because of this Charter, a person may seek any relief or remedy in respect of an act or decision of a public authority on the ground that the act or decision was unlawful, that person may seek that relief or remedy on a ground of unlawfulness arising because of this Charter.

Section 39(2) of the Charter provides that this does not affect the ability of an applicant to obtain judicial review. The convoluted nature of s 39 has been widely criticised.[143] In *Sabet*, Hollingworth J stated that the effect of s 39 was that if an applicant (apart from the Charter) had a right to a remedy, then the applicant could seek the same remedy on the basis that a decision 'was unlawful, because of the Charter'.[144] In that case the applicant sought the remedies of certiorari and injunction against the Medical Practitioners Board on the basis that it had breached natural justice. Hollingworth J held that the 'effect of s 39 is that he may also seek the same relief on the ground that the decision was unlawful under the Charter'.[145] In *Director of Housing v Sudi*,[146] Weinberg JA indicated that it 'was anticipated by the drafters of the Charter that there would be some expansion in the field of existing administrative law remedies as the basis upon which human rights could be enforced'.[147] He also thought that this would encompass the jurisdiction of the Supreme Court to grant the remedies in judicial review, but emphasised that the Charter did not create new causes of action or remedies.[148] These comments suggest that the Charter may be useful in judicial review proceedings for the existing remedies, although ultimately Weinberg JA did not have to decide the point because the power of the Supreme Court to grant remedies was not at issue in *Sudi*. This contrast between the position in the United Kingdom and the (uncertain) position in Victoria demonstrates that whether human rights review will coexist with, or become an element of, judicial review depends greatly on the drafting of the relevant human rights statute. In Victoria, it is clear that human rights review under the Charter does not replace judicial review as a method of protecting individual rights and providing a remedy for a person aggrieved by executive action.

Conclusion

In answer to the question posed in the title of this chapter, there are a number of ways in which judicial review and human rights are 'two sides of the same

---

143 For example, J Gans, 'The Charter's Irredeemable Remedies Provision' (2009) 33 *Melbourne University Law Review* 105.
144 *Sabet v Medical Practitioners Board of Victoria* (2008) 20 VR 414, 430.
145 Ibid.
146 [2011] VSCA 211.
147 Ibid, [217].
148 Ibid, [215]–[217].

coin'. Although judicial review is concerned with the procedure rather than the substance of executive decision-making, there is no shortage of ways in which the courts protect individual rights. The absence of a specific right to administrative justice in Australia does not mean that 'administrative justice' as a concept is foreign to Australian administrative law[149] or that rights have no place in its review mechanisms. Robertson has suggested that the 'fundamental contribution of judicial review to individual rights is to give reality to those rights by means of access to a forum where the lawfulness of decisions and actions can be tested'.[150] Whether rights are expressed as fundamental, common law, or international human rights, they are relevant at many stages of judicial review – from the commencement of an action to the remedies that may be granted.

Overall, it would appear that courts are more comfortable defending fundamental or common law rights, but cautious when using international human rights law. Thus, courts have been vigorous in using fundamental rights in interpreting legislation but have referred to international human rights law more sparingly in the same context. Although the courts have not favoured taking into account international human rights law norms as mandated relevant considerations, they have utilised them in procedural fairness. The decision in *Lam* suggests that *Teoh* may represent the high point in such arguments, but nevertheless the courts have recognised the need to ensure the enhanced fairness of procedures where people's rights are at stake in the context of refugee status determinations. This is illustrated by Gleeson CJ's comment in *Plaintiff S157/2002* that people whose fundamental rights are at risk are entitled to expect fairness.[151] The extent to which a statutory bill of rights at the federal level could change this picture would depend on the content of the Act, particularly the provisions dealing with remedies. Even without such a statute, as the authors of the quotations set out at the beginning of this chapter would recognise, while judicial review may not be the same as human rights review, the protection of rights nevertheless has a central role in judicial review proceedings.

---

149 Administrative justice in Australian administrative law more generally is examined in J McMillan and N Williams, 'Administrative Law and Human Rights' in David Kinley (ed), *Human Rights in Australian Law*, 63 and R Creyke (2007), above n 43.
150 A Robertson, 'Judicial Review and the Protection of Individual Rights' in J McMillan (ed) *Administrative Law: Does the Public Benefit?* (Australian Institute of Administrative Law, 1992) 37, 43.
151 See n 35 and accompanying text.

SECURITY AND FAIRNESS IN AUSTRALIAN PUBLIC LAW

Ben Saul

Introduction

Security concerns raise troubling rule of law questions about the weighing of competing public interests in national security, fairness to affected individuals, the accountability of administrative decision-makers, and public confidence in the openness of justice before the courts. Such concerns habitually emerge in times of crisis, such as during the world wars and the Cold War, and the pall of suspicion often falls most heavily on 'outsiders', whether Germans and Japanese, communists or terrorists. Legal concerns about security were reignited by the heightened security environment after the 11 September 2001 terrorist attacks and recurring political preoccupations with strong 'border protection'.

Many legal doctrines, principles and procedures may apply where national security is raised in administrative decision-making or judicial review proceedings. The content or quality of procedural fairness at common law or under statute may vary. Special statutory procedures may govern the handling of security-sensitive information. The availability and nature of merits review can be affected and non-binding reviewers may displace binding tribunals. Public interest immunity may be invoked to preclude the admissibility of otherwise relevant evidence. The degree of scrutiny brought to bear by judges may diminish out of deference to executive expertise in making security judgements.

The ways in which security concerns are dealt with by the law naturally involve deeply political policy decisions by the legislature and the executive. But they also reflect value choices made by the judiciary in selecting between different interpretative or policy approaches and in deciding where the balance of interests lies in a given case. In most other liberal democracies, the political and value choices made by parliaments, governments and the courts are also circumscribed by the ultimate limits demanded by human rights law, whether statutory, constitutional, regional or international. Australian law persists in maintaining its outlier status, remaining relatively unencumbered by the intrusion of overt human rights principles in the security field, even if public law concerns sometimes cross over with human rights.[1] Australian administrative and judicial proceedings involving security questions are consequently following a different trajectory from their counterparts in legal comparators such as the United Kingdom, Europe, Canada and New Zealand.

This chapter examines two particular legal contexts in which national security issues have generated serious concerns about the fairness of administrative decisions and/or judicial review proceedings: (1) the diminution of procedural fairness to

---

1 Ben Saul, 'Australian Administrative Law: The Human Rights Dimension', in Matthew Groves and HP Lee (eds), *Australian Administrative Law: Fundamentals, Principles and Doctrines* (Cambridge University Press, Cambridge, 2007).

'nothingness' in certain security decisions by the Australian Security Intelligence Organisation ('ASIO'), and (2) the invocation of public interest immunity (also known as Crown privilege) to preclude the admission into evidence of security information. In either case the result may be that an affected person may not know the essence of the case against them, rendering them unable to effectively challenge the executive's claims and its adverse administrative decisions. Independent merits or judicial review of decisions is also severely curtailed by the potential absence of relevant information or evidence, further degrading fairness and accountability.

This chapter also reflects on the proper role of the judiciary in scrutinising security issues and ensuring fairness. It argues that Australian courts have sometimes been unjustifiably deferential to the executive when security is invoked and have chosen (rather than being compelled by the legislature) to unnecessarily sacrifice fairness to individuals. The courts have tended to present security and fairness as irreconcilable in hard cases, without first utilising means available to safeguard security while preserving basic fairness. They have also underestimated their own security expertise or their capacity to acquire it. In so doing they have treated aspects of security as *innately* non-justiciable, when in reality they have chosen to construct security as such. The immunising of executive action from review is a deeply political choice by judges, not inevitable in some 'natural' order of things. Separation of powers arguments also fail to justify the prevailing approach.

This chapter contrasts the Australian approach with that taken in comparable liberal democracies where binding human rights principles apply to security decisions. It demonstrates how a human rights approach results in a more discerning and proportionate weighing of competing public interests in security and fairness. It points to creative ways of recalibrating Australia's approach, such as through the requirement of a minimum irreducible content of procedural fairness in all cases and a 'special advocate' procedure to better balance the public interests in security, fairness, accountability and public confidence.

The vanishing point of procedural fairness

Australian common law imposes a duty to act fairly, by according procedural fairness, in the making of administrative decisions, unless a statute clearly provides otherwise.[2] Procedural fairness may possess a minimum content but identifying what that is has proven difficult, since its content varies significantly according to context. Procedural fairness ordinarily requires prior notice that a decision will be

---

2 *Kioa v West* (1985) 159 CLR 550, 584 (Mason J).

made, disclosure of the substance of the information upon which a decision will be based and an opportunity to respond.[3] Legislation can augment these requirements – a more elaborate articulation of procedural fairness might include a statement of reasons and a right to merits review. Legislation can also fundamentally diminish any common law minima or presumptions, while the common law itself alters the nature of procedural fairness according to the context and circumstances.

The content of procedural fairness reaches its nadir when security is at stake. An example is decision-making by ASIO. ASIO is empowered by the *ASIO Act 1979* (Cth) ('the ASIO Act') to make 'security assessments' in respect of a person, which may result in a non-prejudicial finding (where there are no security concerns), a qualified assessment (where there may be some concerns but no action is recommended), or an adverse security assessment (where ASIO recommends that prescribed administrative action be taken or not be taken).[4] ASIO applies a wide definition of 'security'.[5] Its assessments are used in making a wide range of administrative decisions across government, from visa clearances to employment eligibility.[6]

Section 36 of the ASIO Act provides that the explicit procedural fairness requirements of Part IV of the ASIO Act, including the rights to a statement of reasons and merits review before the Administrative Appeals Tribunal ('AAT'),[7] do not apply to a person who is not an Australian citizen, permanent resident or special purpose visa holder. ASIO accordingly has no statutory duty to provide reasons to such people when they are affected by security assessments. Even for citizens, the content of procedural fairness can be fundamentally reduced by statute.[8]

Disclosure of adverse security information

The scope of any residual common law procedural fairness for those who are not citizens, permanent residents or permanent visa holders has been considered in

---

3 Chapter 10.
4 *ASIO Act 1979* (Cth), s 35.
5 *ASIO Act 1979* (Cth), s 4(a), which includes protecting Australia and its people from domestic or external (i) espionage; (ii) sabotage; (iii) politically motivated violence; (iv) promotion of communal violence; (v) attacks on Australia's defence system; or (vi) acts of foreign interference. The definition also refers to 'the carrying out of Australia's responsibilities to any foreign country' in relation to any of the foregoing threats (s 4(b)) and 'the protection of Australia's territorial and border integrity from serious threats' (s 4(aa)).
6 On the latter, see, eg, *Fisher v Gaisford* (1997) 48 ALD 200 (DFAT officer was held entitled to procedural fairness when his security clearance was suspended).
7 *ASIO Act 1979* (Cth), s 54.
8 See, eg, *ASIO Act 1979* (Cth), ss 37(2) (ASIO must disclose all information it relies upon 'other than information the inclusion of which would, in the opinion of the Director-General, be contrary to the requirements of security'), and 38 (the Attorney-General can withhold notice of the assessment or disclosure of its grounds where necessary to protect security).

many decisions involving foreign visitors and refugees assessed by ASIO to be security risks. ASIO decisions are judicially reviewable,[9] including on procedural fairness grounds. The federal courts also have jurisdiction to review consequential administrative decisions which flow from ASIO security assessments, such as a decision by the Department of Immigration and Border Protection to refuse or cancel visas or to place people in detention.[10]

People who receive an adverse security assessment from ASIO may face the immediate difficulty that they do not know the basis on which the assessment has been made. ASIO has no statutory duty to disclose adverse allegations, evidence or reasons, or even a summary thereof, though it can do so at its discretion. Where people do not know the case against them, it will normally be very difficult, even impossible, to identify any probable or even possible errors of law upon which to legitimately commence judicial review proceedings.

Even if a person manages to commence proceedings, the federal courts have accepted that procedural fairness may be lawfully eviscerated in certain security cases. The *Leghaei* case is instructive. Sheikh Mansour Leghaei entered Australia on a temporary visa in 1994 and was refused a permanent residency visa in 1997 on the basis that he was assessed by ASIO as a risk to security.[11] New adverse security assessments were issued in 2002 and 2004. Leghaei maintained that he did not know the basis of the assessment and was denied procedural fairness. The Federal Court considered the issue in a decision in late 2005. In a decision which excluded confidential parts, Justice Madgwick observed that under the ASIO Act, non-citizen non-permanent residents are not entitled to the procedural fairness rights enjoyed by citizens and permanent residents,[12] namely, rights to receive a statement of reasons for an adverse security assessment, to be notified of an assessment, to merits review and to procedural fairness at the judicial review level.[13] Madgwick J noted, however, that there is an indirect right to receive notification of the existence of the assessment under the *Migration Act* where an adverse security assessment is the basis for cancelling a visa.[14] Where the visa would be directly threatened by

---

9 ASIO decisions are excluded from review under the *Administrative Decisions (Judicial Review) Act 1977* (Cth), sch 1, but are reviewable by the Federal Court under s 39B of the *Judiciary Act 1903* (Cth) and under the original jurisdiction of the High Court by s 75 of the *Australian Constitution*.
10 The High Court has original jurisdiction under s 75 of the *Australian Constitution*. The Federal Magistrates' Court is given the same jurisdiction as the High Court to review 'migration decisions' under s 476 of the *Migration Act 1958* (Cth).
11 The *Migration Regulations 1994* (Cth) excluded visa applicants if they were 'assessed by the competent authorities to be directly or indirectly a risk to Australian national security': *Migration Regulations 1994* (Cth) sch 4, Public Interest Criterion 4002 ('PIC 4002').
12 Under the *ASIO Act 1979* (Cth), s 36.
13 *Leghaei v Director General of Security* [2005] FCA 1576, [70]–[73].
14 Ibid, [73].

an adverse security assessment, the Federal Court found that there is a duty at the primary decision-making phase to afford 'such degree of procedural fairness as the circumstances could bear, consistent with a lack of prejudice to national security'.[15] Such obligation will be 'discharged by evidence of the fact and content of such genuine consideration by the [ASIO] Director-General personally'.[16] The Court found that Parliament had determined that the ASIO Director-General must be trusted to be fair to those against whom an adverse security assessment had been made:

> [R]ecognition and respect must be given to the degree of expertise and responsibility held by relevant senior ASIO personnel in relation to the potential repercussions of disclosure and...usual lack of such expertise on the part of judges (myself included...) and...a degree of faith must, as a practical matter, be reposed in the integrity and sense of fair play of the Director-General. If this is unsatisfactory, the remedy lies in Parliament's hands.[17]

Madgwick J affirmed that 'courts are ill-equipped to evaluate intelligence'.[18] Accordingly, the Court was not in a position to contradict the opinion expressed in confidential affidavit evidence from ASIO. His Honour stated, 'even a sceptical judge out to defend civil liberties and human rights, but without either independent expert assistance or considerable and recent experience of security cases, is not in as good a position as is desirable to make a judgment on the matter'.[19] Madgwick J concluded, after 'having read and had debated the confidential material' before him, that 'genuine consideration' was given by ASIO to disclosure, but that the prejudice to national security meant that 'the content of procedural fairness is reduced, in practical terms, to nothingness'.[20] Leghaei was thus found to have been accorded as much fairness as national security permitted.[21]

The Full Federal Court dismissed an appeal by Leghaei. Parts of that judgment remain confidential, but it is clear the Full Court accepted authority that the balancing of the individual's entitlement to know the case against them with security interests may sometimes produce the 'unsatisfactory' feature that the content of an assessment is withheld from the person,[22] reducing procedural fairness to 'nothingness'.[23] The Full Court acknowledged the risk of 'serious unfairness'.[24] It found, however, that

---

15 Ibid, [83].
16 Ibid, [86].
17 Ibid, [87].
18 Ibid, [84].
19 Ibid, [92].
20 Ibid, [88]. A similar approach was taken in *Soh v Commonwealth* (2008) 101 ALD 310, 328.
21 *Leghaei v Director General of Security* [2005] FCA 1576, [88].
22 *Leghaei v Director-General of Security* [2007] FCAFC 37, [50].
23 Ibid, [51].
24 Ibid, [59].

there was no error of law by the primary judge, who 'did not simply rubber stamp the opinion' of ASIO but had 'satisfied himself that the Director-General had given personal genuine consideration to…whether disclosure would be contrary to the national interest'.[25]

The High Court denied Leghaei's special leave to appeal application, perhaps because the High Court had previously accepted that the sensitive nature of information can affect the content of natural justice. Fairness can be limited to require limited disclosure of confidential information. Limited disclosure is said to take into account the public interest in maintaining confidentiality in information.[26]

The diminution of procedural fairness has bitten hardest in relation to refugees assessed by ASIO as security threats. Between 2009 and early 2013, around 56 people recognised as refugees by Australia were adversely assessed by ASIO and refused protection visas to remain permanently in Australia. All were consequently detained, ostensibly pending removal from Australia, but in circumstances where their removal was practically impossible as it was not safe to return them home, and no other country would admit them. They accordingly faced the prospect of indefinite administrative detention, ruled lawful by the High Court in the different circumstances of a stateless person in *Al-Kateb v Godwin*.[27]

Most of the refugees claim not to adequately know the basis of the security case against them. In the 2012 case of *Plaintiff M47*, one refugee challenged the procedural fairness of the issue of his adverse security assessment. On the facts of that particular case, the High Court found that procedural fairness had not been denied because during interview, ASIO had put specific allegations of involvement with the LTTE (Tamil Tigers) to the refugee, drawn attention to inconsistencies or gaps in the refugee's account, and provided an adequate opportunity to respond and explain discrepancies.[28] The refugee had not been 'left in the dark'.[29] The case turned instead on the invalidity of a migration regulation which relied upon ASIO assessments of protection visa applicants.

It was unnecessary for the High Court to consider the Full Federal Court's finding in *Leghaei* that procedural fairness may be reduced to nothingness in an appropriate (different) case, since on the facts disclosure had been given. The Full Federal Court's decision – that zero disclosure may be lawful in other cases – remains good law and, as explained below, is compounded by the invocation of public interest immunity to preclude the admissibility of critical evidence.

---

25 Ibid, [61].
26 *Applicant VEAL of 2002 v Minister for Immigration and Multicultural Affairs* (2005) 225 CLR 88.
27 (2004) 219 CLR 562.
28 *Plaintiff M47/2012 v Director-General of Security* (2012) 292 ALR 243, [144] (Gummow J), [252] (Heydon J), [380] (Crennan J), [415] (Kiefel J), [505] (Bell J).
29 Language used in *Mahon v Air New Zealand Ltd* [1984] AC 808, 821.

Some judges in *Plaintiff M47* remarked on relevant policy factors in weighing the different interests at stake. French CJ found it unnecessary to decide the procedural fairness point because no valid migration decision had yet been made, but noted that 'the content of procedural fairness will depend upon the part played by the assessment in the exercise of the power in which it is considered and the nature of that power'.[30] Justice Bell similarly recognised that the 'statutory framework within which an administrative decision is made is of course critical to the assessment of the content of procedural fairness',[31] and that the 'particular circumstances of the case' are also decisive.[32] Her Honour also observed that the consequence of an adverse assessment – the refusal of a visa and protracted detention – is 'a consideration which, as the defendants acknowledge, tends to increase the content of the obligation of procedural fairness in the conduct of the assessment'.[33] Also noted were the 'countervailing considerations' argued by the defendants to condition the scope of procedural fairness, namely the restrictive scheme of the ASIO Act and the necessity of secrecy in intelligence and security matters.[34] These were claimed by the defendants to 'militate against any requirement that "issues" be identified to the subject of an adverse security assessment other than at a high level of generality'.[35]

The question whether procedural fairness entails a minimum irreducible level of disclosure in all cases was, however, avoided. As discussed below, the position in Australian law contrasts markedly with legal developments in comparable liberal democracies such as the United Kingdom, Canada and New Zealand, and in Europe, where human rights law demands a higher degree of disclosure (and thus of fairness) even in national security cases.

Exclusion of merits review

The statutory exclusion of merits review of ASIO decisions affecting those who are not Australian citizens, permanent residents or special purpose visa holders originated in a scantly reasoned view expressed by the Royal Commission on Intelligence and Security in 1976, which suggested simply that '[t]he claim of non-citizens who are not permanent residents but who are in Australia to be entitled to such appeal is difficult

---

30 *Plaintiff M47* (2012) 292 ALR 243, [73] (French CJ).
31 Ibid, [498], citing *SZBEL v Minister for Immigration and Multicultural and Indigenous Affairs* (2006) 228 CLR 152, 160.
32 Ibid, [498], citing *Re Minister for Immigration and Multicultural Affairs; Ex parte Lam* (2003) 214 CLR 1, 14 (Gleeson CJ), 16 (McHugh and Gummow JJ); *Applicant VEAL of 2002 v Minister for Immigration and Multicultural and Indigenous Affairs* (2005) 225 CLR 88, 99 (Gleeson CJ, Gummow, Kirby, Hayne and Heydon JJ).
33 Ibid, [497] (Bell J).
34 Ibid.
35 Ibid.

to justify, particularly as they have no general appeal'.[36] The distinction appears to rest on a parochial intuition that those with a stronger citizenship or migration status connection to Australia deserve stronger procedural protections.

That intuition is dubious for two reasons. First, the idea of a fair hearing aims not only to do justice to the individual concerned but also to ensure the accuracy and accountability of public decision-making. Review allows the executive's allegations to be tested and scrutinised, and ensures that security agencies are not over-reaching. Second, a more contemporary understanding of the rule of law and human rights assumes that the law should provide procedurally equal treatment of like situations, absent exceptional justifications. Thus, if the policy concern is to efficiently identify security risks while safeguarding intelligence information, it is hard to see why higher procedural protections ought to be accorded to dangerous Australians who may present equally serious security risks as foreigners. Australians too can be terrorists, spies or saboteurs. That Australians' rights are not statutorily circumscribed in the same manner suggests how removing basic review rights would ordinarily be seen as intolerable.

The Australian Human Rights Commission has criticised the exclusion of review as 'contrary to basic principles of due process and natural justice'.[37] In recent years, many bodies have called for the Administrative Appeals Tribunal to be given merits review jurisdiction over those who are not citizens, permanent residents or special purpose visa holders,[38] just as the Security Appeals Division of the AAT is already empowered to review ASIO assessments of citizens, permanent residents or special purpose visa holders.[39] Extending AAT jurisdiction alone would not provide a fair hearing. At present, even where the AAT's security jurisdiction is available (for instance, to citizens), essential security information can still be withheld, whether through statutory exceptions to the requirement to give reasons, where disclosure would be prejudicial to national security, or due to ministerial certificates to that effect.[40] In addition (as noted above), procedural fairness at common law may still be reduced to nothingness in such proceedings, while (as noted below) public interest immunity may also prevent the admissibility of critical evidence. Merits review may therefore be available in name, but be substantially ineffective.

---

36 Commonwealth, Royal Commission on Intelligence and Security, *Fourth Report* (1976) vol 1, 154.
37 Australian Human Rights Commission, Submission to *Independent Review of the Intelligence Community*, April 2011, 6.
38 Ibid, 6; Inspector-General of Intelligence and Security, *Annual Report 2006–2007* (2007), 12; Inspector-General of Intelligence and Security, *Annual Report 1998–1999* (1999), paras 89–91; Senate Joint Select Committee on Australia's Immigration Detention Network, Parliament of Australia, *Final Report* (2012), 173–5.
39 *ASIO Act 1979* (Cth), s 54.
40 See, eg, *ASIO Act 1979* (Cth), ss 37(2) (ASIO must disclose all information it relies upon 'other than information the inclusion of which would, in the opinion of the Director-General, be contrary to the requirements of security') and 38 (the Attorney-General can withhold notice of the assessment or disclosure of its grounds where necessary to protect security).

Such was the case in *Leghaei*, where merits review was formally available but empty in substance. On conclusion of the Federal Court proceedings, the Migration Review Tribunal was tasked with reviewing the merits of the decision to refuse his visa in the absence of a copy of the security assessment, knowledge of its contents, or any of the information which purportedly supported it. In 2010 the Tribunal affirmed the visa refusal decision, also stating that while it 'is sympathetic to the primary applicant's predicament, it does not have the power to go behind or to examine the validity of the ASIO assessment'.[41] The same result is also possible in respect of Australian citizens, who are equally unlikely to be comforted by the knowledge that a merits tribunal is available but can do nothing for them. The pretence of justice corrodes the rule of law, since governments are able to invoke the formal availability of review to legitimise a deeply unfair process.

In October 2012 a new 'Independent Reviewer', a retired Federal Court judge, was appointed to conduct an 'advisory' review of ASIO security assessments of the refugees mentioned earlier.[42] The Independent Reviewer has access to all material relied on by ASIO in order to determine whether the assessment is an 'appropriate outcome', and will provide her opinion and reasons to the person where possible. Unclassified written reasons will also be provided by ASIO when a person seeks review, but only to the extent not prejudicing security. The Independent Reviewer will periodically review adverse assessments every 12 months in conjunction with ASIO's own reconsideration.

This is an improvement, but does not ensure a fair hearing. Unlike AAT review, the Independent Reviewer's findings are not binding upon ASIO. While disclosure to a person may be improved in some cases, *there remains no minimum content of disclosure in all cases*, which clearly limits a refugee's ability to effectively respond. ASIO may still determine that it is not possible to disclose any meaningful reasons to a person without prejudicing security. This then also prevents further disclosure by the Independent Reviewer. Refugees will continue to receive no notice of allegations prior to decisions being made.

Public interest immunity

It is now clear that in Australia, security decisions are judicially reviewable. That proposition was not self-evident to common law courts historically, which either treated particular sources of security power (such as certain prerogatives) as non-justiciable, or characterised certain subject matter (such as security or foreign

---

41 *N0500729, N9701858* [2010] MRTA 327 (19 February 2010), para 46.
42 Attorney-General's Department, *Independent Review Function – Terms of Reference* (16 October 2012) <http://www.attorneygeneral.gov.au/Media-releases/Documents/IndependentReviewFunction-TermsofReference.pdf>.

affairs) as non-justiciable.[43] In an early Australian case, *Commonwealth v Colonial Combing, Spinning & Weaving*,[44] the High Court invoked English authority known as the *Zamora* principle to hold that '[i]t is unquestionable that "those who are responsible for the national security must be the sole judges of what the national security requires"'.

The High Court later asserted stronger oversight of security decisions. In *Church of Scientology v Woodward*,[45] it accepted that the courts are 'quite capable' of considering whether intelligence is relevantly connected to security in reviewing ASIO decisions. Justice Mason noted that express or implied statutory exclusion of judicial review of security decisions would be unlikely to protect jurisdictional errors or ultra vires acts.[46] In *A v Hayden*, Gibbs CJ described the *Zamora* principle as 'too absolute', and noted that the courts will not defer without question to the judgement of the executive as to what national security requires when seeking immunity.[47] Review extends not only to consideration of documents over which immunity is claimed, but to antecedent matters such as disclosure of the existence of documents[48] or government affidavits arguing for non-disclosure.[49]

The concept of non-justiciability persists not as a complete exemption of security decisions from judicial review, but in a more limited 'public interest immunity' that precludes the admission of particular information into evidence in court.[50] The scope of the immunity is nonetheless very wide where security is involved, raising questions about whether the judiciary has gone far enough in subjecting security decisions to independent scrutiny.

While the courts are not bound by the executive's opinion on security matters,[51] judges have frequently emphasised the need to accord great weight to those entrusted with security decisions.[52] National security has been characterised as a public interest category of special importance.[53] In the context of modern terrorism,

---

43 See Chris Finn, 'The Concept of "Justiciability" in Administrative Law' in M Groves and HP Lee (eds), *Australian Administrative Law: Fundamentals, Principles and Doctrines* (Cambridge University Press, 2007) 143, 147–51.
44 (1922) 21 CLR 421, 422 (Isaacs J).
45 (1982) 154 CLR 25, 61 (Mason J).
46 Ibid, 55.
47 *A v Hayden (No 2)* (1984) 156 CLR 532, 548–9 (Gibbs CJ). The Court found that the Commonwealth owed no enforceable duty to treat as confidential the identities of the ASIS agents, even if it breached (unenforceable) employment contracts.
48 *Alister v R* (1983) 154 CLR 404.
49 *Parkin v O'Sullivan* (2009) 260 ALR 503.
50 *Gypsy Jokers Motorcycle Club Inc v Commissioner of Police* (2008) 234 CLR 532, 556. See also *Parkin v O'Sullivan* (2009) 260 ALR 503, 511.
51 *Church of Scientology v Woodward* (1982) 154 CLR 25, 75 (Brennan J).
52 *A v Hayden (No 2)* (1984) 156 CLR 532, 576 (Wilson and Dawson JJ); *Haj-Ismail v Minister for Immigration and Ethnic Affairs (No 2)* (1982) 64 FLR 112; *R v Bersinic* [2007] ACTSC 46.
53 *Gilligan v Nationwide News Pty Ltd* 101 FLR 139; *R v Lodhi* (2006) 163 A Crim R 508, 571.

it has also been suggested that 'increased deference' may be warranted given that 'the mere publication of even apparently trivial information such as names and occupations could have adverse consequences'.[54]

Deference has a number of consequences for immunity decisions. First, it leads to a presumptively greater weighting of security interests over other public interests. In *Church of Scientology v Woodward*, the High Court acknowledged the need to weigh competing public interests in security and the administration of justice in assessing immunity claims, and such balancing is reflected in evidence legislation.[55] But the Court observed that in security cases:

> discovery would not be given against the Director-General [of ASIO] save in a most exceptional case. The secrecy of the work of an intelligence organisation which is to counter espionage, sabotage, etc is essential to national security, and the public interest in national security will seldom yield to the public interest in the administration of civil justice...[56]

The courts admittedly give special consideration to the interests of a fair criminal trial,[57] though that factor alone is not determinative. Prosecutions have been discontinued to prevent impending disclosure of security information by courts, including where the law of the jurisdiction recognises the human right to a fair trial.[58] It should be noted, however, that administrative decisions can have consequences as invasive as criminal convictions, for instance where a person is indefinitely detained or deported.

Recent statutory intervention in civil and criminal cases has accorded even greater weight to the interests of security, though the statute does not displace public interest immunity at common law (which probably remains more commonly used than the new statutory scheme). Under the *National Security Information (Criminal and Civil Proceedings) Act 2004* (Cth), in considering claims for the non-disclosure of security-sensitive information, a court is directed to take into account (a) the risk of prejudice to national security, (b) the defendant's right to a fair hearing, and (c) other matters it considers relevant. But the legislation requires the court to 'give greatest weight' to the risk of prejudice to national security. In *Lodhi v R*,[59] such statutory guidance as to the weighting of interests was found

---

54 *R v Bersinic* [2007] ACTSC 46.
55 See also *Alister v R* (1983) 154 CLR 404, 412; *R v Lodhi* (2006) 65 NSWLR 573, 585; *Evidence Act 1995* (Cth), s 130(1).
56 *Church of Scientology v Woodward* (1982) 154 CLR 25, 76 (Brennan J).
57 *Alister v Queen* (1984) 154 CLR 404, 414 (Gibbs CJ); *R v Lodhi* (2006) 65 NSWLR 573, 585 (McClellan CJ).
58 *R v Bersinic* [2007] ACTSC 46 (involving the *ACT Human Rights Act*).
59 [2007] NSWCC 360.

to affect the court's balancing exercise, but not so as to undermine the integrity of the judicial process and thereby usurp judicial power under Chapter III of the *Constitution*.

Second, deference results in courts themselves being reluctant to even inspect documents over which immunity is claimed. The power to inspect is not exercised lightly or as a matter of course,[60] or upon a bare assertion by a party that something in the documents may assist them.[61] A strong positive case must be made.[62] This naturally places parties in a catch-22 situation – they cannot compel disclosure unless they know how a document may assist them, but they may not know how a document may assist them unless they can see the document. It is also rather surprising that judges appear to doubt their own trustworthiness – one would hope judges are no more likely to unlawfully disclose state secrets than security officers.

Third, access to documents may be denied to a party's lawyers even where they offer to give binding undertakings of confidentiality not to disclose their contents to others, including their client.[63] It is not determinative that this may lead to a denial of procedural fairness.[64] The courts appear reluctant to trust lawyers, even where lawyers' obligations of confidentiality are backed by criminal penalties for breach and professional discipline. Again, one wonders why lawyers are seen as less dependable than public servants working for ASIO.

The outcome of the presumptively greater weight accorded to security interests is often that competing public interests are resolved wholly in favour of security, and to the extinguishment of fairness to an affected person. As noted in *Church of Scientology v Woodward*:[65]

> It is a test which presents a formidable hurdle to a plaintiff and not only because a successful claim for Crown privilege may exclude from consideration the very material on which the plaintiff hopes to base his argument – that there is no real connexion between the intelligence sought and the topic.

Such 'handicap'[66] is starkly evidenced in recent adverse security assessment cases where ASIO successfully invoked public interest immunity. In *Parkin v O'Sullivan*,[67] the Federal Court upheld ASIO's immunity claim in relation to a security assessment

---

60 *Haj-Ismail v Minister for Immigration and Ethnic Affairs (No 2)* (1982) 64 FLR 112.
61 *Gilligan v Nationwide News Pty Ltd* (1990) 101 FLR 139.
62 Ibid.
63 *R v Khazaal* [2006] NSWSC 1061; *Parkin v O'Sullivan* (2009) 260 ALR 503.
64 *R v Khazaal* [2006] NSWSC 1061.
65 (1982) 154 CLR 25, 61 (Mason J).
66 *Gypsy Jokers Motorcycle Club Inc v Commissioner of Police* (2008) 234 CLR 532.
67 (2009) 260 ALR 503.

leading to the cancellation of the visa of Scott Parkin, an American peace activist. Parkin did not know the basis of the assessment and argued that he could not make his case without access to the documents. The Court observed that this consequence of the balancing of public interests was not exceptional and did not justify admitting the documents.

In *Sagar v O'Sullivan* (2011), the Federal Court rejected an argument that granting immunity would make it difficult or impossible for the affected person to challenge their security decision, thus impermissibly preventing the Court from meaningfully reviewing the decision, controlling executive power and upholding the rule of law. Sagar was an Iraqi refugee detained on Nauru in 2001 under the Howard Government's 'Pacific Solution'. He was assessed as a security risk by ASIO in 2005 and spent five years in detention, including as the sole remaining detainee on Nauru, before being resettled in Sweden.

The Court noted that Sagar's arguments involved 'matters of fundamental importance to the administration of justice in this country' and discussed the rule of law at length.[68] But the Court did not accept 'that the self-imposed constraints which courts have adopted when undertaking the review of security decisions, are somehow incompatible with the rule of law'.[69] While the rule of law required judicial review of security decisions:

> the courts have acknowledged the need for a cautious approach lest their actions might harm national security interests. They have also recognised, without deferring absolutely to any relevant security agency, that such agencies are usually better placed to assess the impact of disclosure of particular material than are the courts.[70]

The Court held that 'no jurisdictional error is made if sensitive security information is withheld from an applicant and the applicant is not, as a result, alerted to prejudicial material on which the decision has been based'.[71] There is thus no minimum floor of disclosure to an affected person, who may not be given notice, reasons, evidence or access to documents sustaining the conclusion that a person is a security risk.

The Australian Law Reform Commission has observed that immunity is a 'blunt' instrument.[72] The Australian Human Rights Commission too has criticised it for

---

68 *Sagar v O'Sullivan* (2011) 193 FCR 311, 325.
69 Ibid.
70 Ibid, 326.
71 Ibid, 325. See also Australian Law Reform Commission, *Keeping Secrets: The Protection of Classified and Security Sensitive Information*, Report No 98 (2004), paras 8.185–8.187.
72 Australian Law Reform Commission, Ibid, para 8.209.

making it 'virtually impossible' to challenge security information.[73] It is no comfort for an affected person to learn from the High Court in *Church of Scientology* that the *Constitution* preserves esoteric jurisdictional interests, but not those of the affected person:

> The fact that a successful claim for [Crown] privilege handicaps one of the parties to litigation is not a reason for saying that the Court cannot or will not exercise its ordinary jurisdiction; it merely means that the Court will arrive at a decision on something less than the entirety of the relevant materials.[74]

The principal justification advanced by the Australian courts for such security deference and weighting is a concern about the relative competence of the executive in security matters. First, the courts feel that they lack security expertise. In *Alister v Queen*,[75] a case involving an alleged terrorist bombing plot by the Ananda Marga organisation, Justice Brennan noted that a court is generally 'ill-equipped itself to evaluate pieces of intelligence obtained by ASIO'. As noted in *Leghaei*, this is true of 'even a sceptical judge out to defend civil liberties and human rights'.[76] Justice Brennan elaborated on the problem in *Church of Scientology v Woodward*:[77]

> But, it may be said, how can the gravity of a security risk be evaluated by a court? It may be necessary to evaluate Australia's relationships with foreign countries, the stability of international affairs, the passion inspired by a particular cause or the likelihood of adherents to the cause taking violent steps in support of it; it may be necessary to evaluate rumour or suspicion as well as proof. It may be reasonable, even necessary, to determine the gravity of a risk by intuition rather than deduction. It may be truly said that the skills and procedures of a court do not fit it to find the point on the scale of gravity of every risk which may be thought to pose a threat to the Commonwealth, the States and Territories and the people thereof, and it may be accepted that a court will not necessarily have or be able to obtain all the evidence needed to allow it to quantify a risk precisely. However, it does not follow that judicial review is excluded.

Second, the courts view security agencies 'as usually better placed to assess the impact of disclosure of particular material than are the courts'.[78] As was explained above, Madgwick J acknowledged in the *Leghaei* case that 'recognition and respect'

---

73 Australian Human Rights Commission, Submission to *Independent Review of the Intelligence Community*, April 2011, 6–7.
74 *Church of Scientology v Woodward* (1982) 154 CLR 25, 61 (Mason J).
75 *Alister v Queen* (1984) 154 CLR 404, 455 (Brennan J).
76 Ibid, [92].
77 (1982) 154 CLR 25, 74.
78 *Sagar v O'Sullivan* (2011) 193 FCR 311.

should be given to the expertise and role of ASIO.[79] But that is no reason for courts to abdicate their role.

Of course security agencies are more expert than judges in security analysis and prediction. But it does not automatically follow that the degree of deference accorded by Australian judges is appropriate. Judges are not asked to review the merits of security decisions, but to review them for errors of law, and to make decisions about the safety of disclosing information. In these contexts, the lack of judicial competence in security matters is arguably overstated.

The courts have tended to present their lack of expertise as intrinsic to the judicial function, as opposed to as being a consequence of habit. Judges routinely evaluate information in a range of expert areas, whether complex corporate transactions, elaborate taxation schemes, mergers and acquisitions, scientific gene patents cases, or assessments of complex environmental impacts. One rarely hears courts objecting that they lack the expertise necessary to perform their assigned statutory or constitutional judicial functions. Many such areas equally require risk assessments, probability judgements, or predictions of impacts.

To be sure, security cases are relatively rare and other expert areas perhaps more common, so judges are on more familiar territory elsewhere. Also, since many judges are drawn from the gene pool of the corporate bar, they bring with them greater knowledge of certain practice areas but not others. Security decisions are also peculiarly politically sensitive because of the legitimacy risks to courts of getting it wrong – no judge wants to be known for making a decision which may lead to the deaths of fellow citizens at the hands of terrorists. None of this justifies the courts in presenting security matters as somehow innately outside judicial expertise. It simply demonstrates that the courts may not be particularly experienced in security issues, or are sensitive about them for political reasons. In other contexts, courts have been quite assertive about their abilities in the security field. In *Thomas v Mowbray*, the High Court upheld the constitutional validity of Australia's anti-terrorism control order scheme. In doing so, the Court found that '[t]he protection of the public as a purpose of decision-making is not alien to the adjudicative process'.[80] Courts were said to have long and often made predictive judgements about various social risks, and a law asking the courts to protect the public from terrorism was not too vague or indefinite as not to be a proper exercise of judicial power. The Court was confident in its ability to process security evidence in deciding to impose a control order on the *merits* of the security case.

If the High Court was right in *Thomas v Mowbray*, it is then awkward or inconsistent for the courts to continue to claim elsewhere that they lack expertise in security and must defer as heavily as they do to the opinions of security agencies.

---

79 *Leghaei v Director General of Security* [2005] FCA 1576, [87].
80 *Thomas v Mowbray* (2007) 233 CLR 307, [108] (Gummow and Crennan JJ).

This is particularly so in other contexts where the court is being asked to do *less* than in control order cases – not to consider the merits of security evidence, but merely to assess the safety of its admissibility or disclosure, or to review for errors of law security decisions already made by the executive.

Deference is one thing; vacating the field another. If judges feel that they lack expertise in a given case, they are surely bound to acquire the necessary expertise to discharge their statutory or constitutional responsibility of judicial review. In *Leghaei*, Justice Madgwick averred that there was a possibility of 'independent expert assistance' to help the court understand the security issues.[81] The special advocate procedure adopted in other democracies is another potential mechanism to assist the courts. Judges have inherent judicial power to control their own proceedings – deference is a choice, not the natural order. Throwing one's judicial hands in the air and declaring that one doesn't understand security cannot be right.

Some judges have been more mindful of the pitfalls of excessive deference and more willing to shed the long historical legacy of non-justiciability which characterised the courts' approach to security. In *Alister v Queen*, Justice Brennan suggested that any balancing of public interests should favour liberty, not security:

> It is of the essence of a free society that a balance is struck between the security that is desirable to protect society as a whole and the safeguards that are necessary to ensure individual liberty. But in the long run the safety of a democracy rests upon the common commitment of its citizens to the safeguarding of each man's liberty, and the balance must tilt that way.[82]

ASIO's nemesis, Justice Lionel Murphy, likewise declared in the *Scientology* case that:

> …it is to be expected that the courts will be astute to ensure the misuse of power is not cloaked by claims of national security. Because of the experience that secret organisations of this kind from time to time misuse their powers in relation to individuals and institutions, it is essential that the judicial process be exerted, no doubt with caution, but if occasion warrants it, firmly, to keep the organization and officers within the law.[83]

The relatively light judicial supervision of security matters is, as the courts themselves have noted, largely 'self-imposed'.[84] It is thus open to the courts to ask more of themselves, including by examining underlying principles rather than

---

81 *Leghaei v Director General of Security* [2005] FCA 1576, [92].
82 *Alister v Queen* (1984) 154 CLR 404, 456.
83 *Church of Scientology v Woodward* (1982) 154 CLR 25, 68–9 (Murphy J).
84 *Sagar v O'Sullivan* (2011) 193 FCR 311, [73].

simply relying on 'the dead weight of past authority'.[85] Parliaments are unlikely to direct them to do more. Human rights principles also chart a different path, as the discussion below of other democracies demonstrates. But first there is a question whether the *Australian Constitution* may demand more of Australian courts.

A lingering constitutional question

While it remains possible for Australian Parliaments to exclude natural justice from the administrative process, it is clear that core elements of fairness cannot be removed from the judicial process. Thus in *International Finance Trust Company*, the High Court found invalid a statutory provision which 'deprives the Court of the power to determine whether procedural fairness...requires that notice be given to the party affected before an order is made'.[86] A NSW law had required a State court exercising federal jurisdiction to receive, hear and determine an application *ex parte* (in a criminal law context). It impermissibly directed the court as to the manner of the exercise of its jurisdiction, and deprived it of an important characteristic of judicial power (fairness between the parties). Similarly, in *South Australia v Totani*, the High Court considered a statute which precluded disclosure to the Federal Magistrates Court of certain factual matters and evidence (including criminal intelligence) in a proceeding to impose a control order. As such it was found to impair 'the decisional independence of the Magistrates Court from the executive in substance and in appearance in areas going to personal liberty and the liability to criminal sanctions which lie at the heart of the judicial function'.[87] Further, it authorised 'the executive to enlist the Magistrates Court to implement decisions of the executive in a manner incompatible with that Court's institutional integrity'.[88]

These cases involved challenges to the validity of statutes and concerned criminal contexts. The ASIO Act does not preclude procedural fairness as such; nor are courts mandated by statute to resolve public interest immunity claims in favour of the executive. A question nonetheless arises whether the *Constitution* limits judges' own powers to reduce procedural fairness to 'nothingness' or to grant public interest immunity where that would leave a person wholly in the dark about the security allegations against them. The right of a party to challenge the

---

85 Chris Finn, 'The Concept of "Justiciability" in Administrative Law' in M Groves and HP Lee (eds), *Australian Administrative Law: Fundamentals, Principles and Doctrines* (Cambridge University Press, Cambridge, 2007) 143, 156.
86 (2009) 240 CLR 319, 355.
87 *State of South Australia v Totani* (2010) 242 CLR 1, 52 (French CJ).
88 Ibid.

case against it, and the idea of equality of arms between the parties, are elements of procedural fairness ordinarily guaranteed in federal courts under Chapter III of the *Constitution*. A party's rights to challenge the case and to enjoy equality of arms necessarily require that a person must know at least the essence or substance of the case against them. In turn that requires that an affected person must be reasonably informed of such case by the provision of sufficient information.

Naturally, the degree of disclosure to an affected person may vary in the circumstances, including because of the need to protect other legitimate interests such as national security. It would be permissible, for instance, for the Commonwealth to protect sensitive information (including the identity of informants and methods of intelligence gathering) from disclosure by only furnishing the person with a redacted summary of reasons or evidence. But it would not be permissible for the Commonwealth to withhold *all* reasons and evidence from the affected person, such that the person cannot know anything in substance of the case against them. To so deprive a person of the essence of the case against them compromises the judicial function and institutional integrity of a federal court, which demands an irreducible minimum of procedural fairness (including disclosure) as a necessary element of judicial process.

The deprivation of basic fairness to a person may also impermissibly implicate the federal courts in the work of the executive, since the fundamental inequality of the parties inevitably means that the court cannot but accept the view of the executive. The deprivation of elementary fairness also seriously undermines public confidence in the independence and impartiality of a federal court *as a court*, instead of as the extended arm of the executive. Absent the provision of such entrenched minimum procedural fairness, a Chapter III federal court cannot be said to be exercising the requirements or characteristics of the judicial function, which are an incident of the exercise of Chapter III judicial power. In short, the court is not acting as a Chapter III court if one party is so unfairly disadvantaged by non-disclosure that there is no genuine equality of arms. The full Federal Court's decision in *Leghaei* was arguably incorrect because it failed to recognise the constitutionally entrenched minimum degree of disclosure. The scope of public interest immunity too is necessarily qualified by the constitutionally entrenched disclosure requirement.

The ascendancy of due process under human rights law abroad

The position under current Australian law in relation to security cases can be starkly contrasted with developments in comparable liberal democracies bound by domestic or regional human rights law. Two key developments are considered: the requirement of a minimum irreducible level of disclosure of information; and the use of a 'special advocate' to enable the confidential testing of security information while safeguarding its secrecy.

An irreducible minimum of disclosure in security cases

The evolution of European human rights law has gradually produced a convergence of due process standards across a range of administrative proceedings. In the United Kingdom, for example, various proceedings involving security issues – such as administrative detention of suspected terrorists and 'control orders' to prevent terrorism – have recently been found to require an irreducible minimum disclosure of information to an affected person. This is the case even where a special advocate procedure exists and provides a means of dealing with further security information which cannot be safely disclosed to an affected individual personally.

Thus in *A v United Kingdom*,[89] the Grand Chamber of the European Court of Human Rights ('ECtHR') held that the 'dramatic impact' of lengthy and potentially indefinite administrative detention of non-citizen suspected terrorists demanded the importation of the fair hearing guarantees of a criminal trial[90] into proceedings challenging the lawfulness of detention.[91] Thus certain non-criminal proceedings which severely impact upon a person's rights were found to attract the higher procedural protections applicable to a criminal trial.

In particular, such guarantees were found to include a minimum degree of disclosure *personally* to a detainee. While the protection of classified information may be justified to protect national security, the ECtHR held that it must be balanced against the requirements of a fair hearing.[92] The starting point is that it is 'essential that as much information about the allegations and evidence against each applicant was disclosed as was possible without compromising national security or the safety of others'.[93] Where 'full disclosure' is not possible, however, a person must still enjoy 'the possibility effectively to challenge the allegations against him'.[94] Further, 'where all or most of the underlying evidence remained undisclosed', 'sufficiently specific' allegations must be disclosed to the affected person to enable that person

---

89 *A v United Kingdom* (2009) 49 EHRR 625.
90 Under article 6 of the *European Convention on Human Rights 1950* (ECHR), equivalent to article 14 of the *International Covenant on Civil and Political Rights 1966*.
91 Otherwise governed by article 5 of the ECHR, which is equivalent to article 9 of the ICCPR.
92 *A v United Kingdom* (2009) 49 EHRR 625, 636.
93 Ibid, 636.
94 Ibid.

to effectively provide his/her representatives (including security-cleared counsel) 'with information with which to refute them'.[95] The provision of purely 'general assertions' to a person, where the decision made is based 'solely or to a decisive degree on closed material' will not satisfy the procedural requirements of a fair hearing.[96] The ECtHR held that the affected person's hearing had been unfair because the case against him was largely in closed material and the open case was insubstantial. This case suggests that a greater degree of procedural protection, including minimum disclosure, is essential where a person is administratively detained for protracted periods, even if not facing a criminal trial.

The UK House of Lords later drew upon that ECtHR decision to specify the minimum disclosure necessary for a fair trial in anti-terrorism 'control order' proceedings. In *Secretary of State for the Home Department v AF*,[97] the House of Lords found that the more stringent standard of fairness applicable in criminal trials applied to control order proceedings, even though such proceedings did not involve a criminal penalty. It held that '[t]he requirements of a fair trial depend, to some extent, on what is at stake in the trial'.[98] The Lords added:

> The controlee must be given sufficient information about the allegations against him to enable him to give effective instructions in relation to those allegations. Provided that this requirement is satisfied there can be a fair trial notwithstanding that the controlee is not provided with the detail or the sources of the evidence forming the basis of the allegations. Where, however, the open material consists purely of general assertions and the case against the controlee is based solely or to a decisive degree on closed materials the requirements of a fair trial will not be satisfied, however cogent the case based on the closed materials may be.[99]

There is a accordingly a converging standard of minimum fair hearing rights in certain non-criminal national security cases as a result of European human rights law, which may demand the higher level of procedural protections recognised in criminal trials due to the serious adverse consequences of detention or control orders. In Britain, such a disclosure requirement has not yet extended to immigration proceedings, but only because Britain is not a party to an additional European protocol which extends due process protections to immigration decisions.[100] British

---

95 Ibid, 637.
96 Ibid.
97 [2010] 2 AC 269, 353.
98 Ibid.
99 Ibid.
100 *Protocol No 7 to the European Convention for the Protection of Human Rights and Fundamental Freedoms* (adopted 22 November 1984, entered into force 1 November 1988, ETS 117); see *W (Algeria) v Secretary of State for the Home Department* [2010] EWCA Civ 898, [32].

judges have expressly acknowledged the resulting unfairness: 'There is no doubt that to deprive anyone, including an alien, of even the essence of the case put against him as to why he is a threat to national security goes against the basic concept of a fair trial'.[101]

Australia is evidently not bound by European human rights law and its international human rights law obligations are configured differently.[102] But the European approach suggests a more progressive way of legally conceptualising the relationship between fairness and security, in relation to both procedural fairness and public interest immunity in Australia. It is also relevant because Australian courts have sometimes invoked English decisions to support their reasons for not disclosing security evidence,[103] yet have tended to omit reference to the human rights law developments there which have precisely altered the contemporary English approach.

Such an approach never permits security interests to extinguish fairness to individuals (as can occur in Australia) but requires a finer, more proportionate balancing of interests. It demands procedures which can accommodate security concerns (by restrictions on security information, and devices such as a special advocate) yet accord the individual some procedural justice,[104] and ensure that security agencies are adequately scrutinised, are held accountable, and act within the law.

It is strongly arguable that security decisions should attract minimum procedural fairness protections because of the often serious consequences of those decisions – whether expulsion of people from a country where they are settled, disruption of employment, denial of travel documents, or interference in family life. As the Canadian Supreme Court observed, the consequences of issuing security certificates there, which may include expulsion to another country, 'are often more severe than those of many criminal charges'[105] or, indeed, control orders or limited preventive detention. The Court further observed that such processes place 'the individual in a critically vulnerable position vis-à-vis the state' and 'confirm the need for

---

101 *W (Algeria) v Secretary of State for the Home Department* [2010] EWCA Civ 898, [43].
102 Even so, in 2013 the United Nations Human Rights Committee found that ASIO's non-disclosure of information to refugees on security grounds contributed to its finding that they were illegally detained under article 9 of the ICCPR: see *F.K.A.G. et al v Australia*, HRC Communication No 2094/2011 (26 July 2013); *M.M.M. et al v Australia*, HRC Communication No 2136/2012 (25 July 2013).
103 In *Leghaei v Director-General of Security* [2007] FCAFC 37, the Full Federal Court endorsed a British decision which stated that courts are not equipped to make counter-terrorism decisions or charged with that responsibility: *A v Secretary of State for the Home Department* [2005] 2 AC 68 (Lord Nicholls). The same passage was invoked in *Sagar v O'Sullivan* (2011) 193 FCR 311.
104 *Al-Nashif v Bulgaria* (2003) 36 EHRR 655, 678.
105 *Charkaoui v Canada (Citizenship and Immigration)* [2008] 2 SCR 326, [54].

an expanded right to procedural fairness, one which requires the disclosure of information'.[106]

The content of procedural fairness in security cases should thus require that a person must always be provided with 'sufficiently specific' allegations so as to allow them to effectively instruct their lawyers in dealing with those allegations. The provision of purely general assertions that a person is a national security risk is insufficient where a security assessment is based solely on closed material. There will of course be dispute about what precise degree of disclosure meets this standard, but the courts can work through those questions as they arise. As the European Court noted in *Chahal v United Kingdom*,[107] the use of confidential material might be unavoidable where national security is at stake, but that does not mean that the executive is free from effective control by the domestic courts whenever they choose to assert that security and terrorism are involved.

There may be rare hard cases where any disclosure would tip off a person to intelligence methods – as where information could only have come from a particular source – and disclosure may unduly compromise intelligence methods or endanger an informant. Such cases are rare. It may be that requiring minimum disclosure in such cases remains a necessary trade-off to ensure fairness, accurate decision-making, and accountability, and to ensure that public confidence is not lost when secret justice replaces the rule of law. As a last resort, where ASIO does not wish to disclose even a summary of the case against a person, it would always have the option of not issuing a security assessment so as to protect its sources, or utilising other means (such as surveillance) to address the threat. That is the price of maintaining elementary justice and the rule of law.

A special advocate procedure for security information

Special advocate procedures were developed in the United Kingdom, Canada and New Zealand[108] in response to human rights law concerns about the non-disclosure of security information that was essential in informing a person of the case against them. The overall purpose of the special advocate is to assist the tribunal or the court to review (on the merits and law respectively) the evidence against a person, by independently testing it when the affected person and their lawyers cannot see all of it for security reasons. It is a mechanism for balancing the individual's fair

---

106 Ibid, [55].
107 *Chahal v United Kingdom* (1996) 23 EHRR 413, 468–9. See also *Al-Nashif v Bulgaria* (2003) 36 EHRR 655, 678.
108 *Special Immigration Appeals Commission Act 1997* (UK) c 68, s 6; *Immigration and Refugee Protection Act* (Canada), SC 2001, c 2, s 85; *Immigration Act 2009* (New Zealand), s 263.

hearing rights while meeting the concerns of security agencies about the protection of security-sensitive information.

In the UK, the exclusion from review of deportation cases involving national security was successfully challenged on human rights grounds as early as 1997,[109] resulting in a new and fairer process before the Special Immigration Appeals Commission ('SIAC').[110] Information cannot be disclosed where it would be contrary to national security. The affected person and their lawyers can be excluded from proceedings. In such circumstances, SIAC may appoint a 'Special Advocate'[111] with 'disclosure' and 'representative' functions.[112] The Special Advocate is appointed to advise SIAC and is not the person's lawyer, although the role is designed to protect their interests.

The 'disclosure' function enables the Special Advocate to challenge the Secretary of State's objection that disclosing material to the affected person would prejudice security. The Secretary of State is not required to disclose material or a summary of it to the person where directed to do so by SIAC, but where disclosure is refused such information cannot be relied upon in the proceeding. The 'representative' function empowers the Special Advocate to view, examine and challenge confidential material which is not disclosed to the affected person, including material which SIAC has not requested to be disclosed to the affected person.

The key drawbacks of the procedure include that the Special Advocate cannot disclose any confidential material to the affected person or receive instructions from them about how to deal with it, thus limiting the person's ability to test any adverse evidence.[113] Special Advocates have 'no access to independent expertise and evidence' and 'lack the resources of an ordinary legal team for the purpose of conducting a full defence in secret and they have no power to call witnesses'.[114] Their appointment also assumes that the person's regular lawyer or barrister cannot be safely entrusted (in confidence) with the evidence, whereas it may be enough to empower a person's lawyers with the Special Advocate's functions – particularly when any breaches of confidence by them could incur criminal penalties. However, Special Advocates might acquire expertise in repeatedly dealing with security information and intelligence methods and thus be a stronger safeguard than less experienced lawyers. The position is also designed not as the person's legal representative, but as an independent office at greater arms-length.

---

109 *Chahal v United Kingdom* (1996) 23 EHRR 413.
110 Under the *Special Immigration Appeals Commission Act 1997* (UK), c 68.
111 *Special Immigration Appeals Commission Act 1997* (UK), c 68, s 6.
112 See, generally, Aileen Kavanagh, 'Special Advocates, Control Orders and the Right to a Fair Trial' (2010) 73 *Modern Law Review* 836, 838.
113 Ibid.
114 Ibid.

Overall the UK's special advocate procedure provides a considerably fairer hearing than in Australia, where there is no provision for a special advocate; the person's lawyers may be excluded from viewing confidential material (in both proceedings about whether to disclose material to the person, and in testing the substance of the evidence); and the affected person may be denied access to any evidence or summary of it. Further, SIAC performs a more active role in decision-making about disclosure of the material or a summary of the material.

The appointment of a 'special advocate' has been contemplated in the context of Australian criminal proceedings, but the procedure has been neither used nor statutorily required in ASIO security assessments or other administrative decision-making or judicial review proceedings. At most, an affected person's lawyers have occasionally been given confidential access to security information through existing legal provisions,[115] as happened in *Leghaei*. In other cases, this was refused.[116]

The Independent Reviewer of ASIO security assessments created in October 2012 admittedly gives a retired judge access to all information relied on by ASIO in making its assessment, when 'merits' reviewing that assessment at a later time. However, that review process is far less protective than a special advocate procedure because it reposes in one inquisitorial person the task of both reviewing the materials and making decisions about them, whereas an advocate assists a tribunal or court to reach an independent decision in a more typical adversarial context. The process remains imbalanced because no-one with access to all of the information is advocating the cause of the person, and the person may remain in the dark about the evidence. Further, the Independent Reviewer mechanism is non-binding, whereas a special advocate procedure would be part of binding tribunal or court processes.

A special advocate procedure could be readily transposed into Australian law. Special advocates would ideally be empowered to: make submissions on the adequacy of the notice and/or reasons provided to the person; test ASIO's claims that information may not be safely disclosed to the person; and make submissions on substantive evidence which cannot be safely disclosed to the person. As in other jurisdictions, the special advocate would be entitled to see all of the information upon which ASIO seeks to rely, and which it seeks to keep confidential (unless authorised by ASIO, the AAT or a federal court to disclose it). If ASIO refused to disclose evidence to the special advocate, it could not rely upon it as a basis for making a security decision.

---

115 See, eg, *Administrative Appeals Tribunal Act 1975* (Cth), ss 39A, 39B (in the exercise of inherent judicial power). See also *National Security Information (Criminal and Civil Proceedings) Act 2004* (Cth).
116 See, eg, *SBEG v Secretary, Department of Immigration and Citizenship* [2012] FCA 277; *Sagar v O'Sullivan* (2011) 193 FCR 311.

Conclusion

This chapter has shown how a human rights approach to administrative justice in security decisions can fundamentally alter the balance of public policy interests. Fairness to an affected person is not necessarily weighed more heavily than public security in such an approach. Security is simply no longer permitted to extinguish everything else. That brings a more discriminating, proportionate and sensitive balancing of interests than the Parliament or the common law may provide.

The diminution of procedural fairness to 'nothingness' in some security cases, and the inadmissibility of even basic evidence due to public interest immunity, can result in practical injustice. It is not stipulating an abstract theory of justice to demand an irreducible minimum degree of disclosure of the essence of a case against a person. While that idea is certainly prescriptive – it is, after all, a minimum condition of justice on a human rights approach – it is not inflexible or inappropriate. It still allows for the adequate protection of security information when coupled with a special advocate procedure. It precludes the total sacrifice of an individual's basic rights for the ostensible public good. It demands only that the law should be sharp, not blunt; an instrument of fairness, not sacrifice.

STATUTORY INTERPRETATION AND ADMINISTRATIVE LAW

Jeffrey Barnes

Introduction: The *Mona Lisa* of the law

In a television documentary discussing Da Vinci's *Mona Lisa*, the renowned Australian art critic, the late Robert Hughes, observed:

> The *Mona Lisa*, the most famous painting in the world…Her image is so familiar that it has been deprived of meaning.[1]

This comment has an unexpected resonance with statutory interpretation. Statutory interpretation is similarly 'so familiar' to all those with an acquaintance with the law. Statutory interpretation is a necessary element in the court's identification of the substantive or procedural statute law it is called upon to apply.[2] It thus 'keys into the whole system of law'.[3] It is particularly entwined in administrative law. Indeed, Professor D G T Williams once opined that 'administrative law is for the courts largely an exercise in statutory interpretation'.[4] Although administrative law in total is much more than statutory interpretation, there cannot be any doubt about their close connection. Chief Justice French of the High Court has suggested that statutory interpretation is central to administrative law because:

> The exercise by public officials of powers conferred upon them by statute is subject to review by the courts where it is asserted that an official has exceeded his or her powers or has purported to exercise the power in a way that is not authorised by the statute. This again involves the judiciary in the exercise of statutory interpretation.[5]

But like the *Mona Lisa*, the familiarity of statutory interpretation does not mean that it is adequately understood in the legal community. Many argue that it is inadequately, if not poorly, understood by some trial courts and elements of the

---

1 R Hughes, 'Robert Hughes: The *Mona Lisa* Curse', ABC1 Television, 12 August 2012.
2 S Gageler, 'Common Law Statutes and Judicial Legislation: Statutory Interpretation as a Common Law Process' (2011) 37 *Monash University Law Review* 1, 1; A Barak, *Purposive Interpretation in Law* (Princeton University Press, 2005) 12–14, making the point that '[e]very text requires interpretation': 12.
3 F Bennion, *Understanding Common Law Legislation: Drafting and Interpretation* (Oxford University Press, 2009) 11, citing F Bennion, *Bennion on Statutory Interpretation: A Code* (LexisNexis, 5th ed, 2008) 8.
4 D G T Williams, 'Statute Law and Administrative Law' [1984] *Statute Law Review* 157, 159.
5 Chief Justice R S French, 'The Judicial Function in an Age of Statutes: 2011 Goldring Memorial Lecture', Wollongong, 18 November 2011, at <www.hcourt.gov.au/publications/speeches/current/speeches-by-chief-justice-french-ac>, 14–15.

legal profession[6] and by many law teachers.[7] The same goes for statute law more generally.[8]

To explore the connection between administrative law and statutory interpretation, we need to ask how, who and why. First, the 'how' plane: *how* is statutory interpretation connected to the functions of administrative law? This connection is explored in three sections of this chapter. The first section examines the function of defining the general ambit of statutory powers. The second examines the determination of the limitations on the exercise of such powers. The third section examines the ascertainment of the effect of non-compliance with a statutory requirement. The second plane is: *whose* interpretations carry legal authority in administrative law matters? The third plane is: *why* are there different judicial interpretations? This matter is discussed in the last section of this chapter.

Defining the ambit of statutory powers

It is a basic administrative law principle that '[a] power to do one thing cannot be validly exercised by doing something different'.[9] Of course, disputes may arise about the meaning of the 'thing', that is, the ambit or extent of the statutory power.

A relatively simple problem is where the court is required to construe a statutory term and the contest is between two grammatical meanings – two meanings in everyday use. An example is *Minister for Immigration and Citizenship v Yucesan*.[10]

---

6 Chief Justice Marilyn Warren and President Chris Maxwell, Letter to Professor S D Clark, Chairman, Law Admissions Consultative Committee, 31 August 2007, in Law Admissions Consultative Committee, *Approaches to Interpretation* (2009) Attachment B at http://www.lawcouncil.asn.au/lacc/documents/discussion_papers.cfm> 2. See also Bennion 2009, above n 3, 1–2.

7 Warren and Maxwell, above n 6, 2; Law Admissions Consultative Committee of the Law Council of Australia, *Approaches to Interpretation* (2009) at <http://www.lawcouncil.asn.au/lacc/documents/discussion_papers.cfm>; K Mason, 'The Intent of Legislators: How Judges Discern It And What They Do If They Find It' (2006) 27*Australian Bar Review* 253, 263; J Steyn, 'The Intractable Problem of the Interpretation of Legal Texts' (2002) 25 *Sydney Law Review* 5, 5; Murray Gleeson, 'Justice Hill Memorial Lecture: Statutory Interpretation', Taxation Institute of Australia, 24th National Convention, Sydney, 11 March 2009, <http://www.hcourt.gov.au/assets/publications/speeches/former-justices/gleesoncj/gleeson11mar09.pdf>; M D Kirby, 'Statutory Interpretation: The Meaning of Meaning' (2011) 35 *Melbourne University Law Review* 113, 117; Bennion 2009 above n 3, 1–2, 180; K Goodall, 'Teaching Statutory Interpretation: Citings of NESSSI in Scotland' (2007) 171 JPN 604 at <http://www.francisbennion.com/2007/nfb/005.htm> 1.

8 W M C Gummow, 'Statutes: The Sir Maurice Byers Annual Address' (2005) 26 *Australian Bar Review* 121, 132.

9 *Paull v Munday* (1976) 9 ALR 245, 251 (Gibbs J).

10 (2008) 169 FCR 202; [2008] FCAFC 110.

In this case the dispute concerned the scope of the words 'have met' in cl 300.214 of the *Migration Regulations 1994* (Cth). It provided that parties to a proposed marriage must 'have met and be known to each other personally'. In the case, the parties concerned had not physically met. They had been introduced by their families and had corresponded using telephone, email and the internet. Did the phrase 'have met' have the narrow meaning of 'have come into each other's company or physical presence',[11] or did it, as the Migration Review Tribunal had held,[12] have the wider meaning of encompassing also 'non-physical person-to-person interactions'? In a problem such as this, the court identifies the relevant interpretative criteria and considers which of the two rival constructions constitutes the legal, that is, the preferred, meaning.[13]

In *Yucesan*, the interpretative choice was between two everyday meanings. A case which illustrates a greater range of interpretative techniques is *ABC Developmental Learning Centres Pty Ltd v Secretary, Department of Human Services*.[14] This case involved a challenge to the purported exercise of a power, by an authorised person under the *Children's Services Act 1996* (Vic), to request answers to specific questions and the provision of certain documents. The relevant parts of s 36(1)(f) of the Act read:

> An authorised officer may at any reasonable time, with such assistants as may reasonably be required, for the purpose of ascertaining whether this Act is being complied with – ...
> **(f)** require a person –
> **(i)** to answer a question to the best of that person's knowledge, information and belief;
> **(ii)** to take reasonable steps to provide information.

Section 46 of the Act created an offence for refusing to answer a question lawfully asked by an authorised officer or to produce a document lawfully required by an authorised officer. The written request followed incidents in two Victorian children's services operated by the applicant, but the request was made to the applicant's head office in Queensland. The applicant replied that it was not legally obliged to comply with the DHS requests because the request made to the head office was not a lawful request under s 36 and attracting liability under s 46. The ambit of the power in this case was limited by the word 'person'. The Department argued that 'person' meant, literally, 'any person at any place'.[15] This construction was challenged by the applicant. The applicant did not, as in *Yucesan*, point to another everyday meaning of 'person' as the favoured construction. It argued that

---

11 Ibid, 206 [10]–[11], 209 [28].
12 Ibid, 204–5 [4].
13 The Court concluded that the narrow meaning was the legal meaning: Ibid, 209 [28]–[29].
14 (2007) 15 VR 489.
15 Ibid, 493 [18].

'an authorised person may only require a person to answer a question or provide information if that person is actually on the licensed premises at the time of the request'.[16] The implication was that the provision ought to be read as if it stated '(f) require a person *on the licensed premises…*'. In this way, the applicant was attempting to show that the enactment and the judicial gloss formed a unified text.[17]

Speaking generally, courts take into account interpretative factors derived from a consideration of four main sources: the provision in question; the Act in which the provision lies; the legislative history of the Bill which became the Act; and the wider context.[18] In the *ABC* case, the Court noted two arguments supporting the wide (Departmental) construction. First, from the provision itself, the Court identified the grammatical sense of 'person', there being no reference to the licensed premises in the relevant paragraph.[19] Second, it could be inferred from the Act as a whole, the Department argued, that the legislative purpose was to protect young children from harm.[20] Against this, several considerations were argued to support a narrower construction.[21] First, the provision in question. All other paragraphs in s 36(1) were expressly restricted to the licensed premises. Similarly also, the heading to s 36 referred to 'Powers of entry'. Second, the remainder of the Act included s 41, which provided that authorised officers could not exercise powers (which included s 36) if they failed to produce, on request, their identity card for the inspection of the occupier of the premises. This requirement suggested that the s 36(1)(f) power was exercised in person on the licensed premises. Other provisions of the Act referred to 'notice in writing' requirements, which was a means to signal when a requirement may be made in writing. Third, the legislative history. The Explanatory Memorandum accompanying the Bill which became the Act had referred in summary form to giving 'powers of entry and inspection'. A member of the Legislative Council (not the responsible Minister) had stated that the Act allowed 'questioning, interviewing and investigating people who are on site'. Finally, the wider context (the common law principle of legality) supported the narrow construction, as the wider construction of the Department potentially infringed on freedom of speech.[22] The Court noted that '[i]f Parliament wishes to give DHS officers broad powers to interrogate any person, no matter who they are or where they are located, orally or in writing, with the threat of prosecution under s 46 if they fail to respond, it must do so in clear and unambiguous language'.[23] It had not done so.

---

16 Ibid.
17 F A R Bennion, *Bennion on Statutory Interpretation: A Code* (LexisNexis, 5th ed, 2008) 504; section 177.
18 S Glazebrook, 'Filling the Gaps' in R Bigwood (ed), *The Statute: Making and Meaning* (LexisNexis, Wellington, 2004) 153, 169–76.
19 (2007) 15 VR 489, 493 [20].
20 Ibid, 493 [19].
21 Ibid, 493–5 [20]–[31].
22 See Chapter 1 for discussion of the principle of legality.
23 (2007) 15 VR 489, 494 [31].

The Court upheld the construction advanced by the applicant and granted declaratory and injunctive relief.[24] Impliedly, the Court found that the factors favouring the literal meaning advanced by the Department were outweighed by the factors favouring the implication advanced by the applicant.

Determining the limitations on the exercise of statutory powers

The *Yucesan* case and the *ABC* case showed that the extent of a statutory power may be established, by a process of interpretation, to have express or implied limitations. The limitations on the exercise of statutory powers may be found, similarly, to be subject to express and implied limitations, as Brennan J explained in an oft-cited passage:

> The consequence is that the scope of judicial review must be defined not in terms of the protection of individual interests but in terms of the extent of power and the legality of its exercise. In Australia, the modern development and expansion of the law of judicial review of administrative action have been achieved by an increasingly sophisticated exposition of implied limitations on the extent or the exercise of statutory power, but those limitations are not calculated to secure judicial scrutiny of the merits of a particular case.[25]

Implied limitations on the exercise of statutory powers arise in a variety of ways in administrative law, such as by the importation of the common law rule of natural justice and the determination of relevant and irrelevant considerations.[26]

Natural justice provides a useful example of the determination of implied limitations. To understand the interconnections between statutory interpretation and the duty to accord natural justice, we need to see how natural justice is viewed from a statutory perspective. From this perspective natural justice is an 'ancillary rule of law'.[27] This term refers to the legal principles and rules, whether common law or statutory, which are implied in a statute for its effectiveness.[28] As Bennion

---

24 Ibid, 490 [4], 495 [32].
25 *Attorney-General (NSW) v Quin* (1990) 170 CLR 1, 36 (Brennan J).
26 The leading case on the determination of implied relevant considerations is *Minister for Aboriginal Affairs v Peko-Wallsend Ltd* (1986) 162 CLR 24. A case which illustrates the determination of whether express considerations are a code is *Roche Products Pty Ltd v National Drugs and Poisons Schedule Committee* (2007) 163 FCR 451.
27 Bennion, above n 17, Part XXIII.
28 Ibid, 1034.

explains, '[i]t is impossible for the drafter to restate in express terms all those ancillary legal considerations which are, or may become, necessary for the Act's working'. Therefore, an Act of Parliament 'is not a statement in a vacuum'.[29] As a result, a legal presumption arises, 'that Parliament is taken to intend general rules of law to apply in the interpretation of enactments so far as relevant'.[30]

Consistent with natural justice being an ancillary rule of law, the High Court has recently acknowledged that, so far as statutory powers are concerned:

> The implication of the principles of natural justice in a statute is...arrived at by a process of construction. It proceeds upon the assumption that the legislature, being aware of the common law principles, would have intended that they apply to the exercise of a power of the kind referred to in *Annetts v McCann*. Observance of the principles of natural justice is a condition attached to such a statutory power and governs its exercise...[31]

The Court therefore rejected the idea that natural justice was simply a free-standing common law doctrine. However, as pointed out in a later case, natural justice is not simply an implication in a statute:

> A debate whether procedural fairness is to be identified as a common law duty or as an implication from statute proceeds upon a false dichotomy and is unproductive.[32]

These passages indicate that the duty to accord natural justice is not solely a common law one nor simply an implication from statute; rather it is both. It is the common law, not legislation, which sets the rules for implication. There are two main steps to the implication. The first step is to determine whether 'the presumption that the principles of natural justice condition the exercise of a statutory power'[33] arises. The court must determine that the power concerned is 'such a statutory power'[34] as gives rise to the presumption.[35]

If this first step is satisfied, as it usually now is, the next step in the implication process is to ask whether the presumption is displaced. It may only be displaced by 'a clear contrary intention'.[36] It is at this point that statutory interpretation

---

29 Ibid, 1033.
30 Ibid.
31 *Saeed v Minister for Immigration and Citizenship* (2010) 241 CLR 252, 258–9 [12]–[13] (French CJ, Gummow, Hayne, Crennan and Kiefel JJ).
32 *Plaintiff S10/2011 v Minister for Immigration and Citizenship* (2012) 290 ALR 616, 640 [97].
33 *Kioa v West* (1985) 159 CLR 550, 619 (Brennan J), approved and applied in *Plaintiff S10/2011 v Minister for Immigration and Citizenship* (2012) 290 ALR 616, 633 [66].
34 *Saeed v Minister for Immigration and Citizenship* (2010) 241 CLR 252, 259 [13].
35 Chapter 10.
36 *Kioa v West* (1985) 159 CLR 550, 609 (Brennan J). See also 584 (Mason J).

comes to the fore. It will be deployed to determine if such an intention arises. However, even here, administrative law doctrine (ancillary law) influences the interpretative task. It is not any intention reached on the balance of probabilities which will suffice (as occurs normally in statutory interpretation). It must be a '*strong* manifestation of contrary statutory intention in order for [the presumption] to be excluded'.[37] To determine whether there is evidence of such an intention, a court identifies, and then gives appropriate weight to, the interpretative factors. As has been seen already, the relevant factors arise from a consideration of: the empowering provision concerned, the Act, the legislative history of the Act, and the wider context.

An example of a case in which the empowering provision was heavily influential is *Plaintiff S10/2011 v Minister for Immigration and Citizenship*.[38] In this case the High Court identified the 'extraordinary nature' of the provisions,[39] namely the 'personal, non-compellable, "public interest" powers'[40] which were conferred upon the Minister, as a basis to exclude the presumption. A court may also infer that the purposes of the legislative provision would be defeated if a hearing were afforded.[41]

As regards the Act as a whole, in a rare case a specific provision of the Act may expressly exclude the rules of natural justice.[42] More commonly, the remainder of the Act may be found as a basis for an implication that the hearing rule is excluded. The Act as a whole may, through 'lengthy and detailed provisions' provide a 'statutory code governing the requirements of natural justice during and in relation to the inquiry';[43] or it may make a statement which is inconsistent with the provision of a fair hearing by way of the common law.[44]

A court may have regard to the legislative history of the Act in question, and give weight to a statement in extrinsic materials. But it would be unusual for it to be determinative. In *Miah*,[45] members of the High Court had regard to a statement in an Explanatory Memorandum accompanying the Bill which became the Act in question. It stated that the Bill 'provides a code for decision-making to replace the current common law rules of natural justice' and aimed to 'replace the uncodified

---

37 Ibid, 585 (Mason J, emphasis added).
38 (2012) 290 ALR 616.
39 Ibid, 639 [96].
40 Ibid, 641 [100].
41 *Edelsten v Federal Commissioner of Taxation* (1989) 85 ALR 226, 233; *Francis v Attorney-General (Qld)* (2008) 100 ALD 600, 606; *Kioa v West* (1985) 159 CLR 550, 586.
42 *Seiffert v Prisoners Review Board* [2011] WASCA 148, [115] (hearing rule).
43 *Edelsten v Health Insurance Commission* (1990) 27 FCR 56, 71. See also *State of South Australia v O'Shea* (1987) 163 CLR 378, 402.
44 *Riverside Nursing Care Pty Ltd v Bishop* (2000) 100 FCR 519, 522 [11]–[13]; *Francis v Attorney-General (Qld)* (2008) 100 ALD 600, 605 [15].
45 *Re Minister for Immigration and Multicultural Affairs; Ex parte Miah* (2001) 206 CLR 57.

principles of natural justice with clear and fixed procedures which are drawn from those principles'.[46] However, by majority, the Court did not find a sufficiently clear contrary intention expressed by the Act.

The wider context beyond the Act and its legislative history takes in the totality of the statute law and the common law.[47] It thus includes constitutional principles such as the separation of powers and the independence of the judiciary. In the natural justice context, a contrary intention may be found if acknowledging a duty to accord natural justice would require the court to venture into 'a political matter',[48] such as 'the area of politically created formulation of and justification for the foreign policy and its sanctions'.[49]

Ascertaining the effect of non-compliance with a statutory requirement

It is common for a legislative drafter to set out requirements which are intended to regulate the exercise of government powers. The requirements may be stated in the empowering provision itself or elsewhere in the Act. If such requirements are breached, the question may arise whether that non-compliance has the effect of invalidating the exercise of the power. Parliament could have provided for the effect expressly, stating that a breach of the requirement invalidates the exercise of the power, or stating that it does not do so. If Parliament has not clearly provided for the effect of non-compliance, the determination of the effect (if any) is an interpretative exercise. As Brennan J explained in *Project Blue Sky Inc v Australian Broadcasting Authority*:

> When the validity of a purported exercise of a statutory power is in question, the intention of the Parliament determines the scope of a power as well as the consequences of non-compliance with a provision prescribing what

---

46 Ibid, 95 [132], 109 [173].
47 Gageler, above n 2, 15.
48 *Aye v Minister for Immigration and Citizenship* (2010) 187 FCR 449, 452 [9] (Spender J).
49 Ibid, 475 [127] (McKerracher J). Other well-known cases in 'the political field' and impliedly excluding the provision of natural justice include *State of South Australia v O'Shea* (1987) 163 CLR 378 (see Brennan J at 411); *Peninsular Anglican Boys' School v Ryan* (1985) 7 FCR 415, 430; *Minister for Arts, Heritage and Environment v Peko-Wallsend Ltd* (1987) 15 FCR 274, 278–9; *Council of Civil Service Unions v Minister for the Civil Service* [1985] AC 374.

must be done or what must occur before a power may be exercised. If the purported exercise of the power is outside the ambit of the power or if the power has been purportedly exercised without compliance with a condition on which the power depends, the purported exercise is invalid. If there has been non-compliance with a provision which does not affect the ambit or existence of the power, the purported exercise of the power is valid.[50]

In the following oft-cited passage from the joint opinion in the *Project Blue Sky* case, their Honours referred to the principal criteria used to determine whether a purported exercise of power is invalidated by the breach of a statutory requirement:

> An act done in breach of a condition regulating the exercise of a statutory power is not necessarily invalid and of no effect. Whether it is depends upon whether there can be discerned a legislative purpose to invalidate any act that fails to comply with the condition. The existence of the purpose is ascertained by reference to the language of the statute, its subject matter and objects, and the consequences for the parties of holding void every act done in breach of the condition.[51]

In the *Project Blue Sky* case the statutory power, the exercise of which was impugned, was one to make a broadcasting standard under s 122 of the *Broadcasting Services Act 1992* (Cth). Standards are to relate to, among other things, 'the Australian content of programs': s 122(2)(b). Section 122(4) provided that 'Standards must not be inconsistent with this Act or the regulations'. The statutory requirement which the plaintiff argued was an essential preliminary, the breach of which invalidated the exercise of the power, was set out in s 160(d) of the Act:

> The ABA is to perform its functions in a manner consistent with:
>
> ...
>
> (d) Australia's obligations under any convention to which Australia is a party or any agreement between Australia and a foreign country.

The agreement which attracted this provision was the Australia New Zealand Closer Economic Relations Trade Agreement, together with the Trade in Services Protocol to the Trade Agreement. Articles 4 and 5 of the Protocol provided that

---

50 (1998) 194 CLR 355, 375 [41].

51 Ibid, 388–9 [91]. The joint opinion referred confusingly to 'a breach of a *condition*' as potentially applicable to both a case where the breach has the effect of invalidity *and* to a case where the breach is found not to have that effect. Compare Brennan J in *Project Blue Sky*, who restricted the word 'condition' to the first case: see 373–5 [37]–[41]. It is respectfully suggested that Brennan J's terminology is clearer since a 'condition' suggests that breach of the requirement *will* result in invalidity. For this reason, in this chapter, I use the more neutral term of 'requirement' to describe the provision whose effect is at issue.

each member State was to allow persons of the other Member State the same access rights to markets as were allowed to its own persons and services. The Australian Broadcasting Authority had made an Australian Content Standard, clause 9 of which declared, among other things, that 'Australian programs must be at least 50% of all programming broadcast between 6.00 am and midnight'. It having been found in the joint opinion that cl 9 of the Standard was in breach of Australia's obligations under Arts 4 and 5 of the Protocol,[52] the interpretative issue arose as to whether as a consequence the Standard was void and of no force or effect.

The joint opinion held that the Standard was not void by reason of a breach of s 160(d).[53] To justify this conclusion their Honours drew on the now familiar sources of interpretative factors: the provision whose effect was at issue, the Act as a whole, and the wider context. As regards *the provision at issue*, the joint opinion was influenced by the nature of the obligations imposed by s 160. These obligations included regulatory policy described in s 4, general policies of the Government notified by the Minister, and directions given by the Minister. Because '[n]ot every obligation imposed by the section has a rule-like quality which can be easily identified and applied', this made the requirements less fit to be regarded as conditions the breach of which was intended to invalidate any act done in breach of the section.[54] As for international conventions and agreements, many of them were 'expressed in indeterminate language as a result of compromises made between the contracting State parties'.[55] As regards *the Act as a whole*, the joint opinion found that the location of the s 160 requirements in the Act was a strong indication that breach of s 160 was not intended to invalidate any act done in breach of that section. This was because s 160 was set out *after* the conferral of the power to make the Standard.[56]

As regards *the wider context*, their Honours considered the presumption that a consequentialist construction be given; that is, it is presumed that a court should assess and take into account the likely consequences of adopting each proposed construction. If the consequences of a construction are more likely to be adverse than beneficent, then that is a factor telling against that construction.[57] Here, the High Court inquired into the consequences of holding void every act done in breach of the requirements in s 160. Their Honours inferred that the likelihood of the ABA breaching its obligations under s 160 was far from fanciful, especially considering that Australia was a party to about 900 treaties. As licensees in many cases 'would have great difficulty in ascertaining whether the ABA was acting consistently with the obligations imposed by s 160', their Honours inferred that '[e]xpense, inconvenience

---

52 Ibid, 386 [84].
53 Ibid, 392–3 [99].
54 Ibid, 391 [95].
55 Ibid, 391–2 [96].
56 Ibid, 391 [94].
57 Bennion, above n 17, 869; Bennion 2009, above n 3, 41–3.

and loss of investor confidence must be regarded as real possibilities if acts done in breach of s 160 are invalid'.[58] Although their Honours had earlier observed that a finding in this context 'often reflects a contestable judgment',[59] the interpretative issue apparently proved in the end not to be difficult to resolve. Their Honours did not cite any factors as indicating that s 160 was merely directory.

The *Project Blue Sky* case shows that interpretative techniques can be applied not only to determine the limitations on the extent or the exercise of a power but also to determine the *effect* of breaching statutory requirements. In essence, what the Court is doing in the latter (*Project Blue Sky* case) is determining what the provision impliedly says about the effect of its breach. As the High Court held in that case, 'the best *interpretation* of s 160 is that, while it imposes a legal duty on the ABA, an act done in breach of its provisions is not invalid'.[60] The criteria the High Court considered in that case – the subject matter of the provision, the language of the Act as a whole, and the consequences of holding void every act done in breach of the requirement – are nothing new so far as statutory interpretation is concerned.

Whose interpretations carry legal authority?

The courts, the executive and the lay person

Courts, the executive and the lay person each enjoy, to varying degrees, legal authority. Clearly, courts have prime and superior authority to interpret the law. The famous statement of this principle was made by Marshall CJ in *Marbury v Madison*:

> It is emphatically the province and duty of the judicial department to say what the law is. Those who apply the rule to particular cases must of necessity espouse and interpret that rule.[61]

The executive's interpretation of the law enjoys presumptive status through the presumption of regularity: 'Where a public official or authority purports to exercise

---

58 (1998) 194 CLR 355, 392 [97]–[98].
59 Ibid, 389 [91].
60 Ibid, 392–3 [99] (emphasis added).
61 (1803) 1 Cranch 137, 177 [5 US 60, 73]. Australian courts have adopted this passage. See, eg, *Attorney-General (NSW) v Quin* (1990) 170 CLR 1, 35 (Brennan J); *Commissioner of Taxation v Indooroopilly Children Services (Qld) Pty Ltd* (2007) 158 FCR 325, 327 [4] (Allsop J, Stone J agreeing).

a power or to do an act in the course of his or its duties, a presumption arises that all conditions necessary to the exercise of that power or the doing of that act have been fulfilled.'[62] That aside, as a general rule, the executive enjoys no special position to influence judicial interpretation, let alone the ability to control the result of interpretation by a court. This reflects the separation of powers in the Australian system, whereby '[t]he authoritative determination of the meaning of a statutory provision is an exercise of the judicial power, not of the legislative power, let alone of the executive power'.[63] Thus, for example, a Minister's speech in Parliament, *after* the enactment of the relevant Bill, is not entitled to any special weight;[64] nor are opinions of agencies such as the Aborigines Protection Board and Crown Solicitor,[65] or an excise bulletin of the Australian Taxation Office.[66] However, as is documented in the standard works,[67] a Minister's second reading speech in the Parliament, an Explanatory Memorandum laid before the Parliament, and law reform reports publicly available at the time of the consideration of the relevant Bill, may be considered by a court under the authority of extrinsic aid legislation[68] or the common law. Some judges would restrict the use of Ministerial second reading speeches under the Acts Interpretation Acts to an indication of the legislative purpose.[69] However, another view is that the Interpretation Acts can be used as evidence of the intended operation or linguistic meaning of the provision in question.[70]

A lay person's 'interpretation' of the law, if it (as often would be the case) reflects the grammatical or ordinary meaning of a provision in question, enjoys

---

62 *Minister for Natural Resources v New South Wales Aboriginal Land Council* (1987) 9 NSWLR 154, 164 (McHugh J).
63 *Harrison v Melhem* (2008) 72 NSWLR 380, 384 [15] (Spigelman CJ).
64 *Dossett v TKJ Nominees Pty Ltd* (2003) 218 CLR 1, 6 [10] (McHugh J). Kirby J did not decide if the Minister's post-enactment statement in the Parliament was admissible: 26 [87]. See also *Waugh Hotel Management Pty Ltd v Marrickville Council* (2009) 171 LGERA 112, 148–9 [146]–[149]. An exception was made for a speech identifying the mischief with which the earlier Bill had been seeking to deal: [146].
65 *State of South Australia v Lampard-Trevorrow* (2010) 106 SASR 331, 377 [217].
66 *Port of Brisbane Corporation v Commissioner of Taxation* (2004) 140 FCR 375, 386 [25].
67 D C Pearce and R S Geddes, *Statutory Interpretation in Australia* (LexisNexis Butterworths, 7th ed, 2011) ch 3; M Sanson, *Statutory Interpretation* (Oxford University Press, 2012) 142–8.
68 *Acts Interpretation Act 1901* (Cth) s 15AB and State and Territory equivalents (except in South Australia).
69 *Harrison v Melhem* (2008) 72 NSWLR 380, 401 [172] (Mason P, Spigelman CJ, Beazley and Giles JJA agreeing).
70 This is the view of Basten JA in *Shorten v David Hurst Constructions Pty Ltd* (2008) 72 NSWLR 211, 217 [27] (*dicta*). It is submitted that Basten JA's interpretation is the better view. In *Re Bolton; Ex parte Beane* (1987) 162 CLR 514, 518 Mason CJ, Wilson and Dawson JJ gave 'serious consideration' to a Ministerial second reading speech that 'unambiguously' asserted the intended operation of the provision in question. Deane J also considered the speech: at 532. See also C Cook et al, *Laying Down the Law* (LexisNexis, 8th ed, 2012) 313, who regard the view taken in *Harrison v Melhem* as 'surprising'.

prima facie weight in the courts. The grammatical meaning is the starting point in the judicial interpretation process,[71] and 'good reason' must be shown for departing from it.[72] Also, if legislation is intended to be accessible to the ordinary person, this will be another factor giving weight to the grammatical meaning.[73]

Administrative law qualifications

Two qualifications are noteworthy. The first relates to the Administrative Appeals Tribunal ('AAT'). As a body bestowed with administrative functions, the AAT does not have judicial power.[74] Although its interpretations might be thought to bear the same features as those of other members of the executive, the reality is otherwise. It is in fact both an administrative institution and a legal institution.[75] Right from the start, it was expected that the Tribunal would create 'law'. The Tribunal was to be established, the Parliament was told, to 'build up a significant body of administrative law and practice of general application'.[76] As its jurisdiction has grown to comprise over 400 areas,[77] its decisions have created de facto precedents for itself[78] and 'administrative norms'[79] for the bureaucracy below it,[80] even though it has not always been consistent.[81]

---

71 *Cooper Brookes (Wollongong) Pty Ltd v Commissioner of Taxation of the Commonwealth of Australia* (1980) 147 CLR 297, 304 (Gibbs CJ); *Chiropedic Bedding Pty Ltd v Radburg Pty Ltd* (2008) 170 FCR 560, 569 [39].
72 *Cooper Brookes (Wollongong) Pty Ltd v Commissioner of Taxation of the Commonwealth of Australia* (1980) 147 CLR 297, 321 (Mason and Wilson JJ).
73 *Re Secretary, Department of Social Security and Diepenbroeck* (1992) 27 ALD 142, 145 [18] (President O'Connor J).
74 *Drake v Minister for Immigration and Ethnic Affairs* (1979) 2 ALD 60, 64.
75 Administrative Appeals Tribunal, cited in J McMillan, 'Merits Review and the AAT: A Concept Develops' in J McMillan (ed), *The AAT – Twenty Years Forward: Passing a Milestone in Commonwealth Administrative Review* (Australian Institute of Administrative Law, 1998) 32, 55.
76 Australia, House of Representatives, 6 March 1975, Mr Enderby (Attorney-General), p 1188, Second Reading Speech to the Administrative Appeals Tribunal Bill 1975 (Cth).
77 The Hon Justice Garry Downes AM, 'Structure, Power and Duties of the Administrative Appeals Tribunal of Australia', Bangkok, 21 February 2006, at <www.aat.gov.au/SpeechesPapersAndResearch/speeches/downes/StructurePowerDutiesFebruary2006.htm> [31].
78 Ibid, [48].
79 *Re Scott and Commissioner for Superannuation* (1986) 9 ALD 491, 499, discussed in D C Pearce et al, *Australian Administrative Law* (LexisNexis, Looseleaf service, 2012) [273A].
80 D Davies, 'The First Twenty Years of AAT Adjudication' in J McMillan (ed) *The AAT: Twenty Years Forward* (Australian Institute of Administrative Law, 1998) 198; A SBlunn, 'The Impact of the AAT on Social Security Administration' in J McMillan (ed) *The AAT: Twenty Years Forward* (Australian Institute of Administrative Law, 1998) 99 (social security); J Dwyer and G Woodard, 'Dreams of a Fair Administrative Law' in S Argument (ed), *Administrative Law and Public Administration: Happily Married or Living Apart Under the Same Roof?* (Australian Institute of Administrative Law Inc, 1994) 197.
81 Pearce et al, above n 79, [273A].

The second qualification arises where a body has a knowledge of the area which specially equips it to provide an answer. In *Corporation of the City of Enfield v Development Assessment Commission*[82] the High Court held that in these circumstances a court could attach weight to the application of the law by an administrative tribunal, including matters going to its jurisdiction.[83] Examples of matters upon which, it has been held, weight can be accorded are a jurisdictional finding of fact by the Development Assessment Commission,[84] and 'an opinion of a planning authority that a particular undefined use has qualities which tend to align it with a particular definition'.[85] An example of a matter *not* raising grounds for giving weight is a specification by a delegate of the Registrar of Aboriginal and Torres Strait Islander Corporations as to what constitutes a 'reasonable period' for showing cause why a determination under s 487-10(1)(a) of the *Corporations (Aboriginal and Torres Strait Islander) Act 2006* (Cth) should not be made.[86]

Why are there sometimes different judicial interpretations?

It is a trite observation that judges in the same case[87] on occasion disagree over the meaning and effect of statutory provisions.[88] As a professor once said, 'Why

---

82 (2000) 199 CLR 135.
83 Ibid, 154–5 [45]–[50].
84 Ibid, 156 [50].
85 *Woolworths Ltd v Maryborough City Council (No 2)* [2006] 1 Qd R 273, 289 [36].
86 *Dunghutti Elders Council (Aboriginal Corporation) RNTBC v Registrar of Aboriginal and Torres Strait Islander Corporations* (2011) 279 ALR 138, 152–3 [61].
87 Some commentators bemoan the fact that judges do not take the same approach in cases on *different statutes*, eg K Hall and C Macken, *Legislation and Statutory Interpretation* (LexisNexis Butterworths, 3rd ed, 2012) 84 [4.3]; S Corcoran, 'Theories of Statutory Interpretation' in S Corcoran and S Bottomley (eds), *Interpreting Statutes* (Federation Press, 2005) 8, 10, 30. With respect, this is asking the wrong question. Different statutes necessarily attract different interpretative criteria. Each statute is unique: G Bowman, 'Sir William Dale Annual Memorial Lecture: The Art of Legislative Drafting' (2005) 7 *European Journal of Law Reform* 3, 4; M D Kirby, 'Towards a Grand Theory of Interpretation: The Case of Statutes and Contracts' (2003) 24 *Statute Law Review* 95, 106, citing P M Perell, 'The Ambiguity Exception to the Parol Evidence Rule' (2001) 36 *Canadian Business Law Journal* 21, 22. The interpretative factors which are relevant turn on 'the particular case' (*Cooper Brookes (Wollongong) Pty Ltd v Commissioner of Taxation of the Commonwealth of Australia* (1980) 147 CLR 297, 320 (Mason and Wilson JJ).
88 It is unclear how often this occurs. Across all matters it has been found that, in cases published in the Commonwealth Law Reports, members of the High Court disagreed as to the orders in 44.62% of cases during the period 1981–2003: A Lynch, 'Does the High Court Disagree More Often in Constitutional Cases?: A Statistical Study of Judgment Delivery 1981–2003' (2005) 33 *Federal Law Review* 485, 497. But High Court cases are inherently more likely

is it so?'. The question seems important. There is a lively literature discussing the elements of judicial reasoning in statutory interpretation.[89] Some commentators question whether the rule of law is being served by statutory interpretation,[90] and suggest non-legal considerations are involved,[91] such as result-orientation.[92]

A number of theories have been advanced to explain different judicial interpretations. One school of thought is Bennion's 'differential readings'.[93] This is the name Bennion gives to 'the phenomenon where different minds conscientiously arrive at different conclusions on the legal meaning'.[94] This school of thought is compatible with the orthodoxy that statutory interpretation is not a mechanical task.[95] The theory does not discount the influence of different value preferences or judicial philosophies[96] informing legal reasoning; indeed it regards such influences as inevitable. Importantly though, judicial reasoning is constrained by the law.[97] It is law which dominates.[98] The ultimate sources of differential readings are variously identified.[99] Bennion refers to 'the human condition',[100] implying that no individual judge thinks exactly the same as another. Kirby J similarly referred to the 'subjective perceptions' involved in ascertaining the legislative purpose from plural and diverse sources,[101] and to the act of judgment being 'in part one of impression'.[102] Various

---

to produce such disagreement. It is possible that some judges who agreed on the orders disagreed on matters such as interpretation. In Lynch's study, 36.11% of cases were resolved by concurrence (agreement on orders but not by way of a joint opinion): 497.

89 For an overview, see J Barnes, 'Statutory Interpretation' in I Freckelton and H Selby (eds), *Appealing to the Future: Michael Kirby and His Legacy* (Lawbook, 2009) 721, 745–9.
90 Sanson, above n 67, 8; J Goldsworthy, 'Parliamentary Sovereignty and Statutory Interpretation' in R Bigwood (ed), *The Statute: Making and Meaning* (LexisNexis, Wellington, 2004) 187, 210.
91 See commentators discussed in Barnes, above n 89, 745–6.
92 Hall and Macken, above n 87, 110 [4.36].
93 Bennion 2009, above n 3, 127–9.
94 Ibid, 18.
95 Gageler, above n 2, 2; *Coleman v Power* (2004) 220 CLR 1, 96 [247] (Kirby J).
96 On judicial philosophies, see A Mason, 'Rights, Values and Legal Institutions: Reshaping Australian Institutions' in G Lindell (ed), *The Mason Papers: Selected Articles and Speeches by Sir Anthony Mason AC KBE* (Federation Press, 2007) 80, 82.
97 Barnes, above n 89, 727, 747, discussing the views of Fiss, Mason CJ, and Kirby J.
98 Mason, above n 96, 82–3.
99 One may be discounted, however. Some writers maintain there is judicial 'discretion', at least in some cases, for example Hall and Macken, above n 87, 94; L Solan, *The Language of Statutes: Laws and their Interpretation* (University of Chicago Press, 2010) 3. Cf Barak above n 2, 38 who says, '[j]udicial discretion operates within the framework of interpretive rules, not outside it'. But this is a misconception: the law confers no formal discretion: Bennion 2009, above n 3, chs 13, 14.
100 Bennion 2009, above n 3, 127.
101 M D Kirby, *Judicial Activism: Authority, Principle and Policy in the Judicial Method – The Hamlyn Lectures Fifty-Fifth Series* (Sweet and Maxwell, 2004) 33. To similar effect is M Gleeson, *The Rule of Law and the Constitution* (ABC Books, 2000) 130.
102 *Hickling v Laneyrie* (1991) 21 NSWLR 730, 738 (Kirby P).

commentators have also pointed to the 'vague'[103] and 'nebulous character'[104] of the interpretative criteria.

A case illustrating differential readings is *Shahi v Minister for Immigration and Citizenship*.[105] The case concerned a refusal to grant a certain visa under the Migration Regulations 1994 (Cth). The applicant had qualified for the visa at the time of the application but not when the application was actually determined (because the visa applicant's son turned 18 years of age during this time). The statutory interpretation question for the High Court was whether the requirement that, at the time of decision, 'The applicant continues to satisfy the criterion in clause 202.211' applied to *all* the criteria in the clause referred to, including the age requirement (the Minister's construction), or to merely one of the criteria, which did not include the age requirement relating to the visa proposer (the applicant's construction). Among other things, the majority emphasised that the result of taking the Minister's construction would be 'capricious and unjust'[106] since an applicant for the visa, having qualified for the visa at the time of the application, could be disentitled merely by a delay in deciding the application. However, the minority, who agreed with the Minister's construction, seemingly gave this consequence less weight, conceding only that there were anomalies and difficulties with both the plaintiff's and the Minister's constructions.[107]

A second school of thought is that judges can disagree in the one case as a result of taking different *approaches*. Here one is not concerned simply with different *conclusions*. That can be the result of differential readings of the same interpretative criteria.[108] Rather, we are concerned with reliance on different interpretative criteria. But how can different approaches in this sense be explained? One explanation – judicial discretion to choose amongst the interpretative criteria as if the law were a smorgasbord – must be discounted: the interpretative criteria are legal and binding,[109] and a judge or other interpreter has a duty to apply relevant criteria to the best of his or her ability.[110]

---

103 W Twining and D Miers, *How to Do Things with Rules: A Primer of Interpretation* (Cambridge University Press, 5th ed, 2010) 243.
104 M D Kirby, 'Statutory Interpretation – Principles and Pragmatism for a New Age' (2007) 19(6) *Judicial Officers' Bulletin* 49, 50.
105 (2011) 283 ALR 448.
106 Ibid, 458 [38].
107 Ibid, 460 [50].
108 Some commentators (eg Sanson, above n 67, 7, discussing Bell J's opinion in *Jemena Gas Networks (NSW) Ltd v Mine Subsidence Board* (2011) 243 CLR 558) equate the conclusion as to meaning with the reasoning approach. But a judge can come to the conclusion that a provision in doubt has a literal meaning after a wide consideration of interpretative factors (as Bell J did in that case). In such a case the judge is not 'formalist'; rather her approach is multifactorial.
109 Barak, above n 2, 47.
110 Bennion, above n 17, 13, 435.

A case which illustrates different approaches is *Minister for Immigration and Ethnic Affairs v Mayer*.[111] In this case, the question was whether a reference, in s 6A(1)(c) of the *Migration Act 1958* (Cth), to a determination by the Minister that 'the Minister has determined, by instrument in writing that he has the status of refugee' was a reference to a past determination of the Minister under a non-statutory power (the Minister's construction), or whether it was to be read as a determination under the statutory provision in which the reference occurred (the applicant's construction). If it was the latter, a right to be given reasons for the refusal to make a determination upon request arose under s 13 of the *Administrative Decisions (Judicial Review) Act 1977* (Cth). By majority, the High Court held that the latter (applicant's) construction was preferable. Both the majority (Mason, Deane, Dawson JJ jointly) and the minority (Gibbs CJ and Brennan J in separate opinions) considered the text of s 6A(1)(c).

Admittedly, part of the explanation for the different interpretations in this case was that the majority and minority took differential readings of the provision in question. The majority read s 6A(1)(c) as operating contemporaneously by virtue of the second 'has' reference in the provision ('has the status of refugee').[112] In contrast, the minority read the provision with emphasis on the first 'has' reference ('has determined'). This indicated to them that the provision assumed a *past* determination of the Minister outside of the Migration Act.[113]

However, the majority also cited certain interpretative criteria which were not cited by the minority in their opinions. The majority gave weight to two consequences of the Minister's construction. The first was that there would be no statutory obligation even to consider whether a determination should be made. The second was that, if the Minister's construction were the law:

> the statutory provisions of par. (c) could be deprived of any effective content by mere administrative decision discontinuing current administrative arrangements or allocating the function of determining whether a person was a refugee to someone other than the Minister.[114]

The latter consideration was elevated by the majority into the status of a general principle.[115] This suggested that the majority (but less so the minority) were influenced by a judicial philosophy that statute law is so important to democracy that references in statute law are presumptively not to be read as dependent for their content on a mere administrative decision. Alternatively, a simpler explanation

---

111 (1985) 157 CLR 290.
112 Ibid, 302.
113 Ibid, 306.
114 Ibid, 301.
115 Ibid, 303.

for the different approaches is that the majority thought of these consequences, whereas the minority simply did not! Or perhaps the minority *did* think of these consequences but regarded them as insignificant – in which case we are back to Bennion's theory of differential readings.

Finally, a third school of thought, advanced by some academics and journalists, is that different judicial interpretations are explained by the fact that different personal values of judges dominate statutory interpretation.[116] For example, it has been said that 'judicial decisions [are] largely unconstrained individualistic policy preferences'[117] and that judges are 'not really constrained by legal language, precedents, rules, doctrines or principles' as interpreters of the law.[118] This school of thought immediately runs into difficulties. First, judges have no discretion conferred by the law. Second, they have no authority to '[act] according to his or her own values or individual views'.[119] Occasions when judges mistakenly do expressly base their decisions on private values (or what the High Court has described as a 'judicially constructed policy'[120]) are comparatively rare. When they occur, the appeal system corrects the error.[121] Third, where is the evidence? One researcher has attempted to use sophisticated statistical techniques ('jurimetrics') to support this school of thought. The researcher found that, statistically speaking, judges' conclusions are highly predictable in the public law arena, the prediction rate being 83% of cases decided in the House of Lords from 1986 to 1995.[122] He claims that 'we have now shown that the actual outcome of cases is entirely compatible with such a theory'.[123] But statistical predictability is also compatible with Bennion's differential readings. Further, cases in the House of Lords are not typical of judging, let alone of all interpretations and applications of statute law, which differ again.[124] The 'evidence' therefore pertains only to the rarefied end of the legal system.

---

116 For examples, see Barnes, above n 89, 745–6.
117 D Robertson, *Judicial Discretion in the House of Lords* (Clarendon Press, 1998) 70. The author acknowledges that statute law does reduce the scope for judicial preferences: 51.
118 R Benson, *The Interpretation Game: How Judges and Lawyers Make the Law* (Carolina Academic Press, 2008) xv.
119 *WBM v Chief Commissioner of Police* (2010) 27 VR 469, 481 [46]. See also Brennan J in *Theophanous v Herald & Weekly Times Ltd* (1994) 182 CLR 104, 143.
120 *Australian Education Union v Department of Education and Children's Services* (2012) 285 ALR 27, 35 [28].
121 As the High Court of Australia did in *Australian Education Union v Department of Education and Children's Services* (2012) 285 ALR 27, 35 [28]; and the full Federal Court did in *Minister for Immigration and Citizenship v Yucesan* (2008) 169 FCR 202, 209 [28] (correcting the Federal Magistrate in that case).
122 Robertson, above n 117, 51.
123 Ibid, 70.
124 J Burrows, 'The Changing Approach to the Interpretation of Statutes' (2002) 33 *Victoria University of Wellington Law Review* 561, 561 makes the point that 'almost by definition, [court cases] are the difficult cases where there are competing arguments about the proper interpretation'.

Conclusion

We recall the observation of Robert Hughes that the *Mona Lisa* is so familiar that she has been deprived of all meaning. Statutory interpretation is so ubiquitous that it might lose meaning if we do not analyse it. In this chapter I have tried to show that the path to better understanding of statutory interpretation as an element in administrative law is by asking three questions: 'How is statutory interpretation connected to the functions of administrative law?'; 'Whose interpretations carry legal authority?'; and 'Why is there occasional disagreement amongst judges?'. The tasks statutory interpretation undertakes include determining the extent of statutory powers (of primary decision-makers as well as of the review bodies under their governing statutes); determining the limitations on the exercise of powers (both express and implied); and ascertaining the effect of non-compliance with a statutory requirement. The 'who' question entails looking at the interpretations of the courts, the executive and the lay person. Australian courts retain overall governance of authoritative statutory interpretation in Australia, assisted by legal advisors looking over their shoulders predicting what a court would hold. The 'why' question leads us into murky waters. But as Bennion points out, we should not exaggerate the capacity of individual judges in the one case to bring about differential readings.[125]

Behind these discernible features of statutory interpretation lies its deeper meaning. The analysis in this chapter shows us that the law of statutory interpretation has a highly flexible structure. While its applications are diverse, remarkably, the basic technique changes little. This is the case whether the issue is, for example, determining the express limitations on the extent of power (*Yucesan*), implied limitations on the extent or the exercise of power (*ABC Developmental Learning Centres*), the exclusion of the presumption that the principles of natural justice condition the exercise of a statutory power (*Plaintiff S10*), or ascertaining the effect of non-compliance with a statutory requirement (*Project Blue Sky*). At the heart of the technique is a form of legal reasoning based on multiple factors,[126] which requires consideration of the provision at issue, the Act as a whole, the legislative history, and the wider context.

The interpretative process is flexible in a number of ways. The interpreter is not bound to apply the same factors in each case; the factors which are relevant 'present themselves'[127] according to the circumstances of the case.[128] And the

---

125 Bennion 2009, above n 3, 128–9.
126 See also F Kyrou, 'Judicial Review of Decisions of Non-Governmental Bodies Exercising Governmental Powers: Is Datafin Part of Australian law?' (2012) 86 *Australian Law Journal* 20, 32 for a defence of 'factor-based' reasoning in public law.
127 Bennion, above n 17, 9.
128 *Cooper Brookes (Wollongong) Pty Ltd v Commissioner of Taxation of the Commonwealth of Australia* (1980) 147 CLR 297, 320 (Mason and Wilson JJ).

interpreter works not only with the statute and the interpretative criteria of the law but, as often happens in administrative law, with ancillary law. Surrounding law which is relevant is implied in a statute unless, on an interpretation, the statute expressly or impliedly excludes it (*Plaintiff S10*). The interpreter's function is not restricted to determining the meaning of particular words; the interpreter may also consider implying statements about the effect of non-compliance with a statutory requirement (*Project Blue Sky*). The interpreter is not bound in all cases to choose amongst the everyday meanings (*ABC Developmental Learning Centres*), although a dispute may turn on such a choice (*Yucesan*). The interpreter has a variety of ways to accommodate the legal meaning. So long as a proposed interpretation is reasonably open and not inconsistent with the text, the interpreter can confirm a grammatical meaning (*Yucesan*), or the interpreter can gloss the text (*Plaintiff S10*; *Project Blue Sky*) or add an implication unifying the legal meaning and the text (*ABC Developmental Learning Centres*).

The underlying structure I have presented is the opposite of what a number of academic commentators are looking for – in vain. They would prefer to see a single interpretative approach or principle.[129] This mistakes both the reality and the strength of statutory interpretation. Statutory interpretation works up from problems[130] rather than imposing a top-down approach. Its very flexibility gives rise on occasions to differences of view. But without this flexibility, interpreters would not be able to accomplish the enormous range of tasks assigned to them in administrative law and elsewhere.

---

129 As pointed out in M Schwarzschild, 'Mad Dogmas and Englishmen: How Other People Interpret and Why' in J Goldsworthy and T Campbell (eds), *Legal Interpretation in Democratic States* (Ashgate/Dartmouth, 2002) 93, 94. For examples of commentaries tending to advocate a single principle, see Sanson, above n 67, 9 T Campbell, 'Legislative Intent and Democratic Decision Making' in N Naffine, R Owens and J Williams (eds), *Intention in Law and Philosophy* (Ashgate/Dartmouth, 2001) 291.
130 Crennan, above n 87, 11–12.

7

STANDING FOR ENVIRONMENTAL GROUPS: PROTECTING PUBLIC AND PRIVATE INTERESTS

Andrew Edgar

Introduction: Standing and interests

The general principle of Australian standing laws is that an applicant is to have a special interest in the subject matter of the proceedings.[1] This is easily satisfied when the applicant has suffered harm to their private rights and interests – particularly if the harm relates to property or financial concerns. Issues tend to arise when applicants bring proceedings claiming to represent other persons with rights and interests that are affected, or when they claim to represent the public interest. This chapter examines the difficulties under the basic rules of standing for environmental groups in bringing proceedings to challenge administrative decisions. It also examines reforms that facilitate environmental groups' access to the courts.

It is convenient to mention at the outset that, technically, there is a variety of standing rules in Australia – the rules vary depending on the remedy being sought. While it is doubtful whether standing rules should differ according to the remedy, it is also commonly accepted that the different tests for standing are converging.[2] The common thread in standing laws is that the applicant has an 'interest' that is regarded as worthy of protection[3] – reflected in Australian law in the special interest test established in *Australian Conservation Foundation v Commonwealth*.[4]

How do applicants with environmental interests push the traditional boundaries of standing rules? A convenient starting point is to examine briefly the characteristics of environmental decisions. Their primary characteristic is that they ultimately concern the acceptability of the environmental impacts of a particular development[5] – a highly subjective administrative judgement. These decisions typically involve balancing social, economic and environmental factors – public interest considerations – and may require the decision-maker to have a degree of expertise, or at least be given expert advice regarding aspects of the decision.

Environmental decisions are also a form of multi-stakeholder governance. For the purposes of standing rules, there are three stakeholder categories for environmental decisions. The first are the developers who apply for approvals and

---

1 *Australian Conservation Foundation v Commonwealth* (1980) 146 CLR 493, 527 (Gibbs J).
2 M Aronson and M Groves, *Judicial Review of Administrative Action* (Lawbook, 5th ed, 2013) 723; *Australian Institute of Marine and Power Engineers v Secretary, Department of Transport* (1986) 13 FCR 124, 132.
3 S M Thio, *Locus Standi and Judicial Review* (Singapore University Press, 1971) 13–14.
4 *Australian Conservation Foundation v Commonwealth* (1980) 146 CLR 493.
5 R Harding, C M Hendricks and M Faruqi, *Environmental Decision Making: Exploring Complexity and Context* (Federation Press, 2009) 236–8.

permits. Their interests can be characterised as maximising development potential.[6] As their property and economic rights and interests are at stake, they have no problem with standing to challenge an adverse decision.

The second category includes neighbours, local residents, and those who may use the area in which the development is to occur. Their interests can be understood as relating to matters such as privacy, solar access, noise and odour impacts, and impacts relating to the aesthetic and recreational qualities of the particular area. These interests may not be within the scope of strict standing laws that require property or economic interests to be directly affected, but are sufficiently personal to not be problematic for standing in the modern era.[7] The terminology used to describe this category is that they are beneficiaries of environmental laws. The issues relating to environmental groups in this context concern whether standing rules permit groups to represent their members for the personal harms that the members are likely to suffer if the development is approved.

The third category includes the individuals and groups who seek to protect the 'environment' – typically in relation to the physical environment or threatened species. Their interests in particular decisions often relate to the way the decision-maker balances environmental considerations against social and economic matters. They are also interested in procedural aspects of decisions such as that public consultation requirements are fully complied with and that expert, scientific material relied on by the decision-maker is well-founded. These interests cannot be regarded as being private or personal – they relate to the public interest in environment protection and good decision-making practices. The individuals and groups in this category can also be regarded as beneficiaries of environmental laws. Of the three categories of stakeholder for environmental decisions, they have the most difficulty in being granted standing.

The stakeholders that test the boundaries of standing rules are therefore the second and third categories. These two categories are most simply distinguished by regarding the second – the local residents and users of a locality – as having *personal or private interests* in the environment that they seek to protect, and the third – typically environmental groups – as seeking to represent the *public interest* in the environment. The line between these categories of beneficiary of environmental laws is crucial to understanding the scope of standing laws. Extending standing to local residents raises minor concerns – extending standing to public interest-based applicants presents fundamental concerns. Moreover, different issues arise for each of these categories as to the basis on which environmental groups may seek standing. Environmental groups may bring proceedings seeking to represent members whose personal interests have been harmed. On the other hand, an

---

6 L A Stein, *Principles of Planning Law* (Oxford University Press, 2008) 199.
7 Eg, *Day v Pinglen Pty Ltd* (1981) 148 CLR 289, 299–300.

environmental group's claim to standing may be based on its representation of the public interest in the environment. In Australian standing law, environmental groups have difficulty being granted standing in both of these contexts.

The structure of this chapter is based on the distinction between the stakeholders who seek to protect private interests and the stakeholders who seek to protect the public interest in the environment. The second part of the chapter examines traditional standing rules that require harm to a person's private rights and interests. It explains how this traditional approach to standing has been extended to facilitate access to the courts for local residents and similar beneficiaries of environmental laws. This is common to Australia, the United States and the United Kingdom. It also examines the way that Australia's standing rules differ from those of the United States and the United Kingdom on whether environmental groups may represent their members whose private interests are affected by a decision. The third part of this chapter examines the steps taken in Australian law to move beyond the traditional scope of standing rules and instead grant access to the courts for those seeking to represent the public interest. The final part of this chapter evaluates the reform options for Australian standing rules.

Private interests

Interests, injuries and environment protection

The baseline for standing rules in common law jurisdictions is that the applicant's private interests are affected by government action. Environmental interests can be protected according to this approach if standing is extended, as it now commonly is, to allow access to the courts for individuals and groups with personal interests in the environment.

The landmark Australian case on standing is the High Court's decision in *Australian Conservation Foundation v Commonwealth* ('the *ACF* case').[8] This case established the special interest test as the primary rule for standing and explained its parameters. The *ACF* case involved a challenge to a decision of the Reserve Bank to approve foreign investment in a tourist resort in central Queensland.[9] The environmental group (the ACF) challenged irregularities in the decision-making procedures and seemed to have a good case because the foreign investment decision was made prior to the necessary environmental impact assessment

---

8 *Australian Conservation Foundation v Commonwealth* (1980) 146 CLR 493.
9 For a detailed explanation of the *ACF* case, see T Bonyhady 'Introduction' in T Bonyhady and A Macintosh (eds), *Mills, Mines and Other Controversies: The Environmental Assessment of Major Projects* (Federation Press, 2010) 8–11.

processes being completed.[10] But the ACF was denied standing. It argued for open standing – that any 'private citizen' should be granted standing to 'enforce public duties unless the court considers it inadvisable that the action should be allowed to proceed'.[11] The majority of the court disagreed, saying that such a test was a matter for Parliament,[12] and settled instead on the special interest test.[13] Justice Gibbs famously referred to an applicant requiring more than a 'mere intellectual or emotional concern', suggesting that a mere interest in compliance with laws is insufficient – there must be some particular advantage to be gained by the applicant if they succeed in the proceedings or a disadvantage if they fail.[14] The ACF's environment protection objects and its participation in the consultation process for the administrative decision were held insufficient to support its claim to standing.[15]

The *ACF* case requires that an applicant's personal rights or interests are harmed in order to be granted standing. The special interest test effectively excludes environmental groups being granted standing on a public interest basis. The special interest test does not, however, exclude standing for all beneficiaries of environmental laws. This is apparent from the decision of the High Court in *Onus v Alcoa of Australia Ltd*,[16] determined soon after the *ACF* case.

The High Court affirmed the special interest test in *Onus*, and accepted that it was satisfied by two Aboriginal women who brought proceedings claiming that an aluminium smelter would interfere with relics in breach of heritage legislation – the *Archaeological and Aboriginal Relics Preservation Act 1972* (Vic). Much of the reasoning in *Onus* sought to distinguish the interest of the applicants from the one held in *ACF*. The applicants' interest in *Onus* was regarded as being different from that of the general public since they lived close by and claimed to be custodians of the particular relics on the site.[17] Justice Stephen referred to them as having 'proximity' with the subject matter of the litigation.[18] The applicants in the *ACF* case were regarded as very different. Justice Gibbs described the ACF as 'a diverse group of white Australians associated by some common opinion on a matter of social policy which might equally concern any other Australian'.[19]

The applicants' interests that were accepted by the High Court in *Onus v Alcoa* can be regarded as an extension of the scope of the rights and interests that can support standing. They were based on the applicants' cultural and spiritual

---

10 *Australian Conservation Foundation v Commonwealth* (1980) 146 CLR 493, 520.
11 Ibid, 528.
12 Ibid, 529 (Gibbs J), 540 (Stephen J), 552 (Mason J).
13 Ibid, 527 (Gibbs J), 547 (Mason J).
14 Ibid, 530.
15 Ibid, 531–2.
16 (1981) 149 CLR 27.
17 See also *Edwards v Santos Ltd* (2011) 242 CLR 421, 436.
18 (1981) 149 CLR 27, 42.
19 Ibid, 37.

connections to a particular area. Importantly, these cultural and spiritual interests were personal to the plaintiffs. The plaintiffs were not claiming to represent the public interest in the protection of the environment. The special interest test is therefore applied in a selective manner with regard to the beneficiaries of a regulatory scheme. The *ACF* case and *Onus v Alcoa* indicate that the line is drawn to exclude access to the courts for those seeking to protect the public interest. The applicants in *Onus* were treated as local residents with direct personal interests affected by the decision.

How does the special interest test as understood in the *ACF* case and *Onus v Alcoa* compare to standing laws in other jurisdictions? It is convenient to start with the United States, since it was referred to in the *ACF* case and the US approach to standing was regarded as similar to the special interest test.[20] Standing rules in the United States are far more complex than in Australia.[21] Yet, like the Australian special interest test, they require an injury that is personal to the applicant. The US position on standing is essentially that there are constitutional requirements – primarily that the applicant has suffered an 'injury in fact' – and there are 'prudential requirements' that may be varied or overridden by legislation.[22] The primary prudential requirement is that the applicant is within the 'zone of interests' that are protected by the particular Act. This requires the applicant to be a beneficiary, or represent a beneficiary, of the regulatory scheme.

The 'injury in fact' requirement serves the same purpose as the special interest test – that the applicant has suffered a particular harm that may be redressed by the court.[23] Like the High Court's decision in *Onus v Alcoa*, it has long been accepted in the United States that applicants can be granted standing to enforce environmental laws on the basis of harm to 'aesthetic, conservational, and recreational' qualities, so long as the applicant is actually 'injured' in these ways.[24] However, unlike in Australia,[25] the injury in fact element is a constitutional requirement that constrains congressional power in relation to legislation that affects the courts.[26] It is therefore

---

20 (1980) 146 CLR 493, 530 (Gibbs J), 540 (Stephen J), 551 (Mason J).
21 For a comprehensive analysis, see R J Pierce, *Administrative Law Treatise* (Aspen Publishers, 5th ed, 2010) ch 16.
22 Ibid 1412–3; *Association of Data Processing Service Organisations Inc v Camp* 397 US 150, 152–3 (1970).
23 P Cane, 'Open Standing and the Role of Courts in a Democratic Society' (1999) 20 *Singapore Law Review* 23, 27.
24 *Summers v Earth Island Institute* 555 US 488 (2009); 129 S. Ct. 1142, 1149 (2009); *Sierra Club v Morton* 405 US 727, 734–5 (1972), 734–5.
25 *Truth About Motorways Pty Ltd v Macquarie Infrastructure Investment Management Ltd* (2000) 200 CLR 591.
26 In particular, standing is controlled by the Article III requirement that courts are limited to 'cases' and 'controversies': *Association of Data Processing Service Organisations Inc v Camp* 397 US 150, 150–51 (1970).

directly related to the separation of powers. This was a major theme of Justice Scalia's famous opinion in the Supreme Court's decision in *Lujan v Defenders of Wildlife*.[27] Scalia J referred to standing in terms distinguishing law from politics. Quoting Justice Marshall in *Marbury v Madison*, he stated that the court's role 'is, solely, to decide on the rights of individuals',[28] and that 'vindicating the public interest...is the function of Congress and the Chief Executive'.[29] While Justice Scalia's reasoning in *Lujan* has been controversial,[30] it serves to highlight the way that traditional standing rules relate to separation of powers concerns. Requiring applicants to have suffered an injury to their personal rights or interests that may be remedied by court action is regarded as a way of ensuring that the courts remain within the scope of judicial rather than political functions.[31]

Standing rules in the United Kingdom have developed in the opposite direction. The test is set out in s 31(3) of the *Senior Courts Act 1981*, and requires that 'the applicant has a sufficient interest in the matter to which the application relates'. While the 'sufficient interest' terminology is very similar to Australian standing rules – in fact, the terminology is sometimes used in Australia[32] – it has been applied very differently in the United Kingdom from the way that the special interest test was applied in the *ACF* case. The United Kingdom courts have taken a liberal approach to standing. The starting point was Lord Diplock's judgment in *Inland Revenue Commissioners v National Federation of Self-Employed and Small Businesses*,[33] often referred to as the '*Fleet St casuals* case', in which he linked a liberal approach to standing with the rule of law. Lord Diplock stated:

> It would, in my view, be a grave lacuna in our system of public law if a pressure group, like the federation, or even a single public-spirited taxpayer, were prevented by outdated technical rules of locus standi from bringing the matter to the attention of the court to vindicate the rule of law and get the unlawful conduct stopped.[34]

The rule of law has continued to influence the United Kingdom courts to provide a broad approach to standing. In two recent cases, *AXA General Insurance Limited*

---

27 504 US 555 (1992).
28 5 US 137, 170 (1803).
29 504 US 555, 576 (1992).
30 See, eg, Pierce, above n 21, 1437–9.
31 Cane, above n 23, 29.
32 *Edwards v Santos Ltd* (2011) 242 CLR 421, 435; *Bateman's Bay Local Aboriginal Land Council v Aboriginal Community Benefit Fund Pty Ltd* (1998) 194 CLR 247, 267; *Croome v Tasmania* (1997) 191 CLR 119, 126–7, 137–8.
33 *Inland Revenue Commissioners v National Federation of Self-Employed and Small Businesses Ltd* [1982] AC 617.
34 *Inland Revenue Commissioners v National Federation of Self-Employed and Small Businesses Ltd* [1982] AC 617, 644.

v HM Advocate[35] and *Walton v Scottish Ministers*,[36] the Supreme Court confirmed that standing may be extended to applicants who have no private interest harmed by the governmental action to bring proceedings to challenge it.[37] In both cases the rationale for this extension was based on the rule of law in the sense explained by Lord Diplock in the *Fleet St casuals* case.[38]

The contrast between the UK approach to standing and the High Court's understanding of the special interest test is stark. While Gibbs J recognised in *Onus v Alcoa* that enforcement of the law is one factor that underlies standing rules, he also recognised that it is outweighed by competing considerations such as not putting others to 'great cost and inconvenience' in defending the legality of their actions, and that requiring the applicant to have a 'direct stake' tends to ensure that there is a real controversy between the parties and therefore supports the adversarial system.[39]

The extended approach to standing in the United Kingdom case has supported proceedings by environmental groups. The great example is the 'Pergau Dam case'.[40] The case was about a decision to grant aid to Malaysia to build a dam, which environmental groups believed would badly damage the environment.[41] The applicant, which was an organisation interested in the way that the United Kingdom provides aid to developing countries, was recognised to have a sufficient interest in the decision to grant aid. The court was heavily influenced by Lord Diplock's statement in *Fleet St casuals* and what was referred to as the 'increasingly liberal approach to standing'.[42] Most significantly, it was apparent that the applicant brought proceedings on a purely public interest basis. This was made clear by the court's reference to it as a 'pressure group'[43] and its acknowledgement that neither the organisation, nor its members, had any 'direct personal interest' in the decision.[44] The acceptance of standing in this context is a substantial step beyond

---

35 [2012] 1 AC 868.
36 [2012] UKSC 44.
37 These cases included some vague qualifications. The first is that a mere busybody may not be granted standing: *Walton v Scottish Ministers* [2012] UKSC 44, [94] (Lord Reed), [153] (Lord Hope); *AXA General Insurance Limited v HM Advocate* [2012] 1 AC 868, 918 [63] (Lord Hope). The second is that extended standing may require courts to focus additional attention on the discretion to refuse a remedy: *Walton v Scottish Ministers* [2012] UKSC 44, [103], [111]–[114] (Lord Carnwath).
38 See *AXA General Insurance Limited v HM Advocate* [2012] 1 AC 868, 952 [170]; *Walton v Scottish Ministers* [2012] UKSC 44, [94].
39 (1981) 149 CLR 27, 35.
40 *R v Secretary of State for Foreign and Commonwealth Affairs, Ex Parte World Development Movement Ltd* [1995] 1 WLR 386.
41 C Harlow, 'Public Law and Popular Justice' (2002) *Modern Law Review* 1, 5.
42 [1995] 1 WLR 386, 390, 395–6.
43 Ibid, 392.
44 Ibid, 394.

the special interest test applied by the Australian High Court in the *ACF* case and the standing rules in the United States.

This brief comparison of Australia's special interest test with the equivalent tests in the United States and the United Kingdom highlights that, although standing rules have similar language, the application of the rules is shaped by different fundamental principles. In the United Kingdom the liberal application of standing rules has been justified on the basis of the rule of law. The approaches of the Australian High Court and the United States Supreme Court emphasise the separation of powers. The rule of law and the separation of powers therefore tend to be competing principles when it comes to standing rules, and courts in different jurisdictions effectively choose which one to favour. While the rule of law rationale for extending standing has tended to support environmental groups' access to the courts in the United Kingdom, the influence of the separation of powers in Australia and the United States tends to operate as a limitation on their access.

Private interests and environmental groups

The extension of standing in the United Kingdom to a form of public interest-based standing effectively overcomes the traditional restrictions on standing for environmental groups. What of Australia and the United States, where general standing rules limit access to the courts to those whose private rights and interests are affected? Do they exclude access for environmental groups? The answer is – not necessarily. A pragmatic method used in Australia is to bring proceedings in the environmental group's name and join as a co-plaintiff an individual who lives near the particular area or has relevant economic interests.[45] If standing for the group is refused, the proceedings can continue in the individual's name. Another possibility is for the environmental group to bring proceedings representing the interests of individuals who are directly affected by the decision. There are conflicting Australian authorities as to whether this is permissible.

The more restrictive approach to environmental groups bringing such proceedings is reflected in a statement by Gibbs J in the *ACF* case. He stated that

> if it is the fact that some members of the [Australian Conservation] Foundation have a special interest – and it is most unlikely that any would have a special interest to challenge the exchange control transaction – it would not follow that the Foundation has locus standi, *for a corporation does not acquire standing because some of its members possess it.*[46] [emphasis added]

---

45 See, eg, M Barker, 'Standing to Sue in Public Interest Environmental Litigation: From *ACF v Commonwealth* to *Tasmanian Conservation Trust v Minister for Resources*' (1996) 13 *Environmental Planning Law Journal* 186, 196.
46 (1980) 146 CLR 493, 531; cf Murphy J (dissenting) 556.

This approach has been applied to environmental groups in later cases.[47] It treats the particular organisation as a separate legal entity[48] – effectively requiring it to show that it has suffered harm to its own interests. This approach excludes environmental groups unless they show that their own property or economic interests are affected. This is, of course, not the basis on which they seek to challenge decisions.

There is another High Court decision that goes the other way. In *Shop Distributive and Allied Employees Association v Minister for Industrial Affairs of South Australia*,[49] the Court accepted that a trade union had standing based on its members having special interests that were affected.[50] While this case reached the opposite conclusion to Gibbs J in *ACF*, it is not clear whether it supports standing for representative organisations more generally, because the respondent conceded that the applicant trade union had the same interest as its members.[51] It may also be the case that trade unions are regarded as a special kind of association as they are subject to specific regulation.[52] Despite such qualifications and uncertainties, many Australian cases have granted standing to environmental groups to represent individuals who have special interests that are affected.[53]

The law of the United States and of the United Kingdom is much clearer on this point. Both jurisdictions accept proceedings brought by environmental groups to protect the private interests of their members. The cases in these jurisdictions also provide the reasons for why it is a beneficial addition to standing rules.

The US Supreme Court has determined that environmental groups *cannot* bring proceedings as 'representatives of the public',[54] but that they can bring proceedings to represent their members whose interests are affected in the required manner. The relevant test requires that the members would otherwise have standing, the interests the group seeks to protect are germane to the organisation's purpose, and the claim does not require participation of the individual members in the

---

47 *Australian Conservation Foundation v South Australia* (1990) 53 SASR 349, 353; *Onesteel Manufacturing Pty Ltd v Whyalla Red Dust Action Group Inc* (2006) 94 SASR 357, 366–9 [23]–[33]; *Clyde Group Incorporated v Minister for Primary Industries and Water* [2007] TASSC 95, [15].
48 E Fisher and J Kirk, 'Still Standing: An Argument for Open Standing in Australia and England' (1997) 71 *Australian Law Journal* 370, 379; Aronson and Groves, above n 2, 748; *Access For All Alliance (Hervey Bay) Inc v Hervey Bay City Council* (2007) 162 FCR 313, 333 [58].
49 (1995) 183 CLR 552.
50 Ibid, 557–9.
51 Ibid, 557.
52 Harlow, above n 41, 5.
53 *Re MacTiernan; Ex parte Coogee Coastal Action Coalition Inc* (2005) 30 WAR 138, 161–2 [99]–[101] (McLure P, Wheeler and Pullin JJA agreeing); *Ex parte Helena Valley/Boya Assn (Inc); State Planning Commission and Beggs* (1990) 2 WAR 422, 437 (Ipp J, Pidgeon J agreeing).
54 *Sierra Club v Morton* 405 US 727, 736 (1972).

lawsuit.[55] This test facilitates standing for groups in a manner that is consistent with the constitutional requirement that applicants are harmed by particular injuries.[56]

The Supreme Court has justified standing for groups as a way of facilitating access to justice for individuals. In *International Union, United Automobile, Aerospace and Agricultural Implement Workers of America v Brock*,[57] the Court stated that, 'the reason people join an organisation is often to create an effective vehicle for vindicating interests that they share with others'. Many academics maintain that this rationale facilitates proceedings to restrain harmful and unlawful actions in a context where individuals are unlikely to bring proceedings on their own. The harm to the affected individuals may be small and the costs and stress of litigation too great for them to bring proceedings themselves.[58]

Courts in the United Kingdom have also accepted standing for environmental groups to represent the personal interests of their members. The case which is commonly referred to is *R v Inspectorate of Pollution; Ex Parte Greenpeace (No 2)*.[59] Greenpeace brought proceedings to challenge the authorisation of radioactive waste discharges from a nuclear reprocessing plant. Otton J accepted that Greenpeace could represent local residents at risk of harm from the radioactive waste.[60] Otton J placed great weight on Greenpeace's capabilities as a litigant and concluded that it possessed expertise that local residents lacked. The experience of Greenpeace in environmental matters, and its access to scientific and technological experts, enabled it to 'mount a carefully selected, focused, relevant and well-argued challenge'.[61] This reasoning suggests that granting standing to groups as representatives of their members' personal interests confirms the expertise of the applicant and therefore effective and efficient litigation processes.[62]

The acceptance in the United States and the United Kingdom of groups having standing to represent their members' personal interests provides a strong reason for Australian courts and legislators to at least review this question. The acceptance by courts of other jurisdictions that this form of standing facilitates access to justice for individuals who are relevantly harmed, and that groups are likely to have access to

---

55 *Hunt v Washington State Apple Advertising Commission* 432 US 333, 343 (1977); *United Food and Commercial Workers Union Local 751 v Brown Group Inc* 517 US 544, 553–6 (1996).
56 Pierce, above n 21, 1542.
57 477 US 274, 290 (1986).
58 Pierce, above n 21, 1538; R Douglas, 'Uses of Standing Rules 1980–2006' (2006) 14 *Australian Journal of Administrative Law* 22, 26–7.
59 [1994] 4 All ER 329.
60 Ibid, 350. He also seemed to accept Greenpeace's claim to be representing the public interest: [1994] 4 All ER 329, 349–50.
61 Ibid. See also *International Union, United Automobile, Aerospace and Agricultural Implement Workers of America v Brock*, 477 US 274, 289 (1986).
62 Ibid.

expertise that is unlikely to be available to individuals, provides strong support for Australian standing rules to move in the same direction. Some scholars suggest that courts should not assume that particular groups actually represent their members' interests. Professor Cane has argued that courts should require groups who claim to represent their members' interests to show that they have internal mechanisms for ascertaining their members' views.[63] This is an important factor that should be considered in any reforms in this area.

Public interests

As we have seen, the restrictions on standing for environmental groups are most apparent under rules by which a personal or private harm is required. Standing laws that go beyond private rights and interests, and instead permit individuals and groups to bring proceedings to protect the public interest, clearly support proceedings by environmental groups to a much greater extent. According to such standing laws, there is no need for an environmental group to represent its members' private interests or injuries – the environmental group will instead have to show that it is an appropriate representative of the public interest. Or, when there is 'open standing', an environmental group is likely to have access to the court without any restriction based on its particular characteristics.

It is convenient before examining these different options for public interest-based standing to mention briefly some recommended general reforms for standing. The Australian Law Reform Commission published reports in the 1980s and 1990s recommending that standing should be extended to forms of open standing, but neither report was implemented.[64] Since then the question of whether there should be general reforms to standing laws tends to arise in the context of reviews of judicial review procedures at the federal level[65] or when States are considering enacting judicial review legislation.[66] The appropriateness of general reforms as opposed to reforms to sector-specific laws, such as environmental legislation, will be examined in the final part of this chapter. This part examines the characteristics of the various forms of public interest-based standing.

---

63 P Cane, 'Standing, Representation, and the Environment' in I Loveland (ed), *A Special Relationship?: American Influences on Public Law in the UK* (Clarendon Press, 1995) 136.
64 Australian Law Reform Commission, *Standing in Public Interest Litigation* (Report No 27, 1985), xxi, 138, 216; Australian Law Reform Commission, *Beyond the Door-Keeper: Standing to Sue for Public Remedies* (Report No 78, 1996), 5.25.
65 Administrative Review Council, *Federal Judicial Review in Australia* (Report 50, 2012) ch 8.
66 NSW Department of Justice and Attorney General, *Discussion Paper: Reform of Judicial Review in NSW* (2011) 15–18.

Representing the public interest

We saw in the second part of this chapter that the terminology of standing laws is fairly common – the applicant has to have a special or sufficient interest or injury – but that the laws are applied in different ways in different jurisdictions. The most striking difference is the application of the sufficient interest test in the United Kingdom to facilitate actions brought by public interest-based applicants. A related development has occurred in Australia, primarily by the Federal Court's decision in *North Coast Environment Council Inc v Minister for Resources*.[67]

The applicant in *North Coast Environment Council* brought proceedings to require the Minister to provide reasons under s 13 of the *Administrative Decisions (Judicial Review) Act 1977* (Cth) for his decision to grant a licence allowing a company to export woodchips. Justice Sackville determined that the North Coast Environment Council satisfied the special interest test, particularly relying on Justice Stephen's reference in *Onus v Alcoa* to standing being a question of determining the applicant's 'closeness' or 'proximity' to the subject matter of the proceedings.[68] Justice Sackville determined this according to the following factors:[69]

- The applicant was a 'peak' organisation representing 44 other environmental groups in a particular region;
- It was recognised by federal and State governments by its participation on committees and by funding;
- It had conducted and coordinated projects and conferences relating to environmental matters; and
- It had made submissions on related environmental issues to the relevant government agency.

Sackville J also held that the Council's interests were 'entirely compatible' with the public interest reflected in the environmental legislation applicable to this case and with the requirement to provide reasons for decisions in the *Administrative Decisions (Judicial Review) Act 1977* (Cth).[70] This linking of the Council's interests with the purposes of the relevant legislation is effectively the same as the 'zone of interest' requirement in United States standing law.

The *North Coast Environmental Council* case has been subjected to criticism regarding the second factor – recognition by government.[71] The concern is that it

---

67 (1994) 55 FCR 492.
68 Ibid, 512.
69 Ibid, 512–13.
70 Ibid, 514–15.
71 *Right to Life Association (NSW) Inc v Secretary, Department of Human Services and Health* (1995) 56 FCR 50, 67; *Access For All Alliance (Hervey Bay) Inc v Hervey Bay City Council* (2007) 162 FCR 313, 333 [63]; *Re MacTiernan; Ex parte Coogee Coastal Action Coalition Inc* (2005) 30 WAR 138, 142–3 [2]–[3].

tends to delegate to the government the court's authority to determine standing.[72] That is, the courts should make their own assessment of an applicant's claim to represent the public interest instead of relying on the government's recognition of the group. In my view, this is a valid criticism. The better factors referred to by Justice Sackville for whether an organisation is an appropriate representative of the public interest are the focus on the group's activities and whether the organisation comes within the zone of interests protected by the Act.

The deeper question raised by the *North Coast Environmental Council* case is whether standing law should extend to permit access to public interest-based applicants, and whether such a reform should be determined by courts rather than legislatures. There is also a concern as to whether it is consistent with the special interest test explained by the High Court in *ACF v Commonwealth* and *Onus v Alcoa*.[73] It is a large step to permit an applicant to represent the public interest and to devise factors designed to ensure that the particular applicant is its proper representative. The orthodox approach is that private interests are to be affected – either property or financial interests, or environmental interests that are personal to the applicant. It is arguably too large a step for a court, and one that is more suitably handled by legislation.

In fact, the Commonwealth Parliament has enacted legislation that includes criteria similar to the *North Coast Environmental Council* case criteria. The most well-known examples are the standing provisions in the *Environment Protection and Biodiversity Conservation Act 1999* (Cth), ss 475 and 487.[74] Those provisions focus on the applicant's activities and whether their concerns are within the relevant zone of interests.[75] The applicant must have engaged in environmental activities or research in the previous two years. The provisions are consistent with the *North Coast Environment Council* case in this respect. For organisations, there is also a requirement for their objects to relate to environment protection[76] – a requirement that has been regarded by the courts as being otherwise irrelevant.[77] These provisions therefore share with the *North Coast Environment Council* case the acceptance of public interest-based standing. They are also concerned to

---

72 Fisher and Kirk, above n 48, 377; *Bridgetown/Greenbushes Friends of the Forest v Department of Conservation and Land Management* (1997) 93 LGERA 436, 446.
73 See Cane, above n 23, 36, that *North Coast Environmental Council* and similar cases pay 'lip service' to the special interest test.
74 These provisions follow extensions to standing by Commonwealth environmental legislation enacted prior to the *Environment Protection and Biodiversity Conservation Act 1999* (Cth): *Endangered Species Protection Act 1992* (Cth), s 131 (now repealed); *Hazardous Waste (Regulation of Exports and Imports) Act 1989* (Cth), s 58A (inserted by Act No 7, 1996).
75 *Environment Protection and Biodiversity Conservation Act 1999* (Cth), ss 475(6)–(7), 487(2)–(3).
76 *Environment Protection and Biodiversity Conservation Act 1999* (Cth), ss 475(7), 487(3).
77 *Australian Conservation Foundation v Commonwealth* (1980) 146 CLR 493, 531 (Gibbs J); *North Coast Environmental Council Inc v Minister for Resources* (1994) 55 FCR 492, 512.

regulate it, but without reliance on the discredited 'recognition by government' factor. They focus instead on the organisation's objects and activities.

Section 27 of the *Administrative Appeals Tribunal Act 1975 (Cth)* ('AAT Act') has been raised as an option that could be used in judicial review legislation.[78] Section 27 deems an organisation to have interests that are affected 'if the decision relates to a matter included in the objects or purposes of the organization'. The deeming provision does not apply if the organisation is formed after the particular decision that is to be reviewed was made, or if the objects provision was inserted after that decision.[79] Groves has highlighted the benefits of s 27 of the AAT Act as including: its simplicity; its resolution of the inconsistent Australian case law as to whether an organisation can have standing to represent its members' interests that are affected by the decision; its alignment of standing for individuals and groups; and that it would be an effective substitute for the various sector-specific standing provisions.[80]

Section 27 of the AAT Act does, however, have limitations if it is to operate as a method for regulating standing for public interest-based applicants. While requiring the organisation's objects to relate to the decision will tend to ensure that its interests are within the 'zone of interests', the provision does not require the organisation to have a track record of activities and research in the relevant area of regulation. This is a beneficial element, required by the *North Coast Environmental Council* case and the provisions of the *Environment Protection and Biodiversity Conservation Act*, if the applicant is claiming standing on a public interest basis, as it helps to confirm that the applicant has a genuine claim to represent the public interest. If, on the other hand, the organisation is representing its members' private interests, a track record in the subject matter of the litigation will support the organisation's ability to bring expertise to the proceedings which, as we saw in the section entitled 'Private interests and environmental groups' above, is one of the justifications for this form of standing.

Australian law has therefore taken some steps towards public interest-based standing. The judicial steps have been controversial for the particular criteria used to determine whether the applicant is a proper representative of the public interest. The larger question of whether public interest-based standing is appropriate is ripe for examination, given that it conflicts with orthodox views regarding standing. My view, which is developed below in the section on reforming standing laws, is that such reforms may be appropriate but are better suited to sector-specific legislation rather than general standing rules.

---

78 See Administrative Review Council, above n 65, 151; NSW Department of Justice and Attorney General, above n 66, 18; M Groves, 'Should the *Administrative Law Act 1978* (Vic) be Repealed?' (2010) 34 *Melbourne University Law Review* 452, 471–2.
79 *Administrative Appeals Tribunal Act 1975* (Cth), s 27.
80 Groves, above n 78, 471–2.

Participation in administrative processes

There is another, more indirect, method for granting public interest-based applicants standing. This is to grant such applicants standing when they have participated in administrative processes related to the challenged decision. The rationale of this form of standing is that the applicant is granted access to the court to protect their participation rights. While this approach has supported standing for public interest applicants in Australian cases, it also has limits which frustrate its use by environmental groups. The difficulty is that it tends to not extend to applicants who have participated in public consultation processes. This is a substantial problem for environmental groups, as public consultation processes are very often used for environmental decisions.

This approach to standing has been accepted when public interest-based applicants have participated in a form of administrative hearing. For example, the High Court accepted in *Sinclair v Mining Warden*[81] that the applicant had standing due to his participation in a mining warden's hearing as a public interest objector,[82] and a consumer organisation was granted standing by the Federal Court in *United States Tobacco Company v Minister for Consumer Affairs* on the basis of its participation at a form of hearing referred to as a 'conference'.[83] On the other hand, the courts have often denied standing based on participation in public consultation processes.[84] The difference seems to be that public consultation provisions may be regarded as merely permitting a person to lodge a submission.[85] Those who participate in administrative hearings, on the other hand, are regarded as entitled to procedural fairness and to enforce relevant statutory procedural requirements.[86] The crucial factor that supports standing therefore seems to be that there are laws of one form or other that provide the participant something more than a mere entitlement to lodge a submission.[87]

In my view, participation in public consultation processes should be accepted as a basis for standing, at least for consultation processes that are required

---

81 (1975) 132 CLR 473.
82 Ibid, 478. See also *Australian Conservation Foundation v Forestry Commission* (1988) 19 FCR 127, 131.
83 (1988) 20 FCR 520, 530–31.
84 (1980) 146 CLR 493, 525, 531 (Gibbs J), 542 (Stephen J), cf 556–7 (Murphy J dissenting). See also *North Coast Environmental Council Inc v Minister for Resources* (1994) 55 FCR 492, 512; *Re Western Australian Planning Commission; Ex parte Leeuwin Conservation Group Inc* [2002] WASCA 150, [51]. Cf *Alliance to Save Hinchinbrook v Cook* [2007] 1 Qd R 102, 105–6 [17]–[21]; *Walton v Scottish Ministers* [2012] UKSC 44, [86]–[88].
85 *Australian Conservation Foundation v Commonwealth* (1980) 146 CLR 493, 525, 531–2.
86 *United States Tobacco Company v Minister for Consumer Affairs* (1988) 20 FCR 520, 530.
87 Eg, public consultation plus a right to appeal the administrative decision supported an environmental group's standing in *Australian Conservation Foundation v South Australia* (1990) 53 SASR 349, 353–5.

by legislation. This approach enables participants to challenge tokenistic administration of consultation processes – a commonly recognised problem.[88] There are numerous potential grounds for challenging statutory public consultation processes. They include breach of public notice requirements and other statutory procedures,[89] and failure to consider submissions.[90] The difference between public consultation processes and other forms of administrative procedure tends to drop away when these grounds are considered. Extending standing to those who have participated in public consultation proceedings also has an advantage over the factors utilised in the *North Coast Environmental Council* case as it involves a smaller, more incremental, change. It is also familiar, at least to environmental lawyers, since standing for merits appeals for environmental decisions is often limited to individuals and groups who have participated in the initial decision-making process.[91]

The possible disadvantage with this extension of standing rules is that it could substantially widen the pool of litigants. There are potentially many individuals and groups that participate in public consultation processes. This risk could be mitigated in a number of ways. There could be an assessment by the court of the genuineness and substantive nature of the applicant's participation in the administrative decision. While this may sound unhelpfully vague and evaluative, it would in practice simply involve assessing the applicant's submission in the consultation process to ensure that it is not just a signature on a petition and that it raises or engages with issues relevant to the particular decision and the regulatory scheme. Any legislative reform should also include time limits on review proceedings, to provide the decision-maker and holders of permits and approvals a degree of certainty.[92]

Open standing

The broadest open standing provisions permit 'any person' to bring judicial review proceedings without qualification. While there are examples of unqualified open

---

[88] J Kane and P Bishop, 'Consultation and Contest: The Danger of Mixing Modes' (2002) 61 *Australian Journal of Public Administration* 87, 88; B Preston, 'Consultation: One Aspect of Procedural Propriety in Administrative Decision-Making' (2008) 15 *Australian Journal of Administrative Law* 185, 192.

[89] *Scurr v Brisbane City Council* (1973) 133 CLR 242.

[90] *Minister for Aboriginal Affairs v Peko-Wallsend Ltd* (1986) 162 CLR 24; *Tickner v Chapman* (1995) 57 FCR 451.

[91] See, eg, *Development Act 1993* (SA), ss 38(12), 86(1)(b); *Environmental Planning and Assessment Act 1979* (NSW), ss 4 (definition of 'objector'), 98; *Planning and Environment Act 1987* (Vic), ss 57, 82.

[92] E Campbell and M Groves, 'Time Limitations on Applications for Judicial Review' (2004) 32 *Federal Law Review* 29, 29–30, 54.

standing provisions, there are usually some qualifications to restrict interference with private interests – that is, the private interests of persons who have been granted licences or approvals that are challenged by public interest-based applicants. As we have seen, the Australian Law Reform Commission has recommended that Australian law move to open standing.[93] Academics have also argued for open standing for review of administrative decisions[94] and for constitutional litigation.[95] Three judges of the High Court even suggested that standing rules could be abandoned in *Bateman's Bay Local Aboriginal Land Council v Aboriginal Community Benefit Fund Pty Ltd*.[96] Gaudron, Gummow and Kirby JJ stated that standing could be dealt with by other principles, such as non-justiciability or staying proceedings on the basis of their being oppressive, vexatious or an abuse of process. Their Honours also indicated that the risk of an adverse costs order would deter plaintiffs.[97]

Despite these comments and suggestions, there has been no legislative or judicial implementation of open standing for judicial review generally. There are, on the other hand, some long-standing examples of open standing in sector-specific legislation such as trade practices[98] and environmental law.[99] While there are constitutional limitations on open standing provisions in the United States,[100] the *Australian Constitution* does not prevent the legislation for open standing.[101]

Open standing with qualifications can have complications. One of these can be seen in the Australian Law Reform Commission's recommendations for open standing. It recommended that there should be two qualifications to standing – standing could be denied firstly if the relevant legislation intends to exclude the particular applicant, or secondly if there would be unreasonable interference with a person having a private interest in the matter.[102] If implemented, the second of the two qualifications would have created difficulties for environmental groups. The Commission explained that this exception would arise when a third party seeks to challenge a decision concerning the entitlements of another party. It fleshed out the exception with an example of an environmental group challenging a coal export licence. The concern was that the licensee would

---

93 Australian Law Reform Commission, *Beyond the Door-Keeper*, above n 64, [5.25].
94 Fisher and Kirk, above n 48; cf Cane, above n 23.
95 P Keyzer, *Open Constitutional Courts* (Federation Press, 2010).
96 (1998) 194 CLR 247.
97 Ibid, 263 [39].
98 *Competition and Consumer Act 2010* (Cth), s 80, formerly the *Trade Practices Act 1974* (Cth), s 80.
99 *Environmental Planning and Assessment Act 1979* (NSW), 123.
100 *Lujan v Defenders of Wildlife* 504 US 555 (1992), 577, 580.
101 *Truth About Motorways Pty Ltd v Macquarie Infrastructure Investment Management Ltd* (2000) 200 CLR 591.
102 Australian Law Reform Commission, *Beyond the Door-Keeper*, above n 64, [5.25].

incur costs and suffer damages due to delay and possible inability to fulfil obligations to purchasers.[103]

The Commission's example suggests that environmental groups would commonly be caught by the exception, as many of the cases brought by them in the 1980s and 1990s involved challenging export licence decisions.[104] This recommendation would therefore have seriously limited environmental groups' access to the courts. Since there is a regulated party with private interests in most public interest proceedings, it may even have undermined more generally the proposal for open standing.[105] This highlights the risk inherent in open standing with qualifications – the qualifications threaten to become the rule rather than the exception.

What of open standing without qualifications? The great example of this form of open standing for judicial review proceedings is s 123(1) of the *Environmental Planning and Assessment Act 1979* (NSW). That section provides that 'any person' may bring proceedings in the Land and Environment Court 'to remedy or restrain a breach of this Act, whether or not any right of that person has been or may be infringed by or as a consequence of that breach'. This provision is sometimes raised as an option when reforms to standing laws are being considered.[106] The history of s 123 shows why standing provisions are often just one part of an accountability system for a particular regulatory scheme.

The initial background reports for what became the *Environmental Planning and Assessment Act 1979* recommended that merits appeal rights should be extended beyond developers to third parties. This was referred to as a measure to support public participation.[107] However, in the period between these reports and the enactment of the *Environmental Planning and Assessment Act 1979*, review rights for third parties were substantially changed. Merits appeals became generally available under the Act for developers but were restricted for third parties to a narrow category of large-scale industrial development. On the other hand, access to the courts for judicial review and civil enforcement was changed to open

---

103 Ibid [4.19]–[4.23].
104 Eg, *Australian Conservation Foundation v Minister for Resources* (1989) 76 LGRA 200; *North Coast Environmental Council Inc v Minister for Resources* (1994) 55 FCR 492; *Tasmanian Conservation Trust Inc v Minister for Resources* (1995) 55 FCR 516; *Margarula v Minister for Environment* (1999) 92 FCR 35.
105 Cane, above n 23, 34–5.
106 Administrative Review Council, above n 65, 147–50; Senate Environment, Communications, Information Technology and the Arts Committee, Parliament of Australia, Environment Protection and Biodiversity Conservation Bill 1998 (NSW); Australian Law Reform Commission, *Beyond the Door-Keeper*, above n 64, [4.39].
107 Minister for Planning and Environment, *Towards a New Planning System for New South Wales* (First Report, November 1974) 21; Minister for Planning and Environment, *Proposals for a New Environmental Planning System for New South Wales* (Second Report, June 1975), 20–21.

standing.[108] Seen in this context, the *Environmental Planning and Assessment Act 1979* includes open standing as a substitute for third party merits appeal rights.

While s 123 may appear to be a bold development of standing rules, in the context of the review system established by the Act as a whole it involved downgrading the form of review available to third parties.

Has open standing under the *Environmental Planning and Assessment Act 1979* been controversial? There is little indication of concerns being raised, but potential problems with open standing are obvious. It can be used by businesses to challenge their competitors' development projects.[109] This illustrates a larger concern that businesses 'game' planning systems by frustrating and delaying competitors' development projects.[110] It highlights one of the disadvantages of open standing provisions: that an applicant's concerns may not be within the 'zone of interests' sought to be protected by the particular Act.

Reforming standing laws: General rules and sector-specific legislation

We have seen so far that orthodox standing rules in Australia require a special interest, most clearly a particular harm to the applicant's private interests. The primary cases, *ACF v Commonwealth* and *Onus v Alcoa*, highlight that the High Court is willing to take a broad view of special interest – one that extends to personal environmental interests such as the risks of harm to heritage items and local amenity but does not extend to applicants seeking to protect the public interest. On the other hand, there have been judicial and legislative reforms to standing that do extend to public interest-based standing. We can turn now to considering the reforms that are appropriate for general standing rules[111] and the reforms that are better suited to sector-specific legislation, such as environmental laws. The view expressed in this section is that the step to public interest-based standing is a reform that is better suited to sector-specific legislation. There are other reforms, however, that are appropriate for general standing rules.

---

108 *Environmental Planning and Assessment Act 1979* (NSW), ss 98, 123.
109 *Franklins Limited v Penrith City Council and Campbells Cash & Carry Pty Limited* [1999] NSWCA 134; *Macquarie International Health Clinic Pty Ltd v University of Sydney* (1998) 98 LGERA 218.
110 Productivity Commission, *Performance Benchmarking of Australian Business Regulation: Planning, Zoning and Development Assessments* (Research Report, April 2011), 345–50.
111 By this I mean standing rules related to the prerogative writs, equitable remedies and statutory judicial review schemes.

There are two reasons for general standing rules to be limited to harm to personal interests. The first is that the private rights and interests limitation better harmonises with the grounds of review. This is most clear with regard to procedural fairness – one of the most commonly argued grounds of judicial review.[112] Australian courts have consistently determined that public interest-based applicants who gain access to courts according to extended standing provisions cannot satisfy the procedural fairness threshold that a personal interest is adversely affected.[113] It may also be the case that a personal interest being affected plays a normative role for another ground that is commonly relied on – the failure to consider relevant considerations – by influencing the intensity of review. On the one hand, harm to *personal* interests is accepted as a reason for a more intense approach to review on this ground.[114] Harm to the *public* interest, on the other hand, may be regarded as an indication that the decision involves policy considerations for which restraint is appropriate.[115] The problem that this raises is that extending standing beyond protecting private rights and interests to protecting the public interest risks making access to the courts run ahead of the grounds of review, since the most commonly relied-on grounds are either off limits or may be applied only on a restrained basis.[116] Extended access to the courts may therefore end up being futile due to the narrow scope of the grounds of judicial review.[117]

The second reason for limiting general standing rules to the traditional tests is that considering whether standing should be extended or not raises questions specific to particular regulatory schemes. In such contexts, legislators consider the combination of accountability mechanisms – most particularly between merits review and judicial review of particular decisions – as we have seen occurred in relation to the *Environmental Planning and Assessment Act 1979*. It may be that the narrowing of the grounds of review in public interest-based proceedings that was referred to in the previous paragraph provides a reason for giving third parties access to merits review.[118] Consideration would also have to be given to whether

---

112 R Creyke and J McMillan, 'Judicial Review Outcomes – An Empirical Study' (2004) 11 *Australian Journal of Administrative Law* 82, 96.
113 *Botany Bay City Council v Minister of State for Transport and Regional Development* (1996) 66 FCR 537, 568; *Wilderness Society Inc v Turnbull* (2007) 166 FCR 154, 177–8 [88]; *Rivers SOS Inc v Minister for Planning* (2009) 178 LGERA 347, 385 [162].
114 *Minister for Aboriginal Affairs v Peko-Wallsend Ltd* (1986) 162 CLR 24, 45; *Tickner v Chapman* (1995) 57 FCR 451, 462.
115 Ibid, 42.
116 Rawlings has explained this effect through the metaphor of a funnel – liberal standing being represented by the wide top part of a funnel while the grounds of review and remedies are represented by the narrow lower part: R Rawlings, 'Modelling Judicial Review' (2008) *Current Legal Problems* 95, 100–02.
117 Cane, above n 23, 29; A Edgar, 'Extended Standing – Enhanced Accountability?: Judicial Review of Commonwealth Environmental Decisions' (2011) 39 *Federal Law Review* 435.
118 See, eg, A Hawke, *Independent Review of the Environment Protection and Biodiversity Conservation Act 1999: Interim Report* (2009), 313–19.

public interest standing should be facilitated for enforcement of the legislation against other members of the public. This raises questions as to whether it is appropriate for members of the public to have an enforcement role – the traditional view being that enforcement is primarily a matter for government.[119] The important point is that there are policy considerations to be weighed up as to the particular mix of legal accountability mechanisms for any regulatory scheme. Accordingly, if special standing laws are thought to be necessary for environmental groups, the appropriate place for them to be located is in environmental legislation.

On the other hand, there is scope for general reforms by relatively small steps. First, confirmation by the High Court of the convergence of the different tests for standing for different remedies would be helpful. This would involve merely confirming Gummow J's reference in *Australian Institute of Marine and Power Engineers v Secretary, Department of Transport*[120] to there being 'broad agreement' between the different remedies, and taking steps to ensure their harmonisation when opportunities arise.

Second, it would be beneficial for the High Court to resolve the inconsistent case law regarding whether an association can have standing to represent its members' interests that are affected in a personal manner. That would involve determining that the High Court's acceptance of this kind of standing in *Shop Distributive and Allied Employees Association v Minister for Industrial Affairs (SA)*[121] supersedes Gibbs J's opposing view in the *ACF* case.[122] We have seen the support from academics for this form of standing.[123] It is also worth noting that courts in the United States and United Kingdom have supported it,[124] as this highlights that in those jurisdictions it has been accepted as being within the appropriate scope of judicial reform.

Third, it would also be a relatively small, and arguably acceptable, step to recognise the extension of standing for individuals and groups who have participated in public consultation processes.[125] The step would remove the distinction between participation in administrative hearings (which supports standing) and participation in public consultation processes (which usually does not). As explained in the

---

119 See, eg, *Bateman's Bay Local Aboriginal Land Council v Aboriginal Community Benefit Fund Pty Ltd* (1998) 194 CLR 247, 276–80 [81]–[91] (McHugh J); *Wide Bay Conservation Council Inc v Burnett Water Pty Ltd (No 8)* (2011) 192 FCR 1, 4–6 [19]–[27]. For discussion and alternative approaches, see Aronson and Groves, above n 2, 728–30; *Humane Society International Inc v Kyodo Senpaku Kaisha Ltd* (2006) 154 FCR 425, 431–2.
120 (1986) 13 FCR 124, 132.
121 (1995) 183 CLR 552, 557–9.
122 (1980) 146 CLR 493, 531.
123 See the second part of this chapter, above.
124 *Hunt v Washington State Apple Advertising Commission* 432 US 333 (1977); *R v Inspectorate of Pollution; Ex Parte Greenpeace (No 2)* [1994] 4 All ER 329.
125 See 'Public interests: Participation in administrative processes' above.

section above on 'Public interests: Participation in administrative processes', there are risks with such a step due to the broadening of the categories of individuals and groups who are entitled to standing. These risks could be managed by a check on the genuineness of the applicant's participation in the consultation processes. Where sector-specific legislation does not include particular standing rules, standing for public interest-based applicants could be determined according to whether they participated in public consultation processes.

There are therefore numerous reforms that are arguably within the scope of appropriate general reforms. The step taken in the *North Coast Environmental Council* case is a much larger step – one that is more appropriate for Parliaments to determine in the context of sector-specific legislation.

Conclusion

We have seen that traditional standing rules, represented in Australia by *Australian Conservation Foundation v Commonwealth* and *Onus v Alcoa*, limit access to the courts to applicants who have private rights and interests that are affected by a decision. Extending standing to environmental groups requires either recognition that the group represents the private rights and interests of its members who are harmed by the decision, or that the group is a proper representative of the public interest. The former is a relatively small step – a pragmatic method for enabling access to the courts for individuals at risk of similar harms. The latter is a large step – one that breaks judicial review's ties to the protection of individual interests.

In Australian law, unlike in the United States, the step to public interest-based standing is constitutionally permissible. There may be good reasons for Parliaments to extend standing on this basis – notwithstanding that procedural fairness may be excluded as a possible ground of review, and that the lack of a harmed private interest may lead courts to employing a restrained form of review. I have argued that such reforms are better suited to sector-specific legislation rather than general standing rules. This is because the private rights and interests limitation is fundamental to judicial review of administrative action. It aligns with other elements of judicial review, administrative law history and judicial values.[126] Moreover, the question of whether standing should or should not be extended by provisions in sector-specific legislation enables standing-related issues to be considered along with the particular combination of accountability mechanisms for review of decisions made under the particular Act. In my view, this is the appropriate context in which public interest standing for judicial review proceedings is to be determined.

---

126 P A Keane, 'Democracy, Participation and Administrative Law' (2011) 68 *AIAL Forum* 1.

PART

JUDICIAL REVIEW

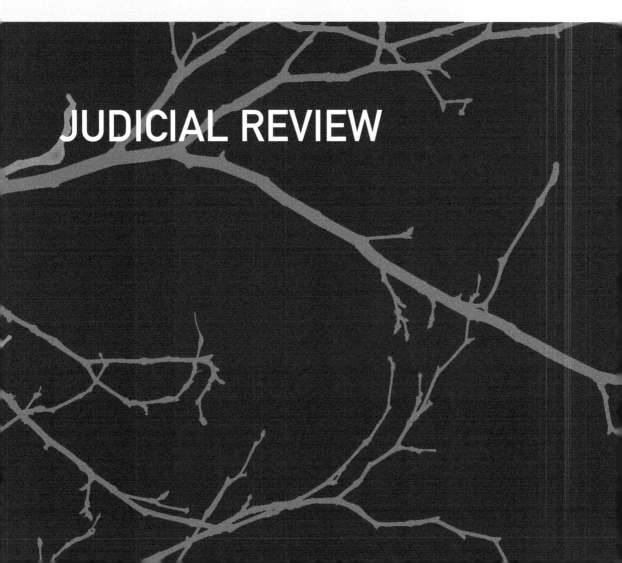

THE CONSTITUTIONAL DIMENSION

Hon Stephen Gageler

Introduction

The *Australian Constitution* came into existence in 1901 in fulfilment of what Sir Henry Parkes had described in his Tenterfield Oration in 1889 as the aspiration to create a 'great national government for all Australia' under which 'great national questions' 'would be disposed of by a fully authorised constitutional authority'.[1] Writing soon after, Professor Harrison Moore noted the 'extraordinary and peculiar' nature of the jurisdiction of courts to 'control' administrative decision-making by 'public officers' and went on to consider 'how far the exercise of judicial control is affected by the existence of a dual system of government over the same persons and territory'.[2]

Given that it is in the nature of a constitution to establish a system of governance, it is hardly surprising that the *Australian Constitution* should have implications for the development of not only the institutional design of the repositories of administrative power but also that branch of Australian administrative law which is concerned with the judicial review of administrative action. What might be thought surprising in hindsight is that, but for the early insight of Professor Harrison Moore and occasional glimpses in reasons for judgment of which his one-time student Sir Owen Dixon was an author or co-author, those constitutional implications went largely unheralded for almost a century, coming to prominence only in the two decades between 1990 and 2010.

Yet the *Australian Constitution* has from the beginning been interpreted and applied within the tradition of the common law. Within that tradition, legal doctrine legitimately develops and nascent implications have been seen often to rise, sometimes later to fall, in response to the stimulus of felt necessities and in the fullness of time.

What follows is a short and deliberately uncritical description of the development of a constitutional conception of the judicial review of administrative action in Australia, together with a brief and deliberately non-committal exploration of some of its implications.

Some matters of history and structure

The basic structure of the *Australian Constitution*, as it came into existence and as it continues today, mirrors in large measure the *United States Constitution* which

---

1 'Sir Henry Parkes at Tenterfield', *Sydney Morning Herald* (Sydney), 25 October 1889, 8, at <www.nla.gov.au/nla.news-article13746899>.
2 W Harrison Moore, *The Constitution of The Commonwealth of Australia* (Maxwell, 2nd ed, 1910) 398–9.

provided its principal inspiration and which in 1901 had sustained a system of government for more than a century. At the national level, Chapters I, II and III provide respectively for the establishment and powers of the Commonwealth Parliament, Commonwealth executive and federal judiciary. At the State level, addressed in Chapter V, what were formerly colonial constitutions are specifically acknowledged and preserved, subject to the *Australian Constitution*, as State constitutions establishing legislative, executive, judicial and other organs of State government.

Chapter III of the *Australian Constitution*, providing for the establishment and powers of the federal judiciary, has been generally understood from at least 1918 to prevent the conferral by the Commonwealth Parliament of judicial power other than on a court,[3] and from at least 1956 to prevent the conferral by the Commonwealth Parliament on a court of any function that is not within or incidental to judicial power.[4] Despite that rigid separation of judicial power, precisely what falls within the concept of judicial power has defied exhaustive definition. The accepted 'truth', however, is that 'the ascertainment of existing rights by the judicial determination of issues of fact or law falls exclusively within judicial power so that the Parliament cannot confide the function to any person or body but a court'.[5] That notion of the exclusive province of judicial power, encompassing the ascertainment of existing rights by the judicial determination of issues of fact or law, has never been doubted to encompass the judicial determination of whatever issues of fact or law may be necessary to the determination and enforcement of the limits and conditions of exercise of any legal power or performance of any legal duty. The High Court, in determining a constitutional case in 1955, accordingly treated as undeniable the proposition that the *Australian Constitution* 'leaves to the courts of law the question of whether there has been any excess of power, and requires them to pronounce as void any act which is ultra vires'.[6] It elaborated:[7]

> In the everyday work of this Court, we are accustomed to examining the validity of Acts of Parliament. Less often does the validity of an executive act come to be considered, but it stands upon the same footing.

Within Chapter III of the *Australian Constitution*, two structural variations from the model of the *United States Constitution* have been significant to the development of what emerged from 1990 as the Australian constitutional understanding of judicial review of administrative action. One is s 75(v). The other is s 73(ii). Both concern

---

3 *Waterside Workers' Federation of Australia v JW Alexander Ltd* (1918) 25 CLR 434.
4 *R v Kirby; Ex parte Boilermakers' Society of Australia* (1956) 94 CLR 254; affirmed *Attorney-General (Cth) v R* (1957) 95 CLR 529.
5 *R v Davison* (1954) 90 CLR 353, 369.
6 *R v Richards; Ex parte Fitzpatrick and Browne* (1955) 92 CLR 157, 165.
7 (1955) 92 CLR 157, 165.

the jurisdiction of the High Court, which s 71 establishes as the 'Federal Supreme Court' and invests irrevocably with the 'judicial power of the Commonwealth'. Section 75(v) is concerned with an aspect of the High Court's entrenched original jurisdiction: it is a constitutional conferral on the High Court of original jurisdiction in any matter in which a writ of mandamus or prohibition or an injunction is sought against an 'officer of the Commonwealth'. Section 73(ii) is concerned with an aspect of the High Court's entrenched appellate jurisdiction: it is a constitutional conferral on the High Court, with only such exceptions and subject only to such regulations as the Commonwealth Parliament may prescribe, of entrenched appellate jurisdiction to hear and determine appeals from all judgments and orders of State Supreme Courts.

The writs of mandamus and prohibition referred to in s 75(v) of the *Australian Constitution* are particular forms of action historically administered at common law in England by the Court of King's Bench. Together with the writ of certiorari, they came to be administered by colonial Supreme Courts during the 19th century, and continued to be administered at common law by State Supreme Courts throughout much of the 20th century by virtue of various charters establishing those Supreme Courts as superior courts of law, each capable of exercising, in its own colony or State, jurisdiction defined by reference to the jurisdiction historically administered in England by the Court of King's Bench. Although plagued, like much of the common law, by overlaps, gaps, obscurities and technical complexities, mandamus, prohibition and certiorari together provided the basic suite of common law remedies known as the 'prerogative writs' which allowed Supreme Courts to supervise the exercise of power by other State courts and other State officers: mandamus to compel the performance of an unperformed duty; prohibition to restrain an unauthorised act; and certiorari to quash the legal effect of an act that was either unauthorised when it occurred or affected by an error of law apparent from the record that was made of it.

The writs of mandamus and prohibition which are able to be issued by the High Court against officers of the Commonwealth under s 75(v) of the *Australian Constitution* took their names and content from the common law. Throughout much of the 20th century, they were referred to as prerogative writs and were, by and large, conceived of in common law terms. Officers of the Commonwealth subject to those writs were held in 1910 to include holders of judicial offices, as well as holders of offices within the Commonwealth executive and holders of offices established under legislation enacted by the Commonwealth Parliament.[8] The practices, principles and terminology that built up around the exercise of the jurisdiction conferred by s 75(v) of the *Australian Constitution* have therefore been

---

[8] *R v Commonwealth Court of Conciliation and Arbitration; Ex parte Whybrow & Co* (1910) 11 CLR 1.

forced to accommodate its application to courts created by the Commonwealth Parliament exercising the judicial power of the Commonwealth as much as to the holders of other officers exercising a wide variety of powers of administration. Writs of mandamus and prohibition under s 75(v) were in practice sometimes directed to Ministers or other officers of the Commonwealth executive. Much more frequently they were directed to members of the Commonwealth Court of Conciliation and Arbitration (for 30 years from 1926 thought to have been validly established by the Commonwealth Parliament as a federal court invested with both judicial power and arbitral power) and later to members of the Commonwealth Industrial Court (established in 1956 as a court invested with exclusively judicial power) and the Commonwealth Conciliation and Arbitration Commission (established in 1956 to exercise arbitral power).

Against that background, Australian administrative law, to the extent that it may have been perceived as a distinct branch of the law at all, was very much perceived throughout most of the 20th century – the first century of the existence of the *Australian Constitution* – as a branch of the common law concerned with the application to administrative officers of the more general jurisdiction of State Supreme Courts and of the High Court under s 75(v) of the *Australian Constitution* to issue prerogative writs. The focus was in large measure on the grounds on which those writs in an appropriate case might be issued or withheld.

There was, at the Commonwealth level, a highly significant legislative reform in 1977 in the form of the *Administrative Decisions (Judicial Review) Act 1977* (Cth) ('ADJR Act'). The ADJR Act empowered the Federal Court of Australia, itself only formed in 1976, to make an order of review in respect of a decision of an administrative character made under a Commonwealth enactment where satisfied that one or more specified statutory grounds of review existed. The ADJR Act provided (and continues to provide) within its field of operation a procedurally simpler and more flexible statutory alternative to the common law writs and to those writs provided for in s 75(v) of the *Australian Constitution*. But the field of operation of the ADJR Act soon came to be narrowed by judicial interpretation[9] and legislative amendment,[10] and its statutory grounds of review were conceived and have always been interpreted and administered as reflections (and in some cases slight modifications) of the common law.[11] The ADJR Act was supplemented by s 39B of the *Judiciary Act 1903* (Cth) which, from 1983, conferred jurisdiction on the Federal Court in substantially identical terms to that conferred on the High Court by s 75(v) of the *Australian Constitution* and which, from 1997, also

---

9 See, eg, *Australian Broadcasting Tribunal v Bond* (1990) 170 CLR 321.
10 See, eg, *Migration Legislation Amendment (Consequential Amendments) Act 1989* (Cth).
11 *Kioa v West* (1985) 159 CLR 550, 576.

conferred on the Federal Court jurisdiction in matters arising under laws made by the Commonwealth Parliament. In relation to matters within its jurisdiction, the Federal Court was given power to make orders and to issue writs of such kinds as the Court thinks 'appropriate'.[12]

Looking then very broadly at the shape of that branch of Australian administrative law which concerned the judicial review of administrative action approaching the last decade of the 20th century, it appeared piecemeal. The various pieces – s 75(v) of the *Constitution*, s 39B of the *Judiciary Act*, the ADJR Act and the prerogative writ jurisdictions of State Supreme Courts – appeared by and large to be based on, or reflective of, the common law.

Emergence of the modern approach

While the pieces have remained, the beginning of a change from the piecemeal common law conception of Australian administrative law can be traced to 1990. One of the cases that came before the High Court by way of appeal from a State Supreme Court that year was a case brought against the Attorney-General of New South Wales by a former magistrate who had sat in the old Court of Petty Sessions, which had just been abolished, and who had not been chosen for appointment to the Local Court of New South Wales established in its place.[13] The question was whether the former magistrate could properly obtain an order from the Supreme Court of New South Wales that would have had the effect of requiring the Attorney-General to determine his application for a position on the Local Court on its own merits without reference to the relative merits of other candidates. The High Court held, by majority, that the former magistrate could not obtain such an order, but just why not was put in different terms by different members of the majority. Sir Gerard Brennan alone went so far as to put it in terms that the making of such an order would involve the Supreme Court exceeding its legitimate constitutional role.

The 'duty and the jurisdiction of the courts', Sir Gerard Brennan said, 'are expressed in the memorable words of Marshall CJ in *Marbury v Madison*'.[14] *Marbury v Madison*,[15] decided by the Supreme Court of the United States in 1803, has always been regarded in Australia as containing, in the judgment of Marshall CJ, a classical exposition of the justification for a court to review the constitutional

---

12 Section 23 of the *Federal Court of Australia Act 1976* (Cth).
13 *Attorney-General (NSW) v Quin* (1990) 170 CLR 1.
14 (1990) 170 CLR 1, 35.
15 5 US 137 (1803).

validity of legislative or executive action.[16] It was in 1990 well known to Australian constitutional lawyers but before then rarely, if ever, mentioned by Australian administrative lawyers. The frequently quoted words used by Marshall CJ in *Marbury v Madison* to justify a court reviewing the constitutional validity of legislative or executive action were these: 'It is, emphatically, the province and duty of the judicial department to say what the law is'.[17] Those were the words quoted by Sir Gerard Brennan. That justification for the court in reviewing the constitutionality of legislative or executive action was then appropriated by Sir Gerard Brennan both to explain and to limit the legitimate role of a court in reviewing administrative action generally. 'The duty and jurisdiction of the court to review administrative action', he went on to say, 'do not go beyond the declaration and enforcing of the law which determines the limits and governs the exercise of the repository's power'.[18] That statement of Sir Gerard Brennan was in time to become accepted as canonical, and to be the outworking of an idea in another statement of his a few years earlier, that '[j]udicial review is neither more nor less than the enforcement of the rule of law over executive action'.[19]

There is a notable similarity between the conception of the duty and jurisdiction of a court to review administrative action so articulated by Sir Gerard Brennan in 1990 and what was explained in the same year by Professor Craig as 'the modern conceptual justification' for judicial review implicit in the 'rule of law', as espoused by Professor Dicey in the context of the unwritten constitution of the United Kingdom.[20] Professor Craig explained that Professor Dicey espoused, as an aspect of the doctrine of the 'omnicompetence' of Parliament, a doctrine of the 'monopoly' of Parliament over 'governmental' or 'public' power.[21] The Diceyan view of the judicial review of administrative action, as Professor Craig put it, 'was designed to ensure that the sovereign will of Parliament was not transgressed by those to whom…grants of power were made':[22]

> If authority had been delegated to a minister to perform certain tasks upon certain conditions, the courts' function was, in the event of challenge, to check that only those tasks were performed and only where the conditions were present. If there were defects on either level, the challenged decision would be declared null. For the courts not to have intervened would have

---

16 *Australian Communist Party v Commonwealth* ('*Communist Party* case') (1951) 83 CLR 1, 262–3.
17 5 US 87, 111 (1803).
18 (1990) 170 CLR 1, 35–6.
19 *Church of Scientology v Woodward* (1982) 154 CLR 25, 70.
20 P P Craig, *Public Law and Democracy in the United Kingdom and the United States of America*, (Oxford University Press, 1990) 21.
21 Ibid, 20.
22 Ibid, 21–2.

been to accord a 'legislative' power to the minister or agency by allowing them authority in areas not specified by the real legislature, Parliament. The less well-known face of [parliamentary] sovereignty, that of parliamentary monopoly, thus demanded an institution to *police* the boundaries which Parliament had stipulated. It was this frontier which the courts patrolled through non-constitutional review.

There are also notable differences from the Diceyan conception. That conception limits judicial review to 'non-constitutional review' – that is, review concerned not with the constitutionality of administrative action, but with the compliance of that action with legislative or common law constraints. Within the context of the *Australian Constitution*, which in common with the *United States Constitution* left no room for legislative omnicompetence, and which had a strong tradition of constitutional judicial review, Sir Gerard Brennan assimilated the conceptual justification for non-constitutional judicial review with the conceptual justification for constitutional judicial review. Non-constitutional judicial review and constitutional judicial review were henceforth manifestations of one and the same constitutional duty of a court to police (declare and enforce) the whole of the law (constitutional and legislative) that limits and conditions the exercise of a repository's power.

Another significant step occurred in 2000 in a migration case brought in the original jurisdiction of the High Court under s 75(v) of the *Australian Constitution*.[23] The High Court there, in effect, adopted the explanation of the duty and jurisdiction of a court given by Sir Gerard Brennan 10 years earlier as the justification for giving a wide interpretation to the original jurisdiction conferred on the High Court itself by s 75(v) of the *Australian Constitution*. The writs of mandamus and prohibition were labelled, with emphasis, 'constitutional writs'. The issue of those constitutional writs was explained wholly in terms of enforcing the law which determines the limits and governs the exercise of a Commonwealth officer's power. For a Commonwealth officer to transgress or fail to act in accordance with the law which determines the limits and governs the exercise of that Commonwealth officer's power was explained as amounting to 'jurisdictional error'. The term 'jurisdictional error' had surfaced only on occasions in the past. From this time 'jurisdictional error' came to be used routinely to describe the necessary condition for a 'constitutional writ' to issue.

A very short step was then taken just three years later in the context of another migration case brought within the original jurisdiction of the High Court under s 75(v) of the *Australian Constitution*.[24] The step was to characterise s 75(v) as introducing into the *Australian Constitution* an entrenched minimum provision of judicial review which was beyond the competence of the Commonwealth Parliament

---

23 *Re Refugee Review Tribunal; Ex parte Aala* (2000) 204 CLR 82.
24 *Plaintiff S157/2002 v Commonwealth* (2003) 211 CLR 476.

to deny. Building on an earlier observation of Sir Owen Dixon concerning the 'impossibility' of the Commonwealth Parliament imposing 'limits upon the quasi-judicial authority of a body which it sets up with the intention that any excess of that authority means invalidity', and the simultaneous deprivation of the High Court 'of authority to restrain the invalid action of the court or body by prohibition',[25] five members of the High Court spelt out 'two fundamental constitutional propositions' which they noted were uncontroversial as between the parties in that case:[26]

> First, the jurisdiction of this Court to grant relief under s 75(v) of the Constitution cannot be removed by or under a law made by the Parliament. Specifically, the jurisdiction to grant s 75(v) relief where there has been jurisdictional error by an officer of the Commonwealth cannot be removed. Secondly, the judicial power of the Commonwealth cannot be exercised otherwise than in accordance with Ch III. The Parliament cannot confer on a non-judicial body the power to conclusively determine the limits of its own jurisdiction.

The constitutionally entrenched minimum provision of judicial review, to the extent that it had come to be declared by the High Court by 2003, was therefore judicial review:

- by the High Court;
- under s 75(v) of the *Australian Constitution*;
- through the constitutional writs of mandamus and prohibition;
- for jurisdictional error;
- in the purported exercise of judicial or non-judicial power by any officer of the Commonwealth.

The High Court cast the constitutional net over Australian administrative law even more widely in early 2010.[27] Ironically, it did so in a case involving not a purported exercise of administrative power but a purported exercise of judicial power by a body constituted under New South Wales legislation as superior court of record having jurisdiction in criminal proceedings to make a decision which, according to a privative clause expressed in the legislation, was to be final and incapable of being appealed against, reviewed or called into question in any other court or tribunal. Holding the privative clause to be constitutionally incapable of preventing judicial review by the Supreme Court of New South Wales, the High Court looked at and linked two things. One was s 73(ii) of the *Australian Constitution* which, in making provision for appeals from State Supreme Courts to the High Court, necessarily recognises and requires the

---

25 *R v Hickman; Ex parte Fox and Clinton* (1945) 70 CLR 598, 616.
26 *Plaintiff S157/2002 v Commonwealth* (2003) 211 CLR 476, 511–12 [98].
27 *Kirk v Industrial Court (NSW)* (2010) 239 CLR 531.

existence of those State Supreme Courts. The other was the historical capacity of the Supreme Court of a State to exercise in that State the jurisdiction historically exercised in England by the Court of King's Bench to issue writs of certiorari, mandamus and prohibition to other courts and officials. The High Court combined those two things to produce the result of constitutionally entrenching judicial review in the States. The steps in its reasoning were these:

- Chapter III of the *Australian Constitution* – s 73(ii) in particular – is predicated on the continuing existence for each State of an institution meeting the description of a State Supreme Court;[28]
- a 'defining characteristic' of a State Supreme Court is its 'supervisory jurisdiction' of determining and enforcing 'the limits on the exercise of State executive and judicial power by persons and bodies other than [the Supreme] Court', that jurisdiction being exercised 'by the grant of prerogative relief or orders in the nature of that relief';[29]
- because 'it would remove from the relevant State Supreme Court one of its defining characteristics', a State law 'which would take from a State Supreme Court power to grant [prerogative relief or orders in the nature of prerogative relief] on account of jurisdictional error is beyond State legislative power'.[30]

The result, reinforced by a holding later in 2010 and repeated in 2012, that 'State legislative power does not extend to depriving a state Supreme Court of its supervisory jurisdiction in respect of jurisdictional error by the executive government of the State, its Ministers or authorities',[31] was to produce a constitutionally entrenched minimum provision of judicial review:

- by Supreme Courts;
- as recognised in s 73(ii) of the *Australian Constitution*;
- through the prerogative writs of mandamus, prohibition and certiorari or their modern statutory equivalents;
- for jurisdictional error;
- in the purported exercise of State executive power or State judicial power by any person or body other than the Supreme Court.

There is, in functional terms at least, an obvious symmetry between what has emerged as the constitutionally entrenched supervisory jurisdiction of a State Supreme Court and the constitutionally entrenched original jurisdiction conferred

---

28 (2010) 239 CLR 531, 580 [96].
29 Ibid, 581 [99].
30 Ibid, 581 [99], [100].
31 *Public Service Association of South Australia Inc v Industrial Relations Commission (SA)* (2012) 289 ALR 1 at 17 [60], citing *State of South Australia v Totani* (2010) 242 CLR 1, 27 [26].

on the High Court by s 75(v) of the *Australian Constitution*. Like the jurisdiction of the High Court under s 75(v), the jurisdiction guaranteed to a Supreme Court under s 73(ii) 'introduces into the *Australian Constitution* of the Commonwealth an entrenched minimum provision of judicial review'.[32] Like the jurisdiction of the High Court under s 75(v), the jurisdiction guaranteed to a Supreme Court under s 73(ii) serves to ensure that there cannot be 'islands of power immune from judicial supervision and restraint'. And complementing the original jurisdiction of the High Court under s 75(v), the appellate jurisdiction conferred on the High Court by s 73(ii) to hear appeals from State Supreme Courts serves to ensure the 'superintendence of [the High] Court as the "Federal Supreme Court" in which s 71 of the Constitution vests the judicial power of the Commonwealth'.[33]

Ambiguities and challenges of the modern approach

What has emerged is an overarching constitutional justification not only for the existence, but also for the minimum scope, of judicial review of administrative action at both the Commonwealth and State levels. The conceptual justification for judicial review at each level is no more and no less than the rule of law itself: the duty and jurisdiction of a court within the limits of its own jurisdiction to declare and enforce the law which determines the limits and governs the exercise of a repository's power. The minimum scope of judicial review at each level, capable always of statutory expansion within constitutional limits, is review for jurisdictional error. The High Court and each State Supreme Court retain within the limits of their respective constitutionally entrenched original jurisdictions an ability to grant appropriate relief to correct a repository of Commonwealth or State power who transgresses or fails to act in accordance with the law which determines the limits and governs the exercise of that power, the High Court through its appellate jurisdiction then exercising ultimate supervision over the entire system. The result: a seemingly singular and elegant constitutional scheme; a new paradigm.

Any new paradigm brings ambiguities and challenges. The ambiguity at the core of the new constitutional paradigm of Australian administrative law lies in its adoption of the opaque terminology of jurisdictional error. The term 'jurisdiction', Felix Frankfurter wrote, 'competes with "right" as one of the most deceptive of legal pitfalls',[34] and is for analytical purposes 'a verbal coat of too many colors'.[35]

---

32 *Plaintiff S157/2002 v Commonwealth* (2003) 211 CLR 476 , 513 [103].
33 *Kirk v Industrial Court (NSW)* (2010) 239 CLR 531 , 581 [99], [98].
34 *City of Yonkers v United States* 320 US 685, 695 (1944).
35 *United States v LA Tucker Truck Lines Inc* 344 US 33, 39 (1952).

To describe 'jurisdictional error' quite properly as a conclusive, not an analytical, label[36] is not necessarily to assent to every aspect of the post-realist insight that the adjective 'jurisdictional' in such a context 'is almost entirely functional', is 'used to validate review when review is felt to be necessary' and is justified only if 'it is understood that the word "jurisdiction" is not a metaphysical absolute but simply expresses the gravity of the error'.[37]

The principal challenge of the new constitutional paradigm lies in unpacking the analysis implicit in the application of the conclusive label of 'jurisdictional error' to produce clear principles of predictable application.

Sir Owen Dixon observed in 1938 that '[i]n the past a tendency may have appeared in the superior courts of common law to adopt constructions of statutes conferring powers on magistrates and others which would result in the withdrawal from their exclusive or conclusive determination matters which we should now think were intended for their decision'.[38] The Kerr Committee, on the other hand, recorded in 1971 a 'tendency of the courts to widen the area in which they may interfere by way of judicial review in cases where the extended doctrine of ultra vires or jurisdictional excess is resorted to'.[39] Those contrasting references, barely thirty years apart, illustrate the reality that tendencies of courts to adopt constructions of statutes having the result of either restricting or expanding the decision-making authority conferred by legislation on repositories of administrative power have varied significantly from time to time and from court to court.

The constitutional paradigm alone does not point to either a restrictive or an expansionist approach to the decision-making authority conferred by legislation on repositories of administrative power. The constitutional paradigm alone similarly does not warrant or sustain an approach to administrative law that so diverges from that which exists elsewhere as fairly to attract the label of 'Australian exceptionalism'.[40] To identify the duty and jurisdiction of a court as being limited to the declaration and enforcement of the law which determines the limits and governs the exercise of a repository's power is necessarily to adopt and maintain a distinction, sometimes difficult and sometimes smacking of a degree of artificiality, 'between acts that are unauthorised by law and acts that are authorised'.[41] It is to

---

36 *SDAV v Minister for Immigration and Multicultural and Indigenous Affairs* (2003) 199 ALR 43, 49–50 [27].
37 *Kirk v Industrial Court (NSW)* (2010) 239 CLR 531, 570–71 [64], quoting Jaffe, 'Judicial Review: Constitutional and Jurisdictional Fact' (1957) 70 *Harvard Law Review* 953, 963.
38 *Parisienne Basket Shoes Pty Ltd v Whyte* (1938) 59 CLR 369, 391.
39 *Commonwealth Administrative Review Committee Report*, Parl Paper No 144 (1971), 13 [33].
40 Cf Taggart, '"Australian Exceptionalism" in Judicial Review' (2008) 36 *Federal Law Review* 1.
41 *Re Minister for Immigration and Multicultural Affairs; Ex parte Lam* (2003) 214 CLR 1, 25 [77], quoting Selway, 'The Principle Behind Common Law Judicial Review of Administrative Action – The Search Continues' (2002) 30 *Federal Law Review* 217, 234.

say nothing, however, of the content of the law which determines the limits and governs the exercise of the repository's power.

Adherence to the foundational principle in *Marbury v Madison* that '[i]t is emphatically the province and duty of the judicial department to say what the law is' necessitates that a court, in circumstances of controversy, fix by judicial determination of fact and law the legal boundaries of the authority delegated to or conferred on a repository of administrative power. Exposition in its country of origin illustrates, however, that the principle is not of itself inconsistent with legislative delegation to a repository of administrative power of a degree of law-making authority so as to produce interstitial interpretative outcomes which must be recognised by courts as legally effective to the extent that they are within the scope of the authority delegated.[42] In language quoted by the High Court in 2000 and stated to be applicable within the Australian constitutional context, it has instead been explained that 'judicial review of administrative action stands on a different footing from constitutional adjudication, both historically and functionally':[43]

> In part no doubt because alternative methods of control, both political and administrative in nature, are available to confine agencies within bounds, there has never been a pervasive notion that limited government mandated an all-encompassing judicial duty to supply all of the relevant meaning of statutes. Rather, the judicial duty is to ensure that the administrative agency stays within the zone of discretion committed to it by its organic act.

The constitutional permissibility of legislative delegation of law-making authority in Australia has never been doubted at the State level and has been accepted at the Commonwealth level since 1931.[44] Doctrinal adherence to the separation of judicial power by Chapter III of the *Australian Constitution* has not been replicated to produce any rigid separation of legislative and executive power by Chapters I and II of the *Constitution*. As explained in 1935 by Sir Owen Dixon:[45]

> The failure of the doctrine of the separation of the powers of government to achieve a full legal operation here is probably fortunate. Its failure to do so may be ascribed perhaps to mere judicial incredulity. For it seemed unbelievable that the executive should be forbidden to carry on the practice of legislation by regulation – the most conspicuous legal activity of a modern

---

42 H P Monaghan, '*Marbury* and the Administrative State' (1983) 83 *Columbia Law Review* 1. See also *City of Arlington, Texas v Federal Communications Commission* 569 US __ (2013).
43 H P Monaghan, '*Marbury* and the Administrative State' (1983) 83 *Columbia Law Review* 1, 33, quoted in *Corporation of the City of Enfield v Development Assessment Commission* (2000) 199 CLR 135, 153.
44 *Victorian Stevedoring and General Contracting Company Co Pty Ltd and Meakes v Dignan* (1931) 46 CLR 73.
45 O Dixon, 'The Law and the Constitution' (1935) 51 *Law Quarterly Review* 590, 606.

government. What otherwise might have been treated as a rigid requirement of the supreme law has been given the appearance of the mere categories of a draftsman. Legal symmetry gave way to common sense.

Common-sense recognition of the practical demands of modern government has also meant that such judicial monopoly as exists in Australia over the ascertainment of existing rights has never been taken so far as to exclude the capacity of others to form and act upon their own judgements about the content of the law that bears upon the taking of action within such area of authority as may be granted to them.[46] To the contrary, the High Court in 1995 unanimously endorsed the statement of Lord Diplock that:[47]

> Parliament can, of course, if it so desires, confer upon administrative tribunals or authorities power to decide questions of law as well as questions of fact or of administrative policy; but this requires clear words, for the presumption is that where a decision-making power is conferred on a tribunal or authority that is not a court of law, Parliament did not intend to do so.

The High Court added:[48]

> The position is, of course, a fortiori in this country where constitutional limitations arising from the doctrine of the separation of judicial and executive powers may preclude legislative competence to confer judicial power upon an administrative tribunal.

Consistent with that understanding as to the scope of legislative power to confer decision-making authority, it has been emphasised that the 'distinction between errors of fact and law' does not 'supplant or exhaust the field of reference of jurisdictional error'.[49] Indeed, it has been steadfastly maintained in Australia that a repository of power may make an 'error of law' (that is, may make a judgment about the content of the law that is different from the judgment that is or would be made independently by a court) that is not 'jurisdictional' (that is, that does not prevent the repository of the power taking action that is legally operative on the basis that the action is within the area of decision-making authority conferred on the repository by the power).[50] Decisions of long standing go so far as to

---

46 *Re Ranger Uranium Mines Pty Ltd; Ex parte Federated Miscellaneous Workers' Union of Australia* (1987) 163 CLR 656, 666; *Precision Data Holdings Ltd v Wills* (1991) 173 CLR 167, 189–90.
47 *Craig v South Australia* (1995) 184 CLR 163, 179, quoting *In Re Racal Communications Ltd* [1981] AC 374, 383.
48 (1995) 184 CLR 163, 179.
49 *Re Minister for Immigration and Multicultural Affairs; Ex parte Applicant S20/2002* (2003) 198 ALR 59, 71 [54].
50 Eg, *R v Taylor; Ex parte Professional Officers' Association-Commonwealth Public Service* (1951) 82 CLR 177, 184.

admit of decision-making authority being so defined as to render valid (within the constitutional limits of Commonwealth legislative power) purported administrative action taken bona fide by a repository of administrative power, provided only that the action relates to the subject-matter of the legislation and that the action can be determined by a court to be reasonably capable of being referable to that power.[51]

Conclusion

When the High Court in 1988 dramatically changed its previously long-held view of the critically important provision of the *Australian Constitution* that guarantees freedom of interstate trade, the High Court went on to explain that the view to which it had then come and which it was then expounding would not 'resolve all problems' but would 'permit the identification of the relevant questions'.[52]

The result of developments since 1990 is that the judicial review of administrative action in Australia irrevocably now has a constitutional dimension which, though it does not resolve all problems, allows identification of the relevant questions. The relevant questions now focus less on grounds upon which a court might issue writs or make other judicial orders and more on the sources and content of the law determining the limits and governing the exercise of an administrator's decision-making authority.

What that constitutional dimension means for the content of Australian administrative law remains to be worked out, in the common law tradition, in the fullness of time.

---

51 Collected in *R v Coldham; Ex parte Australian Workers' Union* (1983) 153 CLR 415, 418. For a view as to the provenance of those decisions, see I Holloway, '"A Bona Fide Attempt": Chief Justice Sir Owen Dixon and the Policy of Deference to Administrative Expertise in the High Court of Australia' (2002) 54 *Administrative Law Review* 687, 691.
52 *Cole v Whitfield* (1988) 165 CLR 360, 408.

AUSTRALIA'S CODIFICATION OF JUDICIAL REVIEW: HAS THE LEGISLATIVE EFFORT BEEN WORTH IT?

Peter Billings and
Anthony Cassimatis*

---

* The authors acknowledge Catherine Drummond and Bianca Kabel for their invaluable research assistance.

Introduction

In Australia, at the federal, State and Territory levels, legislative steps have been taken to enhance the efficacy of judicial review over administrative action. The purpose of statutory codification of judicial review was twofold: first, to enhance access to justice for individuals aggrieved by government action or inaction; and, second, to promote, and affirm the importance of, legal accountability for public administration.[1] This was to be achieved by, *inter alia*:

1. Simplifying the procedures for accessing the courts and applying for judicial review;
2. Codifying the common law grounds for review; and
3. Providing for a right to written reasons in respect of certain administrative decisions.

This chapter examines whether legislative codification has been 'worth it', in view of the rationale underpinning it. Put another way, has codification constrained, or hampered, the law of judicial review in Australia?

Chapter 1 has assessed the role that the Kerr and Ellicott committees played leading up to the enactment of the *Administrative Decisions (Judicial Review) Act 1977* (Cth) ('ADJR Act'). The ADJR Act was 'an important milestone in the evolution of Australian administrative law'.[2] It was the first attempt in Australia 'to codify both the law and much of the procedure of judicial review'.[3] The ADJR Act has been judicially described as 'one of the most important Australian legal reforms of the last century'.[4] Groves has observed that 'during the first decade after its enactment, the ADJR Act was the leading avenue of judicial review and clearly exerted great influence over Australian administrative law'.[5] This assessment is supported by the Administrative Review Council ('ARC') in a report issued in 1989.[6] In that report,

---

1 The importance of a legally accountable public administration is regularly stressed. See: Administrative Review Council, *Federal Judicial Review in Australia* (Report No 50, 2012) 9; Department of Justice and Attorney General, *Reform of Judicial Review in NSW* (Discussion Paper, 2011) 7 [2.7]; Report of a Commission of Inquiry Pursuant to Orders in Council – Commission of Inquiry into Possible Illegal Activities and Associated Police Misconduct (3 July 1989) (the 'Fitzgerald report') (see, especially, [3.4] (Administrative Review) via <http://www.cmc.qld.gov.au/about-us/our-organisation/our-background/fitzgerald-inquiry>).
2 M Groves, 'Should We Follow the Gospel of the *Administrative Decisions (Judicial Review) Act 1977* (Cth)?' (2010) 34 *Melbourne University Law Review* 736, 737.
3 Ibid.
4 *Griffith University v Tang* (2005) 221 CLR 99, 133 [100] (Kirby J). In support of this observation, Kirby J cited the Second Reading Speech by the Attorney-General (Mr R J Ellicott MP) on the Administrative Decisions (Judicial Review) Bill 1977 (Cth): Australia, House of Representatives, Parliamentary Debates (Hansard), 28 April 1977, 1394, 1395.
5 Groves, above n 2, 739.
6 Administrative Review Council, *Review of the Administrative Decisions (Judicial Review) Act: The Ambit of the Act* (Report No 32, 1989).

the ARC set out statistics regarding judicial review applications federally under the ADJR Act but also via s 39B of the *Judiciary Act 1903* (Cth) which corresponds to the High Court's jurisdiction under s 75 of the *Commonwealth Constitution* (see Figure 9.1). The preponderance of ADJR Act applications is striking.

Figure 9.1 Federal judicial review applications[7]

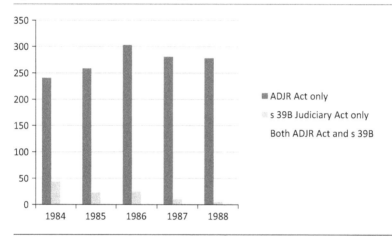

In relation to this first decade, if one bears in mind the empirical evidence that supports the efficacy of federal judicial review,[8] it is difficult to disagree with Kirby J's assessment in *Applicant S20/2002* that 'the effects of the ADJR Act were overwhelmingly beneficial and review of federal administrative action was more commonly pursued under that Act than had been the case under the earlier common law'.[9] Positive assessments of the ADJR Act were also made by bodies charged with recommending law reform in the States,[10] and by the legislatures in the Australian Capital Territory,[11] Queensland[12] and Tasmania.[13]

---

7 Ibid, 18.
8 R Creyke and J McMillan, 'Judicial Review Outcomes – An Empirical Study' (2004) 11 *AJAdminL* 82, 87.
9 *Re Minister for Immigration and Multicultural Affairs; Ex parte Applicant S20/2002* (2003) 198 ALR 59, [157].
10 See Electoral and Administrative Review Commission (Qld) – Report – *Judicial Review of Administrative Decisions and Action* (1990); P Bayne, *Judicial Review in Victoria*, Victorian Attorney-General's Law Reform Advisory Council, Expert Report 5 (1999); and Law Reform Commission of Western Australia, *Report on Judicial Review of Administrative Decisions* (Project No 95, 2002). The Victorian and West Australian governments did not accept these recommendations.
11 *Administrative Decisions (Judicial Review) Act 1989* (ACT).
12 *Judicial Review Act 1991* (Qld).
13 *Judicial Review Act 2000* (Tas).

After its first decade, however, the ADJR Act began to lose its lustre. The Commonwealth Parliament forced migration applicants away from the ADJR Act by excluding migration decision-making from ADJR Act review by the Federal Court. Those applicants were forced to instead use the entrenched jurisdiction of the High Court under s 75(v) of the *Constitution*.

The High Court's expanding jurisprudence in relation to s 75 also highlighted the scope of the Federal Court's jurisdiction under s 39B of the *Judiciary Act 1903* (Cth), particularly when that section was amended in 1997 to replicate, for the Federal Court, the jurisdiction of the High Court under s 75(iii) of the *Constitution*.[14] These developments accentuated the jurisdictional limitations expressly built into the ADJR Act[15] and the limitations that flowed from judicial exegesis on the jurisdictional requirements for ADJR Act review. In 2003, Robertson contrasted the breadth of jurisdiction under s 39B of the *Judiciary Act* with the ADJR Act, and concluded that:

> the AD(JR) Act is not as important as inexperienced pleaders appear to think as they start with its express grounds and apparent jurisdictional and procedural simplicity and chart their course exclusively by those sometimes false lights. Where there is a basis for doubting the applicability of the AD(JR) Act, then ss 39B(1) and 39B(1A) of the *Judiciary Act* should also be relied on.[16]

In terms of judicial exegesis, in 2005, Kirby J referred to the decisions of the High Court in *Neat Domestic Trading Pty Ltd v AWB Ltd* ('*Neat*')[17] and *Griffith University v Tang* ('*Tang*')[18] (Kirby J being in dissent in both cases) as 'an erosion of one of the most important Australian legal reforms of the last century'. The combination of express statutory restrictions and judicial exegesis limiting the applicability of the ADJR Act saw an increasing reliance on non-ADJR Act remedies. Aronson, Dyer and Groves observed in 2009 that s 39B was 'almost always pleaded cumulatively and in the alternative' to claims under the ADJR Act.[19] In 2012, the ARC highlighted the comparative disadvantages of the ADJR Act:

> it is a wise precautionary step for a person commencing judicial review proceedings to do so under s 39B(1), either in addition to ADJR Act proceedings or as an alternative. There are fewer apparent limitations on the right to commence proceedings under s 39B(1) than under the ADJR

---

14 A Robertson, 'The Administrative Law Jurisdiction of the Federal Court – Is the AD(JR) Act Still Important?' (2003) 24 *Australian Bar Review* 89.
15 The 'administrative character' requirement restricts the scope of the ADJR Act more narrowly than the traditional common law and equitable remedies.
16 Robertson, above n 14, 100.
17 (2003) 216 CLR 277.
18 (2005) 221 CLR 99.
19 M Aronson, B Dyer and M Groves, *Judicial Review of Administrative Action* (Lawbook, 4th ed, 2009) 41.

Act. Section 39B(1) requires only that the applicant for relief demonstrate an entitlement to an order of mandamus or prohibition or an injunction against an officer of the Commonwealth. The ADJR Act requires that proceedings concern a 'decision' or 'conduct' of an 'administrative character' made 'under an enactment'... and that the decision not be excluded from review under Schedule 1 of the Act. Stricter time limits also apply to proceedings commenced under the ADJR Act.[21]

The 2012 report of the ARC highlights how much things have changed since the first decade of operation of the ADJR Act. In particular, the contrast between the initial period and the last 10 years (Figure 9.2) demonstrates how dramatic the changes have been. Changes in migration law partly account for this, but limitations in relation to the ADJR Act are another significant factor.

Figure 9.2 First instance judicial review filings in the Federal Court of Australia (excluding appeals)[20]

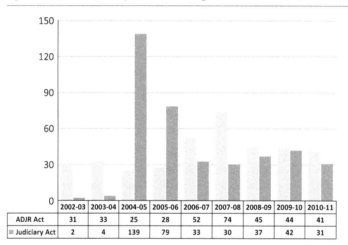

	2002-03	2003-04	2004-05	2005-06	2006-07	2007-08	2008-09	2009-10	2010-11
ADJR Act	31	33	25	28	52	74	45	44	41
Judiciary Act	2	4	139	79	33	30	37	42	31

It is to the jurisdictional requirements of the ADJR Act that attention will now be turned. The provisions of the ADJR Act and judicial exegesis that have prompted criticism from Kirby J and others will be considered, and this will be followed by a consideration of the codified grounds of review. Whilst the enumerated grounds in the ADJR Act have generally been seen as having made a positive contribution, particularly in relation to their educative potential, difficulties nonetheless arise in relation to the codified grounds. This chapter will then consider features of the ADJR Act (and the State and Territory legislation that it has inspired) that are seen as having made important positive contributions to judicial review. The right to

---

20 Ibid, 66.
21 ARC, Report No 50 (2012), above n 1, 74, [4.9] [Footnote omitted].

a written statement of reasons in respect of administrative decisions without the need to commence judicial review proceedings is an important contribution of the ADJR Act. Other procedural reforms include a common test for standing to bring judicial review proceedings, and improvements in relation to the remedial powers of the Federal Court under the ADJR Act. Exclusions from judicial review via the schedules to the ADJR Act, and the State and Territory legislation, have given rise to concerns, particularly in a State context, following the High Court's decision in *Kirk v Industrial Court of NSW* ('*Kirk*').[22] Nonetheless, the procedural benefits of the legislation outweigh its shortcomings.

The ADJR Act's jurisdictional 'flaws and shortcomings'[23]

The ADJR Act (and the State and Territory legislation that it inspired) provides for judicial review of a decision, conduct and failure to decide, where the actual or potential 'decision' is of an 'administrative character' and is made 'under an enactment'. The phrases 'decision', 'administrative character' and 'under an enactment' have all played a part in limiting the scope of review under the ADJR Act.

'Decision'

Judicial exegesis limiting the scope of the ADJR Act can be traced back to the High Court's decision in *Australian Broadcasting Tribunal v Bond*.[24] The High Court in that case sought to avoid the fragmentation of government decision-making that was feared if the word 'decision' in the ADJR Act was interpreted broadly to include substantive steps in a decision-maker's reasoning process, prior to the making of a final decision.[25] Giving a broad construction to the word 'decision' in this context would have both expanded the scope of review and the statutory right to a statement of reasons. According to Mason CJ:

> a reviewable 'decision' is one for which provision is made by or under a statute. That will generally, but not always, entail a decision which is final or operative and determinative, at least in a practical sense, of the issue of fact falling for consideration. A conclusion reached as a step along the way in the course of reasoning leading to an ultimate decision would not

---

22 (2010) 239 CLR 531.
23 Groves, above n 2, 771.
24 (1990) 170 CLR 321.
25 Ibid, 336–7.

> ordinarily amount to a reviewable decision, unless the statute provided for the making of a finding or ruling on that point so that the decision, though an intermediate decision, might accurately be described as a decision under an enactment.
>
> Another essential quality of a reviewable decision is that it be a substantive determination ...[26]

This restrictive approach raises many difficulties.[27] The restrictiveness of this approach can, for example, be avoided in certain circumstances. Three 'escape hatches' have been identified, namely: conduct (interpreted by the High Court to involve matters of *procedure* as opposed to *substantive* determinations) which remains reviewable under the ADJR Act; where substantive 'steps along the way' are 'provided for' by legislation (these are reviewable as 'decisions' on the above approach); and the potential to review substantive 'steps along the way' relying on remedies such as injunctions and the writ of prohibition that are available, *inter alia*, via s 39B of the *Judiciary Act 1903* (Cth).

The difficulties in applying the test in *Bond* have prompted Cane and McDonald to observe that '*Bond* ushered in countless jurisdictional challenges and has generated a large, highly technical and sometimes absurd jurisprudence'.[28] This jurisprudence appears all the more unfortunate when viewed in light of the three escape hatches noted above. The jurisdictional limitation read into the word 'decision' by the majority in *Bond* may also have been unnecessary. The mischief of judicial review being used to fragment government decision-making can be addressed without resort to jurisdictional limitations, by the use of the discretionary powers of the superior courts to dismiss proceedings on the grounds of abuse of process.[29]

'Administrative character'

Restricting the ADJR Act to decisions of an administrative character (and thus potentially excluding the making of subordinate legislation by,[30] for example, Ministers) limited the scope of the ADJR Act more narrowly than, for example, injunctive relief sought via s 39B of the *Judiciary Act 1903* (Cth). There have been

---

26 Ibid, 337.
27 See, eg, M Aronson and M Groves, *Judicial Review of Administrative Action* (Lawbook, 5th ed, 2013) [2.290]–[2.460].
28 P Cane and L McDonald, *Principles of Administrative Law: Legal Regulation of Governance* (Oxford University Press, 2nd ed, 2012) 57–8 [Footnotes omitted].
29 Although the approach of the majority in *Australian Broadcasting Tribunal v Bond* (1990) 170 CLR 321 has a distinct role to play in relation to the statutory right to reasons.
30 Note the capacity to mount indirect challenges to subordinate legislation by challenging administrative decisions purportedly made under invalid subordinate legislation – see, eg, ARC, above n 1, [5.92].

interpretative difficulties in relation to the words 'administrative character',[31] but these pale by comparison with the interpretative difficulties that have arisen in relation to 'decision' and 'under an enactment'.

'Under an enactment'

Reference has already been made to Kirby J's criticisms of the rulings of the majorities in *Neat* and *Tang*. These decisions have been subjected to extensive judicial and academic scrutiny.[32] It is not possible in this chapter to outline all of the arguments for and against the ratios in these decisions.[33] It is perhaps sufficient to note that Gummow, Callinan and Heydon JJ in *Tang* identified two criteria for a decision to be 'under an enactment':

> First, the decision must be expressly or impliedly required or authorised by the enactment; and, secondly, the decision must itself confer, alter or otherwise affect legal rights or obligations, and in that sense the decision must derive from the enactment. A decision will only be 'made…under an enactment' if both these criteria are met. It should be emphasised that this construction of the statutory definition does not require the relevant decision to affect or alter existing rights or obligations, and it will be sufficient that the enactment requires or authorises decisions from which new rights or obligations arise. Similarly, it is not necessary that the relevantly affected legal rights owe their existence to the enactment in question. Affection of rights or obligations derived from the general law or statute will suffice.[34]

The second criterion has posed the most significant impediment for applicants. It proved fatal for the applicant in *Tang*, who was seeking judicial review, under the Queensland equivalent of the ADJR Act, of university decisions to exclude her from a PhD program for alleged academic misconduct. In addition to the difficulty in applying this second criterion,[35] it appears likely that the two disciplinary decisions in this case would have been reviewable had the applicant sought declaratory relief rather than relief via the statutory remedies based on the ADJR Act.[36]

---

31 See, eg, *McWilliam v Civil Aviation Safety Authority* (2004) 142 FCR 74, 83–5. Compare *Schwennesen v Minister for Environment & Resource Management* [2010] QCA 340, [7]–[9] and [33]–[34].
32 See M Aronson, 'Private Bodies, Public Power and Soft Law in the High Court' (2007) 35 *Federal Law Review* 1, and the academic commentary cited therein.
33 For a forthright defence of *Tang*, see P A Keane, 'Judicial Review: The Courts and the Academy' (2008) 82 *Australian Law Journal* 623.
34 *Griffith University v Tang* (2005) 221 CLR 99, 130–31.
35 See, eg, Groves, above n 2, 744–50.
36 Aronson, above n 32, 16, 23; and D J Mullan, *Administrative Law: Cases, Text, and Materials* (Emond Montgomery, 6th ed, 2010) 1016.

Of all of the criticisms of the ADJR Act, this is probably the most telling. The Kerr and Ellicott committees were determined, through their recommendations for statutory reform, to avoid a problem that had bedevilled the traditional judicial review remedies – namely, that an applicant for judicial review might be denied relief, notwithstanding the existence of legal error, because the wrong remedy had been selected.[37] The result in *Tang* suggests that this mischief remains.[38]

The ARC in 2012 recommended that the ADJR Act be amended to address this concern. The ARC recommended that:

> The *Administrative Decisions (Judicial Review) Act 1977* (Cth) (ADJR Act) should provide that, subject to limited exceptions, a person who otherwise would be able to initiate a proceeding in the High Court under s 75(v) of the *Australian Constitution* may apply for an order of review under the ADJR Act. Sections 5, 6, 7 and 13 of the ADJR Act would not apply in those proceedings, but other provisions of the ADJR Act would apply subject to some modifications.[39]

As well as bringing the ADJR Act into closer alignment with s 39B of the *Judiciary Act*, this recommendation is also likely to reduce the risk of an applicant being denied relief for having wrongly chosen the statutory remedies set out in the ADJR Act instead of remedies set out in s 75(v) of the *Constitution*.[40] The ARC's recommendation does not, however, go as far as it could have gone in order to reduce the risk of an applicant choosing the wrong remedy. Had the recommendation included reference to s 75(iii) of the *Constitution*, it would have brought the ADJR Act into even closer alignment with the position under s 39B of the *Judiciary Act*. The Council's recommendation, if implemented as currently framed, would leave the ADJR Act narrower than s 39B(1A) of the *Judiciary Act*.

One of the advantages of the ADJR Act has been the educative effect of its provisions, which, in the context of the grounds of review, have usefully articulated the essence of most, if not all, of the common law grounds of review.[41] Had the words 'decision' and 'under an enactment' been given a broader construction, then the ADJR Act could also have performed this educative function in the context of its

---

37 The Ellicott Committee suggested that if the Kerr Committee's recommendations were implemented, 'a person aggrieved will no longer have to run the risk of applying for the wrong remedy' – Australia, Parliament, Report of the Committee of Review on Prerogative Writ Procedure (Ellicott Committee Report), Parl Paper No 56, 1973, 5–6 [19]. See also, for example, Sir Anthony Mason, 'Administrative Review: The Experience of the First Twelve Years' (1989) 18 *Federal Law Review* 122, 123.
38 M Taggart, '"Australian Exceptionalism" in Judicial Review' (2008) 36 *Federal Law Review* 1, 20.
39 ARC, above n 1, 77.
40 Although not entirely remove the risk, as declaratory relief in *Tang* could potentially have been give under Part 5 of the *Judicial Review Act 1991* (Qld).
41 M Aronson, 'Is the ADJR Act Hampering the Development of Australian Administrative Law?' (2005) 12 *AJAdminL* 79, 91.

jurisdictional requirements. Instead, reliance must now be placed on remedies such as mandamus and prohibition in cases where the ADJR Act does not apply. This is ironic given the hopes expressed in the Kerr and Ellicott committee reports. In the words of the ARC's 1989 report on judicial review, applicants for 'relief under section 39B must run the gauntlet of the technicality and complexity of the rules concerning the prerogative writs'.[42] We now turn to the ADJR Act's codification of the common law grounds of review and the benefits (including their educative effect) of this feature of the ADJR Act.

The codification of the common law grounds of review and the absence of meta-principles

Increasing accessibility, promoting legal certainty and enhancing transparency?

The particular grounds of review, in ss 5 and 6 of the ADJR Act, are regarded as a reflection, in *summary* form, of the grounds on which administrative action ('decisions' and 'conduct', respectively) is susceptible to challenge at common law.[43] The three judicial review statutes inspired by the ADJR Act – the ACT's *Administrative Decisions (Judicial Review) Act 1989*, Queensland's *Judicial Review Act 1991* and Tasmania's *Judicial Review Act 2000* – contain grounds that track the federal provisions.[44]

However, the general statements above are subject to two qualifications: first, in two instances the itemised grounds depart from the common law. Thus, 'errors of law' do not need to appear 'on the face of the record' (ADJR Act ss 5(1)(f), 6(1)(f)). Additionally, the common law was consciously departed from in respect of decisions made without justification (or, 'no evidence') (ADJR Act ss5(1)(h), 6(1)(h)), although the statutory re-iteration of the common law's position – in respect of determinations made without an evidence base – has not clarified matters satisfactorily (see below).

---

42 ARC, above n 6, 30–31.
43 *Kioa v West* (1985) 159 CLR 550, 576.
44 *Accused A v Callanan* [2009] QSC 12, [56].

Second, there are particular statutory grounds that have been applied more generously than their common law counterparts. For example, the ground relating to the non-observance of procedural requirements (ADJR Act ss 5(1)(b), 6(1)(b)) appears to have broader applicability than the common law equivalent; the ground is not tied to procedures regarded as jurisdictional.[45]

No attempt has been made in the legislation to categorise the grounds more abstractly, as has occurred in England with Lord Diplock's 'illegality, irrationality and procedural impropriety' formulation in the *GCHQ* case.[46] The adoption of a more general approach to articulating the basis on which a court may grant relief was recently rejected by the ARC. The ARC concluded that less prescription would undermine the beneficial, educative effect that enumerating the common law grounds has had for decision-makers, practitioners and review applicants.[47]

In addition to claims about increased public accessibility and the educative benefits realised by clearly codifying the grounds, overall, codification of judicial review provides an opportunity to promote legal certainty and rationalise legal principles. Arguably, it also buttresses the democratic legitimacy of judicial review, if it is accepted that the calibration of judicial review principles ought to be the function of the legislature as well as the courts.[48]

Specifying the grounds of review has drawn criticism. Jurists have suggested that enacting grounds of review may artificially stultify the development of the law, leaving Australia lagging behind common law developments overseas.[49] Judges have also warned that codifying the grounds of judicial review has stifled, or arrested, the development of the law.[50] It must also be appreciated that legislative intervention can be motivated by a desire to restrict, as well as promote, access to justice; for example, by way of reducing the available grounds of review or 'ousting' the supervisory jurisdiction of the courts (see below).

---

45 Eg, *Mills v Commissioner of the Queensland Police* [2011] QSC 244 [51], applying s 20(2)(b) of the *Judicial Review Act 1991* (Qld).
46 *Council of Civil Service Unions v Minister for the Civil Service* [1985] AC 374, 410 (Lord Diplock). In Canada, there is a more general approach to listing the grounds on which relief can be sought (s 18.1(4) *Federal Courts Act*, RSC, 1985).
47 ARC, above n 1, 127–30.
48 T Jones, 'Judicial Review and Codification' (2000) 20 *Legal Studies* 517, 520–22; C Saunders, 'Constitutions, Codes and Administrative Law: The Australian Experience' in C Forsyth, M Elliott, S Jhaveri, A Scully-Hill and M Ramsden (eds), *Effective Judicial Review* (Oxford University Press, 2010) 61, 79.
49 J Griffiths, 'Legislative Reform of Judicial Review of Commonwealth Administrative Action' (1978) 9 *Federal Law Review* 42, 69; J Pennell and Y Shi, 'The Codification of Wednesbury Unreasonableness – A Retardation of the Common Law Ground of Judicial Review in Australia?' (2008) 56 *AIAL Forum* 22; Taggart, above n 38, 12.
50 See Pincus J, quoted in Electoral and Administrative Review Commission (Qld) – Report – *Judicial Review of Administrative Decisions and Action* (December 1990), [5.39]; and *Re Minister for Immigration and Multicultural Affairs; Ex parte Applicant S20/2002* (2003) 198 ALR 59, [157], [166].

Aronson doubted that the ADJR Act had retarded the growth of judicial review at common law in Australia. He pointed to, *inter alia*, the development of a 'newly minted ground called "serious irrationality or illogicality"' in *Applicant S20/2002*, and to the 'catch-all' ground in the ADJR Act[51] – namely, administrative action that was 'otherwise contrary to law'.[52] The rationale for this ground was to permit the Act to adapt, 'thereby avoiding the rigidity which might otherwise have set in with real codification or a closed list'.[53] Groves has concluded, however, that this ground, along with the 'abuse of power' catch-all ground, are 'dead letters' due to the almost total lack of applications which have sought to use them.[54]

Aronson's conclusion, that the ADJR Act's 'grounds have proved to be sufficiently flexible to reject the charge of ossification',[55] is supported by Creyke, although in her estimation the ADJR Act's apparent flexibility compromises the values of legal certainty and transparency, thereby negating perceived benefits of codification. Writing 10 years ago, Creyke identified several innovations in the applicable standards of judicial review (such as a failure to give a 'proper, genuine and realistic consideration of the merits' and a 'duty to inquire') as problematical, because the text of the ADJR Act no longer represented an accurate guide to the law.[56]

Yet it would be mistaken to assume that the ADJR Act contained all the heads of judicial review recognised at common law. The Act did not comprehensively and perfectly enumerate all common law grounds, so there was a degree of uncertainty from the outset. Several grounds were omitted, including the common law rule prohibiting delegation of power (now subsumed under ADJR Act, ss 5(1)(c)–(d), 6(1)(c)–(d) and the complex subject of non-fettering of discretionary power and administrative estoppel.[57] Additionally, the common law was, and remains, in a state of flux. Accordingly, any complexities and confusions surrounding common law principles are inherited by the statutory schemes until they are satisfactorily resolved by the judiciary or legislature.

---

51 Aronson, above n 41, 92–3.
52 *ADJR Act 1977* (Cth), ss 5(1)(j), 6(1)(j).
53 Aronson, above n 41, 93.
54 M Groves, 'Substantive Legitimate Expectations in Australian Administrative Law' (2008) 32 *Melbourne University Law Review* 470, 518 (discussing *ADJR Act 1977* (Cth), ss 5(2)(j), 6(2)(j)).
55 Aronson, above n 41, 97.
56 R Creyke, 'Current and Future Challenges in Judicial Review Jurisdiction: A Comment' (2003) 37 *AIAL Forum* 42, 45. Cf. Saunders, above n 48, 75, who concluded that there 'has been relatively little judicial development of the AD(J)R Act grounds'.
57 Griffiths, above n 49, 56, 69. Griffiths stated that important principles were not mentioned in the ADJR Act, albeit the catch-all provisions could capture them; and see EARC, above n 10, [5.37].

Statutory codification and the *Commonwealth Constitution*

Some argue that Australian administrative law is lagging behind other common law jurisdictions. Undoubtedly, judicial review principles in Australia have evolved differently from the way they have evolved in other jurisdictions in recent times. For example, any recognition of 'substantive legitimate expectations' has been resisted in Australia. So has the adoption of a variable standard of 'unreasonableness', where fundamental rights are affected by administrative action, and 'proportionality' as a discrete ground of review.[58] The divergence between Australian and English administrative law is not due, however, to the ADJR Act. A different combination of factors has caused this 'exceptionalism'.[59] Professor Cane has pointed to:

1. Regime change in the 1970s – the creation of the Federal Court with jurisdiction over the ADJR Act, and the Administrative Appeals Tribunal (AAT) – which fragmented administrative law. For Cane, the establishment of the AAT gave the distinction between 'judicial review and merits review a unique and rigidifying significance';

2. The influence of the High Court's (traditional and remedially oriented) 'original jurisdiction' under s 75(v) of the *Commonwealth Constitution*;[60]

3. The lack of an Australian bill of rights. This has meant that, unlike the United Kingdom, human rights have not been a force for renovation of administrative law; and

4. A commitment to conceptualism and historicism on the part of the High Court of Australia under Chief Justice Murray Gleeson (the 'Gleeson court' – 1998–2008).[61]

Scholars have argued that constitutional considerations in Australia have fashioned the grounds, and limits, of judicial review, and that these are the

---

58 See further ARC, above n 1, 135–6, and the authorities referred to therein. See also *SZADC v Minister for Immigration and Multicultural and Indigenous Affairs* [2003] FCA 1497, [24] (special standard of unreasonableness inapplicable in human rights cases); *Sabet v Medical Practitioners Board of Victoria* (2008) 20 VR 414, 422–3 (holding proportionality is not a recognised ground of judicial review).

59 Taggart, above n 38. Taggart also notes that in certain respects it is England that is exceptional; for example, the recognition of substantive legitimate expectations (Ibid, 26–7).

60 Cane and Taggart have both noted that the *Constitution* enshrined the remedies (writs), not the grounds of review; Taggart was unconvinced that the references to the writs warranted the retention of the concept of jurisdictional error (which was abandoned in favour of error of law in the UK and NZ, and which was rejected in favour of codification of the grounds in the judicial review statutes): Taggart, above n 38, 9.

61 P Cane, 'The Making of Australian Administrative Law' (2003) 24 *Australian Bar Review* 114, 133.

primary reason for the differences between English and Australian judicial review principles:

> The Australian conception of judicial review is increasingly fashioned by constitutional considerations, particularly the apparent limits that the separation of powers doctrine imposes upon the scope of judicial review of administrative action. The conception of the judicial function expounded by the High Court draws a clear, arguably rigid, distinction between judicial and merits review. This distinction in turn appears to preclude the adoption of some recent English developments in judicial review, such as the doctrine of substantive unfairness.[62]

The controlling influence of the *Commonwealth Constitution* upon judicial review at the State and Territory level is also clear, notwithstanding the absence of a formal separation of powers at that level. For instance, when considering administrative law reform in 1990, the Electoral and Administrative Review Commission (Qld) had one eye fixed on the limited role of the courts, citing Justice Mason's statement of principle in *Minister for Aboriginal Affairs v Peko-Wallsend Ltd* ('*Peko-Wallsend*')[63] – the gist of that statement being that it is not for the courts to engage in a substantive reconsideration of the exercise of administrative discretion, rather the role for the courts is to set limits on the exercise of that discretion.[64] That statement of principle speaks to the basic distinction between merits and legality that underpins Australian judicial review. So in Queensland – where there is a less stringent application of the separation of powers principle – the reach and content of statutory judicial review was, from its inception, tethered to judicial review at the federal level.[65] The limits on judicial review derived from the *Commonwealth Constitution* by the High Court, evident in seminal cases such as *Peko-Wallsend* and *Australian Broadcasting Tribunal v Bond*,[66] have exerted a powerful guiding influence on the application of statutory review grounds found in the Queensland and Tasmanian legislation.[67] That impact is reinforced by the clear terms of s 16 of the Queensland Act, which forges a direct link between the federal and State statutes.

---

62 Groves, above n 2, 770; and Saunders, above n 48, 64.
63 (1986) 162 CLR 24, 40–41.
64 His Honour cited *Associated Provincial Picture Houses Ltd v Wednesbury Corporation* [1948] 1 KB 223, 238, in support of this proposition.
65 See further M Groves, 'Federal Constitutional Influences on State Judicial Review' (2011) 39 *Federal Law Review* 399.
66 (1990) 170 CLR 321.
67 The examples include: *Gibson v Minister for Finance, Natural Resources and the Arts* [2012] QSC 132, [11]; *Building Professions Accreditation Corporation Tasmania Ltd v Minister for Infrastructure, Energy and Resources* [2005] TASSC 73, [14], [22]; and *Clarence City Council v South Hobart Investment Pty Ltd* [2007] TASSC 16, [44].

Enumerated and emerging grounds of review

There are nine 'principal' codified grounds on which government action may be reviewed – two of which ('improper exercise of power' and 'no evidence') are further sub-divided. The analysis of statutory review grounds below covers highly selective terrain,[68] reflecting particular questions addressed in the recent ARC report on federal judicial review,[69] certain matters singled out in the Electoral and Administrative Review Commission (Qld) report,[70] and relevant academic commentary. This analysis demonstrates the uncertainty regarding the scope of particular codified grounds and the potential for further development of the grounds in the ADJR Act and legislation it has inspired.

(i) Fettering of discretionary powers: Proper, genuine and realistic consideration of the merits

An improper exercise of power arises where there is 'an exercise of discretionary power in accordance with a rule or policy without regard to the merits of the case'.[71] A familiar general rule that informs this statutory ground for review is that, in the application of a lawful policy, 'anyone who has to exercise a statutory discretion must not "shut his (or her) ears" to an application'.[72] This rule requires attention to the facts of each case. As explained in *Khan v Minister for Immigration, Local Government and Ethnic Affairs*,[73] decision-makers must be ready to depart from any applicable policy:

> [W]hat was required of the decision-maker, in respect of each of the applications, was that in considering all relevant material placed before him, he give proper, genuine and realistic consideration to the merits of the case and be ready in a proper case to depart from any applicable policy.[74]

The standard articulated in *Khan's* case is referable to s 5(2)(f) of the ADJR Act, but the question as to whether it has imported a new element of review of general application has proved divisive; uncertainty remains. Creyke identified the 'proper, genuine and realistic consideration of the merits' formula as a novel principle of review in 2003, but its emergence has not been uniformly accepted. Indeed,

---

68 For broader coverage see, generally, Aronson and Groves, above n 27.
69 Administrative Review Council, above n 1, Chapter 7 (Grounds of Review).
70 Electoral and Administrative Review Commission (Qld), above n 10, Chapter 5 (Grounds of Review).
71 ADJR Act 1977 (Cth), ss 5(2)(f), 6(2)(f).
72 *Wiggington v Queensland Parole Board* [2010] QSC 59, [29], citing *British Oxygen Co Ltd v Minister for Technology* [1971] AC 610, 625. See also *ACTEWAGL Distribution v Australian Energy Regulator* (2011) 123 ALD 486, [150]; *Perder Investments v Lightowler* (1990) 21 ALD 446.
73 (1987) 14 ALD 291.
74 Ibid, 292.

recently it was expressly rejected by the Supreme Court of Queensland in statutory review proceedings. Jackson J observed that 'Gummow J was not purporting to lay down a new principle of administrative law in *Khan*'.[75] The Court held that the requirement to give proper, genuine and realistic consideration arises in the context of determining whether a power was exercised inflexibly without regard to the merits of the case – it does not add another legal requirement. By contrast, Robinson's survey of the authorities led him to conclude, on balance, that the requirement was a separate ground.[76] The difficulty presented by the recognition of the 'proper, genuine and realistic consideration of the merits' formula, as a discrete basis for review, is that it invites complaints that effectively go to the merits of an administrative decision. The courts continue to make clear that this is the one issue that remains beyond the scope of their supervisory jurisdiction.[77]

(ii) Raising an administrative estoppel

The absence of a review ground in the ADJR Act relating to the complex subject of administrative estoppel was touched upon by Griffiths, in 1978, in his critical review of the ADJR Act.[78] The absence of any statutory ground of review based upon estoppel is consistent with the general common law principle that the exercise of a public duty cannot be the subject of administrative estoppel.[79] The enforcement of estoppels in the administrative context presents difficulties; the doctrine intersects (and creates tension) with no-fettering principles.[80] The many difficulties and the circumstances in which individuals may seek relief for the disappointment of promises or expectations created by the executive branch are examined in Chapter 11. For present purposes it suffices to say that the statutory omission of administrative estoppel does not mean recognition of the principle is foreclosed as a basis for statutory review. Weeks has opined that, in the light of *Minister for Immigration v Kurtovic*[81] and *Attorney-General (NSW) v Quin*, 'the door to public law estoppel is ajar, if only slightly'.[82] He drew encouragement from the *dictum* of Mason CJ in *Quin's* case:

---

75 *Origin Energy Electricity Ltd v Queensland Competition Authority* [2012] QSC 414, [93]. This approach aligns with, *inter alia*, *Minister for Immigration and Multicultural Affairs v W64/01A* [2003] FCAFC 12, [32].
76 M Robinson, 'State of Play – Administrative Law in Review – State and Territory Perspectives' (2011) 65 *AIAL Forum* 43, 47–8. Cf J McMillan, 'Judicial Restraint and Activism in Administrative Law' (2002) 30 *Federal Law Review* 335, 361–3.
77 See, eg, *Sunshine Coast Broadcasters Pty Ltd v Australian Communications & Media Authority* (2012) 130 ALD 589, [131].
78 Griffiths, above n 49, 56–7.
79 *Orthotech Pty Ltd v Minister for Health* [2013] FCA 230, [58].
80 *Theo v Secretary, Department of Families, Community Services and Indigenous Affairs* [2007] FCAFC 72, [27]–[30].
81 (1990) 21 FCR 193.
82 G Weeks, 'Estoppel and Public Authorities: Examining the Case for an Equitable Remedy' (2010) 4 *Journal of Equity* 247, 255.

> One cannot exclude the possibility that the courts might in some situations grant relief on the basis that a refusal to hold the Executive to a representation by means of estoppel will occasion greater harm to the public interest by causing grave injustice to the individual who acted on the representation than any detriment to that interest that will arise from holding the Executive to its representation and thus narrowing the exercise of its discretion.[83]

This excerpt from *Quin* was referred to with apparent approval, in *Wort v Whitsunday SC*, by Williams JA (with whom the other members of the Queensland Court of Appeal agreed).[84] Furthermore, in *J & MD Milligan Pty Ltd v Queensland Building Services Authority*, the Supreme Court recognised that, in light of *Quin's* case and *Wort v Whitsunday Shire Council*, there were limited exceptions to the general principle that estoppel is not available to prevent the exercise of a statutory duty or a statutory discretion of a public character; however, the pleaded facts did not provide a foundation for an estoppel-based claim.[85] While these cases suggest that declaratory relief may be available when an estoppel is raised, the question of which particular head of judicial review administrative estoppel may be brought under is unresolved. The adaptive 'catch-all' grounds are logical contenders, but the exceptional circumstances in which they might apply is a matter left open. It is at least clear that the 'otherwise contrary to law' ground of review does not permit decisions to be challenged on the basis of 'general unfairness'.[86]

(iii) A duty to inquire?

The ADJR Act, and the legislation it has inspired, contains no reference to 'a duty to inquire', and the juristic basis for a 'duty to inquire' has been described as 'illusive'.[87] However, it is clear that a limited inquisitorial obligation on decision-makers emanates from within the scope of review for 'unreasonable' administrative action for the purposes of statutory review.[88] Or, alternatively, the duty is to be found within the broader, slippery, concept of 'jurisdictional error' at common

---

83 (1990) 170 CLR 1, 18.
84 [2001] QCA 344, [13].
85 [2012] QSC 213. That case was an application to amend a statement of claim, where the plaintiff sought to introduce a new cause of action – estoppel – and declaratory relief.
86 *Minister for Immigration and Ethnic Affairs v Kurtovic* (1990) 21 FCR 193, 220–22.
87 M Smyth, 'Inquisitorial Adjudication: The Duty to Inquire in Merits Review Tribunals' (2010) 34 *Melbourne University Law Review* 231, 247. Compare *Gibson v Minister for Finance, Natural Resources and the Arts* [2012] QSC 132, [132] with *Origin Energy Electricity Ltd v Queensland Competition Authority* [2012] QSC 414, [96]–[97] for differences of opinion on whether the 'proper, genuine and realistic consideration test' can be applied in connection with the relevancy grounds for statutory review.
88 An unreasonable exercise of power constitutes an 'improper exercise of power' for the purposes of statutory judicial review: *ADJR Act 1977* (Cth), s 5(2)(g).

law.⁸⁹ The leading federal authority is *Prasad v Minister for Immigration and Ethnic Affairs*,⁹⁰ where Wilcox J observed that:

> [i]n a case where it is obvious that material is readily available which is centrally relevant to the decision to be made, it seems to me that to proceed to a decision without making any attempt to obtain that information may properly be described as an exercise of the decision making power in a manner so unreasonable that no reasonable person would have so exercised it.⁹¹

Following *Prasad's* case, in *Minister for Immigration and Citizenship v SZIAI*,⁹² ('*SZIAI*') the High Court acknowledged a limited duty to inquire principle at common law. The State courts have drawn upon these cases and advanced collective understanding of the scope and content of this emerging ground in statutory review proceedings. In the Queensland Supreme Court, Henry J stated that 'plainly it would not be enough that a reviewing Court thinks it might have been sounder…to make further inquiries'.⁹³ This and similar jurisprudence establishes that existence and scope of any 'duty to inquire' turns on: (i) whether, as a matter of statutory construction, an implication can be drawn that the decision-maker is required to seek out additional material not provided by the parties;⁹⁴ (ii) the decision-making context⁹⁵ and importance of the administrative action undertaken; and (iii) the nature of the material before a decision-maker.⁹⁶

(iv) Illogical or irrational fact finding

The statutory references to 'unreasonableness' reflect Lord Greene's definition in *Associated Provincial Picture Houses Ltd v Wednesbury Corporation*.⁹⁷ The '*Wednesbury*' principle involves a degree of examination of the reasonableness of a decision, but 'judicial review is not merits review. The issue is whether the exercise

---

89 *Minister for Immigration and Citizenship v SZIAI* (2009) 111 ALD 15, [25]. On jurisdictional error, see Chapter 12.
90 (1985) 6 FCR 155.
91 Ibid, 169–70. See also *Minister for Immigration and Citizenship v Le* (2007) 164 FCR 151.
92 (2009) 259 ALR 436, [25].
93 *Gibson v Minister for Finance, Natural Resources and the Arts* [2012] QSC 132, [133].
94 *Eastman v Miles* [2004] ACTSC 32, [62].
95 *Bezzina Developers Pty Ltd v Deemah Stone (Qld)* [2008] QCA 213, [15].
96 *Cairns City Council v Commissioner of Stamp Duties* [2000] 2 Qd R 267, 274 [29]; and *Videto v Minister for Immigration and Ethnic Affairs* (1985) 69 ALR 342, 353, cited in *Petrie v Queensland Community Corrections Board* [2006] QSC 282, [17] as authority for the proposition that a duty to inquire arises where the material before the decision-maker contains some obvious omission or obscurity that needs to be resolved.
97 *Fares Rural Meat and Livestock Pty Ltd v Australian Meat and Livestock Corp* (1990) 96 ALR 153, 166; *Ashley v Southern Queensland Regional Parole Board* [2010] QSC 437, [2]; *Building Professions Accreditation Corporation Tasmania Ltd v Minister for Infrastructure, Energy and Resources* [2005] TASSC 73, [12]–[13].

of the discretionary power was so unreasonable that no reasonable person could have so exercised it'.[98] Caution or restraint is routinely expressed by the judiciary when applying this ground of review for fear of intruding into the executive's realm.

So, ordinarily, judicial review does not entail a re-evaluation of the factual findings or reconsideration of the merits of administrative action.[99] However, in *Applicant S20/2002* the High Court of Australia recognised that fact-finding processes may be impugned for a want of logic or rationality. It is ironic that this common law companion to *Wednesbury* emerged after the Commonwealth attempted to truncate the available grounds for judicial review. Unreasonableness could not be pleaded by asylum seekers aggrieved by decisions of the Refugee Review Tribunal, due to prohibitions in the *Migration Act 1958* (Cth).[100] Accordingly, it was via the High Court's original jurisdiction that novel administrative law principles were established under the broad concept of 'jurisdictional error', effectively outmanoeuvring legislative prohibitions. The legislative exclusion of the ground of unreasonableness thus sparked the common law growth of an innovative alternative.

The emergence of irrationality or illogicality as heads of review for findings of fact has trickled into statutory judicial review. For example, in *CMC v Assistant Commissioner JP Swindells*,[101] Applegarth J stated that perverse factual findings were reviewable, whether treated as an application of the *Wednesbury* principle or as a related principle that permits judicial review of findings of fact for extreme irrationality or illogicality. Some judges have hesitated to apply these new criteria due to a perceived lack of precision as to the nature and quality of errors characterised as illogical or irrational.[102] Questions about the uncertain nature of this emerging ground were addressed (but not resolved) by the High Court in *Minister for Immigration v SZMDS*.[103] Four judges considered the meaning of 'illogicality or irrationality'. Two different approaches emerged. The approach taken by Gummow A-CJ and Kiefel J questioned 'whether the determination...was irrational, illogical and not based on findings or inferences of fact supported by logical grounds – even if good faith were demonstrated'.[104] Alternatively, Crennan and Bell JJ determined that illogicality or irrationality meant that the decision 'is

---

98 *Bickle v Chief Executive, Department of Corrective Services* [2008] QSC 328, [27]; *Attorney-General (NSW) v Quin* (1990) 170 CLR 1, 36.
99 *Re Minister for Immigration, Multicultural Affairs; Ex parte Applicant S20/2002* (2003) 198 ALR 59, [114].
100 *Migration Act 1958* (Cth), s 476(2)(b).
101 *Crime & Misconduct Commission v Assistant Commissioner J P Swindells* [2009] QSC 409, [11].
102 *Lark v Nolan* [2006] TASSC 12.
103 (2010) 115 ALD 248.
104 *SZNKO v Miniser for Immigration and Citizenship* [2013] FCA 123, [110].

one which no rational or logical decision-maker could have arrived [at] on the same evidence'.¹⁰⁵ These approaches overlap but are subtly different. The latter appears more stringent. As Rares J has explained:

> Even if the decision-maker's articulation of how and why he or she went from the facts to the decision is not rational or logical, if someone else could have done so on the evidence, the decision is not one that will be set aside.¹⁰⁶

The rival approaches to illogical and irrational fact-finding, evident in *SZMDS*, mean the position at common law is ambiguous, which is now reflected in the statutory review setting. State case-law illustrates the point. In *QCoal Pty Ltd v Hinchliffe*,¹⁰⁷ the Queensland Supreme Court applied the definition employed by Crennan and Bell JJ in *SZMDS*.¹⁰⁸ Previously, in *CMC v Assistant Commissioner JP Swindells*, the Supreme Court cited *Applicant S20/2002* with apparent approval. This simply illustrates that the benefits of legal certainty which flow from codification of judicial review principles can be overstated. The judicial review statutes were never intended to be impervious to common law developments. Accordingly they will necessarily embody complexity (and ambiguity) in developing common law principles.

(v) Decisions without justification

The ADJR Act (and State/Territory equivalents) was meant to clarify the circumstances in which particular factual errors were of such magnitude that they were properly regarded as legal errors. In his submission to EARC, Pincus J observed that:

> If <u>anything</u> should be made clear by a specific statement of grounds, it is the extent to which one can ... [consider whether factual findings are correct – sufficiently based in evidence] on judicial review.¹⁰⁹

However, the itemisation of the 'no evidence' ground has not resulted in greater certainty vis-à-vis when factual findings may be judicially reviewed. The interrelationship between the different components of this ground is unsettled at the federal level and 'the case law is unclear on what findings of fact the no evidence ground applies to'.¹¹⁰

---

105 Ibid, [111].
106 *SZOOR v Minister for Immigration and Citizenship* (2012) 202 FCR 1, [15].
107 [2011] QSC 334.
108 (2010) 240 CLR 611, 647–8 [130]–[131].
109 EARC, above n 10, [5.39].
110 ARC, above n 1, 140.

Review, for absence of supporting evidence, is provided for on the basis 'that there was no evidence or other material to justify the making of the decision'.[111] The 'principal' ground is not taken to be made out unless:

a. the person who made the decision was required by law to reach that decision only if a particular matter was established, and there was no evidence or other material (including facts of which the person was entitled to take notice) from which the person could reasonably be satisfied that the matter was established; or

b. the person who made the decision based the decision on the existence of a particular fact, and that fact did not exist.[112]

There are several issues arising in respect of the statutory 'no evidence' ground for review; two are canvassed below to illustrate the uncertainties arising. Arguably the most important problem is whether the requirements found in the two 'limbs' in paragraphs (a) and (b) explain the meaning to be afforded to the principal ground or whether the linkage between the principal ground and paragraphs (a) or (b) is cumulative. The cumulative view of the provisions was adopted in *Curragh Queensland Mining Ltd v Daniel*,[113] whereas in *Minister for Immigration and Multicultural Affairs v Rajamanikkam*,[114] a majority of the High Court appear to favour the explanatory interpretation. What needs to be made clear is that the conditions in ss 5(3) and 6(3) of the ADJR Act establish that the 'principal' ground is made out. This assertion finds support in contemporary case-law on the equivalent statutory provision in Queensland. For example, in *P&O Automotive & General Stevedoring Pty Ltd v Chief Executive, Department of Justice and Attorney-General*, the court stated: 'Section 24 of the JR Act provides that this [principal] ground is not made out unless the decision fits into one of two categories'.[115] Second, there are unresolved questions about the meaning of 'reasonably satisfied' in paragraph (a). In *Garland v Chief Executive, Department of Corrective Services*,[116] Atkinson J cited a passage from the judgment of Mason CJ in *Bond* (with JR Act (Qld) provisions added in square brackets):

> Within the area of operation of par (a) [JR Act s 24(a)] it is enough to show an absence of evidence or material from which the decision maker could reasonably be satisfied that the particular matter was established, that being a lesser burden than that of showing an absence of evidence (or material) to support the decision.

---

111 *ADJR Act 1977* (Cth), ss 5(1)(h), 6(1)(h).
112 *ADJR Act 1977* (Cth), ss 5(3), 6(3).
113 (1992) 34 FCR 212.
114 (2002) 210 CLR 222.
115 [2011] QSC 417, [42]. The Court of Appeal also seems to have embraced the expansive (explanatory) approach in *MBR v Parker* [2012] QCA 271, [61].
116 [2006] QSC 245.

At 359–60 of his judgment, Mason CJ concluded:

> ... a finding of fact will be reviewable on the ground that there is no probative evidence to support it and an inference will be reviewable on the ground that it was not reasonably open on the facts, which amounts to the same thing.[117]

Atkinson J continued by explaining that the 'particular matter that must be established is that the chief executive considers, on reasonable grounds, that generally Mr Garland is a substantial threat to the security or good order of the prison'.[118] Accordingly, Her Honour appears to adopt, and so support, the view that the 'reasonably satisfied' requirement in paragraph (a) constitutes a relaxation of the common law's literal approach to 'no evidence', albeit this more relaxed standard applies only to those particular cases where *facts* (including decision-makers' *opinions* about the existence of relevant facts) *are required by law*.[119] But in *Toulmin v Tasmanian Racing Appeal Board*,[120] the Supreme Court adopted the passage in *Bond* cited above and simply accepted that the 'full implications of the relaxation of the common law's literalism have not been tested'.[121] Re-drafting the 'no evidence' ground could bring the transparency sought by the drafters of the ADJR Act, and provide a more certain guide for judges when determining whether an evidential/factual error should be classified as a legal error. The need for such changes suggests that statutory grounds of review can introduce rather than resolve uncertainty.

Right to reasons

The ADJR Act's creation of a statutory right to a written statement of reasons in respect of administrative decisions is arguably the most significant reform brought about by the legislation. The High Court has held that there is no common law right to reasons for administrative decisions.[122] A statutory right to reasons is therefore a significant reform. Importantly, the right to reasons in the ADJR Act (and in the State/Territory legislation inspired by it) does not require the commencement of judicial review proceedings.[123] Nor does it depend upon showing any form of legal error. The right was intended to ensure general transparency in relation to government decision-making. It follows that an applicant need only show an entitlement to commence proceedings under the Act, not that those proceedings would succeed.

---

117 Ibid, [82].
118 Ibid, [83].
119 Ibid, citing *Australian Heritage Commission v Mount Isa Mines Ltd* (1997) 187 CLR 297, 303.
120 [2009] TASSC 115.
121 Ibid, [34]–[35].
122 *Public Service Board of New South Wales v Osmond* (1986) 159 CLR 656, 662, 667–9.
123 Contrast the position in NSW: see Groves, above n 2, 767.

The right to reasons, being tied to the prerequisites for statutory judicial review (ie, there must be a 'decision' of an 'administrative character' made 'under an enactment' etc), is subject to the same technicality and uncertainty regarding the scope of statutory judicial review considered above.

If the 'decisions' for which reasons must be given were expansively defined, that right could fragment and frustrate government decision-making. Confining the right to final decisions which are of an 'administrative character' provides a sensible limitation. We should also acknowledge the administrative burden imposed on government decision-makers in preparing statements of reasons. The ARC has considered the workload associated with providing statements of reasons under the ADJR Act. The ARC observed:

> Responding to section 13 requests [for statements of reasons] inevitably has an impact on an agency's resources. Sometimes the workload argument is put on the basis that diversion of an undue proportion of an agency's resources to complying with the requirements of the section may prejudice the timeliness and efficiency of the delivery of an agency's services to the public generally.
>
> The evidence that this has in fact happened in areas where there have been relatively high numbers of section 13 requests is hard to find.
>
> ...
>
> A further answer to the workload argument is provided by the statistics concerning the use of section 13.... The statistics [set out in the report] show that the provision of statements of reasons under the section is now only a minor incident of the general administrative process.[124]

The ARC's 2012 report sought to more closely align provisions governing the right to reasons with equivalent provisions in Freedom of Information legislation.[125]

Procedural reforms

In addition to establishing a statutory right to reasons in respect of administrative decisions, the ADJR Act also established a single test for standing to replace the different approaches amongst the common law and equitable remedies. Given that standing has already been addressed in Chapter 7, it is not proposed to revisit the relevant principles here. It is simply noted that a similar approach to standing is applied in relation to joinder under the ADJR Act.

---

124 ARC, *Review of the Administrative Decisions (Judicial Review) Act: Statements of Reasons for Decisions* (Report 33, 1991) 36.
125 ARC, Report No 50 (2012), above n 1, Ch 9.

Another significant contribution of the ADJR Act was the articulation of the remedial powers of the Federal Court (s 16). This remedial power is simple and flexible. Provided the jurisdictional requirements of the ADJR Act are satisfied, the Federal Court (and the Federal Magistrates Court) is given the full range of remedial powers that are necessary in order to undertake legality review. Section 16 of the ADJR Act also avoids the complexity of the common law that flows from the distinction between decisions that are void and those that are voidable. For these reasons, s 16 and the equivalent provisions in the State/Territory legislation are a significant reform.[126]

Exclusions from review

The anomalous exclusion of decisions of the Governor-General must be acknowledged in any assessment of the efficacy of the ADJR Act. Notwithstanding the development of the common law, the exclusion under the ADJR Act remains. By contrast, both the Queensland and the Tasmanian legislation do not exclude judicial review of decisions of their respective State Governors.

The scope and extent of schedule exclusions of review (and the right to reasons) is an important issue. The ARC and other reform bodies (such as EARC in Queensland) have carefully reviewed such exclusions.

In a State context, the High Court's decision in *Kirk*[127] had the potential to create difficulties for the schedule exclusions to the extent that they purported to exclude all review of government action covered by the schedules. In both Tasmania and Queensland, however, it appears that review outside of the legislation inspired by the ADJR Act is still possible, and thus the decision in *Kirk* does not appear to create any special difficulties in relation to schedule exclusions.[128]

Conclusion

Commenting on statutory reform of judicial review in Canada, Professor Mullan offered the following assessment of the relevant judicial review legislation enacted in Ontario:

---

126 See, eg, Groves, above n 2, 762–3.
127 (2010) 239 CLR 531.
128 See *Northbuild Construction Pty Ltd v Central Interior Linings Pty Ltd* [2012] 1 Qd R 525; and *Tasman Quest Pty Ltd v Evans* (2003) 13 TAS R 16, 19–21 [8]–[9]. See now r 623 of the Rules of the Supreme Court (Tasmania). Whilst s 43 of the Tasmanian Act provides that 'the prerogative writs of mandamus, prohibition, certiorari, quo warranto and scirefacias are no longer to be issued by the Court', r 623 of the Rules of the Supreme Court speaks of 'an application for relief *similar to* certiorari, mandamus or prohibition' [emphasis added].

> Probably the most reliable indicator of the success of any exercise in legislative reform is the extent to which it passes the test of time without the need for its parameters having to be established by resort to litigation.... Ontario's *Judicial Review Procedure Act* ... has been a success and, in particular, remedial technicalities seldom intrude in Ontario judicial review litigation so as to prevent the Divisional Court going immediately to the merits of an application for judicial review.[129]

As the above analysis of the jurisdictional requirements demonstrates, on this standard, apart from the first decade of its operation, it is difficult to regard the ADJR Act as an unqualified success. Nonetheless, s 75 of the *Constitution*, together with s 39B of the *Judiciary Act*, provide a means by which to ensure that applicants can avoid the narrowness of the ADJR Act's jurisdictional requirements. As Robertson has suggested, however, the complexity of the position federally will pose problems for 'inexperienced pleaders'.[130] The recommendations made by the ARC in 2012 to incorporate the remedies set out in s 75(v) into the ADJR Act will go some way to addressing these problems, although review along the lines of s 75(iii) of the *Constitution* should also be reflected in the reforms proposed for the ADJR Act.

Notwithstanding the jurisdictional narrowness of the ADJR Act, it has nonetheless been 'worth it'. The ADJR Act's educative potential has no doubt benefited applicants applying under s 75 of the *Constitution*, under s 39B of the *Judiciary Act* and in those jurisdictions that do not have legislation modelled on the ADJR Act.

In our view, overall, the codification of review grounds in the ADJR Act has increased accessibility to review by simply stating the available grounds. The Act has, to a degree, promoted legal certainty, and provided enhanced transparency and flexibility to adapt to the evolving administrative state. While some heads of review do not always speak for themselves, perhaps due to conflicting judicial opinions or because they encompass emerging principles, they do provide more guidance than the common law doctrine of jurisdictional error. The ADJR Act's expansive grounds – 'that the decision was otherwise contrary to law'; and 'any other exercise of a power in a way that constitutes abuse of the power' – point to the adaptive potential of the scheme even if this has yet to be fully realised at the federal level, but there are a few encouraging signs in State Supreme Court decisions.[131] Out of an abundance of caution, statutory recognition of 'any ground of review that may be available at common law' in Australia[132] would, logically, address concerns that statutory review mechanisms might inhibit the law's evolutionary capacity.

---

129 D J Mullan, *Administrative Law* (Irwin Law, 2001) 438.
130 Robertson, above n 14, 100.
131 See, eg: *M v P* [2011] QSC 350, [40]; *Keach v Minister for Health and Human Services* [2006] TASSC 28, [25].
132 See ARC, *Judicial Review in Australia* (Consultation Paper, 2011) [4.71].

10

THE EVOLUTION AND ENTRENCHMENT OF NATURAL JUSTICE

Matthew Groves

Introduction

Natural justice comprises two closely related rules – the rule against bias and the hearing rule. This chapter examines the hearing rule, which governs the procedures that must be adopted in the course of administrative decision-making. The hearing rule requirements have a long common law heritage.[1] They remain crucial to securing the rights of people to fair treatment in the administrative process, but they are limited.

The Australian conception of natural justice is procedural and regulates the fairness of the decision-making process rather than its outcomes. This focus is why some judges have suggested that the doctrine is better described as 'procedural fairness'.[2] The procedural focus of natural justice also reflects the absence in Australia of anything like the 'due process' rights that are constitutionally entrenched in the United States.[3] Australian constitutional principles give far less protection to the rules of fairness. The High Court has accepted that the *Australian Constitution* precludes legislative exclusion of core features of natural justice from the exercise of judicial power.[4] There are, however, no such constitutional prohibitions on legislation excluding or restricting the obligation to observe some or all requirements of procedural fairness outside the courts; but the courts deploy a range of interpretive assumptions against such legislation.

The judicial reluctance to interpret legislation as excluding the rules of natural justice reflects the relentless expansion of the interests to which the duty to observe the rules of fairness applies. This chapter explains the growth of interests that are protected by the requirements of natural justice and how those interests may be regarded as sufficiently affected to attract those requirements. The chapter argues that the expansive approach the courts now take to those issues has made them increasingly reluctant to identify the legislative intention required for the rules of natural justice to be wholly excluded or significantly narrowed.

---

1 The idea that people should be heard before decisions affecting them are made can be traced to at least the start of the 17th century: *Boswell's* case (1606) 6 Co Rep 48B; 77 ER 326; *Bagg's* case (1615) 11 Co Rep 95b; 77 ER 1271, 1275
2 *Kioa v West* (1985) 159 CLR 550, 585 (Mason J), 601 (Wilson J); *Attorney-General (NSW) v Quin* (1990) 170 CLR 1, 53 (Dawson J).
3 This due process right is enshrined in the 5th and 14th Amendments to the *United States Constitution* and codified in the federal *Administrative Procedure Act 1946* (5 USC), s 554. Countries which have a bill or charter of rights usually protect similar interests. See, eg, *Canadian Charter of Rights and Freedoms 1982* (Can), s 7.
4 *Wainohu v State of New South Wales* (2011) 243 CLR 181, 208–15 (French CJ and Kiefel J). Basic procedural rights in the courts, such as the right to be heard and to know the opposing case, cannot therefore be excluded or unduly limited by legislation: *International Finance Trust Co Ltd v New South Wales Crime Commission* (2009) 240 CLR 319, 354–5 (French CJ), 365–7 (Gummow and Bell JJ), 379–81 (Heydon J). The extent to which legislation can limit rather than exclude such rights remains unsettled.

What is fairness and why is it important?

The procedural focus of natural justice reflects a deeply entrenched limit on Australian judicial review. The most widely cited statement of those limits was made by Brennan J in *Quin's* case,[5] where his Honour explained that the 'duty and jurisdiction of the court to review administrative action' extended only to declaring the law. Brennan J took that principle to its logical extreme and concluded that if 'the court avoids administrative injustice or error, so be it; but the court has no jurisdiction simply to cure administrative injustice error'.[6] Some Australian cases have hinted that natural justice could move beyond procedural rules with a requirement that decision-makers must act rationally, must properly respond to whatever case is made, and must base decisions upon probative evidence.[7] These or similar criteria could easily lead courts beyond procedural review, but the possibility has not gained wide acceptance.[8]

The procedural focus in Australia stands in stark contrast to the direction English law took with *Coughlan's* case.[9] Ms Coughlan was seriously injured and needed constant medical care. Government officials broke a promise that she could remain in a particular nursing home for the rest of her life to receive that care. The Court of Appeal acknowledged that public officials sometimes created expectations of substantive rather than procedural benefits, and held that two interrelated tasks fell to the court in such cases. The court could decide if any frustration of the expectation was so unfair that it was an abuse of power. If so, the court had to weigh 'the requirements of fairness against any overriding interest relied upon for the change of policy'.[10] The Court of Appeal held that no such overriding reason was offered in Ms Coughlan's case, so the decision to move her was set aside. This reasoning is vague, but the judicial protection of substantive expectations has flourished in England.[11]

---

5 *Attorney-General (NSW) v Quin* (1990) 170 CLR 1.
6 (1990) 170 CLR 1, 35–6. See also *Neat Domestic Trading Pty Ltd v AWB Ltd* (2003) 216 CLR 277, 288 where Gleeson CJ explained: '[J]udicial review is not an invitation to judges to decide what they would consider fair or reasonable …'.
7 Support for this approach can be gleaned from *Dranichnikov v Minister for Immigration and Multicultural Affairs* (2003) 197 ALR 389.
8 See M Aronson and M Groves, *Judicial Review of Administrative Action* (Lawbook, 5th ed, 2013) 7.30.
9 *R v North and East Devon Health Authority; Ex parte Coughlan* [2001] QB 213. The case and its consequences are examined in Chapter 11.
10 Ibid, 242.
11 *Coughlan*, or its central principle, was cited with approval by the House of Lords in *R v East Sussex County Council; Ex parte Reprotech (Pebsham) Ltd* [2003] 1 WLR 348, [24]; *R (Mullen) v Secretary of State for the Home Department* [2005] 1 AC 1, 30, 41; *YL v Birmingham City Council* [2008] 1 AC 95, 139; and *R (BAPIO Action Ltd) v Secretary of State for the Home Department* [2008] 1 AC 1003, 1015–17, 1025.

The High Court of Australia rejected the substantive enforcement of legitimate expectations well before *Coughlan*. The key case was *Quin*,[12] where an expectation was argued to have arisen from a policy governing appointments to a new lower court which replaced an existing one. Under that policy, the Attorney-General only considered applications for appointment to the new court from members of the old one. Several former magistrates who had not been appointed to the new court argued that the policy and related statements by the Attorney-General created a legitimate expectation that they would receive the same, very favourable, treatment as other members of the old court. A majority of the High Court held that, just as the Attorney could make a policy favourable to former magistrates, he could also change it and adopt a less favourable one.[13] The majority also accepted that undertakings provided by government officials could create procedural obligations in a decision-making process,[14] but stressed that those expectations could not be enforced in any substantive sense.[15] *Quin* both denied the possibility of substantive enforcement of expectations and enabled governments to easily extinguish the source of those expectations.

Any substantive approach to fairness was also implicitly rejected in subsequent High Court decisions confirming a procedural approach to fairness.[16] The High Court examined the point more directly in *Lam's* case, where a majority pointedly disapproved of both *Coughlan* and the substantive enforcement of legitimate expectations. McHugh and Gummow JJ, with whom Callinan J agreed, stressed that the different constitutional structure of Australia limited any use of *Coughlan*; but their Honours' dislike of the English doctrine seemed to extend beyond constitutional reasons.[17]

A procedural conception of fairness is arguably misleading because procedure and substance are interdependent. Fair procedures provide opportunities which, if exercised, influence outcomes. In a widely cited passage, Megarry J explained the benefit of opportunity as follows:[18]

---

12 (1990) 170 CLR 1.
13 Ibid, 23–4 (Mason CJ), 41 (Brennan J), 60 (Dawson J).
14 Ibid, 20–21 (Mason CJ), 40 (Brennan J), 55–6 (Dawson J). The majority judges did not adopt a clear approach to legitimate expectations.
15 Mason J held that substantive enforcement of expectations was inappropriate for judicial appointments, but perhaps not elsewhere: Ibid, 23.
16 *Minister of State for Immigration and Ethnic Affairs v Teoh* (1995) 183 CLR 273, 290–91 (Mason CJ and Deane J), 299, 302 (Toohey J), 313 (McHugh J); *SZBEL v Minister for Immigration and Multicultural and Indigenous Affairs* (2006) 228 CLR 152, 160 (Gleeson CJ, Kirby, Hayne, Callinan and Heydon JJ); *Minister for Immigration and Citizenship v SZJSS* (2010) 243 CLR 164, 177 (per curiam).
17 *Re Minister for Immigration and Multicultural Affairs; Ex parte Lam* (2003) 214 CLR 1, 21–6 (McHugh and Gummow JJ), 48 (Callinan J).
18 *John v Rees* [1970] Ch 345, 402.

the path of the law is strewn with examples of open and shut cases which, somehow, were not; of unanswerable charges which, in the event, were completely answered; of inexplicable conduct which was fully explained; of fixed and unalterable determinations that, by discussion, suffered a change.

Lord Hoffmann recently doubted this possibility, suggesting that:[19]

Most lawyers will have heard or read of or even experienced such cases but most will also know how rare they are. Usually, if evidence appears to an experienced tribunal to be irrefutable, it is not refuted.

Heydon J thought that both judges had exaggerated a little, but acknowledged that both could still be right.[20] Most cases that appear clear cut will, on close inspection, remain clear, but there can be exceptions. Some apparently clear cases become less so when a party is given a full and fair chance to put their own version of events and to also question the case put against them.

The procedures necessary to provide people that full and fair chance to put a case will vary with the circumstances of each case. A key requirement is notice, with sufficient detail to alert those notified to the key issues and adequate time to prepare a response.[21] Other procedural requirements can include rights to: an oral hearing, if there are issues best resolved in a face-to-face hearing, such as the credibility of witnesses;[22] legal representation, where the factual or legal issues are so complex that lay people would struggle to properly address them;[23] call and cross-examine witnesses, where there are disputed accounts of events or facts that are best resolved by directly hearing people;[24] the presence of an interpreter, where a person affected cannot adequately understand English;[25] adjournment of a hearing, if unexpected issues arise and cannot be easily managed.[26] Fairness might also require that some procedures *not* apply. An oral hearing, for example, might fluster a person without

---

19 *Secretary of State for the Home Department v AF (No 3)* [2010] 2 AC 269, 357.
20 *International Finance Trust Co Ltd v New South Wales Crime Commission* (2009) 240 CLR 319, 380–81.
21 *Kanda v Government of Malaya* [1962] AC 322, 337; *Gribbles Pathology (Vic) Pty Ltd v Cassidy* (2002) 122 FCR 78, 104.
22 *Robb & Dale v Chief Commissioner of Police* (2005) 23 VAR 244, 273.
23 *R v Secretary of State for the Home Department; Ex parte Tarrant* [1985] 1 QB 251, 285–6; *Drew v Attorney-General* [2002] 1 NZLR 58, 73–5.
24 That may be hard to achieve if decision-makers cannot force the attendance of unwilling witnesses.
25 *Attorney-General v Udompun* [2005] 1 3 NZLR 204, 225. Fairness may also require the translation of crucial written material: *X v Minister for Immigration and Multicultural and Indigenous Affairs* (2002) 116 FCR 319.
26 In *Minister for Immigration and Multicultural Affairs v Bhardwaj* (2002) 209 CLR 597, 611, Gaudron and Gummow JJ spoke of a failure to grant a 'reasonable request' for an adjournment.

legal qualifications and hamper their ability to put their case. If so, a chance to submit written information might provide a much fairer way for people to make their case. Such examples show that fairness can require different procedures within a hearing, but also different conceptions of what a hearing should be.

The benefits of a procedural conception of fairness are not limited to the apparently 'open and shut' cases Megarry J feared. Fair procedures can foster the legitimacy of decision-making. People are more likely to accept even unfavourable decisions if they accept the fairness of the process by which decisions are made.[27] They may also improve the quality of final decisions by ensuring that decisions are based upon the wider range of information provided by people who exercise procedural rights. These benefits can travel 'upstream' in the administrative process. Officials may review and revise the rules and policies governing decision-making in light of what they learn interacting with people who exercise procedural rights. These upstream benefits of fair procedures strengthen the legitimacy of the officials and agencies that make administrative decisions.[28] Some argue that the practical benefits of fair procedures are not the main purpose of natural justice. Advocates of the 'dignitarian' approach argue that fair procedures have inherent virtue.[29] According to this view, the intangible benefits of fairness are their greatest value.

Questions as to whether procedural fairness should be valued in its own right or for the benefits it provides reflect the instrumental and non-instrumental rationales the doctrine may be given.[30] Those who favour an instrumental rationale point to the benefits of fair procedures, such as increased accuracy in decision-making. Those who favour non-instrumental reasons stress other issues, such as greater participation and more respectful treatment. The requirements of procedural fairness can usually be supported by both instrumental and non-instrumental justifications, and most theorists rely on a combination of the two to justify the doctrine.[31]

The Chief Justice of Australia offered a broader explanation in a speech about the changing levels of protection courts have given to fairness over the last two centuries. French CJ stated that 'procedural fairness is alive and well today in Australia' and explained:

---

27 Psychologists describe this as 'the fair process effect'. See K van den Bos, H Wilke and E Lind, 'When Do We Need Procedural Fairness? The Role of Trust in Authority' (1998) 75 *Journal of Personality and Social Psychology* 1449.

28 T R S Allan, 'Procedural Fairness and the Duty of Respect' (1998) 18 *OJLS* 497, 501.

29 The classic administrative law account is J Mashaw, *Due Process in the Administrative State* (Yale University Press, 1985). See also L B Solum, 'Procedural Justice' (2004) 78 *Southern California LR* 181, 286–9. Lord Millett similarly argued that European civil law systems usually favour utilitarian justifications for fair procedures, but common law systems view procedural fairness as inherently valuable: 'The Right to Good Administration in European Law' [2002] *PL* 309, 312–13.

30 P P Craig, *Administrative Law* (7th ed, 2012) 341–2.

31 L B Solum, 'Procedural Justice' (2004) 78 *Southern California LR* 181.

> There is little doubt that the norms of procedural fairness reach well beyond the confines of the courtroom in judicial proceedings or judicial review of administrative decisions. They are important societal values applicable to any form of official decision-making which can affect individual interests. I do not think it too bold to say that the notion of procedural fairness would be widely regarded within the Australian community as indispensible to justice. If the notion of a 'fair go' means anything in this context, it means that before a decision is made affecting a person's interests, they should have the right to be heard by an impartial decision-maker.[32]

This reasoning confirms that the Australian conception of fairness remains a procedural one, at least for judges and lawyers. It also suggests that the courts are only one arena in which fairness is enforced. The notion that the right to fairness extends 'beyond the confines' of courts implies that courts remain ready to enforce that right but expect bureaucrats to observe it without prompting.

The suggestion of French CJ that the norms of fairness are 'important societal values' is more provocative because it implies the right to fair procedures may exist outside the law. That takes judges beyond their natural terrain. Many commentators criticise courts when they draw upon common law or interpretive principles, on the basis that such cases often lack coherent legal doctrine and do little more than provide a convenient cloak for judges to enforce personal rather than legal values.[33] Those problems are amplified if judges discard the language of the common law and refer openly to wider societal values, because such values are more contestable and something over which judges hold no special expertise or authority. More difficult questions would arise if the courts invoked their perception of social mores to limit the statutory powers granted by Parliaments to decision-makers. What expertise do courts hold to manage such tasks? Can notions such as 'important societal values' be expressed by judges any more clearly than Parliaments do so in legislation?

The interests to which natural justice applies

The duty to observe the rules of natural justice outside the courts was long limited to decision-makers required to 'act judicially'. This principle limited natural justice outside the courts to those processes with similarities to courts. It was swept away

---

32 R S French, 'Procedural Fairness: Indispensible to Justice?' (Sir Anthony Mason Lecture – University of Melbourne Law School Law Students' Society, 7 October 2010) 23.
33 These issues have provoked much debate in England. See T Poole, 'Questioning Common Law Constitutionalism' (2005) 25 *Legal Studies* 142.

by the Privy Council in *Ridge v Baldwin*,[34] which enabled a duty to observe the rules of natural justice to attach to administrative decision-making. New questions arose about the kinds of rights or interests to which this duty might apply. One was a threshold test about precisely what kinds of rights or interests were sufficient to attract the protection of natural justice. The courts have not devised a single definition of the interests used in the threshold test, but the breadth of interests now protected by natural justice confirms that the list is wide and perhaps still widening. Protected interests include immigration status,[35] business reputation,[36] personal reputation,[37] liberty[38] and financial interests.[39] Importantly, the range of protected interests includes benefits that people want, not simply what they already have. That means people who want something from governments, such as a visa or licence, can invoke the protection of natural justice when attempting to obtain that benefit.

Older cases distinguished between 'deprivation' and 'application' and assumed that the interest of those who had, but were then deprived of, a benefit was greater than those seeking the initial grant of a benefit. The classic example was a licence. Greater weight was given to the interest of people complaining of the non-renewal or revocation of a licence than to those whose initial application was refused. The High Court invoked this distinction in *FAI Insurances Ltd v Winneke*.[40] FAI had a licence to provide insurance in the lucrative Victorian workers' compensation insurance market, but was not given notice or a chance to put its views before that licence was revoked. The High Court held that the principles of natural justice required that FAI have a chance to put its case before any decision was made. That finding was greatly influenced by the perception that FAI had a stronger interest because of its existing licence. That approach necessarily placed less value on the interests of applicants for a new licence.[41]

The distinction between application and deprivation cases began to crumble soon after, in the seminal decision of *Kioa v West*.[42] In that case, a majority of the High Court held that an official denied procedural fairness by failing to put prejudicial

---

34 [1964] AC 40. The High Court followed suit in *Banks v Transport Regulation Board (Vic)* (1968) 119 CLR 222.
35 *Kioa v West* (1985) 159 CLR 550, 582 (Mason J), 632 (Deane J).
36 *Ainsworth v Criminal Justice Commission* (1992) 175 CLR 564; *Johns v Australian Securities Commission* (1993) 178 CLR 408.
37 *Annetts v McCann* (1990) 170 CLR 596, 608–09 (Brennan J).
38 *Bromby v Offenders' Review Board* (1990) 22 ALD 249.
39 *FAI Insurances Ltd v Winneke* (1982) 151 CLR 342; *Kioa v West* (1985) 159 CLR 550, 618–19.
40 (1982) 151 CLR 342.
41 Several judges did not exclude the possibility that hearings might not be required for 'new' applicants: 360–61 (Mason J), 376–7 (Aickin J), 394 (Wilson J).
42 (1985) 159 CLR 550. *Kioa* was seminal because of its view on the threshold test. It was also unexpected because the High Court had previously ruled the same power was not subject to natural justice in *Salemi v MacKellar (No 2)* (1977) 137 CLR 396 and *R v MacKellar; Ex parte Ratu* (1977) 137 CLR 461.

allegations to two Tongan citizens before deciding to deport them. Brennan J adopted a view of interests that clearly covered both application and deprivation cases when he held there was an 'almost infinite variety of interests which are protected by the principles of natural justice'.[43] His Honour reasoned that 'any interest possessed by an individual' should attract the protection of natural justice. He explained:[44]

> It is not the kind of individual interest but the manner in which it is apt to be affected that is important in determining whether the presumption [that natural justice be observed] is attracted.

If the important question is not what type of interest people have but the degree to which they might be affected, distinctions between 'application' and 'deprivation' cases have little value. So long as people can demonstrate that they may be affected more than an ordinary member of the public, they can establish sufficient affectation to attract the protection of natural justice.[45] The wider approach to the interests to which the protection of natural justice applies has the further advantage of casting aside technical concepts, such as the legitimate expectation, in favour of a single approach based upon affectation.[46]

The standing of Brennan J's approach remained unsettled following *Kioa*. Many cases referred to 'rights, interests and legitimate expectations', implying that some difference between those terms remained.[47] The issue was never squarely addressed. In *Annetts v McCann*,[48] for example, Mason CJ, Deane and McHugh JJ explained:

> It can now be taken as settled that, when a statute confers power upon a public official to destroy, defeat or prejudice a person's rights, interests or legitimate expectations, the rules of natural justice regulate the exercise of that power unless they are excluded by plain words of necessary intendment.

Such remarks confirmed that the duty to observe the requirements of fairness applied to a wide range of interests that might be affected by public officials but the continued use of several terms to describe those interests raised questions of whether any distinction should be drawn between 'rights, interests and legitimate

---

43 Ibid, 617.
44 Ibid, 619.
45 This reasoning may equate the level of affectation required to attract natural justice with standing, but the issues are distinct: *Griffith University v Tang* (2005) 221 CLR 99, 118 (Gummow, Callinan and Heydon JJ); *Rivers SOS Inc v Minister for Planning* (2009) 178 LGERA 347, [162].
46 (1985) 159 CLR 550, 617–18.
47 *Haoucher v Minister for Immigration and Ethnic Affairs* (1990) 169 CLR 648, 653 (Deane J); *Annetts v McCann* (1990) 170 CLR 596, 598 (Mason CJ, Deane and McHugh JJ).
48 (1990) 170 CLR 596, 598. Mason CJ, Dawson, Toohey and Gaudron JJ made similar remarks in *Ainsworth v Criminal Justice Commission* (1992) 175 CLR 564, 577.

expectations'. At the same time, the High Court never appeared troubled by the point in its growing migration jurisdiction. The issue was examined more directly in two recent such cases. In the *Offshore Processing Case*,[49] the High Court flatly rejected a submission by the Commonwealth that the Minister's decision to grant visa applications made by people offshore from the Australian mainland did not directly affect their rights or interests. The Commonwealth argued that the power was a discretionary one to confer a right. The High Court reasoned that any distinction:[50]

> between destruction, defeat or prejudice of a right, on the one hand, and a discretionary power to confer a right, on the other, proceeds from too narrow a conception of the circumstances in which an obligation to afford procedural fairness might arise.

The Commonwealth sought to revisit the issue soon after in *Kaur's* case.[51] It again invited the High Court to take a restrictive view of the interests to which natural justice applied. The High Court again rejected that invitation and held that the Minister's failure to engage in an exercise of exceptional discretionary powers to grant visas to asylum seekers was apt to adversely affect their interests.[52] Gummow, Hayne, Crennan and Bell JJ approved the following passage of Brennan J from *Kioa*:[53]

> There are interests beyond legal rights that the legislature is presumed to intend to protect by the principles of natural justice. It is hardly to be thought that a modern legislature when it creates regimes for the regulation of social interests – licensing and permit systems, means of securing opportunities for acquiring legal rights, schemes for the provision of privileges and benefits at the discretion of Ministers or public officials – intends that the interests of individuals which do not amount to legal rights but which are affected by the myriad and complex powers conferred on the bureaucracy should be accorded less protection than legal rights.

The approval of this passage does not simply reject a narrow conception of the interests to which the rules of fairness apply. It also confirms that natural justice protects a vast range of the privileges, benefits and advantages within the power of government officials. Perhaps then the phrase 'social interests' used by French CJ better describes that range of benefits. If so, his Honour's suggestion that natural justice embodies 'important societal values' can be understood as a logical one, even if we cannot be precisely sure what those values are.

---

49 (2010) 243 CLR 319.
50 Ibid, 353.
51 *Plaintiff S10/2011 v Minister for Immigration and Citizenship* (2012) 86 ALJR 1019.
52 Ibid, [66], [70].
53 *Kioa v West* (1985) 159 CLR 550, 616–17, quoted in *Plaintiff S10/2011 v Minister for Immigration and Citizenship* (2012) 86 ALJR 1019, [66].

The source of natural justice: common law, statute or both?

Although *Kioa* signalled the start of a simpler and broader test for implying requirements of natural justice, the leading judgments of Mason and Brennan JJ yielded apparently different approaches to the scope of fairness and the decisions to which the threshold test applied. On this latter issue, Mason J explained the test as one applicable to 'the making of administrative decisions'.[54] Brennan J limited his analysis to 'statutory powers'.[55] A test applicable to administrative decisions is wider and can encompass decisions made under prerogative or other non-statutory powers. Uncertainty about the type of decisions to which the threshold test applied was clarified by the acceptance that prerogative and non-statutory powers are amenable to supervisory review.[56]

The apparent differences between Mason and Brennan JJ about the source of any duty to observe the rules of fairness were much messier and only recently resolved. Mason J held that the scope of the duty to observe the requirements of natural justice was:[57]

> a common law duty to act fairly, in the sense of according procedural fairness, in the making of administrative decisions which affect rights, interests and legitimate expectations, subject only to the clear manifestation of a contrary statutory intention.

Brennan J held that any duty to observe the requirements of fairness arose from an implied legislative intent rather than the common law.[58] Subsequent cases interpreted this approach in crude terms, by which the duty to act fairly was solely referable to legislative intent. Brennan J had in fact made clear that legislative intent was to be determined by reference to common law principles of fairness and justice. His Honour suggested that the application and content of the rules of natural justice greatly depended on whether the legislature intended that observance of the rules of fairness be a condition for the valid exercise of the power in

---

54 Ibid, 584.
55 Ibid, 611.
56 This trend began when *Kioa* was decided: *Council of Civil Service Unions v Minister for the Civil Service* [1985] AC 374; *Blyth District Hospital Inc v South Australian Health Commission* (1988) 49 SASR 501, 509; *Minister for Arts Heritage and Environment v Peko-Wallsend Ltd* (1987) 15 FCR 274; *Victoria v Master Builders Association (Vic)* [1995] 2 VR 121.
57 Ibid, 584. Deane J stated a test similar to Mason J: at 632–3.
58 Ibid, 609–11. His Honour's emphasis on statutory intent led him to reject judicially created doctrines used to configure the threshold test, such as 'legitimate expectations': 617–18.

question. He acknowledged that legislative intent was difficult to ascertain when not stated clearly. Brennan J explained that the judicial task of deciphering an implied condition that the exercise of a statutory power required observance of the rules of fairness involved both statutory construction and common law interpretive principles. This explanation went as follows:[59]

> When the statute does not expressly require that the principles of natural justice be observed, the court construes the statute on the footing that 'the justice of the common law will supply the omission of the legislature'. The true intention of the legislation is thus ascertained.

The 'Mason/common law' approach initially attracted more support,[60] but the view of Brennan J slowly gained ascendency as the observance of natural justice was accepted as an implied 'condition' or 'limitation' for the valid exercise of statutory powers.[61] This approach was endorsed by a unanimous High Court in *Saeed v Minister for Immigration and Citizenship*.[62] The Court cited the passage just quoted, and added:[63]

> The implication of the principles of natural justice in a statute is therefore arrived at by a process of construction. It proceeds upon the assumption that the legislature, being aware of the common law principles, would have intended that they apply to the exercise of a power of the kind [of very broad range of interests] referred to in *Annetts v McCann*.

Saeed's case also made clear that the duty to observe natural justice and related interpretive assumptions are deeply embedded in the common law.[64] Subsequent decisions of the High Court have stressed that the foundations of natural justice cannot be viewed as a simple choice between legislative intention and the

---

59 *Kioa v West* (1985) 159 CLR 550, 609.
60 *Attorney-General (NSW) v Quin* (1990) 170 CLR 1, 57–8 (Dawson J); *Annetts v McCann* (1990) 170 CLR 596, 598 (Mason CJ, Deane and McHugh JJ).
61 *Re Refugee Review Tribunal; Ex parte Aala* (2000) 204 CLR 82, 89 (Gleeson CJ), 100–01, 109 (Gaudron and Gummow JJ), 131 (Kirby J), 141–3 (Hayne J); *Re Minister for Immigration and Multicultural Affairs; Ex parte Lam* (2003) 214 CLR 1, 27–8 (McHugh and Gummow JJ), 48 (Callinan J); *SAAP v Minister for Immigration and Multicultural and Indigenous Affairs* (2005) 228 CLR 294, 323 (McHugh J), 354 (Hayne J, Kirby J agreeing); *Applicant VEAL of 2002 v Minister for Immigration and Multicultural and Indigenous Affairs* (2005) 225 CLR 88, 93 (Gleeson CJ, Gummow, Kirby, Hayne and Heydon JJ).
62 (2010) 241 CLR 252.
63 Ibid, 258. A similar approach is used to interpret legislation which affects hearing rights in the courts: *International Finance Trust Co Ltd v New South Wales Crime Commission* (2009) 240 CLR 319, 349 (French CJ).
64 Ibid, 257, 259.

common law. In the *Offshore Processing Case*, the High Court appeared more concerned about the broad approach taken by *Kioa* to the scope of the duty to act fairly, rather than possible differences about the basis of that duty. The Court concluded that it was 'unnecessary to consider whether identifying the root of the obligation remains an open question or whether the competing views would lead to any different result'.[65] It also acknowledged that the requirements of natural justice could be excluded 'by plain words of necessary intendment'.[66] The result is a strong presumption that the rules of natural justice apply to the exercise of statutory powers, and an acceptance that those rules can be excluded or limited by sufficiently clear legislation. The important issue is now not the source of any duty to act fairly but the legislative and factual context, the combination of which determine the scope and content of the requirements of natural justice, and their exclusion or limitation.

That reasoning was confirmed in *Kaur's* case, where Gummow, Hayne, Crennan and Bell JJ suggested that continued questions about the basis of the duty to act fairly served no purpose. They explained:[67]

> the common law usually will imply, as a matter of statutory interpretation, a condition that a power conferred by statute upon the executive branch be exercised with procedural fairness to those whose interest may be adversely affected by the exercise of that power. If the matter be understood in that way, a debate whether procedural fairness is to be identified as a common law duty or as an implication from statute proceeds upon a false dichotomy and is unproductive.

The courts did not end the supposed Mason/Brennan divide by choosing one over the other. They melded the two. The duty to observe natural justice is anchored in the common law, perhaps much deeper than Mason J anticipated. The common law also informs the interpretive process which determines the scope of powers and whether their exercise requires observance of the rules of fairness. Statutory interpretation proceeds on the assumption that Parliaments know and accept these principles. Parliaments may influence or even displace these principles, so long as they do so with sufficiently clear language. Questions of whether natural justice applies and what it requires are both heavily influenced by a blend of common law and statutory influences that should not be separated.

---

65 *Offshore Processing Case* (2010) 243 CLR 319, 352.
66 Ibid, 352, citing *Annetts v McCann* (1990) 170 CLR 596, 598.
67 *Plaintiff S10/2011 v Minister for Immigration and Citizenship* (2012) 86 ALJR 1019, [97] ('*Kaur's* case').

Exclusion of procedural fairness

As the courts have expanded the duty to observe the requirements of natural justice they have acknowledged the ability of Parliaments to limit or exclude those rules by legislation. That strikes a useful middle ground, in which the courts draw upon the common law to supplement or clarify legislative powers but yield to suitably clear legislation. It arguably also moderates the judicial expansion of the doctrine by preserving the ability of legislatures to limit or reverse that expansion and recognising the central role of legislative intention in deciding the application and content of natural justice. The theory of legislative exclusion or limitation has become very difficult to achieve.

The possibility of the legislative exclusion of natural justice was regularly accepted by the courts during the late 1960s and the 1970s.[68] The High Court then adopted a stricter standard which stressed that legislation to exclude natural justice required 'clear manifestation' of that intention,[69] or 'plain words of necessary intendment'.[70] The High Court affirmed that strictness in *Saeed v Minister for Immigration for Citizenship*,[71] where it held that legislation of 'irresistible clearness' was required to exclude a fundamental principle such as natural justice. *Saeed* arguably continued the approach of cases which had stressed that the important question was whether legislation, as construed by the courts, limits or extinguishes the obligation to accord natural justice.[72] But the suggestion that natural justice was not simply a common law principle but a fundamental one, hints that it is more deeply embedded, and therefore more difficult to displace, than was previously thought.

Saeed affirmed another important obstacle to legislative exclusion of natural justice, namely that implication of the duty to observe natural justice is a process of statutory interpretation which assumes that Parliaments are aware of common law principles such as natural justice and intend that they apply to the exercise

---

[68] *Brettingham-Moore v Warden, Councillors and Electors of Municipality of St Leonards* (1969) 121 CLR 509; *Pearlberg v Varty* [1972] 1 WLR 534 (HL); *Furnell v Whangarei High Schools Board* [1973] AC 660 (PC); and *Salemi v MacKellar (No 2)* (1977) 137 CLR 396.
[69] *Kioa v West* (1985) 159 CLR 550, 584 (Mason J).
[70] *Annetts v McCann* (1990) 170 CLR 596, 598 (Mason CJ, Deane and McHugh JJ). See also *Johns v Australian Securities Commission* (1993) 178 CLR 408, 470 (McHugh J); *Jarratt v Commissioner of Police for New South Wales* (2005) 224 CLR 44, 56 (Gleeson CJ), 61 (McHugh, Gummow and Hayne JJ), 88 (Callinan J), 92 (Heydon J).
[71] (2010) 241 CLR 252, 259 (French CJ, Gummow, Hayne, Crennan and Kiefel JJ), citing *Potter v Minahan* (1908) 7 CLR 277, 304.
[72] *Re Minister for Immigration and Multicultural Affairs; Ex parte Miah* (2001) 206 CLR 57, 84 (Gaudron J); and *Re Refugee Review Tribunal; Ex parte Aala* (2000) 204 CLR 82, 101 (Gaudron and Gummow JJ).

of statutory powers.[73] The difficulty for legislatures is that they may never be completely sure what fairness requires until the courts have pronounced upon on the issue. If the requirements of fairness continue to evolve at common law, Parliaments will always struggle to establish or predict those requirements with sufficient clarity to exclude them.

Exclusion of procedural fairness by necessary implication

Natural justice can be excluded by implication, but that possibility remains difficult. The problem was usefully illustrated by *Annetts v McCann*,[74] where the parents of a deceased youth wished to make (through their lawyer) closing submissions to a coronial inquiry into their son's death. The relevant legislation was enacted decades earlier. It enabled coroners to grant interested people the right to legal representation and to cross-examine witnesses, but was silent on closing submissions. The High Court held that the enactment of some procedural rights was insufficient to establish that Parliament had intended to preclude the implication of further rights. This reasoning assumed that Parliament would have addressed the issue in clear terms. That was unlikely because the statute was passed when the duty to act fairly was very narrow and the implication of procedural rights, such as making closing submissions, was inconceivable. The High Court therefore searched for an intention to exclude rights that Parliament had almost certainly thought were inapplicable.

The judicial search for legislative intention will always have an element of artifice, and the problem becomes more acute as legislation ages. There is no easy solution. If courts interpret legislation according to the law as it stood at the time of enactment, administrative law would adopt a level of originalism that constitutional law advocates of that doctrine would envy. Perhaps the solution is to ask whether the application of natural justice, or particular features of the hearing rule, are inconsistent with the proper operation of the statute as it stands at the time the court considers the issue.[75]

The High Court gave little general guidance in *Kaur's* case,[76] when it accepted that the rules of natural justice did not apply to several provisions in the *Migration*

---

73 *Saeed v Minister for Immigration and Citizenship* (2010) 241 CLR 252, 258–9.
74 (1990) 170 CLR 596.
75 M Aronson and M Groves, *Judicial Review of Administrative Action* (Lawbook, 5th ed, 2013) 7.260.
76 *Plaintiff S10/2011 v Minister for Immigration and Citizenship* (2012) 86 ALJR 1019.

Act 1958 (Cth). The relevant powers conferred the Minister with exceptional powers to grant visas to claimants who had unsuccessfully applied through normal channels. Only then could these exceptional powers be exercised. If they were, the Minister had to table in Parliament his reasons why the grant of a visa was in the public interest. French CJ and Kiefel J held that these unusual and highly discretionary powers 'stand apart' from the otherwise closely regulated powers in the Act.[77] Gummow, Hayne, Crennan and Bell JJ also accepted that these powers differed 'radically' from others in the Act.[78] Any legislative intention to exclude natural justice from this regime was faint at best, but one can speculate why the court decided fairness should not apply. The exceptional powers could only be exercised over people who had unsuccessfully sought visas through conventional avenues, all of which were subject to the requirements of fairness. Perhaps the High Court felt that one round of fairness provided a sufficient minimum of fairness that need not be repeated. That possible explanation indicates that the wider context of statutory powers can be as important as the language in which they are expressed.

Express statutory procedures as a form of exclusion

Many statutes include procedural requirements which might otherwise be imposed by the rules of natural justice, such as to give notice or invite submissions. Statutes rarely indicate what effect the inclusion of some requirements is intended to have on the implication of others. An elementary application of legal maxims such as '*expressio unius est exclusio alterius*' ('express mention of one thing excludes another') and '*expressum facit cessare tacitum*' ('express mention of certain things excludes anything not mentioned') might suggest that natural justice was not intended to apply to require observance of any procedures not expressly mentioned.[79] Such maxims have little value since *Annetts v McCann*, where the High Court confirmed that the crucial question was whether a statute contained a clear legislative intention to exclude all or parts of natural justice.[80] The Court stressed that intention could not be inferred 'from the presence in the statute of rights which are commensurate with some of the rules of natural justice'.[81]

---

77 Ibid [30].
78 Ibid, [86].
79 Such reasoning was invoked in *Brettingham-Moore v Warden, Councillors and Electors of Municipality of St Leonards* (1969) 121 CLR 509; and *Salemi v MacKellar (No 2)* (1977) 137 CLR 396, 402 (Barwick CJ), 421 (Gibbs J).
80 *Annetts v McCann* (1990) 170 CLR 596, 598–9 (Mason CJ, Deane and McHugh JJ).
81 Ibid, 598.

The High Court subsequently made clear the point that was implicit in *Annetts*, which was that use of maxims in questions about natural justice requires great care.[82] Maxims alone cannot establish an intention to exclude natural justice. After all, the apparent silence of the legislature is usually ambiguous and could be interpreted as acceptance that the courts can and will invoke common law principles to impose appropriate procedures.[83]

The principle that the enactment of some procedural rights does not preclude the implication of others can be overcome by suitably clear legislation, but the divergent results of cases confirm that the issue depends heavily on statutory context. Some cases have rejected arguments that a detailed procedural regime displaces the requirements of fairness on all matters, holding that the statutory regime may be conclusive on some issues but capable of supplementation by the common law on others.[84] Others have held that detailed procedures governing one aspect of fairness, such as notice, inform rather than displace the requirements of fairness on that issue.[85] Still others have held that legislation governing a particular issue showed an intention to exclude further procedures on that matter.[86]

The stakes are raised when legislation appears to provide an exhaustive code of procedures. Some cases have accepted that 'exhaustive codes' are exactly that.[87] Others implied further hearing rights, if they found the code unfair.[88] Other cases simply held a code was not intended to be exhaustive.[89] The courts sometimes appear mindful of pragmatic reasons when they accept that suitably drafted statutory codes exclude further requirements of fairness. In planning schemes, for example, codes may provide the best way to manage the many competing stakeholders

---

82 *Ainsworth v Criminal Justice Commission* (1992) 175 CLR 564, 575 (Mason CJ, Dawson, Toohey and Gaudron JJ).
83 *Baba v Parole Board of New South Wales* (1986) 5 NSWLR 338, 347 (Mahoney JA) and 349 (McHugh JA); *Re Minister for Immigration and Multicultural Affairs; Ex parte Miah* (2001) 206 CLR 57, 93, 96 (McHugh J), 115 (Kirby J); and *R (Roberts) v Parole Board* [2005] 2 AC 738, [29] (Lord Bingham).
84 *Upham v Grand Hotel (SA) Pty Ltd* (1999) 74 SASR 557 at 567–574 (Doyle CJ and Bleby J).
85 *Telstra Corp Ltd v Australian Competition and Consumer Commission (No 2)* (2007) 240 ALR 135, [221]–[250].
86 *Harris v Great Barrier Reef Marine Park Authority* [2000] FCA 603; *Riverside Nursing Care Pty Ltd v Bishop* (2000) 100 FCR 519, 521–2.
87 *Brettingham-Moore v Warden, Councillors and Electors of Municipality of St Leonards* (1969) 121 CLR 509; and *Baba v Parole Board of New South Wales* (1986) 5 NSWLR 338.
88 *Wiseman v Borneman* [1971] AC 297, 308 (Lord Reid), 309 (Lord Morris), 312 (Lord Guest), 317, 320 (Lord Wilberforce); *Huntley v Attorney-General for Jamaica* [1995] 2 AC 1 (PC). These cases hinted that statutory codes could be presumed to meet the requirements of natural justice, until the court was satisfied otherwise. No clear rule to this effect arose because cases considered whether the code was enacted with the clear intention of excluding natural justice, rather than whether it was fair: *Twist v Randwick Municipal Council* (1976) 136 CLR 106 at 109–10 (Barwick CJ).
89 *J v Lieschke* (1987) 162 CLR 447, 460–61; *Upham v Grand Hotel (SA) Pty Ltd* (1999) 74 SASR 557; *Hill v Green* (1999) 48 NSWLR 161; *State of South Australia v Slipper* (2004) 136 FCR 259.

and issues that regularly arise.[90] The exhaustive nature of codes is sometimes also accepted in 'multi-stage' processes.[91] Such codes may strike a balance between granting procedural rights (at some stage) while ensuring the decision-making process remains manageable.

Statutory or exhaustive codes have a tortured history in migration law. *Re Minister for Immigration and Multicultural Affairs; Ex parte Miah*[92] considered the detailed procedures enacted for refugee decision-making after energetic judicial use of the implication rule. The Explanatory Memorandum which accompanied the Bill containing the code explained that it was a 'procedural code' to 'replace the uncodified principles of natural justice with clear and fixed procedures'. A majority of the High Court held the legislation did not display a sufficiently clear intention to exclude procedural fairness.[93] That finding enabled Mr Miah to rely upon the implication principle in his claim that the Refugee Review Tribunal denied him natural justice by failing to grant him a chance to put his views on adverse materials in a way not covered by the code.

Miah's case confirmed that legislative text is far more important than extraneous materials, such as second reading speeches and explanatory materials, in determining legislative intention. Gaudron J noted that the decisive question was whether the legislation manifested a sufficiently clear intention to exclude the common law duty to observe natural justice, not whether it constituted a code.[94] This focus on substance rather than form meant that Parliament's use of terms such as 'code' had little significance. McHugh J held that inclusion of the word 'code' was 'too weak a reason to conclude that Parliament intended to limit the requirements of natural justice'.[95] His Honour also noted the seeming contradiction that the procedures in issue were included in a section with a heading which stated they were part of a 'code of procedure for dealing fairly, efficiently and quickly' with applications. The Commonwealth was therefore arguing that fairness was removed from a code that was stated to deal 'fairly' with claims.[96]

---

90 *Brooks v Minister for Planning and Environment* (1988) 68 LGRA 91, 99–100; *Grollo Australia Pty Ltd v Minister for Planning and Urban Growth and Development* [1993] 1 VR 627; *Vanmeld Pty Ltd v Fairfield City Council* (1999) 46 NSWLR 78, 113–15.
91 *Huntley v Attorney-General for Jamaica* [1995] 2 AC 1 (PC); *Buonopane v Secretary, Department of Employment, Education and Youth Affairs* (1998) 87 FCR 173.
92 (2001) 206 CLR 57.
93 *Re Minister for Immigration and Multicultural Affairs; Ex parte Miah* (2001) 206 CLR 57, 84–5 (Gaudron J), 95–8 (McHugh J), 111–15 (Kirby J). Gleeson CJ and Hayne J dissented, holding that the code comprehensively covered the obligation to invite submissions on adverse material but no other issues: 73–5.
94 *Re Minister for Immigration and Multicultural Affairs; Ex parte Miah* (2001) 206 CLR 57, 83–4. That point was made about privative clauses in *Plaintiff S157/2002 v Commonwealth* (2003) 211 CLR 476, 499 (Gaudron, McHugh, Gummow, Kirby and Hayne JJ).
95 Ibid, 95.
96 Ibid.

The revised code considered by the High Court in *Saeed v Minister for Immigration and Citizenship*[97] was no longer described as such. Several sub-divisions of the Act contained detailed procedures governing decision-making, including one which stated that the procedures in each were 'taken to be an exhaustive statement of the requirement of the natural justice hearing in relations to the matters it deals with'.[98] Mr Saeed applied for a visa while outside Australia (an offshore visa) rather than while in Australia (an onshore visa). That point was crucial because the High Court held that the section operated to wholly exclude the hearing rule for the 'matters' to which it referred, which were onshore visas. But those 'matters' did not include applications for offshore visas. Accordingly, the statutory procedures were not an exhaustive statement of natural justice for the offshore visa Mr Saeed applied for, so he was able to rely on common law interpretive principles to claim procedural benefits additional to those specified in the sub-division.

Conclusion

The prevailing approach to natural justice makes the doctrine one of wide application. It applies to an extremely wide range of decisions or actions of public officials which may affect people's interests. The variety of interests to which natural justice extends is also broad. These conclusions are elementary and fundamental. They are elementary because they are now so well settled as to provide the starting point in any analysis of the requirements of fairness. They are fundamental because they are deeply entrenched and difficult to displace.

If the territory over which natural justice applies has been comprehensively broadened and secured, one might ask what the next step for natural justice could be. Any movement to a more substantive conception of fairness seems unlikely because Australian courts have devised principles to justify and secure their supervisory jurisdiction which preclude precisely that. A substantive conception of fairness is only one casualty in the wider demarcation of the boundaries of Australian judicial review.

Many other issues remain unclear. One is why courts protect the duty to observe natural justice so fervently. It cannot be simply because the duty is deeply entrenched. After all, it was entrenched by the courts. Any suggestion that courts protect natural justice because it is so fundamental simply begs the question of why they make it so. The courts may not rush to examine that question because any detailed explanation of why natural justice is so fundamental, or exactly what makes a hearing fair or unfair, might draw the courts to move beyond examining fair procedure to fair outcomes.

---

97 (2010) 214 CLR 252.
98 *Migration Act 1958* (Cth), ss 51A(1), 97A(1), 118A(1), 127A(1), 357A(1), 422B(1).

11
HOLDING GOVERNMENT TO ITS WORD: LEGITIMATE EXPECTATIONS AND ESTOPPELS IN ADMINISTRATIVE LAW

Greg Weeks[*]

[*] My thanks to Mark Aronson, John Basten, Leah Grolman and Matthew Groves for comments, and to Sophie Duxson for her excellent research assistance.

Introduction

We make, and break, promises to one another all the time. As every law student knows, to break one's promise does not always result in exposure to legal liability. This may sometimes be as a result of changing times: for instance, the common law action for breach of promise to marry was commonly used in the 19th century but by 1976 had been abolished altogether in Australia, by statute.[1] By contrast, the contractual doctrine of consideration has been required to make room for the power of non-contractual promises and representations in commercial,[2] litigious[3] and other private law circumstances through the development of promissory estoppel.

Sometimes, the nature of the promise or the circumstances in which it was made[4] will be significant but, usually, the identity of the promisor is the most relevant of those circumstances. This contention supports the recent statement by Joseph Raz that 'most undertakings and agreements are much less formally created, arising not so much out of explicit acts of commitment as out of the implied meaning and consequences of an interaction over time'.[5] Rarely is the identity of the promisor of greater significance than when it is the government. The conundrum posed by Raz – 'if promises are binding, if they are cogent ways for people to bind themselves, there must be a reason to do as one promised'[6] – should be presumptively reversed where government is the promisor, given its size and power, not to mention the usual understanding that such power as government has is held as though 'on trust' for the citizenry.[7] In short, where it may be open to discussion whether and why an individual should keep his or her promises, government should need a compelling reason *not* to do so (or alternatively to provide compensation for its failure to do so).

Government has greater capacity to make promises and to create expectations than individuals have.[8] This is simply an extension of the observation that we will generally follow instructions clearly being made by an organ of the state which we

---

1 This cause of action was abolished by the *Marriage Amendment Act 1976* (Cth), s 23. See now *Marriage Act 1961* (Cth), s 111A.
2 *Waltons Stores (Interstate) Ltd v Maher* (1988) 164 CLR 387.
3 *Commonwealth v Verwayen* (1990) 170 CLR 394 ('*Verwayen*').
4 See by way of analogy the law regarding negligent misrepresentation, eg in *Mutual Life & Citizens' Assurance Co Ltd v Evatt* (1968) 122 CLR 556.
5 J Raz, 'Is There a Reason to Keep Promises?' (Columbia Public Law/Oxford Legal Studies Research Paper No 62/2012, 2012) <http://papers.ssrn.com/sol3/papers.cfm?abstract_id=2162656>.
6 Ibid.
7 P Finn, 'Public Trusts, Public Fiduciaries' (2010) 38 *Federal Law Review* 335; R J French, 'Public Office and Public Trust' (Speech delivered at the Seventh Annual St Thomas More Forum Lecture, Canberra, 22 June 2011).
8 The legal effect of such expectations is much harder to identify than the expectations themselves.

would otherwise be likely to challenge or ignore. Consider the uniformed police officer who directs you to drive away from your intended route. Few of us would not comply with such an instruction; absent the uniform and overt trappings of the state, the situation changes radically.[9] Despite this amplified capacity, public law traditionally attached no significance to whether or not administrative action on the part of a public authority would disappoint an expectation on the part of an affected party. Even if that expectation was encouraged by the public authority, this was a matter that could be dealt with only in private law. An estoppel could not be enforced against the public authority such as to limit its discretion or cause it to act contrary to statute.[10]

The origin of legitimate expectations

Lord Denning MR first coined the term 'legitimate expectation' in *Schmidt v Secretary of State for Home Affairs*,[11] at a time when English courts 'were developing the modern law with respect to standing and the range of circumstances which attracted the rules of natural justice'.[12] This is a trite observation which has been made at the beginning of countless discourses on the subject of legitimate expectations, and yet it is an observation which is somewhat misleading. Geo Quinot has noted that '[t]he type of representations creating expectations that has come to be protected by the doctrine of legitimate expectation in South African law has been protected as such in EU law at least since the *Châtillon* case of 1966'.[13] *Schmidt v Home Secretary* was decided some years after *Châtillon*, although this is not to say that it was directly influenced by German or EU law.[14] Lord Denning himself disclaimed any such

---

9 This state of affairs has not translated into police officers owing greater responsibility or being liable in tort simply as a factor of having greater power to intervene: *Stuart v Kirkland-Veenstra* (2009) 237 CLR 215.
10 G Weeks, 'Estoppel and Public Authorities: Examining the Case for an Equitable Remedy' (2010) 4 *Journal of Equity* 247, 248–50.
11 *Schmidt v Secretary of State for Home Affairs* [1969] 2 Ch 149, 170–71 ('*Schmidt v Home Secretary*').
12 *Re Minister for Immigration and Multicultural Affairs; Ex parte Lam* (2003) 214 CLR 1, 16 [47] (McHugh & Gummow JJ) ('*Lam*').
13 G Quinot, 'Substantive Legitimate Expectations in South African and European Administrative Law' (2004) 5 *German Law Journal* 65, 68. The case in question is *Case 54/65: Compagnie des Forges de Châtillon, Commentry et Neuves-Maisons v High Authority of the ECSC* [1966] ECR 185, ('*Case 54/65, Châtillon*').
14 M Cohn, 'Pure or Mixed? The Evolution of Three Grounds of Judicial Review of the Administration in British and Israeli Administrative Law' (2012) 6 *Journal of Comparative Law* 86, 99.

influence, stating that 'it came out of my own head and not from any continental or other source'.[15] The concept used in *Châtillon* is certainly comparable to Lord Denning's 'legitimate expectation' but, naturally enough, those words were not used to describe it.[16] Christopher Forsyth concluded that:[17]

> Lord Denning both invented the concept as far as English law is concerned and he gave the name 'legitimate expectations' to the similar, but not identical, principle that operates in European Law.

It is worthwhile to note that Lord Denning's purpose in *Schmidt* was simply to extend the coverage of procedural fairness to a deportee with an unexpired visa, and was also used as nothing more than a mechanism for expanding procedural fairness in the subsequent case of *Breen v Amalgamated Engineering Union*.[18] As a concept which confers merely procedural rights (in the manner initially intended by Lord Denning), 'legitimate expectation' was never objectionable, in my view, but now has little work to do in any case,[19] since the threshold test of the duty to accord procedural fairness in Australia is extremely broad.[20] Indeed sometimes, in relation to domestic bodies[21] and in the so-called 'club cases',[22] it is broader than the coverage of judicial review's remedies.

The term 'legitimate expectation' has been judicially criticised as a 'fiction'.[23] Barwick CJ icily conceded that it was an 'eloquent phrase', adding (with wholly evident disapproval for its legal purpose), 'I am bound to say that I appreciate its literary quality better than I perceive its precise meaning and the perimeter of its application'.[24] Brennan J later concluded in *Kioa v West* that the term 'legitimate expectation' added nothing to the concepts of rights and interests for the purposes of determining to whom a duty of procedural fairness is owed,[25] noting that

---

15 C F Forsyth, 'The Provenance and Protection of Legitimate Expectations' (1988) 47 *Cambridge Law Journal* 238, 241.
16 Cf S Schønberg, *Legitimate Expectations in Administrative Law* (Oxford University Press, 2000), 118. The words 'legitimate expectation' were subsequently borrowed from English to describe the European concept; see Forsyth, Ibid, 242.
17 C F Forsyth, 'Lord Denning and Modern Administrative Law' (1999) 14 *Denning Law Journal* 57, 62.
18 *Breen v Amalgamated Engineering Union* [1971] 2 QB 175, 191.
19 *Applicant NAFF of 2002 v Minister for Immigration and Multicultural and Indigenous Affairs* (2004) 221 CLR 1, 23 [68] (Kirby J) ('*NAFF v MIMIA*'). See also *Lam* (2003) 214 CLR 1, 16 [47]; 27–8 [81]–[83] (McHugh & Gummow JJ); 45–6 [140] (Callinan J).
20 At common law, this has been so since the High Court's decision in *Kioa* (1985) 159 CLR 550.
21 See J R S Forbes, *Justice in Tribunals* (3rd ed, 2010) ch 3.
22 M Aronson and M Groves, *Judicial Review of Administrative Action* (Lawbook, 5th ed, 2013) [7.410].
23 *Teoh* (1995) 183 CLR 273, 310–14 (McHugh J); cf *NAFF v MIMIA* (2004) 221 CLR 1, 22 [67] (Kirby J).
24 *Salemi (No 2)* (1977) 137 CLR 396, 404.
25 *Kioa* (1985) 159 CLR 550, 617–22.

the appellant's infant child could scarcely be said to have any 'expectation' of a particular outcome.

Professor Aronson has commented that:[26]

> the 'expectation' was often something that the subject had not entertained in fact. Rather, the subject could more accurately be said to have 'naturally'[27] or 'reasonably' assumed a certain course of conduct on the decision-maker's part or taken it for granted.[28] It is submitted that in such cases, it might be more straightforward to talk of 'reasonable assumptions'. Where the decision-maker actually created the relevant expectation in the subject's mind (for example, by promising a certain course of conduct), then it is strictly superfluous to refer to a 'legitimate expectation'. Its legitimacy is not relevant. Its existence is indeed relevant, but only because the decision-maker was its cause. The focus should be on whether the decision-maker's conduct in making and then breaching the expectation was fair in the circumstances.

There can be no doubt that 'legitimate expectation' is a particularly infelicitous piece of judicial expression, but this has caused much more angst than it need have. Administrative law is a field particularly rich in misleading and inaccurate descriptors: the 'improper purpose' ground has nothing to do with propriety; relevance is not the test of whether the 'relevant considerations' and 'irrelevant considerations' grounds have been established; and the ground of *Wednesbury* unreasonableness has nothing to do with 'reasonableness' as that term is used in common parlance; to name just three. Somehow, sufficient people understand these terms of art that doctrinal coherence is able to be maintained. The same ought to have been true of 'legitimate expectations', particularly after *Kioa* extended the obligation to provide procedural fairness to applicants with no legal rights whatsoever. Whether the expression 'legitimate expectation' is considered 'misleading'[29] or as a vital, but rarely utilised, supplement to establishing a right to procedural fairness in the absence of affected 'rights and interests'[30] now makes very little difference. In Australian legal circles, that conclusion is only valid when the focus is on the purely procedural utility of the phrase.[31] As we will see, in most other jurisdictions, such a caveat is unnecessary and the distinction makes very little difference because establishing a legitimate expectation inevitably leads to a substantive remedy.

---

26 M Aronson, 'Private Bodies, Public Power and Soft Law in the High Court' (2007) 35 *Federal Law Review* 1, 5.
27 *Lam* (2003) 214 CLR 1, 30–32 (McHugh & Gummow JJ).
28 Ibid, 45–7 (Callinan J).
29 *Kioa* (1985) 159 CLR 550, 617 (Brennan J).
30 Mason, above n 12, 106–7.
31 *Quin* (1990) 170 CLR 1, 39 (Brennan J).

Perhaps it is the very awkwardness of expression identified with the phrase 'legitimate expectation' which has seen the public law doctrine in England for *enforcing* 'legitimate expectations' often described as 'substantive unfairness'. It is certainly fair to say that whatever controversy continues to surround the term 'legitimate expectation' is now focused predominantly on the suitability of giving such expectations substantive effect, rather than on whether they are a suitable guide to the circumstances in which procedural fairness is owed.[32]

The following section will analyse the approach to the substantive enforcement of legitimate expectations in several jurisdictions. In doing so, it will not distinguish between the term 'legitimate expectation' and the concept of 'substantive unfairness'. Some authors take pains to distinguish the doctrine of legitimate expectations from that of the 'broader principle' of substantive unfairness;[33] others equate them absolutely.[34] Without wanting to give the impression that I prefer one approach to the other, this chapter will, for reasons of facility, use the two terms interchangeably.

The modern law of legitimate expectations

I have chosen to focus on the legitimate expectations regimes in three countries: the UK, Canada and Australia. These are by no means the only jurisdictions in which the concept of legitimate expectations has taken hold.[35] Indeed, legitimate expectations are protected beyond the limits of the common law world; in particular, they are 'deeply rooted in continental [European] law'.[36] The German concept of *Vertrauensschutz*[37] predates the EU law on this subject and, as subsequently

---

32 Cf the *dictum* of Gummow, Hayne, Crennan and Bell JJ that 'the phrase "legitimate expectation" when used in the field of public law either adds nothing or poses more questions than it answers and thus is an unfortunate expression which should be disregarded': *Kaur v Minister for Immigration and Citizenship* (2012) 86 ALJR 1019, 1033 ('*Kaur v MIAC*').
33 See, eg, R Moules, *Actions Against Public Officials: Legitimate Expectations, Misstatements and Misconduct* (Sweet and Maxwell, 2009) 43.
34 See, eg, C Stewart, 'Substantive Unfairness: a New Species of Abuse of Power?' (2000) 28 *Federal Law Review* 617; M Groves, 'Federal Constitutional Influences on State Judicial Review' (2011) 39 *Federal Law Review* 399, 427.
35 In regard to New Zealand, see R Flanagan, 'Legitimate Expectation and Applications: An Outdated and Unneeded Distinction' (2011) 17 *Canterbury Law Review* 283.
36 Cohn, above n 14, 98.
37 See the detailed discussion in Forsyth, 'Provenance and Protection of Legitimate Expectations' (1988) 47 *CLJ* 238, 243–5.

became the case in the EU, successful applicants are able to obtain substantive remedies.[38] Cohn notes that:[39]

> Importantly, the law recognizes that some State actions, not necessarily expressed in a formal obligation, may give rise to enforceable claims of a substantive nature, ensuing from the limitation of their revocation.

England

One of the consequences of Lord Denning's development of the 'legitimate expectations' doctrine was that the limitations imposed by the courts, on arguments that public authorities should be estopped from departing from their representations and undertakings, were rendered less unfair.[40] The degree to which that observation is true has varied from country to country. In Australia, for example, a promise to a prisoner threatened with deportation that the decision-maker will contact his children's carer before deciding whether to deport him would, if not complied with, result at most in the disappointed prisoner's legitimate expectation that the promise would be kept, giving him a right to be heard before the decision to deport him was finally made.[41]

In the UK, however, the doctrine of legitimate expectations has developed to have a more substantial conceptual overlap with the private law doctrine of estoppel. Lord Hoffmann's *dictum* in *Reprotech*, that 'public law has already absorbed whatever is useful from the moral values which underlie the private law concept of estoppel and the time has come for it to stand upon its own two feet'[42] seemed to indicate clearly that the protections that estoppel affords to disappointed expectations resulting from broken promises had become part of the UK law of legitimate expectations.[43] Additionally, this has been treated as a welcome development inasmuch as the public law doctrine of legitimate expectations is more sensitive, and tailored to, the particular context of public law.[44]

---

38 Quinot, above n 13, 68.
39 Cohn, above n 14, 98.
40 Aronson and Groves, above n 22, [7.200].
41 However, it may not even result in that; see *Lam* (2003) 214 CLR 1.
42 *R v East Sussex County Council; Ex parte Reprotech (Pebsham) Ltd* [2003] 1 WLR 348, 66 [35] ('*Reprotech*').
43 Sir Anthony Mason has commented that Lord Hoffmann's *dictum* 'suggests that the role of private law estoppel in English public law, to the extent to which a private law estoppel would not be *ultra vires* the statute, is now subsumed in the doctrine of legitimate expectation, notably in the substantive protection of legitimate expectation, a concept which has no counterpart in Australian public law': A Mason, 'The Place of Estoppel in Public Law' in M Groves (ed), *Law and Government in Australia* (Federation Press, 2005) 160, 179.
44 *R (on the application of Bhatt Murphy (a firm)) v The Independent Assessor* [2008] EWCA Civ 755, [40]; *Reprotech* [2003] 1 WLR 348, [6] (Lord Mackay of Clashfern), [33]–[35] (Lord Hoffmann).

English courts spent a long time moving towards allowing substantive enforcement of legitimate expectations in public law.[45] Lord Denning was particularly prominent in this process, which can be traced back 20 years before the Court of Appeal's decision in *Schmidt v Home Secretary*.[46] In *Robertson v Minister of Pensions*,[47] Denning J considered the plight of a claimant who had placed reliance on the legality of a letter from the War Office, even though the respondent Minister was the proper repository of power. He said:

> The War Office did not refer him to the Minister of Pensions. They assumed authority over the matter and assured the appellant that his disability had been accepted as attributable to military service. He was entitled to assume that they had consulted any other departments that might be concerned, such as the Ministery [sic] of Pensions, before they gave him the assurance. He was entitled to assume that the board of medical officers who examined him were recognised by the Minister of Pensions for the purpose of giving certificates as to attributability. Can it be seriously suggested that, having got that assurance, he was not entitled to rely on it?[48]

Two years later, in *Howell v Falmouth Boat*, the House of Lords overturned the finding in *Robertson* in fairly short order, re-establishing the orthodoxy that an estoppel cannot be enforced against a public authority where it would have the effect of compelling the authority to act *ultra vires*.[49] This point is really no more than an extension of the principle that an estoppel cannot compel an unlawful act either by a public authority or a private actor, which is a matter of public policy.[50] Lord Denning had not given up, though, stating in *Wells*:[51]

> Now I know that a public authority cannot be estopped from doing its public duty, but I do think it can be estopped from relying on technicalities…

By 'technicalities', his Lordship was referring to an 'irregular' procedure by which applicants for planning permission were actively misled. Relying on *Robertson*, Lord Denning considered that the public authority could 'waive' such irregularities

---

45 See the account in C Stewart, 'Substantive Unfairness' in M Groves and HP Lee (eds), *Australian Administrative Law* (Cambridge University Press, 2007) 280, 283–5.
46 Aronson and Groves, above n 22, [6.630].
47 *Robertson v Minister of Pensions* [1949] 1 KB 227.
48 Ibid, 232.
49 *Howell v Falmouth Boat Construction Co*. [1951] AC 837, 845 (Lord Simonds) ('*Howell v Falmouth Boat*'). See also *Minister for Immigration and Ethnic Affairs v Kurtovic* (1990) 21 FCR 193, 211–16 ('*Kurtovic*'); K R Handley, *Estoppel by Conduct and Election* (Sweet and Maxwell, 2006), 22–3.
50 Handley, above n 49, 296.
51 *Wells v Minister of Housing and Local Government* [1967] 1 WLR 1000, 1007 (Lord Denning MR) ('*Wells v Housing Minister*').

and thereby 'render valid that which would otherwise be invalid'.[52] *Wells* has never been overturned, but there is a long and clearly articulated judicial preference for Russell LJ's 'very powerful' dissent,[53] such that '*Wells* is now considered highly dubious'.[54]

This did not prevent Lord Denning from citing his own speech in *Wells* with approval in *Lever Finance*,[55] in which case the Court of Appeal's decision had the effect of further extending the possibility of a statutory authority being estopped from exercising statutory power as a result of representations made by its officers.[56] This was immediately recognised as standing directly in opposition to the previous decision of a Divisional Court in *Southend-on-Sea*,[57] which counsel for the plaintiffs in *Lever Finance* claimed was 'wrongly decided'[58] but counsel for the defendants argued was 'very important'.[59] Lord Denning was not moved, stating that *Southend-on-Sea* and cases like it 'must now be taken with considerable reserve'.[60] His Lordship's basis for this *dictum* was that a public authority should be bound by a representation by one of its officers 'just as much as a private concern would be'. But, of course, this is the point of cases like *Southend-on-Sea* and *Maritime Electric*[61] – the defendant public authorities in those cases cannot be compared to a 'private concern' because they were exercising statutory power, which private concerns generally do not. To allow the representation of an officer not only to bind the public authority, but bind it to operate contrary to its empowering statute, is a bold step and one that cannot be justified by the brief judgments in *Lever Finance*.

The final case which was significant for Lord Denning's continued contribution to the issue of public law estoppel was *HTV Limited v Price Commission*.[62] In *HTV*, Lord Denning held that the limits to a public body's powers included consideration of the fairness requirements inherent in the doctrine of estoppel.[63] Although Lord

---

52 Ibid.
53 *Reprotech* [2003] 1 WLR 348, 357 [30] (Lord Hoffmann); *Western Fish Products Ltd v Penwith District Council* [1981] 2 All ER 204, 223 (Megaw LJ) ('*Western Fish*').
54 Aronson and Groves, above n 22 [6.630] (fn 386).
55 *Lever (Finance) Ltd v Westminster Corp* [1971] 1 QB 222, 230 (Lord Denning MR, Megaw LJ agreeing), 233 (Sachs LJ) ('*Lever Finance*').
56 See J M Evans, 'Delegation and Estoppel in Administrative Law' (1971) 34 *Modern Law Review* 335, 335.
57 *Southend-on-Sea Corporation v Hodgson (Wickford) Ltd* [1962] QB 416 ('*Southend-on-Sea*'); A W Bradley, 'Estoppel – Statutory Discretion – Informal Delegation' (1971) 29 *Cambridge Law Journal* 3, 3.
58 *Lever Finance* [1971] 1 QB 222, 226.
59 Ibid, 225–6.
60 Ibid, 230.
61 *Maritime Electric Co Ltd v General Dairies Ltd* [1937] AC 610 ('*Maritime Electric*').
62 *HTV Ltd v Price Commission* [1976] ICR 170 (Lord Denning MR, Scarman and Goff LJJ agreeing as to the result) ('*HTV*').
63 Aronson and Groves, above n 22, [6.630].

Denning again cited *Robertson*, *Wells* and *Lever Finance*, his approach had become subtly different:[64]

> It has been often said, I know, that a public body, which is entrusted by Parliament with the exercise of powers for the public good, cannot fetter itself in the exercise of them. It cannot be estopped from doing its public duty. *But that is subject to the qualification that it must not misuse its powers*: and it is a misuse of power for it to act unfairly or unjustly towards a private citizen when there is no overriding public interest to warrant it.

Ultimately, the finding that there was generally no capacity for a public authority to break its promises where a private sector body in the same position would be subject to an action seeking to enforce an estoppel was approved by the House of Lords.[65] In *Preston*, Lord Templeman stated that he saw:[66]

> no reason why the taxpayer should not be entitled to judicial review of a decision taken by the commissioners if that decision is unfair to the taxpayer because the conduct of the commissioners is equivalent to a breach of contract or a breach of representation.

In his influential judgment in *Kurtovic*, Gummow J objected strongly to the analogy drawn in both *Preston* and *HTV* between statutory grants of power and the performance of contracts,[67] and this has represented the orthodox view in Australia since. In England, however, the place of estoppel in public law continued until the House of Lords in *Reprotech* took the view that the time had come to replace it with the purpose-built public law doctrine of substantive enforcement of legitimate expectations.

Reprotech came after the arrival of the revolutionary moment for developing a public law remedy in England for failure to adhere to a representation. That moment occurred in *Coughlan*,[68] which made a leap forward, where previous cases had

---

64 *HTV* [1976] ICR 170, 185 (emphasis added).
65 Including by Lord Steyn, who cited *HTV* to support his comment that: 'It is important to bear in mind that the breach involved a deliberate policy decision by the Home Office not to comply with the public law duty. This amounts to an abuse of power and ought to preclude the Home Secretary from relying on his unlawful conduct until notification has taken place. While generally an estoppel cannot operate against the Crown, it can be estopped when it is abusing its powers': *R (Anufrijeva) v Secretary of State for the Home Department* [2004] 1 AC 604, 623 [35].
66 *R v Inland Revenue Commissioners; Ex parte Preston* [1985] AC 835, 866–7, cf *Kurtovic* (1990) 21 FCR 193, 220 (Gummow J). See Weeks, above n 10, 256–7.
67 *Kurtovic* (1990) 21 FCR 193, 210 (Gummow J).
68 *R v North and East Devon Health Authority; Ex parte Coughlan* [2001] QB 213 ('*Coughlan*'). The doctrine of substantive legitimate expectations has since flourished in lower courts but has not been expressly approved by the House of Lords or the Supreme Court, although it

made slow, incremental steps, to hold that the holder of a legitimate expectation may sometimes be entitled to substantive protection of that expectation.[69] The facts of *Coughlan* were 'perfect' for the Court of Appeal to make that leap,[70] but they also demonstrate the shortcomings of looking to the unfairness of a particular outcome to determine whether there has been abuse of power sufficient to invalidate the decision of a public authority.[71]

Ms Coughlan was a severely disabled patient who, along with other similarly disabled patients, was moved to a purpose-built facility run by the National Health Service called Mardon House. These patients were told that this would be their home for life or, alternatively, for as long as they chose. However, within five years, the NHS had made the policy decision that it would close Mardon House and transfer the care of Ms Coughlan to the defendant local health authority. Prior to making this decision, the patients were consulted and allowed to voice their opposition to the proposed change. When the decision was ultimately made to close Mardon House despite the promise made to the patients, Ms Coughlan sought judicial review of the decision and was successful, at first instance, in obtaining an order of certiorari to quash the decision to close Mardon House.

In the Court of Appeal, Lord Woolf MR (with whom Mummery and Sedley LJJ agreed) dismissed the appeal brought by the North and East Devon Health Authority. In doing so, he outlined a taxonomy of three 'categories' of legitimate expectations, and the kinds of remedies which a court exercising a judicial review function would be able to provide in response,[72] the first two of which are utterly uncontroversial.[73] The first category would apply in circumstances where the court requires that the public authority 'bear in mind its previous policy or other representation, giving it the weight it thinks right, but no more, before deciding whether to change course', and would review the decision on the *Wednesbury*

---

has been at least impliedly approved; see, eg, *R (Lumba) v Secretary of State for the Home Department; R (Mighty) v Secretary of State for the Home Department* [2012] 1 AC 245, 275 [69] (Lord Dyson) ('*Lumba v Home Secretary*').

69 The cases in which the possibility of substantive enforcement of legitimate expectations had developed prior to *Coughlan* included: *R v Board of Inland Revenue; Ex parte MFK Underwriting Agencies Ltd* [1990] 1 WLR 1545 (Bingham LJ and Judge J, '*MFK Underwriting*'); *R v Devon County Council; Ex parte Baker* [1995] 1 All ER 73, 88 (Simon Brown LJ) (Court of Appeal); and *R v Ministry of Agriculture, Fisheries, Food; Ex parte Hamble (Offshore) Fisheries* [1995] 2 All ER 714 (Sedley J).

70 Stewart, above n 45, 286.

71 See M Groves, 'The Surrogacy Principle and Motherhood Statements in Administrative Law' in L Pearson, C Harlow and M Taggart (eds), *Administrative Law in a Changing State* (Hart, 2008) 71, 90–97. Groves describes many of the English cases which use the concept of abuse of power as a determinant of validity as 'result in search of a principle': Ibid, 92.

72 *Coughlan* [2001] QB 213, 241–2.

73 M Groves, 'Substantive Legitimate Expectations in Australian Administrative Law' (2008) 32 *Melbourne University Law Review* 470, 478.

standard only.[74] The second category would apply where a promise or practice of a public authority 'induces a legitimate expectation of, for example, being consulted before a particular decision is taken'. Here the court will 'require *the opportunity for consultation* to be given unless there is an overriding reason to resile from it'.[75] The adequacy of reasons given for changing the relevant policy would be assessed by the court itself, 'taking into account what fairness requires', but generally the opportunity for consultation would exhaust the relevance of the expectation.[76]

It was the third category which caused such a revolution in English public law. Lord Woolf stated that, in this category:[77]

> Where the court considers that a lawful promise or practice has induced a legitimate expectation of a *benefit which is substantive*, not simply procedural, authority now establishes that here too the court will in a proper case decide whether to frustrate the expectation is so unfair that to take a new and different course will amount to an abuse of power. Here, once the legitimacy of the expectation is established, the court will have the task of weighing the requirements of fairness against any overriding interest relied upon for the change of policy.

The court held that *Coughlan* fell into this third category as an 'unjustified breach of a clear promise given by the health authority's predecessor to [Ms] Coughlan that she should have a home for life at Mardon House, [which] constituted unfairness amounting to an abuse of power by the health authority',[78] and consequently upheld the order of certiorari granted in the court below to remedy the 'unfairness' to Ms Coughlan. This took the effect of substantively enforcing her legitimate expectation that Mardon House would be her 'home for life' rather than allowing her to have, for example, an additional opportunity to address the defendant public authority as to why Mardon House ought not to be closed.

There are numerous issues at play here. The first is that Ms Coughlan was treated rather badly by the NHS, which had promised her a 'home for life' and duly reneged upon that offer within five short years. Another is that she could not have

---

74 See *Associated Provincial Picture Houses Ltd v Wednesbury Corporation* [1948] 1 KB 223 ('*Wednesbury*').
75 In support of this point, Lord Woolf MR cited *Ng Yuen Shiu* [1983] 2 AC 629.
76 See Groves, above n 73, 478.
77 *Coughlan* [2001] QB 213, 242 (original emphasis).
78 Ibid, 260. Laws LJ later said that 'abuse of power has become, or is fast becoming, the root concept which governs and conditions our general principles of public law. It informs all three categories of legitimate expectation cases as they have been expounded by this court in [*Coughlan*]': *R (on the application of Beghie) v Department of Education & Employment* [2000] 1 WLR 1115,1129 ('*Begbie*'). Nonetheless, it is a phrase which has great potential to confuse: see *Lumba v Home Secretary* [2012] 1 AC 245, 275 [69] (Lord Dyson); *Lam* (2003) 214 CLR 1, 37 [119] (Hayne J).

obtained an equitable remedy, since on the facts she would not have been able to demonstrate detrimental reliance on the NHS' representation, in the sense that she had not altered her position on the faith of it.[79] Lord Woolf made the bald assertion that '[t]he promise was relied on by Miss Coughlan',[80] but with respect, it is not clear from the facts that Ms Coughlan had any genuine alternative to the course of action which she in fact adopted on the faith of the NHS' representation.[81] This issue is more significant than was appreciated in *Coughlan*, or, arguably, since.

In *MFK*, Bingham LJ appreciated that a promise per se was insufficient to bind a public authority to deliver a substantive outcome and that the capacity to grant a remedy would additionally have required detrimental reliance. His Lordship indicated that what was required was something along the lines of the standard for establishing a negligent misrepresentation in tort:[82]

> The doctrine of legitimate expectation is rooted in fairness. But fairness is not a one-way street. It imports the notion of equitableness, of fair and open dealing, to which the authority is as much entitled as the citizen. The revenue's discretion, while it exists, is limited. Fairness requires that its exercise should be on a basis of full disclosure ... it would not be reasonable for a representee to rely on an unclear or equivocal representation. Nor, I think, on facts such as the present, would it be fair to hold the revenue bound by anything less than a clear, unambiguous and unqualified representation.

Lord Woolf said that Bingham LJ's approach 'makes no formal distinction between procedural and substantive unfairness'[83] and, to the extent that it concentrates on the outcome of 'fairness', that much is true. However, Bingham LJ's conclusion, that '[i]f in private law a body would be in breach of contract in so acting or estopped from so acting a public authority should generally be in no better position', indicates that he had in mind at least some substantive operation for a finding of unfairness.[84]

---

79 *Kurtovic* (1990) 21 FCR 193, 196 (Neaves J), 218 (Gummow J). The Full Federal Court rejected Kurtovic's argument that the Minister had, in effect, promised not to deport him if he was convicted of no further criminal offences. See Weeks, above n 10, 252–9.
80 *Coughlan* [2001] QB 213, 253.
81 See Aronson and Groves, above n 22, [6.640].
82 *MFK Underwriting* [1990] 1 WLR 1545, 1569–70. The passage ending with the first sentence of the passage cited above was quoted by Lord Woolf at *Coughlan* [2001] QB 213, 247. His Lordship did not engage with the rest of the passage cited here.
83 *Coughlan* [2001] QB 213, 247.
84 *MFK Underwriting* [1990] 1 WLR 1545, 1569. His Lordship probably also intended to indicate how the requisite level of precision for a representation should be gauged. As Binnie J later commented, '[g]enerally speaking, government representations will be considered sufficiently precise for purposes of the doctrine of legitimate expectations if, had they been made in the context of a private law contract, they would be sufficiently certain to be capable of enforcement': *Canada (Attorney General) v Mavi* [2011] 2 SCR 504, [69] ('*Mavi*').

Where the Court of Appeal in *Coughlan* differed from the Divisional Court in *MFK* is that it did not seek to determine whether or not the public body's unfairness should result in a substantive public law remedy as a result of analogous reasoning of this sort, nor even by assessing the limits of the public body's discretion. Rather, the Court of Appeal held that the disappointment of Ms Coughlan's legitimate expectation, which is to say the fairness of the *outcome* to Ms Coughlan, should be assessed against the public interest more generally.[85]

This is an entirely new and different task from that which had been entered into when public law made a place for the equitable doctrine of estoppel. Furthermore, it is hard to imagine that courts would be able to apply such a test objectively, being a comparison of the claimant's immediate losses consequent on his or her disappointed expectations against the abstract notion of the public interest, in *Coughlan* the interest that the public had in the NHS being run efficiently and cost effectively.[86] That sort of comparison is inevitably weighted against the defendant public body, since it will always be difficult to articulate an 'overriding public interest' to justify the breach of that body's promise.[87]

Where there is no clear guidance about the elements which will ground a finding of abuse of power,[88] there is always a chance that such a finding is not made upon only objective considerations. It is this that has recently caused Professor Forsyth to make the 'sombre reflection' that:[89]

> There is so much uncertainty that there is a real danger that the concept of legitimate expectation will collapse into an inchoate justification for judicial intervention. It sounds so benign – who could be against the protection of legitimate expectations? – but, it seems to me, as sometimes interpreted, the concept often gives little guidance and plays at best a rhetorical role.... The point is that unless the concept is clear, it will be unable to do any of the hard work of deciding whether judicial intervention is apt in any particular case.

---

85 *Coughlan* [2001] QB 213, 246–7.
86 'Where one is dealing with a promise made by an authority a major part of the problem is that it is often not adequate to look at the situation purely from the point of view of the disappointed promisee who comes to the court with a perfectly natural grievance': *R (Bibi) v Newham London Borough Council* [2002] 1 WLR 237, [35].
87 *Coughlan* [2001] QB 213, 254.
88 There has been growing academic disquiet about the meaning (or lack thereof) of the phrase 'abuse of power', which had been employed by Lord Woolf MR in *Coughlan* (at QB 242 [57]) and which Laws LJ subsequently attempted to explain in *R (Abdi and Nadarajah) v Secretary of State for the Home Department* [2005] EWCA Civ 1363, [66]–[69] in terms which relied heavily on a subjective judicial 'sense of fairness' and drew 'no distinction between procedural and substantive expectations'.
89 C Forsyth, 'Legitimate Expectations Revisited' [2011] 16 *Judicial Review* 429, 429.

While the doctrine of substantive enforcement of legitimate expectations is now entrenched in English law, there is some cause for concern that it is not developing along principled lines.

Canada

In *Mount Sinai*,[90] the Supreme Court of Canada rejected the variation of the legitimate expectation doctrine articulated in *Coughlan*, albeit neither as forcefully nor as completely as the High Court of Australia was later to do.[91] Specifically, the Supreme Court rejected the notion that it should be the judiciary, rather than the Minister, which determines whether the public interest overrides substantive enforcement of a legitimate expectation.

The Mount Sinai Hospital Centre was originally established as a facility treating patients suffering from tuberculosis but, in the 1950s, it changed the nature of its services to encompass general respiratory care and began to provide both long-term and short-term care facilities. The government, which provided the Centre's funding, was aware throughout of the facilities and services which were being offered. By 1984, when the Centre was involved in negotiations with the Ministry of Health and Social Services to move to Montreal, it held a permit to provide 107 long-term care beds, but had for 10 years instead provided 57 long-term care beds and 50 intermediary or short-term care beds. The Minister promised the Centre that, once it moved to Montreal, its permit would be altered to reflect the reality of its practice. However, once the Centre had moved to Montreal in 1991, the Minister responded to its formal request to have its permit altered by stating that the Centre would have to continue to operate under the old, unaltered permit. The Centre was not given a further chance to make submissions before this decision was communicated. The government continued to fund the Centre's short-term services, even though they fell outside the scope of the permit. Although unsuccessful at first instance, the Centre succeeded on appeal.

The majority judgment in the Supreme Court, given by Bastarache J, relied essentially upon the interpretation that the Minister's statutory discretion had already been exercised,[92] and consideration of whether that exercise of discretion

---

90 *Mount Sinai Hospital Centre v Quebec (Minister of Health and Social Services)* [2001] 2 SCR 281, ('*Mount Sinai v Quebec*').
91 The Supreme Court's refutation of *Coughlan* was insufficient to allay completely the suspicions of the Australian High Court, in which McHugh and Gummow JJ later commented that the 'Supreme Court of Canada appears to have gone further in allowing...a doctrine [of substantive legitimate expectations] than either Australia or the United States': *Lam* (2003) 214 CLR 1, 22 (fn 49).
92 *Mount Sinai v Quebec* [2001] 2 SCR 281, [101]–[107].

had been validly reversed,[93] therefore making it unnecessary to decide whether the doctrines of substantive unfairness or public law estoppel had any application. Binnie J, whose judgment was also delivered on behalf of McLachlin CJ, preferred to view the relationship (and, crucially, the communications) between the Minister and the respondent Hospital Centre as the vital issue.[94] Like Bastarache J, his Honour found for the Hospital Centre and joined in dismissing the Minister's appeal, leaving in place the order of mandamus issued by the Court of Appeal for Quebec requiring the Minister to issue the permit which had been promised to the Hospital Centre.

Binnie J reached this conclusion without resort to the reasoning used in *Coughlan*, although his Honour did so on a ground that is, in Australia, very nearly as contentious:[95] *Wednesbury* unreasonableness.[96] Moreover, upon closer inspection it becomes clear that Binnie J did not entirely reject a judicial role in determining whether a private interest overrides the public interest,[97] because his Honour was still prepared for the courts to intervene to correct executive decision-making. The difference between *Mount Sinai* and *Coughlan* was that the Court's intervention in the former depended not on the existence of a legitimate expectation but on the Court finding that the decision of the Minister or other executive officer was patently unreasonable (which is to say unreasonable in the *Wednesbury* sense).

Binnie J was at pains to deny this, stating that:[98]

> Where Canadian law parts company with the developing English law is the assertion, which lies at the heart of the *Coughlan* treatment of *substantive* unfairness, of the centrality of the judicial role in regulating government policy.

His Honour quoted Lord Woolf's *dictum* from *Coughlan* that the doctrine of legitimate expectation would only sound in substantive relief 'if there is an overriding public interest. Whether there is an overriding public interest is a question for the court'.[99] Binnie J then stated that:[100]

---

93 Ibid, [108]–[114].
94 Ibid, [4].
95 See G Weeks, 'The Expanding Role of Process in Judicial Review' (2008) 15 *Australian Journal of Administrative Law* 100, 107–11.
96 Binnie J in fact found that the Minister's decision 'was "patently unreasonable" in terms of the public interest': *Mount Sinai v Quebec* [2001] 2 SCR 281, [64].
97 G Huscroft, 'From Natural Justice to Fairness: Thresholds, Content, and the Role of Judicial Review' in C Flood and L Sossin (eds), *Administrative Law in Context* (Emond Montgomery, 2nd ed, 2012) 147, 169–70.
98 *Mount Sinai v Quebec* [2001] 2 SCR 281, [62] (original emphasis).
99 *Coughlan* [2001] QB 213, 249.
100 *Mount Sinai v Quebec* [2001] 2 SCR 281, [63]. His Honour cited the circumstances in which 'unreasonableness' had been found in *Baker v Canada (Minister of Citizenship and Immigration)* [1999] 2 SCR 817.

In Canada, at least to date, the courts have taken the view that it is generally the Minister who determines whether the public interest overrides or not. The courts will intervene only if it is established that the Minister's decision is patently unreasonable in the sense of irrational or perverse or (in language adopted in *Coughlan*) 'so gratuitous and oppressive that no reasonable person could think [it] justified'.[101]

However, the distinction that Binnie J made in the passage extracted above is really one of labelling rather than of substance. His Honour rejected the explicit language and overtly interventionist approach of *Coughlan*, but at the same time allowed for judicial intervention into executive decision-making using the more flexible language of unreasonableness, albeit not under a process which involves a detailed balancing of competing claims.

This was immensely clever because it did not look as if Binnie J was rending Canada's constitutional principles asunder in order to garner ever more power to the courts. His Honour was swift to note that '[a]t the high end [the English cases on legitimate expectations] represent a level of judicial intervention in government policy that our courts, to date, have considered inappropriate in the absence of a successful challenge under the *Canadian Charter of Rights and Freedoms*'.[102] Binnie J did not argue for intervention in these terms, but ensured that a court following his decision in *Mount Sinai* could nonetheless use the flexibility of the *Wednesbury* unreasonableness doctrine to intervene where the court thought it appropriate to do so.

Could Australia follow this reasoning to allow for a level of judicial intervention notwithstanding the constitutional problems identified in *Lam*? As with so many innovations identified in this chapter, it might, but the High Court probably won't.[103] Many of the constitutional considerations which caused the High Court to conclude that it is impossible for Australia to adopt the doctrine of substantive unfairness also led it to restrict *Wednesbury* unreasonableness to 'absurd' decisions (which ensured that the ground rarely succeeded). However, there have been recent hints that Australia's formerly inflexible stance on the correct approach to *Wednesbury* unreasonableness is relaxing somewhat, with a High Court majority commenting that:[104]

---

101 *Coughlan* [2001] QB 213, 247. Lord Woolf MR was referring to the decision of Lord Russell of Killowen CJ in *Kruse v Johnson* [1898] 2 QB 91. His Lordship made it clear, however, that these descriptors all now fall within the meaning of *Wednesbury* unreasonableness.
102 *Mount Sinai v Quebec* [2001] 2 SCR 281, [27].
103 The remark in *Lam* that the 'Supreme Court of Canada appears to have gone further in allowing ... a doctrine [of substantive legitimate expectations]' than Australia clearly took account of this expansionist employment of *Wednesbury*; see *Lam* (2003) 214 CLR 1, 22 (fn 49) (McHugh & Gummow JJ).
104 *Minister for Immigration and Citizenship v Li* (2013) 87 ALJR 618, 639 [74] (Hayne, Kiefel and Bell JJ) (*'MIAC v Li'*).

an obviously disproportionate response [by a decision-maker] is one path by which a conclusion of unreasonableness may be reached.

Australia

Contrary to the way that the law had developed in the UK prior to *Reprotech*, it is uncontroversial in Australia that a representation made on behalf of a public authority that it will perform an act that it has neither statutory nor executive power to perform will be substantively unenforceable,[105] particularly since an official cannot even have ostensible authority which is inconsistent with his or her statutory limitations.[106] Refusal to give substantive effect to an estoppel against a public authority is based on the same principle which holds that soft law cannot be given binding force in Australia because decision-makers are given their discretion by Parliament, and it may not be restricted other than by the terms of the statutory grant of power and the procedural requirements of administrative law.[107]

The proposition, orthodox in the UK, that 'the requirements for legitimate expectation in public law [should] stand separately from private law doctrines such as estoppel...being more sensitive, and tailored to, the particular context of public law'[108] is, on the other hand, far from orthodox in Australia. Indeed, to the extent that the principles of substantive unfairness require a court to weigh substantive unfairness done to an individual against an 'overriding interest' in a public authority being able to disappoint a legitimate expectation, such a process is impossible for an Australian as a matter of public law, for the reasons stated by the High Court in *Lam*.[109] The English proposition, of course, indicates more than that Australia is out of step with the development of the English doctrine of substantive enforcement of legitimate expectations; there is very little point in Australia to talk of such a doctrine standing apart from the equitable doctrine of estoppel, since public law estoppel has been all but a dead letter in Australia for over 20 years.[110]

---

[105] Just as an estoppel cannot give a court or a tribunal jurisdiction that is not permitted by statute: Handley, above n 49, 299. Public authorities are, of course, still subject to estoppel where they are exercising powers held in common with natural persons.

[106] *Attorney-General for Ceylon v AD Silva* [1953] AC 461, 479. See also *Western Fish* [1981] 2 All ER 204.

[107] Further, this merely procedural effect of soft law can also be avoided with sufficient warning that the decision-maker will disregard it: *Lam* (2003) 214 CLR 1.

[108] *R (Grimsby Institute) v Chief Executive of Skills Funding* [2010] EWHC 2134 (Admin) [90].

[109] Sir Anthony Mason has also suggested that it would take a 'revolution in Australian judicial thinking' for a doctrine of substantive unfairness to be recognised: Mason, above n 12, 108.

[110] Although it remains possible that the doctrine retains some life: Weeks, above n 10, 252–9.

Many of the objections which have latterly been raised against the doctrine of substantive unfairness are essentially the same as those which had previously prevented the development of an Australian doctrine of public law estoppel. For example, there is tension between the doctrine of substantive legitimate expectations and the rule against fettering discretions,[111] which mirrors the tension between an estoppel and a statutory discretion of a public character.[112] The *Southend-on-Sea* principle, which has never endured serious doubt in Australia,[113] prevents a court from enforcing an estoppel which would have the effect of fettering a statutory discretion. Indeed, *Southend-on-Sea* and *Maritime Electric*[114] have essentially been treated as axiomatic in Australia for several decades. Those who have argued, as a matter of principle, that the equivalent position in public law should be otherwise have also been wholly unsuccessful.

As is so frequently the case, the conclusive factor in Australia is constitutional.[115] The fact that the separation of powers doctrine, which defines and confines judicial power in equal measure,[116] is entrenched within the *Constitution* has a way of settling many arguments of principle before they start. This is in marked contrast to the English experience. The classic modern exposition of the Australian legal principle is that of Brennan J in *Quin*,[117] which explained the constitutional role of the courts and the necessary limits of that role.[118]

Brennan J's judgment in *Quin* is cited regularly in the Australian High Court, and its constitutional standing is never really contested despite the fact that it does not once 'expressly mention the *Constitution* or a single provision of it'.[119] It is, however, treated as a sufficiently accurate statement of Australia's constitutional structure that its fundamental inconsistency with the Court of Appeal's reasoning

---

111 P Sales and K Steyn, 'Legitimate Expectations in English Public Law: An Analysis' [2004] *Public Law* 564.
112 *Southend-on-Sea* [1962] 1 QB 416, 423 (Lord Parker CJ).
113 In *Kurtovic*, Ryan J stated (at FCR 200) that a dissenting judgment of Windeyer J in which his Honour had distinguished *Southend-on-Sea* was 'significant'; see *Brickworks Limited v The Council of the Shire of Warringah* (1963) 108 CLR 568, 577.
114 Australian courts have also consistently applied *Maritime Electric* [1937] AC 610.
115 See M Taggart, '"Australian Exceptionalism" in Judicial Review' (2008) 36 *Federal Law Review* 1.
116 Groves, above n 73, 507.
117 *Quin* (1990) 170 CLR 1, 35–6. Brennan J further stated that 'if an express promise be given or a regular practice be adopted by a public authority, and the promise or practice is the source of a legitimate expectation, the repository is bound to have regard to the promise or practice in exercising the power, and it is unnecessary to enquire whether those factors give rise to a legitimate expectation. But the court *must stop short of compelling fulfilment* of the promise or practice unless the statute so requires or the statute permits the repository of the power to bind itself as to the manner of the future exercise of the power': Ibid, 40 (emphasis added).
118 Chapter 1.
119 Groves, 'Federal Constitutional Influences' (2011) 39 *Federal Law Review* 399, 402.

in *Coughlan* is as persuasive as the more strident denunciations of *Coughlan* (in *Lam* and subsequently) that Australian and English jurisprudence on the doctrine of substantive unfairness are unlikely to align in the short term. Lord Woolf's *dictum* that a court can weigh 'the requirements of fairness against any overriding interest relied upon for [a] change of policy'[120] is considered highly problematical. An Australian court exercising judicial review cannot simply 'cure administrative injustice', regardless of whether such a course would outweigh the benefits of valid administrative action, because the merits of a decision fall outside its jurisdiction.[121] Similar constitutional reasoning was applied to the concept of abuse of power, as considered by Laws LJ.[122]

Quin was only one of two Australian decisions in 1990 which rejected claims based on public law estoppel. The second was the decision of the Full Federal Court in *Kurtovic*.[123] Those cases are the last notable ones to have considered the concept of public law estoppel in Australia. They are generally viewed as standing against its availability, but neither case in fact completely rejected the possibility of an estoppel being raised against a public authority. To say that the 'clear message of *Kurtovic* and *Quin* is a judicial discomfort'[124] with the principle that an estoppel can *never* be 'raised to prevent the performance of a statutory duty or hinder the exercise of a statutory discretion'[125] possibly states the matter too emphatically, given that there has not been an Australian case since *Kurtovic* and *Quin* which has considered the availability of estoppel in public law proceedings. However, it is true that both Gummow J in *Kurtovic* and Mason CJ in *Quin* were not prepared to state that there could *never* be a case in which public law estoppel would be appropriate, and there has not been a case since which shuts the door that they left open.[126]

This may be explained by the shift of focus, from public law estoppel to substantive unfairness, which occurred after *Coughlan*. There can be no doubt

---

120 *Coughlan* [2001] QB 213, 242.
121 See Groves, above n 73, 507. Interestingly, this reasoning was not applied directly to the issue of substantive unfairness as a ground of judicial review in *Lam*. Rather, it was held that the constitutional issues did not arise because of the limited scope of 'legitimate expectations': *Lam* (2003) 214 CLR 1, 21 [65] (McHugh & Gummow JJ).
122 *Lam* (2003) 214 CLR 1, 23 [73] (McHugh and Gummow JJ), referring to *Begbie* [2000] 1 WLR 1115, 1129.
123 *Kurtovic* (1990) 21 FCR 193.
124 M Allars, 'Tort and Equity Claims Against the State' in P D Finn (ed), *Essays on Law and Government – Volume 2: The Citizen and the State in the Courts* (Lawbook, 1996) 93.
125 Ibid, 86.
126 'The possibility that estoppels may apply in public law is not foreclosed by the current state of authority in Australia': R J French, 'The Equitable Geist in the Machinery of Administrative Justice' (2003) 39 *AIAL Forum* 1, 11.

that the door to substantive enforcement of legitimate expectations in Australian courts has been positively slammed shut,[127] in *Lam* and cases following. The High Court's desire to address the developments consequent on the Court of Appeal's decision in *Coughlan* was emphasised by the fact that Mr Lam had not attempted explicitly to rely on *Coughlan* in the first place.[128] In short, it is generally accepted that *Lam* has definitively taken any doctrine of substantive unfairness off the table in Australia for the foreseeable future.

The plaintiff in *Quin* was in a comparable position to Ms Coughlan in the sense that the decision which affected him 'involve[d] not one but two lawful exercises of power (the promise and the policy change) by the same public authority, with consequences for individuals trapped between the two'.[129] A majority of the High Court was nonetheless prepared to recognise the right of the executive to change its policy.[130] The English cases following *Coughlan* have come to an essentially different view, as Binnie J noted in *Mount Sinai*,[131] and the result of this legal interpretation would cause significant strain on the separation of powers doctrine, particularly where it is constitutionally entrenched.

As in *Quin*, there was an explicit reliance on the nature of the *Australian Constitution* in *Lam*, particularly in the joint judgment of McHugh and Gummow JJ. Their Honours expressly contrasted the constitutional arrangements of the English public law system with that which exists under the written *Australian Constitution* and held that the 'distinction between jurisdictional and non-jurisdictional error which informs s 75(v)'[132] provides a further reason why the role of Australian courts 'does not extend to the performance of the legislative function of translating policy into statutory form or the executive function of administration'.[133] The focus of the court must be on the fairness of the procedure and not on the legitimacy of the expectation,[134] nor the substantive unfairness of the outcome.

Furthermore, absent a bill of rights, a process whereby courts are required to 'balance' public and private interests, as advocated by *Coughlan*, would prima facie represent an unauthorised excursion into the merits by the judiciary under

---

127 Since then, Finn J has held in the Federal Court that it was not open to him even to entertain any cause of action based on a claim that a substantive legitimate expectation was not satisfied: *Rush v Commissioner of Police* (2006) 150 FCR 165, 185 [75].
128 *Lam* (2003) 214 CLR 1, 9–10 [28] (Gleeson CJ).
129 *Coughlan* [2001] QB 213, 244 [66].
130 It was relevant in *Quin* that a change of government (and therefore of Attorney-General) had led directly to the change of policy, cf *Mount Sinai v Quebec* [2001] 2 SCR 281, [28] (Binnie J).
131 Ibid, [24], [26].
132 *Lam* (2003) 214 CLR 1, 25 [77].
133 Ibid, 24–5 [76].
134 Ibid, 36 [111] (Hayne J).

the orthodox Australian reasoning.[135] The balancing exercise which is required of judges under the English doctrine of substantive legitimate expectations was explained by Lord Woolf MR in *Coughlan*.[136]

In Canada, Binnie J made the point that 'fairness' covers an enormous amount of territory, and English cases on substantive legitimate expectations cover 'the full gamut of administrative relief',[137] from cases which 'would fit comfortably within [Canadian] principles of procedural fairness' to a 'level of judicial intervention in government policy' that has hitherto been considered inappropriate absent a successful argument under the *Canadian Charter of Rights and Freedoms*.[138] As I have noted above, in *Mount Sinai*, Binnie J was able to redraft this problem by reference to the doctrine of unreasonableness. Australian courts had been just as reluctant to expand the scope of *Wednesbury* unreasonableness as they were that of legitimate expectations, although *Wednesbury*'s scope may now expand as a result of *MIAC v Li*.[139]

It is also interesting that, in *Lam*, the High Court not only rejected a substantive response to the existence of a legitimate expectation but also took a restrictive approach to the procedural rights that such an expectation may create. The court rejected Mr Lam's application for certiorari, quashing the decision to cancel his visa in part because the existence (and disappointment) of a legitimate expectation that the respondent Minister's delegate would contact the carer of Mr Lam's children was insufficient to demonstrate the absence of procedural fairness. Mr Lam's right to a fair hearing before the Minister's delegate decided to cancel his visa[140] was not denied to him due to the disappointment of his expectation that the delegate would contact his children's carer. This was because, as Gleeson CJ noted,[141] Mr Lam had suffered no 'practical injustice' as the result of the disappointment of his expectation because he was not deprived of the opportunity to put his full case.

The constitutional doctrine of jurisdictional error restricts the availability of remedies under s 75(v) and means that courts lack the jurisdiction to grant a remedy in respect of a legally valid exercise of power, even if it results in

---

135 Cane has pointed out that awarding damages, which is in essence an act of substituting the court's decision for that of the defendant public authority, in public law may amount to a form of merits review in any case: P Cane, *Administrative Law* (Oxford University Press, 5th ed, 2011) 310.
136 *Coughlan* [2001] QB 213, 242 (emphasis in original). See Groves, above n 73, 478–9.
137 *Mount Sinai v Quebec* [2001] 2 SCR 281, [26].
138 Ibid, [27]. McHugh and Gummow JJ approved this passage in *Lam* (2003) 214 CLR 1, 26–7 [80].
139 *MIAC v Li* (2013) 297 ALR 225.
140 *Ng Yuen Shiu* [1983] 2 AC 629, 636.
141 *Lam* (2003) 214 CLR 1, 13–14 [36]–[38].

substantive unfairness. This doctrine will not change in the near future,[142] and the tendencies of Australia's judiciary to prefer constitutional formalism[143] and to focus only on procedure in judicial review proceedings[144] have been noted elsewhere. When Sir Anthony Mason commented that it would take a 'revolution in Australian judicial thinking' to adopt the English approach to substantive enforcement of legitimate expectations,[145] this is the scope of the revolution he was describing. It would require no ordinary revolution for Australia to fall into step with the English jurisprudence following *Coughlan*. Given that the move to provide substantive enforcement of legitimate expectations is even greater where the judiciary is not already performing review on human rights grounds, what would be required is something on the scale of the Industrial Revolution.

Conclusion

There is an appreciable difference between the approaches to legitimate expectations in each of the three jurisdictions I have considered. The UK has embraced substantive enforcement of legitimate expectations as a matter of common law. As has so frequently become the case,[146] Australia will likely stand against the tide of change; it lacks both constitutional capacity and judicial willingness to embrace the required change at this point. Canada has also rejected substantive enforcement of legitimate expectations, but has shown a willingness to achieve the ends of that doctrine by other means.

The developments described in this chapter have done nothing to allay Professor Forsyth's concerns that 'there is so much uncertainty that there is a real danger that the concept of legitimate expectation will collapse into an inchoate justification for judicial intervention'.[147] To varying extents, England and Canada have shown themselves to be comfortable with judicial interventionism. While this may mean that people are disadvantaged because government has promised something which it has not delivered, it also means that any relief such people obtain may not be granted on a principled basis.

This observation does not relate to Australia, which is apt to cause concerns of another type, since Australia has made no developments at all. Professor Taggart's perceptive warning that Australia is out of step with the rest of the common law

---

142 *Kirk v Industrial Court (NSW)* (2010) 239 CLR 531.
143 Taggart, above n 116. This is a problematic label in many ways, which I will not explore here.
144 Weeks, above n 95.
145 Mason, above n 12, 108.
146 Taggart, above n 115.
147 Forsyth, 'Legitimate Expectations Revisited' [2011] 16 *Judicial Review* 429, 429.

world would not, at first blush, appear entirely apt for substantive unfairness because, as Taggart noted, the doctrine is controversial to some extent everywhere and, if anything, it is England which is out of step.[148] It is the *way* in which Australia has rejected substantive enforcement of legitimate expectations (and public law estoppel before it) which concerned Taggart and allowed him to use this issue as part of a broader argument about Australia's legal exceptionalism cum isolationism.[149] In its usual fashion, Australia has fallen back on its written *Constitution* (something which neither England nor New Zealand *can* do) and has used it to 'stop the argument at the point it should begin'.[150] There is no point to constitutional purity if it prevents the law from developing.

How should the law develop to protect the interests of those who have received government promises which are not honoured? One of the risks with any kind of law reform is to assume that the judiciary is the only body which can or should move the law forward. Sometimes it must, because it is the only body with the impetus to shift the *status quo*. As the English are learning, according to Forsyth's lament, this does not always result in the creation of a coherent body of law. Ultimately, law reform which is to be both principled and enduring is best achieved by legislation, ideally following a period of investigation and recommendations from the executive. The judiciary will always have a role in this process; it should not have the dominant, let alone the only, role.

---

148 Taggart, above n 115, 26–7.
149 Ibid, 29.
150 Ibid, 27.

JURISDICTIONAL ERROR AND BEYOND

Mark Aronson*

---

* I am grateful for the advice and assistance I received from Carol Harlow, Matthew Groves, Linda Mulcahy and Tom Poole. My thanks go also to the Law Department of the London School of Economics, for its generous provision of facilities and collegiality whilst I wrote the bulk of this essay.

Introduction

In Australia, every experienced teacher of administrative law knows that their undergraduate classes are liable to go into a tailspin upon first reading the leading cases discussing the concept of jurisdictional error. By contrast, the students will have coped well with their judicial review materials relating to reasonably specific grounds of challenge. That is not to say that the leading cases on the effects of fraud, bad faith, or improper purpose, for example, are all straightforward, but the students will regard the doctrinal difficulties of those cases as being no greater than those in any other area of law that they have encountered. The students will also have coped reasonably well with the massive indeterminacies of the rules of natural justice. But a sizeable proportion of any administrative law class will start to get seriously edgy when they are introduced to the doctrinal distinction between errors of law that are jurisdictional and those that are not, and most of those students will not confine themselves to that particular distinction. They will start asking harder questions.

In terms of the permissible grounds of judicial review, they will ask why we must have *any* distinction between jurisdictional and non-jurisdictional errors, regardless of whether the error in question is one of law, fact or policy. And if (as most of them end up agreeing) the scope of judicial review is to vary according to a number of factors that include whether the error is one of law, fact or policy, their bottom line will be to doubt whether there is any sense at all in expressing those particular variations in the language of 'jurisdiction'. I try to calm them down in so far as their unease boils down to questions of semantics, because I, for one, will not die in any ditch fighting for or against a mere label. In so far as their concerns are more substantive, however, I have to acknowledge that the students are keeping excellent company. England abandoned the terminology of jurisdictional error altogether, and Kirby J (one of Australia's 'great dissenters')[1] regretted that the High Court chose not to follow suit.[2] In each case, however, the reasons were both semantic and substantive.

This chapter will start with the semantics, because however clumsy or strange 'jurisdictional error' may be, it is a term whose former and present meanings need to be sketched before one can move to the more serious (indeed, profound) issues of substance. The second part of this chapter will show that the term has a relatively recent history, that it used to apply only to judicial review of decisions of

---

1 A label frequently applied, but resented by Kirby himself, who prefers 'Great Communicator'. See M Kirby, 'To be a Great Communicator' (a speech delivered in Melbourne on 14 May 2009, and available via the 'Speeches' tab (item number 2354) on <www.michaelkirby.com.au>).
2 *Re Minister for Immigration and Multicultural Affairs; Ex parte Applicant S20/2002* (2003) 198 ALR 59, [121].

inferior courts, and that it used to have a very restricted meaning. From those early days, it now commands the whole field of common law judicial review in Australia.

The next section in the chapter will show that the present meaning of 'jurisdictional error' is now extraordinarily broad. Its reach or scope of application (meaning those to whom it applies) has spread from cases against inferior courts (where 'jurisdiction' once had a reasonably obvious meaning), to all sub-constitutional judicial review, whether the challenged decision be that of a court, a Minister, a bureaucrat or a tribunal. The terminology's content has also expanded, along with its reach. There is a large (and slowly expanding) list of generic grounds for bringing a judicial review challenge, all of which are now sub-sets of 'jurisdictional error'. A 'generic' ground applies generally across broad and diverse areas of administrative practice. Generic grounds might be contrasted with 'innominate' grounds that cannot be generalised beyond their specific statutory environment. That part will give a tentative catalogue of the generic grounds of review presently recognised as constituting (or, more accurately, leading to) jurisdictional error. It will also sketch a number of grounds which have been allowed in some contexts, but with reservations as to whether they are generic.

Moving from the semantics to questions of substance, the part entitled 'Juggling the categories' will demonstrate what everyone realises, whether they be a student or a practitioner – that there is no guarantee that a decision-maker's mistake in one case will count as jurisdictional just because a very similar error was held to have been jurisdictional in an earlier precedent, if the latter concerned a different statutory context. That probably goes without saying as regards the non-generic instances of jurisdictional error, but something needs to be said about the generic grounds. These all exhibit some degree of indeterminacy – an indeterminacy that is considerable in some instances. For example, an error may not be jurisdictional even though it is an error of law; but one must then ask whether that stops it being counted as a jurisdictional error for having 'asked the wrong question', or for having taken a forbidden factor into consideration. Lines must be drawn, but the generic grounds contain few clues as to how we might find or define them, and even fewer clues on dealing with the fact that the generic grounds were never intended to be mutually exclusive. *Anisminic Ltd v Foreign Compensation Commission*[3] ('*Anisminic*') actually affirmed the distinction between errors within and beyond 'jurisdiction'.[4] It did that to get around a privative clause, but in the process, it treated as jurisdictional an error of statutory interpretation that was

---

3 [1969] 2 AC 147.
4 See, eg, [1969] 2 AC 147, 174, where Lord Reid said that judicial review could correct the Commission's misinterpretation of the relevant legislative provision, 'not because the tribunal has made an error of law, but because as a result of making an error of law they have dealt with and based their decision on a matter with which...they had no right to deal'.

obviously within the Commission's legal competence and remit.[5] The English drift from the language of 'jurisdiction' started after *Anisminic* itself, and partly because that case had found it so easy to manipulate the tests.[6] It is one of law's paradoxes that the drift ended by reading *Anisminic* as having itself opposed the distinction between jurisdictional and non-jurisdictional error of law.[7]

The next section will look at a recent discussion of the possibility of legislative restatement of the generic grounds, either to make them even more general, or to abolish the nominate grounds altogether and replace them simply with 'jurisdictional error'.

The malleability of judicial review's principles is not infinite. Lines are drawn that are neither wholly subjective nor the outcome of a consequentialist 'feel' for when intervention is appropriate, and the section in this chapter entitled 'Judicial review's need for margins' briefly explains the need for setting limits to the intensity of judicial review. It is often the case that a body has done what its Act allowed, even though a court might have done it differently, perhaps reaching an entirely opposite result. Not all instances of differences of opinion between the bureaucracy and the courts are instances of mistakes on the bureaucracy's part. In fact, they are usually instances of matters of judgement, evaluation, policy or discretion, where the important thing is for the court to recognise that Parliament gave the final word to the bureaucrat, not the court. Furthermore, even if there was a mistake, it will stand uncorrected by judicial review if it was within the bureaucrat's power to commit. Non-jurisdictional errors of law are the exception to that general rule, but their reviewability at common law is strictly limited as discussed near the end of this chapter, in the section entitled 'Severing the link with jurisdictional error'. Allowing some margin for error is critical to the distinction between judicial review and merits appeal.

'Setting the margins', below, provides an overview of how those margins are set. Australia sets its margins according to principles anchored in the twin considerations of the separation of powers and statutory interpretation. However, statutory interpretation is not always straightforward. Most of judicial review's

---

5 An eminent QC chaired the Commission; see [1969] 2 AC 147, 175 (Lord Morris).
6 Lord Denning said in *Pearlman v Harrow School* [1979] 1 QB 56, 70 that he could call an error of law jurisdictional any time he wanted to grant judicial review, but that he would prefer not to have to use the language of jurisdictional error. He said that it was intolerable that a tribunal or inferior court's legal error should not be corrected. His Lordship's principal concern seemed to be that there were revealed in the instant case two streams of County Court authority, interpreting the same provision in radically different ways.
7 The move was actually made by *R v Hull University Visitor; Ex parte Page* [1993] AC 682. For examples of reading *Anisminic* as having made the move, see: *Boddington v British Transport Police* [1999] 2 AC 143, 154; *R (Cart) v Upper Tribunal* [2012] 1 AC 663, 676, 683, 702; and *Eba v Advocate General for Scotland* [2012] 1 AC 710, 718–19.

generic requirements are *implied* into the bureaucrat's relevant statute. They are rarely to be found in express form, and even where an Act does identify them, it is usually for the purpose of telling us which generic principles do *not* apply.[8] Most judicial review cases are not about the generic (and usually implied) principles, but concern a bureaucrat's breach of some specific statutory requirement that is confined to the particular administrative task in question. And whether the statutory requirement be generic, unique, or somewhere in between, and whether it be express or implied, very few statutes actually say that its breach has the consequence of nullifying the challenged administrative conduct or decision.

It is appropriate at this point to take a broader view of the principles that underlie and guide the grounds of review. Tom Poole writes that there exists at this level a considerable gap between Australian and English judicial review.[9] Cases from both countries resort, as they must, to established principles of statutory interpretation. And in this process, both countries are at least influenced by normative, rule of law considerations. However, the weight accorded to those considerations is far greater in England than in Australia. According to Poole, England is in danger of replacing its rules with principles too broad to be of any real guidance or constraint, turning judicial review into the subjective, manipulable and result-oriented exercise that was meant to have been ditched with the rejection of the terminology of 'jurisdictional error'. Poole sees the Australian cases as going to the other extreme, offering no principles to guide and constrain the operation of the established categories of jurisdictional error, let alone the creation of new categories. He hints that the answer lies somewhere in the middle, and 'Setting the margins' will argue that this middle ground consists of an unavoidably imprecise mix of particularist concerns for statutory interpretation and functionalism on the one hand, and more general normative considerations on the other hand. England's 'rule of law' or 'abuse of power' principles are not just far too broad to stand alone – they have force in only the extreme case. Similarly, there is more justificatory than explanatory force in Australia's location of 'jurisdictional error' within the constitutional principles of the separation of Commonwealth judicial power and the preservation of an inherent feature of State Supreme Courts.

To this point, I will show that the generic principles of jurisdictional error are conclusory, with the result that any finding of such an error has been reached by reference to a number of additional factors, including general principles of constitutional and statutory interpretation, informed by the sense that normative

---

[8] Section 500A(11) of the *Migration Act 1958* (Cth), for example, disapplies the hearing rule of natural justice from a decision taken by the Minister personally to deny entry to a person who would be likely to incite community violence. The Minister has to table such decisions and their accompanying reasons in the Parliament.

[9] T Poole, 'Between the Devil and the Deep Blue Sea' in L Pearson, C Harlow and M Taggart (eds), *Administrative Law in a Changing State* (Hart Publishing, 2008) ch 1.

considerations should not usually be allowed seriously to impair the effective functioning of the statutory scheme under consideration. If 'jurisdictional error' is a conclusory label for all sorts of faults, its consequences are usually more straightforward. Nullity is the usual consequence of a finding of jurisdictional error, and I will show in a later part of this chapter that 'nullity' is itself a court-ordained result. It involves the court in retrospectively nullifying some or all of those consequences of a decision found to have been affected by jurisdictional error, that are relevantly adverse to the applicant.

The section in this chapter on 'The limits to statutory interpretation' addresses issues that have gained more prominence in the last ten years or so. If (as the High Court has said) jurisdictional error is ultimately a matter of statutory interpretation, where does that leave judicial review of non-statutory governmental power? Are there any limits to the legislature's power to tell us which of its requirements are jurisdictional and which are non-jurisdictional? In Australia (in contrast to England), those limits would need to be sourced ultimately to the *Constitution*, but what room is there for reading relevant common law values into the *Constitution*?

Finally, the section 'Severing the link with jurisdictional error' questions the shelf-life of judicial review's linkage to jurisdictional error. Specifically, what would have changed if the High Court had followed the English decision to treat all legal errors as reviewable?

Some history

'Jurisdictional error' is a relative newcomer to judicial review.[10] According to Austlii, its first High Court usage occurred in 1983.[11] However, cognate terms such as 'excess of jurisdiction' and 'want of jurisdiction' made their first public law appearance in High Court judgments as early as 1905.[12] 'Ultra vires' was in common usage at around the same time.[13]

---

10 A detailed account appears in S Gageler, 'Impact of Migration Law on the Development of Australian Administrative Law' (2010) 17 *Australian Journal of Administrative Law* 92. Whilst acknowledging its lengthy antecedents, Gageler explained that the term became ubiquitous almost by accident. A series of cases started to bundle together both implied limitations on statutory power and those that were express, placing them all beneath the umbrella of 'jurisdictional error'. That process led to *Re Refugee Review Tribunal; Ex parte Aala* (2000) 204 CLR 82, which rejected what Gageler called (at 100) the Minister's 'fairly heroic argument' that because the requirements of natural justice stood outside 'jurisdictional error' at federation, they could not be imported into that concept at a later date. At roughly the same time as this series of cases, the High Court also started emphasising that the constitutional duty and function of the courts were restricted to the enforcement of jurisdictional limitations.
11 In *R v Coldham; Ex parte Australian Workers' Union* (1983) 153 CLR 415, 423.
12 In *Mooney v Commissioners of Taxation (NSW)* (1905) 3 CLR 221, 236 and 247 respectively.
13 *R (on the Prosecution of Freeman) v Arndel* (1906) 3 CLR 557, 581.

In substance, 'jurisdiction' and 'vires' currently mean the same thing. They refer nowadays only to a body's *power*, *authority* or *capacity* validly to act, order or decide as they have done; although one can certainly mine the modern cases for the finer distinctions between the words here italicised.[14] This was not always the case, because 'jurisdiction' and 'vires' used to belong to different fields. In earlier times, 'jurisdiction' and its cognates were principally used in discussions about the authority or power of bodies with adjudicative functions; and in even earlier times, those bodies had to be courts or court-like institutions, which were typically constituted by justices of the peace.

An inferior court's 'jurisdiction' could be restricted to a particular district, or to particular classes of persons, or to particular subject matters,[15] but assuming compliance with those restrictions, its 'jurisdiction' originally meant its authority to determine a dispute. On that view of it, a court's jurisdiction was determinable at the outset of a matter, so that once the matter had passed that point, then the inferior court could not 'lose' its jurisdiction, no matter how egregious an error it might have committed thereafter. That 'commencement theory'[16] of jurisdiction had its champion[17] and some notable judicial endorsement,[18] but it was a losing battle with the inexorable expansion of judicial review grounds for things done post-commencement. The House of Lords finally pronounced the theory's death in *Anisminic*,[19] and the High Court did likewise in *Kirk v Industrial Court (NSW)*[20] ('*Kirk*'). In each case, those death notices were long overdue.

'Ultra vires' did not become a well-used legal term in English law until the 19th century, and even then, its original contexts were mostly about the powers

---

14 Eg, *Williams v Commonwealth* (2012) 288 ALR 410, [200]–[203]. Similarly, the High Court distinguishes between 'jurisdiction' and 'power': *Osland v Secretary, Department of Justice (No 2)* (2010) 241 CLR 320, 332.
15 *Berowra Holdings Pty Ltd v Gordon* (2006) 225 CLR 364, 375.
16 Professor Craig's term: P P Craig, *Administrative Law* (Sweet and Maxwell, 6th ed, 2008) 465.
17 D M Gordon, 'The Relation of Facts to Jurisdiction' (1929) 45 *Law Quarterly Review* 459; '*Tithe Redemption Commission v Guynne*' (1944) 60 *Law Quarterly Review* 250; 'Conditional or Contingent Jurisdiction of Tribunals' (1960) 1 *UBC Law Review* 185; 'Book Review of S A de Smith, *Judicial Review of Administrative Action*' (Stevens, 1959) (1960) 76 *Law Quarterly Review* 306; 'Book Review of A Rubinstein, *Jurisdiction and Illegality*' (OUP, 1965) (1966) 82 *Law Quarterly Review* 263; and 'Jurisdictional Fact: an Answer' (1966) 82 *Law Quarterly Review* 515.
18 *R v Bolton* (1841) 1 QB 66; and *R v Nat Bell Liquors Ltd* [1922] 2 AC 128, 151. *Bolton*'s commencement theory was used to judge-proof the magistracy's administration of harsh labour laws: K Costello, '*R (Martin) v Mahony*: The History of a Classical Certiorari Authority' (2006) 27 *Journal of Legal History* 267.
19 [1969] 2 AC 147, 171, 199, 200, overruling the theory's endorsement in *Davies v Price* [1958] 1 WLR 434.
20 (2010) 239 CLR 531, 569–70.

of trustees, or of bodies corporate.[21] Its transition to the wider public law context took some time, and nowadays it means simply that the relevant body (usually not an inferior court, although this is entirely a matter of usage) lacked power validly to do what it has done. In terms of outcome, therefore, it is no different to 'jurisdictional error',[22] which latter term now dominates the Australian judicial review landscape.

An indicative catalogue of generic instances of jurisdictional error

There is no hard-and-fast list of jurisdictional errors. The leading cases have provided examples, and sometimes a catalogue of examples, but these have never been offered as watertight rules. The High Court told us in *Kirk*[23] that there is no 'rigid taxonomy',[24] and that: 'It is neither necessary, nor possible, to attempt to mark the metes and bounds of jurisdictional error.'[25] What counts as a jurisdictional error in one context may be irrelevant in a different statutory setting. For example, it is obvious that warrants to intercept a criminal's phone calls can be granted without first hearing from the criminal. Even the generic grounds (such as procedural fairness in this example) have exceptions.

Nevertheless, one can list the standard judicial review grounds that are not unique to a specific statutory context, and it is convenient to call these the 'generic grounds'. What counts as a jurisdictional error depends on statutory meaning, from which it follows that other grounds will be unique to a specific statute, and some might be appropriate in only a limited number of statutory contexts.

---

21 For a historical account, see H A Street (formerly S B Brice), *A Treatise on the Doctrine of Ultra Vires: Being an Investigation of the Principles which Limit the Powers and Liabilities of Corporations, Quasi-Corporate Bodies and Non-Sovereign Legislatures* (Sweet and Maxwell, 1930). By 1800, 'ultra vires' was in common usage in Scotland in a number of contexts, but its first appearance in the English Reports (online via Commonlii.org.uk) was in *Bank of Australasia v Harding* (1850) 9 CB 662, 679. A similar result appears from an online search of *The Making of Modern Law: Legal Treatises 1800–1926*, a fabulous database of old legal treatises and textbooks at <www.Galenet.galegroup.com>.
22 See, eg, *Enfield City Corp v Development Assessment Commission* (2000) 199 CLR 135, 145; and *Re Refugee Review Tribunal; Ex parte Aala* (2000) 204 CLR 82, 91.
23 *Kirk v Industrial Court (NSW)* (2010) 239 CLR 531.
24 Ibid, 574.
25 Ibid, 573.

The following list of generic grounds draws on the leading cases[26] – sometimes using their own words, and sometimes paraphrasing them. This list has gained some currency,[27] but always on the understanding that it is not exhaustive, but is only indicative. The generic instances of jurisdictional error include:

1. A mistaken assertion or denial of the very existence of jurisdiction.

2. A misapprehension or disregard of the nature or limits of the decision-maker's functions or powers.

3. Acting wholly or partly outside the general area of the decision-maker's jurisdiction, by entertaining issues or making the types of decisions or orders which are forbidden under any circumstances. An example would be a civil court trying a criminal charge.

4. Mistakes as to the existence of a jurisdictional fact or other requirement, when the relevant Act treats that fact or requirement as something which must exist objectively as a condition precedent to the validity of the challenged decision. The fact or requirement is not such a condition precedent if it suffices for the decision-maker to come to its own opinion or satisfaction as to whether it exists. In that case, the opinion is challengeable only on the other grounds in this list.

5. Disregarding relevant considerations or paying regard to irrelevant considerations, if the proper construction of the relevant Act is that such errors should result in invalidity.

6. Some, but not all, errors of law. In particular, if the decision-maker is an inferior court or other legally qualified adjudicative body, the error is likely to be jurisdictional only if it amounts to a misconception of the nature of the function being performed or of the body's powers.

7. Acting in bad faith.

8. Breaching the hearing or bias rules of natural justice.

9. Acting extremely unreasonably, whether in the exercise of a specific procedural power, or in the exercise of the substantive powers either to determine facts or determine an outcome.

---

26 Namely: *Anisminic* [1969] 2 AC 147, 171; *Craig v South Australia* (1995) 184 CLR 163, 176–80; *Re Refugee Review Tribunal; Ex parte Aala* (2000) 204 CLR 82; *Commissioner of Taxation v Futuris Corporation Ltd* (2008) 237 CLR 146, 164–5; and *Minister for Immigration and Citizenship v Li* [2013] HCA 18, 297 ALR 225.

27 Eg, *Commissioner of Taxation v Futuris Corporation Ltd* (2008) 237 CLR 146, 186; *Kirk* (2010) 239 CLR 531, 573; and *Mahmoud v Sutherland* [2012] NSWCA 306, [29].

Other generic grounds might be added. For example, an improper purpose will invalidate the purported exercise of a power that has purposive limits, although one could argue that this already has a home within item 3 above.

Then there are highly specific grounds that are unique to a particular statute. In *Gedeon v Crime Commission (NSW)*[28] ('*Gedeon*'), for example, the Act allowed undercover police to engage in the trade of prohibited drugs, but only if a very senior officer had granted authorisation. The Act specifically prohibited the issuance of authorisations in circumstances where there would be a likelihood of serious risk to someone's health. The authorisation in *Gedeon* had allowed the undercover police to send 3.75 kg of cocaine onto the streets. That was an obvious risk to the health of end-users, and the High Court therefore concluded that the authorisation was invalid.

Somewhere between the two extremes of generic and unique instances of jurisdictional error are a number of errors which permit some extrapolation from their immediate statutory contexts, but only to a limited extent. Administrative decision-makers, for example, are not under any generic duty to inquire. Nevertheless, non-adversarial tribunals might very occasionally need to seek further clarification from a party, or even from some other reasonably obvious and readily available source, if the issue is of central importance and further inquiry would not be too burdensome.[29] In exceptional cases, natural justice might be breached by a merits review tribunal failing to come to grips with a basic element of a party's evidence or application,[30] or where the tribunal's dilatoriness and lack of note-taking have disabled it from having any genuine recall of a witness's credibility.[31] However, these may not be generic grounds. They might exist not in their own right, but as instances of tribunals breaching their statutory obligation to 'hear' an appeal, or to conduct a 'review', or to 'invite' an appellant to appear at a hearing, or to perform their 'core' function of acting within the bounds of reason.[32]

Juggling the categories

The law reports and judgment databases contain thousands of court rulings as to whether this or that administrative error was jurisdictional, and these cases provide

---

28 (2008) 236 CLR 120.
29 *Minister for Immigration and Citizenship v SZIAI* (2009) 111 ALD 15, [25]; and *Minister for Immigration and Citizenship v SZGUR* (2011) 241 CLR 594, 603, 620.
30 *Dranichnikov v Minister for Immigration and Multicultural Affairs* (2003) 197 ALR 389.
31 *NAIS v Minister for Immigration and Multicultural and Indigenous Affairs* (2005) 228 CLR 470.
32 See: *Minister for Immigration and Citizenship v SZJSS* (2010) 243 CLR 164, 175–6; *Minister for Immigration and Citizenship v Li* [2013] HCA 18, 297 ALR 225; and M Aronson and M Groves, *Judicial Review of Administrative Action* (Thomson Reuters, 5th ed, 2013) [3.360], [4.800].

guidance where the same or similar problems arise in similar contexts. Their guidance is obviously limited, however, in the case of the non-generic instances of jurisdictional error. What is almost as obvious is that some caution is needed even where one contends that the error answers to the description of one of the generic grounds of review. This is not just to recall *Kirk*'s warning that the list of generic grounds contains no more than examples, and that there is no hard-and-fast taxonomy. Most of the catalogue's items are themselves either extraordinarily imprecise or obviously incomplete.

The content of procedural fairness, for example, is famously adaptable and variable according to context.[33] Setting the content in any particular case depends on a number of factors – some normative, some highly pragmatic. Gleeson CJ said in *Re Minister for Immigration and Multicultural Affairs; Ex parte Lam*:[34]

> Fairness is not an abstract concept. It is essentially practical. Whether one talks in terms of procedural fairness or natural justice, the concern of the law is to avoid practical injustice.

Further examples come easily. For example, item 1 in my list is entirely circular – it says that there is a jurisdictional error when there is a mistaken assertion of jurisdiction. In any event, courts (or, at least, superior courts of record) have jurisdiction to determine their own jurisdiction. They can be judicially reviewed for going wrong in such cases. However, their wrong decisions will retain their force (their 'validity', if you like) to the moment they are overturned. There is no retrospective nullification in such cases.[35] Item 2 is not to be taken literally – not every mistake is so serious as to amount to a misapprehension of the decision-maker's powers or functions. In the 'classic'[36] words of Jordan CJ, 'there are mistakes and mistakes'.[37] Items 3–5 simply restate the problem, by telling us that the answers lie not in any close analysis of the items themselves, but in statutory interpretation.

Item 6 – the item that probably worries people the most – tells us that only some errors of law are jurisdictional, and that this often turns on whether the decision-maker is a court or court-like body. Distinguishing between judges and bureaucrats makes obvious sense, because we know that a judicial interpretation of a difficult statute will trump a contrary interpretation made by a bureaucrat, even if each was entirely reasonable. But the authority to make non-jurisdictional errors of law is not

---

33 See: *Kioa v West* (1985) 159 CLR 550, 612–13; and *Re Minister for Immigration and Multicultural Affairs; Ex parte Miah* (2001) 206 CLR 57, 94, 115.
34 (2003) 214 CLR 1, 14.
35 *New South Wales v Kable* [2013] HCA 26; 298 ALR 144.
36 Gaudron J's description, in *Re Minister for Immigration and Multicultural Affairs; Ex parte Miah* (2001) 206 CLR 57, 81.
37 *Ex parte Hebburn Ltd; Re Kearsley Shire Council* (1947) 47 SR (NSW) 416, 420.

confined to judges.[38] Having the last word on a question of law does not always turn on whether the speaker is a judge. Even judges are sometimes reviewable for jurisdictional legal errors, as in *Kirk*, where a State Industrial Court had made two very serious errors in its criminal jurisdiction. It had interpreted a criminal offence so widely as to allow convictions without any indication of what the defendants had done wrong. Also, it had allowed the prosecution to call one of the defendants as its witness, in disregard of a fundamental rule of evidence law that accused persons are testimonially incompetent for the prosecution. Being a judge certainly helps in deciding whether a decision-maker has the last word on a question of law, but it is not determinative. Similarly, not being a judge is some indication that the decision-maker lacks the last word, but once again, that is not determinative. The High Court had said in *Craig v South Australia*[39] that whether a body's legal error was jurisdictional turned on whether it was empowered 'authoritatively to determine questions of law', but as *Kirk* pointed out, this was not very helpful.[40]

Kirk also pointed out that the items listed in the catalogue above are not just imprecise or incomplete – they often overlap each other.[41] The Industrial Court's misinterpretation of the criminal offence charged in that case meant that it had misconceived the limits of its functions or powers,[42] and had also led it to make orders that it had no power to make because no offence had been proved.[43] Allowing the prosecution to call a defendant was more than just an error of evidence law. It, too, was a misapprehension of the limits of the Court's powers.[44]

With so many and such open-ended examples of 'jurisdictional error', it is obvious that the term itself is conclusory.[45] It is even more obvious in light of the High Court's recent expansion of the generic 'unreasonableness' ground in *Minister for Immigration and Citizenship v Li* ('*Li*').[46] *Li* is a striking illustration of the consequences of the generic grounds overlapping each other. The Court set aside a tribunal's decision which could well have been different if only the tribunal had acceded to an application for an adjournment. The refusal to adjourn

---

38 See: *Coal and Allied Operations Pty Ltd v Australian Industrial Relations Commission* (2000) 203 CLR 194; *Bodruddaza v Minister for Immigration and Multicultural Affairs* (2007) 228 CLR 651, 675; and *Kirk v Industrial Court (NSW)* (2010) 239 CLR 531, 572–3.
39 (1995) 184 CLR 163, 179.
40 *Kirk v Industrial Court (NSW)* (2010) 239 CLR 531, 573.
41 A point also made in *Minister for Immigration and Multicultural Affairs v Yusuf* (2001) 206 CLR 323, 351.
42 (2010) 239 CLR 531, 574–5 [74].
43 Ibid, 575 [75].
44 Ibid, [76].
45 A view adopted by the Full Court of the Federal Court in *SDAV v Minister for Immigration and Multicultural and Indigenous Affairs* (2003) 199 ALR 43, [27], and described as 'painfully accurate' in S Gageler, 'Impact of Migration Law on the Development of Australian Administrative Law' (2010) 17 *Australian Journal of Administrative Law* 92, 104.
46 [2013] HCA 18; 297 ALR 225.

was variously characterised as wholly unreasonable, bad for failure to give any or sufficient weight to the applicant's stated reasons for her application, and bad for breach of the hearing rule of natural justice.

In one sense, the examples of jurisdictional error *are* its meaning. In another sense, the term serves to limit the competence of any Australian Parliament to diminish the scope of judicial review, because the High Court[47] and all State Supreme Courts have entrenched judicial review jurisdiction.[48] Further again, a finding of 'jurisdictional error' is a staging point, and its usual (although not inevitable) consequence is to render the challenged decision or conduct a nullity.

Legislative reform?

An obvious question at this point is to ask whether we should consider legislative reform in this area. The Administrative Review Council (ARC) recently considered this issue at some length.[49] It noted that most of the grounds of review listed in ss 5–7 of the *Administrative Decisions (Judicial Review) Act 1977* (Cth) ('ADJR Act') were intended merely to restate the common law's generic grounds.[50] The exceptions appear to be threefold. The ADJR Act certainly allows review for *any* error of law (not just those that are jurisdictional).[51] Its 'no evidence' ground was probably meant to go further than its common law analogue, and the ARC wants it to be amended to make that clear.[52] And the ADJR Act's 'procedural error' ground might extend to breaches of non-jurisdictional procedural requirements.[53]

By majority, the ARC concluded that for all its difficulties, it would be unwise for Parliament to do anything more than tinker with the ADJR Act's list of judicial review grounds. The ARC had two principal reasons for this overall conclusion.

---

47 It suffices to refer to s 75(v) of the *Constitution*, which invests original jurisdiction in the High Court in all matters in which mandamus, prohibition or injunction are sought against officers of the Commonwealth.
48 *Kirk v Industrial Court (NSW)* (2010) 239 CLR 531.
49 Administrative Review Council, *Federal Judicial Review in Australia* (Report No 50) (Canberra, 2012) ch 7.
50 Ibid, 126, citing Mason J in *Kioa v West* (1985) 159 CLR 550, 576.
51 Sections 5(1)(f) and 6(1)(f).
52 The ARC recommended amendment to clarify that the ADJR Act's 'no evidence' ground in ss 5(1)(h) and 6(1)(h) can be established if either paragraph of ss 5(3) and 6(3) applies: Administrative Review Council, *Federal Judicial Review in Australia* (Report No 50) (Canberra, 2012) 139–42. The problem case is *Minister for Immigration and Multicultural Affairs v Rajamanikkam* (2002) 210 CLR 222.
53 Sections 5(1)(b) and 6(1)(b), considered in: *Minister for Immigration and Multicultural Affairs v Yusuf* (2001) 206 CLR 323, 341, 372; *Muin v Refugee Review Tribunal* (2002) 190 ALR 601, [169]; and *Re Minister for Immigration and Multicultural and Indigenous Affairs; Ex parte Applicant S134/2002* (2003) 211 CLR 441, 460.

First, 'jurisdictional error' is constitutionally entrenched at both the federal and State levels, so it is beyond repeal. In terms of intelligibility to the profession, however, it is nevertheless a clear loser in any contest with the ADJR Act's generic grounds, which have bedded down and become very well-known. In effect, and even though the ADJR Act's changes to the common law grounds are small, and even though the Act's grounds are an incomplete codification, that statutory restatement now has the considerable advantage of 'incumbency'. The ARC's second reason was that nothing could or should stop the High Court from developing the common law's review grounds, with the ADJR Act picking up any new common law developments via its catch-all grounds.[54]

It is true that none of the ADJR Act's grounds uses the terminology of 'jurisdictional error', although one comes very close[55] and another comes reasonably close.[56] It is also true that the ADJR's Act's lack of any explicit reference to jurisdictional error 'has not led to the sky falling in'.[57] The ADJR Act has at times been criticised for being too particular, and for lacking any overarching or normative statements of higher principle.[58] The ARC considered but unanimously rejected the option of supplementing or even replacing the ADJR Act's existing grounds with a more general set of standards or principles. The Council acknowledged that a list of high-level abstract principles might sometimes provide guidance in the application of more specific grounds of review, and in the development of new grounds. However, it thought that the development and articulation of a set of meta-principles would prove difficult, and would be likely to produce more rather than less complexity in the long run.[59] The ARC's second broad option was to repeal the ADJR Act entirely, and place a short and very general set of principles into the *Acts Interpretation Act 1901* (Cth). Only one Council member supported this option.[60] The dissentient neither listed his general principles, nor gave any indication as to the level of abstraction at which he thought they should be articulated.

---

54 The ADJR Act allows review of 'decisions' that are 'otherwise contrary to law' or that constitute an 'abuse of power': ss 5(1)(j), 5(2)(j). The same grounds appear in s 6 (for review of 'conduct').
55 Sections 5(1)(c) and 6(1)(c) allow challenge on the ground that the decision-maker 'did not have jurisdiction to make the decision'.
56 Sections 5(1)(d) and 6(1)(d) allow challenges to decisions or conduct that were not 'authorised'.
57 M Taggart, 'Australian Exceptionalism in Judicial Review' (2008) 36 *Federal Law Review* 1, 9.
58 Cf *Re Minister for Immigration and Multicultural Affairs; Ex parte Applicant S20/2002* (2003) 198 ALR 59, [157], [166] (Kirby J) with M Aronson, 'Is the ADJR Act Hampering the Development of Australian Administrative Law?' (2004) 15 *PLR* 202, 214–16.
59 Administrative Review Council, *Federal Judicial Review in Australia* (Report No 50) (Canberra, 2012) 126–32.
60 Ibid, 195–200, R Wilkins, briefly rejected by the majority at 72. The debate is pursued in J McMillan, 'Restoring the *ADJR Act* in Federal Judicial Review' (2013) 72 *AIAL Forum* 12; and R Wilkins and B McGee, 'Judicial Review: A Jurisdictional Limits Model' (2013) 70 *AIAL Forum* 20.

Judicial review's need for margins

If, as Jordan CJ said (and as *Kirk* demonstrated), 'there are mistakes and mistakes',[61] and if (as *Kirk* said) there are no hard and fast *rules* for distinguishing between jurisdictional and non-jurisdictional mistakes, why do we bother drawing any lines, and how in fact are they drawn? This section addresses the first question, and the section on 'Setting the margins', below, addresses the second.

Every comparable country accepts that lines must be drawn because judicial review is not a full merits appeal, and the task that is being reviewed was not given to the judicial review court – it was given to the bureaucrat, tribunal or inferior court whose decision or conduct is under challenge. Whilst every country therefore accepts the need for lines, each uses different terminology and techniques to express how they will set these margins.

That lines must be drawn is uncontroversial when it comes to issues of judgement, evaluation, policy or discretion – no judicial review court claims or wants to claim a general appellate power over such matters. The issue that is controversial, and that so agitated Kirby J, is whether it is proper to concede any margin for matters of statutory interpretation, or for questions of law more generally. And on this issue, it is absolutely vital to distinguish between semantics and substance. Australia expresses its margin for tolerable legal errors in the distinction between jurisdictional and non-jurisdictional errors of law. Canada still uses the language of 'jurisdiction', but has returned the meaning of that term to a position very close to its original, 'commencement theory' version. Judicial review for any other reason in Canada (including most instances of legal error) rests on theories of deference to adjudicative tribunals, systemic coherence, fundamental values, and 'legislative supremacy' (by which they appear to mean statutory meaning).[62] Our cases frame the issue in terms of rules, whilst England's cases resort to judicial discretion.

Lord Denning once said that it was 'intolerable' that some errors of statutory interpretation should escape the reach of judicial review,[63] but he clearly did not mean that literally, because he said that he would pick and choose when he would intervene for legal error. Interpretive perfection comes at too high a price. There is no need to treat the answer to every legal question as provisional, subject always to second-guessing by a judge on judicial review. It is only in a highly fictionalised

---

61 *Ex parte Hebburn Ltd; Re Kearsley Shire Council* (1947) 47 SR (NSW) 416, 420.
62 See: *Dunsmuir v New Brunswick* [2008] 1 SCR 190; *R v Conway* [2010] 1 SCR 765; and *Doré v Barreau du Québec* [2012] 1 SCR 395.
63 *Pearlman v Harrow School* [1979] 1 QB 56, 70. See above, n 6.

sense that one can truly say that there can be only one right answer to any question of law. Further, not all questions of law are of equal importance. Nor do all doubts, all genuine questions of law, really need resolution by a superior court. Further again, we are all used to a legal system that has some degree of tolerance for unresolved differences of legal interpretation. Different judges take different views of particular statutes, and so do bureaucrats and tribunals.

Setting the margins

Everyone in fact agrees that it would be dysfunctional to allow judicial review of all legal errors, but different legal systems have different ways of filtering out unwanted or unnecessary challenges. England's filtration system is different from ours. They treat every error of law as theoretically challengeable on judicial review, but they do some major filtering at the stage when challengers need to get permission to proceed with their case. Applications for permission are usually dealt with on the papers. Most applications fail, sometimes because of the triviality of the legal error, and often because of a judicial policy in England that limits litigants to their statutory appeal rights (where available). Australia also requires leave to proceed (originally called a 'rule nisi') for challenges brought in the High Court, the Northern Territory, Western Australia and South Australia,[64] but not elsewhere. The availability of alternative appeal rights is slowly becoming a significant factor in Australia, both where leave is needed and when the courts come to consider whether to exercise their *discretionary* power to deny relief.[65] Aside from the availability of alternative appeal rights, our leave criteria focus not on discretionary filters, but on whether the respondent has a case to answer.

England needs its discretionary filter, if only to prevent its courts being flooded with challenges for any and every error of law, especially since their courts sometimes take a very relaxed view as to what might constitute such an error.[66] For example, the Upper Tribunal's role in relation to the First Tier Tribunal (FTT) is theoretically limited to correcting 'errors of law', but it is allowed to stretch that concept if the FTT is reaching diametrically opposed conclusions in different cases whose facts are essentially the same.[67]

---

64 J Basten, 'Jurisdictional Error After *Kirk*: Has it a Future?' (2012) 23 *Public Law Review* 94, 107–8.
65 See *Elias v Director of Public Prosecutions (NSW)* [2012] NSWCA 302.
66 The Court of Appeal said in *E v Secretary of State for the Home Department* [2004] QB 1044 that it would treat a migration tribunal's error of fact as an error of law if the parties were in agreement that it was a significant error. In reality, this amounted to review for substantive unfairness.
67 *Jones v First Tier Tribunal* [2013] 2 AC 48.

The UK's Supreme Court said in *R (Cart) v Upper Tribunal*[68] ('*Cart*') that its filtering process had to acknowledge the need for rationing judge and tribunal time, and achieve a 'proportionate' balance between functionality concerns and the correction of legal error.[69] The respondent in *Cart* was the upper tier of England's tribunal system. It was headed up by senior judges who could hear internal appeals and even judicial review matters. According to Lord Brown:[70]

> The rule of law is weakened, not strengthened, if a disproportionate part of the court's resources is devoted to finding a very occasional grain of wheat on a threshing floor full of chaff.

Laws LJ's explanation was more blunt when *Cart* had been in the Administrative Court:[71]

> The nature of the judicial review jurisdiction owned by the High Court has an elusive quality, because its limits are (generally) set by itself. In consequence, the distinction between a legal place where the jurisdiction cannot go, and a legal place where as a matter of discretion the High Court will not send it, is permeable: even unprincipled. Ultimately the court is simply concerned to give the jurisdiction the reach, or edge, which the rule of law requires.

Cart rejected an attempt to resurrect the distinction between errors of law that were or were not jurisdictional – a distinction it regarded as unprincipled.[72] However, its turn to the rule of law as its foundational principle provides no greater clarity than the older language of jurisdiction. The real clue lies in its frank balancing between normative and efficiency considerations – a balance that the Canadian Supreme Court used to call 'pragmatic functionalism'.[73] Canada's terminology has since changed,[74] but its current doctrine still balances functionalist and normative concerns.

Kirk also balanced normative and efficiency considerations, but instead of deriving these directly from the rule of law, it drew upon principles of statutory interpretation which were in turn informed by constitutional principles.

Statutory interpretation often requires more than just looking at the legislative text. In judicial review, this is so even if the Act's requirements are unambiguous.

---

68 [2012] 1 AC 663, 688–9.
69 See also M Elliott and R Thomas, 'Tribunal Justice, *Cart* and Proportionate Dispute Resolution' (2012) 71 *Cambridge Law Journal* 297.
70 [2012] 1 AC 663, 700.
71 *R (Cart) v Upper Tribunal* [2011] QB 120, 156.
72 [2012] 1 AC 1 AC 663, 702.
73 *Baker v Canada (Minister of Citizenship and Immigration)* [1999] 2 SCR 817.
74 *Dunsmuir v New Brunswick* [2008] 1 SCR 190.

The relevant Act in *Gedeon*[75] might have made it quite clear that no authority could permit undercover police to trade in forbidden drugs if that would be likely to endanger people's health, but it was not entirely clear that the court was to be the judge of that issue. Section 17(2) of the *Evidence Act 1995* (NSW) was quite clear in *Kirk* that accused persons were testimonially incompetent for the prosecution, but that Act gave no thought to distinguishing which of its provisions were jurisdictional and which were not. In each case, the High Court filled those gaps by exercises of statutory interpretation that necessarily went beyond the bare statutory texts.

Regardless of whether a legal error can be established easily or with difficulty, the important point to note here is that very few Acts actually address the administrative lawyer's question of whether that or any other error is jurisdictional.[76] In the vast bulk of cases, that is for the court to decide, and a number of factors can play a role in making those decisions.

Understood both institutionally and functionally, the constitutional doctrine of the separation of powers has been a major factor in this exercise of statutory interpretation, although it would be a mistake to pin too much directly onto the *Constitution*. Strictly speaking, the separation of powers applies only at the federal level. However, State courts can easily find themselves exercising federal jurisdiction,[77] with the result that they cannot stray too far from federal conceptions of the separation of powers for fear of violating the so-called *Kable* principle. *Kable* forbids them from assuming roles that would substantially impair their institutional integrity.[78] One consequence is a marked reluctance to characterise any issue as jurisdictional to the extent that it has significant policy or political content.[79]

In the field of constitutional interpretation, McHugh J was particularly wary of any direct resort to political or moral principles. He saw constitutional interpretation as starting with the 'natural meaning of the text', and supplemented by implications from the structure of the *Constitution* only so far as 'logically or practically necessary'.[80] In a passage that still has currency,[81] his Honour added:[82]

---

75 (2008) 236 CLR 120.
76 The exceptions usually take the form of a statutory statement that the 'validity' of certain conduct or decisions is not affected by breach of a particular provision. See: *Commissioner of Taxation v Futuris Corporation Ltd* (2008) 237 CLR 146; and L McDonald, 'The Entrenched Minimum Provision of Judicial Review and the Rule of Law' (2010) 21 *PLR* 14.
77 As happened in *Momcilovic v R* (2011) 245 CLR 1, where an accused person's inter-State residence meant that her trial and appeal courts were exercising federal jurisdiction.
78 *Kable v Director of Public Prosecutions (NSW)* (1996) 189 CLR 51.
79 See M Groves: 'Substantive Legitimate Expectations in Australian Administrative Law' (2008) 32 *Melbourne University Law Review* 470; and 'Federal Constitutional Influence on State Judicial Review' (2011) 39 *Federal Law Review* 399.
80 *McGinty v Western Australia* (1996) 186 CLR 140, 231, McHugh J.
81 *Baker v Commonwealth* [2012] FCAFC 121, [45].
82 *McGinty v Western Australia* (1996) 186 CLR 140, 231–2, McHugh J, reference deleted.

> ...I cannot accept...that a constitutional implication can arise from a particular doctrine that 'underlies the Constitution'. Underlying or overarching doctrines may explain or illuminate the meaning of the text or structure of the Constitution but such doctrines are not independent sources of the powers, authorities, immunities and obligations conferred by the Constitution. Top-down reasoning is not a legitimate method of interpreting the Constitution.

A joint judgment of Gummow and McHugh JJ voiced similar concerns:[83]

> In Australia, the observance by decision-makers of the limits within which they are constrained by the Constitution and by statutes and subsidiary laws validly made is an aspect of the rule of law under the Constitution. It may be said that the rule of law reflects values concerned in general terms with abuse of power by the executive and legislative branches of government. But it would be going much further to give those values an immediate normative operation in applying the Constitution.

Although they are linked, one must nevertheless make the point that constitutional and statutory interpretation are not the same thing. When it comes to statutory interpretation, the 'principle of legality' is as standard fare in Australia[84] as it is in England.[85] The principle is sometimes rationalised as a 'democracy forcing' device, requiring Ministers to make their intentions very clear to Parliament when they want their Bills to infringe fundamental rights or values. The legality principle requires narrow readings of many police powers, and other powers that might affect, for example, rights of property or freedom of association or movement. The principle's importance is very clear, although its rationalisation is unconvincing, because the interpretive principle focuses on the legislative drafting itself. Clear drafting can achieve an obnoxious result even where Ministers sneak their offending provisions into Bills without warning Members,[86] and the courts will exploit loopholes in unclear drafting even if the Ministers' malign intentions were clearly stated in their Second Reading speeches.[87] The inescapable conclusion is that in the absence of clear statutory drafting to the contrary, the principles of statutory interpretation (which include the fixing of judicial review's margins) usually provide the indirect route for the operation of rule of law values.

---

83 *Re Minister for Immigration and Multicultural and Indigenous Affairs; Ex parte Lam* (2003) 214 CLR 1, 23 (McHugh and Gummow JJ).
84 *Saeed v Minister for Immigration and Citizenship* (2010) 241 CLR 252, 259; and *Momcilovic v R* (2011) 245 CLR 1, 46–9, 177–8, 200. See D Meagher, 'The Common Law Principle of Legality in the Age of Rights' (2011) 35 *Melbourne University Law Review* 449.
85 *R v Secretary of State for the Home Department; Ex parte Simms* [2000] 2 AC 115, 131.
86 As in *Chang v Laidley Shire Council* (2007) 234 CLR 1, 27, 37.
87 As in *Plaintiff S157/2002 v Commonwealth* (2003) 211 CLR 476; and *Lacey v Attorney General (Qld)* (2011) 242 CLR 573, 582–3, 592, 605–7.

Roughly ten years ago, Gleeson CJ said that it was constitutionally impermissible for judges to elevate their sense of the principles of 'good administration' into judicial review grounds in their own right.[88] That is obviously right, if only because judges are not famously versed in how to manage large departments of state, and also because management styles change with sometimes unsettling frequency. Nevertheless, *Kirk* made it abundantly clear that functionality concerns are central to the process of setting the margins for judicial review. Quoting an American author[89] with evident approval, the joint judgment said that a court's decision to characterise an issue as 'jurisdictional':[90]

> is almost entirely functional: it is used to validate review when review is felt to be necessary...If it is understood that the word 'jurisdiction' is not a metaphysical absolute but simply expresses the gravity of the error, it would seem that this is a concept for which we must have a word and for which the hallowed word is justified.

'Jurisdictional error', therefore, is a conclusory term that is applied as one outcome of a process of statutory interpretation that goes further than the statutory text itself. The separation of powers is one of the background factors in that process, whilst a range of normative and functional considerations operate in the foreground. *Kirk* said that in one sense, the courts set judicial review's margins case by case, context by context, after balancing the competing tensions of enforcing the law and the need for finality of decision-making.[91]

Nullity

'Jurisdictional error' is conclusory, but useful nevertheless. It is not just a term of conclusion. It is also a departure point. Having reached it, one must then ask about its consequences. The usual consequence is a court order that declares or treats the jurisdictionally flawed decision, conduct or omission as a nullity; but what does that mean? 'Nullity' is also a conclusory term, and also useful nonetheless. It has equivalents, such as 'void' and 'invalid'.

Despite the language in some of the cases,[92] there is no point in pretending that 'nullities' have no existence. They exist, which means that there is no such thing

---

88 *Re Minister for Immigration and Multicultural and Indigenous Affairs; Ex parte Lam* (2003) 214 CLR 1, 12.
89 L L Jaffe, 'Judicial Review: Constitutional and Jurisdictional Fact' (1957) 70 *Harvard Law Review* 953, 963 (footnote omitted).
90 (2010) 239 CLR 531, 570–71.
91 *Kirk v Industrial Court (NSW)* (2010) 239 CLR 531, 567–8, 577.
92 Lord Wilberforce said in *Calvin v Carr* [1980] AC 574, 590 that a decision can be 'totally void, in the sense of being legally non-existent'. Cf *Minister for Immigration and Multicultural*

as an 'absolute nullity'. No matter how obviously unlawful a government decision may be, if it adversely affects an individual, then something needs to be done about it. Sometimes the administration itself will fix the problem, withdrawing its decision rather than forcing the adversely affected party to seek help from an external source such as a tribunal, the Ombudsman or the courts.[93] If the party does go to court, then judicial review will try its best to undo any adverse consequences of the decision so far as they affect the individual applicant, but it must sometimes pick and choose which consequences it will reverse.

Some of nullity's consequences are useful. For example, valid and invalid decisions alike lay the foundations for appeals to the AAT, because it would be entirely counter-productive to interpret legislated appeal rights as being limited to instances of valid decisions.[94] AAT decisions frequently replace the decisions from which the appeals were brought, but generally without retrospective effect.[95]

Nullity's consequences are sometimes irreversible in practical terms, and injured parties must then look to see if they can maintain damages actions. Incarceration at the hands of the state is illegal if done pursuant to an invalid order or decision, and injured parties can always seek judicial review, and usually damages as well.[96] I say 'usually', because statute sometimes gives the government party a 'good faith' defence to the tort action, in which case judicial review will be the only remedy.[97] And in the special context of an error as to the jurisdiction of a court (or, at least, of a superior court of record), judicial review is available to overturn the decision, but *not* to treat it as a nullity. That was decided in *New South Wales v Kable*,[98] a High Court decision that studiously avoided the term 'jurisdictional error'.

Two general points need to be made. First, retrospective nullification might be the usual consequence of a finding of jurisdictional error, but even in the usual case, not everything is undone. The court will try to fashion an order that undoes only the consequences that are harmful to the challenger, but even that must be both possible and appropriate. A young policeman who was invalidly forced to

---

Affairs v Bhardwaj (2002) 209 CLR 597, 614–15 (Gaudron and Gummow JJ): 'A decision that involves jurisdictional error is a decision that lacks foundation and is properly regarded, in law, as no decision at all'. That was an interesting formulation, because it denied the decision's legal effect but refrained from denying its existence.

93 *Minister for Immigration and Multicultural Affairs v Bhardwaj* (2002) 209 CLR 597. However, it is usually a difficult judgement call for bureaucrats to decide that their first decisions were jurisdictionally flawed.

94 See *Collector of Customs (NSW) v Brian Lawlor Automotive Pty Ltd* (1979) 24 ALR 307.

95 *Administrative Appeals Tribunal Act 1975* (Cth), s 43.

96 *R v Governor of Brockhill Prison; Ex parte Evans (No 2)* [2001] 2 AC 19; and *R (Lumba) v Secretary of State for the Home Department* [2012] 1 AC 245.

97 The Act in *Ruddock v Taylor* (2005) 222 CLR 612 required immigration officials to detain non-citizens they *reasonably suspected* to be without a current visa. Judicial review falsified their suspicions, but that did not make them unreasonable.

98 [2013] HCA 26; 298 ALR 144.

resign in *Chief Constable of North Wales v Evans*[99] got a declaration that said, in effect, that he had been unlawfully dismissed. The House of Lords sympathised with his plight, but rightly felt unable to make a retrospective order that would have produced the entirely fictitious effect that he had remained in the force during the four years of his litigation, with consequent entitlements to back pay, leave pay, and incremental promotions.

Second, a court might refrain from making *any* order that either declares or treats a decision as a nullity, even though it has agreed with the applicant that the challenged decision was jurisdictionally flawed. If judicial review is refused because the challenger lacks standing to sue, and if no-one with standing wants to sue, the net result is that the flawed decision remains undisturbed. In the High Court's original jurisdiction, for instance, judicial review's remedies can always be refused on discretionary grounds.[100] The remedies might be refused because the applicant took so long to institute proceedings that he or she no longer deserves judicial protection.[101] Delay might also ground discretionary refusal of relief because third parties had already acted in reliance upon the challenged decision.[102] The courts might also refuse to grant judicial review where it would have been more appropriate for the challenger to use statutory appeal mechanisms first. That consideration is especially important in the case of decisions made within a structured hierarchy that has a well-ordered internal appeal structure followed by a full right of access to merits tribunals, the regular courts, or both.[103]

The limits to statutory interpretation

The High Court said in *Project Blue Sky Inc v Australian Broadcasting Authority*[104] ('*Project Blue Sky*') that whether an error is jurisdictional is ultimately a question of statutory interpretation, and added with some understatement that the answer is

---

99 [1982] 1 WLR 1155. Cf: *Commissioner for Railways (NSW) v Cavanough* (1935) 53 CLR 220; and *McLaughlin v Governor of the Cayman Islands* [2007] 1 WLR 2839, in each of which the challenger received back pay.
100 *Re Refugee Review Tribunal; Ex parte Aala* (2000) 204 CLR 82, 89, 105–8, 136–7, 144.
101 *SZKUO v Minister for Immigration and Citizenship* (2009) 180 FCR 438, where the applicant took six years to launch a challenge.
102 See: *R v Australian Broadcasting Tribunal; Ex parte Fowler* (1980) 31 ALR 565; *Re Wakim; Ex parte McNally* (1999) 198 CLR 511, 592; and *Re McBain; Ex parte Australian Catholic Bishops Conference* (2002) 209 CLR 372, 425.
103 *Commissioner of Taxation v Futuris Corporation Ltd* (2008) 237 CLR 146, 172–5; and *Kirk v Industrial Court (NSW)* (2010) 239 CLR 531, 578.
104 (1998) 194 CLR 355, 389.

often unclear. To be clear, I should add that this is no fault of either the legislature for poor drafting, or of the courts for failure to spell out their interpretive principles. Blame is quite inappropriate. No drafting can predict all of the issues that will arise in a regulatory scheme, nor should it try. There was a time when Immigration Ministers sought to reduce their legislation to a rule-bound code with no need for administrative or Ministerial discretion, but they inevitably made a mess of it. Discretion has crept back in, alongside a forest of rules that have multiplied the courts' interpretive tasks. In any event, it is usually good policy to leave to the courts the determination of whether an error is jurisdictional and if so, whether the usual consequences of retrospective nullification should follow. In making those determinations, there is a limit to how much guidance the courts can provide, because solutions in one context might well not apply to a different statutory context.

Project Blue Sky's identification of statutory interpretation as its foundational principle raises at least two major issues. First, it fails to explain judicial review of non-statutory government action. Second, it prompts questions as to whether the High Court will entrench not just its judicial review jurisdiction and the supervisory jurisdiction of the State Supreme Courts, and therefore not just judicial review's remedies, but also some substantive aspects of judicial review's principles.

There is no room here to examine the debate about whether judicial review should extend to non-governmental actors when they are exercising non-statutory power that is 'public' – the *Datafin* question[105] is examined elsewhere.[106] Nor do I have room to discuss the availability of judicial review of government actors exercising public but non-statutory power (sometimes called prerogative power). Federal judicial review of the exercise of non-statutory power must proceed on the assumption that the executive power of the Commonwealth has limits which it is the function of the High Court (in the last resort) to enforce. Those limits are doubtless informed by both inherited and evolving common law rules regarding the exercise of prerogative power, but the common law remains subordinate to the *Constitution*. There are large questions concerning the identification of unalterable limits to the Commonwealth's executive power, and the identification of limits that serve as default principles which statute can change or override. I need merely to note here that if statutory interpretation is the only theoretical basis for 'jurisdictional error', then judicial review of non-statutory public power must at the Commonwealth level seek its theoretical basis in the *Constitution*.

Back in the days when prerogative power was one of the common law's 'no go' areas, the courts said that they could determine whether a prerogative power

---

105 Named after *R v Panel on Take-overs and Mergers; Ex parte Datafin Plc* [1987] QB 815.
106 See M Aronson and M Groves, *Judicial Review of Administrative Action* (Thomson Reuters, 5th ed, 2013) [3.5]–[3.6].

existed, but that they could not set controls on how it was to be exercised.[107] It now appears that the principles of natural justice can sometimes attach to the exercise of prerogative[108] or non-statutory power,[109] and perhaps they might go further and supervise the exercise of some executive powers for fraud, malice or 'improper purpose'. It is difficult to understand how the other generic grounds of review would have any traction in a non-statutory context.[110]

The High Court spoke in *Plaintiff S157/2002 v Commonwealth*[111] ('*S157*') of 'an entrenched minimum provision of judicial review', and there has been some debate as to what exactly might be entrenched. If it were only the remedies for jurisdictional error, then entrenchment would provide little protection against a legislature determined to judge-proof its statutes. Parliament would be free to include 'no invalidity' provisions[112] in its Acts, stipulating, in effect, that breach of the Act's rules or requirements will not result in jurisdictional error. However, *S157* and other cases have raised the possibility that no parliament can give advance authority[113] for government agents to act fraudulently, maliciously, dishonestly, in bad faith, in return for a bribe, or for any other highly improper purpose.[114] Will Bateman has argued against trying to pick and choose between the generic principles that are entrenched and those which Parliament can override. His argument is that the substantive principle that needs entrenching is a prohibition against arbitrary power.[115]

---

107 *Prohibitions del Roy* (1607) 12 Co Rep 63; and *Case of Proclamations* (1611) 12 Co Rep 74, 76.
108 *Council of Civil Service Unions v Minister for the Civil Service* [1985] AC 374. The English cases must be treated with some caution, especially because they have (so far) assumed that legislation can override any prerogative. English judicial review now extends to a number of prerogatives, including prerogative legislation (taking the form of Orders in Council) for overseas territories: *R (Bancoult) v Secretary of State for Foreign and Commonwealth Affairs (No 2)* [2009] 1 AC 453. England's extension of judicial review's reach has usually not been much help to litigants, because the courts pay great respect to the government party's justifications for its actions; see T Poole, 'Judicial Review at the Margins: Law, Power, and Prerogative' (2010) 60 *University of Toronto Law Journal* 81. See also D Mullan, 'Judicial Review of the Executive – Principled Exasperation' (2010) 8 *New Zealand Journal of Public and International Law* 145.
109 *Minister for Arts, Heritage and Environment v Peko-Wallsend Ltd* (1987) 75 ALR 218.
110 See *R v Toohey; Ex parte Northern Land Council* (1981) 151 CLR 170, 219–20.
111 (2003) 211 CLR 476, 513.
112 I take this terminology from L McDonald, 'The Entrenched Minimum Provision of Judicial Review and the Rule of Law' (2010) 21 *PLR* 14, 15.
113 Acts of indemnity for wrongs already committed might be different.
114 *Plaintiff S157/2002 v Commonwealth* (2003) 211 CLR 476, 508; and *Commissioner of Taxation v Futuris Corporation Ltd* (2008) 237 CLR 146, 164–5.
115 W Bateman, 'The *Constitution* and the Substantive Principles of Judicial Review: The Full Scope of the Entrenched Minimum Provision of Judicial Review' (2011) 39 *Federal Law Review* 463.

Severing the link with jurisdictional error

The ADJR Act makes no specific reference to 'jurisdictional error', and indeed three of its grounds appear to have no common law analogue in jurisdictional error.[116] The most prominent of those three is the ground of review for any error of law. That has counterparts in three other Australian jurisdictions,[117] and substantively near-equivalents in two more.[118] Certiorari is a common law remedy that has long been available for non-jurisdictional error of law, on the proviso that the error must appear on the face of the decision-maker's record.[119] Similarly, the injunction and the declaration are not tethered to jurisdictional error.[120]

Subject to the possibilities already discussed of entrenching substantive principles of judicial review, all Parliaments are competent to reverse these instances of judicial review for non-jurisdictional errors. The High Court said twice in *Kirk* that the distinction between jurisdictional and non-jurisdictional errors of law was 'useful'.[121] Given the context, I assume that the utility lies partly in allowing the courts to refrain from overly intrusive review for minor legal errors, and partly in allowing the legislature some voice in setting the margins for allowable error. Judicial review of migration decisions, for example, lies only for jurisdictional error.[122]

It might at this point be asked whether there would have been any practical difference if the High Court had followed the English cases, and decided that all errors of law are jurisdictional at common law, no matter what remedy is being sought. The added reach of judicial review would have required (as in England) more frequent resort to the court's discretionary power to refuse relief,[123] but there

---

116 See above, nn 51–53.
117 See: *Administrative Decisions (Judicial Review) Act 1989* (ACT), ss 5(1)(f), 6(1)(f); *Judicial Review Act 1991* (Qld), ss 20(2)(f), 21(2)(f); and *Judicial Review Act 2000* (Tas), ss 17(2)(f), 18(2)(f).
118 *Administrative Law Act 1978* (Vic), s 10; and *Supreme Court Act 1970* (NSW), s 69.
119 *Craig v South Australia* (1995) 184 CLR 163. Note that in the High Court's constitutional writ jurisdiction under s 75(v) of the *Constitution*, certiorari is an ancillary remedy that lies only for jurisdictional error: *Re McBain; Ex parte Australian Catholic Bishops Conference* (2002) 209 CLR 372; *Bodruddaza v Minister for Immigration and Multicultural Affairs* (2007) 228 CLR 651; and *Commissioner of Taxation v Futuris Corporation Ltd* (2008) 237 CLR 146, 162.
120 See: *Project Blue Sky Inc v Australian Broadcasting Authority* (1998) 194 CLR 355, 393; *Australian Broadcasting Corp v Lenah Game Meats Pty Ltd* (2001) 208 CLR 199, 232, 240–41; *Muin v Refugee Review Tribunal* (2002) 190 ALR 601, [47], [169]; and *Re Minister for Immigration and Multicultural Affairs; Ex parte Lam* (2003) 214 CLR 1, 21.
121 *Kirk v Industrial Court (NSW)* (2010) 239 CLR 531, 576, 581.
122 *Plaintiff S157/2002 v Commonwealth* (2003) 211 CLR 476.
123 Lord Carnwath said in *Walton v Scottish Ministers* [2012] UKSC 44, [103] that the judicial discretion to refuse relief is the 'necessary counterbalance to the widening of rules of standing'.

might be some who would argue that this would have forced the courts to be more articulate as to their criteria for self-restraint. The argument assumes that Australia's distinction between jurisdictional and non-jurisdictional errors of law is so manipulable that it is in substance just as discretionary as the English system. I have two reasons for disagreeing. First, I see no inarticulacy in *Kirk*'s frank balancing of normative and functional considerations. I might add that there is an almost complete lack of transparency in England's major filtering mechanism – the application for permission to proceed is, in effect, a black hole. The vast bulk of such applications are determined on the papers, without the provision of detailed reasons.[124] Second, the High Court has struck a strategically sensible compromise in its decision to allow legislatures some flexibility in cutting off review for minor legal errors. I suspect that if it is compelled to give further definition to that compromise, it might align it to separation of powers principles.

Conclusion

This inquiry into the meaning and operation of the concept of 'jurisdictional error' started with the relatively easy issues, but quickly led to some of administrative law's most difficult questions. That is because the term itself lies at the core of Australian judicial review, with ramifications for the criteria for judicial review challenges to the bureaucracy, and for the consequences in any particular case of having established those criteria.

The term used to have a narrow meaning – authority to commence a process ending in the determination of an issue. And it used to have a narrow field of operation – it applied only in respect of judicial or quasi-judicial bodies or functions. Those constraints have long since gone. These days, jurisdictional errors can be committed at the outset of a process, during it, or at its conclusion, and the process need not be 'judicial' in any sense of that term. Indeed, 'jurisdictional error' is now conclusory – the establishment of any one of the grounds of judicial review that lead to invalidity *is* the establishment of a jurisdictional error.

This chapter contains an indicative list of the generic grounds of review – a list that bears a strong resemblance to the list to be found in the ADJR Act. Each list is

---

[124] See: H Woolf, J Jowell, A Le Sueur, C Donnelly and I Hare, *De Smith's Judicial Review* (Sweet and Maxwell, 7th ed, 2013) 915–23; V Bondy and M Sunkin, 'Accessing Judicial Review' [2008] *Public Law* 647; V Bondy and M Sunkin, 'Settlement in Judicial Review Proceedings' [2009] *Public Law* 237; and V Bondy and L Mulcahy, *Mediation and Judicial Review: An Empirical Research Study* (Public Law Project, London, 2009) (available online at <www.publiclawproject.org.uk>) 17–24. Full reasons are given in three of the four Australian jurisdictions (above n 64) with a leave filter, but most High Court leave applications have no oral hearing.

useful, but they are neither exhaustive nor self-contained. The common law list is not exhaustive because the common law is continually reshaping its grounds and adding to them, and the ADJR Act's list has two 'catch-all' grounds enabling it pick up any new developments at common law. Further, there are necessarily some grounds of review that are not generic, that are instead unique to their particular statutory contexts, which set specific limits to a public official's authority.

The lists of generic grounds are not just non-exhaustive – the grounds themselves are not self-contained. A judge's task in judicial review is to determine the legality of the official's decision or conduct – not to replace it with an order reflecting how the judge would have decided or acted if the administrative task had been entrusted to him or her. In one sense, therefore, judicial review's grounds are all about margins – how to determine the limits within which bureaucrats are free to make their own assessments of facts, policy or value, and even the limits within which they are free to make errors of law that might go uncorrected. Predicting where those margins will be set in any particular context is a necessarily imprecise task. Australian cases say that it all depends, in the long run, on questions of statutory interpretation.

To an English reader, Australia's generic grounds seem too specific, and lacking in any overarching moral or political concept such as 'the maintenance of the rule of law', or 'the prevention of abuse of public power'. Such principles influence the formation and application of our generic grounds – how could they not? – but they are not grounds in their own right. The ARC debated whether to recommend replacing or supplementing the generic grounds with very broad statements of general principle underlying the entire spectrum of government's administrative activity. It wisely decided against that option, which would have been too difficult for too little gain. It was an option that had the real potential to generate a considerable amount of extra complexity.

The fact is that judicial review's grounds (what constitutes 'jurisdictional error') vary across statutory contexts. The subjects of judicial review cannot all be squeezed into a 'one size fits all' model. The cases typically start with the particular statutory context, but add to it general interpretive principles that mould or shape the way we read statutes. Very few Acts actually tell their readers in so many words whether the bureaucracy must obey the particular Act's rules or requirements if decisions made under them are to be valid.

Statutory interpretation is said to be the mainspring of 'jurisdictional error', and of decisions as to the extent to which a court can retrospectively erase the adverse consequences that flow from a jurisdictionally flawed decision, but judges necessarily bring to the task of statutory interpretation an accumulation of legal principles and values. These are used to 'flesh out' statutory texts, as also is a court's sense of the need to strike a balance of sorts between legal values and administrative practicalities.

Complaints that 'jurisdictional error' provides too little guidance are therefore misguided. They boil down to complaints that statutory interpretation can be an imprecise art. Of course it is, in any country, and in administrative law as in any other field of law. Administrative law deals with the administrative state – a huge and multifaceted creature. Statutory interpretation cannot just be about statutory text. The courts have an unavoidable role in filling in the gaps left by the usual failure of legislative drafters to distinguish between mandatory and directory provisions. And in this as in any other field of law involving the interaction of statutory and common law, the courts bring to statutory interpretation their presuppositions as to the spoken and unspoken meaning behind, or qualifying, otherwise plain statutory language.

Aside, perhaps, from the very peculiar context of High Court review of Federal Court decisions, the High Court has told us that 'jurisdictional error' is here to stay – it is the irreducible minimum of the constitutionally entrenched jurisdictions of the High Court itself, and of all State Supreme Courts. The term itself does not appear in the ADJR Act, although that Act stays very close to the common law grounds except when it comes to review for any error of law. 'Jurisdictional error', therefore, has a very long shelf-life, but the frequency with which we need to use that terminology will vary according to whether we are forced beyond statutory restatements of the common law to the common law itself.

PRIVATIVE CLAUSES: POLITICS, LEGALITY AND THE CONSTITUTIONAL DIMENSION

Simon Young*

---

* I would like to acknowledge the work and wisdom of Bill Lane, Richard Hooker and Chris Field, with whom I have worked in the field of administrative law for many years. I am also indebted to the editor of this book, Matthew Groves, for his insightful comments on the draft of this chapter.

Introduction

Privative clauses are essentially a legislative attempt to limit or exclude judicial intervention in a certain field. They have been deployed by parliaments over many years for many reasons – a desire for finality or certainty, a concern about sensitivity or controversy, a wish to avoid delay and expense, or a perception that a matter requires specialist expertise and/or awareness of executive context. Yet a common response from observers is that a broad and undiscerning use of such legislation promotes temporary and specific convenience, and perhaps political expediency, over fundamental legal values.

It has long been acknowledged that to accompany the conferral of a specified public function with a privative clause is something of a contradiction.[1] Parliament is on the one hand conferring (probably well-defined) functions and powers, whilst also providing, in effect, that the recipient may act however it wishes, free from judicial supervision and control. The contradiction here is not trivial. The Diceyan conception of the rule of law sits squarely in one corner[2] and is easily agitated in a system where the executive not only holds administrative power but also tends to dominate the legislature.[3] Also, even the vaguest notion of a 'separation of powers' suggests that there should ultimately be some limit on ouster of judicial intervention in executive decision-making. Yet by the same token, the principles of parliamentary supremacy and the floating ideals of a parliamentary democracy suggest that a clear legislative intention should be respected. Not surprisingly then, the history of privative clauses in Australia is one of acute legal tension. The courts have long read such clauses narrowly, often reciting the relevant foundational legal tenets and presumptions about non-interference with rights or access to the judicial system. Perhaps inevitably, the resistance has been somewhat conceptually scattered.

The principal means by which the courts have evaded privative clauses are discussed in the first section of this chapter. However, it is important to note at the outset that privative mechanisms vary and continue to evolve, and hence constantly present new challenges to judges. There are some reasonably common formulations, for example a direction that any decision by a body is final and conclusive and not to be challenged, appealed or questioned in any court. However, many other versions have been tried, refined and combined over the

---

1 Eg, *Clancy v Butchers' Chop Employees Union* (1904) 1 CLR 181.
2 M Aronson, 'Commentary on "the Entrenched Minimum Provision of Judicial Review and the Rule of Law"' (2010) 21 *Public Law Review* 35, 37.
3 Cf M Aronson and M Groves, *Judicial Review of Administrative Action* (Lawbook, 5th edn, 2013) 17.10.

years – ultimately shading into broader legislative drafting practices that might not immediately seem privative in nature. The various devices employed, beyond the clause which simply declares finality and/or prohibits judicial challenge, include restrictions on specified remedies, restrictions on available grounds of challenge, confinement or redirection of review jurisdiction, 'conclusive evidence' provisions, 'no-invalidity' type provisions, provisions declaring things to have effect 'as if enacted', and time limits.[4]

The expanding constitutional entrenchment of 'jurisdictional error' review, particularly via the decision in *Kirk v Industrial Court (NSW)*,[5] has brought the mechanisms for ouster back to centre stage. How will these devices work in the new constitutional context? There has been a rush of academic interest here because a number of roads now converge at this particular point in administrative law. The pattern of recent commentary suggests a response to *Kirk* of three stages. First, given that standard privative clauses are now unable to protect jurisdictional error from High Court or Supreme Court review, how else might parliaments achieve this? Second, how might the courts legitimately respond to these alternatives? Can the substance of the new constitutional protection be shored up in some way? Finally, how hard should courts and academics work to reinforce this review jurisdiction? The discussion in this chapter will ultimately return to these matters, but first there is some background to traverse.

Traditional interpretative techniques

The courts have largely maintained an awkward but determined resistance to privative provisions.[6] At a basic level, clauses have commonly been restricted to their express scope – for example, their protection confined to the named body (strictly defined) or upheld only against the named judicial remedies.[7] Moreover, they have often been read down to their lesser viable operation – for example, an ousting of 'actions', 'proceedings' or 'appeals', or indeed an immunity from

---

4 See further Administrative Review Council, Discussion Paper: *The Scope of Judicial Review* (2003), Appendix 2, 157ff.
5 (2010) 239 CLR 531.
6 On the techniques employed, see Aronson and Groves, above n 3, 17.3; R Creyke and J McMillan, *Control of Government Action* (LexisNexis, 3rd edn, 2012) 870ff.
7 *G J Coles & Co Ltd v Retail Trade Industrial Tribunal* (1986) 7 NSWLR 503 (improperly constituted tribunal); *Wingecarribee Shire Council v Minister for Local Government* [1975] 2 NSWLR 779 (bar to prohibition and certiorari only). Cf, recently, *Building Insurers' Guarantee Corporation v Owners – Strata Plan 60848* [2012] NSWCA 375.

'liability', may be read so as not to protect the decision-maker from judicial review.[8] Similarly, basic 'final and conclusive' clauses have been read to exclude only appeal (rather than judicial review).[9] And 'no certiorari' clauses have been held to protect only the lesser target of this writ, errors on the record.[10] Of course the plaintiff may also have a part to play in the avoidance of a privative clause. They may, for example, commence proceedings prior to the making of a determination that might be protected,[11] or indeed refashion their arguments to target available remedies or grounds or to focus on particular unprotected aspects of the broader process in train (see below).

Here, also, we find one of the most important functions of the amorphous concept of 'jurisdictional error': even broadly worded privative clauses have frequently been held not to protect such serious error. This is an old methodology,[12] recently described as 'elegant in its simplicity'.[13] A traditional explanation was that a purported ouster of review should not effectively render a power unlimited, by allowing a decision-maker to proceed without interference beyond the expressly defined jurisdiction.[14] Constitutional considerations ultimately broadly reinforced this approach, but the traditional interpretative principle remains in the background, often by some variation on the basic logic that a clause declaring protection for a 'decision' will not apply where there is jurisdictional error because the resulting nullity means there is no 'decision' to protect.[15] Parliaments ultimately developed responses to this logic, such as a privative clause expressed to extend to 'purported decisions'.[16] The High Court at one point cast some doubt upon the textual effectiveness of such an extension,[17] but appears to have acknowledged again its potential role in extending protection[18] (subject of course to constitutional considerations).

There were always conceptual difficulties with the 'jurisdictional error' approach. For example, this interpretative technique was ill-fitting where a privative clause

---

8   *Applicants A1 and A2 v G E Brouwer* (2007) 16 VR 612 (no 'action or proceedings');
    Curruthers v Connolly [1998] 1 Qd R 339 ('protection and immunity', 'no liability').
9   *Hockey v Yelland* (1984) 157 CLR 124.
10 *Anisminic Ltd v Foreign Compensation Commission* [1969] 2 AC 147.
11 *Batterham v QSR Ltd* (2006) 225 CLR 237.
12 *Clancy v Butchers' Chop Employees Union* (1904) 1 CLR 181.
13 W Bateman, 'The Constitution and the Substantive Principles of Judicial Review: The Full Scope of the Entrenched Minimum Provision of Judicial Review' (2011) 39 *Federal Law Review* 463, 470.
14 *R v Commonwealth Rent Controller; Ex parte National Mutual Life Association of Australasia Limited* (1947) 75 CLR 361, 368–9.
15 *Kirk v Industrial Court (NSW)* (2010) 239 CLR 531 (discussed below).
16 *Mitchforce Pty Ltd v Industrial Relations Commission of New South Wales* (2003) 57 NSWLR 212; *Bodruddaza v Minister for Immigration and Multicultural Affairs* (2007) 228 CLR 651.
17 *Batterham v QSR Ltd* (2006) 225 CLR 237, 249.
18 *Kirk v Industrial Court (NSW)* (2010) 239 CLR 531, 582; and the implications of *MZXOT v Minister for Immigration and Citizenship* (2008) 233 CLR 601.

specifically named remedies that were *only* available for jurisdictional error. More importantly, this close traditional (and contemporary) association between privative clauses and 'jurisdictional error' means that the former frequently become entangled in the uncertainties of the latter. Of course the privative clause deserves no sympathy on this front. As will be seen, migration privative devices drove the haphazard resurgence of the notion of jurisdictional error.[19]

A separate approach to privative clause interpretation,[20] the *Hickman* methodology, was prominent in Australia for a long period. This approach involved (as we now understand it) a very strong presumption of reviewability when certain particularly serious errors were identified. *Hickman* itself concerned a privative clause relating to decisions of a coal mining industrial relations board. Dixon J in his separate judgment emphasised that determining the effect of such clauses required reconciliation of the power conferring provisions with the terms of the ouster. Later courts drew a formula from this analysis, which involved inquiry into whether the decision in issue was a bona fide attempt to exercise the power; was related to the subject matter of the legislation; and was reasonably capable of reference to the power conferred (ie did not on its face go beyond power).[21]

These vaguely worded provisos are best understood, from a contemporary viewpoint, as targeting a core selection of jurisdictional errors[22] – sometimes called 'manifest errors'. This formula was keenly recited in decisions for many years,[23] establishing a path of sorts through the privative clause dilemmas. Yet this methodology faded somewhat in application and rationale over time.[24] Besides, there were variations – at least in emphasis – in important restatements,[25] and hence a lingering uncertainty over its precise effect. The High Court has since explained that the *Hickman* principle is essentially just a construction aid to help resolve the statutory contradiction that comes with a privative clause,[26] and indeed is only a first step in ascertaining their effect.

---

19 S Gageler, 'Impact of Migration Law on the Development of Australian Administrative Law' (2010) 17 *Australian Journal of Administrative Law* 92.
20 At least for clauses apparently aimed at protecting jurisdictional error: see Aronson and Groves, above n 3, 17.150.
21 *R v Hickman; Ex parte Fox and Clinton* (1945) 70 CLR 598, 615–17; *Plaintiff S157/2002 v Commonwealth* (2003) 211 CLR 476, 500.
22 C Finn, 'Constitutionalising Supervisory Review at State Level: The End of Hickman?' (2010) 21 *Public Law Review* 92, 103; J J Spigelman, 'The Centrality of Jurisdictional Error' (2010) 21 *Public Law Review* 77, 82.
23 See, eg, *R v Commonwealth Conciliation and Arbitration Commission* (1967) 118 CLR 219; *O'Toole v Charles David Pty Ltd* (1991) 171 CLR 232.
24 Aronson and Groves, above n 3, 17.20.
25 Eg, *R v Murray; Ex parte Proctor* (1949) 77 CLR 387 (Dixon J) as to a second search for 'inviolable' or 'imperative' duties.
26 See the discussion of *Plaintiff S157/2002 v Commonwealth* (2003) 211 CLR 476 below.

The contemporary Australian jurisprudence and commentary on privative clauses was relatively slow in coming. There was for a time a tendency to regard these issues as chiefly a concern of industrial law, where they were long prominent. In addition, the significance of this drafting device was disassembled to some extent, initially at the federal level, by the enactment of the *Administrative Decisions (Judicial Review) Act 1977* (Cth) ('ADJR Act'), which contained a provision negating the operation of pre-existing privative clauses in other legislation and a mechanism by which classes of decision could be excluded from review by the Act's own schedule. But the traditional privative clause did not remain peripheral for long.

Privative clauses and contemporary federal jurisdiction: *Plaintiff S157*

From the early 1990s, accumulating controversies in migration led to a series of Commonwealth legislative initiatives that began to significantly re-shape Australian administrative law.[27] Federal Parliament sought essentially to restrict the Federal Court's extensive capacity (under ADJR Act and general law jurisdiction) to review migration decisions. The original strategy, essentially of substituting a scheme with constricted grounds,[28] did not have great effect, owing to the courts' generous interpretations and the plaintiffs' strategic re-fashioning of arguments (or engagement of the High Court's own s 75(v) jurisdiction).[29] In 2001 the legislature enacted a general, broadly worded privative clause (s 474) that declared finality, prohibited challenge and excluded the key remedies in respect of (broadly defined) 'privative clause decisions'.[30] The Commonwealth argued that this strongly worded clause should substantially confine judicial review, by limiting invalidity to actions which did not satisfy the *Hickman* provisos and thereby effectively expanding the

---

27 See generally E Campbell and M Groves, 'Privative Clauses and the Australian Constitution' (2004) 4 *Oxford University Commonwealth Law Journal* 51.
28 1992 amendments established a new Pt 8 of the *Migration Act 1958* (Cth), declared valid in *Abebe v Commonwealth* (1999) 197 CLR 510.
29 See particularly *Minister for Immigration and Multicultural Affairs v Yusuf* (2001) 206 CLR 323, esp at [77]ff; *Minister for Immigration and Multicultural Affairs; Ex parte Applicant S20/2002* (2003) 198 ALR 59, [74], [146].
30 *Migration Act 1958* (Cth), s 474(1)–(2). See also the then para (da) in Sch 1 of the ADJR Act (exclusion of 'privative clause decisions').

relevant field of lawful activity.[31] The underlying logic was that privative clause protection would always be effective where the *Hickman* provisos were met – reflecting the bolder reading of *Hickman*.

The Commonwealth's position initially gained some traction,[32] but the High Court decision in *Plaintiff S157/2002 v Commonwealth*[33] would unseat much of this reasoning. In these s 75(v) proceedings (alleging breach of natural justice by the Refugee Review Tribunal (RRT)), the plaintiff argued that the s 474 privative clause was invalid in this constitutional setting (a possibility ultimately avoided), while the Commonwealth pressed its power-expansion reading of *Hickman*. The High Court held that the meaning of privative clauses must be ascertained from their terms and any necessary reconciliation with the power-conferring provisions, and that they did not (aided by *Hickman*) effect some automatic expansion of statutory authority or repeal of limits elsewhere stated (here in very expansive legislation).[34] The Court indicated that satisfaction of the *Hickman* provisos was required for privative clause protection to attach, but was not necessarily sufficient. The second step required a search for any (other) inviolable or essential requirements attaching to the power.[35] Yet it was acknowledged that not every statutory limitation must be inviolable (with breaches incapable of protection). The majority observed that some requirements might be construed as not essential to validity.[36] The idea behind this second step – a search for infringement of an inviolable or essential restraint – was not new. This was arguably implicit in *Hickman* itself and further developed thereafter.[37]

Having placed *Hickman* in its proper place, the High Court stressed other rules of construction. Citing the need to read privative clauses narrowly (based on presumptions about parliamentary intentions), and more critically the need to interpret them consistently with the *Constitution* where possible, the joint majority arrived at a somewhat traditional textual restriction of s 474. It was held that a decision involving jurisdictional error was not a 'privative clause decision' to which s 474 attached.[38] The constitutional difficulties attending a broader interpretation of the clause were

---

31 Hansard House of Representatives (26 September 2001), 31559–31561. Cf, eg, *Darling Casino Ltd v New South Wales Casino Control Authority* (1997) 191 CLR 602, 630 (Gaudron and Gummow JJ).
32 At least in the Federal Court: *NAAV v Minister for Immigration and Multicultural and Indigenous Affairs* (2002) 123 FCR 298.
33 (2003) 211 CLR 476.
34 Ibid, 499–501 (Gaudron, McHugh, Gummow, Kirby and Hayne JJ); cf at 493 (Gleeson CJ).
35 Ibid, 488, 512.
36 Ibid, 504, 506.
37 *R v Murray; Ex parte Proctor* (1949) 77 CLR 387; *R v Coldham; Ex parte Australian Workers' Union* (1983) 153 CLR 415; *Mitchforce Pty Ltd v Industrial Relations Commission of New South Wales* (2003) 57 NSWLR 212, 232 (Spigelman CJ).
38 (2003) 211 CLR 476, 505 (it was not a decision 'made under' the Act as required for that category, and perhaps not a 'decision' at all).

significant. It is clear that the Commonwealth Parliament can not deprive the High Court of its constitutional jurisdiction under s 75(v) to supervise jurisdictional error.[39] Whatever the original purposes behind s 75(v), this 'accountability' function of the provision dominated its later history.[40] Significant constitutional difficulties also arise in any attempt by Commonwealth Parliament to confer upon an administrative body a power to conclusively determine the limits of its own jurisdiction.[41]

The majority in *Plaintiff S157* returned then to the notion of a 'reconciliation' of the statutory provisions, as a means of determining whether some failure constitutes a jurisdictional error (thus falling outside s 474 protection). However, their Honours quickly so classified the breach of natural justice claimed here, simply based on earlier precedent.[42] Interestingly, Gleeson CJ proceeded further on this path, noting that the question of whether an RRT decision in breach of natural justice was unprotected by the privative clause depended on a construction of the statute as a whole, which here made it clear that this was a breach of an indispensable condition on the power.[43] This late methodological divergence between Gleeson CJ and the joint majority was maybe not just a matter of judicial stamina. The lead-up reasoning of all of these judges obviously reflects some conflation of the search for 'essential' limitations and the notion of jurisdictional error,[44] but while this association is ever more frequently seen, it is one which is as yet incomplete given the ongoing influence of the pre-mixed formulas from *Craig v South Australia*[45] and presumptions about the status of certain errors. The latter were on display in *Plaintiff S157*, in the joint judgment. At base, this divergence perhaps reflects a lingering tension between what may be termed 'internal' (ie derived from the statute at hand) and 'external' conceptualisations of jurisdictional error. To some extent this is an old dichotomy, lining up with the well-worn debate between 'ultra vires theorists', who emphasise statutory boundaries, and 'common law theorists', who emphasise the deeper historical and conceptual roots of the law.[46] Yet it would seem that this opposition might be heavily implicated in the

---

39 (2003) 211 CLR 476, 482, 498, 500, 505ff and 513.
40 See M Groves, 'Outsourcing and s 75(v) of the Constitution' (2011) 22 *Public Law Review* 3; J Stellios, 'Exploring the Purposes of Section 75(v) of the Constitution' (2011) 34 *University of NSW Law Journal* 70.
41 (2003) 211 CLR 476, 484, 505; cf *R v Kirby; Ex parte Boilermakers' Society of Australia* (1956) 94 CLR 254; *R v Coldham; Ex parte Australian Workers' Union* (1983) 153 CLR 415.
42 Ibid, 506–08, cf 496.
43 Ibid, 490–91, 494. Cf *Re Minister for Immigration and Multicultural and Indigenous Affairs; Ex parte Akpata* [2002] HCA 34.
44 Ibid, 504–7 (Gaudron, McHugh, Gummow, Kirby and Hayne JJ. Cf the implications of Gleeson CJ's comments at 486, 489–90, 493.
45 (1995) 184 CLR 163.
46 See further D Meyerson, 'State and Federal Privative Clauses: Not So Different After All' (2005) 16 *Public Law Review* 39.

very contemporary uncertainty over jurisdictional error. And it is very relevant to emerging questions about how legislatures can respond to the constitutional entrenchment of jurisdictional error review and how courts in turn might react.

Plaintiff S157 also read down a time limit on High Court review proceedings (s 486A – similarly attaching to a 'privative clause decision').[47] Yet subsequently, in *Bodruddaza v Minister for Immigration and Multicultural Affairs*,[48] the Court examined an amended s 486A that clearly sought to cover jurisdictional error and hence brought the constitutional issue into sharper relief.[49] The new s 486A was ruled invalid because it subverted the constitutionally entrenched right under s 75(v) to seek review before the High Court. The Court held that a decision on the validity of the clause required consideration of its substance or practical effect, not merely its form. Particular reference was made to the time limit here being inflexibly calculated from decision notification, and to the potential difficulties which applicants may face in identifying reviewable errors within the period so set. This case was perhaps the high point of the High Court's shoring up of its judicial review jurisdiction. Amendments which attempted to restrict the High Court's power of remittal (in a complicated confinement of review options) were subsequently ruled *valid* by the High Court in *MZXOT v Minister for Immigration and Citizenship*.[50]

The s 75(v) backstop has some important limits. One is that the reach of this jurisdiction, and hence the federal supervisory guarantee, is limited by the notion of 'officer of the Commonwealth' which remains of uncertain application in the context of corporatised and outsourced federal activity.[51] A point of broader significance is the uncertain position of the Federal Court after *Plaintiff S157*. Notwithstanding its varying role in migration over recent years, the Federal Court is a key player in judicial review more broadly (including via its general law jurisdiction). Yet while the traditional textual confinement of s 474 was very relevant to Federal Court matters at the time,[52] that Court is not a direct beneficiary of much of the constitutional reasoning in *Plaintiff S157* (or indeed in the *Kirk* decision on State Supreme Courts, discussed below). Obviously the Federal Court has a range of traditional interpretative tools at its disposal for the evasion of privative clauses;

---

47 (2003) 211 CLR 476, 495, 509–10; cf Callinan J at 537.
48 (2007) 228 CLR 651, 671–2.
49 Note the express extension of the provision to 'purported' decisions (defined by reference to failures to exercise or excess of jurisdiction).
50 (2008) 233 CLR 601 (arguments about undue burdens on the High Court and constitutional implications failed). See further L Burton, '*MZXOT v Minister for Immigration & Citizenship*: Last stop on Route 75(v)?' (2009) 16 *Australian Journal of Administrative Law* 115.
51 Groves, above n 40.
52 *Plaintiff S157/2002 v Commonwealth* (2003) 211 CLR 476, 511.

however, it may not be easy to find for it some greater protection of its judicial review function.[53]

It should also be remembered in any consideration of the Federal Court that its ADJR Act jurisdiction (although no longer significant in the migration context[54]) was initially reinforced by the inclusion of a provision[55] effectively negating, for ADJR Act purposes, the operation of pre-existing privative clauses (ie those enacted before 1 October 1980). The significance of this provision has obviously declined with the passage of time. Also, the ADJR Act has a 'Schedule 1' (now sizeable) which operates to expressly exclude various classes of decisions from ADJR Act review – including a broad swathe of migration decisions.[56]

Privative clauses and contemporary State jurisdiction: *Kirk*

Following *Plaintiff S157*, there was deliberation on the relevance of this decision to the operation of privative clauses at State level.[57] The traditional interpretative mechanisms obviously continued to apply, and the *Hickman* principle was generally assumed to have a role,[58] but inevitably there was discussion of grander potential restrictions on State legislative ouster.[59] There was quite a distance to travel here. In Australia there was a reasonably settled assumption that skilled State drafting could produce a privative clause that did effectively exclude review of jurisdictional error. A passage from *Darling Casino Ltd v New South Wales Casino Control Authority*,[60] identifying only the narrower *Hickman* standard as the ultimate

---

53 See, eg, the implications of the reasoning in *MZXOT v Minister for Immigration and Citizenship* (2008) 233 CLR 601 (re the current ss 476 and 476A of the *Migration Act 1958* (Cth)); cf *Abebe v Commonwealth* (1999) 197 CLR 510; *Minister for Immigration and Multicultural Affairs v Eshetu* (1999) 197 CLR 611.
54 See now ADJR Act, s 3 and Sch 1 (cl (da) and (db)).
55 ADJR Act, s 4. See also *Judicial Review Act 1991* (Qld), s 18; *Judicial Review Act 2000* (Tas), s 15; *Administrative Decisions (Judicial Review) Act 1989* (ACT), s 4; *Administrative Law Act 1978* (Vic), s 12.
56 See the cross-references to the broad definitions in ss 474(2) and 5E of the *Migration Act 1958* (Cth). See also *Aye v Minister for Immigration and Citizenship* (2010) 187 FCR 449.
57 M Sexton and J Quilter, 'Privative Clauses and State Constitutions' (2003) 5 *Constitutional Law and Policy Review* 69.
58 *Maitland City Council v Anumbah Homes Pty Ltd* (2005) 64 NSWLR 695.
59 On the difficulties here, see Meyerson, above n 46.
60 (1997) 191 CLR 602, 634 (Gaudron and Gummow JJ).

supervisory preserve, is often referred to in this regard. This thinking lingered. In the post-*Plaintiff S157* NSW decision of *Mitchforce Pty Ltd v Industrial Relations Commission of New South Wales*,[61] Spigelman CJ referred to *Darling Casino* and noted that at State level the *Hickman* principle operated 'by a process of statutory construction without constitutional overlay'.[62] So while a privative clause clearly seeking to protect jurisdictional error would run aground in the federal (s 75(v)) context,[63] it was thought that a State equivalent may be more effective.[64]

The point arrived squarely before the High Court in the 2010 case of *Kirk v Industrial Court (NSW)*.[65] This case marked a significant advance in the collaboration between administrative law and constitutional law in Australia because the High Court effectively replicated for State Supreme Courts the constitutional protection afforded to its own s 75(v) jurisdiction. This major step perhaps should not have been unexpected,[66] and indeed was predicted by some.[67] In administrative law terms, *Kirk* goes some way towards closing a circle as regards the resilience of judicial review jurisdiction in Australia. In constitutional law terms it is part of a broader story of the emerging constitutional personality of State Supreme Courts.[68]

Kirk concerned an occupational health and safety prosecution in the NSW Industrial Court. The proceedings were potentially protected by a privative clause declaring such decisions final and prohibiting judicial intervention by any relief or remedy (s 179 of the *Industrial Relations Act 1996* (NSW)). The High Court found the proceedings to be flawed by reason of a lack of particularisation in the statement of charges[69] and the prosecution's calling of Kirk as a witness, contrary to *Evidence Act* restrictions.[70] Both were identified as 'jurisdictional errors'.[71] From that point, it was determined that the Supreme Courts' supervisory jurisdiction over the errors was constitutionally protected. The Court confirmed that

---

61 (2003) 57 NSWLR 212.
62 Ibid, 229 (Spigelman CJ).
63 *Bodruddaza v Minister for Immigration and Multicultural Affairs* (2007) 228 CLR 651.
64 (2003) 57 NSWLR 212, 230, 233 (Spigelman CJ).
65 (2010) 239 CLR 531.
66 J Basten, 'The Supervisory Jurisdiction of the Supreme Court' (2011) 85 *Australian Law Journal* 273, 278.
67 See Spigelman, above n 22; cf also eg Campbell and Groves, above n 27.
68 See, eg, *Wainohu v State of New South Wales* (2011) 243 CLR 181; *Condon v Pompano Pty Ltd* [2013] HCA 7.
69 (2010) 239 CLR 531, 553ff (French CJ, Gummow, Hayne, Crennan, Kiefel and Bell JJ).
70 Ibid, 565.
71 Ibid, 573. It was also noted, at 575, that both of these errors appeared 'on the face of the record' as that expression must be understood in light of ss 69(3)–(4) of the *Supreme Court Act 1970* (NSW). This had no bearing here, but importantly the majority flagged an impending reassessment of the common law's confined understanding of the scope of the 'record'.

Chapter III of the *Constitution* requires there to be a body fitting the description 'Supreme Court of a State'. It is beyond the power of a State, it was said, to alter the constitution or character of its Supreme Court so that it ceases to meet the constitutional description.[72] Most importantly, and more controversially,[73] it was said that a defining characteristic of State Supreme Courts is the power to confine inferior courts and tribunals within the limits of their authority via the grant of relief on grounds of jurisdictional error (which is ultimately subject to High Court supervision by s 73 appeals).[74] Particular reference was made in this context to 'accepted doctrine' at the time of federation, the importance of this Supreme Court review function as regards State executive and judicial power, and the fact that loss of this mechanism would create 'islands of power' immune from supervision and restraint. Consequently, the court declared that a State privative clause which purports to strip the Supreme Court of this function of correcting jurisdictional error is beyond State legislative power.[75]

The High Court majority ultimately took its new constitutional principle, as well as the traditional tools of strict textual interpretation, back to the privative clause in issue and concluded that it should be read down.[76] The privative clause did not, and could not validly, exclude the jurisdiction of the Supreme Court to grant relief via certiorari, prohibition or mandamus to enforce the limits of the Industrial Court's statutory authority. It did not on its proper construction, therefore, exclude certiorari for jurisdictional error.

As adverted to above, the constitutional foundation of *Kirk* (in fact its reliance on both the history and constitutional text) has been questioned. And some point out that this is a further promotion of the judiciary over the executive and legislature, when even the protection accorded to s 75(v) jurisdiction, on which *Kirk* builds, sits awkwardly with its original purposes.[77] Yet ultimately, few seem to question the prospective worth of *Kirk*, and the High Court would be highly unlikely to ever relinquish the public law symmetry it has now achieved through replication of the s 75(v) constitutional guarantee. Former Chief Justice Spigelman has described the result in *Kirk* as a matter of 'gravity'; the product of ongoing constitutional 'pull' upon State administrative law.[78]

---

72 Ibid, 566, 578–9.
73 N Gouliaditis, 'Privative Clauses: Epic Fail' (2010) 34 *Melbourne University Law Review* 870.
74 (2010) 239 CLR 531, 566–7, 580. The principle clearly extends to executive decision-making more broadly.
75 Ibid, 566–7, 581. Protection of non-jurisdictional error (including that appearing on the face of the record) is not beyond power: 581.
76 Ibid, 581–2.
77 R Sackville, 'The constitutionalisation of State administrative law' (2012) 19 *Australian Journal of Administrative Law* 127, 129ff.
78 Spigelman, above n 22, 77.

Subsequent lower court decisions have begun exploring the various implications of the *Kirk* decision, as regards prosecutorial and evidentiary practice and of course State legislative capacity. In the latter regard, *Kirk* might seem to have delivered a death blow to the old assumption that determined State Parliaments could exclude review of jurisdictional error. The decision in *South Australia v Totani*[79] confirmed that bolder contemporary drafting techniques, such as the extension of privative clauses to 'purported decisions', now suffer the same difficulties in the State Supreme Court context as they do in the context of original High Court review. There are deeper issues to be explored here about the manner in which 'jurisdiction' might be defined by legislatures. The High Court took a small step into these issues in the recent case of *Public Service Association of South Australia Inc v Industrial Relations Commission (SA)*,[80] reading a limited express *exception* to the protection of a State privative clause (namely an exception for 'excess or want of jurisdiction') as including a failure to exercise jurisdiction. It was said that the reading of such provisions must take into account the incapacity of States to take from Supreme Courts their authority over jurisdictional error; and that the expression in issue was 'apt to include jurisdictional error, rather than merely some species of jurisdictional error'.[81] The implications of more fundamental legislative manipulation of 'jurisdiction' are considered below.

What is left of the old *Hickman* principle? Following *Plaintiff S157* (and before the constitutional override arrived at the State level), important State cases had applied the aggregated *Hickman* approach: privative clause protection was apparently understood to depend upon satisfaction of the *Hickman* provisos and compliance with any inviolable or 'essential' limitations. In *Mitchforce*,[82] for instance, Spigelman CJ found that a boldly worded privative clause protected a serious error of a State Industrial Relations Commission – on the basis that the error was not in breach of the *Hickman* provisos or any inviolable limit. Yet following *Kirk*, it seems that *Hickman* (with its focus on a narrow category of particularly serious error – now only a subset of jurisdictional error, it seems) is of little relevance at State level because the effectiveness of a privative clause turns essentially, for constitutional reasons, upon the existence (or not) of jurisdictional error in its full form. Obviously *Hickman* had been similarly undercut in the federal (s 75(v)) context by *Plaintiff S157*, but its emerging redundancy was clearer in

---

79 (2010) 242 CLR 1. See also *Wainohu v State of New South Wales* (2011) 243 CLR 181, 195.
80 (2012) 289 ALR 1.
81 Ibid, [60], [65] (Gummow, Hayne, Crennan, Kiefel and Bell JJ) (hence questions of invalidity per se did not arise: at [53]).
82 *Mitchforce Pty Ltd v Industrial Relations Commission of New South Wales* (2003) 57 NSWLR 212, [92]. Cf *Maitland City Council v Anumbah Homes Pty Ltd* (2005) 64 NSWLR 695.

Kirk. By the time of *Kirk*, the bolder, constitution-evading reading of *Hickman* could no longer be viably pressed.

Hickman may remain as an echo to remind us of the seriousness of the errors it identified, and the courts' historically uncompromising approach in that context. Indeed it may retain a theoretical presence via the remote possibility that some error might prove to be not 'jurisdictional' but still fall foul of its provisos. But it can no longer offer to drafters and decision-makers the possibility of a 'safe harbour'[83] for all but these serious errors (which, as noted above, was always a brave reading). Importantly, however, if the constitutional guarantee of jurisdictional error review does not somehow leak through to the Federal Court, one implication is that this court may conceivably provide a final refuge for the *Hickman* methodology, albeit in its clarified form.

As in the case of the federal (s 75(v)) guarantee, some interesting issues arise as to the precise reach of *Kirk* beyond traditional public sector boundaries. There is not, in the State general law context, a cornerstone phrase such as 'officer of the Commonwealth' to be interpreted (or perhaps reinterpreted) for these purposes. However, there are common law principles concerning the application of judicial review in private sector contexts (arising particularly from decisions such as *R v Panel on Take-overs and Mergers; Ex parte Datafin Plc*[84]) which remain at present surprisingly unsettled in the Australian context.[85]

Finally, the handling of the notion of 'jurisdictional error' in *Kirk* is an interesting, albeit less-discussed, aspect of the decision. The majority candidly explored the tension and uncertainty in the concept. They discussed the key decision in *Craig v South Australia*,[86] with its generic formulas for the identification of such error,[87] but emphasised that there is no 'bright line test' and that *Craig* provided not a rigid taxonomy but just examples. Yet ultimately the Court did not stray far from the formulas of *Craig*, identifying jurisdictional errors in the mistakes alleged (lack of particularisation and evidentiary breaches) simply in terms of those formulas.[88] This juxtaposition of predictive formulas and admissions of uncertainty might just reflect the fact that the Court was focused on bigger issues and perhaps concerned to preserve flexibility in this field. Alternatively, it might reflect the fact that the errors here returned the Court to the harder end of the jurisdictional error

---

83 Aronson and Groves, above n 3, 17.150.
84 [1987] QB 815.
85 See Groves, above n 40; *CECA Institute Pty Ltd v Australian Council for Private Education and Training* (2010) 30 VR 555; *Chase Oyster Bar Pty Ltd v Hamo Industries Pty Ltd* (2010) 78 NSWLR 393.
86 (1995) 184 CLR 163.
87 (2010) 239 CLR 531, 573–4.
88 Ibid, 573–5.

classificatory task,[89] after the matters before it had for some years accumulated around reasonably well-worn categories. Going one step further yet, perhaps the reasoning here echoes with the same important conceptual tension that seemed to be visible in *Plaintiff S157*; a tension between the 'internal' (statute and context-specific) conceptualisation of jurisdictional error and the 'external' (pre-mixed or predictive) one.

Alternative mechanisms for restricting judicial review

These questions about the nature of jurisdictional error are fast losing their abstraction. In the wake of *Kirk's* extended entrenchment of 'jurisdictional error' review, attention has been firmly focused on what parliaments might now do to *redefine* 'jurisdiction' or remove substantive limits on powers. And following this closely is the issue of how the courts might respond – are there limits on such legislative efforts? These are now the 'important imponderables'.[90] Answers might begin to emerge in the abstract, but these dilemmas must ultimately be examined in their fuller political and institutional context.

The legislative devices that might carry on the work of the traditional privative clause include 'no-invalidity' clauses, the exclusion of grounds of review, the imposition of time bars or procedural obstacles, or simply the conferral on decision-makers of more broadly stated powers and discretions. Some of these options are now being termed 'plenary provisions' by some – that is, mechanisms for excluding substantive limits on power.[91] Beyond the more obvious ouster devices, with a broader sweep we could include strategies such as the wider use of 'subjective jurisdictional facts' or 'jurisdictional opinions' (to lessen the judicial scrutiny of compliance with jurisdictional conditions), or indeed the 'outsourcing' of decision-making (to tap into lingering uncertainty on the reach of judicial review).[92]

The hobbled traditional privative clause may continue to play an indirect role. It may, for example, conceivably be an indicator that a jurisdictional condition is a subjective one (ie entrusted in large part to the decision-maker's judgement).[93]

---

89 As revealed by the different conclusions below: see *Kirk* (2008) 173 IR 465.
90 Basten, above n 66, 298.
91 See Bateman, above n 13, 467.
92 See in this regard Groves, above n 40. Cf recently *Plaintiff M61/2010E v Commonwealth* (2010) 243 CLR 319.
93 Cf, however, the somewhat inverse effect in *Fish v Solution 6 Holdings Ltd* (2006) 225 CLR 180, 194.

More importantly, on one view it is a legitimate participant in the reconciliation of provisions that delimit the unprotectable category of 'jurisdictional error' in the particular context. The logic of such an approach was apparently acknowledged in *Plaintiff S157*[94] and (albeit less clearly) in *Kirk*.[95] This methodology has been doubted in some quarters – perhaps in part because it carries echoes of the discredited reading of *Hickman*. Yet an approach that acknowledges a privative clause when identifying the precise jurisdictional tipping point[96] would seem to be quite different from an approach that reads such a clause as an automatic expansion of jurisdiction out to the limits of a narrow pre-set class of serious error. Perhaps the more important problem with this methodology, as Aronson and Groves have noted, is the difficulty of finding actual examples of its application.[97]

The courts' likely responses to the various drafting devices noted above, in the contemporary constitutional and political climate, are not in all cases obvious. The no-invalidity clause – declaring that specified errors or failures do not affect the validity of a decision – has been a particular focus in the post-*Kirk* commentary. Such clauses might seem to side-step constitutional constraints (by redefining jurisdictional limits on a power rather than ousting judicial supervision), and have drawn a more moderate response from the High Court than privative clauses. In *Re Minister for Immigration and Multicultural and Indigenous Affairs; Ex parte Palme*,[98] the type of procedural error in question (failure to comply with a succeeding obligation to give reasons) and a clause declaring that such failure did not affect the validity of the actual decision (a visa cancellation) prompted the majority to conclude that failure did not impeach the decision for jurisdictional error (in s 75(v) proceedings).[99] A similarly soft context presented itself in *Federal Commissioner of Taxation v Futuris Corporation Ltd*,[100] where in the face of a carefully constructed appeal regime the Court held that a more generally targeted no-invalidity clause (re non-compliance with the relevant Act's provisions) meant that errors to which it was directed did not go to jurisdiction (so as to attract a writ under s 75(v)). The term 'assessment' (to which the no-invalidity provision applied) was, however, read down to exclude 'conscious maladministration'.[101]

---

94 (2003) 211 CLR 476, 504, cf 486, 490–91, 506. Cf also *Batterham v QSR Ltd* (2006) 225 CLR 237, 249.
95 *Kirk v Industrial Court (NSW)* (2010) 239 CLR 531, 579.
96 Aronson and Groves, above n 3, 17.170.
97 Ibid, 17.40, 17.170. For a pre-*Kirk* example (that would need some adjusting) see *Mitchforce* (2003) 57 NSWLR 212.
98 (2003) 237 CLR 146 at 161ff (Gleeson CJ, Gummow and Heydon JJ).
99 This finding drew upon *Project Blue Sky Inc v Australian Broadcasting Authority* (1998) 194 CLR 355.
100 (2008) 237 CLR 146, 156–7 (Gummow, Hayne, Heydon and Crennan JJ).
101 Perhaps an echo of the *Hickman* first proviso: see J Basten, 'Jurisdictional error after Kirk: Has it a future?' (2012) 23 *Public Law Review* 94, 101.

There is a general consensus that there must be a limit to the effectiveness of a no-invalidity clause, beyond the basic point that it might logically not protect against correction or containment in some way of lesser 'unlawfulness'.[102] There seems little doubt that an Act can effectively declare that breach of a particular statutory requirement does not affect validity – as one observer has pointed out, such a provision appears merely to state expressly the intention that would be searched for in a *Project Blue Sky* analysis.[103] Indeed such deliberate legislative focus on identifying the essential and inessential conditions on a power would seem to be useful.[104] A general validation (for any error) raises more interesting issues.[105] For one, it is conceivable that the deeper-set conventional review grounds might not be so easily buried (see further below). More broadly, it has been suggested, for example, that no-invalidity and privative clauses are the same in practical effect,[106] and the determination of validity is itself an essential part of the constitutionally protected judicial role;[107] or that the constitutional notion of 'jurisdictional error' cannot be 'hollowed out' and that parliaments at both levels are at least prevented from conferring a power without limits sufficient to render it 'non-arbitrary'.[108] The possibility that the expanding constitutional dimension of 'jurisdictional error' somehow alters its meaning, or produces a new variant of the concept, has been raised not infrequently in recent years. However, there appear to be differing views on whether this new dimension draws the old concept away from its foundations in basic statutory interpretation[109] or pushes it further in that direction.[110]

The device of excluding specific grounds is one with which all administrative lawyers – particularly those working in migration – are familiar. Natural justice, or at least the fair hearing rule, has on occasions been pulled out at the roots in a legislative scheme (that is, declared in some manner not to apply). It is not an easy drafting exercise,[111] but there has been little doubt that fair hearing principles can be so excluded from administrative decision-making processes. The recent West Australian decision in *Seiffert v Prisoners Review Board*[112] answered a constitutional

---

102 As to the potential reach here of the s 75(v) injunction see, eg, *Commissioner of Taxation v Futuris Corporation Ltd* (2008) 237 CLR 146, 162; cf *Plaintiff S157/2002 v Commonwealth* (2003) 211 CLR 476, 482–3, 508. See also the reasoning in *Project Blue Sky* itself.
103 A Robertson, 'Commentary on "the entrenched minimum provision of judicial review and the rule of law" by Leighton McDonald' (2010) 21 *Public Law Review* 40, 42.
104 Basten, above n 66, 298.
105 See, eg, L McDonald, 'The Entrenched Minimum Provision of Judicial Review and the Rule of Law' (2010) 21 *Public Law Review* 14.
106 Cf *Bodruddaza v Minister for Immigration and Multicultural Affairs* (2007) 228 CLR 651.
107 Finn, above n 22, 106.
108 Bateman, above n 13.
109 Sackville, above n 77, 133.
110 Bateman, above n 13, 487.
111 See, eg, *Saeed v Minister for Immigration and Citizenship* (2010) 241 CLR 252.
112 [2011] WASCA 148, [111] (Martin CJ).

objection to this, in the State context, with the explanation that it defines the duties of the decision-makers rather than seeks to oust supervisory jurisdiction. This history of the important ground of natural justice casts a sizeable shadow over attempts to elevate other grounds to some higher status.

Aspects of natural justice and other grounds have been expressly excluded at the point of defining permissible challenges — most notably (albeit not with great effect) in respect of the Federal Court's jurisdiction under the 1990s migration regime. It seems a simple provision which declares that a decision 'may not be challenged on ground x' will run into difficulties since *Plaintiff S157* and *Kirk* (in the High Court and State Supreme Court contexts respectively), if 'ground x' is determined to be a jurisdictional error in the circumstances. Similar considerations arise where a clause excludes review *except for* certain grounds, and the exception is insufficient to cover the constitutional guarantees of review.[113] Drafters are now perhaps less likely to contemplate such provisions. More difficult is the scenario where a no-invalidity clause is attached to a particular ground, or the limit inherent in the ground is otherwise somehow substantively removed. As indicated above, instinct might tell us (now with an uncertain constitutional tinge) that some grounds have deeper footings — that they reach somewhat beyond the specific statutory terms and intentions. However, most grounds are closely attached to statutory terms, making their extrication from statutory intent (including a no-invalidity clause) difficult. Also, as a number of observers have noted for some time now,[114] if some grounds are destined for higher status, which ones and why? And could the select list (and the grounds themselves) still evolve?

The High Court has given some signals in this context. As noted above, 'conscious maladministration' was set apart to some extent in *Futuris* (which is particularly relevant to arguments of bad faith). In *Plaintiff S157*, reference was made (in the context of the conventional privative clause there) to the continued availability of injunctive relief under s 75(v) for 'fraud, bribery, dishonesty or other improper purpose'.[115] However, the reasoning relied in part upon the first proviso of *Hickman* (in its re-rationalised form), and *Hickman's* operation beyond conventional privative clauses might be unpredictable. Moreover, the Court's reference to the possible constitutional invalidity of the clause (should *Hickman* fail to preserve High Court supervision over such matters) was perhaps simply

---

113 Cf *Public Service Association of South Australia Inc v Industrial Relations Commission (SA)* (2012) 289 *Administrative Law Review* 1.
114 J Kirk, 'The entrenched Minimum Provision of Judicial Review' (2004) 12 *Australian Journal of Administrative Law* 64; S Gageler, 'The Legitimate Scope of Judicial Review' (2001) 21 *Australian Bar Review* 279.
115 *Plaintiff S157/2002 v Commonwealth* (2003) 211 CLR 476, 408.

a reminder that the jurisdiction conferred by s 75(v) cannot be removed, rather than an indication that the limits on the decision-making power below cannot be re-defined. Yet perhaps the comments in *Futuris*, and the reference there (in the context of a no-invalidity clause) to the comments in *Plaintiff S157*, do take 'conscious maladministration' of these various types some way towards having a special status.[116] Aronson and Groves suggest that such status might also logically attach to errors that need correction in order to prevent a failure of the demarcation between laws or regulatory bodies.[117] Of course, in the case of decisions made and powers exercised by actual courts, constitutional principles potentially attach more directly to shore up conventional administrative law limits.

With respect to the imposition of time bars or other practical obstacles to review (the former being particularly important in the State context), the courts do appear to have the recipe for a principled response. These devices pose a lesser conundrum given that they would apparently be seeking simply to obstruct the constitutionally guaranteed jurisdictional error review, rather than to undermine it by any redefinition of 'jurisdiction'. In the High Court decision in *Bodruddaza v Minister for Immigration and Multicultural Affairs*[118] – the sequel to *Plaintiff S157* – the Court looked to 'whether directly or as a matter of practical effect' the time bar provision in issue so curtailed or limited the right or ability to seek relief under s 75(v) that it was 'inconsistent with the place of that provision in the constitutional structure'. *Bodruddaza* has a relatively sharp edge, casting some doubt over any absolute bar in the s 75(v) context (given the variety of exigencies that may present themselves in particular cases). The *Kirk* decision might seem to allow extension of this methodology to the State context; however, it must be remembered that the courts (prominently at State level) have a long history of some tolerance of time bars (pre-*Kirk*).[119] Besides, the federal constitutional guarantee may not necessarily operate in exactly the same way in the State translation.[120]

Obiter in *Plaintiff S157* raised some further possible responses to broad ouster devices. It was suggested that the conferral of too open-ended a power might lack the 'hallmark of the exercise of legislative power', namely the determining of 'the content of a law as a rule of conduct or a declaration as to power, right or duty'.[121] It was also observed in *Plaintiff S157* that a federal power conferred in

---

116 As to the special case of fraud, see Z Meyers, 'Revisiting the purposes of judicial review: Can there be a minimum content to jurisdictional error? (2012) 19 *Australian Journal of Administrative Law* 138.
117 Aronson and Groves, above n 3, 17.40.
118 (2007) 228 CLR 651, 671, 676.
119 Aronson and Groves, above n 3, 17.7, 17.210. Cf Spigelman, above n 22, 89ff.
120 See, eg, J Knackstredt, 'Judicial Review after *Kirk v Industrial Court (NSW)*' (2011) 18 *Australian Journal of Administrative Law* 203, 212.
121 (2003) 211 CLR 476 512ff.

too open-ended a manner may thereby lack connection with a constitutional head of power, and that this was something a court might not repair without rewriting the statute (not a judicial function).[122] Yet the point might seem to be somewhat hypothetical given that an open-ended conferral of power could usually offer up the connection to a constitutional head without detracting much from its purpose of evading administrative law limits. Another separation of powers argument of relevance here is the well-cited but underexplored notion that Parliament cannot confer on a non-judicial body the power to conclusively determine the limits of its own jurisdiction.[123] The reach and usefulness of this idea in the context of broad attempts at ouster has been questioned,[124] and of course all separation of powers arguments necessarily lose much in any translation across to the State level.

One point to emphasise, at this stage of the debate, is that the inclusion of alternative appeal or review rights in conjunction with the attempted ouster (eg, as in *Futuris*) appears to strengthen the legislature's position on many of the arguments outlined above.[125] For example, it perhaps evades a characterisation of the power as 'arbitrary', makes it harder to suggest that the Parliament has conferred a power to 'conclusively' define jurisdictional limits, and might conceivably avoid the fundamental constitutional opposition by retaining an ultimate path back to superior court supervision.[126]

Conclusion

As Justice Sackville has noted, the 'field of conflict' between courts and parliaments has shifted.[127] The High Court has drawn and extended a constitutional bottom line, protecting for itself and for State Supreme Courts a jurisdiction over 'jurisdiction'. The challenge for legislatures now, it seems, is to disentangle themselves from old drafting habits and the vague search for *Hickam's* lost 'safe port', and to look for space within the constitutional guarantees to effect substantive removal of administrative law limits and the redefinition of 'jurisdiction'. The apparent task for courts is to devise responses. This task is not a small one. Is the protected court role to enforce the limits of jurisdiction, or to define them? Is it to ensure that Parliament's design is respected, or to ensure compliance with some particular methodology or standard? And from where and how will any unassailable administrative law

---

122 Ibid, 512ff.
123 Ibid, 484, 505.
124 Bateman, above n 13.
125 On the courts' greater tolerance of ouster in this context, see Aronson and Groves, above n 3, 17.8.
126 Basten, above n 66, 275.
127 Sackville, above n 77, 137.

limits be derived? Some sizeable theoretical, precedential and practical dilemmas crowd into these questions. However, as noted at the outset of this chapter, a third dimension has appeared in the debate. While the administrative lawyer naturally tends to assume that there will be wild new legislative attempts at ouster, and proceeds from the position that there must be clear limits, questions are now being asked about the appropriateness of these starting points.

Can we assume that legislatures will necessarily press hard on the constitutional guarantees in inappropriate circumstances? In the first place, the clarity of drafting required in any attempted ouster or removal of substantive limits (and the likely context of such attempts) may well ensure that the legislature's design is exposed to very real political and public scrutiny. It should also be remembered that the evasion of courts by the conferral of undefined powers will often come at some expense to the clarity and security of the underlying political purposes, and to administrative coherence and efficiency. Moreover, it is possible that our predictions about future legislative tactics might be skewed somewhat by the administrative extremes of recent times. The intractable political controversies in the area of migration have in the last two decades produced an unprecedented raw interplay between politics and law. This recent context should be kept in mind as regards the motives and will that we attribute to the Australian legislatures more generally.

The arguments for a robust judicial response to legislative ouster, direct or indirect, have been well rehearsed in this field of law – drawing as they do upon some fundamental tenets of our legal system. Yet there are also factors which suggest that some caution is in fact appropriate here. First, as mentioned above, the law has certainly already imposed on parliaments (in various ways) the requirement that their desire to depart from significant administrative law conventions must be expressed with 'irresistible clearness',[128] and no doubt the usefulness of this methodology is not yet exhausted. The same might be said of the mechanism of statutory 'reconciliation'. Whatever broad attempt at ouster is dropped in, administrative law is skilled at finding implied purposes and limits on power which might well invite some 'reconciliation' and hence rationalisation of the ouster mechanism.

It should also be remembered (against our Diceyan instincts) that effective legislative ouster of judicial review does not necessarily leave executive power in an accountability vacuum, even where specific appeal avenues have not been provided. It has been pointed out at the highest levels that in contemporary legal debates over executive performance, we forget too quickly the potential of a diligent Parliament, rigorous media, and the sophisticated oversight provided by

---

128 *Saeed v Minister for Immigration and Citizenship* (2010) 241 CLR 252, 259.

proliferating integrity bodies.[129] Indeed we perhaps tend to overstate the purposes, capacity and effectiveness of judicial review in this regard, and the neutrality and universality of the standards and values it imposes.[130] The temptation to do so has been great in recent years, given the contests faced by judicial review in the overbearing field of migration. But again, we should be mindful of this recent context as we consider future responses to legislative ouster more generally, and particularly the size of the legal counterweight actually required.

The maturing collaboration between administrative law and constitutional law in Australia is of considerable theoretical and practical importance, and the task ahead, of giving it principled and sustainable meaning, is a sizeable one. Ultimately, there may need to be some acceptance that the 'immutable' constitutional jurisdiction must to some extent take its shape on a case-by-case basis. There are potential risks in overstating the constitutional guarantee, and searching too determinedly and too abstractly for clear and fixed limits on legislatures. Apart from the broad implications for governmental balances of power, as Justice Basten has recently noted, there is a need to protect the 'political legitimacy' of the entrenched supervisory jurisdiction and avoid prompting a questioning of the judiciary's own accountability.[131]

---

129 See, eg, R S French, 'The Executive Power' (2010) 12 *Constitutional Law & Policy Review* 5; J McMillan, 'Re-thinking the Separation of Powers' (2010) 38 *Federal Law Review* 423.
130 Basten, above n 66.
131 Ibid, 299.

PART

BEYOND THE COURTS

14

THE INTEGRITY BRANCH: A 'SYSTEM', AN 'INDUSTRY', OR A SENSIBLE EMERGING FOURTH ARM OF GOVERNMENT?

AJ Brown

Introduction

The integrity branch of government consists of those permanent institutions, established with a degree of political independence under a constitution or by statute, whose function is solely or primarily to ensure that other governmental institutions and officials exercise the powers conferred on them for the purposes for which they were conferred, and in the manner expected of them, consistent with both the legal and wider precepts of integrity and accountability which are increasingly recognised as fundamental to good governance in modern liberal democracies.[1]

Recognising the reality and potential of the integrity branch is especially important to administrative law. As the 'law of public accountability',[2] administrative law does not operate in a legal vacuum in the same way as other specialist areas of law. Administrative lawyers know that the most effective forms of relief for citizens aggrieved by official decision-making often lie not in remedies 'at law', but in the administrative investigation and resolution of complaints by an ombudsman, or merits review by a tribunal. Where legal questions do become central to a dispute or action, they often revolve around questions of the powers that were (or are) available to decision-makers and how those powers should be exercised in accordance with constitutional or statutory limits, conditions or responsibilities. Ever since Ian Thynne and Jack Goldring's seminal work, *Accountability and Control: Government Officials and the Exercise of Power*,[3] it has been clear in Australia that modern systems of public integrity encompass mechanisms of constitutional and administrative law, public administration and management, and financial accountability. As if these did not together define a big enough field, integrity systems also encompass the processes used to regulate the personal integrity, conduct and misconduct of individuals, right through to the criminal law.

Accordingly, while administrative lawyers recognise their role as focused in only some of these areas, they usually recognise the close relationships between what

---

1 On the meaning of the term 'integrity' as used here, see AJ Brown, 'What is a National Integrity System?: From Temple Blueprint to Hip-Pocket Guide' in B Head, AJ Brown and C Connors (eds), *Promoting Integrity: Evaluating and Improving Public Institutions* (Ashgate, 2008) 33; J Spigelman, 'The Integrity Branch of Government' (2004) 78 *Australian Law Journal* 72.
2 AJ Brown, 'Putting Administrative Law Back into Integrity, and Putting the Integrity Back into Administrative Law' (2007) 53 *Australian Institute of Administrative Law Forum* 32.
3 I Thynne and J Goldring, *Accountability and Control: Government Officials and the Exercise of Power* (Lawbook, 1987).

they do and this wider integrity system. Similarly, to practising public lawyers who work in and around this system, the 'core' integrity institutions[4] that function at its heart are fairly easily recognisable as constituting an identifiable 'branch' of our governmental system as a whole. The roles of these integrity institutions closest to the traditional areas of administrative law – such as ombudsmen, information commissioners, and independent merits review tribunals – are dealt with in specific chapters of this book. Other institutions not dealt with, such as anti-corruption agencies and auditors-general, nevertheless remain just as integral to the role and functioning of the integrity branch; and, as will be discussed, are of course also themselves subject to the rule of law, with which all administrative lawyers are concerned.

This basic description of the integrity branch is not uncontroversial, however. Moreover, the healthy evolution and functioning of the integrity branch are not things to be taken for granted – rather, nationally and internationally, they demand ongoing scrutiny and careful deliberation by policymakers, integrity professionals (including administrative lawyers) and the wider community. This chapter explains what the integrity branch is, and why it is significant that we now conceptualise it as a 'branch'. First, some clarification is attempted as to what the branch is, to distinguish more clearly between the institutions that form this 'branch', and the 'integrity system' of which the branch is the core part. Next, we confront recent debates over whether it assists public accountability to see these institutions as forming a 'fourth' branch of government in constitutional terms, as opposed to a mere administrative convenience within the executive. The fourth part of the chapter deals with an important question about the practical role and operations of these institutions: when and why do we regard the integrity branch institutions as requiring the high degree of statutory independence which is their single greatest hallmark? This discussion is informed by contrasting views, including those of Spigelman (former Chief Justice of NSW)[5] and Gummow (a former High Court Justice),[6] and a recent review of some of Queensland's most significant integrity branch legislation – the *Crime and Misconduct Act 2001 (Qld)* – led by former High Court Justice Ian Callinan.[7] This review usefully points to the practical

---

4 On the meaning and role of 'core' integrity institutions, see Brown, above n 2, 39–45.
5 Spigelman, above n 1.
6 W M C Gummow, 'A Fourth Branch of Government?' (2012) 70 *AIAL Forum* 19.
7 I D F Callinan and N Aroney, *Review of the Crime and Misconduct Act [Qld 2001] and Related Matters: Report of the Independent Advisory Panel*, Queensland Government, Brisbane, 28 March 2013 (Redacted Version: Parliamentary Paper 5413T2447, Parliament of Queensland, 18 April 2013); see <www.justice.qld.gov.au/cmareview>.

implications and risks of the different ways in which the above questions might be answered.[8]

The basic description of the integrity branch with which the chapter commenced can help resolve some of the confusion that surrounds this quasi-constitutional idea. But there are also practical implications for the effectiveness of the integrity system as a whole, including administrative law, in how we conceive and choose to institutionalise the integrity branch. Recognising that it does exercise a distinctive, fourth type of governmental functions and powers, and that it does or should operate with a degree of constitutional protection, may help resolve these questions.

What is the integrity 'branch'?

In Australia, and more broadly in liberal democratic systems, the notion of an 'integrity branch' of government has many origins. Some of these relate to increased awareness among policymakers during the 1990s that a range of long-standing and more recent institutions can, or should, combine to form an integrity 'system' – the distinction between 'branch' and 'system' being an issue to which we will return. In 1996, Transparency International published the first edition of its sourcebook, noting that in addition to the traditional tripartite division of governmental power between three main branches – legislative, executive and judicial – many other institutional 'pillars' were also vital to the promotion and maintenance of integrity in the use of official power.[9] These ranged from the permanent public service, as something distinct from the political executive, to bodies such as an ombudsman, 'supreme audit institution', anti-corruption agencies, a free media and other non-government actors.

---

8 These issues were included in a related presentation, 'The Health of the Integrity Branch', in *Integrity in Administrative Law Making*, National Administrative Law Conference, Australian Institute of Administrative Law, Adelaide, 19 July 2012. The same conference produced many valuable perspectives on the integrity branch in Australia, drawn on below, including: D Solomon, 'What is the Integrity Branch?' (2012) 70 *AIAL Forum* 26; R Creyke, 'An "Integrity" Branch' (2012) 70 *AIAL Forum* 33; J Wenta, 'The Integrity Branch of Government and the Separation of Judicial Power' (2012) 70 *AIAL Forum* 42; J Kinross, 'The Transmission of the Public Value of Transparency through External Review' (2012) 71 *AIAL Forum* 10; C Wheeler, 'Review of Administrative Conduct and Decisions in NSW since 1974: An Ad Hoc and Incremental Approach to Radical Change' (2012) 71 *AIAL Forum* 34; and C Field, 'The Fourth Branch of Government: The Evolution of Integrity Agencies and Enhanced Government Accountability' (2013) 72 *AIAL Forum* 24.

9 J Pope, *Confronting Corruption: The Elements of a National Integrity System (The TI Source Book)* (Transparency International, 2000).

This internationalised description of a multi-institutional, multi-branched system borrowed significantly from the types of integrity reforms developed in Australia in the early 1990s, especially in Queensland. It was supplemented by Transparency International's parallel assessment of what most anti-corruption activists were trying to achieve in less-developed countries.[10] The description also captured a trend that influential political scientists such as Guillermo O'Donnell had been observing internationally, in newer or revitalised democracies – that good governance efforts were based on the institutionalisation of a more developed concept of 'horizontal accountability' between institutions than had gone before in Western and post-Western political theory:

> [F]or this kind of [horizontal] accountability to be effective there must exist state agencies that are authorized and willing to oversee, control, redress and/ or sanction unlawful actions of other state agencies. The former agencies must have not only legal authority for proceeding in this way but also, de facto, sufficient autonomy with respect to the latter. This is, of course, the old theme of the division of powers and the system of checks and balances. It includes the classic institutions of the executive, the legislative and the judiciary; but in contemporary polyarchies it also extends to various overseeing agencies, ombudsmen, accounting offices, *fiscalias*, and the like.[11]

This concept of horizontal accountability was central to the multi-institutional framework of the TI 'national integrity system'. However, it is an indicator of a genuine trend when many voices arrive at similar destinations without necessarily directly informing one another. A senior Australian public servant, Bruce Topperwein, was perhaps the first to articulate in legal circles the fact that these developments pointed to a distinct integrity branch or arm of government.[12] In constitutional circles, the argument that 'the credible construction of a separate "integrity branch" should be a top priority for drafters of modern constitutions' came of age shortly after with Ackerman's article, 'The New Separation of Powers'.[13] In Australia, the concept received a boost in the 2004 National Administrative Law Lecture delivered

---

10 See N Preston, C Sampford and C Connors, *Encouraging Ethics and Challenging Corruption: Reforming Governance in Public Institutions* (Federation Press, 2002); J Pope, 'National Integrity Systems: The Key to Building Sustainable, Just and Honest Government' in B Head, AJ Brown and C Connors (eds), *Promoting Integrity: Evaluating and Improving Public Institutions* (Ashgate, 2008) 13.
11 G O'Donnell, 'Horizontal Accountability in New Democracies', in A Schedler, L Diamond and M Plattner (eds), *The Self-Restraining State: Power and Accountability in New Democracies* (Lynne Rienner, 1999) 29, 39.
12 B Topperwein, 'Separation of Powers and the Status of Administrative Review' (1999) 20 *AIAL Forum* 1. See also Creyke, above n 8, 36.
13 B Ackerman, 'The New Separation of Powers' (2000) 113 *Harvard Law Review* 642, 694–6.

by the then Chief Justice of New South Wales, Jim Spigelman AC, arguing that a range of bodies effectively functioned as a 'fourth branch' of government alongside the legislature, executive and judiciary:

> [T]here have been a number of candidates for a 'fourth branch' designation over the years. The number does not matter. The idea does. The primary basis for the recognition of an integrity branch as a distinct functional specialisation, required in all governmental structures, is the fundamental necessity to ensure that corruption, in a broad sense of that term, is eliminated from government. However, once recognised as a distinct function, for which distinct institutions are appropriate, at a level of significance which acknowledges its role as a fourth branch of government, then the idea has implications for our understanding of constitutional and legal issues of broader significance.[14]

The 'fourth branch' is not to be confused with the 'fourth estate', a term used to describe the role of the media as reporters upon what were once seen in the Westminster tradition as the three estates of Parliament (the Lords Spiritual, Lords Temporal and Commons).[15] Nevertheless, the fact that a free, well-functioning media is often recognised as a pillar of national integrity systems reinforces the trend towards multiplicity in the number of institutions upon which public integrity depends.

It would be a mistake to say, however, that recognition of this fourth, integrity branch of government is supported by a constitutional consensus, or has been free of confusion. At a basic level, there are different accounts of which institutions actually make up this 'branch' – is it a few, or many? The wide range of governmental institutions that play integrity roles has been confirmed, empirically, by 'national integrity system assessments' conducted in over 80 countries in the past decade or so.[16] As part of an exploratory Australian assessment in 2004, a network analysis of NSW Government public institutions of functional importance to integrity, compiled through interviews of senior executives of 20 line agencies, identified around 14 such institutions (see Figure 14.1).

This multiplicity of agencies is sometimes advanced as a positive good. For example, the Australian Government recently presented its 'multi-agency approach to combatting corruption', depicted in Figure 14.2, as a particular strength of its system, as against the idea of trying to simplify or consolidate institutional

---

14 Spigelman, above n 1, 725.
15 Solomon, above n 8, 30–31.
16 For current national integrity system assessment work internationally, see <www.transparency.org/whatwedo/nis>.

Figure 14.1 Relationships between NSW public sector agencies and integrity agencies[17]

	ICAC	Omb	Aud-Gen	Prem	Courts	Parl	Police	ADT	HCCC	PIC	OCG	Other 1	Other 2	Other 3	Total
Agency 3	+	++	+		++	++		+			+	++	++	++	10
Agency 18	++	+	++	++	++	++	+	++		+		+			10
Agency 7	++	++	++	++	++	+	++	+				++			9
Agency 9		+	+	++	+	+	+			+		+	+		9
Agency 13	++	++	+		++		++	+	++	++		++			9
Agency 4	++	++	++	+	+		++	++			+	++			8
Agency 8	++	++	++	++			+		++		+	++			8
Agency 16	+	++	++	++	++	+		+		++					8
Agency 17	++	++	++	++	+	++	++	+							8
Agency 20	++	++	++	++	++	++		+				+			8
Agency 19	++	++	+	+		+	++	+							7
Agency 10	++	+	++	++	++	++									6
Agency 11	++		++			+	++		++			+			6
Agency 5	++		+	++	++		+								5
Agency 6	++	+	++	++	+										5
Agency 12	+	+	+			+						++			5
Agency 14	+	++	+	+				++							5
Agency 1	++	++		+		+									4
Agency 2	++	++	+		+										4
Agency 15															0

Notes:
++ indicates 'very important' to the agency.
+ indicates 'fairly important' to the agency.
The 'Other' columns refer to 'very' or 'fairly' important integrity agencies and organisations not listed in the interview schedule/questionnaire but raised by the respondent.

arrangements through the creation of any new, 'overarching' integrity or anti-corruption body.[18] Sixteen different agencies are identified as relevant. Not long before, John McMillan, the then Commonwealth Ombudsman, included many of the same but also several additional agencies in his description of the Commonwealth integrity system, including military disciplinary bodies, the inspector-general of taxation, and the Australian Human Rights Commission.[19]

---

17 Source: R Smith, 'Mapping the New South Wales Public Integrity System' (2005) 64 *Australian Journal of Public Administration* 54, 57 (Table 2); also published as Table 7 in AJ Brown, C Sampford et al., *Chaos or Coherence? Strengths, Opportunities and Challenges for Australia's Integrity Systems*, Final Report, National Integrity Systems Assessment (NISA), Transparency International Australia and Griffith University, December 2005; available at <www.transparency.org.au/wp-content/uploads/2012/08/nisa_final.pdf>, 27.

18 Attorney-General's Department, *Discussion Paper: Australia's Approach to Anti-Corruption*, prepared as part of the development of the National Anti-Corruption Plan, March 2012, 12. See also Government Response (February 2012) to Parliamentary Joint Committee (ACLEI), *Inquiry into the Operation of the Law Enforcement Integrity Commissioner ACT 2006: Final Report*, Parliamentary Joint Committee on the Australian Commission for Law Enforcement Integrity (July 2011).

19 J McMillan, 'The Ombudsman and the Rule of Law' (2005) 44 *AIAL Forum* 1, 11–12.

Figure 14.2 Multi-agency approach to anti-corruption (Australian Government)[20]

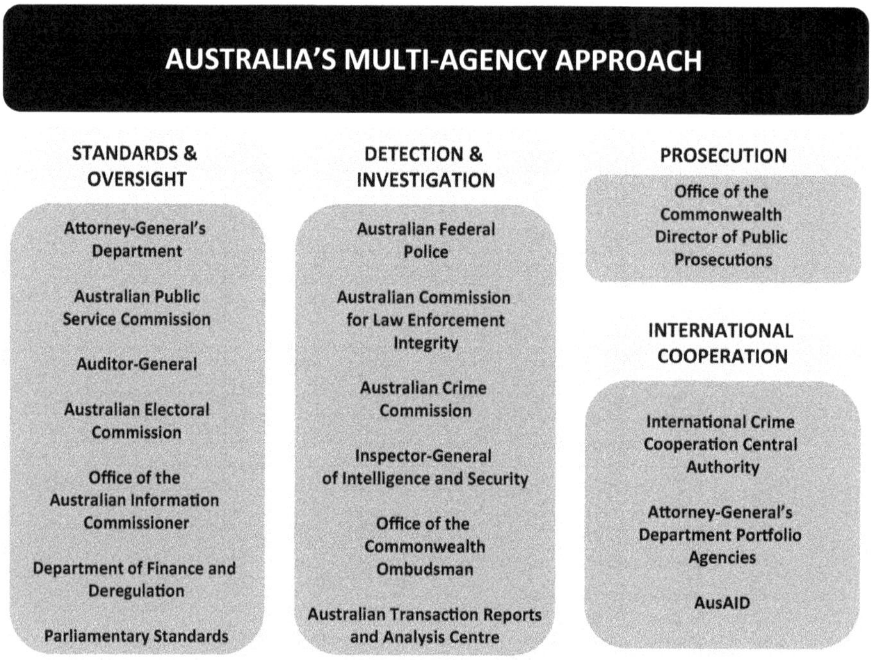

AUSTRALIA'S MULTI-AGENCY APPROACH

STANDARDS & OVERSIGHT
- Attorney-General's Department
- Australian Public Service Commission
- Auditor-General
- Australian Electoral Commission
- Office of the Australian Information Commissioner
- Department of Finance and Deregulation
- Parliamentary Standards

DETECTION & INVESTIGATION
- Australian Federal Police
- Australian Commission for Law Enforcement Integrity
- Australian Crime Commission
- Inspector-General of Intelligence and Security
- Office of the Commonwealth Ombudsman
- Australian Transaction Reports and Analysis Centre

PROSECUTION
- Office of the Commonwealth Director of Public Prosecutions

INTERNATIONAL COOPERATION
- International Crime Cooperation Central Authority
- Attorney-General's Department Portfolio Agencies
- AusAID

This same institutional multiplicity can be a problem. In their report of the review of Queensland's *Crime and Misconduct Act 2001*, Callinan and Aroney identified a similar number (15) of statutory office-holders, agencies and institutions as involved in the State's public integrity system.[21] However, where most previous analyses of the system had described the presence of multiple agencies in positive terms,[22] Callinan and Aroney described this as an 'extraordinary multiplicity' of agencies and officials,[23] giving rise to 'serious questions' of complexity and inefficiency.

---

20 Attorney-General's Department, *Discussion Paper*, above n 18, 12.
21 Callinan and Aroney, above n 7, 6–7. The non-exhaustive list of 15 statutory office-holders, agencies and institutions identified as having 'functions primarily of maintaining or adjudicating on, of overseeing, of promoting integrity in the public sector, or of investigating conduct which is said to run counter to it', were the: Ombudsman; Integrity Commissioner; Privacy Commissioner; Information Commissioner; Coroner; Public Service Commission; Auditor-General and the Queensland Audit Office (QAO); Public Interest Monitor; CMC; Queensland Civil and Administrative Tribunal (QCAT) (quasi-judicial); Health Quality and Complaints Commission; Electoral Commissioner; Parliamentary Crime and Misconduct Commissioner (Parliamentary Commissioner); Parliamentary Ethics Committee; Parliamentary Crime and Misconduct Committee (Parliamentary Committee).
22 See Preston et al., above n 10; Brown, Sampford et al., above n 17, 21–3.
23 Callinan and Aroney, above n 7, 6–7, 128.

They saw such a large number of offices and bodies as undesirable. They also criticised 'the overlap in functions which this inevitably produces, and the potential problems this creates in terms of cost and the burden on public administration, and on those subjected to their activities'.[24] They reported that the result was not an integrity 'system' but an 'integrity industry' which was 'new and expensive', 'bloated, inefficient and thriving', 'burgeoning and excessive' and 'over-elaborate'.[25] Callinan and Aroney's recommendations to rectify this situation, however, did not involve any reduction or consolidation in the number of institutions, but rather a rationalisation of some potential overlaps between them, by way of contraction of the role of the Crime and Misconduct Commission (CMC) to involve less prevention, less education, and no research; a reduction in staff within line agencies dedicated to internal integrity matters (eg, the Ethical Standards Units); and a consolidation of power in the Public Service Commission to set and maintain standards of proper conduct.[26]

Are all such institutions part of the 'integrity branch'? Many of them are simply conventional departments of the executive, or courts, or committees, or staff of parliaments; many of them also have other functions besides public integrity. Indeed, the more institutions that are added, the more the concept of the integrity branch starts to look like the entire governmental system. The fact that the modern institutionalised integrity framework is so basic to the operations of government, and therefore also so large and all-pervading, tends to fuel arguments that there is, or should be, no distinct integrity 'branch'. So what then are we talking about?

Fortunately, there is a relatively simple explanation. From the integrity system assessment work conducted in Australia, and internationally, together with other similar evaluations in OECD countries, we can see that these long lists of institutions may be important to the operation of the integrity *system*, but do not necessarily define which institutions are members of the integrity *branch*. Integrity systems can be seen as reliant on a range of both 'core' institutions (generalist or specialist), established solely or primarily to carry out integrity functions; and 'distributed' integrity institutions which are embedded in the internal accountability and governance systems of every organisation (whether through the Ethical Standards Units targeted by the Queensland review above, or other types of management system favoured by the same review). Figure 14.3 captures this larger matrix. On one view, all these institutions can be seen as part of the integrity system; but only the core institutions in the hatched quadrant might potentially qualify as members of the 'branch'. By way of comparison, much the same can be said of the legal

---

24 Ibid, 8.
25 Ibid, 9, 144, 204 and 215 respectively.
26 Ibid, ch 8 (128ff).

Figure 14.3 Key integrity institutions by sector and level[27]

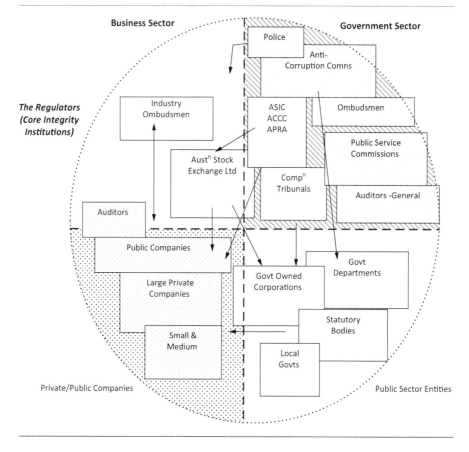

system – a complex, all-pervading web, operating wherever legal obligations are salient or legal practitioners or advisors tread, but in which only the most core institutions (the courts) constitute the judicial 'branch' of government.

These distinctions are important. Creyke has noted that there can be a lamentable lack of clarity from commentators and analysts as to when they are referring to the integrity *system*, and when they are discussing the integrity *branch*. This problem 'leads to confusion about what standards, institutions, individuals or bodies are being discussed', and has 'clouded the debate'.[28]

---

27 Taken from AJ Brown, 'The Australian National Integrity System Assessment (NISA): Towards a Framework Methodology', Paper to 'Integrating Integrity' Workshop, Griffith University, November 2003; Brown, above n 1, Figure 3.1.
28 Creyke, above n 8, 35.

It has also fuelled arguments that it is impossible or inappropriate to identify any distinct branch at all. In fact, empirical work and the way these institutions increasingly organise themselves make it relatively easy in Australia to identify the institutions that are candidates for the branch. In Queensland, the branch is most clearly defined by the five 'integrity commissioners', who over the last fifteen or so years have come to coordinate themselves as an Integrity Committee: namely, the Ombudsman, Auditor-General, chair of the Crime and Misconduct Commission, Information Commissioner (overseeing and reviewing public access to information), and Integrity Commissioner (a statutory office providing ethical scaffolding to parliamentarians and senior public servants).[29] In Western Australia, there are also five core offices, which have also chosen to organise themselves for several years as an Integrity Coordinating Group. Four are the same: the Ombudsman, Auditor-General, chair of the Corruption and Crime Commission, and Information Commissioner. There is no Integrity Commissioner in WA. The fifth member is the Public Sector Commissioner – a position predated by, and now incorporating, the significant integrity functions role of a separate Public Sector Standards Commissioner.[30]

All jurisdictions now have similar institutions. In NSW, the network analysis mentioned above identified the Ombudsman, Auditor-General, and Independent Commission Against Corruption (ICAC) as clearly most important to the system.[31] At the time, there was no Information Commissioner, but one now exists; parliamentary integrity functions were (and are) at least partly covered by the ICAC's jurisdiction. The Premier's Department (which at the time included public service commission functions), parliamentary committees, courts, police and the administrative decisions tribunals were rated as forming a group of agencies of considerable, but secondary, importance for the system as a whole, with other more specialist or sectoral agencies following behind.

In all jurisdictions, whether or not the public service commission is integral to the group seems to depend not only on whether one exists, but on its degree of independence and whether it has statutory responsibilities for setting and maintaining ethical standards, as opposed to simply serving as the executive's workforce, training and human resource management agency. Despite the importance afforded to this body by the *Crime and Misconduct Act* reviewers, for example, Queensland and other jurisdictions have gone through long periods with no Public Service Commission at all.

---

29 J Kinross, 'The Transmission of the Public Value of Transparency through External Review' (2012) 71 *AIAL Forum* 10.
30 Field, above n 8, 25.
31 Smith, above n 17, 55; Table 1.

Similarly, while merits review tribunals do not figure as centrally in the integrity branch list, this may be due to their relatively recent creation at State level, together with their overlap with judicial functions – to be further discussed shortly. They can be seen as more central to the Commonwealth Government's integrity branch, where the Administrative Appeals Tribunal is as old as the Ombudsman, and where its President sits with the Ombudsman and others as an *ex officio* member of the Administrative Review Council. The Commonwealth also differs in other respects. Its integrity branch includes the Inspector-General of Intelligence and Security, covering an area of administration which exists only at the national level; and while since 2006 it has included a dedicated anti-corruption body for federal law enforcement agencies,[32] there continues to be much debate over the comparative lack of central review and oversight applied to other federal agencies' handling of official misconduct.[33] Consequently, the Commonwealth integrity system has been described as less coherent.[34]

How the integrity branch institutions' roles and jurisdictions are configured, and how they coordinate their handling of complaints, cases, matters, standard-setting, research, education and training are all vitally important questions for those at the coalface of public administration and of administrative law. Issues of clarity, efficiency and effectiveness obviously arise. Australia's first national integrity system assessment pointed to the need for 'an active strategy' to ensure effective policy coordination between the significant 'players' in the integrity field, and found that 'in contrast to Australia's fairly widespread reputation for having well-organised integrity systems', there were real questions of 'policy and operational coherence in the implementation and long-term institutionalisation of integrity programs'.[35] Small surprise, then, that in their recent review Callinan and Aroney found much

---

32 Australian Commission for Law Enforcement Integrity, established under the *Law Enforcement Integrity Commission Act 2006* (Cth), whose jurisdiction commenced with the law enforcement functions of the Australian Federal Police and Australian Crime Commission, but which since 2010 has been extended by regulation to include a wider range of such functions in more agencies, including the Australian Customs and Border Protection Service. See Parliamentary Joint Committee (ACLEI) (2011), above n 18.

33 See AJ Brown, 'Federal anti-corruption policy takes a new turn...but which way?: Issues and options for a Commonwealth integrity agency' (2005) 16 *Public Law Review* 93. Some experts describe it as 'increasingly difficult' to argue against the role of general purpose anti-corruption bodies as 'essential institutions': T Prenzler and N Faulkner, 'Towards a model public sector integrity commission' (2010) 69 *Australian Journal of Public Administration* 251, 260.

34 P Roberts, 'Don't Rock the Boat: The Commonwealth National Integrity System' (2005) 64 *Australian Journal of Public Administration* 48.

35 C Sampford, R Smith and AJ Brown, 'From Greek Temple to Bird's Nest: Towards a Theory of Coherence and Mutual Accountability for National Integrity Systems' (2005) 64 *Australian Journal of Public Administration* 96, 101.

to criticise in the alleged inefficiency of Queensland's integrity system.[36] However, the logic of the integrity branch is reinforced by the fact that the small number of core integrity institutions involved align closely with what reviewers such as Callinan and Aroney identify as the 'three fundamental and very simple elements of "integrity"...honesty, fairness and openness',[37] which they fear may otherwise be overwhelmed by a proliferation and bureaucratisation of integrity processes. Honest conduct is, of course, the primary concern of an anti-corruption and official misconduct agency. Fairness is a primary concern of ombudsmen and merits review tribunals. Openness is the primary concern of information commissioners. If one accepts that integrity should, like justice, not be allowed to become an over-elaborate concept, but rather be embedded 'as an obvious element of overall diligence',[38] we can see why not only ombudsmen but auditors-general and public sector standards commissioners are also members. In other words, the limited membership of the branch reinforces the basic shared purpose of its existence.

A constitutional branch?

While many institutions have roles in the integrity system, the integrity branch can be seen as consisting of a small number of permanent institutions whose function is solely or primarily to ensure that other governmental institutions and officials exercise the powers conferred on them for the purposes for which they were conferred. Even more hotly contested than its efficiency, however, is the question of whether recognition of the existence of an integrity branch has, or should have, constitutional implications. This question need not impede many of the practical benefits of recognising the role and needs of the branch, even as a mere administrative phenomenon. As noted by WA's Ombudsman, Chris Field:

> [W]hat is less contestable is that we can identify a very mature...framework of agencies, functions and activities in our system of government that has at its heart the protection and promotion of institutional and personal

---

36 See especially Callinan and Aroney, above n 7, 142–3. Here, the reviewers unfortunately assume that to accept a multi-institutional approach as being a strength of the system 'is to risk assuming that "more is better", rather than critically to assess their merits and especially their efficiency, utility and necessity'. This is not only factually incorrect, but overlooks what is perhaps the key issue, which is whether it is better for the legislated roles of integrity agencies to overlap slightly, with those overlaps then able to be minimised or managed administratively – or for them to be hermetically sealed as separate, which risks gaps in power and jurisdiction which are more difficult, if not impossible, to bridge administratively.
37 Ibid, 8.
38 Ibid, 215.

integrity.... [T]here is no need for any constitutional contortions to identify, and critically analyse, an integrity framework of government.[39]

Nevertheless, as the then Commonwealth Ombudsman and Inspector-General of Intelligence and Security wrote, the growing 'familiarity of this model of independent review should not detract from the profound nature of this change'.[40] So how profound is it, and why does it matter?

It matters because, as will be demonstrated in more detail below, the precept on which parliaments have created the 'fourth branch' institutions is quite distinct from those informing the design of conventional executive agencies, or indeed other policy-specific statutory and regulatory authorities. Moreover, as well as deliberately granting a higher degree of independence to such bodies than to any other executive or statutory agencies, parliaments have chosen, in these bodies, to create some unique mixing and blurring of what would otherwise be considered the three traditionally separate types of governmental power. So far, too little attention has been paid to whether this actually represents a discrete constitutional development. Confusingly, even proponents of the integrity arm as a 'fourth branch' of government seem to see this idea as something of a bridge too far. Spigelman's argument for the integrity branch, for example, still described 'the three recognised branches of government, including the Parliament, the head of state, various executive agencies and the superior courts' as the key institutions through which the 'fourth' branch did its work.[41] This prompted Queensland's Integrity Commissioner, Dr David Solomon, to describe the fourth branch as 'not a separate, distinct branch' because the institutions as defined by the traditional constitutional matrix already 'collectively constitute the integrity branch of government.... [T]here would be no advantage in trying to remove those functions [from the existing three branches] and send them off to a fourth branch'.[42]

So is there a distinct integrity branch? We have seen that there is, in administrative terms. But if we do not believe it to have any constitutional implications, why discuss it as being an emerging 'fourth branch', rather than simply a subset of the executive? Some insight can be found in the views of those who argue that there is simply no constitutional scope for a fourth branch in a democracy based on the Montesquiean division of legislative, executive and judicial power; or that even if there was, such a development would have no value. In 2012, Justice Gummow directly rejected Spigelman's proposition that the fourth branch idea might have wider benefits or provide a 'broader context' to inform constitutional

---

39 Field, above n 9, 28.
40 J McMillan and I Carnell, 'Administrative Law Evolution: Independent Complaint and Review Agencies', (2010) 59 *Admin Review* 35.
41 Spigelman, above n 1; Creyke, above n 8.
42 Solomon, above n 9, 26, 32.

and administrative law. Gummow thought the concept offered 'little utility and some occasion for confusion'.[43] Possibly, he was rejecting the notion that the judicial function should ever allow anything much, outside the law, to inform its role.[44] What he did make clear was his view that if any branch of government was an integrity branch, it was the existing third, judicial branch. Commonwealth administrative law, properly understood, was simply 'a subset of constitutional law'; questions of whether public power was being exercised with integrity ultimately came back to the authority of the High Court as the peak arbiter of whether government officials and agencies were acting within power.[45] Even more importantly, Justice Gummow's perception of the fourth branch assumed that those suggesting such a designation thought judicial oversight of integrity institutions would no longer apply – an idea he then correctly rejected:

> It remains open to the Federal and State legislatures to create by statute organisations and bodies to oversee good governance and investigate corruption and malpractice. But those entities and their members cannot be placed by the enabling legislation in islands of power where they are immune from supervision and restraint by the judicial branch of government.[46]

Why Justice Gummow made this assumption, or why he might think that the integrity branch could not exist as a separate arm of government unless immune from judicial review, is unclear. Others also raise the spectre of the potential unaccountability of such bodies. In their review of the CMC Act, Callinan and Aroney observe that since the CMC is not subject to the 'same degree of scrutiny' as agencies with similar powers, 'the question arises: *Quis custodiet ipsos custodes?* [who shall guard the guardians?]'.[47] But there is no question that integrity branch agencies are generally subject to the same rule of law that applies to all executive agencies and statutory authorities. In fact, Justice Gummow answers his own question by detailing how the existing tripartite structure provides 'in significant respect for the oversight of each of the three branches of government by the other two'.[48] This is exactly the type of 'horizontal' or 'mutual' accountability discussed earlier, which explains how the modern system works, and indeed, on which we should expect to rely irrespective of whether we conceive governmental power as divided between three branches or four, or even more. Figure 14.4 explains this shift from a focus on 'vertical

---

43 Gummow, above n 6, 19.
44 For an entrée to this much larger issue, see AJ Brown, *Michael Kirby: Paradoxes & Principles* (Federation Press, 2011) 359–75.
45 Gummow, above n 6, 20.
46 Ibid, 24.
47 Juvenal, *Satire VI* (attributed); see Callinan and Aroney, above n 7, 25.
48 Gummow, above n 6, 21.

Figure 14.4 (a) Formal models of two conceptions of trust[49].

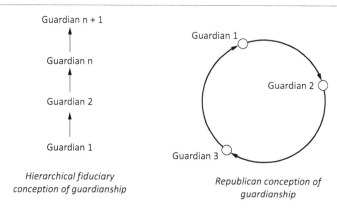

Hierarchical fiduciary conception of guardianship

Republican conception of guardianship

(b) A model of mutual accountability[50].

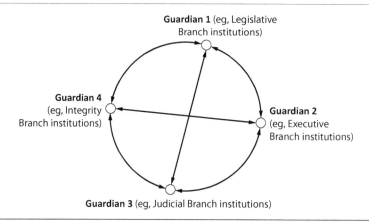

accountability', which imperfectly seeks to trace authority from the people to the parliament to other institutions in a hierarchical fashion; to a more sophisticated understanding of the intricate checks and balances between major institutional branches, all of which owe their authority to the people (usually to at least some degree via the parliament, or directly via the constitution) in a variety of ways; and all of which help oversee the others, again in a variety of ways.

From this, it can be seen that the fact that the third branch has vital integrity roles on questions of law does not in itself answer the question of whether there is, or should

---

49 J Braithwaite, 'Institutionalizing Distrust, Enculturating Trust' in V Braithwaite and M Levi (eds), *Trust and Governance* (Russell Sage Foundation, 1998) 354. See Sampford et al., above n 35, 98 (Figure 1).
50 Adapted from Sampford et al., above n 35, 99 (Figure 2).

be, a fourth branch. The roles of these branches remain distinct. The separation of judicial power ensures that the third branch stands alone. No fourth branch is likely to subsume it any time soon. But the judicial branch is also different because, even if the courts are crucial to public integrity, they differ from integrity branch institutions because they are not established solely or even primarily for that purpose. The rest of the executive branch can also be distinguished from the integrity branch, even when agencies have significant integrity roles, because these regulatory roles are either an intrinsic part of general management or apply sectorally to all institutions and citizens. They are not solely or primarily public integrity functions (examples include discrimination, rights protection, child protection and law enforcement generally).[51] The role of the judicial branch is also broad, involving dispute resolution and determination of law across all areas of society; public integrity constitutes but a small proportion of the work of the judicial branch as a whole, relative to general criminal, civil and commercial law. Even in the High Court, constitutional (including administrative law) cases amount to an average of only around 40 per cent of annual caseload, in terms of cases going to full judgment.

Justice Gummow's assumption that only the judicial branch can act as ultimate overseer of integrity agencies is also not empirically correct. The judicial branch is important, but it is parliaments which have developed the primary machinery for directly ensuring the accountability of integrity agencies on a day-to-day basis, through neither the executive nor the judiciary, but through a unique new range of mechanisms (special parliamentary committees, and parliamentary commissioners, officers, monitors or inspectorates) over the last 20 years.[52] These developments remain a 'work in progress', and deserve ongoing scrutiny and improvement,[53] but they underscore the fact that mutual accountability truly is multi-dimensional, not only in theory but also in practice.

In fact, more than anything else, it is this direct relationship between the legislative and integrity branches which explains why we see the emergence of the integrity branch as constitutionally significant. Like Gummow, Callinan and

---

51 Ackerman argued that there should not only be a fourth integrity branch, but a fifth 'regulatory branch' to recognise the particular position of this parallel breed of independent statutory agencies: see Ackerman, above n 13, 696–7.
52 In Queensland, this special parliamentary oversight was part of the design recommended by the Fitzgerald Inquiry: see Callinan and Aroney, above n 7, 30. This arrangement had antecedents in most jurisdictions in the oversight and support of auditors-general by parliamentary public accounts committees over many decades; and was paralleled by the establishment of parliamentary committees in most States to oversee Ombudsman's offices, a development described in NSW (where the Joint Parliamentary Committee was only established in 1990, 15 years after the office) as one of the most significant changes increasing the independence of the office from the executive: see Wheeler, above n 8, 39.
53 See Callinan and Aroney, above n 7, 24, 35–6, 195–8 and 218–9 (Recommendations 11 and 16).

Aroney were careful to make clear that bodies such as Queensland's CMC are not 'a constitutionally established fourth arm of government, distinct from the Legislature, the Executive and the Judiciary...By its nature, the CMC is a part of the Executive'.[54] Yet they accurately acknowledge that such agencies are quite different from most, if not all, of their counterparts, even if most form part of the executive and exercise aspects of the executive power of the State. As 'auxiliary precautions' added to the constitutional system in support of the continuing quest for government to maintain control over itself,[55] the integrity branch institutions go beyond the 'distinct roles played by the fundamental institutions of Parliament, the Executive and the Courts', since 'most...are also creatures of statute, enacted by the Parliament and responsible to the Parliament or one of its committees, rather than to the Premier, Cabinet or other Ministers of State'.[56] In other words, they exercise executive power, but are given statutory and institutional independence from the executive. Unlike other regulatory agencies, they report only and directly to Parliament itself. In this, we have a form of executive power deliberately configured so as to minimise the role of the executive in determining how it is used. These unique relationships sometimes have constitutional reinforcement. For example, the Victorian Ombudsman's status as an officer of the Parliament is expressly reflected in the State Constitution, fulfilling all the 'fourth branch' hallmarks noted by Ackerman and others. At the Commonwealth level, Gummow observes that s 97 of the *Constitution* requires 'the review and audit by law of the receipt and expenditure of money on account of the Commonwealth', confirming that the Auditor-General has not simply an executive, but a constitutional function.[57] But if not constitutionally, this status is often demonstrated legislatively – for example, in State legislation confirming that Ombudsmen are not mere executive creations but 'parliamentary commissioners for administrative investigations'.[58]

To make matters even more complex, there is also increasing reason to see integrity branch institutions as exercising powers that are not simply executive in nature, even if their constitutional origin lies with the executive. Some integrity

---

54 Ibid, 25.
55 Ibid, 23, quoting US federalist James Madison.
56 Ibid, 23–4.
57 On the alternative term 'mutual accountability' see R Mulgan, *Holding Power to Account: Accountability in Modern Democracies* (Palgrave McMillan, 2003) 232.
58 Even in NSW, the Ombudsman has travelled a long road to achieve statutory confirmation that he acts for the people, as an officer of the Parliament, rather than being part of the executive – see Wheeler, above n 8. It is only the Commonwealth Ombudsman, by comparison with his or her State counterparts, who often continues to be treated as subservient to the executive as opposed to independent of it, increasingly out of keeping with the office's expanding roles and public expectations.

agencies are charged by Parliament with roles relating to the integrity of Parliament itself and its members. The idea that this represents the executive exercising oversight of the Parliament – rather than the other way around – has been described as sitting 'somewhat uncomfortably' with 'the principle of Parliamentary sovereignty upon which the Westminster system of Parliamentary democracy ... is based'.[59] The discomfort disappears if we regard this as being not executive power at all, but simply the power of the Parliament being applied to itself through a new form of statutory mechanism.

There are similar long-standing dilemmas over the ways that executive and judicial power intersect in the exercise of many integrity functions. Peak administrative review tribunals, such as the Commonwealth AAT and the newer State Civil and Administrative Tribunals (CATs), are strong candidates for inclusion in the integrity branch. In theory, their statutory powers too have been regarded as administrative or executive. In practice we continue to recognise them as 'quasi-judicial', especially when they are led by actual judicial officers, deemed by a legal fiction to be only acting administratively in a personal capacity, as *persona designata*.[60] Even at the Commonwealth level, the question of what power they are exercising becomes even more complex when they are granted authority to overturn decisions for errors of fact and law. There is a complex doctrine of 'incompatibility' for determining when the conferral of executive and policy roles on judicial officers inappropriately compromises judicial power. Examining how this doctrine applies to integrity functions, Wenta confirms that judicial scrutiny and authorisation of executive warrants can survive the doctrine; as can judicial leadership and membership of administrative review tribunals.[61] Less clear is the status of 'quasi-judicial investigations', such as royal commissions, or standing anti-corruption and anti-crime commissions – here, it is 'difficult to reach a confident conclusion' as to the likely effect of the doctrine.[62] However, if we distinguish between those types of commission which solely or primarily exercise an integrity function, and commissions charged with helping find answers to wider questions of public policy (eg, *ad hoc* inquiries into management of a natural disaster, or institutional child abuse), there may be a clearer result. Such integrity functions appear to occupy a different category, more similar to the other two identified by Wenta, as generally compatible with judicial office.

---

59 B McClintock, 'Independent review of the *Independent Commission Against Corruption Act 1988*: Final Report' (2005) para 5.7; see Callinan and Aroney, above n 7, 25.
60 See AJ Brown, 'The Wig or the Sword?: Separation of Powers and the Plight of the Australian Judge' (1992) 21 *Federal Law Review* 48; F Wheeler, 'The Separation of Judicial Power and Progressive Interpretation', in HP Lee and P Gerangelos (eds), *Constitutional Advancement in a Frozen Continent* (Federation Press, 2009).
61 Wenta, above n 8, 54–8.
62 Ibid, 56.

Another alternative would be to acknowledge that what is being fulfilled here by judicial officers is not an executive function in a personal capacity, nor a judicial function, but an integrity function. In other words, recognising such an integrity function as a distinct field of governmental power in its own right, interrelated with but different from our conventional categories of power, could help solve multiple problems. Rather than simply three basic kinds of governmental power – the power to make law, the power to execute law, and the power to adjudicate disputes concerning the application of the law[63] – perhaps there are actually four, including also the power to ensure integrity in the manner that laws are made, executed and adjudicated upon. It can be, and has been, said that on such issues, we may not be wiser than our ancestors.[64] And yet it is part of our history that fields of power we now regard as distinct and separate – such as judicial power – have emerged over time out of other fields of power. It would seem strangely anti-historical to see it as impossible that new classifications of power might grow out of one or more of the three traditional branches we have now. If it makes sense to distinguish the functions and powers of the integrity branch in this way, it is sensible to acknowledge that we are – or perhaps should be – dealing with a distinct fourth branch of institutions, in constitutional terms.

Independence: When, why and how?

Whether or not the integrity branch is seen as a fourth, constitutional arm or something less, it is clearly the independence of integrity agencies from those institutions whose integrity they are charged with maintaining which represents their most important feature. Apart from their shared purpose, this independence defines the agencies that make up this branch. Even when uncertain about whether there is a fourth branch, for example, Solomon identifies the crucial feature of the integrity branch institutions as being statutory recognition that they 'should have the appropriate degree of independence from government, or at the very least, operational autonomy'.[65] As we have seen, independence is never absolute, for any branch of government – even High Court judges may be removed from office by the Parliament, in cases of incapacity or proven misbehaviour. Integrity branch appointments are similar, except usually for much shorter, limited terms. Given that it is overwhelmingly the executive that controls the legislature, more than

---

63 This phrasing is from Callinan and Aroney, above n 7, 20.
64 Gummow, above n 6, 20.
65 Solomon above n 8, 32. See also Wheeler, above n 8, 38–9, 55–6.

the other way round,[66] vital implications flow from the statutory standards that are set for how integrity agencies may conduct themselves in practice. On one hand, the Parliament is always free to limit the powers of an integrity agency that it has created, or to abolish it altogether, subject to any constitutional protection; on the other, it typically remains central to the statutory purpose and political legitimacy of such agencies that they have the freedom to investigate what they see fit, as they see fit, and to report when and what they see fit (subject to law). The principles that govern the judicial branch's independence for similar purposes, in administering justice according to law, have evolved over a long period of time, not least through conflict, tension and controversy. What principles should apply to define the independence of the integrity branch?

This more basic, practical question is playing out large in Australia's integrity branches, due to significant shifts in the way in which governments and parliaments are approaching the powers of their anti-corruption agencies. This is no accident – Chris Field has noted that the 'institutionalising of tackling corruption' has been 'the most visible, and sometimes controversial, aspect of the move by the state to fortifying integrity in government' over the past 20 years.[67] To understand the tensions, and their serious implications, it is enough to focus on one important example of the statutory powers of such agencies: their degree of independent discretion as to whether and when to make information public, or use publicity, as part of their activity. Two types of power are involved: the power to conduct public hearings as part of an inquiry, akin to 'royal commission' powers; and the power to make other public statements regarding the receipt of complaints or the conduct of investigations, even when the matter is only being assessed for investigation, or otherwise being investigated in private. Choices regarding the role and nature of such powers represent one of the most crucial design questions for any such institutions.[68]

On the first issue, the original policy presumption embedded in the NSW ICAC Act 1988 was that investigative hearings would ordinarily be held in public, such was the importance accorded to the role of public exposure in the investigative and educative functions of the Commission. Subsequent amendments to the ICAC's legislation have increased its flexibility and reduced the use of public hearings to instances where the Commission deems this to be in the public interest – but the Commission's legislation directs it to a fairly open and balanced set of

---

66 See, eg, Sir Gerard Brennan's influential description of the theoretical world in which the parliament controlled the executive as 'virtually destroyed': (1990) 65 *Australian Law Journal* 32.
67 Field, above n 8, 25.
68 See AJ Brown and B Head, 'Institutional Capacity and Choice in Australia's Integrity Systems' (2005) 64 *Australian Journal of Public Administration* 84, 91.

criteria for making this decision, preserving its independent discretion as to when to use this powerful tool.[69] Queensland's CMC, and WA's Corruption and Crime Commission were established with a somewhat reverse approach, but one now comparable in substance and effect.[70] However, against what appeared to be this relatively settled policy approach, two States have more recently adopted quite different settings – reflecting a clear desire by governments to wind back the breadth of discretion available to such commissions as to how to conduct their investigations. In Victoria, the Independent Broad-based Anti-corruption Commission (IBAC), created in 2011, may only conduct a public hearing where satisfied on reasonable grounds that (i) 'there are exceptional circumstances' for doing so, being something of a reversal of the presumption that public hearings are a good way to expose corruption; and (ii) no 'unreasonable damage' to a person's reputation, safety or wellbeing will result, being rather different from a discretion to balance the competing public interests.[71] The South Australian Government's *Independent Commissioner Against Corruption Act 2012* provides no discretion to the agency to conduct public hearings. All examinations must be undertaken in private.[72] Across Australia, therefore, the independent discretion available to this type of integrity agency now ranges from considerable to none. If one accepts that their statutory purpose and the basis of their political legitimacy is similar – as one should, from the public statements of the governments concerned – it seems unlikely from the perspective of either policy or principle that both positions can be right.

A similar conundrum is raised by the second issue, of other public statements regarding the receipt, assessment or investigation of complaints, where a similar constriction may be occurring. In general, it has been accepted that an integrity agency must have its own discretion to inform those it deems need to know, including the media or general public, about its own activities, where reasonably satisfied that this is in the public interest, and provided it is following statutory procedures and observing procedural fairness. For example, the Commonwealth Ombudsman will ordinarily conduct even major investigations in private and must normally follow laborious procedures before an investigation report may eventually become public (which occurs after an agency has refused to accept the Ombudsman's findings or recommendations, after which a Minister is required to table the report in Parliament). But the Ombudsman also has a power to make

---

69 See Callinan and Aroney, above n 7, 66; *Independent Commission Against Corruption Act 1988* (NSW), s 301.
70 See Callinan and Aroney, above n 7, 40, 66.
71 *Independent Broad-based Anti-corruption Commission Act 2011* (Vic), s 117(1).
72 *Independent Commissioner Against Corruption Act 2012* (SA), s 7(4)(a)(i). See also Sch 2, s 3(3).

information (including such reports) public, subject only to limited constraints, when and where he or she considers this to be in the public interest.[73]

Even the new SA legislation allows the ICAC to make 'public statements' in connection with particular matters, if, in the Commissioner's opinion, 'it is appropriate to do so in the public interest' having regard to sensible criteria.[74] This somewhat offsets an otherwise very prescriptive set of constraints upon the Commission, or indeed any person, from 'directly or indirectly' disclosing any information in connection with any 'complaint, report, assessment, investigation, referral or evaluation' under the Act – other than complainants, persons involved in investigations, a range of official bodies, and 'any other person of a class prescribed by the regulations'.[75] In other words, apart from the discretion to make 'public statements', the SA Act removes any general discretion to make information public other than to the extent that the executive and legislature might choose to extend those categories through subordinate legislation. It is noteworthy, too, that the SA legislation was modelled on the Commonwealth legislation creating the Australian Crime Commission – a criminal investigation body, squarely exercising executive power in a traditional sense, and not a public integrity agency.

This development is again especially significant because it has been recommended by Callinan and Aroney as the basis for amendment of the Queensland *Crime and Misconduct Act 2001*. This would make it a criminal offence for anyone, including the CMC, to make public any information about a complaint 'without the prior written consent' of any person who is the subject of a complaint or investigation – without even the balancing prerogative of a suitable power to make public statements, as is possible in South Australia.[76] The only other exceptions would be if the investigation proceeded by way of public hearing, or if the release is 'authorised by the Supreme Court in advance' based on 'a compelling public interest'. The reform is advanced on the basis that it would reduce both the incentive for, and impact of, malicious and vexatious complaints, and thus also help reduce a reportedly excessive complaint load by preventing complainants and others from using the mere fact of a complaint or an investigation to unjustly damage personal

---

73 See *Ombudsman Act 1976* (Cth) s 35A. Note, however, the more recent insertion of a power in the role of Attorney-General to certify that the Ombudsman may not publish certain information relating to the Australian Crime Commission or Australian Commission for Law Enforcement Integrity: ss 35B, 35C.
74 *Independent Commissioner Against Corruption Act 2012* (SA), s 25.
75 *Independent Commissioner Against Corruption Act 2012* (SA), s 54(2)(j). See, generally, ss 54, 56.
76 Callinan and Aroney, above n 7, 112; see Recommendation 8 at 216; and at 108: 'Though [SA] section 25 deserves consideration, section 56 directly tackles the root cause of the concerns the CMC has with its need to make public statements'.

reputations. As it happens, it also addresses the primary controversy which led the government to commission the review, being the CMC's decision to publicly affirm that it was assessing allegations of misconduct against a particular political leader, who then became Premier in 2012.[77] It is doubtful that the solution would be workable, given the impracticability of the restrictions, which on Callinan and Aroney's account surpass any such restrictions on other investigative bodies such as the police. However, the key point is that rather than preserving the independence of the agency by imposing a balanced discretion, the independent discretion to make information public would simply be removed.

Such debates, and the legislative options being pursued or canvassed for the powers of integrity agencies in such matters, highlight the need for more sophisticated principles. If governments and parliaments cannot get them right for themselves, perhaps these principles will eventually need to come from the courts, in deciding what kinds of limitations of discretion are incompatible with the statutory purposes and consequences of the independence inherent to such agencies' functions. While no political leader is ever likely to do anything but affirm this independence in principle, this small case study shows that, in practice, its creation and maintenance requires clear recognition of the unique place and role of such agencies. The desire of some officeholders to escape or lessen the burden of integrity oversight is inevitable, but should not become a de facto policy trend away from the very basic purpose for which such agencies were established. There is always a balance to be struck in legal theory, but without clear overarching principles, there is no guarantee that it will be struck in political practice. Irrespective of where the precise balance is to be struck on individual questions, the fact that these are integrity agencies – and not mere creatures of executive policy and preference, like other statutory agencies – should remain front and centre in the calculation. Indeed, if it would serve to help us remember this, these may provide yet further reasons why the continued constitutionalisation of the fourth branch is desirable.

Conclusion

Why do we have an integrity branch, and allocate such a high degree of policy importance and public resources to having well-developed integrity systems? In

---

[77] For the circumstances that triggered the review, see S Wardill, 'Newman puts watchdog on notice', *The Courier-Mail* (Brisbane), 11 October 2012; D Hurst, 'Spin check: CMC a "political weapon"', *Brisbane Times* <brisbanetimes.com.au>, 16 October 2012. Despite the centrality of this issue to the review, the review report refers to it only obliquely: see Callinan and Aroney, above n 7, 74, 82–3.

Queensland, Callinan and Aroney concluded that the alleged 'proliferation of people, agencies, schemes and legislation to ensure integrity by public servants' has occurred because 'there must have been, still is perhaps, an apprehension of widespread dishonesty and unethical behaviour in public administration, and a contagion in respect of which the proliferation of such arrangements is the only antidote'.[78] In fact, as Callinan and Aroney also recognise, a wider and more positive answer lies in the long recognition of liberal democratic practitioners that diffuse auxiliary precautions against the corruption of power are inherently and naturally required, to contain the risks of that otherwise inevitable outcome. More recently, Professor Braithwaite has explained that, in the age of institutions, the 'institutionalisation of distrust' is actually fundamental to how we 'enculturate trust' in the way in which power is exercised.[79] The people want to trust their institutions, most of the time; and most of the time they do trust their institutions. In Australia, their institutions serve them well, most of the time. But this positive state of affairs is maintained, at least in part, because of the people's confidence that if this trust was abused, or their legitimate rights and expectations were being contravened, someone would listen, or notice, and do something about it.

It is the political, statutory, and perhaps constitutional role of the integrity branch to ensure this public confidence. An analysis of the nature and legal position of the integrity branch institutions – Ombudsman, Auditor-General, Information Commission, anti-corruption body (or bodies), administrative review tribunal(s), and public sector standards commissioners – provides some justification for considering that clearer constitutional recognition of their shared function and independence may be advantageous. Irrespective, the growing reality of the integrity branch's role provides an important set of organising principles for administrative law practitioners. It provides strong reminders that administrative law remedies may not simply be legal, but multi-faceted; and that individual complaints and causes of action play their role within a broader framework for keeping government honest, open, fair and diligent. Whether any of the integrity branch institutions will truly be able to help deliver public accountability and administrative justice, like judicial branch ones, depends on whether their intended powers, independence and capacity actually aligns with the statutory purposes and political rhetoric surrounding their establishment. Like an effective judicial branch, the ongoing health and effectiveness of the integrity branch should not be taken for granted.

---

78 Callinan and Aroney, above n 7, 8–9.
79 Braithwaite, above n 49.

15

THE OMBUDSMAN

Anita Stuhmcke

> the basic purpose of an Ombudsman is provision of a 'watchdog' designed to look into the entire workings of administrative cases ... [he or she] can bring the lamp of scrutiny to otherwise dark places even over the resistance of those who would draw the blinds. If [his or her] scrutiny and reservations are well founded, corrective measure can be taken in due democratic process, if not no harm can be done in looking at that which is good.
>
> *Re Ombudsman Act* (1970) 72 WWR 176, 190, 192 (Milvain CJ)

Introduction

The riddle for legal observers is not whether the ombudsman institution is a success. If proliferation and evolution are measures of success, the Australian ombudsman institution is the 'poster child' for administrative law institutions. Since their original introduction to Australia in the 1970s, to provide a mechanism for individual citizens to complain about government administration, public Ombudsmen[1] now review a wide range of government action. Their jurisdiction includes: deaths in custody; oversight of the police force; monitoring of whistleblowing legislation; and auditing of records for telecommunication interception. The institution itself has also been adapted to provide a forum for complaint handling across private industry and large organisations. Calls have recently been made for the creation of a vast array of new ombudsmen, including an internet ombudsman[2] and a supermarket ombudsman,[3] and for ombudsmen to cover sport, the arts, gambling, crime, franchising and the motor industry.[4]

In the face of such success, the real riddle for legal observers is why ombudsmen are effective at all in resolving disputes. As lawyers and students of law we are well primed to accept, largely without question, the effectiveness of legal institutions such as courts, which make orders and provide binding remedies in the resolution of disputes. It follows that we will be more sceptical in our appreciation of institutions, such as the government Ombudsman, which make recommendations

---

1 Due to general usage, the plural 'Ombudsmen' is used throughout this paper.
2 A Sharp, 'Rudd flags Internet Ombudsman', *The Age* (Melbourne), 27 February 2010, <www.theage.com.au/national/rudd-flags-internet-ombudsman-20100226-p97l.html>.
3 M Paish, 'Retailers reject AFGC's anti-competitive regulatory proposals', *AFN Food for Thought* (Melbourne), 23 May 2012, <www.ausfoodnews.com.au/2012/05/23/retailers-rejects-afgc%E2%80%99s-anti-competitive-regulatory-proposals.html>.
4 The calls for new kinds of Ombudsmen are so regular that some have suggested the title of 'Ombudsman' should be regulated: J McMillan, 'What's in a name?: The use of the term "Ombudsman"' (Presentation to ANZOA Conference, 22 April 2008). In Australia the use of the title 'Ombudsman' is not restricted to the original statutory office of government Ombudsman except in South Australia: see *Ombudsman Act 1972* (SA), s 32, <www.ombudsman.gov.au/files/22_April_2008_Whats_in_a_name_use_of_the_term_Ombudsman.pdf>.

that are neither legally enforceable nor binding. This scepticism is arguably reflected in the historical treatment of the Ombudsman, which is often relegated to last place in administrative law textbooks, rarely the focus of rigorous critical independent analysis, and often subject to disparaging word plays on the Swedish title of the office (such as 'Ombudsmouse', Ombudsboob' and 'Ombudsflop').[5] The challenge for legal observers is to put aside such anachronistic views and ask why Ombudsmen have become central to the landscape of Australian dispute resolution.

Our riddling must therefore begin, and perhaps end, with the observation that government Ombudsmen are markedly different from the traditional dispute resolution institutions of courts and tribunals. The form of review undertaken by Ombudsmen may overlap with the judicial review in the courts and merits review in tribunals, but it is not the same as either. Described as 'unique',[6] with 'a unique role to play in scrutinising the conduct of government agencies',[7] Ombudsmen may, like courts and tribunals, look at whether a decision is lawful and correct, and yet assess the correctness of the decision according to broader principles of fairness and reasonableness.[8] Such standards are both derived from, and aiming to serve and improve, the broader system of government administration, rather than being applied to promote the interests of either the citizen or the government.

This chapter investigates Ombudsman practice and the evolving jurisdiction of the institution. The chapter begins by briefly examining the reasons for the introduction of Australian Ombudsmen. The second part of the chapter then explains the institutional differences between Ombudsmen, and courts and tribunals, as being both jurisdictional and operational. Having established that the ombudsman institution itself is essentially different from courts and tribunals, the next section of the chapter then further explains this divergence through an assessment of Ombudsman practice. The chapter's third section begins with an examination of how an Ombudsman goes about the core business of individual complaint handling. Using two individual complainant case studies, some of the more intangible qualities associated with the ombudsman model are revealed and norms of Ombudsman practice identified. This part of the chapter explains the unique criteria, often described as the principle of 'fairness and reasonableness', which is applied by Ombudsmen to assess administrative decision-making. Ombudsman performance is then critiqued in the next section, by identifying how the core role of individual

---

[5] R Gregory, 'The Origins and the Development of the Ombudsman Institution in the United Kingdom' in G Drewry and C Blake (eds), *Law and the Spirit of Inquiry* (Kluwer, 1989) 86.
[6] *Ainsworth v Ombudsman* (1988) 17 NSWLR 276, 283 (Enderby J).
[7] *Commissioner of Police v Ombudsman* (Unreported, NSW Supreme Court, 9 September 1994) 29 (Sackville AJ).
[8] Eg, see *Ombudsman Act 1976* (Cth), s 15(1): 'unreasonable, unjust, oppressive or improperly discriminatory' or that the action was 'otherwise, in all the circumstances, wrong'.

complaint handling is being augmented and perhaps irrevocably changed. Australian Ombudsmen have been granted extended jurisdiction by governments, but many are also utilising their own operational discretion to emphasise particular functions. It is possible that the ongoing ad hoc accumulation of roles and divergence of functions within Ombudsman offices will operate to the disadvantage of the fundamental aims of the institution. An issue which is raised, but left unanswered, in this chapter is whether the increasing emphasis in some government Ombudsman offices upon systemic reform, audit and the traversing of public and private areas of complaint resolution are matters of policy solution convenience for government, rather than an effective outcome for the institution itself.

Setting the scene: The derivation of Australian Ombudsmen

The international history of the development of the institution of ombudsman is one of adaptation. The model has been transplanted and modified to suit the needs of the political institutions of each individual country. The result is that numerous and diverse ombudsman offices now exist on every continent. The modern ombudsman institution is universally accepted as originating from the creation of the Swedish Parliamentary Ombudsman (Riksdagens ombudsman) in 1809.[9] The Swedish model is the basis for the public law Ombudsmen that now exist in every Australian jurisdiction.[10] These offices were established in the 1970s, following the introduction of the institution to the English-speaking common law world in New Zealand in 1962, and then the United Kingdom in 1967.

---

9 This is the official name of the institution, but it is more commonly known as 'JO' or the 'Justitieombudsman': see the Swedish website of the Parliamentary Ombudsman, <www.jo.se>.

10 The Commonwealth Ombudsman was established in 1976 by the *Ombudsman Act 1976* (Cth), and all of the State Ombudsmen were also established in the 1970s. The first Australian government Ombudsman was established in Western Australia by the *Parliamentary Commissioner Act 1971* (WA), soon followed in South Australia by the *Ombudsman Act 1972* (SA), then Victoria by the *Ombudsman Act 1973* (Vic), in Queensland by the *Parliamentary Commissioner Act 1974* (Qld) (now replaced by the *Ombudsman Act 2001* (Qld)), in New South Wales by the *Ombudsman Act 1974* (NSW), and in Tasmania by the *Ombudsman Act 1978* (Tas). In the Territories, the Northern Territory Ombudsman was established by the *Ombudsman (Northern Territory) Act 1978* (NT) (now replaced by the *Ombudsman Act 2009* (NT)) and the Australian Capital Territory Ombudsman by the *Ombudsman Act 1989* (ACT).

As in New Zealand and the United Kingdom, the move to introduce Ombudsmen in Australia was political and legal rather than populist. The catalyst for the introduction of Ombudsmen in Australian jurisdictions was generally a change in government, as 'parties in opposition were in favour of establishing an Ombudsman while parties in power were against the proposal'.[11] This was the case in Western Australia, the site of the first Australian Ombudsman, where a change of government facilitated Premier John Tonkin (who as Opposition leader had three times unsuccessfully sought to establish an Ombudsman's office) in introducing legislation in 1971 to create the first State Ombudsman in Australia.[12]

This pattern of a government change ushering in a new Ombudsman office highlights the constitutional nature of the traditional Swedish institution – that it is intended to be independent of the executive.[13] In terms of constitutional theory, Dicey would have it that representative government ensures that laws made by Parliament are in accord with the will of the electorate, and that Parliament's control over the executive ensures that decisions are made by a parliamentary majority and not by an executive decision.[14] The expansion of government activities over the last hundred years has, however, made a 19th century parliamentary structure inadequate for monitoring wide areas of government performance. The undermining of the traditional watchdog role of Parliament has occurred in numerous areas. For example, modern day Parliament has been forced to delegate law-making authority to the executive. Statutes passed by Parliament often contain general terms, leaving the operational details to regulations drawn up by the executive through the grant of discretionary powers. In Australia the party system has also transferred power from the legislature to the executive, which again has led to an expansion of the executive. Without being overly cynical, this explains why the call for Ombudsmen has traditionally come from political parties that are not the government of the day. After all, accountability of government is always attractive for a party in opposition.

More nobly, perhaps, the call for an Ombudsman may be explained by a desire to uphold the Australian democratic tradition. Access to justice and effective resolution of citizen complaints are essential to a healthy democracy.[15] In the

---

11 Senate Standing Committee on Finance and Public Administration, *Review of the Office of the Commonwealth Ombudsman* (December 1991) 7.
12 Ibid.
13 The word 'intended' is used here as most Australian Ombudsman are not established as officers of Parliament. For a recent discussion of the negative impact of this on the Commonwealth Ombudsman, see J Wood, 'Time for an independent Ombudsman', *Inside Story*, 31 February 2012, <inside.org.au/time-for-an-independent-ombudsman/>.
14 A V Dicey, *Introduction to the Study of the Law of the Constitution* (Palgrave Macmillan, 10th ed, 1960).
15 Access to Justice Taskforce, *A Strategic Framework for Access to Justice in the Federal Civil Justice System: A guide for future action*, Attorney-General's Department, September 2009, <www.ag.gov.au/LegalSystem/Pages/Accesstojustice.aspx>.

Westminster tradition, the expectation is that government should be accountable to the people – this check on power is the product of the electorate's grant of power to government.[16] The introduction of the ombudsman institution into Australia was seen as a necessary addition to the doctrine of ministerial responsibility and the existence of an independent judiciary. The growth of the welfare state, and the consequential increased government intrusion into our private lives, creates the need for an impartial and efficient forum to consider complaints against government administrators.[17] The office of Ombudsman may thereby be characterised as a necessary part of a framework of administrative review which aims to achieve administrative accountability through correcting defective decisions and assuring the public that the rule of law is safeguarded.[18]

Traditional Ombudsman jurisdiction: Complaint handling and own motion investigation

The core role of the Ombudsmen – which is to hold the executive accountable – is reflected in the key function of the office: that is, providing a complaint resolution option for any person aggrieved by an act or omission in the carrying out of government administration.[19] This core function explains why the jurisdiction and remedies of Ombudsmen over administrative decisions is different from that of courts and tribunals. For example, an individual may wish to complain about the rudeness of a government decision-maker, delay or lack of clarity in decision-making, or other similar issues for which one would not normally seek formal judicial redress. Ombudsmen have no determinative powers. They can only recommend a course of action, but often use this power to suggest a course of

---

16 Administrative Review Council, *The Contracting Out of Government Services*, Report No 42 (1998) ch 2.
17 I G MacLeod, 'The Ombudsman' (1966–67) 19 *Administrative Law Review* 93, 93; L Hill, *The Model Ombudsman: Institutionalising New Zealand's Democratic Experiment* (Princeton University Press, 1976) 5.
18 Commonwealth, *Commonwealth Administrative Review Committee Report*, Parl Paper No 144 (1971) [354], [364].
19 This part of the chapter refers to the following sections (excluding schedules) which cover the jurisdiction of the Ombudsman in each jurisdiction: *Ombudsman Act 1976* (Cth), ss 3, 3A, 5, 6; *Parliamentary Commissioner Act 1971* (WA), ss 4, 4A, 13, 14; *Ombudsman Act 1972* (SA), ss 3, 5, 13–15; *Ombudsman Act 1973* (Vic), ss 2, 13, 14; *Ombudsman Act 2001* (Qld), ss 7–10, 14–16, 18; *Ombudsman Act 1974* (NSW), ss 5, 12–14; *Ombudsman Act 1978* (Tas), ss 3, 4, 12, 14–16; *Ombudsman Act 2009* (NT), ss 3, 10–14; *Ombudsman Act 1989* (ACT), ss 3, 5, 6.

action that would not arise in courts and tribunals, such as that the executive make ex gratia payments to complainants.

The procedure of an Ombudsman is also very different from that of courts and tribunals. Ombudsmen are intended to provide a free, fast and impartial mechanism to resolve disputes between the bureaucracy and members of the public. Thus an Ombudsman avoids the expense, time, formality and difficulty of approaching a court or tribunal for review.

The core function of resolving the grievances of individual people is supplemented by a power that enables an Ombudsman to examine problems of wider scope. Ombudsmen can do this by conducting own motion investigations – the investigation of defective administrative problems when no specific complaint has been made.[20] This power provides a means to rectify systemic problems in public administration, and has been characterised as a proactive approach to prevent future complaints, which will over time 'lift the standard of government performance'.[21]

Each Australian Ombudsman has legislative authority to perform these dual roles. While the adaptation of the institution into each Australian jurisdiction has been slightly different, the function common to each of the nine Australian Ombudsmen is to use these roles to review government 'action', which broadly translates into review of 'the full gamut of activity that is undertaken by governments'.[22] The scope of investigation is thus defined broadly to include a decision, act, recommendation, proposal to act, or refusal or failure to act.[23] Rudeness, lost records and poor service are all examples of actions which an Ombudsman may investigate on the basis that they may be unlawful, unreasonable, unfair, improperly discriminatory or otherwise wrong. This function of investigating an 'action' sets Ombudsmen apart from the formal justice mechanisms of tribunals and courts, as it means that Ombudsmen may conduct investigations even if no administrative decision has been made at all. Thus an Ombudsman may intervene to prevent a harmful and lengthy dispute from arising, or may be involved in the process of administrative decision-making itself. In this sense, even though an Ombudsman may be reacting to an individual complainant, the action of the Ombudsman is proactive. This is

---

20 As to the own motion powers, see: *Ombudsman Act 1976* (Cth), s 15; *Parliamentary Commissioner Act 1971* (WA), s 25; *Ombudsman Act 1972* (SA), s 25; *Ombudsman Act 1973* (Vic), s 23; *Ombudsman Act 2001* (Qld), s 49; *Ombudsman Act 1974* (NSW), s 26; *Ombudsman Act 1978* (Tas), s 28; *Ombudsman Act 2009* (NT), s 14; *Ombudsman Act 1989* (ACT), s 18.

21 Commonwealth Ombudsman, *Annual Report* (2003–04) 2; M Oosting, 'The Ombudsman: A Profession' in L Reif (ed), *The International Ombudsman Yearbook* (Brill, 1997) 80.

22 D Pearce, 'The Jurisdiction of Australian Government Ombudsman' in M Groves (ed), *Law and Government in Australia* (Federation Press, 2005) 110.

23 J McMillan and R Creyke, *Control of Government Action* (LexisNexis, 3rd ed, 2012) 201.

essentially different from merits review and judicial review, which can provide solutions only *after* decisions are made.[24]

There are, however, limits upon the jurisdiction of the Ombudsman. An Ombudsman may not investigate all matters which concern government decision-making. The legislation governing an Ombudsman will always specify that particular agencies and decision-makers are outside the jurisdiction of the office.[25] In addition to explicit legislative exclusion of agencies from Ombudsman jurisdiction, the government 'action' which is reviewable by the Ombudsman is generally described in Australian legislation to be an action concerning a 'matter of administration'. Exactly what a 'matter of administration' means has been left largely to Australian Ombudsmen themselves, with occasional incursions by courts. These judicial incursions have caused ambiguity, which reflects the separation of powers doctrine. If this doctrine is applied strictly to define a 'matter of administration', it would mean that an Ombudsman could not investigate administrative decisions related to a judicial or a legislative matter. The leading Victorian decision of *Glenister v Dillon*[26] interpreted the phrase 'a matter of administration' narrowly, so that it referred to the arm of government performing the action rather than to the nature of the action being performed. In that case the delay in bringing prisoners to trial was held to be the responsibility of the judicial arm of government and therefore not a matter of administration. It followed that any matter of administration undertaken by the legislative or judicial arm of government could not be investigated by the Victorian Ombudsman. Australian Ombudsmen largely ignore the *Glenister* decision,[27] casting strong doubt over the authority of the case.[28] Subsequent decisions by Canadian courts have distinguished *Glenister* and interpreted 'administration' broadly, allowing the Ombudsman to investigate everything done by government authorities in the implementation of government policy.[29]

There is also ambiguity as to whether government policy is a 'matter of administration' and thus subject to Ombudsman investigation. This issue arose squarely in the Victorian case of *Booth v Dillon (No 2)*,[30] where the court held that the issue of where prisoners slept in a Victorian prison, and the related issue of resource allocation, were questions of policy and not administration. Dunn J

---

[24] Judicial review is possible where an official fails or refuses to make a decision, but such cases are fairly rare.
[25] Eg, judicial officers are excluded from the jurisdiction of all Australian Ombudsmen except for the SA Ombudsman.
[26] [1976] VR 550.
[27] See, eg, the Victorian Ombudsman, *Annual Report* (2010) 89 (detailing a case study investigating administrative errors in the Victorian Magistrates Court).
[28] W B Lane and S Young, *Administrative Law in Australia* (Thomson Reuters, 2007) 406.
[29] See, eg, *Re British Columbia Development Corp v Friedmann* [1984] 2 SCR 447.
[30] [1976] VR 434.

conceded that any distinction between policy and administration was difficult to draw 'because no clear line of demarcation exists between what is involved in policy and what is involved in administration'. He concluded that determining:

> whether the young prisoners in 'J' Division should be required to sleep in dormitories or be locked in individual cells is a matter of policy, and not a matter of administration. It obviously involves consideration of a number of matters of policy as to the most appropriate method of dealing with young prisoners.[31]

The wider issue under investigation in *Booth*, which was sexual violence in prison, was ultimately held in *Booth v Dillon (No 2)* to be outside the jurisdiction of the Victorian Ombudsman. In practice, this and similar decisions[32] have been largely ignored by Australian Ombudsmen, who nevertheless frequently make recommendations for policy change as well as making submissions to government for legislative and policy reform.

The observation that judicial decisions which limit jurisdiction have been 'ignored' by Ombudsmen highlights the importance of discretion. Ombudsmen exercise discretion at every stage of their work. An example is the process of complaint resolution.[33] Initially an Ombudsman may use discretion to decline or accept a complaint.[34] Once the decision to investigate is made, the approach taken is generally one of efficiency and informality. Powerful legislative provisions give all Australian Ombudsmen discretion to use wide investigatory powers to obtain information and make inquiries as they see fit. The powers that an Ombudsman has the discretion to use include: compelling the production of information and the giving of testimony; examining witnesses under oath; and entering and inspecting government premises.[35] The exercise of discretion also exists at the finalisation of an investigation, where an Ombudsman, again subject to differing requirements as to notification of findings,[36] may make broad recommendations for change.

---

31 Ibid, 439.
32 Such as the decision of the SA Supreme Court in *Salisbury City Council v Biganovsky* (1990) 54 SASR 117.
33 Variation in complaint investigation methods has been described as 'startling': W Gwyn, 'The Conduct of Ombudsman Investigations of Complaints' in G Caiden, *International Handbook of the Ombudsman: Evolution and Present Function* (Greenwood Press, 1983) 81.
34 The legislation in each jurisdiction broadly states the grounds upon which an Ombudsman may refuse a complaint to include: where there is an alternative avenue of review or another mechanism can deal with the complaint more effectively; where the nature of the complaint is such that it is frivolous or vexatious or investigation is not warranted; and where the complainant does not have a substantial interest in the matter.
35 See, eg, *Ombudsman Act 1976* (Cth), ss 9, 13, 14, 36.
36 For a discussion of this in the Commonwealth jurisdiction see *Chairperson, Aboriginal and Torres Strait Islander Commission v Commonwealth Ombudsman* (1995) 63 FCR 163.

This use of discretion extends beyond individual complaint handling to wider operational choices as to the direction and focus of the institution. Ombudsmen are funded by government and, as with all justice institutions, resource allocation drives operational choices. For example, over the last 10 years the office of the Commonwealth Ombudsman has doubled in size through the conferral of new functions such as wider immigration review powers.[37] This growth has led the Commonwealth Ombudsman to place more emphasis upon own motion investigations, which comprise the traditional dual function of the jurisdiction of Australian Ombudsmen.

Finally, discretion also exists as to the delivery of outcomes of own motion or individual complaint investigations. As previously noted, an Ombudsman makes recommendations which are non-binding and do not substitute for that of the original decision-maker, which is why Ombudsmen are sometimes lampooned as 'toothless tigers' or as 'fly swatters' rather than 'lion tamers'. In order to have recommendations accepted, an Ombudsman will rely largely upon powers of persuasion. Persuasion failing, the discretionary powers left to Ombudsmen in all Australian jurisdictions are generally to report the agency's lack of co-operation to Parliament or to the media. The greatest power of sanction available to the Commonwealth Ombudsman lies in ss 16 and 17 of the *Ombudsman Act 1976*.[38] If the agency has not acted upon Office recommendations, the Ombudsman may make a report to the Prime Minister under s 16, and to Parliament under s 17. This power is used sparingly because 'experience indicates that the Ombudsman's formal reporting powers, conferred pursuant to sections 16 and 17 of the *Ombudsman Act*, have not had the persuasive value that the Parliament might have expected when the legislation was enacted'.[39]

Thus the ultimate power of an Ombudsman may be characterised as the power of suggestion. It is this very absence of formal legal power which is viewed by some commentators to be 'the genius of the Ombudsman idea...that the holder of the office has full authority to investigate and pass judgment, but no power to enforce'.[40] As Enderby J noted in *Ainsworth v Ombudsman*:

---

37 J McMillan, 'How Ombudsmen Review and Influence Public Administration', Paper delivered to the International Intelligence Review Agencies Conference, Sydney, March 2010, <www.ombudsman.gov.au/files/10_March_2010_How_Ombudsmen_review_and_influence_public_administration.pdf>.

38 In addition, s 35A of the *Ombudsman Act 1976* allows reports to be released in the public interest.

39 Submission by the Commonwealth Ombudsman to the Senate Standing Committee on Finance and Public Administration, *Review of the Office of the Commonwealth Ombudsman*, submitted on 28 February 1991, 44.

40 G B McClellan, 'The Role of the Ombudsman' (1968–69) 23 *University of Miami Law Review* 463, 463, citing Anderson, 'The Scandinavian Ombudsman' (1964) 52 *American-Scandinavian Review* 408.

> It has always been considered that the efficacy of [his or her] office and [his or her] function comes largely from the light [he or she] is able to throw on areas where there is alleged to be administrative injustice and where other remedies of the Courts and the good offices of the members of the Parliament have proved inadequate. Goodwill is essential. When intervention by an Ombudsman is successful, remedial steps are taken not because orders are made that they be taken, but because the weight of its findings and the prestige of the office demands that they be taken.[41]

At first blush, this absence of formal powers would seem to have little practical benefit for a complainant as, unlike binding decisions of formal legal redress, the recommendations of an Ombudsman are non-enforceable. For some individual complainants, however, this lack of formal legal power is of considerable benefit in so far as it facilitates retention of formal legal rights, meaning that an individual complainant dissatisfied with the Ombudsman's decision may instigate actions through formal dispute resolution mechanisms such as courts and tribunals. Further, dissatisfied complainants may seek review of the Ombudsman investigation through the courts.[42]

Assessing Ombudsman practice: The application of the principle of 'fair and reasonable'

The name 'ombudsman' means 'representative',[43] but the possibility that an Ombudsman may be subject to legal proceedings commenced by both complainants and by government departments suggests that Ombudsmen neither represent the complainants nor the agency complained about. Rather, an Ombudsman impacts

---

41 (1988) 17 NSWLR 276, 283–4.
42 See *McGuirk v NSW Ombudsman* [2008] NSWCA 357, where an applicant was denied standing because success in his application would not bring any personal advantage or disadvantage. This also applies to government agencies who have litigated with respect to clarification or restriction of the powers of the Ombudsman: see *Chairperson, Aboriginal and Torres Strait Islander Commission v Commonwealth Ombudsman* (1995) 63 FCR 163.
43 The word 'ombuds' is a Swedish word meaning representative or agent of the people or a group of people. The word's origin is found in the Old Norse *umbuds man*, meaning representative. The first preserved use in Swedish is from 1552. H H Kircheiner, 'The Ideological Foundation of the Ombudsman Institution' in Caiden, above n 33.

upon the relationship between the governing and the governed by improving the fairness and justness of administration. This is the democratic strength of an Ombudsman – that they are responsible to both the individual citizen and the state, yet independent and impartial in the pursuit of good governance:

> [T]he basic idea is what makes the ombudsman institution so beautiful and powerful – that rational men [sic], the administrator, the individual citizen, and the ombudsman, can reason together to arrive at a rational and legal conclusion which is beneficial to the people. Many people are surprised that the concept works, but it works because most administrators, most individuals, and the Ombudsman share the same objective – to arrive at a fair and equitable decision in each case.[44]

As this part of the chapter will explain, 'fair and equitable' (more commonly referred to with respect to Ombudsmen as 'fair and reasonable') applies to both the approach taken by an Ombudsman to determine a complaint and the subsequent measure applied by the Ombudsman to the administrative decision-making involved in that dispute. 'Fairness and reasonableness' thus refers to both the procedure and the standards applied throughout the investigation rather than to the outcome.

Any exploration of the practice of an Ombudsman should ideally begin with their annual reports. Just as courts record decisions in published cases, Ombudsmen document their practice in Annual Reports. These reports are important public documents, required by legislation, recording key aspects of performance such as complaint statistics and the result of own motion investigations, and allows an Ombudsman to 'draw attention to problems that cannot simply be solved by an Ombudsman's investigation'.[45] Larry Hill has noted that an Ombudsman:

> has tasks that are in a structural sense highly patterned and repetitive, although in substance every complaint is unique. The work is analogous to a court's activities: complaints are lodged, some sort of deliberative investigative process – involving various political actors – occurs, and a ruling is made which disposes of the case. Over time, a clear a pattern of relationships develops, including the growth of a body of 'case law'.[46]

The following two case studies, selected from Annual Reports of the Tasmanian and Commonwealth Ombudsmen, illustrate the 'case law' of Ombudsmen:

---

44 H S Doi, 'Reply', Paper presented at *Conference of Australian and Pacific Ombudsman*, Wellington, New Zealand, 19–22 November 1974, 10.
45 Commonwealth Ombudsman, *Annual Report* (1979–1980) 25.
46 Hill, above n 16, 41.

CASE STUDY 1[47]

Mr P placed a bet with TOTE Tasmania that Spain would win the 2010 World Cup one goal to nil, and as it turned out this was the final result of the match. TOTE refused to pay, arguing that because the goal was scored in extra time it was not liable to pay, as bets were only paid for results at the conclusion of normal time. These rules were not easily accessible on the TOTE website by customers such as Mr P.

When the Ombudsman pointed this out to TOTE, it undertook to amend its website to improve accessibility to the information, and decided on this occasion to pay out Mr P's bet.

This example demonstrates the value of the Ombudsman in improving government administration. In one sense the Ombudsman acted as a 'consultant' to government, revealing a problem in risk management for TOTE. The resulting improvement of the TOTE website not only allows for due process and an individual use of the agency which is fair and equitable, but also means that TOTE will not be exposed to any future legal claims on this topic. One individual complaint has thus changed the experience of many, and has minimised the legal exposure of this government agency (which has since been privatised) to expensive and time-consuming law suits. In another sense the independence of the Ombudsman investigation legitimises the course of action taken by TOTE. The availability of independent scrutiny enhances the processes of the agency because 'in checking on the validity and reasonableness of administrative decisions, the Ombudsman also legitimises those decisions and thereby strengthens the bureaucracy'.[48]

Importantly, the norms of good administration used by an Ombudsman may be higher, at least in terms of quality of service, than legal requirements applied by courts in judicial review. On the facts, there is no legal requirement for the decision made by TOTE to pay out Mr P's bet. The decision made by TOTE to pay out the bet is legitimated not through legal doctrine but by application of the principle of 'fairness and reasonableness'. The result for Ombudsman practice is that there may be a range of possible remedies to apply to resolve a dispute. This spectrum of choice arises as 'the very concept of "unfairness" is very wide, and permits reasonable people to disagree'.[49] The flexibility of the 'fairness and

---

47 Ombudsman Tasmania, *Annual Report* (2010–2011) 28–29.
48 Commonwealth Ombudsman, *Annual Report* (1987–1988) 3.
49 *Norwich v Financial Ombudsman Service Ltd* [2002] EWHC 2379, [77].

reasonableness' principle is illustrated in this Case Study through the *non-legal* nature of administrative norms.

Finally this Case Study illustrates the significant advantage for the individual of lodging a complaint through an Ombudsman. The only other alternative available to Mr P without the Tasmanian Ombudsman would have been the courts. Legal action is difficult to access, slow, expensive and complex. It normally does not provide quick, effective and simple resolution of citizen disputes with government. The Australian Law Reform Commission explained:

> Society and the profession have wrongly been caught up in a rhetoric that often equates expense and formality with importance and quality... The counterweight to the institutional desire to provide an idealised form of individualised justice is the obligation to apply the limited resources available within the civil justice system in such a way as to meet the instances and areas of greatest need... The proportionality principle is associated with the philosophical theories of 'distributive justice'.[50]

In this case, Mr P achieved a result that he would not easily have achieved acting alone. Not only is an Ombudsman able to resolve a matter with an organisation at a higher level than with a harassed customer service member, but the Ombudsman also provides a proportionate response to those who are dissatisfied with government decision-making.

CASE STUDY 2[51]

In 1996, Shahraz Kayani, from Pakistan, was accepted in Australia as a refugee. On 2 April 2001, nearly four and a half years after his family's first application to join him in Australia had been lodged, Mr Kayani's frustration and loss of hope of ever being reunited with his wife and daughters led to a desperate and tragic act of self-immolation outside Parliament House in Canberra. He died within three months, from infection caused by his burns.

The report resulting from the investigation into the complaint made by Shahraz Kayani before his death was damning. The Ombudsman stated that 'the

---

50 Australian Law Reform Commission, *Managing Justice: Continuity and Change in the Federal Justice System* (ALRC Report 89, 1999) [1.91]–[1.93].
51 Commonwealth Ombudsman, *Annual Report* (2001–2002) 87. For the full report see R McLeod, 'Report on the Investigation into a Complaint about the Processing and Refusal of a Subclass 202 (Commonwealth Ombudsman, 2001) (Split Family) Humanitarian Visa Application Report under section 35A of the *Ombudsman Act 1976*, August 2001, 1, <www.ombudsman.gov.au/files/investigation_2001_07.pdf>.

history of this case is one of administrative ineptitude and broken promises ... the decision-making process surrounding his wife's application to come to Australia was affected by error, and possibly, bias or prejudice'.[52] The Department of Immigration and Multicultural and Indigenous Affairs (DIMIA) did not accept all findings of the report.[53] The report made little difference to the plight of the Kayani family. Three months after her husband's death, and eleven months after being assured of expeditious treatment, Ms Yasmin's application still had not been finalised. The family was refused entry to the country on the anniversary of his death.[54]

This Case Study differs markedly from the first. It demonstrates the value of the Ombudsman as a moral and ethical compass for government administration. Here, the role of an Ombudsman in correcting the power imbalance between the governors and the governed is one of overseeing the integrity and humanity of government action.[55] This has been described as an intangible quality associated with the Ombudsman model, 'an institutionalised form of public consciousness'.[56] The ombudsman institution is part of public administration, and is thus able to commend and condemn government action from a vantage point both within and outside the system of government decision-making. As observed by the Ombudsman in his public report into this complaint: '[F]rom an administrative viewpoint, the handling of this case is a tragic reminder to all Government officials that in applying bureaucratic processes and procedures, they should never lose sight of the human dimension of their work'.[57]

This Case Study illustrates both the vulnerability of individual citizens to government administration and how an Ombudsman may, without assisting the individual complainant, nevertheless improve the wider system of government administration. In this Case Study the agency ultimately failed the test of what is fair and reasonable. While the Ombudsman was unable to resolve the complaint of Mr Kayani, he found that the agency failed norms of good administration as to: the expectation that a citizen's affairs will be handled with reasonable speed, particularly in a situation such as this where the administrator knows that delay

---

52 Commonwealth Ombudsman, *Annual Report* (2001–2002) 87.
53 Ibid, 87–8.
54 'Ruddock continues persecution of Kayanis', *The Green-Left Weekly*, 29 May 2002, <http://groups.yahoo.com/group/Ausnews/message/4791>.
55 C Lewis, Ombudsman of Ontario, Canada, 'The view from the Ombudsman's Chair' 2001 <http://www.soar.on.ca/docs/speaker_docs/SOS-01_Lewis.PDF>.
56 P Birkinshaw, *Grievances, Remedies and the State* (Sweet and Maxwell, 1994) 245.
57 McLeod, above n 51.

will impact adversely upon the individual's interests; the obligation to give correct advice to a citizen and to do so without prejudice; and the fact that agencies have an obligation to correct deficiencies in administrative decision-making, even when the resource implications are adverse. In these situations it may be expensive and difficult for an agency to rectify a problem, but it is clearly appropriate that this cost be borne by the agency which caused the problem, rather than the citizen who did not. This then is how the Ombudsman applies, creates and improves norms of good administration – through exposing the defective administration and articulating what the norms of good administration should be.

Both Case Studies show that the role of the Ombudsman in determining what is fair and reasonable may be segregated into two interrelated stages. First, the investigation itself must be fair and reasonable. For example, the NSW Ombudsman website gives a guarantee of service, to:

- consider each matter promptly, fairly and provide clear reasons for our decisions
- where we are unable to deal with a matter ourselves, explain why, and identify any other appropriate organisations where we can
- help those people who need assistance to make a complaint to the Ombudsman
- add value through our work.[58]

Second, in order to be relevant and have impact, the standards of administration applied to government decision-making must also be fair and reasonable. According to American theorist Roscoe Pound, an equitable approach to dispute settlement will have the decision-maker 'be free to deal with the individual case so as to meet the demands of justice between the parties and accord the reason and moral sense of ordinary men'.[59] In the context of an Ombudsman investigation, the 'reason and moral sense' applied is not that of 'ordinary men' but rather that of developed principles, standards and rules of what an Ombudsman believes to be good administration. Quite simply, without principles of good administration there can be no maladministration; and further, without acceptance of those principles by the bureaucracy there will not, as was shown in Case Study 2, be a fair and reasonable process applied by agencies.

The difference in outcomes between the Case Studies underscores the importance of agency acceptance of the administrative norms of Ombudsman practice. In both Case Studies the Ombudsman said what *ought* to happen – a consideration involving intangible qualities of fairness, equity, reasonableness and justice, as well as more concrete considerations of law and policy. Ultimately,

---

58 See NSW Ombudsman website at <www.ombo.nsw.gov.au/what-we-do/about-us>. Less tangible concepts such as the vision, mission, purpose and values of an Ombudsman are also emphasised by the office. Values include concepts such as integrity, impartiality, fairness, adding value, and respect.
59 *Introduction to the Philosophy of Law* (Yale University Press, 1959) 63.

however, such norms of good administration must be accepted as being fair and reasonable by the administrators themselves. In Case Study 1 the bureaucracy went further than legally necessary to assist the complainant, and in Case Study 2 they fell horribly short. This demonstrates the artistry of Ombudsman practice – to maintain independence from government administrators while simultaneously setting fair and reasonable standards under which those same administrators are to function. To be effective in improving government administration, Ombudsmen must ensure not only compliance with the basic norms of the authority with political power, but also that those same administrative norms are subject to ongoing and substantive review, revision and renewal.

This process of administrative norm creation and application thus involves considering more, or perhaps at least something other than the legality of decision-making. Characterised increasingly as 'integrity review',[60] this normative role ensures that Ombudsmen will set standards and clarify the requirements for good decision-making for government administrators. Ultimately the public derives benefit from the observance of those principles. Langbroek and Rijpkema have coined a name for this contribution of Ombudsmen to the growth of a body of norms of good administration – 'Ombudsprudence'.[61] This demarcation of a particular body of theory to explain Ombudsman decisions helps to clarify that Ombudsman dispute resolution takes place 'between internal conflict resolution mechanisms of the administration and external conflict resolution offered by courts'.[62] As is apparent from the Case Studies, Ombudsmen apply norms of good administration side by side with correctness of legal decision-making. That said, what is fair and equitable does not mean 'according to law', as an Ombudsman does not enforce existing rights, but creates new expectations between the parties with regard to the fairness of the case.[63] In this context Ombudsmen appeal to a higher ethical, just, consistent and fair normative decision-making framework which centres on a co-operative approach to good administration *as it applies to the individual*, rather than with reference to the coercive approach of consolidation or refinement of legal principles a court might apply.

---

60 A Stuhmcke, 'Ombudsmen and Integrity Review' in L Pearson, C Harlow and M Taggart (eds), *Administrative Law in a Changing State: Essays in Honour of Mark Aronson* (Hart, 2008) 349.
61 P M Langbroek and P P Rijpkema, 'Demands of Proper Administrative Conduct: A Research Project into the *Ombudsprudence* of the Dutch National Ombudsman' (2006) 2 *Utrecht Law Review* 81.
62 M Remac and P Langbroek, 'Ombudsman's Assessments of Public Administration Conduct: Between Legal and Good Administration Norms', <unpan1.un.org/intradoc/groups/public/documents/nispacee/unpan049015.pdf>.
63 S Cohen, 'Fair and Reasonable – An Industry Ombudsman's Guiding Principle' (2009) *AIAL Forum* 63, 26.

Increasing jurisdiction: The sign of a thriving institution?

Against this backdrop of investigative approach, we can now assess the significance of the very real change currently occurring in the operation of Ombudsman offices.[64] In 2012 the New Zealand Ombudsman, which was the genesis of all English-speaking offices, celebrated its 50th anniversary. That Ombudsman issued the following statement:[65]

> The Ombudsmen are increasingly seen as an appropriate 'home' for overseeing key democratic measures and initiatives aimed at safeguarding the rights of individuals and increasing government transparency. In an environment where it is recognised that savings can be made using existing institutions to deliver new measures and initiatives, we are aware that the Ombudsmen may be asked to perform additional functions.

This premonition of things to come reflects the significant jurisdictional changes that Australian Ombudsmen too have undergone.

As this part of the chapter will discuss, since the introduction of the institution into Australia 40 years ago, Ombudsmen too have become increasingly differentiated from both their own original functions and from more formal legal institutions, such as courts and tribunals. For example, Hill noted in 1976 that, although the New Zealand Ombudsman 'has the power to be self-activating, nearly all of his investigations are initiated by citizens' complaints'.[66] By contrast, in 1998–99 Professor Kenneth Wiltshire observed during his review of the Queensland Ombudsman (which led to legislative change in 2001) that 'the lot of the modern ombudsman is not simply to open the door, the switchboard and the mail each day and respond to complaints which waft in, many of which have common causes elements and generic causes'; rather the emphasis of the office is to be 'proactive, systemic, and preventative in its orientation'.[67]

This jurisdictional change has been imposed upon Ombudsmen through external legislative mandate. Successive governments, to varying degrees across all Australian jurisdictions, have passed legislation creating an ad hoc expansion of

---

64 For an international overview of such change see T Buck, R Kirkham and B Thompson, *The Ombudsman Enterprise and Administrative Justice* (Ashgate, 2011).
65 New Zealand, Office of the Ombudsman, Statement of Intent for period 1 July 2011 to 30 June 2014, 9.
66 Hill, above n 17, 79.
67 K Wiltshire, *Report of the Strategic Review of the Queensland Ombudsman* (Queensland Government, 1998) 32.

Ombudsman functions.[68] For example, the Commonwealth Ombudsman currently describes itself as having four major statutory roles:[69] complaint investigations; own motion investigations; compliance audits; and immigration detention oversight. The office notes, however, that 'handling complaints and conducting own motion investigations are traditional ombudsman activities; they account for most of the work done by the office'.[70]

The New South Wales Ombudsman has experienced an even greater expansion of functions. That office's role has been increased by successive NSW Parliaments to now cover an extraordinary range of activities, including: oversight of police investigation of complaints about police officers; Freedom of Information complaints; auditing of records of bodies authorised to intercept telecommunications; complaints about the provision of community services by both public and private organisations; coordinating the work of the Official Community Visitors; oversight of the system for dealing with allegations against people who work with children (in both public and private organisations); convening and supporting the NSW Child Death Review; reviewing the causes and patterns of the deaths of children in care; reviewing the implementation of legislation giving greater powers to police; determination of Witness Protection appeals; oversight of controlled operations; oversight of compliance by law enforcement agencies with the *Surveillance Devices Act 2007*; oversight of powers to conduct covert searches; and oversight of the implementation of whistleblowing legislation.[71]

While the NSW Ombudsman provides the strongest example of jurisdictional expansion, other State and Territory jurisdictions are not immune. The Victorian Ombudsman, for example, was granted the power to inquire into whether an administrative action of a public authority is incompatible with a human right.[72] This express human rights mandate transforms the Victorian Ombudsman into a human rights Ombudsman and marks a new focus of an Australian government giving a classical Ombudsman a human rights protection oversight role. This means the Victorian Ombudsman is the first sub-national human rights or hybrid Ombudsman in Australia.[73] A quite different example, which also alters the character of the office from a classical public Ombudsman to something new, is the conferral upon the

---

68 C Wheeler, 'Review of Administrative Conduct and Decisions in NSW since 1974: An ad hoc and Incremental Approach to Radical Change' (2012) 71 *AIAL Forum* 34.
69 Commonwealth Ombudsman, *Annual Report* (2011–2012), Chapter 1.
70 Ibid.
71 Wheeler, above n 68.
72 This jurisdiction is a consequence of the *Charter of Human Rights and Responsibilities Act 2006* (Vic).
73 L Reif, *The Ombudsman, Good Governance and the International Human Rights System* (Martinus Nijhoff Publishers, 2004) 2–11, 393.

Western Australian and Tasmanian Ombudsmen of a private industry Ombudsman role – as the Energy Ombudsmen for gas and electricity.[74]

While significant, external legislation is only partly responsible for the changing role and functions of Australian Ombudsmen. The other important contributor is the use of discretionary internal allocation of resources by Ombudsmen to place emphasis upon chosen functions. For example, as previously noted, the use of own motion inquiries has significantly increased over the lifetime of the Commonwealth Ombudsman. This is an intriguing development, as the choice to do so is discretionary in the sense that there has been no external mandate by way of government legislation or any other explicit imperative to do so. Interestingly, it has coincided with a modification in the approach to handling individual complaints, where there is now an increased use of discretion to refer complainants to the 'first resort' of the agency complained about rather than to the Ombudsman.

A fear of irrelevance and a history of struggling to secure necessary government resources may partially explain the motive of Ombudsmen in taking on new functions and placing increased emphasis on others. This change and expansion of jurisdiction may therefore be a deliberate strategy to ensure that Australian Ombudsmen 'make themselves politically and managerially indispensable'.[75] The current NSW Ombudsman argues that adaptation is both necessary and desirable because:

> We need to accept that change will happen, and we need to be the driver of this change, to look for better and more effective ways to operate, to re-shape the Ombudsman model to keep pace with community needs and expectations, to explore and question – to see as possible what we have previously thought was not. This will be essential if we are to remain relevant. ... We have evolved from a reactive complaint handling body into a forward-thinking, strategic, community focussed and proactive office. Using the core principles of our Swedish heritage, building on them, developing them to meet the needs and circumstances of our own community. Placing them in today's context and planning for tomorrow.[76]

The accuracy of the above comments may be reflected in the ripples occurring across the wider landscape of accountability organisations which keep the executive in check, such as auditors-general, privacy commissioners and corruption commissioners. The increase in powers of existing agencies and the introduction

---

74 For classifications of the offices into three models of Ombudsman see: A Stuhmcke, 'The Evolution of the Classical Ombudsman: A View From the Antipodes' (2012) 2 *International Journal of Public Law and Policy* 83.
75 W B Lane and S Young, *Administrative Law in Australia* (Thomson, 2007) 474.
76 B Barbour, 'Actions Speak Louder than Words: An Ombudsman's Office and Children', Speech delivered at *IOI World Conference Stockholm*.

of new accountability mechanisms to keep executive governments in check have led to calls for recognition of a new fourth branch of government.[77] This branch, called the 'integrity branch' of government, would include institutions such as the Ombudsman. It is hoped that such constitutional recognition of integrity agencies would improve government accountability, as constant revision of the landscape of dispute resolution is necessary to guard against both complacency and the dangers of unchecked growth in the jurisdiction of the institutions, such as the ombudsman institution, which control government action.[78]

Conclusion

Reforms to the Australian legal system have altered the management framework of formal legal institutions, such as courts and tribunals, through the introduction of operational mechanisms such as caseload targets and staffing.[79] The impact of such reforms is undeniably great, but they have not altered the fundamental philosophy of our legal institutions. The same argument can be made for the Ombudsman – that the additional roles have not altered the institution. Indeed, Snell has characterised many of the new functions of Ombudsmen as falling into a category he describes as 'fire prevention'.[80] Snell argues that the 'fire prevention' functions of Ombudsmen are those which are disengaged from that of the complainant because they are not 'based solely or primarily on intelligence gained from previous complainants'.[81] This differs from the traditional roles originally characterised by Harlow and Rawlings as 'fire-fighting' and 'fire-watching', where 'fire-fighting' is the reactive response made by Ombudsmen to individual complainants and 'fire-watching' is a systemic investigation based upon previous individual complaints.[82]

---

77 J J Spigelman, 'The Integrity Branch of Government' (2004) 78 *Australian Law Journal* 724.
78 The Ombudsman is of course not a perfect mechanism for access to justice. For example, studies of Ombudsman complainants both in Australia and overseas show that, despite community education initiatives and outreach programs run by Ombudsmen, complainants remain largely middle-class and advantaged. See S van Roosbroek and S Van de Walle, 'The Relationship between Ombudsman, Government, and Citizens: A Survey Analysis' (2008) *Negotiation Journal* 287, 298; A Stuhmcke, 'Australian Ombudsman and Human Rights Ombudsman' (2011) 66 *AIAL Forum* 48.
79 See, eg, the changes to the NTT: Moira Coombs, 'National Native Title Tribunal Reform', <www.aph.gov.au/About_Parliament/Parliamentary_Departments/Parliamentary_Library/pubs/rp/BudgetReview201213/CourtReforms>.
80 R Snell, 'Australian Ombudsman' in M Groves and HP Lee (eds) *Australian Administrative Law: Fundamentals, Principles and Doctrines* (Cambridge University Press, 2007) 104.
81 Ibid.
82 C Harlow and R Rawlings, *Law and Administration* (Cambridge University Press, 3rd ed, 2009) 528.

Accepting that this is currently the case, it is nevertheless clear that a looming issue for policy makers, legislators, citizens, the bureaucracy and Ombudsmen, is 'a danger in Australia that the original purpose for the establishment of the office is being lost'.[83] Diversification and proliferation of functions does not automatically mean an Ombudsman will be more effective in ensuring good administration. Ombudsmen were originally intended to guard quality performance in public administration, and the proliferation of functions may be conferred by a government with that aim in mind and with the best of intentions, such as to fine-tune institutions to consolidate a democratic structure.[84] However, the issue is not one of good intention, but whether the increased functions enhance or detract from the contribution an Ombudsman makes to democratic processes and administrative justice. The degree of success an Ombudsman will have in building good governance necessarily depends on a number of legal, political, financial and social factors affecting the institution. Weaknesses in one or more of these areas may occur from time to time, and will need to be remedied if the institution is to continue to operate effectively. In short, a watching brief must be kept on the institution to ensure it remains a riddle worth solving.

---

83 See Pearce, above n 22, 138.
84 L Reif, 'Building Democratic Institutions: The Role of National Human Rights Institutions in Good Governance and Human Rights Protection' (2000) 13 *Harvard Human Rights Journal* 23, 23.

16

FREEDOM OF INFORMATION: A NEW ERA WITH OLD TENSIONS

Judith Bannister

Introduction

Access to information is fundamental to all areas of administrative law. Indeed, the very early origins of prerogative writs have been characterised in terms of information access: 'certiorari was essentially a royal demand for information'.[1] The relationship between the citizen and the state is one of unequal power that modern administrative law helps to redress. Access to information is crucial to that process. The duty to disclose adverse information is central to the procedural fairness that government decision-makers must accord to persons whose interests are directly affected by their actions.[2] Once a decision has been made, providing reasons is essential if affected people are to properly understand whether the decision may be susceptible to administrative or judicial review.[3]

Public access to information is also central to the administrative law goals of executive accountability and improving the quality, efficiency and effectiveness of government decision-making. In modern democracies, governments are obliged to disclose information in a wide range of circumstances, including: answering parliamentary questions; disclosing evidence to independent inquiries and to courts; and many official reporting obligations. This chapter will focus upon one particular system of information disclosure: the rights of citizens to access government documents granted by Commonwealth and State freedom of information statutes. It will provide an overview of those statutes and their recent reforms, and identify some key areas of ongoing concern.

The story of freedom of information in Australia has been one of high ideals, cautious legislative reform and often disappointing implementation. It is over 30 years since freedom of information was first introduced in Australia.[4] The Commonwealth and some Australian States have recently implemented major reforms, but other jurisdictions retain their 'first generation'[5] statutes. In the reformed jurisdictions there is a new era, with expectations of greater openness. Reforms such as stronger presumptions in favour of disclosure, proactive publication, and oversight by information commissioners, have all contributed to a renewed commitment to open government. How successful these reform projects will be will depend upon how some old tensions are managed. These old tensions, which

---

1 H Woolf, J Jowell, A Le Sueur, C Donnelly and I Hare, *De Smith's Judicial Review* (Sweet and Maxwell, 7th ed, 2013) 857.
2 *Kioa v West* (1985) 159 CLR 550.
3 There is no common law right to reason: *Public Service Board of New South Wales v Osmond* (1986) 159 CLR 656. Statutory rights now exist. See, eg, *Administrative Decisions (Judicial Review) Act 1977* (Cth), s 13; *Administrative Appeals Tribunal Act 1975* (Cth), s 28.
4 *Freedom of Information Act 1982* (Cth) commenced operation 1 December 1982.
5 See below, nn 21–22.

arose when freedom of information was first introduced, focus upon fundamental differences about the scope and objects of open government.[6]

Whilst the concept of open government is generally accepted, disagreements regularly emerge over how the schemes should operate. How is the public interest in open and accountable government to be weighed against competing public interests that at times require secrecy be maintained? How are those public interests to be assessed, and who gets the final say in that process? Who should bear the costs?

Before considering these ongoing issues, it is important to place this discussion of information access in context. Freedom of information legislation as we know it today is a relatively recent and quite revolutionary innovation for a system of government administration with a long tradition of secrecy.

Official secrecy

It is tempting to approach any account of open government in Australia by focusing upon the failures, and to highlight the cover-ups and exemption claims so beloved of newspaper headline writers.[7] However, before critiquing the Australian freedom of information schemes, old and new, it is worth recalling how open Australian governments are today when compared with 30 or 40 years ago, before freedom of information was an accepted part of the administrative law landscape. The shift in attitudes of Ministers and public servants that has been demanded in the new era of open government was once described by Justice Kirby as 'nothing short of revolutionary'.[8]

Before the last quarter of the 20th century, secrecy was the accepted norm in Australian government. Australian public administration inherited a culture of secrecy from England.[9] In her 1967 comparison of freedom of information in the United States and Anglo-Australian official secrecy, Enid Campbell observed:

> The right of public servants to perform their functions anonymously and *in camera* and the right of executive departments to treat their records as

---

6 For an early discussion by the Queensland Information Commissioner of the 'tension between the objects which the FOI Act seeks to attain, and the tradition of secrecy', see *Eccleston and Department of Family Services and Aboriginal and Islander Affairs* (1993) 1 QAR 60, 87.
7 See, eg, M Owen, 'One sentence – all you are allowed to know about plans for $1.7bn Marj', *The Advertiser* (Adelaide), 22 November 2007, 7.
8 *Osland v R* (2008) 234 CLR 275, 303.
9 Which was strengthened throughout the British Empire by official secrets legislation. The history of secrecy in Australian public administration was discussed in *Osland v The Queen* (2008) 234 CLR 275, 301–3 (Kirby J).

confidential are so firmly rooted in our political tradition that it may be hard to imagine how any form of government could function properly without them.[10]

This secrecy was sometimes justified as being an essential feature of our Westminster system of government.[11] Public disclosure was thought to undermine good administration. The 1976 Royal Commission on Australian Government Administration reported that one in ten of the submissions received by the Commission criticised the way the bureaucracy gathered, used and mostly failed to disseminate information. The Commission warned of the dangers of departments 'regarding as "their own" information they obtain in the course of their work'.[12]

Governments are far more open today, but there is still a strong pressure to maintain secrets in some areas. In its 2009 report on secrecy laws, the Australian Law Reform Commission (ALRC) identified 506 secrecy provisions in 176 pieces of primary and subordinate legislation.[13] Of these, approximately 70 per cent created criminal offences. Around three-quarters of those criminal offences were indictable offences.[14] Equitable obligations of confidence,[15] common law obligations of fidelity in employment, and public service regulations and codes of conduct[16] also impose duties not to disclose information that has been obtained or generated by public officials.

Of course, governments produce vast quantities of material that is intended for public release, ranging from public education programmes to 'spin', and governments strategically manage information with publication.[17] Quite different issues arise when information is created or compiled with no intention to publish it. Compelled disclosure of sensitive information is where the real tensions arise. If one takes a long view, the battle over freedom of information has been about control over when to publish. The historical archival record will one day be disclosed.[18] The difficult question is: who is to determine what is to be disclosed now? The idea that members of the public, pesky journalists, or opposition parliamentarians can

---

10 E Campbell, 'Public Access to Government Documents' (1967) 41 *Australian Law Journal* 73, 73. See also J Spigelman, *Secrecy: Political censorship in Australia* (Angus & Robertson, 1972).
11 Commonwealth, Royal Commission on Australian Government Administration, *Report* (1976) 350.
12 Ibid, 346.
13 Australian Law Reform Commission, *Secrecy Laws and Open Government in Australia* (Report 112, 2009) Ch 3.
14 Ibid, 3.20–3.21.
15 *Commonwealth v Fairfax* (1980) 147 CLR 39.
16 *Public Service Act 1999* (Cth), s 13(10); Public Service Regulations 1999 (Cth), reg 2.1.
17 For a discussion of the strategic management of information by government, see G Terrill, *Secrecy and Openness* (Melbourne University Press, 2000) 196.
18 See, eg, *Archives Act 1983* (Cth).

compel publication of an official document before the author is ready, or before the matter is relegated to history and the officials involved have had time to retire or die, is a significant shift in power that came with freedom of information in the 1980s in Australia.

Freedom of information has re-characterised official documents as a national resource.[19] Public access to that resource is facilitated by modern information technologies, new approaches to licensing public sector information (PSI)[20] and the statutory access schemes discussed in this chapter. The extent to which that resource is truly available to the public has been debated since the laws were introduced.

First generation freedom of information laws

Freedom of information was introduced at a Commonwealth level in Australia in 1982.[21] The States and Territories followed over the next two decades.[22] These are the 'first generation'[23] of freedom of information laws in Australia, and they granted every person a legally enforceable right to obtain access to government documents, subject to a range of exemptions. Freedom of information was heralded as an important advance,[24] but almost from its inception the legislation was criticised for failing to meet its proclaimed ideals. The practical experiences of regular FOI applicants were of delays, excessive costs and routine reliance upon broadly worded exemptions.[25] Freedom of information worked reasonably well for private

---

19 *Freedom of Information Act 1982* (Cth), s 3(3).
20 Government 2.0 Taskforce, *Engage: Getting on with Government 2.0* (2009); Office of the Australian Information Commissioner, *Principles on open public sector information: Report on review and development of principles* (2011). See discussion in J Bannister, 'Open Government: From Crown Copyright to the Creative Commons and Culture Change' (2011) 34 *University of New South Wales Law Journal* 1080.
21 *Freedom of Information Act 1982* (Cth) commenced operation 1 December 1982. For a history of these developments see Terrill, above n 17, ch 6.
22 *Freedom of Information Act 1982* (Vic); *Freedom of Information Act 1989* (NSW) (now replaced); *Freedom of Information Act 1989* (ACT); *Freedom of Information Act 1991* (SA); *Freedom of Information Act 1991* (Tas) (now replaced); *Freedom of Information Act 1992* (Qld) (now replaced); *Freedom of Information 1992* (WA). The Northern Territory did not join the ranks until 2002: *Information Act 2002* (NT).
23 In 2008, Snell spoke of the first generation FoI laws, and advocated a new generation: R Snell, 'Opening up the mindset is key to change', *The Public Sector Informant* November 2008, 10–11.
24 Commonwealth Attorney-General, *Freedom of Information Act 1982: Annual Report for the period December 1982 – June 1983* (1983) xi.
25 Queensland FoI Independent Review Panel, *The Right to Information: Reviewing Queensland's Freedom of Information Act* (2008) 299–300. Journalists using the system complained of an enduring culture of secrecy: Australia's Right to Know Coalition, *Report of the Independent Audit into the State of Free Speech in Australia* (2007) 89.

citizens seeking access to, or amendment of,[26] their own personal information, but applicants seeking access to sensitive policy-related documents found the system far less effective.[27]

Sir Anthony Mason described freedom of information as a 'substantial disappointment'[28] when discussing the reforms that established the modern system of Australian administrative law in the 1970s following the Kerr Committee's recommendations.[29] Although not a recommendation of the Kerr Committee, freedom of information is often grouped alongside the establishment of the Administrative Appeals Tribunal and the Commonwealth Ombudsman, and the classification of the grounds of judicial review in the *Administrative Decisions (Judicial Review) Act 1977* (Cth), as part of the major reforms that transformed Australian administrative law in the last quarter of the 20th century.

Concerns about the implementation of the freedom of information regimes began very early. Only five years after commencement of the Commonwealth Act, the Senate Standing Committee on Legal and Constitutional Affairs reported complaints about the 'attitude' of government agencies towards disclosure.[30] In 1996 the ALRC and the Administrative Review Council (ARC) recommended reform of the Commonwealth Act to ensure a pro-disclosure approach to interpretation of the provisions.[31]

The operation of State schemes has also been criticised. In 2000, for example, the South Australian Parliament Standing Legislative Review Committee concluded that the South Australian Act was 'problematical at best and a failure at worst'.[32] More recently, the Victorian Ombudsman[33] and Western Australian Information Commissioner[34] have reviewed the legislation in those jurisdictions.

---

26 *Freedom of Information Act 1982* (Cth), Part V: procedures for amendment and annotation of personal records.
27 See M Paterson, *Freedom of Information and Privacy in Australia* (LexisNexis, 2005) 499.
28 A Mason, 'The 30th anniversary: A Judicial Perspective' (2007) 58 *Admin Review* 13, 14.
29 Commonwealth Administrative Review Committee, *Report*, Parl Paper No 144/1971 ('the Kerr Committee Report). See also R Creyke and J McMillan (eds), *The Kerr Vision of Australian Administrative Law* (Australian National University Centre for International and Public Law, 1998).
30 Senate Standing Committee on Legal and Constitutional Affairs, *Freedom of Information Act 1982: Report on the Operation and Administration of the Freedom of Information Legislation* (1987) 12.
31 ALRC and ARC, *Open Government: A Review of the Federal Freedom of Information Act 1982 ARC* (ALRC Report 77, 1995 and ARC Report 40, 1995) 11.
32 South Australian Parliament, *Report of the Legislative Review Committee concerning the Freedom of Information Act 1991* (2000); Discussed in R Snell, 'Freedom of Information: The Experience of the Australian States – an Epiphany?' (2001) 29 *Federal Law Review* 343, 353–4.
33 Ombudsman Victoria, *Review of The Freedom of Information Act* (2006).
34 Western Australia. Information Commissioner, *The Administration of Freedom of Information in Western Australia* (2010).

These official reviews have been accompanied by criticisms from the media and other users.[35]

There is now a significant disparity between those jurisdictions that have introduced reforms and those that have not. There have been some limited reforms over the years in the jurisdictions that retain their first generation statutes. For instance, in 2004, South Australia removed ministerial certificates that enabled Ministers to establish 'conclusively' that documents were exempt from disclosure and that limited the scope of external review of that decision.[36] Victoria has recently introduced an Information Commissioner.[37] Despite these variations, South Australia, Western Australia, Victoria and the Australian Capital Territory all essentially retain their original freedom of information statutes. The Northern Territory did not pass its first freedom of information legislation until 2002 and so, it might be said, is on a generational cusp.[38]

Second generation: A reform miscellany

After a series of reviews and reports,[39] there are now new or radically amended statutes in Queensland,[40] New South Wales,[41] Tasmania[42] and the Commonwealth[43].

---

35 Australia's Right to Know Coalition, *Report of the Independent Audit into the State of Free Speech in Australia* (2007) 89. Journalists are a major user group interested in accessing politically sensitive information, and the media play an important role in the process. See M Paterson, 'The Media and Access to Government-Held Information in a Democracy' (2008) 8 *Oxford University Commonwealth Law Journal* 3.
36 Along with some other changes, including limiting the exemption for Cabinet documents to those documents specifically prepared for Cabinet: *Freedom of Information (Miscellaneous) Amendment Act 2004* (SA). On the Commonwealth experience, see *McKinnon v Secretary, Department of Treasury* (2006) 228 CLR 423. Conclusive certificates have not been included in the new statutes in Queensland, New South Wales and Tasmania, and have been removed at the Commonwealth level: *Freedom of Information (Removal of Conclusive Certificates and Other Measures) Act 2009* (Cth).
37 *Freedom of Information Amendment (Freedom of Information Commissioner) Act 2012* (Vic).
38 *Information Act 2002* (NT).
39 ALRC/ARC Report, above n 31. See Commonwealth Ombudsman, *Scrutinising Government – Administration of the Freedom of Information Act 1982 in Australian Government Agencies*, Report No 2 (2006); Queensland FoI Independent Review Panel, *The Right to Information: Reviewing Queensland's Freedom of Information Act* (2008) 299–300; New South Wales Ombudsman, *Opening Up Government: Review of the Freedom of Information Act 1989* (2009) 36; Tasmanian Department of Justice, *Strengthening Trust in Government – Everyone's Right to Know: Review of the Freedom of Information Act 1991* (Directions Paper, 2009).
40 *Right to Information Act 2009* (Qld).
41 *Government Information (Public Access) Act 2009* (NSW).
42 *Right to Information Act 2009* (Tas).
43 A major revision of the old statute: *Freedom of Information Act 1982* (Cth).

The reforms that have introduced the second generation statutes have been focused upon culture change.[44] This acknowledges that no matter how creative the legislative reform, it is the practical application, and the attitude of agency staff to transparency, that will ultimately determine outcomes. New objects clauses now emphasise the pro-disclosure intentions of the legislation, with references to: democracy, accountability, public participation, better informed decision-making, and proactive publication.[45] Many of these have been the rationales for open government since freedom of information was introduced in Australia,[46] but the stated objects have taken on a more modern hue. For instance, the new objects section in the Commonwealth statute recognises government information as a national resource that is to be managed for public purposes. The nomenclature has evolved from 'official secrets' to 'public sector information' (PSI).[47] The intention is that an institutional culture of openness will evolve in the same way.[48]

The second generation freedom of information jurisdictions have adopted quite different approaches to achieve this common objective of culture change. A major reform at the Commonwealth level has been the appointment of the Information Commissioner and Freedom of Information Commissioner, with roles in merits review of agency decisions, as well as guidance on compliance and procedures. New South Wales has also established an Information Commissioner, and Queensland has retained the position originally established under the old legislation,[49] but now with enhanced functions.[50] Standing out from this group is Tasmania, where the Ombudsman has retained a review role for freedom of information.[51]

An innovation that particularly characterises the reformed jurisdictions is proactive disclosure. From its beginning, freedom of information has imposed upon agencies an obligation to publish information concerning their functions and powers, the kinds of documents they hold, and the manuals, rules and

---

44 J McMillan, 'Freedom of Information Reforms and Cultural Change' (Paper presented at UNESCO Conference to mark World Press Freedom Day, Brisbane, 2 May 2010).
45 *Freedom of Information Act 1982* (Cth), s 3; *Government Information (Public Access) Act 2009* (NSW), s 3; *Right to Information Act 2009* (Tas), s 3.
46 See the purposes and benefits of FoI legislation listed by the Commonwealth Attorney-General in 1983: Commonwealth Attorney-General, *Freedom of Information Act 1982: Annual Report for the period December 1982 – June 1983* (1983) xi.
47 Government 2.0 Taskforce, *Engage: Getting on with Government 2.0* (2009); Office of the Australian Information Commissioner, *Principles on open public sector information; Principles on review and development of principles* (2011).
48 The Queensland, New South Wales and Tasmanian legislatures have also abandoned the term 'freedom of information' and now use 'right to information' or 'public access'. I will continue to use 'freedom of information' throughout this discussion.
49 Western Australia and the Northern Territory also have information commissioners.
50 All these statutory bodies also have privacy commissioner positions. See Chapter 17.
51 South Australia is the other jurisdiction where the Ombudsman, rather than an information commissioner, conducts merits review of freedom of information decisions.

guidelines they use in making decisions. The consequence of failure to publish this information is that members of the public are not to be subjected to any prejudice that they could have avoided had the information been published.[52] Despite some publication, the first generation laws focused primarily upon applications for access. This has been described as the 'pull' model, where access is granted in response to specific requests.[53] The new approach to information publication[54] promotes proactive disclosure, and requires agencies to anticipate the information needs of the public by publishing routinely requested material.[55] Disclosure logs add a new dimension.[56] When agencies make documents available in response to a freedom of information application, they then publish the documents, or an account of them, on a website.

Different approaches to exemptions

A significant example of the miscellany of approaches with the new statutes is the way the exemption criteria are dealt with, and the various approaches to the public interest test. All freedom of information regimes balance competing public interests. They weigh the desirability of open and accountable government against the need to sometimes maintain secrecy in order to protect public interests in national security, law enforcement, the administration of justice, personal privacy, commercial confidentiality and so forth. Some agencies are entirely excluded from freedom of information.[57] For the agencies[58] that are covered, not all documents in their possession can be accessed. The right granted to all persons (there is no standing test) is the right to obtain documents of agencies or Ministers, other than exempt documents.[59]

The traditional approach has been to incorporate extensive lists of exemptions in the statutes. Tasmania and the Commonwealth have retained categories of

---

52 *Freedom of Information Act 1982* (Cth), s 10.
53 Paterson, above n 27, 12.11.
54 *Freedom of Information Act 1982* (Cth), s 8(2)(g); *Government Information (Public Access) Act 2009* (NSW), Part 3.
55 A 'push' model: Paterson, above n 27, 12.11.
56 *Freedom of Information Act 1982* (Cth), s 11C; *Government Information (Public Access) Act 2009* (NSW), ss 25–26; *Right to Information Act 2009* (Qld), ss 78–78B.
57 For instance at the Commonwealth level agencies such as the Auditor-General, Australian Government Solicitor, and Australian Security Intelligence Organisation (ASIO): *Freedom of Information Act 1982* (Cth), sch 1 part I. Also with respect to particular commercial activities, sch 2 part II.
58 Agencies are variously defined in the statutes. Commonwealth agencies include departments or prescribed authorities, which are bodies established for a public purpose: *Freedom of Information Act 1982* (Cth), s 4. Official documents in the possession of Ministers are also covered.
59 *Freedom of Information Act 1982* (Cth), s 11 and Part IV.

exemptions, albeit reformed, but Queensland and New South Wales have adopted new approaches, weighing competing public interests. In all jurisdictions there has been a concerted attempt to change the language and culture of freedom of information.

Queensland agencies and Ministers must decide to give access to requested information unless giving access would, on balance, be contrary to the public interest.[60] The decision-making process for determining whether disclosure is contrary to the public interest is set out in a series of steps,[61] with guidance provided in Schedule 4 on factors favouring disclosure, factors favouring nondisclosure, and irrelevant factors. That there are factors that may cause a public interest harm does not, of itself, mean that the balance will weigh against disclosure.[62] Decisions must be approached with a pro-disclosure bias.[63]

The Queensland legislature has made it clear that grounds for refusing access are to be interpreted narrowly.[64] There is, however, a range of exempt information that the Queensland Parliament has determined it would be contrary to the public interest to disclose.[65] Some old favourites are to be found in the list, such as information concerning Cabinet or the Executive Council, and national or State security information. It is, therefore, possible to mount the same kinds of arguments that have been run for decades in relation to certain sensitive areas such as Cabinet material. There are also unusual specific exemptions, such as budgetary information for local governments.

In New South Wales the public interest test is also central to the Act. There is a general public interest and presumption in favour of disclosure.[66] The statute does not refer to exemptions,[67] and the right to access is expressed in terms of there being a right to access unless there is an overriding public interest against disclosure.[68] Agencies are required to identify public interest considerations both in favour of and against disclosure, weigh them up and determine where the balance lies.[69] There is an exhaustive list of factors against disclosure in the statute, along with a list of irrelevant factors that must not be considered.[70] The Act provides

---

60 *Right to Information Act 2009* (Qld), ss 23, 48(1), 49(1).
61 *Right to Information Act 2009* (Qld), s 49.
62 *Right to Information Act 2009* (Qld), s 49(4).
63 *Right to Information Act 2009* (Qld), s 44(4).
64 *Right to Information Act 2009* (Qld), s 47(2)(a).
65 *Right to Information Act 2009* (Qld), ss 47–8, Sch 3.
66 *Government Information (Public Access) Act 2009* (NSW), ss 5, 12.
67 Except in relation to exemptions under interstate freedom of information.
68 *Government Information (Public Access) Act 2009* (NSW), s 9(1).
69 *Flack v Commissioner of Police, New South Wales Police* [2011] NSWADT 286, [19].
70 *Government Information (Public Access) Act 2009* (NSW), ss 14(2), 15.

some examples of public interest considerations in favour of disclosure that do not limit decision-makers in any way.[71] Other matters in favour may be considered along with guidelines from the Information Commissioner.

However, in New South Wales there are some matters that have been taken out of this balancing process. There are conclusive presumptions of an overriding public interest against disclosure of some material.[72] Again, there are some old favourites, including: overriding secrecy laws, Cabinet and Executive Council information, legal professional privilege, contempt, law enforcement, and some specific matters such as information relating to adoption and Aboriginal heritage.

The Commonwealth Act has retained categories of exemption that are familiar from the old legislation, but they have been divided into two kinds: outright exemptions that have no public interest test attached, and conditional exemptions that are subject to a public interest test.[73] For the outright exemptions, the legislature has determined in advance that it is against the public interest to disclose this information.[74] These exemptions include Cabinet documents, and documents affecting national security and law enforcement.[75]

The starting point for the Commonwealth statute is that conditionally exempt documents will be made available, subject to a public interest test. There is a strong public interest in disclosure. The Act provides:

> The agency or Minister must give the person access to the document if it is conditionally exempt at a particular time unless (in the circumstances) access to the document at that time would, on balance, be contrary to the public interest.[76]

Attempts have been made in the Commonwealth statute to increase the exemptions that are conditional and so subject to a public interest test. For instance, personal privacy, business affairs and research exemptions are now conditional upon a public interest test.

The preference for disclosure is reinforced by the fact that there are factors listed in the Commonwealth Act favouring disclosure, such as promoting the objects of the legislation and informing public debate, and irrelevant matters that must not be taken into account, for instance that disclosure might cause the

---

71 *Government Information (Public Access) Act 2009* (NSW), s 12.
72 *Government Information (Public Access) Act 2009* (NSW), s 14(1), Sch 1.
73 See, respectively, *Freedom of Information Act 1982* (Cth), s 11A(4), Pt IV Div 2 and s 11A(5), Pt IV Div 3.
74 ALRC, above n 13, 550.
75 *Freedom of Information Act 1982* (Cth), Pt IV, Div 2.
76 *Freedom of Information Act 1982* (Cth), s 11A(5).

government embarrassment. However, no factors are listed that favour withholding the information and agencies are given no assistance from the legislature on how to identify factors against disclosure.[77]

Like the Commonwealth, the Tasmanian Act has retained categories of exemption – those that are not subject to the public interest test,[78] and those that are.[79] The Tasmanian legislation also includes lists of matters that are relevant,[80] and irrelevant,[81] to assessment of the public interest.

Some old tensions

Many aspects of the reforms discussed above have widespread support – the presumptions favouring disclosure, oversight and guidance offered by information commissioners, and proactive release of information, are all working towards generally accepted objectives of open government. In the jurisdictions that have not undertaken reform these developments are watched with great interest, and calls are being made for similar reforms.[82] However, many tensions still exist concerning how the reformed regimes operate. This is more than resistance from recalcitrant bureaucrats or the enthusiasm of opposition politicians that evaporates in office. There are fundamental questions that freedom of information regimes old and new have struggled to answer; I have selected four of these questions to discuss for the remainder of this chapter.

Who bears the costs?

The costs of administering freedom of information processes, and who should bear those costs, are issues that continue to cause ongoing tension in all jurisdictions. Government agencies do not absorb the full cost of freedom of information. The level of application fees and processing charges, and the basis upon which they are calculated, vary between jurisdictions. For instance, search and retrieval time may be charged, and additional charges may be applied for the time taken to make decisions. Copying and postage charges are also applied.

---

77 But see Australian Information Commissioner, *Guidelines*; *Part 6 Conditional Exemptions*, Step 4: Identify the factors against disclosure.
78 *Right to Information Act 2009* (Tas), Pt 3 Div 1.
79 *Right to Information Act 2009* (Tas), Pt 3 Div 2.
80 *Right to Information Act 2009* (Tas), Sch 1.
81 *Right to Information Act 2009* (Tas), Sch 2.
82 See, eg, South Australia: D Jean, 'Forcing open government', *The Advertiser* (Adelaide), 6 March 2012, 19.

These processing charges can add up to significant amounts. Invariably, they are not calculated on a full cost recovery basis, but even the amounts that are charged can have a significant deterrent effect upon applicants. Fees and charges are sometimes imposed at lower rates when individuals are seeking their own personal information.[83] In some jurisdictions applicants can seek reductions in charges on the grounds of financial hardship to the applicant, or because access to the document in question is in the public interest.[84] Substantial charges are invariably interpreted by applicants as a ruse to avoid disclosure, but the costs to agencies can also be significant. The use of large and complex freedom of information applications by law firms, as a form of discovery, has been identified as a particular problem for agencies.[85]

Charges are not just about partial cost recovery. They can also encourage agencies and applicants to work collaboratively. Charges can focus applicants' minds on what information is really required. At the Commonwealth level, no charge is payable if an agency does not make a decision on a request within the time limits.[86] This encourages timely responses by agencies, or at least penalises tardy ones.

Poor information management can lead to significant costs for government agencies, and also for individuals seeking access to documents. In their 1995 review of freedom of information, the Australian Law Reform Commission and the Administrative Review Council recommended that FoI charges be based upon the number of documents released, rather than on the processing time, to avoid penalising applicants for inefficient information management practices and reluctance to disclose on the part of government agencies.[87]

The ability to challenge costs and seek their reduction in the public interest, with independent external review, is an important system for defusing many of these tensions. Proactive disclosure of commonly requested information[88] is also a significant development, and avoids individual applicants paying the costs of retrieval. However, disclosure logs pose a particular problem in relation to charges. Individual applicants may resent paying for access when the results of their applications are going to be published to the world at large.[89] It may be appropriate

---

83 See, eg, Freedom of Information (Charges) Regulations 1982 (Cth), reg 5.
84 *Freedom of Information Act 1982* (Cth), s 29 (5).
85 Australian Information Commissioner, *Review of Charges under the Freedom of Information Act 1982; Report to the Attorney-General* (2012) 39.
86 Freedom of Information (Charges) Regulations 1982 (Cth), reg 5.
87 ALRC/ARC Report, above n 31, [14.14]–[14.15]. See also Australian Information Commissioner, above n 85, 36.
88 *Freedom of Information Act 1982* (Cth), s 8(2)(g).
89 The Australian Information Commissioner has considered the reduction of fees in the public interest in relation to disclosure logs, and recommended that a greater public benefit should be required than mere publication: Australian Information Commissioner, above n 85, 72.

for commercial entities to pay the full costs of access when the information sought has a particular value in private enterprise. However, when disclosure is sought for information which informs the public at large, and facilitates government accountability, the costs to individual applicants should be minimal.

Who has the final word on the public interest?

References to the public interest in freedom of information require a decision-maker to make a discretionary value judgement, as it inevitably does when this phrase is used.[90] A major tension over the years has concerned who gets the final word on whether disclosure is, or is not, in the public interest. For exemptions that do not include a public interest test, or when there are conclusive presumptions against disclosure,[91] Parliament has already had the final word.

Third parties who have a special interest in official documents, either because they are the subject of the information or have supplied the documents to government, have a particular interest in influencing the outcome of access applications. They are entitled to be consulted before disclosure, but they do not make decisions about release or have a veto of any kind, although they can have appeal rights.[92]

Decisions are made initially within agencies by Ministers, principal officers of agencies or their delegates.[93] As administrative decisions, errors of law are, of course, subject to judicial review,[94] but the battle over the last word has inevitably been over the scope and availability of external merits review.

Conclusive certificates were once a part of the freedom of information landscape across Australia, but they are slowly being abolished.[95] These certificates were generally signed by Ministers or heads of departments and established, without the need for further proof, that a document contained exempt material or that

---

90 Exercise of the discretion is confined by the subject matter, scope and purpose of the legislation: *Osland v Secretary, Department of Justice* (2008) 234 CLR 275, 323; *Osland v Secretary, Department of Justice (No 2)* (2010) 241 CLR 320, 329.
91 *Government Information (Public Access) Act 2009* (NSW), s 14(1), Sch 1.
92 *Freedom of Information Act 1982* (Cth), s 54M(3).
93 See for instance: *Right to Information Act 2009* (Qld), ss 30–1; *Freedom of Information Act 1982* (Cth), s 23. If made by delegates there are internal review procedures: *Freedom of Information Act 1982* (Cth), part IV.
94 *Shergold v Tanner* (2002) 209 CLR 126.
95 Conclusive certificates are no longer included in the reformed jurisdictions and were also removed in South Australia: *Freedom of Information (Miscellaneous) Amendment Act 2004* (SA).

disclosure was contrary to the public interest. The certificates could oust or severely restrict the scope of merits review. Once a certificate was issued, review could be limited to determining whether or not there were reasonable grounds for the claims made in the certificate.[96] The decline of these certificates does not preclude other ways to show deference to the initial assessment of the public interest by agencies and Ministers.

There is a good deal of variation in how external merits review is dealt with across the various jurisdictions. There is a trend towards information commissioners, but a different approach can be found in the two jurisdictions that utilise Ombudsman's review of freedom of information decisions (Tasmania and South Australia). While Ombudsmen generally make recommendations, in these States the Ombudsmen have powers to substitute their own decision for those of the agency or Minister in freedom of information cases.[97]

It cannot be assumed that all freedom of information merits review bodies have the same roles and powers. For instance, while the Queensland and Commonwealth Information Commissioners have powers to substitute their own decisions for those of the agency or Minister,[98] in New South Wales, the Information Commissioner makes recommendations to the agency on review.[99]

Examples can also be found where Parliament requires external review bodies to defer to agencies and Ministers when assessing the public interest, at least initially. For instance, in South Australia when the Ombudsman or District Court is advised of an agency's or Minister's assessment of the public interest, they must uphold that assessment unless satisfied that there are cogent reasons for not doing so.[100]

In New South Wales there is some sensitivity in relation to Cabinet and Executive Council information when an agency determines there is an overriding public interest against disclosure. The Administrative Decisions Tribunal is initially limited to deciding whether there were reasonable grounds for the agency's claim, at least until the Premier has had a chance to be heard. If not satisfied that there were reasonable grounds after examining all the evidence, the Tribunal can substitute its own decision on the matter.[101]

---

96 See *McKinnon v Secretary, Department of Treasury* (2006) 228 CLR 423 on the certificates that once operated at the Commonwealth level.
97 *Freedom of Information Act 1991* (SA), s 39(11); *Right to Information Act 2009* (Tas), s 47(1)(k).
98 *Right to Information Act 2009* (Qld), s 105; *Freedom of Information Act 1982* (Cth), s 55K.
99 *Government Information (Public Access) Act 2009* (NSW), s 92. The NSW Administrative Decisions Tribunal has review jurisdiction: s 100.
100 *Freedom of Information Act 1991* (SA), ss 39(9), 40(7).
101 *Government Information (Public Access) Act 2009* (NSW), s 106. There are also restrictions on the Information Commissioner's ability to access Cabinet information: *Government Information (Information Commissioner) Act 2009* (NSW), s 30.

The heavy-handed conclusive certificates are slowly being removed, but merits review bodies are still required to exercise caution in relation to some sensitive information. That parliaments still favour caution is apparent from the way sensitive areas, including Cabinet documents and high level policy deliberations, are dealt with – there are ongoing tensions over the scope and operation of these exemptions.

Should absolute protection of classes be limited?

Exemptions from disclosure in freedom of information can be characterised in various ways. It is common to distinguish, as the Commonwealth Act now does, between absolute exemptions and qualified or conditional exemptions, the latter being subject to a public interest test.[102] Distinctions can also be drawn between class based exemptions and harm or prejudice based exemptions.[103] For exemptions expressed in terms of the harm or prejudice that disclosure may cause, it is not enough to treat documents as being of a particular kind – it is necessary to look at the content of the documents and the context surrounding disclosure. So, for instance, documents may not be exempt simply because they relate to law enforcement or national security matters, but only if disclosure could reasonably be expected to prejudice a criminal investigation, or cause damage to the security of the Commonwealth. Harm based exemptions are generally expressed in terms of a reasonable expectation of the adverse effect.[104] These exemptions may also be subject to a public interest test, weighing the harm of disclosure against other public interests favouring disclosure. Even when there is no public interest test, if an exemption is expressed in terms of the harm caused, the content of the document and the impact of disclosure must be assessed.

Class based exemptions have the potential to be very wide-ranging, and have been particularly problematic in freedom of information.[105] Once a document has been categorised as falling within a class, there is no requirement to consider whether any harm will be caused by disclosure, and so no need to consider the content of specific documents. If an exemption is expressed in terms of a class of documents, but is then subject to a public interest test, then the content of the documents must at least be considered to determine whether disclosure would be contrary to the public interest. The circumstances surrounding access to the

---

102 See P Coppel, *Information Rights: Law and Practice* (Hart Publishing, 3rd ed, 2010) 450–54.
103 Coppel, Ibid, 457–9.
104 *Attorney-General's Department v Cockcroft* (1986) 10 FCR 180, 190; *McKinnon v Secretary, Department of Treasury* (2006) 228 CLR 423, 445–6; *Apache Northwest Pty Ltd v Department of Mines and Petroleum* [2012] WASCA 167, [60].
105 ALRC, above n 13, 549.

document must be considered. A public interest test can help to ameliorate the rigidity of the class.

If, however, a broad class of material is given absolute protection, there is a real risk that far more material is kept secret than the public interest would require. The quintessential example of an absolute class claim is Cabinet documents.[106] Over the years, the extensive protection granted to Cabinet documents has been particularly controversial, and critics have revelled in the idea of trolley loads of documents being wheeled around Cabinet rooms in order to claim confidentiality.[107] Restrictions have been introduced in some jurisdictions to limit, to some extent, the scope of the exemption to the core of the Cabinet process, by restricting it to documents created for the dominant purpose of submission to Cabinet.[108] However, the absolute protection granted is still very strong.

The convention of collective responsibility in Cabinet explains the extent of the protection granted.[109] Cabinet confidentiality ensures that Ministers can be candid during discussions, and this strengthens the collective decision-making process. However, Cabinet confidentiality is no longer sacrosanct; the courts now refuse to accept bold assertions from government that access to Cabinet documents must always be refused. Any disclosure of evidence to the courts in public interest immunity cases must be decided on the basis of detriment to the public interest.[110] That issue is determined by the courts.[111] In the public interest immunity cases before the courts, the public interest being weighed against protection of high level policy development and decision-making processes is the proper administration of justice. The courts can diminish the risk to state affairs by restricting access to documents that are produced in court. Freedom of information disclosure is to the world at large, and the impact of disclosure cannot be controlled in the same way. Nevertheless, there is no reason in principle why the exemption of

---

106 *Freedom of Information Act 1982* (Cth), s 34. Executive Council documents are another example.
107 See, eg, the ABC comedy series *The Hollowmen*. The Senate, Finance and Public Administration References Committee, *Independent Arbitration of Public Interest Immunity Claims*, February 2010, 27. For reference to the practice of taking documents into the Cabinet room to obtain protection in Queensland, see Queensland FoI Independent Review Panel, *The Right to Information: Reviewing Queensland's Freedom of Information Act* (2008) 107.
108 *Freedom of Information Act 1982* (Cth), s 34; *Government Information (Public Access) Act 2009* (NSW), Sch 1 cl 2.
109 Documents recording the actual deliberations of Cabinet have a pre-eminent claim to confidentiality that will be paramount 'in all but quite exceptional situations': *Commonwealth v Northern Land Council* (1993) 176 CLR 604, 618.
110 *Sankey v Whitlam* (1978) 142 CLR 1, 41–2, Gibbs ACJ. Public interest immunity was once known as crown privilege: *Commonwealth v Northern Land Council* (1993) 176 CLR 604.
111 Ibid, 38, Gibbs ACJ.

Cabinet documents could not to be subject to a public interest test.[112] What is being protected is the efficient working of government. When the matter being considered is no longer current or controversial, the risks of injury become slight.[113]

Rather than consider the public interest on a case-by-case basis, some jurisdictions have limited the length of time for which the Cabinet documents exemption operates.[114] This makes documents available well before the 20 or 30 years that is otherwise the time taken for the records to become available in the archives.[115] However, release upon anniversaries, whether that is 10, 20, 30 or 50 years, takes no account of the subject matter of Cabinet discussions. There is certainty in knowing that documents are secret for a set period, but no reasoned assessment of the true impact of disclosure in a particular case. The underlying issue is the one raised above: who gets the final say? When absolute protection is granted to classes of documents, or when there are conclusive presumptions against disclosure, Parliament has the final word.

How should we deal with claims of future harm?

As well as collective decisions in Cabinet, high level policy advice to Ministers and deliberations within agencies are also sensitive. Tensions surrounding the preservation of the decision-making processes of government are not easily resolved, because it can be difficult to disentangle protected public interests from political and personal interests. As discussed above, most freedom of information exemptions involve consideration of the damage that public release of particular information might cause. This can be because the exemption is expressed in terms of likelihood of harm, or because the weighing of public interests includes quantifying the harm that public release may cause. When the potential harm from release flows from the specific content of the document, the issue concerns present harm. For example, could an ongoing police investigation be jeopardised? Could sensitive security information be disclosed? Might an individual be harmed by disclosure of personal information?

Some of the most difficult tensions in freedom of information decision-making arise when arguments are made about future harm – specifically, the argument that release of particular information now, which in itself will cause no specific

---

112 This argument was made in the submission by Assoc Prof Moira Paterson, Faculty of Law, Monash University, to the Hawke *Review of Freedom of Information* (2013).
113 *Sankey v Whitlam* (1978) 142 CLR 1, 97 (Mason J).
114 10 years for Cabinet documents: *Right to Information Act 2009* (Qld), sch 3 cl 2; *Government Information (Public Access) Act 2009* (NSW), sch 1 cl 2; *Right to Information Act 2009* (Tas), s 26.
115 See open access periods, for instance: *Archives Act 1983* (Cth), s 3(7); *State Records Act 1998* (NSW), s 50. However, see Cabinet notebooks: *Archives Act 1983* (Cth), s 22A.

harm, will prejudice the future supply of information or the future decision-making processes of government. This is not a question of timing of release. If the content of a specific document might cause harm now but be uncontentious shortly thereafter, this can be accommodated.[116] The statutes allow for deferred release if it is in the public interest to do so – for instance if a decision is about to be made or announced, or the material will soon be presented to parliament or published.[117] The public interest is also assessed in terms of access to a document at a particular time,[118] and can be reassessed in future applications.

Difficult tensions emerge over claims of future harm, because refusal to release uncontentious documents now is based on speculation that maintaining confidentiality will protect future flows of information or candid advice. If the public interest against disclosure is not determined with reference to the specific documents being sought, there is a real risk that what you end up with looks very much like a class based exemption,[119] and that needs to be closely examined.

Specific references to the harm of future supplies of information are scattered throughout the statutes in the wording of exemptions and matters relevant to the public interest. These include future supplies of commercial and confidential information to government from third parties,[120] and informants supplying information to police.[121] These factors concern the flow of information from external third-party sources. Parliament is sanctioning the suppression of documents that could inform the public and facilitate open government, not because of the information they disclose, but to reassure future informants about confidentiality and protect future information flows.

The obligations and motivations of future information sources that are being reassured by official secrecy must be examined. Is the supply of information to government purely voluntary?[122] If it is, and if the possible loss of confidentiality is likely to discourage disclosure, future sources will need protection. A clear example

---

116 If a document is exempt at one point in time, it may not be at another point in time: *Tunchon v Commissioner of Police, New South Wales Police Service* [2000] NSWADT 73.
117 See, eg, *Freedom of Information Act 1982* (Cth), s 21.
118 *Freedom of Information Act 1982* (Cth), s 11A (5).
119 Paterson, above n 27, 296. See discussion in *Crowe and Department of the Treasury* [2013] AICmr 69 [53].
120 *Right to Information Act 2009* (Qld), sch 4 (7) (8); *Freedom of Information Act 1982* (Cth), s 47G.
121 *Government Information (Public Access) Act 2009* (NSW), s 14(2). The list of public interest factors against disclosure in the Commonwealth OAIC Guidelines anticipate that there is a public interest in protection of future sources of information and that impeding future information flows may be a factor weighing against disclosure in a particular case: Office of the Australian Information Commissioner, *Freedom of Information guidelines* [6.29] (g), (h), (i).
122 Compelled disclosure of information to government, for instance sensitive personal information, should clearly be protected.

of this is police informants – confidentiality is extremely important to them; they have a choice whether or not to come forward; and their information may be of great significance. In such cases there will be a strong public interest in maintaining secrecy to protect future information supplies.

Police informants can be contrasted with third parties who supply information to government in exchange for some commercial benefit, and who understand in advance that dealing with government means dealing with an entity that is subject to public accountability mechanisms. Clearly some business information and trade secrets need to be protected from disclosure. However, arguments along the lines that a culture of openness might jeopardise future supplies of information from businesses should be closely questioned; if there are lucrative deals to be struck then people will continue to do business with open and accountable governments.[123]

The most contentious argument for secrecy based upon future harm does not concern third-party informants, but public service advice and the need to ensure 'frankness and candour'.[124] This asserts that disclosure now of existing documents about past deliberations will cause the following harm: 1) the quality of advice will be diminished in the future because public servants will hold back; and 2) records will not be kept properly and so be available in the future. Concern to protect frank and fearless advice was apparent from the very early days of freedom of information in Australia, and continues through to the present day,[125] although not without criticism.[126] The argument that disclosure is contrary to the public interest if it is likely to 'inhibit frankness and candour in future pre-decisional communications' was the third of the *Howard*[127] factors that have had such a major influence on public interest analysis in freedom of information, particularly in relation to high level policy and decision-making processes. The new approaches to the public interest test in the reformed jurisdictions have declared some of the *Howard* factors to be irrelevant. Risks of embarrassment to senior figures and condescending views on the ability of the public to understand complex information are no longer

---

123 This point has been discussed by the South Australian Ombudsman and District Court: *Daycorp Pty Ltd v Parnell* [2011] SADC 191 [97].
124 See R Snell 'The Ballad of Frank and Candour: Trying to Shake the Secrecy Blues From the Heart of Government' (1995) 57 *Freedom of Information Review* 34; Paterson, above n 27, [7.15].
125 The issue was specifically mentioned in the terms of reference for the Hawke review: N Roxon, Attorney-General, *Review of the Freedom of Information Act 1982 and the Australian Information Commissioner Act 2010 Terms of Reference*; <www.ag.gov.au/consultations/pages/reviewoffoilaws.aspx>.
126 Senate Standing Committee on Constitutional and Legal Affairs, *Freedom of Information Report* (1979) [2.72].
127 *Re Howard and Treasurer of the Commonwealth* (1985) 3 AAR 169, 178.

reasons for refusing access to information about government,[128] but protecting 'frankness and candour' has not been expressly excluded.

Even before the statutory reforms, external review bodies were reluctant to accept *Howard* factor arguments without specific evidence of harm.[129] The public service has a duty to provide frank, comprehensive advice along with a duty to maintain good record keeping systems.[130] These public service obligations to supply information and maintain records can be contrasted with third-party sources who do not have a duty to provide, or even an interest in providing, information to government. It is professionally compromising to public servants to suggest that they will ignore their statutory obligations in the future unless they are promised confidentiality in the present. There is no doubt that it is essential to the administration of government that frank and fearless advice is provided by public servants. The question is whether transparency undermines the availability of that advice, and so diminishes the decision-making process to the point where it is contrary to the public interest to disclose.

One answer to lingering concerns that freedom of information will undermine future deliberative processes of government is that the documents being sought by applicants today are in fact there. The agencies may still be reluctant to disclose on occasion, but they have continued to record their robust deliberative processes. At the Commonwealth level, all documents created after 1 December 1982 have been written by their authors in the knowledge that they are in a new era of open government, and yet the documents are there. It can be argued that records are not as candid as they might otherwise have been, but the pre-FoI archival records show that even in a time of confidential communications, not everything was committed to paper. Then, as now, details of discussions were sometimes missing from minutes,[131] and there are memos that refer to conversations, obviously recalled by the participants, that no one has documented. Waiting for documents to enter the 30-year (soon to be 20-year) open access period,[132] in the hope that they may be a little more comprehensive, is likely to leave everyone disappointed.

---

128 *Freedom of Information Act 1982* (Cth), s 11B(4); *Government Information (Public Access) Act 2009* (NSW), s 15; *Right to Information Act 2009* (Qld), Sch 4 Part 1; *Right to Information Act 2009* (Tas), Sch 2.
129 See, eg, *Re Eccleston and Department of Family Services, Aboriginal & Islander Affairs* [1993] 1 QAR 60. ALRC/ARC, above n 31, [9.16].
130 For a recent discussion see *Re Mullett and Attorney-General's Department* [2012] AATA 103.
131 Terrill, above n 17, 103–4.
132 See open access periods, for instance: *Archives Act 1983* (Cth), s 3(7); *State Records Act 1998* (NSW), s 50.

Conclusion

Freedom of information in Australia is in transition. There have always been high ideals and grand objectives, but the day-to-day implementation has been difficult. There have been important recent attempts at reform in some jurisdictions, but their success will depend upon how some old tensions are managed. These are tensions that have remained unresolved since freedom of information was first introduced, and include: fundamental differences about the scope and objects of information access; who decides what is in the public interest; and how open government is paid for. It is essential that these tensions are identified and acknowledged if the reforms are to achieve their stated objectives.

PRIVACY

Moira Paterson

Introduction

Just as governments are obliged to allow access to information on request, they are also required to maintain the privacy of the personal information that they hold. Privacy is the neglected aspect of information management because it is not well understood. This is in part because privacy as a concept is difficult to understand and partly because the regulatory framework which regulates it is complex.

This chapter is concerned with the privacy of information that is handled by government agencies. Information privacy – or data protection, as it is more commonly described in Europe – is frequently confused with related concepts such as secrecy and confidentiality. However, it differs from them in important respects. Privacy may require secrecy as an aspect of information security, but it is much broader and more flexible in its scope. It may also overlap with confidentiality where personal information is received in a context which imposes an obligation to treat it as confidential, but it extends much more broadly. Its key focus is on the ability of individuals to exercise control over the handling of their identifiable personal information. It therefore has a critical role to play in establishing appropriate boundaries between citizen and government.

Privacy is accepted internationally as a human right. Article 17 of the International Covenant on Civil and Political Rights proscribes 'arbitrary or unlawful interference with an individual's privacy, family, home or correspondence' and has been interpreted as requiring, among other things, 'the implementation of basic data protections'.[1] However, the protection of personal information creates practical difficulties in the light of increasing imperatives to accumulate and share personal information. These difficulties have become more acute as a result of increasing imperatives for a more 'joined-up' mode of government service delivery.[2]

This chapter is concerned primarily with the *Privacy Act 1988* (Cth) ('Privacy Act') and the way in which it regulates Commonwealth public sector agencies.[3] It also provides a brief overview of State and Territory information privacy laws. Other laws which protect privacy include: laws which regulate telecommunications interceptions and certain uses of surveillance devices;[4] laws which restrict data

---

1 Human Rights Commission, *General Comment 16*, issued 23 March 1998 [7]–[10].
2 This concept is discussed in detail in V Bogdanor (ed), *Joined-Up Government* (Oxford University Press, 2005).
3 *Privacy and Personal Information Protection Act 1998* (NSW); *Information Act 2002* (NT); *Information Privacy Act 2009* (Qld); *Personal Information Protection Act 2004* (Tas); *Information Privacy Act 2000* (Vic). Government agencies in the ACT are bound by the *Privacy Act 1988* (Cth).
4 See *Telecommunications (Interception and Access) Act 1979* (Cth); *Listening Devices Act 1992* (ACT); *Surveillance Devices Act 2007* (NSW); *Surveillance Devices Act 2000* (NT); *Invasion of*

matching by Commonwealth government agencies; and spent convictions laws, which impose restrictions on the handling of criminal records information.[5]

Privacy also receives some indirect protection via the common law – in particular via the action for breach of confidence, which protects personal information that is imparted in circumstances that impose duties of confidentiality.[6] Australia still lacks any specific protection for privacy along the lines of that offered via a privacy tort in New Zealand[7] or the extended action for breach of confidence in the United Kingdom.[8] However, the High Court has cleared the way for such a development,[9] and the traditional action for breach of confidence has recently been expanded to allow for mental distress damages.[10]

The Commonwealth Privacy Act

Background

The Privacy Act was enacted in 1988, primarily to alleviate public concerns that had arisen in the context of a failed attempt to introduce a compulsory national identification card (the 'Australia Card')[11] and the subsequent introduction of tax file numbers for use as unique identifiers.[12] It originally applied only to the handling of personal information by Commonwealth government agencies and to the collection, use and disclosure of tax file numbers ('TFNs') by TFN recipients.

Commonwealth agencies were regulated via a set of Information Privacy Principles ('IPPs'), which were broadly derived from a set of principles developed

---

Privacy Act 1971 (Qld); *Listening Devices Act 1991* (Tas); *Surveillance Devices Act 1988* (Vic); *Surveillance Devices Act 1998* (WA).

5 *Crimes Act 1914* (Cth), Part VIIC.
6 The ingredients of this action are summarised in *Commonwealth of Australia v John Fairfax & Sons* (1980) 147 CLR 39, [51] (Mason J).
7 *Hosking v Runting* [2003] 3 NZLR 385.
8 *Campbell v MGN* [2004] 2 AC 457.
9 *Australian Broadcasting Corp v Lenah Game Meats Pty Ltd* (2001) 208 CLR 199. For a further discussion see D Lindsay, 'Playing Possum? Privacy, Freedom of Speech and the Media Following *ABC v Lenah Game Meats Pty Ltd*; Part II: The Future of Australian Privacy and Free Speech Law, and Implications for the Media' (2002) 7 *Media and Arts Law Review* 161.
10 N Witzleb, '*Giller v Procopets*: Australia's privacy protection shows signs of improvement' (2009) 17 *Tort Law Review* 16.
11 This is discussed in G Greenleaf, 'The Australia Card: Towards a National Surveillance System' (1987) 25 *Law Society Journal (NSW)*, available at <ssrn.com/abstract=2195493>.
12 See M Jackson, 'Data Protection Regulation in Australia after 1988' (1997) 5 *International Journal of Law and Information Technology* 158.

by the OECD[13] in a bid to develop a commonly accepted international benchmark for protecting the privacy of identifiable personal information. The IPPs imposed limitations on the collection, use and disclosure of personal information, imposed requirements to maintain the quality and security of information collected, and gave individuals rights of access and amendment in relation to their own personal information.

The Privacy Act was extended in 1990 to regulate the handling of personal consumer credit records,[14] and in 1994 to cover Australian Capital Territory agencies.[15] It was further extended in 2000 to regulate information handling by some private sector organisations (including government contractors) via a separate set of National Privacy Principles ('NPPs').[16] The NPPs regulated information handling in a similar manner to the IPPs but also contained additional principles which: allowed individuals, where practicable, to enter into transactions on an anonymous basis; limited the use of unique identifiers assigned by public sector agencies; restricted the transborder flow of personal information; and imposed additional limitations on the uses of more sensitive categories of personal information.

In 2006 the Australian Law Reform Commission (ALRC) was given a reference to consider the extent to which the Privacy Act continued to provide an effective framework for the protection of privacy in Australia.[17] This inquiry resulted in a three-volume report, containing 295 recommendations for reform.[18] A key outcome of this reform process has been the enactment of the *Privacy Amendment (Enhancing Privacy Reform) Act 2012* (Cth), which commences in March 2014. This made a number of key changes to the Act, including: amalgamating the public/private sector principles into a single set of Australian Privacy Principles ('APPs'); changes to some definition sections; and changes to the powers of the Privacy Commissioner. These changes are discussed below.

Objectives and interpretation

The historical development of the Privacy Act makes it clear that its intention is to facilitate the handling and processing of information while ensuring appropriate protection for privacy. Its objects clause in s 2A refers to eight objectives, including: promoting the protection of the privacy of individuals; recognising that the

---

13 'OECD Guidelines on the Protection of Privacy and Transborder Flows of Personal Data' (1980).
14 *Privacy Amendment Act 1990* (Cth).
15 See *Australian Capital Territory Government Service (Consequential Provisions) Act 1994* (Cth).
16 *Privacy Amendment (Private Sector) Act 2000* (Cth).
17 See <www.alrc.gov.au/inquiries/privacy/terms-of-reference>.
18 ALRC, *For Your Information: Australian Privacy Law and Practice* (ALRC Report 108, 2008).

protection of the privacy of individuals is balanced with the interests of entities in carrying out their functions or activities; promoting responsible and transparent handling of personal information; and facilitating the free flow of information across national borders, while ensuring that the privacy of individuals is respected.

The requirements in the Act operate in relation to two categories of information – 'personal information' and 'sensitive information'. Both of these terms are defined in s 6(1) with reference to individuals who are living.

'Personal information' was originally defined as 'information or opinion (including information or an opinion forming part of a database), whether true or not, and whether recorded in a material form or not, about an individual whose identity is apparent or can reasonably be ascertained, from the information or opinion'. The latter part of that definition has now been changed so that it refers to 'information or an opinion about an identified individual, or an individual who is reasonably identifiable', and there is no longer any requirement that the individual should be identifiable *only from the information or opinion*. As explained by the ALRC in recommending this change, this reformulation means information will now qualify as 'personal information' if it relates to an individual who can be identified from information in the possession of an agency or organisation, or from that information and other information the agency or organisation may access without 'unreasonable cost or difficulty'.[19] In that respect the criterion of reasonableness requires consideration of 'the cost, difficulty, practicality and likelihood that the information will be linked in such a way as to identify him or her'.[20] Other key factors to note about this definition are that it does not require any assessment of whether information is 'private', that it includes opinions (as opposed to factual information), and that it applies even when that opinion or information is factually incorrect.

'Sensitive information' is a sub-set of 'personal information' which receives additional protection in relation to collection. It encompasses information about a person's health, racial or ethnic origin, political opinions, membership of political organisations, religious beliefs or affiliations, philosophical beliefs, membership of a professional or trade association or trade union, sexual preferences or practices, criminal record, biometric templates and biometric information that is to be used for the purpose of automated biometric verification or biometric identification.[21]

The expression 'health information' is also defined.[22] It includes information or an opinion about: an individual's health or disability at any time; and information about health service provision (including an individual's expressed wishes about

---

19 Ibid, [6.55].
20 Ibid, citing with approval the description used in a submission by Microsoft Asia Pacific.
21 The latter two categories were added in 2012.
22 See s 6(1).

future provision of health services) and donations of body parts and substances. In addition, all personal information collected in relation to provision of a 'health service' is deemed to be health information.

Health information is generally regulated in the same way as other categories of personal information (and subject to the additional protection available to sensitive information), although there are some provisions which differentiate it (for example, via specific exceptions to privacy principles). However, the operation of the Privacy Act in relation to health information is affected by a number of guidelines, including guidelines which deal with the use of information held by Commonwealth agencies in the conduct of medical research.[23]

The majority of the obligations under the Act apply in cases where an entity 'collects' or 'holds' personal or sensitive information. The Act provides that an entity collects personal information only if it 'collects the information for inclusion in a record or generally available publication'.[24] It also provides that an entity holds personal information if the entity 'has possession or control of a record that contains the personal information'. The expression 'record' means a document, or an electronic or other device.[25] To qualify as a record, information must be recorded in some form.[26]

Scope

The privacy obligations in the Act apply to APP entities, which are forbidden from doing an act, or engaging in a practice, that breaches an APP. A body qualifies as an 'APP entity' if it is a public sector 'agency' or a private sector 'organisation'.[27] The term 'agency' is broadly defined. It includes federal government Ministers, public service departments and courts, bodies and offices established for public purposes under federal legislation, and various other federal office-holders.[28] However, a number of agencies are excluded either totally or in relation to specific documents and activities. These exclusions are similar to those applicable to the *Freedom of Information Act 1982* (Cth), and several are defined with reference to the latter.[29]

---

23 See NHMRC, 'Guidelines Issued Under section 95 of the Privacy Act' (2000). These can be accessed at <http://www.nhmrc.gov.au/guidelines/publications/e26>.
24 See definition in s 6(1).
25 See the definition of 'record' in s 6(1). The word 'document' has the same meaning as in the *Acts Interpretation Act 1901* (Cth), s 2B.
26 Likewise, the term 'generally available publication' is defined with reference to 'a magazine, book, article, newspaper or other publication': see s 6(1).
27 See the definition of 'entity' in s 6(1). 'Agency' is also defined in s 6(1) and 'organisation' is defined in s 6C.
28 See definition in s 6(1).
29 These received detailed consideration by the Federal Court in *Rivera v Australian Broadcasting Corporation* (2005) 144 FCR 334 (in relation to a broadcast by the respondent)

The requirement to comply with individual APPs is made subject to some generalised exceptions which fall into two groups – 'permitted general situations' and 'permitted health situations'. The rationale for this approach is to remove and group together exceptions which would otherwise add to the complexity of individual APPs.

The APPs

The Privacy Act operates by reference to a set of APPs which regulate the handling of personal information by establishing what may be described as 'fair information handling practices'. These principles apply to both agencies and organisations, although some of them impose specific obligations that apply only to agencies or organisations. There are some circumstances in which an act or practice of an agency will be treated as an act or practice by an organisation. These are set out in s 7A and include where any agency falls within the list of bodies excluded from the operation of the Freedom of Information Act in respect of their commercial activities.[30]

The Privacy Act also contains provision for entities which wish to do so, to develop and apply for the registration of an APP code which sets out an alternative set of rules which provide for at least an equivalent level of privacy protection.

The APPs are largely adapted from the private sector NPPs, and therefore contain a number of matters that were not previously dealt with in the public sector IPPs. However, they are generally more complex than the NPPs and contain some novel features not previously found in either set of principles. They have been ordered so as to reflect the general way in which information is handled.

The generalised exceptions

The principles regulating the collection, use and disclosure of personal information in general are subject to a number of exceptions in respect of 'permitted general situations', set out in a tabular form.[31] (These are referred to in this chapter as exception 1, 2, 3 etc, based on their numbering within the table.) Some apply to entities generally, but some are confined to either agencies or organisations. These exceptions apply to collection, use and disclosure of personal information (referred to collectively in this chapter as 'information handling') and are based on a number of tests: some require merely that a body 'has reason' to believe

---

and in *Nicholson v Federal Privacy Commissioner* [2010] FMCA 716 (in relation to the status of the Adult Multicultural Education Service). See Chapter 16.
30 See Chapter 16.
31 See s 16A(1).

or suspect certain facts, others require some reasonable belief, and others again impose purely objective tests based on reasonableness.

The first two of these exceptions apply generally to entities and in relation to government-related identifiers as well as to personal information more generally. Exception 1 applies where it is 'unreasonable' to obtain an individual's consent and the entity 'reasonably believes' that the information handling is 'necessary' to lessen or prevent a serious threat to the life, health or safety any individual or to public health or safety more generally. Exception 2 applies where an entity 'has reason to suspect' unlawful activity or misconduct relating to its functions or activities and 'reasonably believes' that the information handling is 'necessary' to enable it to take appropriate action.

The next three exceptions also apply to entities generally, but they are confined, in their application, to personal information. Exception 3 applies where an entity 'reasonably believes' that the information handling is 'reasonably necessary' to assist any person or body to locate a person who has been reported as necessary and the information handling complies with specified rules.[32] Exceptions 4 and 5 apply respectively where the information handling is 'necessary' for the establishment, exercise or defence of a legal or equitable claim, or for the purposes of a confidential alternative dispute resolution process.

The final two exceptions are more limited in their application. Exception 6 is confined to agencies and applies where an agency 'believes' the information handling is 'necessary' for its diplomatic or consular functions or activities. Exception 7 is available only to the Defence Force and applies where it 'reasonably believes' that the information handling is necessary for specified defence-related matters, provided that they occur outside Australia and its external territories. The exceptions for permitted general situations are supplemented by a further set of exceptions for permitted health situations.[33] These are confined to organisations and apply to information handling involving health information.

The preliminary principles

The first two principles are contained in Part 1, which is titled 'Consideration of personal information privacy'. The rationale for making them precede the others is to reinforce that the development of information privacy policies and procedures should precede any collection or handling of personal information.

APP 1 requires entities to develop open and transparent policies to manage their handling of personal information consistently with their obligations under

---

32 See s 16(2).
33 See s 16B.

the Act. Privacy codes must contain specified information, including: the kinds of personal information collected and held; how that information is collected and held; the purposes for which it is collected, used and disclosed; information about procedures for seeking access to and amendment of personal information and making complaints about breaches of APPs; and information about mechanisms for and details about overseas transfers of information.

APP 2 follows with additional requirements to provide for anonymity and pseudonymity. These requirements are new to government agencies and require that individuals should, where practicable, be provided with the option of not identifying themselves, or of using a pseudonym, when dealing with an agency in relation to particular matters. This would be the case, for example, where an individual wishes to make a generalised query about entitlements. The requirement does not, however, apply when the entity is required or authorised by law, or by an order of a court or tribunal, to deal with individuals who have identified themselves. The latter would include where an individual is required to authenticate their identity in order to safeguard the privacy of their own personal information.

Collection of personal information

The next set of privacy principles deals with the collection of personal information. These principles deal with the collection of personal information and with the unsolicited receipt of personal information. The restrictions on collection apply only in relation to the collection of information for inclusion in a record or generally available publication.[34] It follows that modes of collection which do not result in permanent capture are not subject to regulation. It should also be noted that personal information is deemed to have been solicited if an entity requests another entity to provide it, or to provide a kind of information in which that personal information is included.[35]

APP 3 contains separate tests for sensitive information and other categories of personal information. In the case of the latter, it requires that an agency must not collect the information unless that collection is reasonably necessary for, or directly related to, one or more of the agency's functions or activities.[36] (The requirements

---

34 See the new definition of 'collects' in s 6(1) . The terms 'record' and 'or generally available publication' are also defined in s 6(1).
35 See the new definition of 'solicits' in s 6(1).
36 APP 3.1.

relating to organisations are more stringent: they may collect information only where it is reasonably necessary for one or more of their functions or activities.[37])

The collection of sensitive information is more restricted than was previously the case under the IPPs, although it is subject to a number of important exceptions. Unless one of the exceptions is applicable, an agency must not collect sensitive information about an individual unless that individual consents and the information is reasonably necessary for, or directly related to, one or more of the agency's functions or activities.[38] (The test for organisations is again slightly narrower and requires that information is reasonably necessary for one or more of the organisation's functions or activities.[39])

Collection of sensitive information by an agency is not subject to these restrictions if it is required or authorised by or under an Australian law or by an order of a court or tribunal, or if a 'permitted general situation' exists in relation to its collection. There are also further exceptions for enforcement bodies,[40] for organisations that collect health information,[41] and for non-profit organisations.[42]

APP 3 also contains two further requirements that apply in relation to personal information generally. An entity must collect information only by lawful and fair means,[43] and must collect it directly from the individual unless it is unreasonable or impracticable to do so. An agency may collect information otherwise than from the individual concerned only with the individual's consent, or if such collection is required or authorised by law or by an order of a court or tribunal.[44]

APP 4 deals with the situation where an entity receives personal information which it has not solicited, and creates new obligations for agencies. It requires an initial determination as to whether or not (solicited) collection of that information would have been permitted under APP 3. If such collection would not have been permitted and the information is not contained in a 'Commonwealth record',[45] the information must be destroyed or de-identified, as practicable, but only if it is lawful and reasonable to do so. Otherwise, its handling is subject to the requirements in APPs 5 to 13 in the same way as would have been the case had it been collected in compliance with APP 3.

The last of the collection principles, APP 5, contains requirements to notify the individuals to whom personal information relates (referred to in this chapter

---

37 APP 3.2.
38 APP 3.3(a)(i).
39 APP 3.3(a)(ii).
40 APP 3.4(d).
41 APP 3.4(c).
42 APP 3.4(e).
43 APP 3.5.
44 APP 3.6.
45 'Commonwealth record' has the same meaning as in the *Archives Act 1983* (Cth): see s 6(1). It means a record that is created or received in the course of APS employment.

as 'information subjects') about specified matters. It requires notification at or before the time when information is collected or, if that is not practicable, as soon as practicable afterwards. An entity must take such steps (if any) as are reasonable in the circumstances to notify the information subject of such of the specified matters as is reasonable in the circumstances. This qualified language envisages the possibility that notification may be impracticable in some situations, and that the nature of the steps taken and the content of communications with information subjects may vary according to the circumstances. For example, it may not be practicable to notify individuals whose images have been collected by CCTV, even if the information is sufficiently identifiable to qualify as personal information.

The range of matters specified as requiring notification is broader than was the case under IPP 2. It includes: the identity and contact details of the collector; the facts and circumstances of collection (where the information is collected indirectly and an individual may be unaware of the collection); the fact that the collection is required or authorised by law or by an order of a court or tribunal (where that is the case); the purposes for which the information has been collected; the main consequences for the information subject if some or all of the information is not collected; details of other persons or bodies to whom the collecting entity usually discloses information of that kind; that its privacy policy contains information about the exercise of access and amendment rights and complaints procedures; and whether it is likely to disclose the personal information to overseas recipients (and, if so, and if practicable to do so, the countries in which recipients are likely to be located). Compliance with notification requirements is an important means of ensuring that decisions by information subjects to disclose their personal information are made on an informed basis, that information subjects whose information is collected indirectly are aware of the fact of collection, and that information subjects generally are aware of their rights of access and amendment and of available complaints mechanisms.

Dealings with personal information

The next set of principles regulates dealings with personal information. It contains a general set of rules which regulate the use and disclosure of personal information collected, and separate rules regulating direct marketing by organisations and dealings with government-related identifiers.

APP 6 imposes limitations on the use and disclosure of personal information (other than uses and disclosures by organisations for direct marketing purposes or dealings by organisations with government-related identifiers).[46] It is premised on the fact that information has been collected for some particular purpose (referred to as the 'primary purpose'), and requires that it should not be used or disclosed for a different purpose (referred to as the 'secondary purpose'), except with the consent of the information subject.[47] The rationale for this limitation is one of fairness. The collection of personal information is constrained by requirements based, in part, on the purposes of collection, and there is a requirement that individuals should be made aware of these purposes either at the time of collection or at least later. It follows that the information should be handled accordingly and that consent should be obtained for dealings involving different purposes.

The limitations in APP 6 are subject to a number of important exceptions, including exceptions for related purposes which would reasonably be expected by the information subject. The scope of these related purpose exceptions varies according to whether or not the information is sensitive information. In the case of sensitive information, use or disclosure for the related purpose is permitted only if that purpose is directly related to the primary purpose of collection. In the case of personal information that is not sensitive information, the other purpose must simply be related to the primary purpose (and therefore includes purposes that are indirectly related).

There are also exceptions for uses or disclosures which are required or authorised by law or an order of a court or tribunal,[48] which fall within the permitted general situations or permitted health situations exceptions,[49] or which an entity 'reasonably believes' are ' reasonably necessary' for one or more enforcement-related activity conducted by, or on behalf of, an enforcement body.[50] There is also an exception which permits the disclosure of biometric information or biometric templates to an enforcement body in accordance with guidelines issued by the Office of the Australian Information Commissioner ('OAIC').[51]

APPs 7 and 9 contain separate rules which regulate the use and disclosure of personal information for direct marketing purposes, and the adoption, use and disclosure of government-related identifiers,[52] respectively. These are confined in their application to organisations, although APP 7 permits contracted service providers for Commonwealth contracts to use or disclose personal information for

---

46 APP 6.7.
47 APP 6.1. (See APP 6.6 in relation to the rules which apply where the information was collected by a related body corporate.)
48 APP 6.2(b).
49 APPs 6.2(c) and 6.2(d). The latter exception is relevant only to organisations and requires compliance with APP 6.4.
50 APP 6.2(e). If this exception is relied upon, the entity must make a written note of the use or disclosure: see APP 6.5.
51 APP 6.3.
52 The terms 'identifier' and 'government related identifier' are defined in s 6(1).

the purpose of direct marketing if certain conditions are met. It should also be noted that acts or practices of an agency may be treated as those of an organisation in certain circumstances, including where any agency is excluded from the operation of the Act in respect of its commercial activities.[53]

APP 8 deals with transborder data flows. It requires an entity to take such steps as are reasonable in the circumstances to ensure that an overseas recipient does not breach the APPs (other than APP 1) before disclosing any personal information to them.[54] That requirement does not, however, apply if the entity reasonably believes that the recipient is subject to a law or binding scheme that has the effect of protecting the information 'in a way that is substantially similar to the way in which the APPs protect it' or if the information subject is informed about the transfer and consents to it. There are also further exceptions for disclosures required or authorised by law, or by order of an Australian court or tribunal, where permitted general situations exist, for disclosures by agencies that are required or authorised under an international information sharing agreement and for certain law enforcement activities.

Integrity of personal information

The next two principles are designed to ensure the integrity of personal information collected. They contain requirements relating to information quality and information security. APP 10 deals with issues of quality, in relation to both collection of personal information and subsequent dealings with it. It requires entities to take such steps, if any, as are 'reasonable in the circumstances' to ensure the information they collect is 'accurate, up-to-date and complete'. It also contains a further requirement to take identical measures to ensure that the personal information it uses or discloses is accurate, up-to-date, complete and relevant, as assessed by the purpose of the use or disclosure. The privacy rationale for this requirement is to ensure that individuals are not unfairly affected by decisions based on poor-quality data.

The other principle in this category is APP 11, which requires entities to take such steps as are 'reasonable in the circumstances' to protect personal information from misuse, interference and loss and from unauthorised access, modification or disclosure. The rationale for this provision is a dual one: to ensure that information does not fall into the wrong hands and to ensure that individuals are not affected adversely by decisions based on data that is incomplete or incorrect. Agencies are no longer required to protect information disclosed to third parties providing

---

53 See s 7A.
54 APP 8.1.

services to the agency, as the latter are now subject to identical obligations under the APPs. (Obligations concerning transfer to bodies located outside Australia are regulated by APP 9, as discussed above.)

Access and amendment rights

The next two principles relate to access and amendment rights. The ability of an information subject to seek access to his or her personal information is an important aspect of information privacy and is closely linked to the notification requirements. It allows an individual who is aware that his or her personal information has been collected to be fully informed of the nature and extent of the information held and to request its amendment if it does not comply with the quality requirement in APP7.

APP 12 requires an entity which holds personal information about an individual to provide him or her with access to that information on request.[55] However, it is intended that the Freedom of Information Act will continue to provide the primary avenue for the exercise of these access rights.[56] This means that whether or not an individual is able to access his or her records is determined having regard to the exemptions in the Freedom of Information Act, rather than the exceptions in APP 12.3.[57] This is made clear in APP 12, which provides that the requirement to provide access is subject to an exception – namely, where an agency is required or authorised to refuse to give the individual access to the information by an Act providing for access by persons to documents.

An agency must respond to a request within 30 days after it is made, must provide access in the manner requested by the information subject, if it is reasonable and practicable to do so,[58] and must provide access free of charge.[59]

If an entity refuses to provide access to the information requested, or in the manner requested, by the information subject, it must take such steps, if any, as are reasonable in the circumstances to give access to the information in a way which meets its own needs and those of the individual.[60] This may include the provision of information via an intermediary.[61]

---

55 APP 12.1.
56 OAIC, *Australian Privacy Principles and Information Privacy Principles – Comparison Guide* (2013) 17, at <http://oaic.gov.au/publications/guidelines/privacy_guidance/comparison_guide_APP_IPP.pdf>.
57 See Chapter 16.
58 APP 12.4.
59 APP 12.7. In the case of an organisation, any charges imposed must not be excessive and must not apply to the making of requests: see APP 12.8.
60 APP 12.5.
61 APP 12.6.

An entity that refuses to provide access to personal information requested, or in the manner requested, must give the information subject a written notice which includes specified information, including its reasons for refusing access (unless it would be unreasonable to provide them) and details of applicable complaints mechanisms.[62] Circumstances where it would be unreasonable to provide reasons would include the situation where the reasons would shed light on information which forms the basis for the exemption on which the refusal of access is based.

APP 13 requires an entity, on request by an information subject whose personal information it holds, to take such steps as are reasonable in the circumstances to correct that information and to ensure, having regard to the purpose for which it is held, that the information is accurate, up-to-date, complete, relevant and not misleading. This principle provides for similar grounds to those set out in the provisions in the Freedom of Information Act relating to the amendment of personal information, except that it allows for amendment based on relevance (a ground that is not available under the Freedom of Information Act). The inclusion of this ground in the Privacy Act is consistent with its internal logic, which is to limit the use and disclosure of personal information with reference to the purposes which have justified its collection.

APP 13 also contains a separate requirement for an entity to correct any personal information that it holds about an individual if it is satisfied, having regard to purposes for which the information is held, that the information is inaccurate, out-of-date, incomplete, irrelevant or misleading. The latter obligation is closely related to that in APP 10.

There is a further requirement for an entity, if requested to do so by an information subject, to take such steps, if any, as are reasonable in the circumstances, to pass on details of any amendment to other entities to which it has previously disclosed the information (in uncorrected form). This new requirement is subject to an exception where to do so would be impracticable or unlawful. The ability to request that corrected information is passed on in this way provides an important means for individuals to minimise any potential adverse consequences arising from the use of uncorrected information about them.

An entity which refuses an information subject's request for amendment must provide him or her with a written notice that sets out specified matters, including the reasons for the refusal (except to the extent that it would be unreasonable to do so) and details of available complaints mechanisms.[63] It must also, if requested to do so by the information subject, take such steps as are reasonable

---

62 APP 12.9. See also 12.10 in relation to refusals by organisations based on grounds of commercial sensitivity.
63 APP 13.3.

in the circumstances to associate with information that was the subject of the unsuccessful request for amendment, a statement that information is inaccurate, out-of-date, incomplete, irrelevant or misleading.[64] This must be done in such a way that will make the statement apparent to users of the information.[65] The ability to request an annotation serves an important role in enabling individuals to ensure that their views about deficiencies in their personal records are brought to the attention of decision-makers who have made decisions about them based on those records.

Tax file numbers

Some agencies may also have obligations relating to the handling of tax file numbers. The Act also required (and still requires) tax file number recipients to comply with a set of binding Tax File Number Guidelines which restrict the collection and disclosure of TFNs and their secure storage and disposal.[66] The TFN requirements in the Privacy Act are supported by provisions in other legislation which criminalise unauthorised dealings with TFNs.[67]

Agencies may also have related obligations arising under the *Data-matching Program (Assistance and Tax) Act 1990* (Cth). This regulates the use of TFNs in comparing personal information held by the Australian Taxation Office and by agencies, such as Centrelink and the Department of Veterans' Affairs, which provide government benefits. The current guidelines came into effect in February 1995. Data matching without use of TFNs is regulated via a set of advisory guidelines issued by the Privacy Commissioner for voluntary adoption by government agencies. An act or practice which breaches Part 2 of the *Data-Matching Program (Assistance and Tax) Act*, or of the guidelines in force under it, constitutes an actionable interference with privacy of the individual for the purposes of the Privacy Act.

Privacy codes

The Act contains scope for entities, including agencies, or the Commissioner to develop binding codes of practice about information privacy, called APP codes.[68] These must set out how one or more of the Australian Privacy Principles are to be

---

64 APP 13.4.
65 Ibid.
66 The Tax File Number Guidelines 2011 can be accessed at <www.comlaw.gov.au/Details/F2011L02748>.
67 These are contained in the *Taxation Administration Act 1953* (Cth) and parts of the *Income Tax Assessment Act 1936* (Cth).
68 The provisions relating to codes are found in Part IIIB of the Act.

applied or complied with; they may also impose additional requirements to those imposed by the APPs, or deal with other specified matters. If the Commissioner includes an APP code on the Codes Register, any breach of its terms constitutes an interference with the privacy of an individual (with the same consequences that apply in relation to breaches of the APPs or the TFN requirements).

Public interest determinations

The Commissioner has power to authorise non-compliance with specific requirements of the Act on public interest grounds by making a determination that an act or practice which may constitute a breach of an APP, or of an approved APP code, shall be regarded as not breaching that principle or approved code for the purposes of the Act. The Commissioner is required to maintain a register of public interest determinations.[69]

Enforcement and oversight by the Information Commissioner

The Privacy Act was originally administered and enforced by the Privacy Commissioner. When the government decided to create a new Freedom of Information Commissioner, it was decided to combine both of these oversight functions within a new office, the Australian Information Commissioner ('OAIC').[70]

The OAIC is responsible for oversight and enforcement of the Act. The Commissioner's functions are grouped within the Act according to whether they foster compliance (via the provision of guidance),[71] monitor compliance[72] or support compliance (via the provision of advice).[73] The Information Commissioner also has privacy responsibilities under other legislation, including the *Data-matching Program (Assistance and Tax) Act 1990* (Cth), the *National Health Act 1953* (Cth), the *Crimes Act 1914* (Cth) and the *Telecommunications Act 1997* (Cth).

The Act is enforced primarily via a complaints-based system, although the Information Commissioner also has power to conduct audits to assess entities'

---

69 This can be accessed at <www.oaic.gov.au/privacy/applying-privacy-law/privacy-registers/public-interest-determinations/>. Applications for new determinations are listed on the consultation page of the OAIC's website: see <www.oaic.gov.au/news/consultations.html>.
70 The new regime was implemented by the *Australian Information Commissioner Act 2010* (Cth).
71 See s 28.
72 See s 28A.
73 See s 28B.

maintenance of personal information,[74] to require provision of privacy impact assessments[75] and to conduct 'own motion' investigations.[76]

An individual may complain to the Commissioner about an act or practice that may be an interference with his or her privacy.[77] Complaints may also be made on a representative basis.[78] If a complaint is made, the Commissioner must investigate it.[79] However, the Commissioner has discretion not to investigate, or not to investigate further, in specified circumstances, including where the respondent has not yet had an adequate opportunity to deal with the complaint or has dealt, or is dealing, adequately with the complaint.[80] The Commissioner may also conduct preliminary inquiries to decide whether or not to investigate a matter.

The vast majority of complaints that are accepted are resolved by way of conciliation,[81] but the Commissioner also has the power to make determinations enforceable via the Federal Magistrates' Court or the Federal Court.[82] If the Commissioner finds that a complaint is substantiated, he or she may make one or more of the following declarations: a declaration that the respondent should not repeat conduct that constitutes an interference with the complainant's privacy; a declaration that a respondent must take specified steps to ensure that the conduct complained of is not repeated or continued; a declaration that the respondent should perform any reasonable act or course of conduct to redress any loss or damage suffered by the complainant; a declaration that the complainant is entitled to a specified amount of compensation; or a declaration that it would be inappropriate for any further action to be taken in the matter.[83]

In *Re Rummery and Federal Privacy Commissioner and Department of Justice and Community Safety*,[84] the AAT was required to consider a determination in which the Privacy Commissioner found that there had a been an interference with the complainant's personal privacy, but nevertheless decided that he was not entitled to any financial compensation. In finding in favour of the applicant and awarding him $8000, the Tribunal was influenced by the fact that the Privacy Act

---

74 Section 33C.
75 Section 33D(1). A 'privacy impact assessment' means a written assessment that identifies the impact an activity or function might have on the privacy of individuals and sets out recommendations for managing, minimising or eliminating that impact: see s 33D(3).
76 Section 40.
77 Section 36.
78 Section 38.
79 Section 40.
80 Section 41.
81 Conciliation is now specifically dealt with in s 40A.
82 Sections 55A and 62. The procedures for investigations and enforcement are contained in Pt V of the Act.
83 *Privacy Act 1988* (Cth), s 52.
84 [2004] AATA 1221.

specifically provides for compensation for injury to a complainant's feelings and for humiliation, and that once loss was proved, there would need to be some good reason shown to as to why compensation for that loss should not be awarded. This decision articulates a set of principles to be applied in determining whether financial compensation is appropriate in a particular case.[85] These include: that awards should be restrained but not minimal; that principles of damages applied in tort law may provide assistance in measuring compensation; that aggravated damages may be awarded in appropriate cases; and that compensation should be assessed having regard to the complainant's reaction and not to the perceived reaction of the majority of the community or of a reasonable person in similar circumstances.

The Commissioner's power to make declarations is now supplemented by an additional power: to seek civil penalty orders ranging from $110 000 up to $1.1 million on application to a court. Civil penalties are available where an entity does an act or engages in a practice which is a serious interference with the privacy of an individual, or where the entity repeatedly does an act or engages in a practice that is an interference with the privacy of one or more individuals.[86] The Act provides a non-exhaustive list of matters that the court must take into account in determining the pecuniary penalty, including: the nature and extent of the contravention and any loss or damage suffered because of the contravention; the circumstances in which the contravention took place; and whether or not the entity has previously been found by a court to have engaged in any similar conduct.[87]

Finally, the Commissioner also now has power to accept written undertakings by entities.[88] If an undertaking is breached, the Commissioner may apply to the Federal Court or the Federal Magistrates' Court for an order directing the entity to comply with the undertaking, pay compensation, or any other order the court considers appropriate.[89]

AAT review

The Privacy Act provides for very limited rights of appeal.[90] Prior to its amendment in 2012, the main avenue available was to apply to the Commonwealth Administrative Appeals Tribunal for review of determinations involving agencies that relate to

---

85 Those principles were applied by the Information Commissioner in *'D' and Wentworthville Leagues Club* [2011] AICmr 9 (9 December 2011).
86 Section 13G.
87 Section 80W(6).
88 Section 33E.
89 Section 33F.
90 See s 96.

compensation and expenses.[91] This review function arises only where there has been a determination made[92] and has to date been exercised on one occasion only, because there have been very few determinations made.[93]

The Act also now also provides for right of appeal in relation to decisions by the Information Commissioner to make determinations. [94]

Enforcement by the courts

As discussed above, the Privacy Act confers jurisdiction on the Federal Magistrates' Court and the Federal Court in relation to three specific matters arising from the exercise of the Information Commissioner's powers: the enforcement of determinations; the award of civil penalties; and the enforcement of written undertakings given to the Commissioner.

Section 98 also provides a right to apply to the Federal Magistrates' Court or the Federal Court for injunctive relief to restrain a person from engaging in conduct that constituted, or would constitute, a contravention of the Act.[95] That provision was originally interpreted as not being available as a source of action in respect of breaches of the privacy principles in the Privacy Act. However, in *Seven Network (Operations) Limited v Media Entertainment and Arts Alliance*,[96] the Federal Court held that it was open to the appellant to apply for an injunction to restrain breaches of the Privacy Act in circumstances where it had not previously made any complaint to the Privacy Commissioner. In arriving at this conclusion, Gyles J expressed the view that ss 55A and 62, which deal with the enforcement by the Federal Court of determinations by the Privacy Commissioner, pointed against a restrictive view of s 98, which provides a more general right to injunctive and declaratory relief. He also pointed out that it is by no means uncommon for there to be concurrent statutory remedies.

The Act also contains, in Part VIII, provisions which were designed to supplement the redress available to plaintiffs who sue agencies at common law in relation to breaches of confidence involving their personal information. These allow for a confider to recover damages from a confidant in respect of a breach of an obligation of confidence with respect to personal information,[97] but only where

---

91 The scope of this review right is considered in detail in *Re Epifano and Privacy Commissioner* [2010] AATA 489.
92 *Wijayaweera v Australian Information Commissioner* [2012] FCA 99.
93 *Re Rummery and Federal Privacy Commissioner* [2004] AATA 1221.
94 Section 96(1)(c). This applies to a power under decision under subsections 52(1) or (1A) to make a determination or declaration.
95 *Ibarcena v Templar* [1999] FCA 900; *Gao v Federal Privacy Commissioner* [2001] FCA 1683.
96 (2004) 148 FCR 145.
97 Section 93.

there is an obligation capable of enforcement by some kind of court order under the common law.[98]

The collateral consequences of breaches of the Act

There have been cases in which applicants have sought unsuccessfully to use alleged breaches of the Privacy Act as a means of collateral challenge.

For example, in *Phillips v Military Rehabilitation and Compensation Commission*,[99] alleged breaches of the Act were raised as a basis for invalidating a decision concerning the appellant's entitlement to receive compensation for incapacity. The court concluded that there had not been any breaches of the Act, so it was unnecessary for it consider the issues as to whether breaches of the Privacy Act were capable of rendering such a decision invalid.

In another case, a defendant appealed against a conviction in part on the basis that evidence used to prosecute him should not have been admitted because it was obtained in alleged contravention of the Privacy Act.[100] This argument was rejected in part because the alleged breach did not attract any criminal sanctions.

State and Territory information privacy laws

The Privacy Act is supplemented by information privacy laws which apply in all States other than South Australia and Western Australia, and also apply in the Northern Territory. The *Privacy Act 1988* (Cth) applies to ACT government agencies and is administered by the OAIC. However, the handling of health records (including by public sector agencies) is regulated by a sui generis health records regime.[101] These State and Territory privacy laws operate on a similar basis to the Commonwealth regime, requiring compliance with sets of privacy principles that regulate the handling of identifiable, or potentially identifiable, personal information. However, they differ considerably in terms of their content and scope.

---

98 See *Michael James Austen v Civil Aviation Authority* (1994) 33 ALD 429.
99 [2006] FCA 882.
100 *C Cockerill & Sons (Vic) Pty Ltd v County Court of Victoria* [2007] VSC 182 (31 May 2007).
101 *Health Records (Privacy and Access) Act 1997* (ACT). This requires compliance with a set of privacy principles in Schedule 1 and is regulated by the ACT Health Services Commissioner.

The *Privacy and Personal Information Protection Act 1998* (NSW) applies to NSW public sector agencies and requires them to comply with a set of IPPs contained in Part 2 of the Act. It does not apply to health records, which are governed by separate health records legislation.[102] The Act is administered by the NSW Privacy Commissioner, who also has power to investigate and conciliate privacy breaches by organisations and individuals who are not public sector agencies.

The handling of personal information by Queensland government agencies is regulated by the *Information Privacy Act 2009* (Qld). This requires agencies, other than health bodies, to comply with a set of IPPs. Health bodies are required instead to comply with the Commonwealth Privacy Act. The Information Privacy Act is enforced by the Queensland Office of the Information Commissioner.

In the case of Tasmania, the handling of personal information by public sector bodies is regulated by the *Personal Information Protection Act 2004* (Tas). This requires compliance with a set of Personal Information Protection Principles in Schedule 1. The Act is administered by the Tasmanian Department of Justice and provides for review by the Tasmanian Ombudsman.

The regime in Victoria is similar to that in New South Wales. The *Information Privacy Act 2000* (Vic) applies to Victorian public sector agencies and requires them to comply with a set of IPPs contained in Schedule 1. It does not, however, apply to health records, which are instead governed by separate health records legislation.[103] The Act is regulated by the Office of the Victorian Privacy Commissioner.

The position is the Northern Territory differs in that privacy is regulated via a combined law which also regulates freedom of information and the archiving of public records. The *Information Act 2002* (NT) requires compliance with a set of IPPs in Schedule 2, and is enforced by the Northern Territory Information Commissioner.

Conclusion

While the common law now provides for improved privacy protection via the action for breach of confidence, there is a clear need for legislative protection. The first and most comprehensive public sector protection was provided by Commonwealth

---

102 *Health Records and Information Privacy Act 2002* (NSW). This regulates the handling of information in both the private and public sectors and requires compliance with a set of Health Privacy Principles in Schedule 1. It is regulated by the New South Wales Privacy Commissioner.
103 *Health Records Act 2001* (Vic). This regulates the handling of information in both the private and public sectors and requires compliance with a set of Health Privacy Principles in Schedule 1. It is regulated by the Victorian Health Services Commissioner.

legislation which was followed by the enactment of broadly similar legislation in most States and in the Northern Territory. These developments illustrate that governments now clearly accept that privacy is a valuable right, even if it is not always explained precisely in the language of human rights. The enactment of comprehensive privacy laws both recognises and strengthens the expectation that most people rightly have about the management by government of information. The privacy principles on which they are based, including the new Commonwealth APPs which will take effect in 2014, provide an important framework of principles which both regulate and guide governments and their agencies.

Although privacy legislation and privacy principles include some limited rights of review and appeal, there is clearly less litigation about privacy than occurs in other areas of administrative law. The low level of litigation arising from information privacy laws is in part due to the limited nature of the rights available, but it is arguably also due to the role of specialist oversight bodies in privacy law. Privacy legislation typically imposes wide-ranging obligations upon the agencies that handle personal information, and creates specialist independent agencies to oversee and enforce those obligations. Regulatory oversight by specialist commissioners is an important feature of privacy laws, which rely on education and persuasion as well as complaints-based enforcement, thereby allowing for more proactive regulation. The specialist commissioners created to regulate privacy are empowered to monitor compliance with privacy legislation and to provide wider guidance to governments and their agencies about compliance with their privacy obligations. Dispute resolution takes place primarily via conciliation, although there is scope for commissioners to make determinations and to award compensation where appropriate. These features of privacy legislation show how it comprises a unique element of our administrative law framework.

18

TRIBUNALS AND MERITS REVIEW

Robin Creyke

Introduction: What is a tribunal?

Tribunals are bodies 'which stand on the frontiers between law and administration'.[1] They 'provide specialised machinery for the adjudication of cases that would otherwise be decided by the civil courts'.[2] The first tribunals emerged in the 17th century in England, when a judicial power was given to Commissioners of Customs and Excise. Among others, a specialist tax tribunal was set up in England towards the end of the 18th century, and in the 19th century, adjudicative functions in areas unfamiliar to the courts, such as railways and canals, were allocated to bodies outside the court system.[3] Nonetheless, for the most part tribunals are a 20th century phenomenon.[4]

There have been various attempts to describe a tribunal – a task made more difficult by the variety of bodies which bear that label. The Australian Law Reform Commission (ALRC) defined tribunals in these terms:

> a body which is not a court but carries out a mix of judicial or quasi-judicial tasks. The term covers a wide spectrum of bodies, both in terms of the subject matter dealt with and the processes used.[5]

The *Administrative Law Act 1978* (Vic), s 2, defines a 'tribunal' as:

> a person or body of persons (not being a court of law or a tribunal constituted or presided over by a Judge of the Supreme Court) who, in arriving at the decision in question, is or are by law required, whether by express direction or not, to act in a judicial manner to the extent of observing one or more of the rules of natural justice.

The definition in the Constitution of the Council of Australasian Tribunals (COAT) is:

> any Commonwealth, State, Territory or New Zealand body whose primary function involves the determination of disputes, including administrative review, party/party disputes and disciplinary applications but which in carrying out this function is not acting as a court.

---

1 R E Wraith and P G Hutchesson, *Administrative Tribunals* (Allen & Unwin, 1973) 13.
2 *Tribunals for Users – One System, One Service: Report of the Review of Tribunals by Sir Andrew Leggatt* ('Leggatt Review') (UK Stationery Office, 2001) [1.6].
3 New Zealand Law Commission, *Tribunals for New Zealand*, Issue Paper 6 (2008) [1.2]–[1.7].
4 Ibid, [1.1], [1.2], [1.8]–[1.10].
5 Australian Law Reform Commission, *Review of the Adversarial System of Litigation: Federal Tribunal Proceedings* (Issues Paper 24, 1998) 2.1.

The definitions are subtly different but they reflect core aspects of the tribunal, including: that there is a spectrum of models which governments can adopt; that a tribunal is not a court, but like a court it resolves disputes in the public or private sectors by the application of rules; and that, as a body with an adjudicative function, it is expected to operate in a fair, independent and impartial fashion, but beyond that its procedures are at its discretion. Although there are many private sector tribunals, the focus of this chapter is on tribunals which resolve disputes between individuals, or companies, and government.

Tribunals' place in the machinery of government

As the definitions indicate, tribunals are adjudicative bodies but they are intended to be different from courts. That raises two issues: 'Where do tribunals fit in the tripartite system of government?'; and 'What makes a tribunal distinctive?'. Historically, in England, the first major discussion of the tribunal phenomenon was that tribunals should be seen as 'machinery provided by Parliament for adjudication rather than as part of the machinery of the administration'.[6] That view has persisted, and today, in England and Wales, tribunals are generally regarded as part of the judicial branch of government. Senior members of tribunals are known as tribunal judges and, for the most part, tribunals are seen as specialist judicial bodies which decide disputes in particular areas of law.

In Australia, the tendency, principally for constitutional reasons, has been the reverse. Tribunals are viewed as part of the executive, not the judicial arm, of government.[7] Although tribunals may have judicial members, they are generally not called judges when acting as adjudicators in a tribunal. At the same time, the need for tribunals to be independent casts doubt on their placement in the executive. In the late 1980s Curtis suggested that tribunals occupy a 'no man's land'.[8] A similar view was expressed by Bayne, who said that tribunals straddle both the executive and the judicial arm.[9] The most recent view is that tribunals in Australia are part of a fourth, 'integrity', arm of government and that they operate alongside other independent monitoring and accountability bodies such as Ombudsman offices,

---

6 *Report of Committee on Administrative Tribunals and Enquiries* ('Franks Committee Report') (Cmnd 218, 1957) 9.
7 Australian Law Reform Commission, above n 5, 12.2; *Commonwealth Administrative Review Committee* (1971) ('Kerr Committee Report') [61], [89].
8 L Curtis, 'Crossing the Frontiers Between Law and Administration' (1989) 58 *Canberra Bulletin of Public Administration* 56.
9 P Bayne, 'Tribunals in the System of Government' (1990) 10 *Papers on Parliament* 1, 3.

anti-corruption commissions, public service commissions, auditors-general, and information and privacy offices.[10]

Distinctive features

Typical characteristics of a tribunal are that it:

- has legal authority to make decisions on disputed claims;
- is independent from the decision-maker, be it a Minister or an agency, the decisions of which are reviewed;
- holds public hearings;
- has an obligation to give reasons for decisions;
- possesses members with expertise in the matters being reviewed; and
- is subject to the supervisory or appellate powers of a court.[11]

To that list could be added that it is established by statute,[12] and that there is a predominant emphasis on negotiated dispute resolution, that is, the settlement of a dispute following an alternative dispute resolution (ADR) process rather than through a formal hearing followed by a decision.

These characteristics are exemplified by the latest multi-purpose State tribunal, the Queensland Civil and Administrative Tribunal (QCAT), the objectives for which include that it:

- provides decisions which are independent and impartial;
- adopts a more inquisitorial approach than courts to dispute resolution;
- has a large and flexible membership with specialist expertise; and
- is accessible, fair, just, economical, informal and quick.[13]

There are some other significant features of Australian tribunals which distinguish national from State or Territory tribunals.[14] Federal tribunals may not exercise federal judicial power under Chapter III of the *Constitution*, which means they may not make determinative findings of law, their decisions are always subject to judicial supervision, and they cannot enforce their own decisions.[15]

---

10 Key Centre for Ethics, Law, Justice and Governance, Griffith University, and Transparency International, *Chaos or Coherence? Strengths, Opportunities and Challenges for Australia's Integrity Systems: National Integrity Systems Assessment (NISA) Final Report* (2005) 119–21.
11 Eg, the characteristics of QCAT (Second Reading Speech, Queensland Civil and Administrative Tribunal Bill, *Hansard*, 19 May 2009, 349–51).
12 *Owen v Menzies* [2012] QCA 170, [10].
13 Second Reading Speech, above n 11, 349–51 .
14 *R v Kirby; Ex parte Boilermakers' Society of Australia* (1956) 94 CLR 254; *Kable v Director of Public Prosecutions (NSW)* (1996) 189 CLR 51.
15 Kerr Committee Report, above n 7, [89]; Australian Law Reform Commission, above n 5, [3.4]–[3.6]; *Brandy v Human Rights and Equal Opportunity Commission* (1995) 183 CLR 245, 269.

Pre-hearing dispute resolution

Another feature that is distinctive of tribunals is their growing interest in avoiding the formal hearing as the principal dispute settlement process, in favour of pre-hearing agreed settlement processes described compendiously as ADR process models. Tribunals have generally been quicker than courts to embrace ADR processes. However, this is a relatively recent development. There was little attention in the *Report of the Commonwealth Administrative Review Committee* (Kerr Committee Report) to solving disputes outside the hearing process. The Kerr Committee Report in the early 1970s was the precursor to the development of the modern Australian administrative law system – notably, the notion of a general purpose, rather than specialist, administrative appeals tribunal. Nonetheless, as Professor Whitmore, one of the architects and principal authors of that report pointed out, the Committee envisaged that, prior to a hearing, there would be 'some research work coupled with a proposed procedure whereby parties to a dispute would be encouraged to exchange written statements and to confer with a view to settlement'.[16] This was the genesis of the preliminary conference, which has become a mainstay of the processes of many tribunals.

Many more procedures for pre-hearing dispute settlement have been devised and introduced since then. Such procedures are standard in many tribunals.[17] Conciliation, mediation, case appraisal and neutral evaluations have entered the lexicon. Their use has been encouraged at the Commonwealth level by recent Attorneys-General and is enjoined nationally by the Model Litigant Principles under the *Legal Services Directions 2005* (Cth), backed up by costs orders, as well as by injunction in the legislation of some tribunals. For example, it is compulsory in the compensation jurisdiction before the Administrative Appeals Tribunal (AAT),[18] and 'where appropriate' in applications to QCAT,[19] exemplifying the position in the major general purpose and multi-purpose tribunals in Australia.

What has not been publicised sufficiently is the significance of this move. As an example, of the over 8000 alternative dispute, interlocutory and formal hearings conducted by the AAT in 2011–12, only 11 per cent were hearings.[20] The AAT

---

16 H Whitmore, 'Administrative Law in the Commonwealth: Some proposals for reform' (1972) 5 *Federal Law Review* 7, 16.
17 ACT: ACAT Act, Div 5.3; Cth: AAT Act, Part IV Div 3; NSW: ADT Act, Part 4; Qld: QCAT Act, Part 6 Divs 2–4; SA: *District Court Act 1991*, ss 31–2; Tas: *Magistrates Court Act 1987*, s 15AE; Vic: VCAT Act, Part 4 Div 5; WA: SAT Act, Part 4 Div 2.
18 *Safety, Rehabilitation and Compensation Act 1988* (Cth).
19 *Queensland Civil and Administrative Tribunal Act 2009* (Qld) (QCAT Act), ss 4(b), 69, 75; Justice Alan Wilson, 'QCAT Hybrid Conferencing Processes: ADR and Case Management' (2011) 67 *Australian Institute of Administrative Law Forum* 80.
20 *Administrative Appeals Tribunal Annual Report 2011–2012*, 174.

is not alone. In QCAT, 45 per cent of minor civil matters and 62 per cent of non-minor civil disputes were finalised through mediation in 2011–12.[21] In VCAT, over 1700 matters were finalised through mediation or compulsory conferences in 2011–12.[22] WA's State Administrative Tribunal resolved 57 per cent of contested matters in its commercial and civil stream, and 70 per cent in its development and resources stream, using 'facilitative measures' in 2011–12.[23]

So rather than hearings being the locus for dispute settlement, the preponderance of applications to at least the major Australian tribunals are finalised following consensual settlement processes. These figures indicate that it is the pre-hearing, not the hearing, processes of tribunals that are the engine rooms of their processes for settling disputes. This aligns with government policies which enjoin the virtues of cheaper, personalised, more accessible and speedy justice.

At the same time, there are critics of this movement, not least because the content and processes of such proceedings are confidential. As a consequence they fail to provide guidance to the executive, particularly as to the meaning and application of the legislation under which government decision-making is conducted.[24] Since this is one of the prime functions tribunals perform, the failure to give clear and authoritative rulings on issues involved in disputes has been argued to over-emphasise the interests of users of the system at the expense of the general public interest.[25] This criticism reflects the reality that government decisions have application to citizens generally, not just the individual who disputes an outcome.

There are also other advantages to holding public hearings. As identified by the Administrative Justice and Tribunals Council in England and Wales, they include:

> transparency, the scope for testing contested evidence and the maintenance of public confidence. There are also less tangible attributes of participation, including dignity of the individual and democratic legitimacy.[26]

---

21 *Queensland Civil and Administrative Appeals Tribunal Annual Report 2011–2012*. Although he said the statistics need refining, Justice Alan Wilson, President of QCAT, estimated that between 50 per cent and 60 per cent of Administrative Review cases are expected to settle prior to a hearing: Wilson, above n 19, 85 (fn10).
22 *Victorian Civil and Administrative Appeals Tribunal Annual Report 2011–2012*, 22. These figures do not include matters which were finalised after removal of matters over which VCAT had no jurisdiction or which were withdrawn.
23 *WA State Administrative Tribunal Annual Report 2011–12*, 10–11.
24 Administrative Justice and Tribunals Council, *Putting It Right – A Strategic Approach to Resolving Administrative Disputes* (June 2012), [129].
25 Ibid, citing M Adler, 'Tribunal Reform: Proportional Dispute Resolution and the Pursuit of Administrative Justice' (2006) 69 *Modern Law Review* 695.
26 Ibid, [122].

The upshot is that while both the formal hearing and reasons of tribunals, as well as the ability to resolve matters outside a hearing, remain essential justifications for their existence, consensual dispute resolution is likely to be an increasingly important feature of the tribunal model.

Distinguishing tribunals from courts

Their distinctive characteristics also serve to differentiate tribunals from the other principal form of body for dispute resolution, courts. The Australian Law Reform Commission noted simply that: 'Tribunals provide decision making and dispute resolution processes which are "alternative" to traditional court proceedings'.[27] What makes a tribunal 'alternative' was not explored. However, their distinctive character can be identified in: the extent of their jurisdiction, that is, generally to decide the merits of the dispute; the different processes by which their roles are performed; their membership; and the fact that unlike courts, tribunals are invariably set up by statute. Tribunals' merit review function means that they are able to reconsider all aspects of the decision under challenge.[28] Most of these features are discussed in more detail later in this chapter.

Other characteristics which distinguish tribunals from courts are that: tribunals are more accessible for users since their procedures are less formal than courts; they may adopt an inquisitorial role in their dispute handling; their membership includes those with specialist, not necessarily legal, expertise; and their members generally have specific knowledge or experience of the principles of administrative law.[29]

Despite these discriminating features, it is often difficult to decide whether a body is a tribunal or a court, either for all, or some only, of its functions. That is a consequence of the often haphazard growth of tribunals, which has not been accompanied by the development of guidelines or principles which determine whether a body is a court or a tribunal. The result is that the categorisation of the body is only found from an analysis of its statutory powers and functions. Recent cases have identified over twenty factors which are relevant to that

---

27 Australian Law Reform Commission, above n 5, [12.2].
28 Kerr Committee Report, above n 7, [89] and Ch 14.
29 Leggatt Review, above n 2, [1.10]–[1.13]. See, for a succinct list, Tasmanian Office of the State Service Commissioner, *Report of the Review of Administrative Appeals Processes* ('Vines report') (2003) 28.

categorisation. Commonly the question is decided by finding that the body is not a court and hence it must, by default, be a tribunal. So it is the characteristics of a court which are often the focus of such inquiries. That does not simplify the task, since deciding whether the body is a court is equally problematic.

The issue has practical consequences, since the powers and functions of courts and tribunals, and their intended method of operation, differ – often markedly. The distinction is important for at least three reasons: there are constitutional implications – for example, if the body is a court according to Chapter III of the *Constitution*, it can exercise the judicial power of the Commonwealth. That may be important, for example, in deciding whether a State tribunal has authority over a federal officer.[30] If a State tribunal is not a Chapter III 'court' it cannot exercise federal judicial power,[31] but this does not prevent it from exercising State judicial power.[32] A State tribunal which is found to be a Chapter III court must also not offend the *Kable* principle:[33] that is, it must exhibit institutional integrity.[34] Key characteristics in favour of a State or Territory tribunal being a court in this constitutional context are that the body is a 'court of record',[35] and that it has independence and impartiality.[36]

A second issue is whether the powers being exercised by the body are executive or judicial in nature. That will affect whether it is subject to judicial review, in those jurisdictions where a statute dealing with judicial review provides that the supervisory jurisdiction is restricted to decisions 'of an administrative character'.[37] Finally, there are functional consequences, such as whether the body enjoys litigation privilege or legal professional privilege, and financial consequences, particularly the heavy costs in settling whether the body is a court or a tribunal if this question has to be litigated.

---

30 *Commonwealth v Anti-Discrimination Tribunal (Tas)* (2008) 169 FCR 85.
31 *Jomal Pty Ltd v Commercial & Consumer Tribunal* [2009] QSC 3; *Owen v Menzies* [2012] QCA 170; *Commonwealth v Anti-Discrimination Tribunal (Tas)* (2008) 169 FCR 85; *Sunol v Collier (No 1)* [2012] NSWCA 14.
32 *Trust Co of Australia (t/a Stockland Property Management) v Skiwing Pty Ltd (t/a Café Tiffany's)* (2006) 66 NSWLR 77, [74] (Basten JA, Handley JA and McDougal JA agreeing).
33 *Kable v Director of Public Prosecutions (NSW)* (1996) 189 CLR 51. See also *K-Generation Pty Ltd v Liquor Licensing Court* (2009) 237 CLR 501; *Gypsy Jokers Motorcycle Club Inc v Commissioner of Police* (2008) 234 CLR 532.
34 *Owen v Menzies* [2012] QCA 170, [53] (McMurdo P, De Jersey CJ agreeing).
35 *Owen v Menzies* [2012] QCA 170, [10] (De Jersey CJ), [49], [52], [61] (McMurdo P). Muir JA agreed with De Jersey CJ and McMurdo P.
36 *North Australian Aboriginal Legal Aid Service Inc v Bradley* (2004) 218 CLR 146, 152 (Gleeson CJ); *Owen v Menzies* [2012] QCA 170, [19] (De Jersey CJ), [49] (McMurdo P).
37 See *Administrative Decisions (Judicial Review) Act 1977* (Cth), s 5; *Administrative Decisions (Judicial Review) Act 1989* (ACT), s 5; *Judicial Review Act 1991* (Qld), ss 4, 31; *Judicial Review Act 2000* (Tas), s 4.

Varieties and advantages of tribunals

Varieties of tribunals

The growth in the role of government after the First World War led to economic and social pressures for more government regulation, services and income support. This led to an upsurge in the volume of executive decisions affecting citizens, producing in turn a significant increase in disputes with government. In order to relieve the courts of that adjudicative burden, it was often cheaper, faster and more efficient to establish a tribunal to manage those disputes.

The effect has been for tribunals to abound in Australia and elsewhere. Typically, the tribunals in a State or Territory would be set up to hear appeals or to make primary decisions. The body might comprise a public official, a Minister, a professional, occupational or business body which hears complaints or appeals from disciplinary decisions, and specifically named boards.[38]

There has been no estimate of the number of tribunals in Australia then or now. However, as an example, a 1996 taskforce on Western Australian tribunals identified at least 54 such bodies – a number which had increased by 2002 when the next report into tribunals in that State appeared.[39] The Leggatt Review into tribunals in the United Kingdom in the early 2000s identified some 137 bodies which provided specialised machinery for the adjudication of cases, and that was only a subset of the number which performed adjudicative services in the UK civil law system.[40] These numbers indicate the popularity of the tribunal model of adjudication.

Advantages of tribunals

The tribunal model is a flexible one. A feature of tribunals is that their jurisdiction is granted solely by legislation. Parliaments therefore have the ability to tailor what decisions are subject to tribunal review – an advantage which aids efficiency and is often attractive to government. Tribunals can also be set up for a variety of functions, and in many different forms: as appeal bodies; primary decision-makers; with multiple functions, only one of which is dispute resolution; or on a temporary basis

---

38 For a discussion of the kinds of bodies which could be classified as national tribunals, see S Skehill, *Strategic Review of Small and Medium Agencies in the Attorney-General's Portfolio* (2012) ('Skehill Review') [7.5]–[7.10].
39 *Western Australian Civil and Administrative Review Tribunal Taskforce Report on the Establishment of the State Administrative Tribunal* (2002) 29.
40 Leggatt Review, above n 2, [1.6].

to make decisions about disputes concerning the allocation of funds, for example, raised after a natural disaster. The many kinds of bodies which perform tribunal functions are a reflection of the fact that tribunals are often created in order to meet an immediate policy need. The result is that there is a spectrum of bodies designated as tribunals with benefits which accrue to government and to the aggrieved citizen.

Another advantage of the tribunal model is that the body can be set up when 'functions require a level of separation from government, to ensure objectivity'[41] and to avoid any perception of lack of impartiality.[42] As indicated earlier, many tribunals also offer a range of dispute resolution options. These pre-hearing means of reaching a solution reduce the cost of tribunal operations and often lead to more sustainable outcomes for the parties involved. Guidelines for the kinds of matters or circumstances which favour use of alternative dispute resolution rather than a hearing have been drawn up by the Administrative Justice and Tribunals Council.[43]

Tribunal systems in Australia

Historically, tribunals have been developed on an 'as needs' basis. This was often a decision made ad hoc, and did not provide guidance as to what matters were more appropriately dealt with by courts or by tribunals. This has produced bodies which often had little in common. However, beginning with the creation of the AAT in the 1970s, with its taking over of the functions of many national tribunals and, in the last ten to fifteen years, the moves in the States and Territories to amalgamate their civil and administrative tribunals and courts, this proliferation of ad hoc tribunals has been stemmed. The moves, made largely for cost and efficiency reasons, have changed the tribunal landscape in Australia.

Categories of tribunals

Tribunals can be classified in various ways: specialist versus general jurisdiction or multi-purpose tribunals; first and second tier tribunals; public and private (or domestic) tribunals; and primary decision-making or review tribunals.

Specialist tribunals

Initially, as the historical overview indicated, all tribunals had a specialist function. Examples are the eponymous NSW Consumer, Trader and Tenancy Tribunal, and

---

41 *Review of the Corporate Governance of Statutory Authorities and Office Holders* (2003) ('Uhrig Review') 7.
42 Skehill Review, above n 38, 9.
43 [UK] Administrative Justice and Tribunals Council, *Putting It Right – A Strategic Approach to Resolving Administrative Disputes* (2012) [134], Appendix A.

the Dust Diseases Board of Queensland, which dealt with diseases from exposure to asbestos as well as other dust-related claims. Federal specialist tribunals have been established in high volume dispute areas such as income support, migration, veterans' entitlements and professional, usually medical, services.

General or multi-purpose jurisdiction tribunals

Tribunals which deal with a spread of matters, the general jurisdiction, or multi-purpose tribunals, are more recent in origin. The model began with the establishment of the Commonwealth's Administrative Appeals Tribunal (AAT), which began operating in 1976. The AAT has jurisdiction across government, provided that an agency allocates authority for the AAT to reconsider its decisions.[44] Matters the AAT deals with are as diverse as the rates of shared care payments for children when parents have separated; the licensing of migration agents; whether national disability plans for the profoundly disabled are 'reasonable and necessary'; security assessments; compensation for work-related injuries; accreditation of certain education institutions; and rights to income support and other entitlements.

The multi-purpose civil and administrative tribunals (CATS) which have emerged in the States and Territories combine extensive civil, administrative, disciplinary, human rights, and often guardianship and management of property jurisdictions.

First or second tier tribunals

It has been accepted that in high volume jurisdictions it can be efficient to filter disputes through an independent, first tier tribunal before offering a second, or later, hearing by a general jurisdiction tribunal. The notable examples nationally are the first tier specialist tribunals: namely, the Social Security Appeals Tribunal, the Veterans' Review Board, and in some areas of migration law, the migration review tribunals, from which an appeal lies to the general jurisdiction of the AAT.

A variation of this practice is for a multi-purpose tribunal to have primary decision-making and second tier review functions. The appeals are heard by more senior members of the tribunal.[45] Examples are the Appeals Panel of the NSW Administrative Decisions Tribunal (ADT), which hears appeals from its first instance panels. There are restrictions on that right of appeal: the appeal may only be on a question of law, unless leave is given by the Appeal Panel to review the merits.[46] Other

---

44 *Administrative Appeals Tribunal Act 1975* (Cth) (AAT Act), s 25.
45 *ACT Civil and Administrative Tribunal Act 2008* (ACT) (ACAT Act), s 81(3); *Administrative Decisions Tribunal Act 1997* (NSW) (ADT Act), s 24(1); *Queensland Civil and Administrative Tribunal Act 2009 (Qld)* (QCAT Act), s 166(1).
46 ADT Act, s 113(2).

multi-purpose tribunals which have an appeal panel are the ACT Civil and Administrative Tribunal (ACAT)[47] and the Queensland Civil and Administrative Tribunal (QCAT).[48]

Public and private tribunals

Public tribunals review decisions made by government, such as land planning matters, freedom of information decisions and applications for citizenship. Tribunals, however, also exist to make decisions or to review matters outside government. These private sector matters include professional, occupational and disciplinary decisions such as accreditation of professional qualifications, for example by bodies such as law societies, and building and tenancy disputes. These tribunals, as mentioned earlier, are not the prime focus of this chapter.

Primary decision-making and review tribunals

Independent tribunals can make primary decisions about matters such as guardianship, or mental or other health matters. Formerly these decisions were the function of courts, but since 1986 they have progressively been undertaken by tribunals. Frequently, there is a right of review of such decisions by a general jurisdiction tribunal or a multi-purpose tribunal.

National, State and Territory systems

Tribunals have been established in Australia since the 19th century. From the early 1900s there were specialist tribunals to adjudicate in areas such as tax, valuations of property for gift duty purposes, promotion and discipline decisions within the public service, film censorship, customs and excise, and veterans' entitlements.[49] The increasing reliance on specialist tribunals led to such an increase in their number, with attendant costs, that steps were taken progressively by governments to rein in that growth and to either bring these tribunals under a single roof where possible (often called co-location), or to amalgamate them into one institution.

National system

The amalgamation of tribunals was initiated in the Commonwealth with the Kerr Committee Report recommending the establishment of the body which became the Administrative Appeals Tribunal. The AAT has a general merits review jurisdiction, which has expanded steadily so that jurisdiction is now granted to it by over

---

47 ACAT Act, ss 9(1)(b), (2).
48 QCAT Act, s 42(1).
49 *Commonwealth Administrative Review Committee* (1971) ('Kerr Committee') [18].

400 different pieces of legislation. A list of the jurisdictions is found in *The Australian Administrative Law Service* (LexisNexis, looseleaf) or on the AAT website (www.aat.gov.au). The initial preference at the national level was for a single tribunal, with limited exceptions in some specialist areas,[50] but despite this ambition, not all specialist tribunals were folded into the AAT when it was established, and a number of tribunals designed for a specific purpose have subsequently been set up and have been retained largely, but not entirely, in high volume areas.[51]

An attempt was made at the beginning of 2000 to amalgamate all major national tribunals into a body to be called the Administrative Review Tribunal, but the legislation was not passed by the Senate. A suggestion was also made to reintroduce a similar body,[52] but the government did not accept that recommendation.[53] At the same time, the government indicated that 'except in exceptional circumstances, no new Commonwealth merits review body should be established' and that 'any new merits review jurisdiction should be conferred on the AAT'.[54]

States' and Territories' systems

The States and Territories have followed the same pattern of ad hoc growth of specialist tribunals, followed by proposals to amalgamate tribunals into a single tribunal. However, as they are not shackled by the constitutional limitations which exist nationally due to the strict separation of executive and judicial functions, the general jurisdiction model adopted by the Commonwealth has been modified in the States and Territories. Instead of the amalgamation of purely administrative review bodies, as has occurred nationally, several States (Queensland, Victoria and Western Australia) and the ACT have each combined their civil and administrative tribunals and created the so-called CATS.[55]

New South Wales amalgamated some of its administrative tribunals into the Administrative Decisions Tribunal (ADT) in 1997,[56] and in 2001 set up a mega tribunal – the Consumer, Trader and Tenancy Tribunal (CTTT) – with extensive civil jurisdiction. In 2012, the government announced that it intended to establish an NCAT (NSW Civil and Administrative Tribunal).[57] The NCAT will combine some

---

50 Ibid, [353], [recommendation 18, [390]].
51 R Creyke and J McMillan, *Control of Government Action* (LexisNexis, 3rd ed, 2012) [3.2.21].
52 Skehill Review, Recommendation 7.1, xxi.
53 Hon Nicola Roxon MP, Attorney-General, 'Review of Attorney-General Portfolio Agencies Released' (Media Release, 6 June 2012) 2.
54 Ibid, 3.
55 ACAT Act; QCAT Act; VCAT Act; SAT Act.
56 ADT Act.
57 Greg Smith SC, NSW Attorney-General, 'Consolidation of NSW tribunals' (Press Release, 26 October 2012).

25 existing tribunals including the ADT and the CTTT. The legislation for NCAT has been passed, and it is planned for NCAT to begin operation on 1 January 2014.[58]

In July 2012, the SA Attorney-General, The Hon John Rau, promised to introduce a SACAT, a promise which has now been implemented.[59] At present, in South Australia there is an Administrative and Disciplinary Division of the District Court, amalgamating the administrative review and disciplinary appeals functions of previous separate bodies.[60] Tasmania too has an amalgam of jurisdictions of former tribunals located in a court, the Tasmanian Magistrates Court, operating in its Administrative Appeals Division.[61] There is no tribunal or court with general jurisdiction in the Northern Territory. Instead, administrative review, disciplinary and occupational licensing appeals, tenancy and land valuation, and other civil matters are heard in a variety of courts and tribunals. The Attorney-General and Minister for Justice announced in 2013 that he has called for a report into the creation of a centralised Administrative Appeals Tribunal.

Relationship of tribunals with courts

Appeal from tribunals

There is generally a right of appeal against decisions of tribunals. Some tribunal systems provide a right of appeal on the merits. That appeal can be within a tribunal – for example, to an appeal panel – or it can be externally, to another tribunal. However, in all jurisdictions there is a right of appeal to the courts either on a 'question', 'error', or 'matter', of law. For example, an appeal from the AAT to the Federal Court can be made on 'a question of law'.[62]

The courts have identified subtle distinctions between the various statutory appeal rights. For example, it has been decided that an appeal 'on *a question of law*' is narrower than an appeal that merely *involves* a question of law.[63] Whatever the extent of appeal rights granted under these provisions, the courts have been increasingly strict about refusing to hear appeals on what are in substance errors of fact, not law.[64] The justification at the federal level rests on constitutional

---

58 *Civil and Administrative Tribunal Act 2013* (NSW).
59 Hon John Rau, SA Attorney-General, 'Keynote speech' (delivered at the AIAL National Conference, Adelaide, July 2012).
60 *District Court Act 1991* (SA), s 7.
61 *Magistrates Court (Administrative Appeals Division) Act 2001* (Tas).
62 AAT Act, s 44.
63 *Comcare v Etheridge* (2006) 149 FCR 522, 527 (Branson J, Spender and Nicholson JJ agreeing); *Birdseye v Australian Securities and Investment Commission* (2003) 76 ALD 321, [10]–[18] (Stone and Branson JJ); *TNT Skypack International (Aust) Pty Ltd v Federal Commissioner of Taxation* (1988) 82 ALR 175, 178 (Gummow J).
64 *Comcare v Etheridge* (2006) 149 FCR 522, 527 (Branson J, Spender and Nicholson JJ agreeing); *Birdseye v Australian Securities and Investment Commission* (2003) 76 ALD 321, [10]–[18] (Branson and Stone JJ).

grounds: namely, the separation of judicial (legal issues) and executive power (factual issues).

Merits review

Concept and scope

As the report of the Kerr Committee put it in recommending the introduction of a general jurisdiction merits review tribunal for Australia: 'The basic fault of the entire structure [of administrative law in Australia in the 1970s] is...that review cannot as a general rule, in the absence of special statutory provisions, be obtained "on the merits" – and this is usually what the aggrieved citizen is seeking'.[65] The AAT was set up to remedy that defect. Thus it was surprising that the legislation for the AAT contained no definition of 'merits review'. Instead it was left to the tribunal itself to determine what it meant, as it did in a number of early decisions.[66]

Merits review distinguishes tribunals from courts in that it permits the tribunal to re-examine the facts, the law and, if appropriate, any policies relevant to the decision. Generally, courts review decisions solely on the basis that the decision is unlawful: that is, the decision-maker has not complied with legal principle. Whether the facts have been found accurately is not typically a role for judicial review. Much less is a supervisory court able, as a general rule, to take account of applicable policy.[67] So the exercise of merits review encompasses all aspects of the decision and is considerably broader than the judicial review role of courts.

Bennett has defined the distinction between merits review and judicial review as follows:

> A merits review body will 'stand in the shoes' of the primary decision-maker, and will make a fresh decision based upon all the evidence available to it. The object of merits review is to ensure that the 'correct or preferable'[68] decision is made on the material before the review body. The object of judicial review, on the other hand, is to ensure that the decision made by the primary decision-maker was properly made within the legal limits of the relevant power.[69]

---

65 Kerr Committee Report, above n 7, [58].
66 Eg, *Re Greenham and Minister for Capital Territory* (1979) 2 ALD 137; *Re Drake and Minister for Immigration and Ethnic Affairs (No 2)* (1979) 2 ALD 634.
67 P Cane, 'Judicial Review in the Age of Tribunals' [2009] *Public Law* 479, 494–5.
68 *Drake v Minister for Immigration and Ethnic Affairs* (1979) 2 ALD 60, 68.
69 D Bennett, 'Balancing Judicial and Merits Review' (2010) 53 *Admin Review* 3, 4.

'Correct or preferable' standard of merits review

The general standard for deciding the merits of the original decision is whether it is 'correct or preferable'. So the tribunal must decide whether the facts have been found correctly, whether the correct legal provision or principle has been identified and correctly applied, and – where the decision involves an exercise of judgement, typically where the decision-maker must be satisfied that statutory criteria have been met – whether the decision is the preferable one in the circumstances.[70] This has been described as 'administrative second thoughts',[71] or via the more colourful metaphor, 'standing in the shoes' of the original decision-maker.[72]

The expression 'correct or preferable' has a chequered history. It was coined in 1979,[73] and was adopted faithfully thereafter until the mid-1990s. However, the *Better Decisions* report in 1995 referred to the test as 'correct and preferable'.[74] As a consequence, the 'correct and preferable' test was expressly adopted in legislation governing the ADT in 1997,[75] the SAT in 2004[76] and QCAT in 2009.[77] Subsequently, however, the original formulation 'correct or preferable' was endorsed by the High Court.[78] No studies have been conducted to assess whether the different formulations have had an impact on outcomes in cases.

The 'preferable' element of the expression involves an exercise of judgement. What factors should be taken into account in making that judgement has, until recently, not been explored. However, in 2011 this gap was filled by a panel of the AAT led by Downes, the former President of the Tribunal. They concluded that the judgement involved in deciding what was 'preferable' could be informed by resort to community standards.[79] It remains to be seen whether the reliance on community standards to inform the decision-maker as to what is 'preferable' will be generally accepted.

---

70 *Collector of Customs (NSW) v Brian Lawlor Automotive Pty Ltd* (1979) 24 ALR 307, 335; *Shi v Migration Agents Registration Authority* (2008) 235 CLR 286, 299–300, 302 (Kirby J), 315 (Hayne and Heydon JJ), 325, 327–8, 332 (Kiefel J, Crennan J agreeing on this issue).
71 *Re Pastoral Lease No 531* (1970) 17 FLR 356, 360.
72 Used first in *Re Costello and Secretary, Department of Transport* (1979) 2 ALD 934, 943. See also *Budworth v Repatriation Commission* [2001] FCA 317, [51].
73 *Drake v Minister for Immigration and Ethnic Affairs* (1979) 46 FLR 409, 419.
74 Administrative Review Council, *Better Decisions: Review of Commonwealth Merits Review Tribunals*, Report No 39 (1995) (Better Decisions report) viii, ix.
75 ADT Act, ss 63(1), 115(1).
76 SAT Act, s 27(2).
77 QCAT Act, s 20(1).
78 *Shi v Migration Agents Registration Authority* (2008) 235 CLR 286, 298, 307 (Kirby J), 314–15 (Hayne and Heydon JJ), 324–5, 327–8 (Kiefel J, Crennan J agreeing on this point).
79 *Re Rent to Own (Australia) Pty Ltd and Australian Securities and Investment Commission* (2011) 127 ALD 141; *Re Visa Cancellation Applicant and Minister for Immigration and Citizenship* [2011] AATA 690.

The 'correct or preferable' standard is widely used but is not the only standard for tribunals. For example, the Superannuation Complaints Tribunal is required to review decisions according to whether they are 'fair and reasonable' in the circumstances,[80] and decisions about the suitability of a disability plan under the National Disability Insurance Scheme legislation are to be decided on the basis of what is 'reasonable and necessary'.[81] These differing merits review standards illustrate another flexible element of the tribunal model.

Other features of merits review are that, again unlike judicial review, a tribunal is generally not restricted to the material before the original decision-maker, that person's reasons, or the grounds on which review is sought.[82] In exercising its role, the tribunal may receive fresh evidence. As Deane J said in relation to the AAT in *Drake v Minister for Immigration and Ethnic Affairs*:

> The question for the determination of the Tribunal is not whether the decision which the decision maker made was the correct or preferable one on the material before him. The question for determination of the Tribunal is whether that decision was the correct or preferable one on the material before the Tribunal.[83]

The consequence is that the tribunal, as an independent decision-maker,[84] may take account of information not before the original decision-maker, and of developments – for example, deterioration or improvement of a medical condition or of behaviour[85] – since the initial decision was made. For this reason, merits review is often referred to as *de novo* review, that is, review afresh. This flexibility can be a significant advantage in tribunal review.

Mode of operations

Procedure and evidence

Tribunals were set up to operate differently from courts. Defining merits review is as much about the way in which disputes are settled, and about who is to

---

80 *Superannuation (Resolution of Complaints) Act 1993* (Cth), ss 37(6), 37(4).
81 *National Disability Insurance Scheme Act 2013* (Cth), s 34.
82 *Re Greenham and Minister for Capital Territory* (1979) 2 ALD 137; *Re Control Investments and Australian Broadcasting Tribunal (No 3)*(1981) 4 ALD 1; *Re Dennison and Civil Aviation Authority* (1989) 19 ALD 607. See also J McMillan 'Merit Review and the AAT: A Concept Develops' in J McMillan (ed), *The AAT – Twenty Years Forward* (Australian Institute of Administrative Law, 1998) 41–4.
83 *Drake v Minister for Immigration and Ethnic Affairs* (1979) 2 ALD 60, 68.
84 The courts regularly stress that this independence influences the AAT's functions. See, eg, *Shi v Migration Agents Registration Authority* (2008) 235 CLR 286, 327 (Kiefel J).
85 Eg, *Shi v Migration Agents Registration Authority* (2008) 235 CLR 286.

settle them, as it is about the criteria that are applied in settling those disputes. So the procedural rules applying in tribunals are critical. As with most aspects of tribunals, there is a spectrum of procedural models – from an adversarial, court-like or judicial model to those which rely solely or heavily on alternative dispute resolution mechanisms such as arbitration or mediation, and those which are made on the papers.

In many tribunals the accent is upon flexibility and informality in procedure. Three statutory provisions commonly found in the legislation of tribunals, relating to their procedure, epitomise their distinct role. The first is that tribunals are not bound by the rules of evidence and can decide what procedure they will adopt at their discretion; the second is that tribunals are intended to be inquisitorial as appropriate in their conduct of matters; and the third requires that tribunals operate in a manner which is 'fair, just, economical, informal and quick'. These principles do not mean, however, that the tribunal is not bound to observe natural justice.[86]

Rules of evidence

The intention was that the rules of evidence were not to apply in tribunals.[87] The formal rules of evidence were seen as time-consuming, expensive, a barrier for self-represented litigants, and inappropriate for the accessible, cheap and informal mode of operations envisaged for tribunals. As the Kerr Committee noted when recommending the body which emerged as the AAT: 'Lawyers should be prepared to reconcile themselves to techniques of analysis and investigation which are different from those in the common law courts'.[88] The minimum requirement for the AAT, and for subsequent tribunals which have been set up on a similar model, was that the tribunal 'shall inform itself as to the issues involved in such manner as it thinks fit, but procedures should be adopted to ensure that all material facts and matters of expert opinion are brought to the attention of the parties before a final decision is reached'.[89] In other words, there was an obligation on tribunals to develop procedures tailored to the matters they had to decide, and adapted to be exercised by individuals acting for themselves, to reflect the interventionist role envisaged for tribunals.[90]

The provisions do not mean, however, that the evidentiary rules that apply in courts, based as they are on well-tried principles, should not also guide the tribunal when appropriate. The rules, after all, represent the wisdom garnered over

---

86 Eg, VCAT Act, s 98(1).
87 Kerr Committee Report, above n 7, [295(g)].
88 Ibid, [334].
89 Ibid, [295(h)].
90 G D S Taylor, 'Access to Administrative Justice' (Paper presented to the conference *Australian Lawyers and Social Change II*, Canberra, 18–20 May 1979) 7.

centuries in countries with a common law judicial system about fair adjudicative process.[91] They are the method of inquiry 'best calculated to prevent error and elicit truth'.[92] As has been said, the rules of evidence impose 'a legal discipline on the administrative process'.[93] Nonetheless, the flexibility of process permitted tribunals has impacted on their operation and, for example, permits acceptance of evidence which would not be permissible in a court. The test adopted in tribunals is relevance, not whether the rules of evidence permit its use.[94] Nonetheless, the freedom not to be bound by the rules of evidence does not free a tribunal from adherence to the rules of fair process.[95]

Despite the permission for tribunals to operate differently from courts in relation to their procedures, lawyers' familiarity with courts' evidential rules inevitably means that they have been prone to adopt them in tribunals as well. This has led to what has been described as 'creeping legalism'.[96] While acknowledging that a level of formality has advantages, there have also been criticisms of this tendency.[97] In relation to VCAT, for example, the adoption of more formal legal process was perceived to be undermining public confidence in the tribunal.[98] The Skehill Review also expressed the opinion that 'the AAT should not seek to be "Court-like" – it should unashamedly seek to be "tribunal-like" – that is, less formal'.[99] At the same time, the Review accepted that the processes and procedures of a tribunal needed to be tailored to the type of matter being dealt with.

'May inform itself'

In addition to being free not to follow the rules of evidence, a tribunal is also often statutorily permitted to 'inform itself in any way it thinks fit'.[100] As Maxwell P said in *Weinstein v Medical Practitioners Board of Victoria*: 'The words "may inform itself..." were plainly intended to have work to do'.[101] The expression intended tribunals' hearings to be free of 'the judicial paradigm', and to ensure that their

---

91 *R v War Pensions Entitlement Appeals Tribunal; Ex parte Bott* (1933) 50 CLR 228, 256.
92 *Re Gee and Director-General of Social Services* (1981) 3 ALD 132; *Re Roche & Commonwealth of Australia* (1998) 16 ALD 787.
93 Australian Law Reform Commission, *Review of the adversarial system of litigation: federal tribunal proceedings* IP 24 (1998) [12.20].
94 *PQ v Australian Red Cross Society* [1992] 1 VR 19, 37–8.
95 *Weinstein v Medical Practitioners Board of Victoria* (2008) 21 VR 29, 37–8.
96 Bell, above n 16, 21, 26.
97 Australian Law Reform Commission, above n 93, [12.12]; Skehill Review, [7.53].
98 Bell, above n 16, 26.
99 Skehill Review, [7.54].
100 Eg, VCAT Act, s 52(1)(c). AAT Act, ss 2A, 33; ACAT Act, ss 8, 26; ADT Act, s 73(3); QCAT Act, s 28; VCAT Act, s 98(1)(d); SAT Act, s 32(2). For commentary see *Minister for Immigration and Multicultural Affairs v Eshetu* (1999) 197 CLR 611, 628.
101 *Weinstein v Medical Practitioners Board of Victoria* (2008) 21 VR 29, 37–8.

work 'was stamped with an inquisitorial character'.[102] Permission for tribunals to be more inquisitorial or investigative than courts was also recognised by French CJ and Kiefel J in *Minister for Immigration v SZGUR*,[103] when their Honours stated that 'the term "inquisitorial" has been applied to tribunal proceedings to distinguish them from adversarial proceedings and to characterise the tribunals' statutory functions'.

The Victorian Court of Appeal has noted that 'the essence of inquisitorial adjudication lies in the active participation of an impartial investigator from the earliest stages of the proceedings. The investigator has primary responsibility for defining the issue and is able to supervise the gathering of evidence'.[104] As the High Court noted too, of the Refugee Review Tribunal, but in words which are applicable to other tribunals when exercising their review function: 'the Tribunal was bound to make its own inquiries and form its own views upon the claim which the appellant made'.[105] The extent to which a tribunal should do so will turn upon the issues, the level of financial support for tribunal investigation, the willingness of the parties to undertake the evidence-gathering, and the provisions of its legislation.

There is a spectrum of ways in which the inquisitorial functions can be exercised. These range from that adopted in migration tribunals, which have a dedicated research team to identify and provide to members information about the circumstances in countries, for example, from which people have fled claiming persecution, to those tribunals which can call for and pay the fees to obtain further evidence, to the active, interventionist role of members personally questioning witnesses at a hearing.[106] Generally, however, tribunals have not been resourced to provide a fully fledged inquisitorial system of the kind which exists in many continental civil based systems of law.[107]

'Must act according to substantial justice'

The statutory provisions often provide that tribunals should 'act according to substantial justice and the merits of the case'. This expression reflects the need for tribunals to comply with natural justice as a minimum standard of fair process in all their dealings.[108]

---

102 Ibid, 38.
103 (2011) 241 CLR 594, 603.
104 *Weinstein v Medical Practitioners Board of Victoria* (2008) 21 VR 29, 37–8.
105 *Applicant VEAL of 2002 v Minister for Immigration and Multicultural and Indigenous Affairs* (2005) 225 CLR 88, 99.
106 N Bedford and R Creyke, *Inquisitorial Processes in Australian Tribunals* (AIJA, 2006); M Groves, 'The Duty to Inquire in Tribunal Proceedings' (2011) 33 *Sydney Law Review* 177; M Smyth, 'Inquisitorial Adjudication: The Duty to Inquire in Merits Review Tribunals' (2010) 34 *University of Melbourne Law Review* 230.
107 Australian Law Reform Commission, *Managing Justice* (Report No 89, 2000), [9.54], [9.62]–[9.63], [9.94 and recommendation 122]. That report usefully examines the meanings of 'inquisitorial' and 'adversarial' at [1.111]–[1.134].
108 Eg, *Migration Act 1958* (Cth), s 353 (MRT), s 420 (RRT); QCAT Act, s 28(2); SAT Act, s 2(2)(b); VCAT Act, s 98(1); ADT Act, s 73(3).

'Fair, just, economical, informal and quick'

The statutory purposes of many Australian tribunals contain this litany of objectives. They can be argued to be inconsistent in that being 'fair', that is, compliant with principles of natural justice, is not always possible while being 'informal' or 'quick'; and being quick may also lead to minimal standards of fair process. As the Administrative Review Council noted in the *Better Decisions* report: 'Achieving a procedural approach that provides fairness while promoting as far as possible the other objectives of merits review is a continuing challenge to all participants in the administrative review system'.[109]

Membership of tribunals

One of the key advantages of the tribunal model is the ability for its members to have a variety of qualifications and expertise. As the Kerr Committee noted, this 'would ensure that particular knowledge of the area of administration which produced the decision under review would be available to the tribunal'.[110] The greater expertise is perceived to produce better decisions because it broadens the experience which members bring to bear on decisions, particularly regarding factual matters, and having non-lawyers on a panel may make it easier for some users to present their cases.[111] The policy of appointing members with expertise appropriate for their areas of review puts pressure on tribunals with multiple areas of jurisdiction. Nonetheless, the advantages have been appreciated and the practice applies generally in tribunals in Australia.

Despite the emphasis on having a spread of experience and knowledge, it is also common for tribunals to have a judge at their head as a presidential member. That is the position in the AAT, and in all the multi-purpose tribunals except ACAT. The justification is that a judge can lend authority and respect to the tribunal, that judicial independence is a valuable attribute on the occasions when a tribunal makes decisions that are against current government policy, and that judicial experience is advantageous in handling complex legal issues. There are also procedural issues for some tribunals in that an appeal from a presidential member can go direct to a full court, thus obtaining an authoritative ruling on a contentious issue and limiting the costs to parties.[112]

---

109 Better Decisions report, above n 74, [3.9].
110 Kerr Committee Report, above n 7, [292].
111 Leggatt Review, above n 2, [1.12], [7.19].
112 Ibid, [1.12].

Impact of tribunal jurisprudence

Tribunals were established to be a cheaper, less formal and more accessible form of adjudication. The figures for applications finalised in tribunals indicate that these objectives are being met. In the 2012 financial year at the national level, the major tribunals[113] finalised over 30 000 matters,[114] while in the States and Territories, the principal tribunals collectively completed close to 200 000 applications.[115] Compare that figure with the number of applications finalised by the Federal Magistrates Court, the Federal Court and the High Court, of 18 546[116] – a number in which civil and administrative cases is only a subset – and it is apparent that the tribunals nationally are indeed the workhorse of civil and administrative law adjudication in Australia. A similar but even more striking picture would be displayed in the States and Territories. As Leggatt said of the system of tribunals in England and Wales, which collectively heard about a million cases a year at the time of his report, and which could equally be said pro rata of Australian tribunals: 'That number of cases alone makes their work of great importance to our society, since more of us bring a case before a tribunal than to any other part of the justice system'. The consequence is, as he said, that '[t]heir collective impact is immense'.[117]

The reality is that even though tribunal decisions do not in theory have precedential effect, in practice it is their decisions that are the substantial source of interpretation and administrative law principle applying to and accepted by citizens and by the executive. Tribunals enable citizens to test the legality and merits of government decisions that affect them, and are doing so with reasonable speed, efficiency and sensitivity to diverse users, applying flexible processes, and at a generally affordable cost. In that regard it can be said that tribunals are indeed the effective face of justice to the majority of Australians.

Conclusion

Despite being relative newcomers to the world of settling disputes, tribunals have already demonstrated their credentials as effective adjudicators. Not only do they shoulder the bulk of the dispute handling role, but they do so with flexibility, a

---

113 AAT, SSAT, VRB, MRT and RRT.
114 2012 annual reports of the AAT, SSAT, VRB, MRT and RRT.
115 2012 annual reports of ACAT, ADT, CTTT, QCAT, SAT and VCAT.
116 2012 annual reports of Federal Magistrates Court, the Federal Court and the High Court.
117 Leggatt Review, above n 2, [1.1].

greater depth of experience, and an ability to take into account all the factors impinging on a challenged decision which exceeds that of the courts. They have pioneered means of resolving disputes suitable for high volume areas such as traffic infringements or refugee claims, been at the forefront of moves to provide solutions to disputes other than through the traditional adversarial methodologies, and have exhibited a willingness to do so in ways which are attuned to the needs of particular users. They are prepared to hold hearings in intensive care units in hospitals, in nursing homes and mental health institutions, after hours for those in the workforce, and to accommodate users in regional and remote places. They do so not only by travelling to those remote and regional centres, but also by using a multitude of electronic mechanisms, including telephones, videoconferencing, SMS and Skype, and they are progressively developing tribunal electronic access points or portals which will enable users to access information, particularly as to the stage their claim has reached.

At the same time, federally tribunals have been hampered by their constitutionally ambiguous position, in the no man's land between the executive and the judicial arms of government. That has restricted their ability to devise for themselves an identity to match their achievements. That position is slowly being rectified, not least by their placement in the increasingly accepted 'fourth' arm of government. Moves to rectify this situation are the more essential because it is often the output from tribunals which guides the executive in its decision-making, and the public in its willingness to seek tribunal review. The development of their distinctive place in the adjudicative world is the challenge for Australian tribunals in the 21st century.

19

'FAIR IS FOUL AND FOUL IS FAIR': MIGRATION TRIBUNALS AND A FAIR HEARING

Linda Pearson

Introduction

It is beyond question that tribunals are required to comply with procedural fairness. Adjudicative tribunals are clearly subject to the implication that the powers conferred on them by statute are to be exercised with procedural fairness to those whose interests may be adversely affected.[1] Most also have an express statutory direction requiring them to act fairly.[2] The requirements of procedural fairness, namely that the person affected have a fair hearing: that is, be provided an opportunity to make their case and to respond to relevant adverse material; and second, that the decision-maker maintain a mind open to persuasion, are settled, at least in the abstract. What is required to constitute a 'fair' hearing in the circumstances of any decision-making process is, of course, another issue. This chapter asks how tribunals can ensure a 'fair' decision-making process when the capacity of the person to participate in a meaningful way in that process is compromised.

This issue is equally important for courts, but may be more complex for tribunals because they lack many of the procedural safeguards that come with formal evidentiary requirements and a formal onus of proof, or the power to appoint someone to act on behalf of an applicant,[3] and may be subject to specific legislated procedural requirements. This chapter focuses on the migration tribunals, whose task it is to review decisions made by departmental delegates of the Minister for Immigration; and on two potential impediments to meaningful participation, being psychological impairment, and language. That is not, however, intended to suggest that these issues are not relevant and significant for other tribunals, including those exercising original jurisdiction in matters such as appointment of substitute decision-makers,[4] or that other potential barriers to participation, such as cultural issues, are not important.[5]

The principal Commonwealth tribunals, namely the Administrative Appeals Tribunal (AAT), Social Security Appeals Tribunal (SSAT), Refugee Review Tribunal (RRT), Migration Review Tribunal (MRT) and Veterans Review Board (VRB) have

---

1 *Saeed v Minister for Immigration and Citizenship* (2010) 241 CLR 252; *Plaintiff M61/2010E v Commonwealth (Offshore Processing Case)* (2010) 243 CLR 319; *Plaintiff S10/2011 v Minister for Immigration and Citizenship* (2012) 86 ALJR 1019.
2 For example, s 2A of the *Administrative Appeals Tribunal Act 1975* (Cth) provides: 'In carrying out its functions, the Tribunal must pursue the objective of providing a mechanism of review that is fair, just, economical, informal and quick'.
3 For example, appointment of a guardian ad litem, or a tutor under rule 7.18 of the *Uniform Civil Procedure Rules 2005* (NSW), or a case guardian under Part 6.3 of the *Family Law Rules 2004* (Cth).
4 For example, appointment of a guardian or financial manager under the *Guardianship Act 1987* (NSW).
5 U Jayasinghe and R Hearn McKinnon, 'Sexual and Gender-Based Persecution and Tribunal Decision-Making: Challenges for Decision-Makers When Social and Cultural Mores Intersect with Administrative Review' (2008) 15 *Australian Journal of Administrative Law* 213.

in common the core function generally described in their legislation as being to 'review' the decision the subject of the application to the tribunal.[6] The nature of the decisions subject to review, and the powers of each tribunal in undertaking that review, vary. There is considerable procedural diversity among merits review tribunals, and there is no single template or model.[7] Whether or not it is, or has ever been, accurate to describe some tribunals as operating according to an 'adversarial' or 'inquisitorial' model, the point is that some jurisdiction-specific tribunals, such as the SSAT, MRT and RRT, have many inquisitorial features, and also that the generalist AAT adjusts its procedures according to the nature of the proceedings or the parties.[8] Labels are not necessarily helpful, or determinative, and the nature of any tribunal's functions is to be found in its legislation.[9]

The nature of the review task was explored in relation to the AAT by the High Court in *Shi v Migration Agents Registration Authority*,[10] where Kiefel J described the merits review task as requiring that the Tribunal reach its conclusion as to what is the correct decision by: conducting its own, independent, assessment and determination of the matters necessary to be addressed; addressing the same question that the original decision-maker was required to address; and, where the decision to be made contains no temporal element (as opposed to a decision where the Tribunal is limited to deciding the question by reference to a particular point in time), enabling the Tribunal to take into account evidence of matters occurring after the original decision in the process of informing itself.

Shi was unusual in its focus on the AAT, in contrast to the more regular consideration by the High Court (and the other federal courts) of questions arising from review of decisions of the specialist migration tribunals (the MRT and RRT). Judicial review of migration decisions has dominated federal judicial review both in numerical terms[11] and in the development of administrative law principles

---

6 *Minister for Immigration and Citizenship v SZIAI* (2009) 259 ALR 249, [18], referring to s 414 of the *Migration Act 1958* (Cth). See also *Administrative Appeals Tribunal Act 1975* (Cth), s 25; *Social Security (Administration) Act 1999* (Cth), s 142; *Veterans' Entitlements Act 1986* (Cth), s 135 .

7 R Creyke, 'Where Do Tribunals Fit into the Australian System of Adjudication?' in G Huscroft and M Taggart (eds), *Inside and Outside Canadian Administrative Law: Essays in Honour of David Mullan* (University of Toronto Press, 2006) 81–3.

8 N Bedford and R Creyke, *Inquisitorial Processes in Australian Tribunals* (AIJA, 2006); M Groves, 'The Duty to Inquire in Tribunal Proceedings' (2011) 33 *Sydney Law Review* 177, 181–2.

9 In *Minister for Immigration and Citizenship v SZIAI* (2009) 83 ALJR 1123, [18], the High Court noted that the label 'inquisitorial' as applied to the RRT does not carry its full ordinary meaning, and merely delimits the nature of the Tribunal's ordinary functions. See also M Aronson and M Groves, *Judicial Review of Administrative Action* (Thomson Reuters, 5th ed, 2013) 512–14.

10 (2008) 235 CLR 286, 327–8.

11 Administrative Review Council, *Federal Judicial Review in Australia* (Report 50, 2012) 65–9; S Gageler, 'Impact of migration law on the development of Australian administrative law' (2010) 17 *Australian Journal of Administrative Law* 92, 92.

generally.[12] Specific issues such as the extent of the statutory obligation to provide an opportunity for comment on adverse information, the relationship between the statutory procedural code and common law procedural fairness requirements, and the extent, if any, of an obligation on either tribunal to consider using the investigative powers conferred by the legislation, have been actively ventilated in the federal courts for some time.

Migration tribunals

Migration decision-making is a natural starting point for considering the question posed at the beginning of this chapter, for a number of reasons. The capacity of an applicant to participate meaningfully in the decision-making process can be of critical importance in refugee decision-making in particular, where, in the absence of corroborating documentary evidence, the credibility of the applicant may be determinative of whether their claims of past or feared future persecution are believed. The same can be said of some matters determined by the MRT: for example, whether a person is in a spousal relationship with another. It is not uncommon for those claiming to meet the criteria for protection – either that they hold a well-founded fear of being persecuted for reasons of race, religion, nationality, membership of a particular social group or political opinion in their country of nationality, or there is a real risk that if returned they will suffer significant harm – to have some psychological impairment such as post-traumatic stress disorder, which may affect their ability to participate.[13] Both the MRT and RRT adopt procedures that are as close to inquisitorial as are available in merits review tribunals, and, at least for the MRT, with a limited role for representatives,[14] which places added significance on what the applicant says at the hearing itself. Both rely heavily on the assistance of interpreters in conducting hearings. As a consequence,

---

12 Gageler, above n 11, 93.
13 A study conducted on use of expert psychological assessments in refugee decision-making found that 62 per cent of the sample of 52 applicants met diagnostic criteria for post-traumatic stress disorder; 67 per cent for major depressive disorder; and 55 per cent for both disorders: J Hunter, Z Steel, L Pearson, M San Roque, D Silove, N Frommer and R Redman, *Tales of the Unexpected and Refugee Status Decision-making: Managing and Understanding Psychological Issues Among Refugee Applicants* (UNSW, 2010) 25.
14 Section 366A of the Migration Act applies to MRT hearings, and provides that an applicant is entitled to have another person present at a hearing to assist him or her; however, the assistant is not entitled to present arguments to the Tribunal or to address the Tribunal unless the Tribunal is satisfied that, because of exceptional circumstances, the assistant should be allowed to do so.

the question posed in this chapter is of crucial significance for decision-making by the migration tribunals.

The challenge is whether it is possible to disentangle principles applicable to administrative decision-making generally from those dependent on the detail of migration legislation and the factual context of migration decision-making, and whether those parameters detract from the tribunals' capacity to provide a fair hearing.

In reviewing migration decisions, the courts have required adherence to the specific elements of the legislative framework, against a background of frequent shifts in migration legislation. Those shifts, and the influence of migration law on the development of administrative law principles more generally, have been comprehensively traced by the former Solicitor General, in themes which he described as discretion (1901–89); prescription (1989–92); limitation (1992–2001); and privation (2001–03); to the present targeted tinkering.[15] Of particular significance for the issues addressed in this chapter were the period of limitation on the grounds of judicial review (in particular, the exclusion of breach of procedural fairness other than actual bias) from 1994 to 2001, which led to litigation testing the boundaries of other legislative requirements;[16] and the addition in 2002 of provisions stating that the procedural requirements for decision-making by delegates, the MRT and RRT, were an exhaustive statement of the requirements of the natural justice hearing rule, which generated litigation concerning the extent to which there remained room for the implication of additional procedural fairness obligations based on the common law.[17]

The *Migration Act 1958* (Cth) requires the MRT and RRT to 'pursue the objective of providing a mechanism of review that is fair, just, economical, informal and quick', and to 'act according to substantial justice and the merits of the case'.[18] Two additional obligations currently imposed on the MRT and RRT by the Migration Act are particularly relevant. The first is the obligation imposed on the tribunals to 'invite the applicant to appear…to give evidence and present arguments relating to the issues arising in relation to the decision under review',[19] which raises issues

---

15 Gageler, above n 11.
16 See, eg, *Minister for Immigration and Multicultural and Indigenous Affairs v Yusuf* (2001) 206 CLR 323 (obligation to give reasons); *Minister for Immigration and Multicultural Affairs v Eshetu* (1999) 197 CLR 611 (on whether the obligation in s 420, to act according to substantial justice, imposed substantive obligations).
17 In *Saeed v Minister for Immigration and Citizenship* (2010) 241 CLR 252, the High Court adopted a narrow reading of the provision in identifying the extent of the specific 'matters' it dealt with.
18 Sections 353 (MRT) and 420 (RRT).
19 Sections 360 (MRT) and 425 (RRT).

as to the relationship between the invitation and the hearing that follows. Second, the obligation imposed on the tribunals in applying the provisions relating to their conduct of a review, to 'act in a way that is fair and just',[20] which has generated divergence of views on the content, and consequences of breach, of that obligation.

Invitation to a hearing

The Full Court of the Federal Court in *Minister for Immigration and Multicultural Affairs v SCAR*[21] considered the obligation imposed by s 425 to invite the applicant to appear to give evidence and present arguments, in a context where the applicant for a protection visa had, at the time of its hearing, and unbeknownst to the RRT, been medicated and was suffering extreme distress after being informed of his father's death. The RRT had found that his evidence concerning a number of aspects of his claims was vague, confused and implausible, and that he was not a credible or reliable witness. On judicial review, the primary judge held that the applicant had not been in a fit state to represent himself, and because of his emotional and medical condition, had been treated (albeit innocently) unfairly, and there had not been a bona fide attempt to exercise the Tribunal's power.[22]

On appeal, the Full Court agreed that there had been jurisdictional error, based on a failure to comply with s 425. The Court noted that s 425 did not require that the Tribunal actively assist the applicant in putting his or her case, nor to carry out an inquiry in order to identify what that case might be. It did, however, impose an objective requirement on the Tribunal: namely, an obligation to provide a 'real and meaningful' invitation to appear to give evidence and present arguments. Compliance with s 425 was a precondition to the valid exercise of jurisdiction, and failure to comply with its requirements involved a jurisdictional error.

The decision in *SCAR* has not met with universal approval.[23] The divergence of views within the Federal Court was captured in the judgments of French and

---

20 Sections 357A(3) (MRT) and 422B(3) (RRT). Sections 357A and 422B are part of Part 5 Div 5 and Part 6 Div 4, which provide for the conduct of review for the MRT and RRT respectively, and were inserted by the *Migration Legislation Amendment (Procedural Fairness) Act 2002* from 4 July 2002 to provide that the Divisions, and specified provisions, are 'taken to be an exhaustive statement of the requirements of the natural justice hearing rule' in relation to the matters they deal with. The latter limitation is important, the High Court in *Saeed* concluding that while those provisions entirely exclude the hearing rule for the matters to which they refer, the statutory procedures are not an exhaustive statement of natural justice for applications not expressly included. See Chapter 10.
21 (2003) 128 FCR 553.
22 Ibid, 557.
23 *SZLBE v Minister for Immigration and Citizenship* [2008] FCA 1789, [23] (Middleton J).

Graham JJ in *Minister for Immigration and Multicultural Affairs v SZFDE*.[24] Graham J held that s 425 required an appropriate invitation followed by a corresponding hearing at which the opportunity to give evidence and present arguments was afforded to an applicant; however, any shortcomings of the Tribunal in respect of the provision of a corresponding hearing would fall to be determined according to the rules of natural justice, and such shortcomings would raise issues which were separate and distinct from the sufficiency of the invitation required by s 425. In so far as *SCAR* requires more of an invitation to appear than compliance with the terms of the Act, Graham J concluded it was plainly wrong and should not be followed.[25] French J disagreed, holding that while there may be room for debate about the reasoning in *SCAR*, it was not plainly wrong; in any event, the scope of the obligation to extend an invitation to the hearing was not critical to the determinative question in that case.

The determinative question in *SZFDE* was the effect of the fraud of the family's agent in persuading them not to appear before the RRT, which meant that SZFDE's application for review of the refusal of her claim for protection was decided without a hearing. The High Court noted that the importance of the statutory obligation in s 425 to invite applicants to a hearing was amplified by a further provision which stated that this and other procedural obligations were 'taken to be an exhaustive statement' of the hearing rule 'in relation to the matters it deals with'. The Court explained:

> An effective subversion of the operation of s 425 also subverts the observance by the Tribunal of its obligation to accord procedural fairness to applicants for review. Given the significance of procedural fairness for the principles concerned with jurisdictional error, sourced in s 75(v) of the Constitution, the subversion of the processes of the Tribunal in the manner alleged by the present appellants is a matter of the first magnitude...

In *SZFDE* the fraud of the agent had subverted the operation of s 425, and s 426A which permitted the Tribunal to make a decision on the review in the absence of an appearance, both provisions of central importance for the legislative scheme for the conduct of review. The stultification of the operation of the natural justice provisions in the Act meant that the Tribunal was disabled from the due discharge of its imperative statutory functions with respect to the conduct of the review, and the Tribunal had failed to discharge its duty to conduct a review.[26]

---

24 (2006) 154 FCR 365.
25 Ibid, 417.
26 (2007) 232 CLR 189, 206. For a discussion of *SZFDE*, see M Groves, 'The Surrogacy Principle and Motherhood Statements in Administrative Law' in L Pearson, C Harlow and M Taggart (eds), *Administrative Law in a Changing State: Essays in Honour of Mark Aronson* (Hart Publishing, 2008) 71–97.

In *Minister for Immigration and Citizenship v SZNVW*,[27] Keane CJ noted that in the context of those proceedings it was not necessary to enter into the controversy as to the correctness of the reasoning underlying *SCAR*.[28] Emmett J noted that the Court was not invited to hold that the decision was clearly wrong, but to distinguish it.[29] Perram J noted that *SCAR* presently represents the established jurisprudence of the Federal Court but was careful to confine that case. He held that the analysis in that case turns not on whether an applicant was afforded a fair hearing, but rather depends on a characterisation of the quality of the invitation given to the applicant in light of the hearing which in fact took place: did the Tribunal conduct a review?[30]

The answer to that question in *SZNVW* was 'yes'.[31] In *SCAR* the Tribunal had been oblivious to the facts which established that the applicant did not have a full and fair opportunity to present his case; here, the applicant had provided a statement from a psychologist, and had sought to rely on his psychological problems first to explain his delay in applying for a visa, and then as a possible explanation for what might otherwise be regarded as unsatisfactory aspects of his evidence. Section 425 did not require the Tribunal to press an applicant to call further evidence of his psychological problems or expand his arguments relating to the ramifications of his problems for any aspect of the case he sought to present.[32]

Section 425 requires an 'invitation'. In *SCAR* the Court noted that s 425 was not a code setting out all the requirements for a fair hearing by the RRT, being directed at the invitation, rather than the hearing itself; however, compliance with s 425 was 'a necessary condition and element of a fair hearing by the Tribunal'.[33] In *SZNVW*, Perram noted the curiosity of grafting the obligation onto the requirement for an invitation, which s 425 provides, rather than onto any obligation to conduct a hearing, for which the legislation did not provide: s 414 imposes the basal requirement to conduct a 'review', but that need not involve a hearing.[34] Despite these reservations, the requirement that the invitation be meaningful, in the sense of providing an application with a real chance to present his or her case, has received confirmation in the High Court decision in *Minister for Immigration v Li*,[35] where Hayne, Kiefel and Bell JJ referred with approval to *Applicant NAHF of 2002 v Minister for Immigration and Multicultural and*

---

27 (2010) 183 FCR 575, 585.
28 Ibid.
29 Ibid, 588.
30 Ibid, 594–5.
31 Ibid, 586 (Keane CJ); 588 (Emmett J); and 594 (Perram J).
32 Ibid, at 582 (Keane CJ).
33 (2003) 128 FCR 553, 561.
34 (2010) 183 FCR 575, 595.
35 (2013) 297 ALR 225, [61].

Indigenous Affairs[36] for the proposition that scheduling a hearing on a date which, to the Tribunal's knowledge, would not permit an applicant to have sufficiently recovered from an incapacity to attend would not fulfil the duty imposed by s 425 and s 360.

Acting in a way that is 'fair and just'

Sections 357A(3) and 422B(3), which provide that in applying the provisions relating to the conduct of review, the MRT and RRT must 'act in a way that is fair and just', were enacted in 2007, after the decision in *SCAR*. *SZNVW* did not consider whether the addition of s 422B(3) had affected the application of *SCAR* and its reasoning based on s 425 of the Act.[37] The issue which has subsequently arisen for consideration is whether all those provisions, together with the legislative direction in ss 353 and 420(1) that the Tribunals provide a mechanism of review that is 'fair, just', have substantive content.

In *Minister for Immigration and Citizenship v SZMOK*,[38] the argument was that the RRT had failed to accord procedural fairness and comply with s 422B(3) by failing to warn the applicant that it would reject a number of documents provided by him after the hearing. Those documents were translations of what were asserted to be false charges brought against the applicant in Bangladesh, which the applicant had raised for the first time at the hearing. Emmett, Kenny and Jacobson JJ were satisfied that the Tribunal had simply said it would consider any documents provided, and it did so; there was no failure to comply with the provisions of Div 4 in the Tribunal's conduct of the review, and no failure to comply with s 425; and there was nothing unfair or unjust in the way in which the Tribunal applied Division 4 in its conduct of the review. In the course of reaching that conclusion, the Court considered whether the introduction of s 422B(3) had impinged on the operation of s 422B(1). The Court held that s 422B(3) should be understood as an exhortative provision in the same way as s 420(1), and should not be understood as creating a procedural requirement over and beyond what was expressly provided for in Division 4;[39] it was not a free-standing obligation;[40] and in the context where it is possible that the procedural powers in Division 4 could be used in ways that were not fair, s 422B(3) 'might be understood as restoring fairness and justice as a procedural concept'.[41]

---

36 (2003) 128 FCR 359.
37 Perram J noted that no argument had been advanced that the insertion of s 422B(3) impacts on the continuing relevance of *SCAR*: (2010) 183 FCR 575, 594.
38 [2009] FCAFC 83.
39 Ibid, [15].
40 Ibid, [16].
41 Ibid, [18].

A different view was taken in *Minister for Immigration and Citizenship v Li*.[42] The MRT had refused to allow an adjournment to enable the applicant to pursue a review by the relevant skills assessing authority of an adverse skills assessment, satisfaction of which was one of the criteria for the grant of a Skilled – Independent Overseas Student (Residence) visa. Greenwood and Logan JJ departed from the reasoning in *SZMOK*, holding that s 353 (the analogue of s 420) did contain substantive requirements;[43] and that the same conclusion necessarily followed in relation to the prescription of fairness in s 357A(3) (the analogue of s 422B(3)).[44] The description of s 420 as 'exhortative' in *Eshetu* had to be understood against the statutory context of the time, which then included the limitations on the grounds of review in s 476, and the resolution of the relationship between s 420 and the then s 476 in terms of the permissible grounds of review.[45] The repeal of the then s 476 did not mean that the substantive requirements in s 420 in respect of the conduct of a review had disappeared or could be ignored, and did not mean that non-observance of those requirements could not constitute jurisdictional error; and further, s 353 was a requirement imposed on the Tribunal in the discharge of its core function of reviewing decisions.[46]

Greenwood and Logan JJ relied on *Bhardwaj* as authority for the proposition that an unreasonable denial of a request for an adjournment is one way in which an applicant for review can be denied an opportunity to be heard and thereby the rules of natural justice breached; and that when a tribunal fails in this way to offer an opportunity to be heard, it fails to discharge the core statutory function of reviewing the decision of the Minister or his delegate.[47] They continued:

> Necessarily, where the MRT behaves in this fashion it has also not met the requirement of providing a mechanism of review that is 'fair' (s 353) or 'acted in a way that is fair and just' (s 357A(3)). It may well be that these particular provisions add nothing to the general law ground of a denial of procedural fairness which can constitute jurisdictional error for the purposes of s 75(v) of The Constitution. On reflection, and with the benefit of expressly considering both *SZMOK* and *SZGUR*, we consider that this is the better way to view the prescriptions for 'fairness' found in s 353 and s 357A(3).

---

42 (2012) 202 FCR 387.
43 Ibid, 393.
44 Ibid, 394. Collier J disagreed, holding (at [83]) that s 357A(3) is an exhortative provision which does not create a procedural requirement over and beyond the express provisions of Part 5 Div 5 of the Act.
45 Ibid, 391–3.
46 Ibid, 393, referring to *Minister for Immigration and Citizenship v SZGUR* (2011) 241 CLR 594 at [19] (French CJ and Kiefel JJ, Heydon and Crennan JJ agreeing).
47 Ibid, 395, citing *Minister for Immigration and Multicultural Affairs v Bhardwaj* (2002) 209 CLR 597.

> Even if these sections are only declaratory, they are not, in our respectful opinion, thereby to be consigned to the status of aspirational statements, as opposed to requirements. It is just that, as with the general law error ground, neither can have any particular content divorced from the circumstances of a particular case or the statutory context in which they appear.

The appearance afforded to an applicant by the invitation under s 360 'must be meaningful, not perfunctory, or it will be no appearance at all', and an unreasonable refusal of an adjournment will not just deny a meaningful appearance, it will mean that the MRT has not discharged its *core* statutory function of reviewing a decision, and that failure constitutes jurisdictional error.[48]

Greenwood and Logan JJ concluded that the refusal to adjourn denied the applicant a reasonable opportunity to present her case, and that was a denial of procedural fairness amounting to jurisdictional error. Collier J held that the failure properly to consider the application for an adjournment was an error going to jurisdiction, on the basis that it amounted to a failure to give the applicant a reasonable opportunity to present evidence and argument within the meaning of s 360.[49]

The decision of the High Court on appeal in *Li* has gone some way towards resolving some of these issues, while raising others.[50] French CJ described s 353 as having a 'facultative rather than restrictive purpose'.[51] Gageler J held that s 357A(3) and s 353 'are couched in language that is broad and best seen to be exhortatory or aspirational'.[52] However, for Gageler J, while a 'mere erroneous application' of the requirements of those provisions would not amount to a failure to comply with a requirement essential to the valid performance of the duty to review a decision, their 'neglect' did; and that neglect need not be the result of bad faith but could be the product of unreasonableness.[53] Hayne, Kiefel and Bell JJ referred to the reasoning in *SZMOK*, and the conclusion that a breach of the requirements of s 375A(3) might not have the same consequences as a breach of common law procedural fairness obligations, but noted that the Federal Court had not considered the role of s 75(v) of the *Constitution*. While expressly declining to determine what s 357A(3) requires, and what might be a consequence of a breach of that requirement, their Honours went on to hold that even if s 357A(3) by itself had no consequence for the ultimate decision of the Tribunal, 'it might nevertheless be concluded that the

---

48 Ibid, 395.
49 Ibid, 413.
50 In particular, the place of rationality and reasonableness in lawful decision-making, and the discussion by the plurality of the potential for jurisdictional error outside error based on a specific ground of review: see Chapter 12.
51 [2013] HCA 18, [15].
52 Ibid, [96].
53 Ibid, [97].

purpose of s 360(1) was not met'; it was, however, not necessary to determine the appeal on that basis.[54]

The focus on particular statutory requirements for the lawful conduct of the review required to be provided by the migration tribunals, in particular the invitation required by s 425 and s 360, is central to the approach of the courts in examining how those tribunals can provide a fair hearing for an applicant with psychological impairment, or for whom communication requires the assistance of an interpreter.

Psychological issues

Psychological impairment arising from past trauma, or from other factors, including illnesses such as depression, can impact on fitness to participate in the decision-making process. Trauma can impact upon a person's ability to give coherent oral evidence, through memory impairment, poor presentation, and difficulties in the reporting of information. Traumatic stress responses can lead to increased likelihood of errors in the recounting and reporting of experiences, which can manifest in: discrepancies in accounts across repeated interviews; reduced specificity of traumatic memory, leading to reporting of overgeneralised memories; increased attention towards central as opposed to peripheral aspects of traumatic events; and avoidance of intrusive traumatic memories, numbing, and dissociation.[55] Such responses can be significant for decision-makers, who generally focus, where credibility is in issue, on consistency, coherence, spontaneous disclosure of important information, and demeanour.[56]

Evidence as to an applicant's psychological condition or presentation can be relevant in asylum decision-making in relation to the fitness of the applicant to give evidence, or as corroborative of claims of past persecution or trauma.[57] It can be relevant in assisting the decision-maker to determine how to evaluate the evidence given – for example, in providing an explanation for apparent inconsistencies or delayed disclosure. It can also be relevant in assisting the decision-maker to understand what procedural accommodations, such as frequent breaks, should be made. The presence of a psychological condition does not of itself preclude meaningful participation in a hearing process, and the supporting evidence will

---

54 Ibid, [62], [86].
55 Hunter et al., n 13, 24. See also J Herlihy and S Turner, 'The Pyschology of Seeking Protection' (2009) 21 *International Journal of Refugee Law* 171–92.
56 Hunter et al., n 13, 16. See also C Rousseau, F Crepeau, P Foxen and F Houle, 'The complexity of determining refugeehood: A multidisciplinary analysis of the decision-making process of the Canadian Immigration and Refugee Board' (2002) 15 *Journal of Refugee Studies* s 43.
57 *Minister for Immigration and Citizenship v MZYHS* [2011] FCA 53.

need to make clear the connection between the condition and any asserted barrier to participation.[58]

SCAR is authority for the proposition that a meaningful invitation to appear, give evidence and present argument requires that the applicant is in fact in a fit state to represent himself or herself. In *NAMJ v Minister for Immigration and Multicultural and Indigenous Affairs*,[59] Branson J reasoned that, while the requirement was likely to intend that a tribunal hearing proceed notwithstanding some measure of psychological distress or disorder in the applicant, there is a point at which an applicant's psychological state would render a tribunal hearing a nullity. Branson J was reluctant to attempt to formulate an exhaustive test of 'fitness' to take part in a tribunal hearing: fitness would have to be assessed having regard to the particular circumstances of each case, including the intended purpose of the hearing and the support and assistance available to the applicant.[60] In the circumstances of the case before her Honour, the applicant needed the capacity to understand that the Tribunal was concerned that he had apparently advanced two separate sets of claims, and considered that his credibility was for that reason suspect; and he further needed the capacity to understand and respond to the questions put by the Tribunal concerning his experiences in his country of nationality and the process by which his claim to a protection visa had been prosecuted in Australia.[61]

The applicant NAMJ was accompanied to the RRT hearing by a registered migration agent and an individual from a social welfare organisation. He provided two expert reports to the RRT, one from a clinical psychologist who expressed the opinion that he was unable to competently give evidence due to his chronic psychological impairment, and the other, received after the hearing, from a professor of general practice who noted that the applicant exhibited severe psychological symptoms and signs consistent with post-traumatic stress disorder and depression, including psychomotor retardation and some slowness of speech when answering questions, but no evidence of neurological deficit. In determining whether the invitation to appear at the Tribunal had been meaningful, Branson J had regard to the two expert reports; to oral evidence given by the psychologist, who had listened to the tapes of the Tribunal hearing; and to the report of the hearing contained in the reasons of the Tribunal. The Tribunal reasons indicated that the applicant engaged in extreme behaviour at times, but not consistently, during the hearing. Branson J concluded that the extreme behaviour was not sufficiently persistent to prevent the member of the Tribunal from conducting the hearing as required by the Act, nor was it sufficient of itself to prevent the applicant from

---

58 *Minister for Immigration and Citizenship v SZGUR* (2011) 241 CLR 594, 620–21 (Gummow J).
59 (2003) 76 ALD 56.
60 Ibid, [58].
61 Ibid, [59].

giving evidence and presenting arguments to the Tribunal. The other evidence supported a conclusion that at the time of the hearing the applicant exhibited symptoms consistent with those described by the professor of general practice. Branson J was not satisfied, however, that the applicant's psychological condition was such as to deprive the hearing conducted by the RRT of the meaning which the Act intended it to have.

It is not apparent from the judgment in *NAMJ* whether the tapes of the Tribunal hearing or a transcript were available. However, the recorded reasons of the RRT included a detailed description of the applicant's presentation and the steps taken by the Tribunal member to ensure that the applicant understood the questions asked. Branson J noted that the Tribunal member should be assumed to have experience in interviewing individuals under stress and in making a judgement as to the fitness of the applicant to take part in the hearing, and so weight should be accorded by the reviewing Court to the view taken by the Tribunal member.

Central to the decision in *NAMJ* was the application of the accepted principle that the onus of establishing that he was unfit to take part in the Tribunal hearing was on the applicant. It is for the applicant to determine what evidence he or she wishes to rely upon, and that may be of particular significance given the limited extent to which the Tribunals might be under any obligation to exercise their powers of inquiry in obtaining assessments or reports relating to an applicant's psychological state.[62] *SCAR* and *SZNW* confirm that whatever is the extent to which s 425 requires a 'meaningful' invitation, or extends to the nature of any hearing, it does not require a Tribunal to press a claimant to call evidence as to whatever psychological problems he or she may seek to rely upon.[63]

The significance of this is illustrated in *SZMSA v Minister for Immigration and Citizenship*.[64] The RRT was advised that an applicant could not participate in a hearing scheduled for September 2007 due to poor health, being 'Post-Traumatic Stress Disorder and Major Depression'. A psychiatrist advised that he may be ready to participate in about two months' time, depending on his response to medication. The RRT arranged through Health Services Australia for an assessment by a psychiatrist, who reported in October 2007 that the applicant had presented with features consistent with a major depressive episode on a background of post-traumatic stress disorder, and was currently unfit to participate in a hearing. The Tribunal invited the applicant to attend a hearing in April 2008, and the applicant indicated that he wished to attend. That hearing was postponed at the

---

62 *Minister for Immigration and Multicultural and Indigenous Affairs v SGLB* (2004) 207 ALR 12; *Minister for Immigration and Citizenship v SZGUR* (2011) 241 CLR 594; M Groves, 'The Duty to Inquire in Tribunal Proceedings' (2011) 33 *Sydney Law Review* 177.
63 *SZMSF v Minister for Immigration and Citizenship* [2010] FCA 585, [20] (Flick J).
64 [2010] FCA 345.

Tribunal's request until July 2008, and the applicant attended and participated. On review, a transcript of the RRT hearing was in evidence, which supported the Tribunal's assessment that the applicant's answers to questions had been responsive and detailed. The fact that the applicant suffered from depression and post-traumatic stress disorder and continued to receive treatment was relevant to, but not determinative of, his fitness to participate in the hearing in July 2008. It was significant that there had been no request to postpone that hearing or the one scheduled for April 2008, and that no medical report was adduced to support an assertion that the applicant was not fit to participate in the July 2008 hearing.

There was no suggestion in *SCAR* that the applicant's inability to participate meaningfully in the hearing process was other than a temporary response to his father's death, and the obvious response to a temporary incapacity such as that would be to reschedule the hearing. That is one of a range of procedural responses open to the Tribunals, although one that needs to be considered against the Tribunals' time standards, which include 90 days from receipt of the Department's documents to a decision in protection visa refusals.[65] The MRT and RRT have developed *Guidance on Vulnerable Persons*,[66] which outlines steps that might be taken to address the needs of individuals who face particular difficulties in the review process, including those who have experienced physical or psychological abuse or trauma, or with mental illness or emotional disorder. Options to assist such persons to participate effectively at a tribunal hearing include encouraging the person to be supported during the hearing, allowing reasonable procedural accommodations, providing breaks or adjournments, or holding a second hearing if the person is becoming emotionally distressed. The *Guidance* outlines particular strategies to assist if impairments are associated with psychological and psychiatric conditions, noting that such impairments might include impaired attention and concentration, disturbances in form and content of mood, or memory impairment. The *Guidance* suggests consideration of alternative means of obtaining evidence, for example by allowing evidence through video conferencing, or taking evidence from family members or close friends, if a person has difficulty in providing oral evidence in person, or is highly agitated or unable to provide coherent evidence.

The *Guidance*, and the authorities, do not provide an answer for a Tribunal faced with an applicant for whom a psychological impairment is so extreme that it is simply not possible for them to participate, even if the hearing is postponed or adjourned. Groves has suggested that a consequence of *SCAR* might be that if

---

65 The High Court decision in *Minister for Immigration and Citizenship v Li* (2013) 297 ALR 225, on appeal from a review of a MRT decision not subject to that time frame, would appear to require a Tribunal member to expressly address such considerations in considering the exercise of discretionary powers including the power to adjourn a review.
66 Available at <www.mrt-rrt.gov.au/Conduct-of-reviews/Legislation,-policies-and-guidelines.aspx>.

a valid hearing could not occur so long as the applicant was unfit to appear to give evidence, the Tribunal may not be able to discharge its central function.[67] While there would, applying *NAMJ*, be no jurisdictional barrier (in the sense of a threshold competency requirement) to the RRT proceeding with a review in those circumstances, there remains the practical issue of how it should go about it. In *SZMSF v Minister for Immigration and Citizenship*,[68] Flick J suggested that when a disability becomes so severe that it denies a party an opportunity to be heard, or to be effectively heard in a meaningful manner, 'difficult factual judgments [may] need to be made'.

Language

Procedural fairness may require in some circumstances that a person be permitted to use an interpreter at a hearing; whether that extends to a right to an interpreter in administrative decision-making more generally is another issue.[69] Tribunal legislation and practice may address the issue. The MRT, for example, is required to provide an interpreter at the request of a person appearing before the Tribunal, unless it considers that the person is sufficiently proficient in English, or even if there is no request, if it considers that the person is not sufficiently proficient in English.[70] In contrast, the RRT *may* direct that communication with a person during his or her appearance proceed through an interpreter, if the person is not proficient in English.[71] In practice, an interpreter is provided by the Tribunals, at their expense, for the majority of hearings.[72]

The courts accept that a person with reasonable knowledge of English for some purposes will not necessarily be sufficiently proficient to give evidence in a hearing in support of an application vital to his or her prospects.[73] When inviting an applicant to a hearing, the MRT and RRT ask the applicant to specify if an interpreter is requested, and endeavour to provide an interpreter of a particular gender, dialect, ethnicity or religion if such a request is made by the applicant

---

67 M Groves, 'Do Administrative Tribunals Have to be Satisfied of the Competence of Parties Before Them?' (2013) 20 *Psychiatry, Psychology and Law* 133, 136.
68 [2010] FCA 585, [32].
69 Aronson and Groves, above n 9, 577.
70 Migration Act, s 366C. That does not require the MRT to provide an interpreter for *all* oral communication with an applicant, only when the applicant is giving evidence: *Minister for Immigration and Citizenship v Le* (2007) 164 FCR 151.
71 Migration Act, s 427(7).
72 In 2011–12, for 58 per cent of MRT and 83 per cent of RRT hearings, in 84 languages and dialects: *Annual Report 2011–12*, vii.
73 *Perera v Minister for Immigration and Multicultural Affairs* (1999) 92 FCR 6, [35].

or where the Tribunals consider it appropriate.[74] Even if the applicant does not request an interpreter, the Tribunals may arrange for an interpreter to be present at the hearing to interpret if the member considers that the applicant is not sufficiently proficient in English.[75] The Tribunals prefer to use interpreters accredited at Interpreter level or above with the National Accreditation Authority for Translators and Interpreters (NAATI), but NAATI does not accredit all languages, at all levels.[76] Interpreters are expected to be independent, and the Tribunals will not engage an interpreter specifically requested by name by the applicant or their representative.[77]

Access to an interpreter is one thing; ensuring an adequate interpretation is another. Adequate interpretation takes on particular significance in asylum decision-making, where credibility is often critical.[78] The interpreting task has been described as being in essence 'to get the real meaning of what's being said across',[79] which includes 'the meaning of words in context, the appropriate use of language according to tongue, culture and situation'.[80] Interpreting requires not simply a literal word for word translation, and the interpreter may be required to convey a meaning of a word or phrase in one language for which there may be no precise or similar equivalent in another.[81] The courts have attempted to state general principles applicable to tribunal proceedings. In *Perera v Minister for Immigration and Multicultural Affairs*,[82] Kenny J explained:

> there is rarely an exact lexical correspondence but, even so, some interpretations are better than others. Whilst the interpretation at a Tribunal hearing need not be at the very highest standard of a first-flight interpreter, the interpretation must, nonetheless, express in one language, as accurately as that language and the circumstances permit, the idea or concept as it has been expressed in the other language.

---

74 MRT and RRT, *Interpreter Handbook*, 2011, 8.
75 Ibid.
76 S Hale, *Interpreter Policies, Practices and Protocols in Australian Courts and Tribunals A National Survey* (AIJA, 2011) 20.
77 That approach is not universal. In her study of current interpreting practices in Australian courts and tribunals, Hale noted in many instances a lack of appreciation of the importance of competent interpreters in ensuring accuracy and fairness, and that issues of impartiality were often overlooked when using the services of non-professional interpreters such as a friend, family member, or another litigant: Hale, n 76, 17.
78 *Long v Minister for Immigration and Multicultural Affairs* [2000] FCA 1172.
79 *R v Watt* [2007] QCA 286, [39].
80 S Hale, *The Discourse of Court Interpreting: Discourse Practices of the Law, the Witness and the Interpreter* (2004), cited in A Hayes and S Hale, 'Appeals on Incompetent Interpreting' (2010) *Journal of Judicial Administration* 119, 127.
81 M Barnett, 'Mind Your Language: Interpreters in Australian Immigration Proceedings' (2004) 10 *University of Western Sydney Law Review* 109.
82 (1999) 92 FCR 6, 19.

Kenny J suggested that relevant criteria include: continuity, such that breaks in interpretation and mere summaries of a proceeding would not be acceptable; impartiality; precision; competency; and possibly contemporaneousness.[83] In *WAIZ v Minister for Immigration and Multicultural Affairs*,[84] Carr J confirmed that the interpreting must be complete: in that case, the Court found that as a consequence of a break in the telephone transmission, a relevant question had not been properly translated; the breakdown in transmission at that critical point effectively prevented the applicant from giving his evidence in relation to a matter of considerable significance for his claim and, in turn, for the Tribunal's decision, and as a consequence, there was an unwitting jurisdictional error.

In some instances, the courts have had no difficulty in accepting that interpretation has been inadequate: for example, where the applicant requested a Punjabi interpreter, as that was the language he spoke best, and part of the hearing was conducted in Hindi;[85] or where the interpreter interpreted the word 'persecution' as 'prosecution' throughout the hearing.[86] Other circumstances are more complex, and not every lapse in interpreting standards will invalidate a decision.[87] The courts generally rely on the transcript of the Tribunal proceedings, and in some instances, on evidence from other interpreters.[88] In *Perera*, Kenny J found that, considering the transcript as a whole, the applicant's evidence was repeatedly unresponsive, at times incoherent and inexplicably inconsistent with other evidence given, and there were departures from the standard of interpretation required in the interpretation of his evidence on matters crucial to the application.[89] The courts are concerned with whether answers given to Tribunal questions are responsive, or show confusion or misunderstanding, and whether any such problems are critical having regard to the reasoning, findings and conclusions of the Tribunal.[90] Inadequate interpreting that compromises the reliability of what is communicated between the Tribunal and an applicant can render unreliable the basis of the Tribunal's findings; where those findings are directly related to the Tribunal's conclusions, that can constitute a denial of procedural fairness.[91]

---

83 Ibid.
84 [2002] FCA 1375, [73].
85 *STPB v Minister for Immigration and Multicultural and Indigenous Affairs* [2004] FCA 818.
86 *SZLDY v Minister for Immigration and Citizenship* [2008] FMCA 1684.
87 (1999) 92 FCR 6, 23–4; *SZQUH v Minister for Immigration and Citizenship* [2012] FCA 1265, [19].
88 A study of 50 court and tribunal appeals based on inadequate interpreting found that in the majority of cases, the adequacy of the interpreting was assessed by the monolingual judge based on the transcript alone: Hayes and Hale, above n 80, 126.
89 (1999) 92 FCR 6, 23.
90 *Mazhar v Minister for Immigration and Multicultural Affairs* [2000] FCA 1759, [39].
91 *STBP v Minister for Immigration and Multicultural and Indigenous Affairs* [2004] FCA 818, [25], applying *SCAR*.

In *Perera*, Kenny J held that absent an interpreter, the Tribunal would not afford a person who is not proficient in English an effective opportunity to give evidence, and it would be deprived of jurisdiction; if it proceeded, the Tribunal would be in breach of the then s 476(1)(b) (or s 476(1)(c) or (e)).[92] The terms of s 425, and s 476, have been amended since *Perera*. In *Mazhar v Minister for Immigration and Multicultural Affairs*,[93] Goldberg J held that the amendment of s 425 after *Perera*, which formerly required the RRT to 'give the applicant the opportunity to appear before it to give evidence', and now requires the RRT to 'invite the applicant to appear before the Tribunal to give evidence and present arguments', did not alter the obligation. The invitation to appear 'must not be a hollow shell or an empty gesture', and if the Tribunal knows an applicant requires an interpreter, and provides an interpreter whose interpretation is such that the applicant is unable adequately to give evidence and present argument, it has not fulfilled its obligation under s 425.

The invitation required by s 425 is critical, and the more recent cases confirm that lapses in interpreting may result in jurisdictional error where the errors deprive the applicant of a real opportunity to give evidence and present arguments which s 425 requires, and which is a precondition to the exercise by the Tribunal of its jurisdiction.[94]

As is the case for psychological impairment, it is not difficult to envisage a circumstance where it may be impossible for a Tribunal to provide a sufficiently competent interpreter who is independent from the parties, either because the language or dialect is so uncommon, or because the recognised accrediting bodies simply do not accredit interpreters to the appropriate level. Given the reliance on s 425 as a precondition to the exercise of jurisdiction, it is arguable that as is the case with psychological impairment, a Tribunal may be faced with the position that it is simply not possible for it to discharge the statutory obligation to review.

What is a fair hearing?: Conclusions

The courts have necessarily framed their consideration of psychological and language barriers to participation before the migration Tribunals in terms of the obligations imposed by the Migration Act, rather than from the common law requirements of procedural fairness, as a consequence of the direction in ss 357A and 422B that the statutory procedures are an exhaustive statement of the requirements of the hearing rule. That is subject to the qualification that the courts

---

92 *Perera* (1999) 92 FCR 6, 16–17.
93 [2000] FCA 1759, [31].
94 *SZQUH v Minister for Immigration and Citizenship* [2012] FCA 1265, [19].

are careful to identify what are the 'matters' with which Division 5 of Part 5 and Division 4 of Part 7 deal.[95]

The issue is whether, notwithstanding the care taken to distinguish any obligations arising from the statutory provisions from general law obligations, there is at the heart of cases such as these a more broadly applicable notion of what a 'fair' hearing requires that is not bound up in the specific provisions of the Migration Act, or the statutory requirement to 'review'.

The experience of judicial review of decisions made by the Independent Merits Review (IMR) reviewers suggest that that may be so. The IMR scheme was established in 2008 to provide review of decisions made by departmental delegates in respect of claims for refugee status made by persons who arrived in places excised from the Australian migration zone, and for whom there was no right to review by the RRT. The IMR process was conducted by persons engaged by an independent contractor, and their function was to make a recommendation about whether Australia had protection obligations to the claimant; a departmental officer would then prepare a submission to the Minister. In *Plaintiff M61/2010E v Commonwealth*,[96] the High Court held that the assessment and review processes were undertaken for the purpose of the Minister considering whether to exercise the statutory power to permit an application for a protection visa; and it followed from the consequence upon the liberty of the claimant, who was detained until the conclusion of that process, that procedural fairness was required. In *Plaintiff M61/2010E*, two of the three errors identified in the review process related to procedural fairness, being a failure to deal with one of the claims made, and a failure to put before the plaintiff the substance of matters that the reviewer knew of and considered might bear on whether to accept the plaintiff's claims. The specific obligations, and limitations, imposed under the Migration Act on the RRT in putting information to an applicant did not apply to the IMR process, and there had been a denial of procedural fairness.

The mental health of a claimant was at issue in *MZYRX v Minister for Immigration & Citizenship*,[97] where the Court had medical records of the applicant post-dating those before the reviewer, and two psychiatric reports prepared some time after the IMR interview. Whelan FM held that they were admissible, but that the weight to be given to the evidence had to be considered in light of the fact that neither psychiatrist was asked to evaluate the capacity of the applicant to participate in an IMR interview conducted at an earlier time. Whelan FM noted that,

---

95 *Saeed v Minister for Immigration and Citizenship* (2010) 241 CLR 252; *Minister for Immigration and Citizenship v Li* (2013) 297 ALR 225, [18] (French CJ).
96 (2010) 243 CLR 319.
97 [2012] FMCA 723.

while *SCAR*, *SZNVW* and *NAMJ* were decided by reference to s 425 of the Migration Act, there was no suggestion that similar considerations were not relevant when similar problems arose in IMR.[98] The Court was, however, unable to determine that the degree of impairment suffered by the applicant was such as to render him incapable of understanding and answering questions, nor that the unreliability of his answers was solely a function of his mental state.

Additional support comes in the judgment of French J in *Minister for Immigration and Multicultural Affairs v SZFDE*,[99] where his Honour explained that the cases had established that:

> procedural unfairness affecting a person's right to a hearing before an administrative tribunal can be a ground for judicial review without any fault on the part of the tribunal. Whether there has been a reviewable failure of procedural unfairness will depend upon the circumstances. On the basis of the cases discussed above, it may arise where:
> 1. By reason of a psychiatric or other medical condition a party has a significantly diminished capacity to participate in the oral hearing.
> 2. The party does not attend at an oral hearing for reasons beyond his or her control and of which the tribunal is unaware. This circumstance is likely to be of practical significance where the tribunal makes its decision at the hearing or before any explanation for non-attendance could reasonably have been proffered by the applicant. Example of its application might arise where a person is involved in a traffic accident on the way to the hearing or is taken suddenly ill and is unable to appear or notify the tribunal of his or her pending non-appearance.
> 3. As a result of the conduct of a third party, the tribunal is misled on a question which is of significance to the outcome of the hearing.
> 4. A third party fails to provide the tribunal and the person to be affected by the decision with documents in its possession or power which would be favourable to that person. There may be a question whether this is a case of procedural unfairness or, in the case of the Tribunal, one better considered under the heading of failure to comply with statutory procedures.

It is clear from those examples, and the High Court's confirmation of the approach of French J in *SZFDE*,[100] that a failure to provide a fair hearing does not depend on any finding of fault on the part of the decision-maker.

---

98 Ibid, [57].
99 (2006) 154 FCR 365, 391–2.
100 *SZFDE v Minister for Immigration and Citizenship* (2007) 232 CLR 189.

More recently, the High Court's decision in *Li* provides an alternative approach, not based on procedural fairness. The MRT had proceeded to finalise its review of a decision to refuse a Skilled – Independent Overseas Student (Residence) visa, despite a request by the applicant's migration agent that it wait until the result of a requested review by the relevant skills assessment authority of its negative skills assessment. In considering whether the MRT had properly exercised the discretionary power conferred by s 363(1)(b) of the Migration Act to 'adjourn the review from time to time', the Court held that the Tribunal had acted unreasonably. Hayne, Kiefel and Bell JJ held that it was not apparent which of the possible errors of taking into account an irrelevant consideration, giving too much weight to the fact that Ms Li had had some opportunity to present evidence and argument and insufficient weight to her need to present further evidence, or failing to have regard to the purposes for which the statutory discretion in s 363(1)(b) was provided in arriving at its decision, was made, but the result itself bespoke error. In the circumstances of the case, it could not have been decided that the review should be brought to an end if all relevant and no irrelevant considerations were taken into account and regard was had to the scope and purpose of the statute. The MRT had not discharged its function of deciding whether to adjourn the review according to law, and had not conducted the review in the manner required by the Act. There are grounds for caution, however, arising from Gageler J's reminder that *Wednesbury* unreasonableness is a stringent test and that *Li* was a rare case, and more specifically from the circumstances of the case itself. The adjournment sought was for a specific purpose articulated by Li's migration agent, and the requested review was based on grounds conceded by the Minister to have been coherent; and the Tribunal did not articulate expressly the reasons for refusing to delay the decision. *Li* may have a limited role to play where potential barriers to participation are unknown to the Tribunal.

The accepted understanding of the obligation to provide a fair hearing includes at least adequate notice that an adverse decision may be made; disclosure of relevant and credible adverse material or information; and the opportunity to put forward evidence or submissions.[101] It is central to this understanding that the term 'hearing' is not limited to an oral process involving at a minimum the person affected and the decision-maker, or a single event. In administrative decision-making to which the common law principles apply, an oral 'hearing' may not be essential;[102] it may not be essential that the decision-maker is the person who 'hears' the person affected;[103] and the decision-making process to which procedural fairness applies

---

101 P Cane and L McDonald, *Principles of Administrative Law: Legal Regulation of Governance* (Oxford University Press, 2nd ed, 2012) 124.
102 Aronson and Groves, above n 9, 563–6.
103 Ibid, 555–9.

may start before any 'hearing' and continue until the moment of decision.[104] Of course if there is an oral hearing, additional issues arise: for example, whether the person affected is entitled to have someone speak on their behalf,[105] or whether witnesses are to be subject to cross-examination.[106]

In the absence of any contrary legislative requirements, the common law principles would not preclude a tribunal faced with an applicant for whom there are psychological or language barriers to participation deciding to invite the person affected to present evidence and submissions in writing, with such assistance as the person requires or prefers. The difficulty is that the courts generally consider that an oral hearing, with the opportunity for the decision-maker to observe the person, is of assistance where there are conflicting issues of fact to resolve, or where credibility needs to be assessed,[107] and that will often be the case in review of migration decisions. One answer may be to combine a face-to-face hearing with a subsequent opportunity to provide detailed written submissions. It may even be appropriate in extreme circumstances to not even attempt an oral hearing, if some alternative means of enabling participation can be identified. In *SZFDE*, French J noted that the statutory scheme applicable to the RRT requires that an invitation to attend an oral hearing be extended where the Tribunal is unable to come to a decision favourable to the applicant on the papers, so that the content of procedural fairness in relation to the right to be heard there involves an oral hearing. His Honour then posed the question of whether, 'if a written case has been put and considered, there is by loss of the oral hearing any "practical unfairness"'.[108] That may be the kind of 'difficult factual judgment' that Flick J had in mind in *SZMSF*. The possibility that such an approach may be open may emerge from continued consideration of what 'fair and just' means in ss 357A(3) and 422B(3). Hayne, Kiefel and Bell JJ in *Li* appear to have provided support for the approach adopted in *SZMOK* – that it constitutes the 'restoration' of fairness and justice and qualifies the application of the legislated procedural steps – in preference to the artificial focus on the invitation required by s 425. While that flexibility would be open on the common law principles, the additional time required, and the possibility that the person may not have access to assistance to prepare or respond adequately to written submissions, might make this an unattractive option. It is unlikely, however, that the courts would countenance a situation where a tribunal could not carry out the required 'review'.

---

104 *Applicant NAFF of 2002 v Minister for Immigration and Multicultural and Indigenous Affairs* (2004) 221 CLR 1.
105 Aronson and Groves, above n 9, 567–73.
106 Ibid, 583–6.
107 Ibid, 565.
108 (2006) 154 FCR 365, 391, referring to *Re Minister for Immigration and Multicultural Affairs; Ex parte Lam* (2003) 214 CLR 1.

Perhaps the response is ultimately a pragmatic one, based in part on the reluctance of the courts to require tribunals to undertake inquiries other than in limited circumstances, and on the limited role of the courts in judicial review. Tribunals are not required to ensure that all available arguments are put or that an applicant presents his or her best case.[109] It would be unfortunate, however, if the task for a challenger of establishing that he or she was unfit to take part in a hearing, whatever procedural adjustments or accommodations might be made, or that the interpretation was inadequate at a sufficiently fundamental level, is simply one that could not be met.

---

109 *Re Minister for Immigration and Multicultural and Indigenous Affairs; Ex parte Applicant S134/2002* (2003) 211 CLR 441; *Minister for Immigration and Citizenship v SZIAI* (2009) 259 ALR 249.

abuse of power, 243
Administrative Appeals
Tribunal, 11–12, 15, 23,
96, 192, 268, 312, 319,
353, 397, 397, 402, 410,
413, 418
 as administrative and legal
institution, 132
 freedom of information
determinations and,
388–9
 function of, 11–12
 influence on judicial review,
22–3
 jurisdiction, 11, 403, 404–5
 merits review and, 16–17,
407
 merits review jurisdiction on
non-citizens and, 101
 nature of review task and,
418–19
 objective of, 11
 Security Appeals Division,
101
administrative decision-making
 ascertainment of fact and,
44–5
 bias and. *See* bias
 discretion and, 44
 relevant considerations and,
80–82
*Administrative Decisions
(Judicial Review) Act
1977*, 8–11, 181–2
 'administrative character'
and, 186–7
 codification of grounds of
review and, 10–11
 contrast to *Judiciary Act*,
183–4
 'decision' and, 185–6
 'duty to inquire' and, 196
 efficacy of, 182–3
 exclusion of migration cases
from, 8
 exclusion of refugee
claimants from, 19
 exclusions from review
under, 203
 explicit reference to
jurisdictional error and,
261, 272, 275
 international human rights
obligations and, 81–2
 judicial review and, 8–9
 jurisdictional requirements
and, 184–5
 recommended reforms to,
188
 right to statement of reasons
and, 9–10
 'under an enactment' and,
187–9
administrative detention, 99
administrative estoppel, 191,
231
 grounds of review and,
195–6
administrative justice
 right to, 72–3, 77, 92
 right to in international
human rights law, 73,
76, 84
 themes and values of, 36–7
administrative law
 definition, 26
 emergence of modern
approach to, 170–5
 exceptionalism of, 192
 good faith and. *See* good
faith
 influence of *Constitution*
on, 4
 new. *See* new administrative
law
 perception of as branch of
common law, 169
 public–private distinction
and. *See* public–private
distinction
 rationality and. *See*
rationality
 relationship between citizen
and state and, 67
 relevant considerations and,
80–2
 rule of law and, 27–33
 statutory interpretation and,
38–41
administrative power
statutory interpretation and,
41
Administrative Review Council,
7, 9, 11, 181, 183, 188,
189, 190, 194, 202, 203,
204, 260–1, 312, 353,
360
Administrative Review
Tribunal, 7, 405
administrative tribunal systems
 first or second tier, 403–4
 general or multi-purpose
jurisdiction, 403
 national, 404–5
 primary decision-making
and review, 404
 public and private, 404
 specialist, 402–3
 states' and territories', 405–6
administrative tribunals,
16, 23
 accountability mechanisms
for, 6–7
 advantages of, 401–2
 alternative dispute resolution
process and, 396, 397
 appeal from, 406–7
 continuum of administrative
decision-making and, 35
 definitions of, 394–5
 distinctive features of, 396
 distinguished from courts,
399–400
 'fair, just, economical,
informal and quick' and,
413
 impact of jurisprudence of,
414
 independence of, 12
 inquisitorial function of, 35,
418
 judicial review of, 34
 'may inform itself' and,
411–12
 membership of, 413
 migration tribunals. *See*
migration tribunals
 'must act according to
substantial justice' and,
412

place of in government, 395–6
pre-hearing dispute resolution and, 397–9
rules of evidence and, 35, 410–11, 417
varieties of, 401
weight of application of law by, 133
alternative dispute resolution, 396, 397
asylum seekers, 85, 198
Australian Law Reform Commission, 74, 75, 106, 151, 157, 339, 351, 353, 373, 374, 394, 399
Australian Privacy Principles, 373, 375–6, 392
APP 1, 377–8, 382
APP 2, 378
APP 3, 378–9
APP 4, 379
APP 5, 379–80
APP 6, 380–1
APP 7, 381–2, 383
APP 8, 382
APP 9, 381, 383
APP 10, 382, 384
APP 11, 382–3
APP 12, 384
APP 13, 384
privacy codes and, 376, 385–6
Australian Security Intelligence Organisation, 95
Independent Reviewer of security assessments and, 102, 117
procedural fairness and, 96
security assessments. *See* security assessments

bad faith, 37, 42
bias, 37, 47
apparent or apprehended, 47
rule against, 206
bill of rights
lack of, 72, 86, 192, 244

bills of rights
statutory interpretation and, 87–9
statutory, impact of on judicial review, 86–91
Bland Committee, 8, 11, 13, 14

codification of grounds of review, 10–11, 353
accessibility, legal certainty and transparency and, 189–91
Constitution and, 192–3
criticism of, 190–1
Ellicott Committee and, 10
enumerated and emerging, 194–201
purpose of, 181
commercial confidentiality, 59–60, 356
Committee of Review of Prerogative Writ Procedures. *See* Ellicott Committee
Committee on Administrative Discretions. *See* Bland Committee
common law, 9, 10, 23, 25, 37, 169
grounds of review at, 77, 188
illogical and irrational fact-finding and, 199
interaction with statute law, 40
judicial review at, 5–6, 189–90
perceived relationship to administrative law, 169
privacy and, 372, 392
procedural fairness and, 125, 215, 216–17, 434
protection of rights and freedoms under, 40, 41, 78, 79, 92
tradition of private sphere and, 68
writs of mandamus and prohibition and, 168

Commonwealth Administrative Review Committee. *See* Kerr Committee
Commonwealth Conciliation and Arbitration Commission, 169
Commonwealth Court of Conciliation and Arbitration, 169
Commonwealth Industrial Court, 169
Commonwealth Ombudsman, 12–13, 312, 335, 344, 345, 353
establishment of, 13
relationship with executive, 13
role of, 13
conscious maladministration, 291, 293–4
Constitution
codification of grounds of review and, 192–3
executive power of Commonwealth and, 31–2
influence on administrative law, 4
new administrative law and, 16–21
official powers under, 32
procedural fairness and, 110–11
rule of law and, 28
structure of, 166–8
unfettered discretion and, 30–1
constitutional interpretation, 265–6
difference from statutory interpretation, 266
constitutions, State
separation of powers and, 32
courts
access to, human rights cases and, 72–6
approach to standing and, 76
authority of in statutory interpretation, 130

courts (*cont.*)
  distinguished from administrative tribunals, 399–400
  enforcement of freedom of information matters by, 389–90
  non-disclosure of security information and, 104
  public–private distinction and, 56
  resistance to privative clauses by, 278–9
  role in judicial review, 193
  security cases and, 95

data protection. *See* privacy
Datafin principle, 53–4, 55–6, 270
discretionary power, 5, 7, 23, 30, 45, 186, 191, 198
  fettering of, 194–5

Electoral and Administrative Review Commission (Qld), 193, 194, 199, 203
Ellicott Committee, 8, 9, 14, 181, 188, 189
  codification of grounds of review and, 10
environmental decisions characteristics of, 141
environmental groups, standing for
  individuals with special interests and, 149
  open standing and, 151, 156–9
  participation in administrative processes and, 155–6
  property or economic interests and, 148–9
  public-interest based, 151, 152–4
  special interest test, Australia, 143–5
  special interest test, United Kingdom, 146–8

special interest test, United States, 145–6
stakeholder categories, 141–3
errors of law
  judicial review and, 263–4
  jurisdictional. *See* jurisdictional errors
  non-jurisdictional. *See* non-jurisdictional error
  statutory interpretation and, 264–5
estoppel, 196, 226, 232, 237
  administrative. *See* administrative estoppel
  enforcement of, 233
  private law, 230
  promisory, 225
  public law, 195, 232, 233, 242, 243, 247
exclusions of procedural fairness, 292–3
  express statutory procedures and, 220–3
  High Court of Australia and, 218–19
  necessary implications and, 219–20
  statutory codes and, 221–2
executive power, 77, 271
Federal Circuit Court of Australia, 8
Federal Court of Australia, 169
  articulation of remedial powers of, 203
  original jurisdiction, 9, 34, 183
  review of magistrates' decisions by, 34

Federal Magistrates' Court, 8, 387, 388, 389, 414
fourth branch of government. *See* integrity branch
fraud, 48, 271, 293
freedom of information, 14, 59
  AAT review and, 388–9
  Cabinet documents and, 364–5

claims of future harm and, 365–9
classes of documents, absolute protection and, 363–5
conclusive certificates and, 361–2, 363
cost absorption and, 359–61
disparity amongst jurisdictions, 354
distinguished from privacy, 14
duty of public servants and, 368
early regimes, criticism of, 353–4
enforcement of by courts, 389–90
exemptions, differing approaches to, 356–9
laws. *See* freedom of information laws
ombudsmen and, 362
open government and, 349–50, 359, 366, 368
'overriding public interest' test and, 61
proactive disclosure and, 355–6
public interest test and, 356, 357, 358, 359, 361–3, 363, 363–4, 367–8
roles and powers of review bodies and, 362
Freedom of Information Act 1982, 14
  'conditionally exempt' documents and, 60–1, 358
  exemptions from, 60–1, 358
  reforms to, 14
freedom of information laws
  first generation, 352–4
  second generation, 354–6

General Counsel for Grievances, 7, 8, 13
good faith, 37, 38, 41–4
  definition, 41
  independence of, 42

442 Index

government
  integrity branch of. *See*
    integrity branch
  place of tribunals in, 395–6
  roles of branches of, 316–7
government power, 225, 171
  contractual, public-private
    distinction and, 51–3
  public, 51
  See also public power
grounds of review
  decisions without
    justification, 199–201
  'duty to inquire', 197
  fettering of discretionary
    powers, 194–5
  illogical or irrational fact
    finding, 197–9
  raising an administrative
    estoppel, 195–6
*Guidance on Vulnerable
  Persons*, 430

hearing rule, 206, 219
  procedural fairness, 420
High Court of Australia
  appellate jurisdiction, 168,
    175
  development of judicial
    review and, 17–21
  exclusions of procedural
    fairness and, 218–19
  implied principles of
    procedural fairness and,
    125
  jurisdictional error and, 259,
    259–60
  legitimate expectation and,
    82
  migration cases and, 8, 19,
    214, 219–20
  original jurisdiction, 4, 8, 19,
    29, 168, 172, 175, 192,
    198, 269, 281
  privative clauses and, 19–20
  security decisions and,
    103
  Wednesbury test of
    unreasonableness and,
    240–1

honesty of purpose, 42
horizontal accountability, 305,
  315
human rights
  access to courts and, 72–6
  access to justice and, 72–3
  bills of rights and, 86–91
  fundamental, 78
  law, international. *See*
    international human
    rights law
  law, relevant considerations
    and, 80–2
  privacy and, 371
  remedies and, 84–6
  security and, 94
  statutory interpretation and,
    78

Independent Merits Review
  scheme, 435–6
information privacy. *See*
  privacy
Information Privacy Principles,
  372–3
integrity branch, 346
  as constitutional branch of
    government, 313–20
  as distinct branch of
    government, 314–15
  description of, 302, 304
  development of, 305–6
  horizontal accountability
    and, 305
  independence of, 320–4
  institutions comprising,
    306–7
  jurisdictional organisation of,
    310–13
  power to conduct public
    hearings and, 152, 321,
    322
  power to make public
    statements and, 321,
    322–4
  problems of institutional
    multiplicity and,
    308–10
  relationship to executive
    branch, 317–20

international human rights
  law, 72, 78
  legitimate expectations and,
    83–3
  presumption that domestic
    law conforms with, 78–9
  procedural fairness and,
    82–3, 111–17
  relevant considerations and,
    80–2
  remedies and, 84–6
  right to administrative justice
    in, 73, 76, 84
International Privacy
  Principles, 379, 380

judicial power, 110
  definition, 167
judicial review, 21, 27, 34, 43
  ADJR Act and, 8–9, 169–70
  'an administrative character'
    and, 76
  at common law, 5–6, 189–90
  availability of, 68–9
  codification of grounds
    of. *See* codification of
    grounds of review
  constitutional and non-
    constitutional, 172
  constitutional entrenchment
    of, 20, 192–3
  decisions of Governor-
    General and, 203
  development of, 17–21
  Diceyan conceptions of,
    171–2
  distinction between merits
    review and, 407
  errors of law and, 263–4
  exclusions from, 203
  government contractual
    powers and, 52–3
  grounds of review and. *See*
    grounds of review
  housing associations and, 63
  influence of AAT on, 22–3
  limits on, 172–3, 174, 175,
    193, 207, 251, 271
  'made under an enactment'
    and, 56, 57, 76

judicial review (*cont.*)
  magistrates' decisions, 34
  margins and, 262–7
  ministerial decisions and, 34
  'modern conceptual justification' for, 171
  of administrative tribunals, 34
  principal object of, 34
  private bodies and, 54–5, 64, 66
  privative clauses and. *See* privative clauses
  proceedings, substantive arguments in, 77
  public power and, 53–4
  remedies and. *See* remedies
  role of courts in, 193
  statutory bills of rights and, 86–91
  substantive legitimate expectations and, 192
  unreasonableness and, 45–6
judicial review jurisdiction
  limits of, 51–6
  statutory conferrals of, 56–9
jurisdiction
  'commencement theory' of, 254
  meaning of, 254
jurisdictional error, 20, 172, 173, 174, 175–6, 178, 196, 198, 245, 278
  as conclusionary label, 252–3, 267
  distinction between non-jurisdictional error and, 262, 272
  generic grounds and, 250–1, 256–74
  generic instances of, 255–7
  High Court of Australia and, 259–60
  history of, 253–5
  'juggling' of categories in, 257–60
  legislative reform and, 260–1
  'manifest errors' and, 280
  migration cases and, 272

nullity and. *See* nullity
present meaning of, 250
privative clauses and. *See* privative clauses, 34, 279–80
statutory interpretation and, 251–2, 253, 269–71, 274–5
justiciability, 73–4
  approach of courts to, 76

Kerr Committee, 5–6, 8, 9, 11, 13, 14, 176, 181, 188, 189, 353
  recommendations, 7
Kerr Report, 5–7, 12–13, 397, 404, 407, 410, 413

legal error, 199, 201
legislative intention, 39
legislative power. *See* statutory power
legitimate expectations, 21, 47
  Australia, 233, 241–6
  Canada, 241, 245
  controversy over meaning of, 227–9
  England, 230–8
  Lord Denning and, 226–7, 230, 231, 231–2, 232–3
  origin of, 226–9
Lord Denning, 31, 226–7, 230, 231–2, 232–3, 262

magistrates' decisions
  judicial review of, 34
mandatory detention, 79
merits review, 21–22, 23, 34
  Administrative Appeals Tribunal and, 16–17, 407
  'correct or preferable' standard of, 408–9
  distinction from judicial review, 407
  exclusion of, security cases and, 100–2
migration cases
  exclusion from ADJR Act, 8
  jurisdictional error and, 272

migration law
  declaration of specified country and, 80
  s 474 privative clause and, 281–3
  shifts in, 420
Migration Review Tribunal, 102, 122, 417, 418, 420, 424, 430
  obligations of, 420–1
  provision of interpreters at, 431
migration tribunals, 419–21
  acting in a 'fair and just' way and, 424–7
  competency of interpreter service and, 433–4
  fair hearing and, 434–9
  Guidance on Vulnerable Persons and, 430
  invitation to a hearing before, 421–4
  language issues and, 431–4
  provision of interpreters at, 431–2
  psychological issues and, 427–31
ministerial responsibility
  principle of, 6

National Privacy Principles, 373, 376
national security. *See* security
natural justice. *See* procedural fairness
new administrative law, 4
  ambiguities and challenges of, 175–9
  as system of administrative responsibility, 15
  Constitution and, 16–21
  reforms of, 5–8, 16
New South Wales
  Ombudsman, 344, 345
no-invalidity clauses, 290, 291–2

non-jurisdictional error, 251, 259
  distinction between jurisdictional error and, 262, 272, 273
non-justiciability, 73–4, 103, 157
nullity
  consequences of, 268
  court orders and, 269
  jurisdictional errors and, 267–9
  retrospective, 268

Office of the Australian Information Commissioner, 14, 381, 386–8, 390
Ombudsman, Commonwealth. *See* Commonwealth Ombudsman
ombudsmen
  annual reports of, 337
  assessment of performance of, 336–42
  core role of, 331–2
  democratic strength of, 336–7
  derivation of, 329
  'fair and reasonable' and, 337, 341–2
  freedom of information and, 362
  increasing jurisdiction by, 343–6
  'matter of administration' and, 333–4
  own motion investigation and, 332, 335, 345
  power of suggestion and, 335–6
  'private' industry, 62–3
  range of, 327
  reasons for introduction of, 330–1
  scope of investigation by, 332–3
  'unique' role of, 328
  use of discretion by, 334–5

open government
  freedom of information and, 349–50, 359, 366, 368
  official secrecy and, 350–2
outsourcing, 50, 62, 65

parliamentary sovereignty, 27
personal information, 371, 372–3
  access and amendment rights to, 383–5
  collection of, 378, 379–80
  damages from breach of, 389–90
  dealings with, 380–2
  integrity of, 382–3
  Privacy Act 1988 and, 372, 374, 375
prerogative power, 51
  procedural fairness and, 271
privacy
  as a human right, 371
  Australian Privacy Principles and. *See* Australian Privacy Principles
  common law and, 372, 392
  distinguished from freedom of information, 14
  information privacy principles and, 372–3
  International Privacy Principles and, 379, 380
  laws, State and Territory, 390–1
  National Privacy Principles and, 373, 376
  Office of the Australian Information Commissioner and, 14, 386–8, 390
  privacy codes and, 376, 385–6
  public interest determinations and, 386
  tax file numbers and, 372, 385, 386
Privacy Act, 131
  background to, 372–3
  breaches, collateral consequences of, 390

exceptions to, preliminary principles, 377–8
  generalised exceptions to, 376–7
  health information and, 374–5
  objectives and interpretation of, 373–5
  personal information and. *See* personal information
  scope of, 375–6
  sensitive information and. *See* sensitive information
privatisation, 50, 62, 65
privative clauses, 34–5, 42, 73, 173
  access to courts and, 75–6
  alternative mechanisms to, 290–5
  approach of courts to, 76
  contemporary federal jurisdiction and, 281–5
  contemporary State jurisdiction and, 285–90
  contradiction of, 277
  definition, 277
  Hickman principle and, 280, 281–2, 285 288–9, 295
  High Court of Australia and, 19–20
  jurisdictional error and, 279–80
  Plaintiff S157 and, 281–5
  procedural fairness and, 283
  resistance to by courts, 278–9
  traditional interpretative technques and, 278–81
  See also conscious maladministration; no-invalidity clauses
procedural fairness, 22, 37, 38, 40, 41, 46–8, 63, 68, 69, 94, 95–6, 255, 257, 258, 417
  Australian conception of, 206, 211
  common law and, 125, 215, 216–17, 434
  Constitution and, 110–11

procedural fairness (*cont.*)
  exclusion of. *See* exclusions of procedural fairness
  hearing rule and. *See* hearing rule
  implied legislative intent and, 215–16
  implied limitations and, 124–6
  implied, principle of, High Court of Australia and, 125
  interests applicable to, 211–14
  international human rights law and, 82–3, 111–17
  judicial process and, 110
  prerogative power and, 271
  privative clauses and, 283
  procedural conception of, 207–10
  provision of interpreters and, 431
  security cases and, 95, 96, 95–100, 101
  source of, 215–17
  standing and, 160
  threshold test for, 215, 227
  value of, 210–11
proportionality, 21, 192
public interest immunity
  security cases and, 102–10
  security information and, 95
public power, 171
  See also government power
public sector information, 352, 355
public–private distinction, 50–1, 57
  attempts to redefine, 64–7
  'conditionally exempt' documents and, 60–1
  courts and, 56
  difficulties with, 62–4
  liberal tradition and, 67–9
  'overriding public interest' test and, 61
  statutory bills of rights and, 89–91
  statutory conferrals of judicial review jurisdiction and, 56

Queensland Civil and Administrative Tribunal, 396, 397, 404, 408

rationality, 37, 38, 44–6
  definition, 44
  statutory power and, 44
reasonableness,
  independence of, 42
  See also unreasonableness
reasons, right to. *See* statement of reasons, right to
refugee claimants, 419
  Independent Merits Review scheme and, 435–6
  restriction of review rights of, 19
Refugee Review Tribunal, 282, 283, 412, 417, 418, 419, 420, 424, 430, 435
  obligations of, 420–1
  provision of interpreters at, 431
  unreasonableness plea and, 198
remedies, 84
  human rights cases and, 84–6
  wrong choice of by applicant and, 188
responsible government, 26
  doctrine of, 6
rule of law, 39, 41, 71, 78, 101, 171, 175, 252, 264, 303, 315
  administrative law and, 27–33
  Constitution and, 28
  Diceyan conceptions of, 27–8, 277
  State Supreme Courts and, 29–30

security
  consequences of judicial deference to, 104–6
  courts and, 95
  human rights and, 94
  public interest immunity and, 102–10
security assessments, 96
  adverse allegations and, 97
  adverse, disclosure of, 96–100
security cases
  exclusion of merits review from, 100–2
  High Court of Australia decisions and, 103
  irreducable minimum of disclosure in, 112–15
  judicial response to, 108–10
security information
  impossibility of challenge to, 107
  lawyer confidentiality and, 105
  non-disclosure of, courts and, 104
  power to inspect, 105
  public information immunity and, 95
  special advocate procedure for, 115–17
sensitive information
  collection of, 378–9
  Privacy Act 1988 and, 374, 375
separation of powers, 12, 16, 28–9, 77, 95, 177–8, 193, 242, 251, 252, 265, 277
  State constitutions and, 32
Skehill Review, 411
Special Immigration Appeals Commission (UK), 116–17
standing, 73, 141, 202
  approach of courts to, 76
  environmental groups. *See* environmental groups, standing for
  habeas corpus and, 85
  open, 144, 151, 156–9
  'person aggrieved' definition and, 74–5
  procedural fairness and, 160

446 Index

recommended reforms for, 151, 159–62
tests for, Australia, 74–5, 141, 143, 185
tests for, United Kingdom, 146, 150
tests for, United States, 145, 149–50
State Administrative Tribunal (WA), 398
State Supreme Courts
prerogative writs and, 168, 170, 174
rule of law and, 29–30
supervisory jurisdiction of, 174, 270
statement of reasons, right to, 9–10, 185, 201–2
statutory interpretation, 38–41, 59, 77–80, 262
administrative power and, 41
ascertaining effect of non-compliance with statutory requirements and, 127–30
authority of courts and, 130
authority of executive in, 130–1
authority of lay person in, 131–2
determining meaning of terms and, 121–3
difference from constitutional interpretation, 266–6
differences in judicial interpretation and, 133–7
errors of law and, 264–5
human rights and, 78
jurisdictional error and, 251–2, 253, 269–71, 274–5
statutory bills of rights and, 87–89
use of extrinsic materials in, 123, 131
statutory power, 38, 39, 40, 56, 57, 77
ascertaining effect of non-compliance with, 127–30
defining the ambit of, 124
determining limitations on exercise of, 124–7
implied limitations on, 124–7
rationality and, 44
statutory authorities and, 232
substantive unfairness. *See* legitimate expectations

tax file numbers, 372, 385, 386
terrorism, 85–6, 103
Transparency International, 305
treaties, 72, 74, 78, 79
legitimate expectations and, 83

ultra vires
meaning of, 254–5
unreasonableness, 46, 90, 192, 197, 198, 228, 234, 239, 240
judicial review and, 45–6
legislative exclusion of grounds of, 197–8
See also Wednesbury test of unreasonableness; reasonableness

Victorian Civil and Administrative Tribunal, 398, 411
Victorian Ombudsman, 344

Wednesbury test of unreasonableness, 437, 245
High Court of Australia and, 240–241
See also unreasonableness
writs
certiorari, 32, 168, 174, 234, 235, 245, 272, 287, 349
common law, 169
constitutional, 33, 34, 172
habeas corpus, 32, 84–6
injunction, 75
mandamus, 29, 32, 34, 75, 168, 172, 173, 174
prerogative, 168, 169, 170, 174, 349
prohibition, 33, 34, 75, 168, 172, 173, 174, 186

For EU product safety concerns, contact us at Calle de José Abascal, 56-1º,
28003 Madrid, Spain or eugpsr@cambridge.org.

www.ingramcontent.com/pod-product-compliance
Ingram Content Group UK Ltd.
Pitfield, Milton Keynes, MK11 3LW, UK
UKHW030806060825
461487UK00019B/1720